Y

Theatre Guide

David Wood
David Holman
Penny Cardagh
Nona Sheppard

BLOOMSBURY
Theatre
Guide

TREVOR R. GRIFFITHS &
CAROLE WODDIS

BLOOMSBURY

For Gay Clifford

American Consultant Editor: Mira Felner

First published 1988
This edition published 1991

Bloomsbury Publishing Limited,
2 Soho Square,
London W1V 5DE

Picture Acknowledgements
All photographs © Donald Cooper except: Neil Bartlett © Mike Laye; Brecht © Martha Swope; Pierre Corneille © T. Charles Erickson; Horton Foote © David S. Talbott; Beth Henley © Gerry Goodstein; Henrik Ibsen © Dan Nutu; Marie Jones © Sarah Ainslie; Garson Kanin © The Cleveland Playhouse; Kaufman and Hart © Richard Feldman; Harry Kondoleon © Gerry Goodstein; Lesbian Theatre (*Belle Reprieve*) © Amy Meadow; Romulus Linney © Richard Trigg; Molière (*Tartuffe*) © Simon Annand; Performance Art (The Wooster Group) © Louise Oligny; Shakespeare (*A Midsummer Night's Dream*) © T. Charles Erickson; Shakespeare (*The Taming of the Shrew*) © Martha Swope; Joshua Sobol © Gerry Goodstein; Sophocles © Joan Marcus; Steinbeck © Brosilow Photography; Wendy Wasserstein © Gerry Goodstein; Tennessee Williams © Michael Tighe; August Wilson © Gerry Goodstein; George C. Wolfe © Jay Thompson.

British Library Cataloguing in Publication Data
A CIP catalogue record for this book is available from the British Library.

ISBN 0 7475 0990 5

10 9 8 7 6 5 4 3 2 1

Designed by Geoff Green
Typeset by Florencetype Ltd, Kewstoke, Avon
Printed in Great Britain by Richard Clay Ltd, Bungay, Suffolk

Contents

Introduction

This is a theatre reference book with a difference because it concentrates on the writers, the plays and the companies you are actually likely to be able to see in the theatre now, rather than those who get into theatre reference books because they have always been in theatre reference books, even though no one has done their plays for the last hundred years. Its other unique feature is a cross-referencing system that allows you to find other plays or authors who have tackled similar topics, share similar interests or offer marked contrasts to the one you started with; and when you look at those further entries you will find more cross-references that can lead you on a sometimes surprising journey of discovery that will give added enjoyment to your appreciation of theatre.

We hope the result is a work that communicates some of the enthusiasm and pleasure all of us who contributed to the book have had from our theatre-going, and that it is a useful guide to the contemporary theatre scene. Theatre, after all, is to be enjoyed, whether that means something to stretch the imaginative and intellectual sinews or escapism; and it always reflects the society in which it takes place, for good or ill, directly or indirectly, positively or negatively, and so offers a way of taking the temperature of a nation.

The success of the *Theatre Guide*'s first edition has given us the opportunity to expand and update its already comprehensive coverage to include many more plays and dramatists, particularly from the USA and Britain. One of the unique features of the *Guide*, its stress on the contemporary theatrical repertory, gives us the opportunity to consider all writers as contemporary figures and to back some hunches about emerging writers and trends. In comparison with the first edition, a number of entries have been expanded, reduced, or even dropped, to reflect our developing judgements of the subjects of those entries. Sadly, some of the British companies included in the first edition have been dropped because they are no longer working as a result of their funding's having been withdrawn, and we have generally reduced the entries for other companies to make room for more individual writers. We have again concentrated on dramatists and on non-music theatre, since it is impossible to do justice to music-theatre and dance within the scope of one book, although we have not drawn the boundaries so rigidly as to exclude those who have made significant contributions in more than one area.

In making our choices of entries for this book we were aware that we would appear to be privileging dramatists and plays over the other vital aspects of the production process. In fact, we share the dramatist Bryony Lavery's view that 'a play is a wonderfully nutty fruit cake . . . made up of the script, the directors, actors, audience, technicians . . . it's what happens the night we were all there for the performance', but we also know that what gets handed down as theatre, what gets remembered, is often to do with what gets published; if it's not printed it doesn't exist.

When we talk about our cultural heritage, the 'our' tends to refer to white middle-class heterosexual men; the female voice and women's experience of life, like those of black, Asian and gay communities and people with disabilities, is under-represented. Within the limitations of space and the need to span the range of international theatre, we have tried to do a little to redress that balance. Our choices are inevitably subjective – particularly as regards very new writers and companies of promise and we have not included writers who work mainly for television – but part of the fun for us was to try to pick out those who would make a lasting contribution, as well as those whose reputations are secure; and remember that no matter how fringe or minority some of our choices may appear today, and how idiosyncratic the juxtaposition of the tried and established with the burgeoning talents may seem, the unknowns of today may be the Harold Pinters, Caryl Churchills and August Wilsons of tomorrow, because film and television feed off the theatre. Live theatre, with all the challenges of entertaining an audience who are actually there with you sharing the same space, is the place where playwrights go to serve their apprenticeship and to renew their spirits (if not their bank balances).

Trevor R. Griffiths
Carole Woddis
March 1991

How to use this book

This book is divided into an alphabetical list of over 300 main entries (which cover individual dramatists, some theatre companies, areas of theatre such as Pantomime and important directors/theorists) and an index of play titles, companies and theatre people.

If you know an author's name you can look it up in the main alphabetical list or in the index. If you know a play's title you can look it up in the index. A ▷ in front of a dramatist's or company's name indicates that they have their own main entry.

Each main entry for an individual writer follows a standard format with a list of plays, discussion of the writer and a list of cross-references. For most writers there is also a key play selected by the contributor for more detailed treatment and for a few major writers there may be more than one key play. We have tried to make the dates of plays as accurate as possible but in some cases there is uncertainty about the exact order of composition and/or production of plays: the dates given are, wherever possible, those of the first public appearances of plays whether in production or in print or in some cases, particularly living playwrights, when written. In the case of writers' dates of birth and death there are also some areas of uncertainty (and some living writers, or their agents, have been unwilling to release information); wherever there is doubt we have reflected it in the use of c by the doubtful date. We have not tried to include all the plays written by each writer or a comprehensive list of film, television, radio, translation and adaptation, or other writing credits but we have tried to draw attention to those that form a significant part of a writer's output. Similarly we have not aimed to be inclusive in our coverage of awards won by writers. In the case of foreign language plays we have tried to include familiar English titles where these exist and literal translations where they don't. We have also tried to track down alternative titles and revised versions of plays going under different titles wherever possible, but a glance at the entry for John Byrne will show the scope of the problem.

The authors acknowledge the helpful suggestions of Ruby M. Cohn in response to the first edition, and would be grateful if any corrections to matters of fact and suggestions for inclusions in future editions were sent to them care of the publishers.

a

ABBENSETTS, Michael [1938–]
Guyanaian dramatist, now living in the USA

Plays include:
Sweet Talk (1973), *Alterations* (1978), *Samba* (1980), *In the Mood* (1981), *The Dark Horse* (1981), *El Dorado* (1983), *Outlaw* (1983)

Michael Abbensetts was the first Caribbean writer to have a television series in Britain with *Empire Road* (1978). Before that he had already had success with *Sweet Talk*, *Alterations*, a television play *The Museum Attendant* and radio plays. The secret of Abbensetts' success was his ability to write situation comedies whose characters and human predicaments struck a common chord, and where colour was not the predominant theme. They appeared therefore to have a universal appeal. However, under the comic, often genially satirical veneer, they revealed bitter legacies of colonialism and emigration as seen through the frustrations, aspirations, and tragedies of the ordinary British black-man-in-the-street. He dealt with marital problems (*Sweet Talk*), and the price to pay for ambition (*Alterations*), with the pathos of individuals who have seen better days (*Samba*), and with those who fought for the 'mother country' (*In the Mood*).

With the increasing sense of black consciousness in Britain, Abbensetts' gentle humour lost favour in the 1980s, but he continues to write successfully in the USA and *Sweet Talk*, his most popular play, has been produced in Nigeria (The World Black Arts Festival; 1977), New York, Kenya, Canada, and throughout the Caribbean.

Try these:
▷Mustapha Matura, ▷Edgar White, ▷Derek Walcott, particularly for examining painful personal legacies of colonialism; ▷Hanif Kureishi and ▷Mustapha Matura for 'mother country' disillusionment; ▷Trevor Rhone for a similar use of sit-com; ▷Tunde Ikoli, ▷Caryl Phillips, and Felix Cross and David Simon's *Blues for Railton* have all focused on the British black experience; for American equivalents, Samm-Art Williams; ▷African-American Theatre.

ABBOTT, George [1887–]
American writer and director and producer of musicals

Plays and musicals include:
Three Men on a Horse (with John Cecil Holm; 1935), *On Your Toes* (with Rodgers and Hart; 1936), *The Boys from Syracuse* (based on ▷Shakespeare's *Comedy of Errors*; 1938), *Beat the Band* (with George Marion Jr; 1942), *Where's Charley?* (1948), *A Tree Grows in Brooklyn* (with Betsy Smith; 1951), *The Pajama Game* (with Richard Bissell; 1954), *Damn Yankees* (with Douglas Wallop; 1955), *Fiorello* (with Jerome Weidman; 1959), *Tropicana* (1985), *Frankie* (based on *Frankenstein*; 1989)

Author or co-author of over fifty plays and musicals, and a legendary director and producer, George Abbott sums up the Broadway musical in its heyday. Like a eulogy to the great American dream, an evening with Abbott paid homage to the vivacity of the entrepreneurial spirit. It was ebullient, full of slick one-liners and showbiz razzmatazz, and put together with brilliant efficiency. Like all good farceurs, Abbott spins his plays and musicals on the corniest of plots – in *Damn Yankees*, it is a losing baseball team; in *Three Men on a Horse*, it is a natural gift for winning. But there is often a twist: *Damn Yankees* also has a touch of *Faust* thrown in (the baseball fan sells his soul to the devil), whilst *The Pajama Game* may be about boy meets girl but she's a shop steward and he's the management stooge out to stop her from earning a few cents more an hour. As one might expect, a good moral message gets stirred in along with the comedy.

Abbott was also responsible for producing and directing some of Broadway's greatest classics, such as *Pal Joey*, *Call Me Madam* and *On Your Toes*. All these seem endurably buoyant and, as revived recently in London, have been more successful than his own shows. On the other hand, *The Boys from Syracuse* bombed on its last outing in London. Abbott hasn't slowed down even as he rounds the bend of a century-long life. In 1985 he premièred a workshop version of his new musical, *Tropicana*; in 1987 he directed a Broadway revival of his 1926 musical, *Broadway*; and in 1989 he opened a new musical off-Broadway. Based on *Frankenstein*, *Frankie* takes place in Manhattan and East Hampton, Long Island's fashionable summer resort town.

Three Men on a Horse

Three Men on a Horse, a happy mix of farce, parable and sentiment, is a classic of its kind, with its downtrodden copywriter, who also happens to have a way of predicting horse-race winners, plus a large supporting cast of kind-hearted gamblers, brassy blonde, long-suffering but loyal wife (and the inevitable butt of comedy, the dragon mother-in-law). *Three Men on a Horse* cleverly ridicules the American obsession with winning, turning it equally into a celebration of generous moral decency and the triumph of the little man over the system.

Try these:
Frank Loesser's *Guys and Dolls* for its similarly bright array of gamblers and low-life characters; ▷Brecht's *Schweik in the Second World War* for its triumph of the 'little man'; ▷Kaufman and ▷Hart for more celebrations of the amiable eccentric; ▷Timberlake Wertenbaker for Faustian bargains.

ADAMOV, Arthur   [1908–1970]
French dramatist

Plays include:
La Parodie (*The Parody*; 1950), *La Grande et la Petite Manoeuvre* (*The Great and the Small Manoeuvre*; 1950), *Le Professeur Taranne* (*Professor Taranne*; 1953), *Le Ping-Pong* (*Ping-Pong*; 1955), *Paolo Paoli*

(1957), *Printemps 71* (*Spring of 71*; 1962), *Sainte Europe* (*Holy Europe*; 1966), *Off Limits* (1968)

Adamov made a precarious literary living in Paris in the 1920s and 1930s, when he was a friend of Artaud and linked with the Surrealists. His plays are most often put on by non-professional or university groups, and they usually try the short and Kafkaesque dream play *Professor Taranne*; but there are more interesting possibilities in his later work. His 1950s plays are dream-like and obsessional, dealing with his urges to suicide, fear of impotence, and general masochism, and his name then tended to be bracketed with those of ▷Beckett and ▷Ionesco. However there are signs of his later political interests in *Ping-Pong*, in which two men spend their lives developing a better electric pin-ball machine, a heavy-handed symbol for capitalism.

With the coming of the Algerian War he turned to political plays, notably *Paolo Paoli*, which uses the trade in ostrich feathers and rare butterflies to make anti-capitalist points about the *Belle Epoque*. In the 1960s he wrote plays on the Paris Commune and on apartheid, a satire on de Gaulle's France, and an interesting and complex full-length play set in the USA at the time of the Vietnam War. This was *Off Limits*, built around a series of parties where the middle-aged drink and the young take dope, each scene interrupted by games and agit-prop sketches. This would be worth trying in English, but expensive, as would Planchon's collage of his work, *A.A. Théâtres d'Adamov*.

Try these:
▷Strindberg for the early dream plays; ▷Ionesco for writing as a liberation from personal neurosis; ▷Brecht for the later political plays; ▷Trevor Griffiths' *The Party* for another party at a time of political strife; ▷Megan Terry's *Viet Rock*, for an anti-Vietnam American satire; ▷Jean-Claude Van Itallie's *America Hurrah* for more anti-US satire.

ADAPTATIONS AND ADAPTERS
The tradition of translating/adapting/reworking plays by other authors in other languages is almost as old as the theatre itself – witness the 'identical twins' plot that is found (inter alia) in Plautus, the *commedia dell'arte*, ▷Goldoni, ▷Dario Fo, and ▷Shakespeare

George C. Wolfe's mask and puppet adaptation of Brecht's *The Caucasian Chalk Circle*, set in a Haiti-like Caribbean island for New York Shakespeare Festival's Public Theatre in 1990

(twice). However, the more proprietorial attitude to literary works of the last two centuries has meant that modern translations of contemporary plays have been attempts to make the work of foreign authors accessible to a public which cannot understand them in the original rather than springboards for something fresh – though the frequency with which works are described as 'adaptations' and the tendency to share the task of translation between two people, one of whom can understand the original and one of whom can write plays, makes one wonder about the fidelity of the English versions.

Attempts to put novels on the stage (as opposed to the Shakespearean habit of taking his plots where he could find them) date back to the Victorian era, when they were primarily 'the play of the book', mostly run up by the resident hack for an audience unaccustomed to reading for pleasure; this market vanished with the rise of the cinema. (*Ben Hur*, for instance, started as a novel and was made into a very successful melodrama before it became a film.) In recent years, however, there have been a remarkable number of adaptations of novels, 'classic' and otherwise, aimed at an audience of much greater sophistication than their Victorian predecessors. The earliest (and one of the longest) was probably the Science Fiction Theatre of Liverpool's *Illuminatus*, which opened the Cottesloe in 1977; the paradigm the ▷RSC's *The Life and Adventures of Nicholas Nickleby*, adapted by ▷David Edgar in 1979; the most disastrous was ▷Mike Alfreds' *The Wandering Jew*, at the ▷National Theatre in 1987 (the melodramatic acting style was carefully worked out, but the plot wasn't up to it); and the culmination of this tendency is surely ▷Peter Brook's *The Mahabharata*, which manages to contain a massive Indian epic within nine hours of superb narrative theatre. Together with shorter and more manageable adaptations of novels such as ▷Christopher Hampton's superb transmutation of Laclos' *Les Liaisons Dangereuses* (1985), these adaptations seem to meet a basic need for story-telling that is not satisfied by most modern playwrights. They are sometimes produced as a collective effort by a writer and a company; they tend to be long, and to move between narration and impersonation, because of the amount of plot which has to be got in; staged non-illusionistically, because the original author set his/her scenes with no eye to dramatic practicability; full of bravura acting and furious doubling, for the same reason; and, at their best, very exciting indeed.

Aside from these adaptations from novels, there have been a growing number of translations, free and otherwise, from foreign plays in recent years: plays by ▷Racine, ▷Schiller, ▷Lessing, and other authors previously thought untranslatable and/or unactable have been successfully presented, and added to the well-known stock of ▷Ibsen and ▷Chekhov. A number of translators' names recur frequently: Tony Harrison became well-known for his brilliant translation and updating of *The Misanthrope* in 1973, and his later translations and adaptations for the ▷National Theatre – *Phaedra Britannica* (1975, set in British India), *The Oresteia* (1981), and *The Mysteries* (presented all together at the Lyceum in 1985) – have been equally successful. He has a fine line in knotty, colloquial verse ('Batter, batter the doom-drum, but believe there'll be better' went his Anglo-Saxon line in *The Oresteia*, where the ▷RSC's *The Greeks* had the more mellifluous 'Cry sorrow, sorrow, but let the good prevail'); and he happily engages with the most 'untranslatable' authors. The same is true of Robert David Macdonald, who has been prepared to tackle, generally for the ▷Glasgow Citizens' Theatre, ▷Racine's *Phedra*, ▷Lorca's *The House of Bernarda Alba*, ▷Schnitzler's *Intermezzo*, and ▷Goethe's *Faust* (both parts), usually working from the original, which is by no means true of most translators; he has also joined the novel-adapters with such unlikely authors as Proust. Christopher Hampton has translated ▷Horváth for the ▷National Theatre (*Tales from the Vienna Woods*, 1977, and *Don Juan Comes Back from the War*, 1978); and Adrian Mitchell has translated ▷Calderón (*The Mayor of Zalamea*, ▷National Theatre 1981, and *Life's a Dream*, ▷RSC 1984), as well as ▷Gogol's *The Government Inspector* (▷National 1985). One should also mention John Fowles, ▷Dusty Hughes, and ▷John Mortimer's speakable versions of ▷Feydeau, (notably *A Little Hotel on the Side*, National 1984); the list of works now made available is long and encouraging, and currently nothing looks impossible. However, one could wish that more of these plays would enter the repertoire, rather than being done once only to acclamation and then forgotten again.

Perhaps because of America's relatively short history and, therefore, early lack of a strong playwriting tradition, US directors, writers, and producers have resourcefully and

Robert Wilson's haunting production for American Repertory Theatre of Ibsen's *When We Dead Awaken*

frequently turned to novels for dramatic fodder for almost 200 years. One of the late 18th-century producer William Dunlop's most successful plays was his free adaptation of Sterne's *Tristram Shandy*, appropriately retitled *The Father, or, American Shandyism*. By far the most commercially popular adaptation of a novel was Aiken's mid-19th century dramatization of *Uncle Tom's Cabin* (in 1900 there were literally hundreds of touring theatre companies performing the epic both in the US and abroad).

Modern Broadway musical creators have been especially adept at reworking bestselling books. The trend is typified by Hammerstein's groundbreaking *Show Boat* (1927) adapted from Edna Ferber's novel of the same name and William Hauptman's rousing *Big River* (1985) adapted from Mark Twain's *The Adventures of Huckleberry Finn*).

Resident theatres have successfully commissioned a number of notable adaptations: Steppenwolf Theater produced Frank Galati's Tony Award-winning version of Steinbeck's *The Grapes of Wrath* (Galati taught the art of oral interpretation at North-western University, spawning a following of like-minded theatremakers); Adrian Hall, former artistic head of Trinity Rep. in Providence, R.I. and Dallas Theater Center in Texas (the two theatres he used to run simultaneously) created crackling adaptations of Robert Penn Warren's *All the King's Men* (1987) and Jack Henry Abbott's account of prison life *In the Belly of the Beast*. Hall also dramatized Dickens' *A Christmas Carol*, which Trinity (like many resident theatres, in a myriad of adaptations) mounts annually to the delight of the box office managers.

The Mark Taper Forum in Los Angeles sponsors a literary cabaret called the Itchey Foot (where George C. Wolfe's *Spunk*, an adaptation of Zora Neale Hurston's stories, originated). And a number of small theatres around the USA are devoting themselves to creating theatrical works from literary media – especially in Chicago-City Lit Theater originated cartoonist Lynda Barry's *The Good Times Are Killing Me*; Organic Theater has adapted everything from Ray Bradbury and Kurt Vonnegut to Roald Dahl. Meanwhile, in Philadelphia, Novel Stages has dramatized Damon Runyon stories, Zola's novel *The Earth*, and other works of fiction.

But perhaps no other theatre in the US relies more on adaptations than theatres devoted to young audiences. Almost every classic children's book has been dramatized – The Children's Theatre in Minneapolis has staged Dr. Seuss, *Little Women*, and turned Beatrix Potter's tales into a Christmas pageant; the Arkansas Arts Center Children's Theatre has mounted ambitious productions of Washington Irving's *The Legend of Sleepy Hollow* and William Golding's *The Lord of the Flies*; and there are more examples, too numerous to list here.

ADSHEAD, Kay   [1954–]
British dramatist

Plays include:
Thatcher's Women (1987)

Like ▷Sharman Macdonald's *When I Was a Girl I Used to Scream and Shout*, *Thatcher's Women* is a first play by an actress/writer. Kay Adshead's play, presented originally by the Paines Plough company. It shows definite traces of television influences in its story of a northern middle-aged wife, pushed reluctantly to the south of England and into prostitution by her husband's unemployment. One of a rash of plays on similar topics inspired (*sic*) by the 'Thatcher decade' and showing the effect of economic policies impinging on private lives. Adshead's is a spirited if uneven play – a kind of School in Unsentimental Education or How I Learned to Stop Feeling and Just Play The Game.

Try these:
Julia Schofield's *Love on the Plastic* and ▷Peter Terson's *Strippers* make similar links between unemployment and female exploitation; ▷Marlane Meyer's *Etta Jenks* for an American parallel. For contrast see *Stars in the Morning Sky* by Alexander Galin, a more melodramatic view of prostitutes; Caroline Kara, an American actress-turned-writer wrote *The Early Girl* starring Demi Moore, which played at Circle Rep. in 1986 and takes place in a legal house of prostitution in Nevada. ▷Debbie Horsfield for a contemporary northern ambience; Paines Plough for other new writers.

AESCHYLUS   [c 525–456 BC]
wrote the earliest surviving Greek tragedies

Plays include:
The Persians (472 BC), *The Seven Against Thebes* (469 BC), *The Oresteian Trilogy* (458 BC), *The Suppliant Women, Prometheus Bound* (dates unknown)

Aeschylus is credited with two of the major innovations in Greek drama: the introduction of a second actor (which made possible dialogue that did not involve the chorus, thus opening the way for greater dramatic flexibility); and the reduction in size (and therefore importance) of the chorus. *The Persians* is particularly interesting for presenting the recent defeat of the Persians at the Battle of Marathon, from a sympathetic viewpoint.

Aeschylus' tenuous hold on the current repertory derives almost entirely from *The Oresteian Trilogy*, the only complete trilogy to survive from the Classical Greek theatre. It tells the story of the royal house of Atreus in which crime breeds crime over the generations until the goddess Athene intervenes to substitute reconciliation and justice for the blind process of revenge. Peter Hall directed a memorable all-male version for the ▷National Theatre in 1981, adapted by ▷Tony Harrison.

Try these:
▷Aristophanes, ▷Euripides, Menander and ▷Sophocles wrote the other surviving Greek plays; ▷T. S. Eliot's *The Family Reunion* updates the Orestes myth to 1930s England and ▷Eugene O'Neill's *Mourning Becomes Electra* updates it to New England.

AFRICAN-AMERICAN THEATRE

Like other alternative theatre movements in the USA, African-American theatre exploded in the 1960s, when the Civil Rights movement in general, and the leadership and subsequent assassinations of Martin Luther King and Malcolm X in particular, spurred the black community into action.

African-American theatre, however, has roots in minstrelsy – the movement can be traced back to the 1820s. The first African-American theatre group was the African Grove Theater, which produced vaudeville-style entertainment for popular audiences. Then, in the 1930s, ▷Langston Hughes' WPA-funded Harlem Suitcase Theater attracted a lot of attention with its ambitious productions.

Throughout the 1940s and 1950s, there was an increse in the number of productions by African-American playwrights, even though theatre was still generally controlled by white producers, directors, and the demand of a predominantly white audience. Mercury Theater productions of Richard Wright's *Native Son* (1941) and ▷Lorraine Hansberry's *A Raisin in the Sun* (1959) serve as two notable bookends on this period. However, while most of the plays written during these two decades subtly suggested that racial inequalities existed, and some of the plays were even angry in tone, none had the ripping vigour of protest that was exhibited by the plays that would shock America in the next decade.

In the 1960s, militant playwrights like Leroi Jones (later to become ▷Amira Baraka) and ▷Ed Bullins attacked the white establishment and called for blacks to return to their African roots. Baraka's *The Baptism*, *Dutchman*, and *The Slave* were all staged in 1964 and 1965. In 1966 the actor/director/playwright Douglas Turner Ward's editorial in *The New York Times* demanded an African-American theatre that would produce plays by, for, and about African-Americans, and which would train a generation of black actors, writers, and theatre artists. His call was answered by the Ford Foundation whose financial support helped jump-start the Negro Ensemble Company (NEC). Meanwhile, Baraka left New York and established his own theatre called Spirit House in Newark, New Jersey, where many of his subsequent plays were premiered.

There's no underestimating the importance of Baraka's move to form his own independent theatre and Ward's success with NEC for subsequent generations of African-American theatre troupes. In 1989 about 180 black theatre companies attended the First National Black Theater Festival. Representatives from theatres all over the country gathered, including Jomandi from Atlanta, Penumbra from Minneapolis, the NEC from New York, Woodie King Jr's New Federal Theater, Crossroads Theater from New Brunswick, New Jersey, and the Oakland Ensemble Theater. These theatres all maintain diverse identities and ask different questions about the role of African-American theatre. Some work on non-hierarchical bases, using collaborative techniques and 'no star' rehearsal programmes; others are primarily concerned with nontraditional casting (Crossroads Theatre offered all-black versions of ▷Mamet's *American Buffalo* and Pielmeier's *Agnes of God*) before producing premières like *Black Eagles* and *The Colored Museum*, both of which transferred to off-Broadway venues;

still others, like Penumbra, focus on adopting classics for African-Americans.

Black playwrights now work in both the mainstream white American theatre (the resident not-for-profit system and Broadway) and the avant-garde. ▷Ntozake Shange's 'choreopoem' *for colored girls who have considered suicide when the rainbow is enuf* (1974) was an example of a smashing commercial Broadway success. More recently, resident theatres have provided a spring-board for ▷August Wilson, whose narrative cycle about twentieth-century black America – *The Piano Lesson, Ma Rainey's Black Bottom, Fences, Joe Turner's Come and Gone* – started at Yale Repertory Theatre, then toured regional venues throughout the country before settling for commercial runs on Broadway (and appearing in London with some success at various venues: the RNT's production of Ma Rainey's *Black Bottom* being a particular triumph.) Other playwrights such as ▷Steve Carter, Ron Milner, ▷Richard Wesley, and ▷Samm-Art Williams have had work successfully produced in the 1980s. Charles Fuller won the Pulitzer Prize in 1982 for *A Soldier's Play*, produced by the NEC and subsequently made into a major film.

Working in more avant-garde forms are performers like John O'Neal and Robbie McCauley. O'Neal's one-man show *Sayings from the Life of Junebug Jabbo Jones* incorporates raucous and wily elements into a storytelling structure. In 1989 McCauley performed *Indian Blood*, a piece that dealt with the historical connections and betrayals between the black and native American communities. In 1989 Suzan Lori-Parks' won an Obie for her first play produced in New York (actually at BACA, a Brooklyn experimental venue) *Imperceptible Mutabilities in the Third Kingdom*. Her follow-up the next year, *The Death of the Last Black Man in the Whole Entire World* (1990), uses skittish minimalism to address issues of racism and stereotyping. And ▷Adrienne Kennedy, whose obsession with the lost American dream began with *Funnyhouse of a Negro* (1962) is still writing in the 1990s.

Some African-American performers, playwrights and theatre groups worry that their significance may be weakened by the mainstream theatre's adoption of multiculturalism and have tried to expand their work to include a 'rainbow coalition' theatre. Other artists and theatres are retrenching and continue to fight stereotypes while celebrating difference.

▷George C. Wolfe, one of a triumvirate of new artistic associates at New York Shakespeare Festival's Public Theater, first came to prominence with his eclectic and sophisticated *The Colored Museum*, which satirises some of the treasured icons of black American playwriting, including the work of ▷Baldwin, Baraka, and Shange. His adaptation and direction of three Zora Neale Hurston stories (*Spunk*) received critical kudos and Obies when produced at the Public in the 1989–90 season. Shange, meanwhile, honed the dramatic adaptation of her book *Betsey Brown* with white director ▷Emily Mann at the McCarter.

The Lincoln Center Theater's revival of Langston Hughes' and Zora Neal Hurston's folk musical *Mule Bone* in 1991 sparked controversy when production plans were announced. Critics of the play argued that Hughes' use of black dialect projected a negative image of African-Americans. Its advocates claimed that blacks have spoken differently from whites, and that this should be pointed out. In any case, the disagreement seems a healthy one and the production is further evidence of mainstream theatre's renewed interest in exploring African-Americans' cultural heritage, even while artists like Parks and Wolfe are intent on blazing new paths for the future.

Try these:
▷Black Theatre in Britain; ▷Asian Theatre in Britain; ▷Yiddish and Jewish-American theatre for parallels and contrasts.

ALBEE, Edward   [1928–]
American dramatist

Plays include:
The Zoo Story (1959), *The Death of Bessie Smith* (1960), *The Sandbox* (1960), *Fam and Yam* (1961), *The American Dream* (1961), *Who's Afraid of Virginia Woolf?* (1962), *Tiny Alice* (1964), *A Delicate Balance* (1966), *Box and Quotations from Chairman Mao Tse-Tung* (1968), *All Over* (1971), *Seascape* (1975), *Counting the Ways* (1976), *Listening* (1976), *The Lady from Dubuque* (1980), *The Man Who Had Three Arms* (1983), *The Marriage Play* (1988), *Three Tall Women* (1991)

The adopted grandson of Edward Franklin Albee, a vaudeville theatre owner and manager, Albee leaped to the forefront of the

American theatre scene in the 1960s with his early plays. *Zoo Story*, *The American Dream*, and *The Sandbox*, evocative of early ▷Ionesco and ▷Beckett both in style and thematic exploration of alienation, provided the United States with a playwright in the tradition of the European avant-garde. His subsequent plays – *Who's Afraid of Virginia Woolf?*, *Tiny Alice*, and *A Delicate Balance* are more Pinteresque in style, raising the question of whether or not Albee found his own voice or has remained derivative in form and content. In recent years, Albee has been less prolific, preferring to spend his time directing his own works and teaching. He is vehement in his protection of the playwright against directorial excess and has had an active voice in public debate on the subject of stage interpretation.

Who's Afraid of Virginia Woolf?
Albee's commercial success is largely based on *Who's Afraid of Virginia Woolf?*, performed on Broadway by Uta Hagen and Arthur Hill, and later in the film version by Elizabeth Taylor and Richard Burton. The play takes place in a small college town and focuses on the relationship between a professor and his wife, the daughter of the college president, as they drag a young faculty couple into their elaborate power games. The play explores the force of fantasy, as the amorphous boundaries between appearance and reality are taxed during vicious marital sparring.

Try these:
▷John Guare's *The Loveliest Afternoon of the Year* for terror in New York's Central Park; ▷Arthur Miller's *Death of a Salesman* for another view of the defunct American dream; ▷Christopher Durang, ▷Tennessee Williams, ▷Beth Henley for American explorations of dysfunctional families.

ALFREDS, Mike [1934–]
British adapter, director

Long before ▷David Edgar's famous adaptation of Dickens' *Nicholas Nickelby* for the ▷RSC, the art of adapting novels and producing them as vivid ensemble stage pieces had become the hallmark of Mike Alfreds' work at Shared Experience. London-born Alfreds, who trained in the States at Carnegie-Mellon, and spent five years in Israel as a director/lecturer, founded Shared Experience

in 1975, pioneering a style by which prudent text cutting re-emphasised the strong narrative line of his dramas. Early successes included his adaptation of Dickens' *Bleak House* and Evelyn Waugh's *A Handful of Dust*. Such an approach used a minimum of props and relied heavily – and with great success – on superb imitative skills by his actors, often taking on many different characters in one piece.

Other adapters involved during Alfreds' time at Shared Experience included ▷Timberlake Wertenbaker (▷Marivaux's *Successful Strategies* and *False Admissions*), and Fidelis Morgan and Giles Havergal (Samuel Richardson's *Pamela*). Alfreds worked for a short time at the ▷National Theatre successfully directing *The Cherry Orchard* for the Ian McKellen/Edward Petherbridge group, but had less luck with his five-hour version of the ▷Goldoni trilogy *Countrymania*, and the impressive but equally lengthy *The Wandering Jew*, adapted by ▷Michelene Wandor from Eugene Sue's 19th-century novel. Alfreds is now Director of Cambridge Theatre Company. Giles Havergal also made an excellent job of adapting Elizabeth Bowen's *The Heat of the Day* with Felicity Browne for Shared Experience; Nancy Meckler, Shared Experience's new director, has adapted ▷Euripides' *The Bacchae*; Jatinder Verma for his many adaptations of Asian and European classics; ▷Ken Campbell for a similar though more anarchic tradition of adaptations; ▷Adaptations and Adapters; ▷Olwen Wymark.

ALRAWI, Karim [1953–]
Anglo-Egyptian dramatist

Plays include:
Aliens (1980), *Before Dawn* (1981), *Sink the Pink* (1982), *Migrations* (1982), *Divide and Rule* (1983), *In Self Defence* (1983), *Fire in the Lake* (1985–87), *A Colder Climate* (1986), *A Child in the Heart* (1987), *Promised Land* (1988), *Crossing the Water* (1991)

One-time writer-in-residence at both the Royal Court and Theatre Royal, Stratford East, Alrawi was one of only two dramatists in Britain in the early 1980s writing about the effects of racism (the other was ▷Hanif

Kureishi) from a non-Caribbean point of view. Brought up in Egypt (he can remember the bombing of Suez), Alrawi went to Britain at the age of 14 to live in Hackney in London's East End, and has never forgotten the sense of dislocation the move produced in him or the racial prejudice he experienced in English schools. His plays have always, one way or another, attempted to dissect the experience of being a migrant in Britain. Reviewers have not always been kind to Alrawi, sometimes with justification when polemics have got in the way of imagination. He remains, however, a dramatist of flair and passion, one willing moreover to speak out for the cultural underdog.

Migrations (an Arts Council John Whiting Award winner and a reworking of the earlier *Before Dawn*) looked at issues of religion and culture, integration and local-authority corruption through the eyes of an old Jewish stall holder, his young Pakistani assistant in Brick Lane, and the dilemmas of his sister. *A Colder Climate* was a bold, not altogether successful, attempt to comment on Thatcher's Britain, showing racism and National Front attitudes filtering through into the behaviour of a group of contemporary East End characters. *A Child in the Heart* for ▷ Joint Stock (he was part of its management team before its demise) typically pulled no punches in its criticism of the West's cultural exploitation of the Third World, but was a bit of a sprawl. However, in its almost Old Testament insistence on sticking to Tribe, it was consistent with Alrawi's ongoing concern with the nature of cultural identity.

Alrawi has also written radio plays and two screenplays for the British Film Institute.

Try these:

Hanif Kureishi's *Borderline* for images of National Frontism and Asian girls in conflict with their traditional culture; ▷Harwant Bains' *The Fighting Kite* and *Blood* for further British Asians' experience; for images of the East End, ▷Barrie Keeffe's *My Girl* and ▷Tony Marchant's *The Lucky Ones*; Jonathan Falla's *Topokana Martyr's Day* also dealt with questionable motives of giving charity to the Third World; ▷Mike Leigh's *Greek Tragedy* showed a Greek immigrant community in Sydney at the end of their tether; ▷Arthur Miller for immigrants and the sense of community.

ANOUILH, Jean   [1910–1987]
French dramatist

Plays include:
Le Bal de Voleurs (*Thieves' Carnival*; 1932), *La Sauvage* (*The Restless Heart*; 1934), *L'Eocadia* (*Time Remembered*; 1940), *Le Rendezvous de Senlis* (*Dinner with the Family*; 1941), *Eurydice* (*Point of Departure*; 1941), *Antigone* (1942), *Medée* (*Medea*; 1946), *Roméo et Jeanette* (*Romeo and Jeanette*; 1946), *L'Invitation au Château* (*Ring Round the Moon*; 1947), *Ardèle ou La Marguerite* (*Ardèle: The Cry of the Peacock*; 1948), *La Répétition ou L'Amour Puni* (*The Rehearsal*; 1950), *La Valse des Toréadors* (*Waltz of the Toreadors*; 1952), *L'Alouette* (*The Lark*; 1953), *Pauvre Bitos ou le Dîner de Têtes* (*Poor Bitos or the Masked Diner*; 1956), *L'Honneur de Dieu* (*Becket*; 1959)

Anouilh's popularity and influence were at their height in the immediate post-war period. Known for his exquisite craftsmanship, in later years his work appeared to take on a whimsical tone. But in a theatre career that spanned over half a century, he covered a wide range: from the controversial *Antigone*, written against a background of the German occupation (some saw it as an apologia for the Nazis, others as a statement against them), to *Number One*, a self-pitying portrait about the ageing playwright facing up to solitude and old age. Anouilh himself categorised his plays into *pièces roses* (rosy, such as *Dinner with the Family* or *Time Remembered*), *pièces noires* (dark, which include the three Greek-based tragedies, *Eurydice* or *Point of Departure*, *Antigone*, and *Medea*, as well as *Romeo and Jeanette*), *pièces brillantes* (sparkling, such as *Ring Round the Moon*), *pièces grinçantes* (grating, *Ardèle* or *Waltz of the Toreadors*), and *pièces costumées* (costume or historical plays such as *Becket*, or *The Lark* (about St Joan). Anouilh's plays seem haunted by certain private and obsessive concerns; the corruption of innocence, the pain of human existence, its ugliness and compromise, the incompatibility of happiness with purity, the clash between the inner and outer worlds, the conflict between past and present, and later in life, loneliness. Above all, as Harold Hobson put it, talking about *Antigone*, there was bitterness and regret at the contrast between 'what life could be and what life was'.

Anouilh's early plays, however, show the bitterness leavened by laughter and strongly

influenced by the form and gloss of ▷Mari-
vaux (for example, the Pirandellian play-
within-a-play (*The Rehearsal*), where behind
brilliant comic dialogue you can detect a typical Anouilh confrontation between purity and
the artifice of the aristocratic world. Again, in
Ring Round the Moon, Anouilh's crippled old
lady exploiting her power by re-arranging the
lives of those around her is another veneer for
the playing out of a deeper battle between
power and money on the one hand, and
poverty and purity on the other.

Anouilh's heroines or heroes frequently
sacrifice themselves for a nobler cause; Becket
and Joan in *The Lark* are both martyrs to their
faith and purity, a theme re-enacted not only
in *Antigone* but also by Orpheus and
Eurydice, Romeo and Jeanette, and even
Medea. *Poor Bitos* on the other hand, about
the humiliation of a smug communist deputy
at a party where the guests are dressed in
Revolutionary costume, is also seen by some
as Anouilh's self-portrait etched in self-
disgust.

Although Anouilh is staged less often now,
the success of the 1990 revival of *The
Rehearsal* in London is a reminder of the qualities of his plays that made such a great impression in the 1940s and 1950s.

Antigone

Antigone follows ▷Sophocles but is typical
Anouilh in its heroine's option for the purity
of death rather than the muckiness and
compromise of life. Sophocles' version dices
with the conflict between secular and divine
law (another, more modern and interesting
reading could see it as a re-assertion of the
female and instinctual over man-made law),
but Anouilh's Antigone is not so much the
victim of an unjust law as a martyr to purity.
Creon argues with her and, unlike Sophocles'
Creon who is thoroughly guilt-stricken for the
trail of tragedies his decisions have provoked,
Anouilh's Creon is a thoroughly modern prag-
matist who puts duty – upholding the security
of the state – above personal emotion. To what
extent Anouilh sympathises with Creon's response remains a question for conjecture.

Try these:
▷Sophocles' *Antigone* for the original;
▷Pirandello; ▷Sartre's *Les Mouches* for
another war-time play subversively attac-
king the Vichy regime; ▷George Bernard
Shaw for another treatment of *St Joan*;

▷Terence Rattigan for other personal
pains treated with similar skill.

ARBUZOV, Aleksei Nicolaevich
[1908–]
Russian dramatist, actor and director

Plays include:
Tanya (1939), *It Happened in Irkutsk*
(1959), *The Promise* (also known as *My
Poor Marat*; 1965), *Tales of Old Arbat*
(1970), *An Old Fashioned Comedy* (also
known as *Do You Turn Somersaults?*; 1978)

A prolific playwright who ranges from 'Brechtian' techniques to the sentimental, melodramatic and near vaudeville, Arbuzov's first big
success was *Tanya*. His most popular play in
the USSR is probably *It Happened in Irkutsk*,
a personal drama set against the construction
of a power station in Siberia, using a
Brechtian chorus, but in the West he is best
known for *The Promise*, (a 1966 Oxford
Playhouse production by Frank Hauser, with
Judi Dench, Ian McShane and Ian McKellen,
had subsequent successful runs in London
and New York). Like many of his plays it
spans a long period, presenting the interaction
of a woman and two men – would-be doctor,
poet and bridge-builder – in Leningrad in
1942, at the time of post-war reconstruction
(1946) and post-Stalin (1959) in the same
Leningrad flat. Though the development of
their romantic relationships is somewhat predictable it is the most tightly written of his
plays.

Try these:
▷Hugh Whitemore's *The Best of Friends*
for an affectionate look at English friend-
ships over a long time span; ▷Robert
Holman's *Today* for contrasting views of
English idealism pre- and post-war;
▷Barry Collins' *The Strongest Man in the
World* for a personal drama set ostensibly
in the Soviet community; Peter Arnott's
White Rose, an elegant, somewhat
Brechtian play about a female Russian
fighter pilot; ▷Chekhov and ▷Brecht for
contrast.

ARCHER, Robyn   [1948–]
Australian writer, singer, cabaret performer

Plays in the UK include:
The Pack of Women (1981), *A Star is Torn*
(with Rodney Fisher; 1982), *Cut and
Thrust* (1986), *The Colony Comes a Cropper*

(being a new Act II added on to the one-act *The Colony* by Marivaux; for Monstrous Regiment; 1990)

Archer is best known to theatre audiences in Britain for her cabaret shows (both presented at the Drill Hall in London), and most of all for her success with the one-woman show *A Star is Torn*. Originally premiered in Australia in 1979, this musical compilation of legendary torch-song singers was intended as an antidote to the usual treatment of – and apparently insatiable appetite for – recycling the tragic stories of female stars (recent subjects for musicals include Jean Seberg and Billie Holiday). Archer's approach to the lives of such as Edith Piaf, Judy Garland, Janis Joplin and Billie Holliday was to reassess them as talented women, victimised as much for stepping outside the prescribed boundaries of their sex as by their own 'self-destructive' impulses. Critics were divided as to how far Archer was successful in this, but all agreed that it confirmed her amazing musical range and versatility. By contrast, *A Pack of Women* and *Cut and Thrust* closely followed the format of Brecht and the political cabarets of Berlin in the 1930s, mixing prose, poetry, song and outspoken political comment with varying degrees of success. Her attempt to wed some of that outspokenness and humour into a dramatic context, with a contemporary second act for ▷Marivaux's one-act play *The Colony*, didn't quite live up to expectations. Full of clever *bon mots* and sexually subversive, it tailed off rather more into a whimper than a bang.

She has created nearly a dozen major stage-shows, operas and cabarets (she is also the author of several children's books) and her recordings of songs by Brecht, Weill and Eisler are now regarded as classics. As a songwriter, her lyrics at their best satirise domestic and public sexism with uncompromising, cheeky *joie de vivre*. But her concerns are global, and the art of the political cabaret, as she says, is not just the short 30-second or 2-minute item but the way they are placed, 'enabling one piece to inform and illuminate what goes before and after it'.

Try these:
▷Pam Gems' *Piaf* for contrast; ▷Marivaux's *The Colony* for the original; ▷Brecht for political cabaret; ▷Christopher Hampton's *Tales from Hollywood* and Nigel Gearing's *Berlin Days, Hollywood*

Nights for other images of Brecht and his librettist, Hanns Eisler; see also ▷Cabaret. See *Lady Day at Emerson's Bar and Grill* by Lanie Robertson for conventional but commercially successful treatment of Billy Holliday.

ARDEN, John   [1930–]

English dramatist and collaborator with ▷Margaretta D'Arcy

Plays by John Arden include:
All Fall Down (1955), *The Waters of Babylon* (1957), *Live Like Pigs* (1958), *Serjeant Musgrave's Dance* (1959), *The Happy Haven* (1960), *The Business of Good Government* (1960), *Ironhand* (1963), *The Workhouse Donkey* (1964), *Armstrong's Last Goodnight* (1964), *Ars Longa, Vita Brevis* (1965), *Left Handed Liberty* (1965), *The Royal Pardon or, The Soldier Who Became an Actor* (1966), *The True History of Squire Jonathan and His Unfortunate Treasure* (1968), *The Hero Rises Up* (1968), *Harold Muggins is a Martyr* (1968), *The Ballygombeen Bequest* (1972), *The Island of the Mighty* (1972), *The Non-Stop Connolly Show* (1975).

Plays written in collaboration with ▷Margaretta D'Arcy:
The Happy Haven (1960), *Ars Longa, Vita Brevis* (1965), *The Royal Pardon or, The Soldier Who Became an Actor* (1966), *The Hero Rises Up* (1968), *Harold Muggins is a Martyr* (1968), *The Ballygombeen Bequest* (1972), *The Island of the Mighty* (1972)

For plays written by ▷Margaretta D'Arcy with John Arden see her entry.

Barnsley born, a student of architecture and, in his own words, 'a product of English public schools and three years as a conscript in Scotland', Arden began writing plays at university. Considered one of the most influential political playwrights of his generation, Arden's output has been indelibly influenced by his meeting with ▷Margaretta D'Arcy in 1955.

Most of Arden's major stage plays appeared in a ten-year period from the late 1950s to the late 1960s, ceasing abruptly after a famous if painful controversy over the RSC's handling of *The Island of the Mighty*, when Arden declared he would never write again for the stage. Instead both his and to some extent D'Arcy's recent work has been more or less devoted to radio, culminating in *Whose is the Kingdom?*, the 1988 nine-part BBC radio series on early Christianity, a theme which has run through several of his plays. Always a moralist, Arden's dissenting voice has increasingly swung away from the earlier anarchic detachment where there are no heroes (even the so-called pacifism of *Serjeant Musgrave's Dance* is hotly disputed by some commentators, who feel it is difficult to decide which side Arden's sympathies are on), through political activism to revolutionary socialism by the late 1970s. Others, however, argue that the seeds of Arden the revolutionary were implicit from the beginning, particularly in the fact that the plays were usually sparked off by historical and contemporary political events. *Armstrong's Last Goodnight*, for example, though set in 16th-century Scotland, was inspired by the Congo War and intended as an analagous, moral parable on the subject of violence. Written in Lowland verse, it emerged as a rumbustious, sardonic study in *realpolitik*, opposing the urbane politician (Lindsay) with the highland rebel, Johnny Armstrong.

Arden, from the beginning, rejected naturalism and though his plays were *about* social, political and economic issues – small town corruption (*The Workhouse Donkey*), the welfare state (*Live Like Pigs*), violence and militarism (*Serjeant Musgrave's Dance*) – his use of bold, imagistic techniques – epics, parables, sometimes grotesque comedy – and the fact that they have an obvious polemical intent, inevitably led to Arden being compared with ▷Brecht, an influence he has always denied. Yet other observers, playing the influence game, detect a kinship with ▷Ben Jonson and ▷Aristophanes in such plays as *The Workhouse Donkey*. Arden/D'Arcy's work, with its increasingly anti-English, pro-Irish and community stance – *The Hero Rises Up* is an anti-heroic view of Nelson; *The Ballygombeen Bequest*, an attack on absentee landlordism in Ireland; *The Non-Stop Connolly Show*, a pro-Irish Republican epic which, according to Arden's biographer, Albert Hunt, should be regarded as a masterpiece – has come under increasing censorship. To the overall impoverishment of British theatre, their work remains outside the mainstream.

Serjeant Musgrave's Dance

Set in a bleak mining town in northern England in the 1880s, a small group of soldiers invade a village ostensibly on a recruiting drive. But the men are deserters, and their leader, Serjeant Musgrave, who has become fanatically anti-war, is as terrifying in his religious zeal as the evil against which he inveighs: he demands the death of twenty-five local townspeople to match the death of a local boy who died in a colonial war and who was the trigger, in reprisal, for the death of five men. A male-oriented play, where women are seen either as whores (sexual and dangerous) or mothers (asexual and comforting), it seems hard in retrospect to see it as anything other than a passionately pacifist, anti-imperialist play.

Try these:
▷Peter Barnes for similar epic treatments of historical subjects; ▷John Osborne's *A Patriot for Me* for another army play with echoes of male sexual fear of women (also *Look Back in Anger*); for contrasting treatment of a national hero (*The Hero Rises Up* which debunks Nelson), ▷Terence Rattigan's *Bequest to the Nation*; for scrutiny of American national figures, ▷Arthur Kopit's *Indians*; for a different handling of local small town corruption, ▷Gogol's *The Government Inspector*, ▷Peter Flannery's *Our Friends in the North*; ▷Community Theatre.

ARDREY, Robert   [1908–]
American scientist and dramatist

Plays include:
Thunder Rock (1939), *Jeb* (1946), *Shadow of Heroes* (1958)

Probably best known today for his scientific theory of 'the territorial imperative', Ardrey worked for most of his career as a dramatist. His place in the current repertory depends entirely on *Thunder Rock*, which receives occasional starry revivals – the most recent being a television vehicle for actor Charles Dance. The play, first staged at the beginning of World War II, is an atmospheric allegorical piece in which a lighthouse keeper's encounters with the spirits of shipwrecked travellers rekindle his fighting spirit. *Jeb*, an investigation of the operations of racism in the American South, was uncomfortably enough in advance of its time to be commercially unsuccessful.

Try these:
▷Pirandello's *Six Characters in Search of an Author* for its use of 'unfinished' characters; ▷David Edgar's *Maydays* deals with the Hungarian uprising which is the subject of *Shadow of Heroes*; ▷African-American Theatre; J.M. Barrie's *Mary Rose* for ghosts.

ARISTOPHANES   [c 450–385 BC]
Greek comic dramatist

Surviving plays:
The Acharnians (425 BC), *The Knights* (424 BC), *The Clouds* (423 BC), *The Wasps* (422 BC), *Peace* (421 BC), *The Birds* (414 BC), *Lysistrata* (411 BC), *The Thesmophoriazousae* (410 BC; sometimes called *Women at the Festival* or *The Poet and the Women* or *Women at the Thesmophoria*), *The Frogs* (405 BC), *Ecclesiazousae* (392 BC; sometimes called *Women in Parliament*), *Plutus* (388 BC; also called *Wealth*).

Aristophanes' plays, the only surviving representatives of Greek Old Comedy, are infrequently performed in the contemporary professional theatre, probably because their blend of topical satire, punning and lyricism poses major difficulties for translators, while the need for a chorus poses economic difficulties. *Lysistrata* has attracted a number of productions because of its concentration on sexual politics, although it is far from a feminist play. When it is produced, the warring Athenians and Spartans are often translated into the American Civil War period or presented as English and Scots. The most interesting modern adaptation is Stephen Sondheim's and Burt Shevelove's 1974 musical version of *The Frogs*, staged originally in a swimming pool at Yale University with a cast including ▷Christopher Durang, Meryl Streep and Sigourney Weaver. In this adaptation ▷Shaw and ▷Shakespeare replace Aeschylus and Euripides. It was given its European premiere by an amateur cast in London in 1990.

Try these:
▷Aeschylus, ▷Euripides, ▷Sophocles for Greek tragic drama; Plautus and Terence for Roman comedy; Theatre Workshop's *Oh What a Lovely War* for a play blending popular forms; ▷Community Theatre.

ARRABAL, Fernando   [1932–]
Spanish dramatist born in Spanish Morocco, who writes in French

Plays include:
Les Deux Bourreaux (*The Two Executioners*; 1958), *Le Cimetière des Voitures* (*The Vehicle Graveyard*; 1964), *Fando et Lis* (*Fando and Lis*; 1964), *L'Architecte et l'Empereur d'Assyrie* (*The Architect and the Emperor of Assyria*; 1967), *Et ils Passerent des Menottes aux Fleurs* (*And They Put Handcuffs on the Flowers*; 1969)

Arrabal's voluminous output of plays (which has continued into the 1990s) reflects his nightmarish childhood, during which his father mysteriously disappeared from prison at the beginning of the Spanish Civil War and his mother tried to behave as though his father had never existed. Unresolved difficulties over this, plus a strict Spanish Catholic upbringing, have led to a number of sado-masochistic plays filled with disturbing images of torture, suffering, blasphemy and eroticism, often involving members of the same family, at which one is horrified to find oneself laughing. Arrabal's Théâtre Panique takes the Theatre of Cruelty label over-literally! Directors with a strong visual sense, such as Victor García and ▷Charles Marowitz, have responded with enthusiasm to these dramatisations of private fantasies. García directed *The Architect and the Emperor of Assyria* (translated by Jean-Norman Benedetti) for the ▷National Theatre in 1971; it was played with some brio by Jim Dale and Anthony Hopkins as two men stranded on a desert island, playing a series of games, exchanging roles of master and slave, mother and child, victim and executioner, until finally one eats the other. The play owes something to ▷Artaud and ▷Beckett, but also to Lewis Carroll, whom Arrabal greatly admires.

Try these:
▷Artaud, with whom his name was often associated in the 1960s; ▷Pirandello for role-swapping; ▷Genet for role-playing; ▷Derek Walcott's *Pantomime* is a variation on the master/slave theme.

ARTAUD, Antonin   [1896–1948]
French actor, director, theorist

Works include:
Jet de Sang (*Jet of Blood*, play; 1925), *La Coquille et le Clergyman* (*The Seashell and the Clergyman*, filmscript; 1927), *Les Cenci* (*The Cenci*; 1935), *Le Théâtre et son Double* (The Theatre and its Double; 1938 incorporating his *First* and *Second Manifestos of the Theatre of Cruelty*; 1931–35)

It is possible, but misleading, to regard Artaud as the archetypal mad genius. Badly affected by meningitis when young, he spent much of his life struggling against an addiction to drugs, and much of the rest in lunatic asylums. He is also one of the most important and seminal theatrical thinkers of the century, with a considerable (but disputed) influence on a wide variety of authors and especially directors. He was, incidentally, a very powerful actor (he can be seen to mesmeric effect as a monk in Dreyer's film *La Passion de Jeanne d'Arc*, and as Marat in Abel Gance's *Napoléon*); he was expelled from André Breton's Surrealist movement for being inadequately committed to Communism; his actual stage output is small, though he mounted four productions with the Théâtre Alfred Jarry, 1927–9, including Vitrac's *Victor* and ▷Strindberg's *The Dream Play*, and in 1935 he put on his own version of *The Cenci* at the Folies Wagram, with little success. He also wrote the filmscript for the Surrealist film *La Coquille et le Clergyman*.

His principal theoretical work, *Le Théâtre et son Double*, influenced by his partial understanding of performances of Cambodian and Balinese dance, recommended a 'total theatre' that would use sound, light, gesture, and visual image rather than relying on the written or even the spoken word, to disturb fundamentally the imagination and subconscious of audience and actors alike; it has in different ways influenced Barrault, ▷Peter Brook, ▷Charles Marowitz, Grotowski, ▷Adamov, ▷Arrabal, ▷Genet, Pip Simmons, Julian Beck, and the Open Theatre – partly because it is full of memorable but somewhat gnomic pronouncements which one can interpret to suit one's own inclinations (eg 'We are not free, and the sky can still fall on our heads; and the theatre exists to remind us of this fact').

Artaud's life is sometimes treated as myth (as with ▷Dylan Thomas and Marie Lloyd) and used as matter for plays, such as ▷Marowitz's *Artaud at Rodez* and *The Asylum of Antonin Artaud*, by Mike Downey and Dennis Akers (1986), which dwelt on the drug-induced madness rather than the 'illuminated genius' (▷Peter Brook's phrase).

Jet of Blood
The text is less than four pages long, but manages to touch on many obsessions – Artaud's and our own. It would be very un-Artaudian to describe the plot, but the following stage directions give the flavour:

'The Whore bites God's wrist. An immense jet of blood shoots across the stage, and we can see the Priest making the sign of the cross during a flash of lightning that lasts longer than the others.'

'An army of scorpions comes out from under the Nurse's dress and swarms over her sex, which swells up and bursts, becoming glassy and shining like the sun. The Young Man and the Whore flee.'

Nonetheless, it was included in the ▷Peter Brook ▷Charles Marowitz Theatre of Cruelty season at LAMDA in 1964, and student groups attempt it from time to time.

Try these:
▷Peter Weiss for a dramatist and La Mama for a group influenced by Artaud's ideas; ▷Performance Art for attempts to realise the idea of total theatre; ▷Claudel for impossible stage directions (*The Satin Slipper*, etc); ▷Expressionism for a non-illusionistic approach to theatre.

ASIAN THEATRE IN BRITAIN
Asian theatre in Britain is like an iceberg – while relatively few groups are visible from the white mainstream, a significant amount goes on in the privacy of separate language groups. At the last public gathering – for the Alternative Festival of India in 1982 – work on display came from groups working in Malayalam, Tamil, Bengali, Hindi/Urdu, Punjabi, Gujarati and English, with another in the wings in Marathi. Although it is hard to be categorical across the board, there have been noises of disquiet from some areas of the movement: Gujarati theatre (a busy movement when it was imported from East Africa) has questioned its own tendency to turn back to India for its material – a fact, it has been suggested, that connects with the decline in interest among the young born or largely brought up in Britain.

Secondly it should be realised that much of what is really 'Asian theatre' goes, in Britain, by another name. The great Indian source-book of performance, the second-century Bharata Natya Shastra, does not make the kinds of distinction between theatre, mime and dance that the West does. Indian dancers are accomplished mime artists: Pushkala Gopal and Unnikrishnan, for instance, took ▷Shakespeare's *The Taming of the Shrew* in 1990 and reinterpreted it through Indian dance techniques and cross-references to Indian customs.

The English language theatre, recognised by Western eyes as bona fide 'theatre', is a recent growth with few locally derived works to its name. Dilip Hiro's *To Anchor a Cloud*, a sumptuous costume drama in the mid-1950s, was one of few to give the increasing body of Asian actors and actresses a vehicle. ▷Hanif Kureishi's *Outskirts* and *Borderline* were the first major works to base themselves firmly in the life of British Asians today and they share, with other developments in the field, highly political roots. His characters exist in a 1980s limbo, without a history and with a future that has to be determined by their own fighting qualities.

Tara Arts Group, started in 1977 in reaction to the racial murder of Gurdip Singh Chaggar, was formed by young Asians from different community backgrounds. Its early devised plays were crisply agit-prop treatments of racism at school (*Fuse*, 1978) and hypocrisy at home (*Playing with Fire*), its themes deriving directly from the realities of the Asian experience and covering issues like old age and mental disturbance. Increasingly Tara has come to see form as vital and has set out to create a distinctive style that takes in traditional Indian dramaturgy, rejects the Western watertight compartments, and creates a fusion between Indian classics (like *The Little Clay Cart*) and modern concerns. This reached a particularly successful point with *Tartuffe* in 1990. Strictly speaking, this was a production of the ▷National Theatre, under its educational programme. However, Tara's artistic director, Jatinder Verma – the lynchpin of the group since its start – used his invitation to direct to stage an essentially Tara production, using Tara performers and the house style, at its best in this version of the ▷Molière classic. Set in the court of the 17th-century Mughal emperor Aurangzeb, *Tartuffe* combined music and dance with the text. Anjana Batra's choreography incorporated the spirit of North Indian Kathak court dance: she encouraged the cast to work within the idiom of the dance rather than use it as decoration.

Other professional developments have been slow to take off. The Hounslow Asian Co-operative (HAC) has held its ground, albeit tenuously. The British Asian Theatre, active in the 1970s and 1980s, has turned its attention more to film and video. The Asian Theatre Co-operative, which started off flamboyantly in the 1980s with plays by Farrukh Dhondy and H.O. Nazareth, has fallen silent. However, signs exist of new developments. The dual-language plays – in English and Gujarati – of Jyoti Patel and Jezz Simons (*Prem, Kirti, Sona and Ba* and *Subahoshaan*) have indicated the strengths of a fusion of language and attitudes. Multilingualism also formed the basis of another venture, Tamasha Theatre, brainchild of Sudha Bhuchar and Kristine Landon Smith. Its first production in 1989 – an adaptation of Mulk Raj Anand's classic novel *Untouchable* – was done in both English and Hindi versions. Set in an Indian village, it handled well a broad panorama of characters, and a moral concerning prejudice that is unfortunately as relevant today as it was when the novel was first published in 1934.

Try these:
For more plays reflecting experiences of being British and Asian, see ▷Karim Alrawi, ▷Harwant Bains and Farrukh Dhondy; see also ▷Community Theatre; ▷Peter Brook's production of the Mahabharata has popularised an Indian classic for Western audiences.

AUDEN, W.H.
(Wystan Hugh)   [1907–72]
British poet, dramatist and critic

ISHERWOOD, Christopher
(William Bradshaw)   [1904–86]
British novelist, dramatist and screenwriter

Joint plays include:
The Dog Beneath the Skin; or, Where is Francis? (1936), *The Ascent of F6* (1937), *On the Frontier* (1938).

Although both produced theatre work independently, their best known plays are the jointly written verse dramas of the 1930s. *I Am a Camera* and the musical *Cabaret* are

Nizwar Karanj as Tartuffe in Jatinder Verma's highly successful transposition of Molière's *Tartuffe* to Moghul India. Royal National Theatre Mobile production, 1989–91

based on Isherwood's Berlin stories but are not his dramatisations.

Left-wing intellectuals from elitist Oxbridge backgrounds, Auden and Isherwood were politicised by the Depression, the Spanish Civil War and by living in Germany. All their joint work, and Auden's *Dance of Death*, set out to attack capitalist power and bourgeois values; *Ascent of F6*, with its protagonist clearly modelled on T.E. Lawrence, added elements of mysticism as well. Their style is not naturalistic and suggests strong Brechtian influence. Despite the evident homosexual content in some of both men's other work, these verse dramas do not explore such themes. The Dog Beneath the Skin is a morality in verse which makes use of a chorus, song and dance, masks, cabaret, and a Master of Ceremonies to present the life of a man-sized dog as it passes from owner to owner through a society peopled with caricatures – a general, financier, churchman, etc. Savagely satirical in its time, it may seem naive when set against contemporary polemics.

Try these:
▷Brecht, who compared these plays with ▷Aristophanes, for his influence; for other modern verse drama, ▷T.S. Eliot, ▷Christopher Fry, Ronald Duncan; for socialist plays in the epic tradition, ▷Edward Bond, ▷David Edgar, ▷Howard Brenton, ▷Caryl Churchill, Henry Livings; also ▷Terry Johnson's underrated *Cries from the Mammal House* for a disenchanted view of the contemporary male using an animal metaphor; ▷Alfred Jarry for a similarly eclectic dramaturgy.

AYCKBOURN, Alan   [1939–   ]
British dramatist/director

Plays include:
Mr Whatnot (1963), *Relatively Speaking* (1967), *How the Other Half Loves* (1969), *Time and Time Again* (1972), *Absurd Person Singular* (1972), *The Norman Conquests* (comprising: *Table Manners, Round and Round the Garden, Living Together*; 1973), *Absent Friends* (1974), *Confusions* (1974), *Bedroom Farce* (1975), *Just Between Ourselves* (1976), *Joking Apart* (1979), *Ten Times Table* (1977), *Sisterly Feelings* (1979), *Taking Steps* (1980), *Suburban Strains*

(1981), *Season's Greetings* (1982), *Way Upstream* (1982), *It Could Be Any of Us* (1982), *Making Tracks* (1983), *Intimate Exchanges* (1984), *A Chorus of Disapproval* (1985), *Woman in Mind* (1985), *A Small Family Business* (1987), *Henceforward* (1987), *Man of the Moment* (1988), *Invisible Friends* (1991), *Wildest Dreams* (1991)

Ayckbourn is now one of Britain's most commercially successful playwrights, with regular West End and repertory productions, frequent televisations, and commissions both as writer and director. His work has also become a staple for resident and community theatres in the US. He has written over thirty plays to date, but says of himself that he is a 'director who writes, rather than a writer who directs'.

After starting his theatrical career as an actor and stage-manager with Donald Wolfit's company, he moved to Stephen Joseph's Studio Theatre Company in the early 1960s, where he began directing and writing with Joseph's encouragement. Many of his most successful plays began at Scarborough where, as Artistic Director of the Library Theatre, he writes a new play annually for their repertory season. Many of these have transferred to London, but he continues to base his work in Scarborough.

A superb theatrical craftsman, his plays are often constructed around a tour de force of staging: *The Norman Conquests* is a trilogy of plays, each of which stands on its own, and presents the same events from the garden, sitting room and dining room; *How the Other Half Loves*, *Absurd Person Singular* and *Bedroom Farce* each present more than one household on stage simultaneously; *Way Upstream* launched a riverboat onto the ▷National Theatre stage; *Sisterly Feelings* offers alternative versions for the central section of the play. His plays have their roots in the tradition of farce rather than in experimental theatre, an allegiance confirmed by the staging of *Intimate Exchanges* by Ray Cooney's Theatre of Comedy company. He has, however, stretched the boundaries of comedy and farce as his work has developed; increasingly, the comings and goings of married couples are injected with a note of black comedy, and social groups are fraught with suggestions of the darker arenas of human interchange. The social niceties of the tea party in *Absent Friends* are disrupted by the inability of the participants to cope with the idea of death, and in *Just Between Ourselves* and *Woman in Mind*, what begins as the familiar comic theme of a sterile marriage transforms into tragedy as the wife descends into catatonia and breakdown. One (male) critic has hailed Ayckbourn as the best contemporary feminist playwright for *Woman in Mind*; while this is clearly arguable, Ayckbourn is one of the theatre's sharpest observers of contemporary suburban values. Ayckbourn's success might be accounted for in that his work is challenging, but within strict limits; his subject matter has tended to be middle-class values and lifestyle under threat (but not too much), while his dramatic form plays with theatrical convention but is always firmly rooted in the familiar structures of farce and West End comedy.

Bedroom Farce

Bedroom Farce, the first of Ayckbourn's plays to be produced at the ▷National Theatre, deals with simultaneous stories, presenting four couples whose dramas interweave around the housewarming party of Malcolm and Kate. Three of the households are on stage, and the action moves from bedroom to bedroom; sometimes all three are presented at once. The potential for farce is explored in the shifts in the occupancy of the bedrooms, but the bedroom of one couple, whose relationship is on the verge of collapse, is a significant absence in the play – an absence which constructs an awareness of the bleakness that underlies the comedy.

Try these:
Brian Rix, ▷Ray Cooney as two of the most celebrated exponents of contemporary farce, the conventions of which Ayckbourn liberally exploits; ▷Michael Frayn's *Noises Off* as one of the funniest and cleverest examples of theatrical sleight-of-hand; ▷Feydeau is a French nineteenth-century equivalent, and perhaps some of ▷Labiche; ▷De Filippo is a European equivalent; ▷Tom Stoppard as another juggler of theatrical conventions; ▷Neil Simon as the nearest American equivalent.

b

BABE, Thomas [1941–]
American dramatist

Plays include:
Kid Champion (1974), *Mojo Candy* (1975), *Rebel Women* (1976), *Billy Irish* (1977), *Great Solo Town* (1977), *A Prayer For My Daughter* (1977), *Fathers and Sons* (1978), *Taken in Marriage* (1979), *Salt Lake City Skyline* (1980), *Kathleen* (1980), *Buried Inside Extra* (1983), *Planet Fires* (1984), *Demon Wine* (1987), *A Hero of Our Time* (1988)

Buffalo-born and Harvard-educated, and one of America's toughest, most independent playwrights, Babe has yet to achieve the recognition he deserves. Associated with Joe Papp's Public Theatre off-Broadway, where many of his plays began, he is interested both in revisionist treatments of history (*Fathers and Sons* and *Salt Lake City Skyline* are about Wild Bill Hickok and union organiser Joe Hill, respectively) and in closer-to-home, more domestic themes. In *A Prayer For My Daughter*, arguably his best-known work, a Sergeant Kelly ignores the suicidal telephone calls of his own daughter to concentrate on the young murder suspect, Jimmy, whom he starts treating as a kind of aberrant 'daughter'. *Taken in Marriage*, which brings a quintet of women together in a New Hampshire church hall to attend a marriage rehearsal fraught with domestic volatility, and *Buried Inside Extra*, a play about journalists which inaugurated the Royal Court's exchange with the Public, are best seen as vehicles for actors, who tend to rip into Babe's roles with abandon. *Planet Fires* was premiered at the GeVa Theatre in Rochester, New York, directed by John Henry Davis. That production moved to the Mark Taper Forum in Los Angeles in 1986.

Try these:
▷Arthur Kopit's *Indians* and much of ▷Sam Shepard and ▷Romulus Linney for iconoclastic views both of history and of the American West; ▷Hecht and McArthur's *The Front Page*, Stephen Wakelam's *Deadlines,* and ▷David Hare and ▷Howard Brenton's *Pravda* for alternative dramatic treatments of journalism.

BAGNOLD, Enid
(Lady Roderick Jones) [1884–1981]
British novelist and dramatist

Plays include:
The Chalk Garden (1955)

Author of *National Velvet* (filmed in 1944 with Elizabeth Taylor) and numerous other successful novels, *The Chalk Garden* was the most successful of her original plays. A typical 'Haymarket play' of the 1950s, when the Theatre Royal was the showcase for star-studded (in this case Edith Evans and Peggy Ashcroft) middle-class theatre with its heart in the right place, it is well tailored, well characterised and with only sufficient undermining of entrenched attitudes to make the audience feel already more enlightened than the characters, as the governess, who brings life to the household and garden of eccentric Mrs St Maugham, is exposed as a convicted murderess.

Try these:
▷N.C. Hunter, ▷Dodie Smith, ▷William Douglas Home for plays of a similar type; ▷Lillian Hellman's *The Children's Hour* for another play of domestic revelation; also ▷Ibsen for plays of family revelation.

BAINS, Harwant [1963–]
British dramatist

Plays include:
The Fighting Kite (1987), *Blood* (1989)

Bains has been hailed as a possible successor to ▷Hanif Kureishi, much to his irritation ('Just because I've got a brown face and write plays . . .'). It's hard, though, to avoid the comparison. Southall-based, and son of Indian parents, Bains takes up some of the same issues the young Kureishi and, to some extent, ▷Karim Alrawi explored in the early 1980s: racial violence and cultural identity. Bains' first play, *The Fighting Kite*, a sprawling, episodic account of a racial attack in Southall had its share of stereotyped cut-outs of National Front skinheads but handled the emotional response of its young, second-generation British Asians to their sense of alienation (neither 'English' nor accepted back on the Indian subcontinent) with subtlety and sensitivity. His second play, *Blood*, a violent political thriller, received harsh treatment at the hands of some critics who found the language and plot bordering on the crudely sensational. But others applauded the ambitious scope of the play which tried to chart the legacy of India's bloody Partition of 1947 through the fate of two contrasting young Punjabi Sikh brothers who settle in Britain.

Try these:
▷Kureishi's *Borderline* and *Outskirts* for an earlier handling of racial violence; ▷Alrawi's *A Colder Climate* for another view of East End racial tension; ▷David Edgar's *Destiny* for a bold attempt to pinpoint the rise of post-war British fascism; Farrukh Dhondy's *Vigilantes* offered an exploration of the problems of cultural identity within the first generation of the British Bangladeshi community. For Afro-Caribbean equivalents ▷Edgar White's *The Nine Night*, ▷Caryl Phillips' *Strange Fruit*; for a female view of being young, black and British ee ▷Jackie Rudet's *Money to Live*. For a view of linkage between violence, history and dehumanisation, ee ▷Peter Flannery's Jewish equivalent in *Singer*; ▷Behan's *The Hostage* and many plays on prison treatment have made a similar observation; for a contrasting view, ▷Martin Sherman's *Bent*; ▷African-American Theatre.

James Baldwin's theatrical reputation rests on his two early plays, both of which struck a lasting chord at their New York debuts, and one of which (*The Amen Corner*) made London history in March 1987 as the first-ever all-black non-musical British production to open in the West End (where, sadly, it losts its £150,000 investment). In *Blues For Mr Charlie*, Baldwin told an unforgettable tale of racial poison based on a true story – a white jury's acquittal, in 1955, of two white men who murdered black Chicagoan, Emmett Till, in Mississippi. In *The Amen Corner*, which was performed briefly at Howard University in 1955, and opened on Broadway in 1965, Baldwin drew on his own background as the son of a Harlem minister to depict the crumbling domestic life and fading religiosity of Sister Margaret Alexander, the censorious pastor of a 'storefront' Harlem church. An avowed homosexual, perhaps best-known for his novels, the expatriate Baldwin, who spent much of his later life in France, was a vociferous champion of civil liberties and of both sexual and racial equality. Interestingly, however, in an interview before his death, he played down the importance of race in his plays, saying with customary wryness: '*The Amen Corner* is not about black people or white people. It's about the people in the play.'

Try these:
▷Amiri Baraka for a raised temperature level; in the 1980s ▷George C. Wolfe (*The Colored Museum* takes satiric aim at Baldwin's dramatic style); the plays of ▷Ed Bullins, and Louis Peterson's *Take a Giant Step*; ▷August Wilson for detonating treatments of racism, especially *Ma Rainey's Black Bottom*; ▷Lorraine Hansberry's *A Raisin in the Sun* for an early view of America's black community confronting racism; Kalamu Ya Salaam's *Black Love Song No 1* for another contemporary satirical swipe at American black stereotypes, produced under the white yoke.

BALDWIN, James   [1924–87]
American dramatist

Plays include:
Blues For Mr Charlie (1964), *The Amen Corner* (1965), *A Deed From the King of Spain* (1974)

BARAKA, Amiri (Leroi Jones)
American dramatist   [1934–]

Plays include:
A Good Girl is Hard to Fine (1958), *Dante* . (1961), *Dutchman* (1964), *The Baptism* (1964), *The Slave* (1964), *The Toilet* (1964),

J-E-L-L-O (1965), *Experimental Death Unit No 1* (1965), *A Black Mass* (1966), *Slave Ship: A Historical Pageant* (1967), *Madheart* (1967), *Arm Yrself or Harm Yourself!* (1967), *Great Goodness of Life (A Coon Show)* (1967), *Home on the Range* (1968), *Resurrection in Life* (1969), *Junkies Are Full of (SHH . . .)* (1970), *Bloodrites* (1970), *A Recent Killing* (1973), *The New Ark's a Moverin'* (1974), *Sidnee Poet Heroical or If in Danger of Sun, the Kid Poet Heroical* (1975), *S-1* (1976), *The Motion of History* (1977), *What Was the Relationship of the Lone Ranger to the Means of Production?* (1979), *At the Dim' Cracker Party Convention* (1980), *Boy & Tarzan Appear in a Clearing* (1981), *Money* (1982), *Primitive World* (1984), *The Life and Life of Bumpy Johnson* (book for the musical; 1990)

Baraka's plays seek to engage the black community by confronting it with an image of its own acquiescence or by elaborating myths of a heroic past or a revolutionary future. In his manifesto, *The Revolutionary Theatre*, Baraka proclaimed that theatre 'should force change; it should be change.' *The Dutchman*, *The Slave*, and *The Toilet* (set in a high-school toilet, a tapestry of festering bigotry brought to the boil) mark the beginning of the black revolutionary theatre of the 1960s. *Slave Ship* traces the black experience from Africa to America. Using a series of vignettes, the play shows the murderous conditions of the Middle Passage, the brutalisation of blacks by both blacks and whites, and attempts to organise black revolts. Baraka has since moved away from an exclusively black nationalist position to embrace a form of Marxism. *Boy and Tarzan* shifts focus by showing present-day African leaders as greedy and corrupt. Their oppressive behaviour has been' learned from white colonists. Currently, Baraka is working on a play incorporateing jazz music by Hal Roach that explores the historical relationship between gangsters and black entertainers in such places as Harlem's Cotton Club.

The Dutchman

Dutchman is the best received of Baraka's work. Clay, a well-dressed, black intellectual is accosted on a subway train by Lulu, a white bitch goddess. When her advances are politely rebuffed, she verbally emasculates her victim and ridicules his white middle-class dress and demeanour. Clay articulately counters her racial stereotyping. He describes the music of a Bessie Smith or a Charlie Parker as the expressions of neurotics who suppress their rage 'to keep from being sane.' In a sense Clay in his three-button suit proclaims his own spiritual death, a fact which does not escape Lulu, who moves rapidly in for the kill with a drawn switchblade. She quickly disposes of Clay's dead body before approaching another young black man boarding the train. Since *Dutchman*, there have been more black plays written and produced than in the previous 130 years of American black theatre history.

Try these:
▷Lorca and ▷Strindberg (especially *Miss Julie*) for often explosive theatrical rituals; ▷Miguel Pinero's *Short Eyes* and ▷David Rabe's *Streamers* as 1970s equivalents to *The Toilet*, in which constricted environments heighten racial tension; ▷George C. Wolfe's *The Colored Museum*, Kalamu Ya Salaam's *Black Love Song No 1* and ▷Ntozake Shange's *Spell No 7* for equivalent rage, 1980s-style; ▷August Wilson, ▷Richard Wesley, ▷Samm-Art Williams for somewhat gentler chronicles of racism and the black experience; for British equivalents, ▷Barry Reckord; ▷Mustapha Matura, ▷Caryl Phillips; Gabriel Gbadamosi's *No Blacks, No Irish* shows racism and prejudice in 1950s England; Ed Bullins and ▷Adrienne Kennedy as other African-American playwrights emerging in the 1960s.

BARKER, Howard   [1946–]
British dramatist

Plays include:
Cheek (1970), *No One Was Saved* (1970), *Alpha Alpha* (1972), *Claw* (1975), *Stripwell* (1975), *That Good Between Us* (1977), *Fair Slaughter* (1977), *The Hang of the Gaol* (1978), *The Love of a Good Man* (1978), *The Loud Boy's Life* (1980), *No End of Blame* (1981), *The Poor Man's Friend* (1982), *Victory* (1983), *A Passion in Six Days* (1983), *Crimes in Hot Countries* (1983), *The Power of the Dog* (1984), *Scenes from an Execution* (radio, 1984; staged, 1989), *The Castle* (1985), *Downchild* (1985), *Women Beware Women* (reworking of ▷Middleton's play; 1986), *The Possibilities* (1988), *The Last Supper* (1988), *The Bite of the Night* (1988), *Seven Lears* (1989)

One of a generation of British dramatists deeply concerned with political and social issues, Barker has never received the degree of critical acclaim given to some of his contemporaries, probably because his interest in the psychopathology of capitalism and patriarchy leads him to deal in much of his work with the grotesque and the distorted, often in highly scatalogical language. At his best Barker is a brilliant and provocative writer; at his worst he can be numbingly verbose. His plays firmly eschew naturalism in favour of an incisive and theatrically inventive cartoon-like style which juxtaposes private desires with public postures and aims for psychological and sociopolitical truth rather than the texture of everyday life. He shares with ▷John Gay and ▷Brecht a crucial perception of the apparent identity of interest between criminal and politician and the inherent corruptions of capitalism. The 'criminal' strand in his work is well represented by, for example, *Alpha Alpha* (a study of two brother patterned on the Kray twins), *Claw* (in which the hero acts as procurer for the Home Secretary) and *Stripwell*, with its judge faced both with the criminal activities of his son and a man he sentenced returning for revenge.

Barker is a history graduate and many of his plays also pursue an interest in historical moments and their lessons for the present. *Victory*, subtitled punningly 'Choices in Reaction', a fine example of this second strand, deals with the aftermath of the Restoration of Charles II, mixing historical and stereotypical characters in an extraordinary evocation of the collapse of the ideals of the Commonwealth. The play is notable for a brilliant explanation of the nature and contradictions of capitalism involving Charles himself, a banker called Hambro, Nell Gwynne, the skull of the parliamentarian Bradshaw, and a large store of gold.

A third significant strand is concerned with specifically Labour party themes, as in *The Loud Boy's Life*, *Downchild* and *A Passion in Six Days* (a dramatic cantata about a Labour Party conference).

The Castle

The Castle is an extraordinary meditation on issues of gender, power, rational and emotional knowledge, war and peace, in which a returning Crusader confronts the peaceful female community established by his wife in his absence. The battle lines, both medieval and contemporary, are drawn between creativity and destruction in confrontations and dialogue that are brilliantly imagined and draw to the full on Barker's ability to write with a poetic density of language, comic as well as tragic, which uses everyday idiom as much as architectural imagery to create an extraordinarily flexible language. In Nick Hamm's original ▷RSC production there were superb performances from Penny Downie as the fecund matriarch, Harriet Walter as her lesbian lover, Ian McDiarmid as the returning Crusader and Paul Freeman as his castle building architect.

Try these:

▷Howard Brenton shares many of Barker's preoccupations and much of his approach to writing for the theatre; ▷David Edgar has also tackled similar issues, particularly in *Destiny* (fascism and Labour reactions to it) and *Maydays* (opposition to totalitarian impulses); ▷Peter Flannery has looked at corruption and the Labour party in *Our Friends in the North*; ▷Ibsen's *The Master Builder* also uses architecture metaphorically; ▷Peter Barnes uses an inventive rhetorical style reminiscent of Barker, particularly in *Leonardo's Last Supper*; ▷Timberlake Wertenbaker's *The Grace of Mary Traverse* explores capitalism and the present through the past; ▷Pam Gems, ▷Caryl Churchill, ▷Deborah Levy and ▷Aphra Behn have all explored the relationships of gender and power to capitalism.

BARNES, Peter   [1931–]
British dramatist

Plays include:
The Time of the Barracudas (1963), *Sclerosis* (1965), *The Ruling Class* (1968), *Leonardo's Last Supper* (1969), *Lulu* (from ▷Wedekind; 1970), *The Bewitched* (1974), *Frontiers of Farce* (adaptations from ▷Feydeau and ▷Wedekind; 1976), *Noonday Demons* (1977), *Laughter* (1978), *Red Noses* (1985), *Sunsets and Glories* (1990)

Much of Barnes' theatre work successfully achieves the aim he stated in the published text of *The Ruling Class*, 'to create by means of soliloquy, rhetoric, formalised ritual, slapstick, song and dances, a comic theatre of contrasting moods and opposites, where everything is simultaneously tragic and ridiculous'. Barnes generally confronts wider political issues, emulating the broad scale, richness of character and theatricality of ▷Ben Jonson, though eschewing his values. He has also 'adapted' a number of Jacobean plays, including Jonson's *The Alchemist*, *The Silent Woman*, *Bartholomew Fair*, *Eastward Ho* and *The Devil is an Ass* (in which nearly half of the material is new). Other adaptations include ▷Feydeau farces; *Laughter* opens with a custard pie slammed in the face of an author and the vitality of music hall humour jostles, sometimes uncomfortably, with the harsh cruelties which Barnes depicts to make emotive attacks on the use of power by the State, the Church and big business. On its first production *The Ruling Class* was hailed as 'a pivotal play' by critic Ronald Bryden, and Harold Hobson placed it on a level with *Waiting for Godot*, *Look Back in Anger* and *The Birthday Party* but Barnes' later work has been less rapturously received. A passionate attack on Toryism, class and privilege, *The Ruling Class* presents a rampaging madman who inherits an earldom and believes he is God. It shows his return to 'sanity', confirmed when he makes a pro-hanging and pro-flogging speech to his cobwebbed fellow peers in the House of Lords. *Leonardo's Last Supper* is an imaginative debate about the value of art, set in a charnel house where da Vinci's corpse revives.

Red Noses was Barnes' first play in London for seventeen years. The ▷RSC's seven-year delay in producing it is evidence of how uncomfortable some can feel about his work. Set in France at the time of the Black Death, *Red Noses* is populated by roaming bands of guilt-ridden flagellants, red-nosed comics who confront disease with laughter and are tolerated by the Church because they keep the people cheerful. When the plague abates and their performances begin to become subversive they are ruthlessly squashed. Barnes is not a polemicist and, though the bold and epic scale of the play gives marvellous opportunities to performers, its characters' hope that 'every jest should be a small revolution' is not answered.

Much of Barnes' recent work has consisted of small-scale pieces for radio.

Try these:
▷Edward Bond, (especially *We Come to the River*); ▷Steven Berkoff for outrage; ▷Alan Bennett for satire; ▷David Hare and ▷Howard Brenton's *Pravda*, ▷Peter

Nichols' *The National Health*, and *Privates on Parade* for contemporary satires on an epic scale; ▷Nick Dear, ▷Arthur Kopit, ▷George C. Wolfe for historical debunking; ▷John Whiting's *The Devils* and ▷Robert Bolt's *A Man For All Seasons* for treatments of historical aberrations without the satire.

BARRIE, (Sir) James Matthew
British dramatist and novelist   [1860–1937]

Plays include:
Ibsen's Ghost (1891), *Walker, London* (1892), *The Professor's Love Story* (1894), *The Little Minister* (1897), *Quality Street* (1902), *The Admirable Crichton* (1902), *Peter Pan* (1904), *What Every Woman Knows* (1908), *The Twelve Pound Look* (1910), *Dear Brutus* (1917), *The Truth About the Russian Dancers* (1920), *Mary Rose* (1920), *Shall We Join the Ladies?* (1922), *The Boy David* (1936)

Barrie, born of a poor Scottish family, went South after leaving Edinburgh University. He started his career as a journalist, then struck gold with the novel of *The Little Minister* in 1891 and wrote prolifically and very successfully through the Edwardian era and beyond. Although Dorothy Tutin added an edge to the whimsical sexism in a recent West End revival of *What Every Woman Knows*, *Mary Rose*, with its odd mixture of innocence, fantasy, and slightly sinister unquiet spirit, and the equally whimsical toing and froing of the classes in *The Admirable Crichton* surface from time to time, in recent years *Peter Pan* has been the only one of Barrie's many plays to be revived regularly. His one-act plays, such as *Ibsen's Ghost*, *The Twelve Pound Look*, and the tantalising first act of the thriller, *Shall We Join the Ladies?* are often more effective than the full-length ones and well worth reviving.

Peter Pan
The plot centres on Peter Pan (the Boy Who Never Grew Up), who flies off to the Never Never Land with the Darling children (Wendy, John and Michael), leaving their father to take refuge in the dog kennel. After defeating the Pirates, they return to Bloomsbury with the Lost Boys, leaving Peter to forget all that has happened and wait for the next generation of Darlings. Recent Broadway revivals featured Sandy Dennis and Olympic gymnast Cathy Rigby. The play is a

Regina Pong, Neil Bartlett and Ivan in *A Vision of Love Revealed in Sleep*, one of the most original pieces of theatre to hit London in recent years. It went through three different incarnations in three different locations from 1986–1990

Freudian's delight and must have bewildered a great many children over the years. Captain Hook, however, remains one of the great bravura parts.

Try these:
▷G.B. Shaw for class issues in *The Admirable Crichton*; ▷Joe Corrie offers a rather different Scottish sensibility; the use in *Mary Rose* of a ghostly spirit has parallels, from ▷T.S. Eliot in *The Family Reunion* to ▷Louise Page's *Salonika*, though none treat it with the almost touching feyness of Barrie.

BARRY, Philip   [1896–1949]
American dramatist

Plays include:
A Punch for Judy (1921), *You and I* (1923), *The Youngest* (1924), *In a Garden* (1925), *White Wings* (1925), *John* (1927), *Paris Bound* (1927), *Cock Robin* (with Elmer Rice; 1928), *Holiday* (1928), *Hotel Universe* (1930), *Tomorrow and Tomorrow* (1931), *The Animal Kingdom* (1932), *The Joyous Season* (1934), *Bright Star* (1935), *Spring Dance* (1936), *Here Come the Clowns* (1938), *The Philadelphia Story* (1939), *Liberty Jones* (1941), *Without Love* (1942), *Foolish Notion* (1945), *My Name is Aquilon* (1949), *Second Threshold* (completed posthumously by Robert Sherwood; 1951)

Born in Rochester, New York, Barry defined a kind of American comedy of manners which the British find in ▷Noël Coward. Educated at Yale and Harvard, he wrote about the sophisticated set of which he was a part, but not without healthy criticism of upper-class complacency and snobbery. His two best-known plays make his bemused contempt clear, even as they introduce the so-called 'Barry girl', a clear-headed, no-nonsense rich kid who is more on the ball than her posh surroundings might suggest. In *Holiday*, the self-made Johnny Case becomes engaged to the heiress Julia Seton only to find he has more in common with her younger sister Linda, who shares his desire for a 'holiday' from rampant materialistic pursuits. In *The Philadelphia Story*, later made into the stage and screen musical *High Society*, the moneyed divorcée Tracy Lord forsakes the dour stiff she's supposed to marry for a man defined more by his personality than his social position. Not all Barry's plays treat the mores of

the well-heeled: *John* is a Biblical tragedy; *Cock Robin*, written with Elmer Rice, a comic mystery; and *Liberty Jones*, an allegory. But he remains best-known for his social satire on the swells among whom he moved so easily.

Try these:
▷Noël Coward for a British equivalent to Barry's deceptive dark domestic frivolity, specifically *Private Lives* as a play about divorcés getting back together; ▷George Kaufman for comparable sophistication; ▷Tina Howe, Dennis McIntyre, Richard Greenberg and ▷A.R. Gurney for modern chroniclers of American class; also ▷Neil Simon; ▷Alan Ayckbourn for another British parallel.

BARTLETT, Neil   [1959–]
British performer, director and dramatist

Plays include:
Antibody (1983), *Dressing Up* (1983), *Pornography* (1985), *A Vision of Love Revealed in Sleep* (1986), *Sarrasine* (1990)

'The most tumultuous, the least categorisable talent to emerge in the 80s' is how Jim Hiley has described the emergence of Neil Bartlett. Chichester bred iconoclast – 'a very beautiful, very deadly place, a beautiful place to leave' – Bartlett has undoubtedly brought a subversively bright spark to a decade otherwise short on radical excitement and bravura. A determinedly anti-establishment figure, despite his first in English from Magdalen College, Oxford and a directors' traineeship at the Bristol Old Vic, much of his work has been in collaboration with friends, designer Robin Whitemore and Nicolas Bloomfield, Leah Hausman, and Simon Mellor with whom he set up his own company, Gloria, in 1988 – fulfilling a promise Bartlett made to himself in drama school to retain autonomy over his own creativity. He has, nonetheless, also won plaudits for dazzling translations of Racine (*Berenice*, at the National Theatre) and Moliere (*Le Misanthrope* for Red Shift and *School for Wives* for Annie Castledine at Derby Playhouse). As a director, he was responsible for Theatre de Complicite's *More Bigger Snacks Now*, and Annie Griffin's equally mould-breaking solo shows, *Blackbeard the Pirate* and *Almost Persuaded*, her country and western music satire. *Antibody* was one of the first plays to deal with AIDS in Britain, but *Dressing Up* began his highly flamboyant explorations into drag, followed, after *Pornography*, with *A Vision of Love Revealed in Sleep* and *Sarrasine* – two of the most extraordinary theatrical spectacles to have burst on the British public since Lindsay Kemp first came to prominence. As Carl Miller has written: 'Bartlett drags high and low culture into creative collusion', an entirely suitable pun on a process that has relocated drag from the small gay cognoscenti fraternity into a broader dramatic arena. Both spectacles featured performer Bette Bourne in ways which fused high art with low camp, and made points about the importance of the living presence of the performer, the nature of artifice and reality and the politics of gay persecution.

Bartlett's visual theatre uses text, image and music in contrapuntal abundance – satirising itself even at its most outrageous, and delighting in the contradiction. He is, nonetheless, equally at home in the quieter waters (structurally speaking) of the novel; his homage to Oscar Wilde, *Who Was That Man?* and his contemporary account of gay life, *Ready to Catch Him Should He Fall*, have both been warmly received.

A Vision of Love Revealed in Sleep

Sleep was originally performed by Bartlett, onstage throughout and naked, as a solo show in a disused warehouse. This studied and luxurious tribute to an all but forgotten Jewish Victorian painter and poet, Simeon Solomon – a friend of Rossetti, Swinburne and Pater who was disgraced and reduced to poverty after being caught in a public toilet with a labourer – was actually taken from Solomon's own erotic prose poem. Reflecting the imagery of the poem through Bartlett's own nakedness, and merging his own circumstances with those of Solomon, it became a witty and moving 'hymn' to art, homosexual love and defiance; Solomon's own refusal to apologise was apparently one of the reasons Bartlett was attracted to his subject. In later incarnations Bartlett was joined by three drag queens – heightening the production's wonderful mix of 'high art' with 'low culture'. The sight and sound of Bette Bourne singing Cole Porter's 'In the Still of the Night' remains an indelible memory and comment on the emotional repercussions of AIDS.

Try these:
Lindsay Kemp for theatre of divine outrage; ▷Genet, ▷Michel Tremblay for mixing the sacred and profane; ▷Robert Lepage and ▷Peter Brook for director/auteurs who also favour an ongoing work-in-progress approach; ▷Noel Greig and Philip Osment for contrasting gay sensibility; ▷Gay Theatre, ▷Performance Art.

BEAUMARCHAIS, Pierre Augustin Caron de   [1732–99]
French dramatist

Plays include:
Eugénie (1767), *Les Deux Amis* (*The Two Friends*; (1770), *Le Barbier de Séville* (*The Barber of Seville*; 1775), *Le Mariage de Figaro* (*The Marriage of Figaro*; 1784), *Tarare* (1787), *La Mère Coupable* (*The Guilty Mother*; 1792)

As well as being a dramatist, Beaumarchais was a watchmaker, musician, financier, courtier, pamphleteer, gun-runner and secret agent, in all of which he achieved some distinction but no lasting success. He wrote two very good plays (*The Barber of Seville* and its sequel *The Marriage of Figaro*) which might be more often performed in English had they not also been the bases of two superlative operas. The first has a plot that can be described in a few lines – old guardian, young ward, young nobleman in disguise, clever servant to help him – the second would need several pages to describe, and combines non-stop comic invention with sharp social satire. *The Marriage of Figaro* is possibly unique in being a successful sequel; there is a third in the series, *The Guilty Mother*, which has a strange combination of elevated moral tone and prurient plot (the Almavivas have come to live in France because of the Revolution, and like to be known as Citoyen and Citoyenne; the hero finds that he is the illegitimate son of the Countess and Chérubin, the latter having been killed in the wars, and so he can marry the Count's illegitimate daughter by the gardener's daughter). There was going to be a fourth episode of this increasingly depressing story, but Beaumarchais died first.

Try these:
▷Marivaux for eighteenth-century French comedy (though their language and approach are very different, Marivaux being a natural miniaturist and Beaumarchais a poster artist); ▷Feydeau

for the complications of plot in *The Marriage of Figaro*; ▷von Horvath for updating and development in *Figaro Gets a Divorce*.

BEAUMONT, Francis   [1584/5–1616]
English Renaissance dramatist, collaborator with ▷John Fletcher

Plays include:
The Knight of the Burning Pestle (1607), *Philaster* (with Fletcher; pre 1610), *The Maid's Tragedy* (with Fletcher; pre 1611)

Although Beaumont is traditionally associated with Fletcher, his place in the contemporary repertory rests largely on his own *The Knight of the Burning Pestle*. A lively blend of satire at the expense of middle-brow taste, this uses plays within plays, popular songs, apparent interruptions from the audience, romance and melodrama in a heady mixture which has maintained its appeal because the tastes and attitudes it confronts are easily recognisable today. It is not surprising that it attracted Michael Bogdanov, a director with a penchant for the freewheeling, who staged the last major British revival, for the ▷RSC in 1981. There was something of a Beaumont and ▷Fletcher revival at that time with successful productions of *The Maid's Tragedy*, a love, honour and duty tragedy, by both the ▷Glasgow Citizens' and the ▷RSC, but there has been little recent interest.

Try these:
▷Dekker's *Shoemaker's Holiday*, ▷Heywood's *Fair Maid of the West* and *Four Prentices of London* (the prime object of Beaumont's parody) are more complimentary to citizen taste than ▷Middleton's *A Chaste Maid*, which shares more of Beaumont's standpoint; ▷Ben Jonson's *Bartholomew Fair* and ▷Shakespeare's *The Merry Wives of Windsor* also offer portraits of the middle classes from this period; there are many plays about theatre companies and interrupted performances including ▷Sheridan's *The Critic*, ▷Pirandello's *Six Characters in Search of an Author* and Tom Stoppard's *The Real Inspector Hound*.

BECKETT, Samuel   [1906–89]
Irish/French dramatist and novelist

Plays include:
Waiting for Godot (1953), *Endgame* (1957), *All That Fall* (1957), *Act Without Words I* (1957), *Krapp's Last Tape* (1958), *Embers* (1959), *Act Without Words II* (1959), *Happy Days* (1961), *Words and Music* (1962), *Cascando* (1963), *Play* (1963), *Eh Joe* (1966), *Come and Go* (1966), *Breath* (1969), *Not I* (1972), *That Time* (1976), *Footfalls* (1976), *Ghost Trio* (1976), . . . *But the Clouds* . . . (1977), *A Piece of Monologue* (1980), *Ohio Impromptu* (1981), *Rockaby* (1980), *Quad* (1982), *Catastrophe* (1982), *Nacht und Träume* (1983), *What Where* (1983)

Born in Ireland of Anglo-Irish parents, Beckett went to Paris in the late 1920s where he worked for a while as secretary to James Joyce and later as a lecturer in English. In 1938 he settled in Paris, where he lived until his death, writing both in French and English and translating his own work into English. He was active in the French Resistance during World War II, and was awarded the Nobel Prize for Literature in 1969.

Beckett began writing as a critic; his first published work was a piece on *Finnegan's Wake*, written at Joyce's request. In 1931 he produced a study of Proust, he then wrote verse, short fiction and novels and turned to drama, he said, for 'relaxation'. *Waiting for Godot* arrived in England at a period in which there was a growing interest and awareness of non-realist forms of drama and of the innovations of European theatre. A play in which two tramp-clown figures wait for Godot, who never arrives, it was greeted with both mystification and acclaim. Beckett denied that it is a Christian allegory; it is a firmly atheist play.

Martin Esslin claimed Beckett as the figure who brought Absurdism to public attention, but Beckett himself did not accept that characterisation, nor can his considerable output and the range of his experiments in drama be neatly categorised. Beckett himself consistently refused to explain his work, continuing to direct and to produce drama that defies easy definition. Existentalism, Christian allegory and nihilism have all been employed as theoretical accounts of Beckett's work, but he has said only, 'I meant what I said'. To reduce the stark and complex imagery and language of Beckett's œuvre to a single 'meaning' would be to diminish their power.

Billie Whitelaw, one of the leading exponents of Samuel Beckett's work, as the immobilised Winnie in his own production of his *Happy Days*, Royal Court, 1979

Beckett's work is full of powerful images which are not referred to or explained, often images of human immobility: in *Play*, the three voices are trapped in jars; Winnie of *Happy Days* is gradually buried up to her neck in sand; in *Endgame*, one of the characters cannot walk, another cannot sit. These images can be seen as metaphors for inescapable traps; in Beckett's plays, as in ▷Sartre's *Huis Clos*, there is literally no way out.

Beckett's plays became increasingly minimalist in their exploration of the limits of the dramatic form. In *Acts Without Words* he produced the works with no verbal language, only sounds, and in a television piece in which actors silently moved around a floor diagram, he raised the question of what a 'play' is; at what point does drama cease to be drama and become dance or mime? He also wrote a number of monologues, most memorably for women: *Not I*, *Rockaby*, and *Footfalls*, which was written for Billie Whitelaw. The setting, timing and direction of a Beckett play are as integral as the text; his stage directions are extremely precise. In *Footfalls* the character is described as 'compulsively pacing', but the footfalls are not arbitrary, they are minutely scripted: 'starting with right foot (r) from right (R) to left (L) . . .'. Beckett places enormous demands upon the performer, but Whitelaw says, 'I think if that is what he's written, that is what he wants. And I think it's up to anyone who's actually doing his work to follow that as faithfully as they can'.

Despite the difficulty of much of Beckett's work, he is not as obscure as is often thought; his plays are full of comic invention and punning. He had a fascination with clowning (his one film, *Film*, 1965, was made with Buster Keaton): *Waiting for Godot* employs comic routines which are worthy of Laurel and Hardy.

Endgame

The four characters of *Endgame* exist in a bare set, with only two small windows. Two of them are locked in a symbiotic relationship: Clov cannot sit, Hamm, blind and impotent, cannot stand; they hate, but need each other, in a pairing that echoes the master/servant relationship of Pozzo and Lucky in *Waiting for Godot*. The senile Nell and Nagg are encased in dustbins, their concerns only the immediately physical. In a bitter image of a marriage, unable to reach one another but to scratch,

Nagg wistfully reminisces about the erotic (a theme also explored in *Krapp's Last Tape*). The claustrophobic world of the play is never specified, the world outside the room only available through the telescope through which Clov sees a barren landscape (Joanne Akalaitis set the play in a subway station and was forced by Beckett to put a disclaimer in the programme). Written in 1958, with nuclear war felt as a very real threat, one possibility is that this is a post-holocaust world. The only clue Beckett offered is his reply to an actor that 'the play doesn't happen only in one person's mind'. The play is full of theatrical references: Clov and Hamm evoke Caliban and and Prospero in ▷Shakespeare's *Tempest*; Hamm (who often sounds Shakespearean) is a reference to 'ham' acting (and to Hamlet?); at one point Clov turns his telescope directly onto the audience and reports: 'I see a multitude in transports of joy'.

Not I

Not I is a stunning visual theatrical effect; the short play is performed on a darkened stage on which only a shadowy draped figure and a spotlighted mouth are visible. The draped figure moves slightly during the course of the play, while the mouth babbles a fragmented and pain-filled discourse. Actress Billie Whitelaw has described the experience as 'falling backwards into Hell, emitting cries'. It is enormously demanding for an actress – when Whitelaw was confronted with the script she told Beckett: 'You've finally done it, you've written the unlearnable and you've written the unplayable'. When she asked Beckett if the character was dead he responded 'Let's just say you're not quite there'.

Try these:
▷Ionesco and ▷Genet were seen with Beckett to represent a European 'Theatre of the Absurd'; ▷Stoppard's *Rosencrantz and Guildenstern are Dead* clearly owes a great deal to *Waiting for Godot*; Robert Wilson for prescripting performers' movements in fine detail; ▷Harold Pinter has obviously been influenced by Beckett; for contrast on the master/servant relationship, see ▷Derek Walcott's *Pantomime*, in the context of the Robinson Crusoe/Man Friday relationship.

BEHAN, Brendan [1923–64]

Irish dramatist, journalist, house-painter and alcoholic

Plays include:
The Quare Fellow (1954), *An Gaill* (reworked as *The Hostage*; 1958), *Richard's Cork Leg* (1972)

A member of the IRA at fourteen, sent to Borstal for three years, sentenced at nineteen to fourteen years jail for political offences and attempted murder, Behan drew on his own life for his autobiographical books *Borstal Boy* (1958) and *Confessions of an Irish Rebel* (1965) and early radio plays which Alan Simpson adapted for the Pike Theatre Club, Dublin. His first stage play *The Quare Fellow*, set in a prison on the eve of an execution, was 'developed' by ▷Joan Littlewood for a new version presented by Theatre Workshop (1956) and in the West End, and had an important effect on attitudes to imprisonment and capital punishment. *An Gaill*, commissioned by the Irish language society Gael Linn, and reworked by Theatre Workshop as *The Hostage*, presents a picaresque set of characters in a brothel used as an IRA safe house where a British soldier is held prisoner. Much of its success was due to the Workshop's style of songs, repartee and audience confrontation. *Richard's Cork Leg*, a political comedy about fascism, was left unfinished and completed by Alan Simpson in 1972.

Behan's own curtain speeches, colourful behaviour and alcoholic interviews attracted as much media attention as his plays on both sides of the Atlantic. Although Behan claimed: 'I'm not a postman . . . I don't deliver messages', both plays have a great deal to say to their audiences and the Theatre Workshop productions affected attitudes both to the topics discussed and to ways of presenting theatre.

Try these:
For plays on Irish politics, see ▷Sean O'Casey, ▷Brian Friel, ▷Frank McGuiness, ▷Seamus Finnegan; ▷Genet's *The Balcony* for a rather different use of a brothel setting; for plays on prison brutality, *In the Belly of the Beast, Fortune and Men's Eyes* and *Short Eyes*, and, for a female view, *Clean Break*.

BEHN, Aphra [1640–1689]

English dramatist and novelist

Plays include:
The Forced Marriage (1670), *The Rover* (1677), *The Lucky Chance* (1686), *The Feign'd Curtizans; or A Night's Intrigue* (1678), *The Roundheads; or The Good Old Cause* (1681), *The City-Heiress; or Sir Timothy Treat-All* (1682), *The Emperor of the Moon* (1687)

The first woman to earn her living by the pen, Aphra Behn was renowned both for her wit and her prolific output. In her lifetime she was one of the most frequently performed playwrights, comparable with ▷Dryden, ▷Wycherley or ▷Congreve and actually left behind eighteen separate plays, as well as novels and some poetry anthologies. An early champion of a woman's right to free expression – Virginia Woolf suggested that 'all women together ought to let flowers fall upon the tomb of Aphra Behn . . . for it was she who earned them the right to speak their minds' – she was consistently vilified by male critics for daring to write as bawdily as they did. After the opening of *The Lucky Chance* an accusation of indecency brought from her a typically robust plea to be accorded the same freedom to write as that enjoyed by men. Her plays deal with subjects familiar to Restoration audiences fattened on a diet of elegant debauchery; double standards in high places; sexual intrigue; and cuckoldry. She wrote tragi-comedies, historical comedies, political lampoons and, with the *commedia dell'arte* based *The Emperor of the Moon*, is credited with a forerunner to the English ▷pantomime.

After two-and-a-half centuries of neglect, Behn is beginning to enjoy a small renaissance: *The Lucky Chance* was revived by the Women's Playhouse Trust (1981) and *The Rover* (1986) by the ▷RSC, and by the Goodman Theatre in Chicago (1988–9). Modern audiences enjoy her plays particularly for their good humour and energy, whilst recognising her early feminist claims for equality in relationships between the sexes. A night with Behn is still a good night out and her plays have as much to offer as those of her better known male contemporaries.

Try these:
Other Restoration playwrights such as ▷Congreve, ▷Etherege, ▷Wycherley, ▷Farquhar, ▷Vanbrugh; ▷Edward

Bond's *Restoration* and ▷ Caryl Churchill's *Serious Money* for modern similarities; also ▷Timberlake Wertenbaker's *The Grace of Mary Traverse* for a similar concern for women in their social context, using a historical setting.

BENNETT, Alan   [1934–]
British dramatist and actor

Plays include:
Forty Years On (1968), *Getting On* (1971), *Habeas Corpus* (1973), *The Old Country* (1977), *Enjoy* (1980), *Kafka's Dick* (1986), *Single Spies* (*An Englishman Abroad*, televised 1983, and *A Question of Attribution*, 1988)

Bennett first attracted attention as a writer and performer in revue on the Edinburgh Fringe, especially with *On the Fringe* with Jonathan Miller, Dudley Moore and Peter Cook which had long runs in London and New York. *Forty Years On* seemed to please everyone, a 'good night out' and a clever satire with songs which analyses Britain in the twentieth century via a revue put on by a boarding school (much of it began life as pastiches of literary and other styles). *The Old Country*, a cerebral discussion of national identity through the image of a British defector living in the USSR, made more demands on audiences.

Enjoy manages to be illuminating about class values, town planners, the generation gap, sexual politics, and fashionable sociology in a play that continually surprises. An ageing working-class couple in the North of England, living in a house due for demolition, and due for removal to a new estate, are visited by an apparently female social worker who, the audience does not realise, is actually their son in drag. Proud of their children, they try to play it his way, and they also boast of their prostitute daughter: 'She's exceptional. You won't find girls like her on every street corner.' *Kafka's Dick*, in which Kafka, his parents and his publisher materialise in the suburban home of a would-be biographer, found appreciative audiences among ▷Royal Court literati but failed to transfer to the West End.

Bennett is a very funny writer, adept at using the techniques of farce and music hall, especially in *Habeas Corpus*, but, while he will find humour in the predicament of cancer patients, geriatrics, Jewish mothers, social workers' cases or homosexual spies, his

characters are not butts for laughter. His own comment on one of his television creations that, 'by the end . . . you understand why she is like that and you sympathise with her', is true of them all. He has an uncannily accurate ear for the richness of real speech, evident most recently in his six-part television monologue series, *Talking Heads*, and in *Single Spies*, a double bill about two English spies, Guy Burgess and Anthony Blunt, which includes an appearance by Elizabeth II. *The Old Crowd* and *The Insurance Man* have explored techniques outside the apparent naturalism of most of his other television plays. His screenplays include the ▷Orton biography *Prick Up Your Ears* (1986).

Try these:
John Dighton's *The Happiest Days of Our Lives* for broad satire on the English public school system; also ▷Simon Gray's *Butley*, ▷Christopher Hampton's *The Philanthropist*; ▷Peter Nichols, and ▷Joe Orton for satirists of social mores; ▷Michael Wilcox's *Lent* for linking the school play with homosexuality; ▷Julian Mitchell's *Another Country* for homosexuality and spies.

BERKOFF, Steven   [1937–]
British actor and dramatist

Plays and adaptations include:
The Penal Colony (1968), *Metamorphosis* (1969), *The Trial* (1970), *Agamemnon* (1973), *The Fall of the House of Usher* (1974), *East* (1975), *Greek* (1979), *The Murder of Jesus Christ* (1980), *Decadence* (1981), *One Man* (1982), *West* (1983), *Harry's Christmas* (1985), *Kvetch* (1987), *Sink the Belgrano!* (1986)

Berkoff is as widely known as a performer as he is a writer. He studied mime in Paris with the École Jacques Le Coq, an emphasis very evident in his performances and plays, which rely as much for their impact on movement as on language. After working in repertory theatre Berkoff went on to found the London Theatre Group, where he began to direct and to develop adaptations from literature into theatre. Kafka and Edgar Allan Poe were favoured authors for this treatment, which often involved Expressionistic sets and acting style. The London Theatre Group also developed a version of ▷Aeschylus' *Agamemnon*, and Greek tragedy became an informing prin-

Aphra Behn's *The Lucky Chance*, successfully revived by Jules Wright for The Women's Playhouse Trust at the Royal Court in 1984 after some 250 years of neglect. Front left: Alan Rickman; front right: Paul Bacon; rear, left to right: Christopher Fairbank, Harriet Walter, Jonathan Adams

ciple of Berkoff's own writing. His first original play was *East*, which used a juxtaposition of street language with high tragedy and blank verse to produce a vitriolic and abrasive account of East End life. *Greek* employed the Oedipus myth to polemicise about mothers, marriage and women. *West* rewrote the Beowolf legend into a scabrous attack on the British upper classes and was (ironically) a great success in the West End, as was his Royal National Theatre revival of his adaptation of *The Trial* in which he starred with Anthony Sher. In 1989 he directed *Coriolanus* starring Christopher Walken at the Public Theater in New York to much acclaim.

Metamorphosis

Metamorphosis was the most successful of the London Theatre Group's productions. Kafka's tale of a young man who wakes up to discover he has been transformed into a beetle becomes a sustained scream of rage against the constraints of conventional society in Berkoff's hands. First performed with Berkoff at the Round House in 1969, *Metamorphosis*, which is highly stylised using acrobatics and mime to powerful effect, toured extensively in Britain and overseas. The play was revived (with another performer, Tim Roth, as the young man, and with Berkoff in the role of the father; and was seen on Broadway starring Mikhail Barishnikov) at London's Mermaid Theatre in 1986, and is now, as a spectacular showcase for an actor, a regular feature of the Edinburgh Festival.

Try these:
▷Alan Bennett's *Kafka's Dick* is a wildly imaginative, but very Bennett-like play on fame and literature, in which Kafka is omnipresent; ▷Lindsay Kemp, is as idiosyncratic and unique in his performance style; ▷Jim Cartwright's *Road* uses language as explosively; the ▷Capek brothers' *Insect Play* is another insect-infected metaphor for society.

BERNARD, Jean-Jacques
[1888–1972]
French dramatist

Plays include:
Martine (1922), *L'Invitation au Voyage* (*Invitation to the Journey*; 1924), *Le Printemps des Autres* (*Other People's Springtime*; 1924), *Le Roy de Malousie* (*The King of Malousie*; 1928), *La Louise* (*Our Louise*; 1930), *A La Recherche des Coeurs* (*Searching for Hearts*; 1931), *Les Soeurs Guedonec* (*The Guedonec Sisters*; 1931), *Jeanne de Pantin* (1933), *Nationale 6* (*Highway No 6*; 1935), *Deux Hommes* (*Two Men*; 1937), *Le Jardinier d'Ispahan* (*The Gardener of Ispahan*; 1939)

Writing just prior to the generation of ▷Cocteau, Genet, and ▷Giraudoux, Bernard is the best-known examplar of the 'theatre of the inexpressible', a French school of writers including Denys Amiel and Charles Vildnac in which it's our unspoken dialogue that resonates, not the words themselves ('subtext', as acting teachers might put it). In *Martine*, the story of the peasant girl Martine's misplaced attraction for a callow upper-class journalist, Julien, the play proceeds inevitably to its sad ending, as Martine's passivity hardens into a tacit acknowledgment of perpetual rejection (see Claude Goretta's film *The Lacemaker* for a contemporary update on this theme). *Nationale 6* tells a similar story whereby an ordinary provincial girl is done in by an overactive imagination, and in *Les Soeurs Guedonec*, two spinsters pass a miserable holiday in complete silence, accompanied by three loud orphan children.

Try these:
▷Chekhov, ▷Harold Pinter, and ▷Samuel Beckett for transmuting the 'inexpressible' into art rather than just an end in and of itself; equally, ▷Robert Holman and ▷Marguerite Duras for the 'inexpressible' recall of past emotions; for treatments of class clashing, see ▷Chekhov's *Three Sisters*.

BETTI, Ugo
[1892–1953]
Italian dramatist and judge

Plays include:
Il Paese delle Vacanze (*Summertime*; 1942), *L'Aurola Bruciata* (*The Burnt Flowerbed*; 1942), *Curruzione al Palasso di Giustizia* (*Corruption in the Palace of Justice*, also translated for radio as *The Sacred Seals*; 1949), *La Regina e gli Insorti* (*The Queen and the Rebels*; 1951)

Some Italian critics considered Betti's later plays even better than those of ▷Pirandello, whose influence is evident in his work. Betti's themes are moral and in the wider sense, religious: his translator Henry Reed suggested that his major theme was 'man's fatal disregard of God'. Carefully plotted and well-constructed in a conventional way, his plays tend to be set in rather unlocalised symbolic settings, though the dialogue is naturalistic. His interest is in the personal and ethical problems of his protagonists rather than any political dialectic: the rebels in *The Queen and the Rebels* or the contending powers in *The Burnt Flowerbed*, for instance, are abstractions without identifiable ideologies. His concerns in these plays are the sacrifice by which a prostitute saves the live of a worthless queen and so herself gains 'queenly' virtues, and a similar self-sacrifice intended to destroy the cynicism of a former politician.

Try these:
▷Genet's *The Balcony*; ▷Pirandello; ▷Barry Collins' *Judgement* for moral enquiry; ▷Anouilh, Montherlant, ▷Giraudoux for ethical discussions.

BILL, Stephen [1948–]
British dramatist

Plays include:
Girl Talk (1977), *The Old Order* (1979), *The Final Wave* (1979), *Piggy Back Riders* (1981), *The Bottom Drawer* (1982), *Naked in the Bull Ring* (1985), *Over the Bar* (1985), *Crossing the Line* (1987), *Curtains* (1987), *Over a Barrel* (1990), *Stitched Up* (1990)

Relatively unrecognised nationally until the success of *Curtains*, which won three awards when it was produced at the Hampstead Theatre in 1987, Stephen Bill has a solid record of regional successes in the UK, including *The Old Order*, for which he won the 1979 John Whiting Award. Set in Birmingham, *Curtains*, an acutely observed savage comedy about a family birthday celebration which turns into a wake, presents an everyday situation of a family's attitudes to the problems of ageing and to euthanasia in terms which are memorably comic as well as horrific. It is a well-crafted, almost old-fashioned play which uses the familiar devices of the family gathering and the unexpected return of the prodigal to unlock themes and to analyse the roots of situations. However, its sombre material is unlikely to make it a popular favourite, as the shortness of its West End run sadly indicates.

Try these:
▷Alan Bleasdale and ▷Willy Russell use Liverpudlian settings and ▷John Byrne uses Glaswegian settings in similar ways to Bill's use of Birmingham; ▷Sophocles' *Oedipus* for family reunions that go wrong; ▷Sam Shepard's *Buried Child* for calamitous consequences of a prodigal's return; contemporary dramatists who share some of Bill's preoccupations are ▷Alan Ayckbourn, ▷Joe Orton and ▷Marsha Norman (*Night Mother*); other contemporary dramatists from Birmingham are ▷Alan Drury and ▷David Rudkin.

BLACK THEATRE IN BRITAIN

Afro-Caribbean theatre began in Britain at the end of the 1960s with the emergence of Temba and the Dark and Light Theatre Club (founded by Frank Cousins, in Brixton). But it really took off in the early 1970s, when a number of black artists from the Caribbean and Africa, then living in London, got together at the Keskidee Centre in north London. From that gathering of directors, performers and writers, including ▷Edgar White, Amadu Maddy, Rufus Collins, Malcolm Fredericks, Yvonne Brewster, Anton Phillips, T Bone Wilson, Carmen Munroe, Linton Kwesi Johnson and many more emerged from the nucleus of today's British black theatre community.

Up until 1982, black theatre in Britain was more or less dominated by male writers. Errol John's *Moon on a Rainbow Shawl* (1956, revived in 1988, directed by Maya Angelou) was the first black play to win a drama award and was followed by a steady stream of writers including Barry Reckord, Mustapha Matura, Farrukh Dhondy. Tunde Ikoli, Caryl Phillips whose plays (as Far Rodrigues had noted in the *Alternative Theatre Guide 1985–86*) amounted to a theatre of protest against apartheid, the racism of British society, imperialism, police brutality and economic exploitation.

After 1982, black theatre began to reflect a different set of preoccupations – sexism, violence against women, young women's aspirations – as companies staged the work of young women writers. For example, Black Theatre Co-operative (BTC) presented Jacqueline Rudet's first play and Temba her second, while Jackie Kay's *Chiaroscuro* was the product of encouragement from Theatre of Black Women, and a reading at Gay Sweatshop's GS × 10 workshop festival. Paulette Randall emerged like the founders of Theatre of Black Women, Bernandine Evaristo and Patricia Hilaire, emerged from the ▷Royal Court's Young Black Writers festival, and her *Fishing* formed part of the first Black Theatre Season, set up by Anton Phillips, at the Arts Theatre in 1983. Now there are well over thirty companies operating with a variety of styles, scale and focus, reflecting the diversity of the black experience in Britain today, many of them members of the Black Theatre Forum which meets as a talking shop to hammer out and develop 'a black aesthetic' (in the words of Yvonne Brewster. The musicals of Felix Cross (*Mass Carib*, *Glory!* and *Blues for Railton*), and the plays of Edgar White (*The Nine Night*) and Dennis Scott (*Echo in the Bone*) seen in Britain in the 1980s exemplify a stream of black writing engaged in self-examination of Caribbean roots, particularly through ritual. Trevor Rhone's comedies of Jamaican life also became favourites with black British audiences and Michael Abbensett's *Sweet Talk* opened the way to the first black British television sitcom *Empire Road*. Some companies are equally interested in exploring timeless themes about personal relationships, whilst multicultural re-interpretations of the classics by Temba's Alby James (*Romeo and Juliet* and *Ghosts*) and Yvonne Brewster's Talawa company (*The Importance of Being Earnest* and *Antony and Cleopatra*) are indicative of a feeling that black theatre has come of age and wishes to address itself as much as to the classics, as well as exploring the black experience. On the other hand, younger companies like Double Edge whose 'house' writer Amali Nephtali deals with the problems of ordinary British black youth from a Rastafarian perspective and the Women's Troop of Black Mime Theatre (who use text with mime) are quite clearly speaking from their own black experience and addressing specifically young, black audiences.

Black theatre in Britain has also been subject to various influences from abroad. In the mid-1980s, some of the work of black American women writers also began to appear in Britain with BTC's revival of Lorraine Hansberry's *A Raisin in the Sun* and the Women's Playhouse Trust's premiere of Ntozake Shange's *Spell No 7* (her *for colored girls who have considered suicide when the rainbow is enuf* was seen in Britain in 1983). In 1989, Endesha Ida Mae Holland's touching account of three young women growing up in the Deep South, *From the Mississippi Delta*, showed a return to a more lyrical strain of black writing whilst two plays of August Wilson, *Ma Rainey's Black Bottom* and *Joe Turner's Come and Gone* suddenly found a certain popularity in London. The steady flow of black theatre companies from South Africa and neighbouring black states to Britain throughout the 1980s probably did more than anything else to bring home the horrors and realities of living under the apartheid system to British audiences, both black and white. These productions combined old-style agit-prop with dynamic physicality and self-mocking humour. The Market Theatre of Johannesburg under ▷Athol Fugard also produced the extraordinary *Woza Albert* by Percy Ntwa, Mbongeni Ngema and Barney Simon and *Sizwe Bansi is Dead* by Fugard, John Kani and Winston Ntshona and in 1988, the equally poignant, *Sophiatown*. Plays by women's groups like the South African Vusisizwe Players' *You Strike the Woman, You Strike the Rock*, Saira Essa's *You Can't Stop the Revolution*, the Jamaican Sistren collective and Poppie Nongena also showed a theatre of resistance that emphasised women's collective strength – and in the case of Poppie Nongena won over many hearts through the sheer beauty of its songs, taken from the black townships. A further, quite different African dimension has also been introduced with British productions of the epic plays of Nigerians Wole Solinyka, Ola Rotimi (*The Gods Are Not To Blame*, a re-working of the Oedipus legend beautifully directed by Yvonne Brewster) and Yemi Ajibade (*Fingers Only* and *Waiting for Hannibal*). British black theatre has survived many financial and artistic vicissitudes. Dwindling public subsidy, the stillborn aspirations of the Roundhouse project, and the hardening political climate which has seen the positive gains of the mid-1980s gradually rolled back are now affecting all areas of the black theatre community who are struggling simply to survive. Alby James, Anton Phillips (Carib Theatre's founder), Malcolm Fredericks (of BTC), comparative newcomer Denise Wong (of the Black Mime Theatre) and the indefatigable Yvonne Brewster somehow manage to keep the light shining. The excitement of younger writers like Amali Nephtali, whose *Ragamuffin* re-worked ▷Genet's *The Blacks* to relate it to the contemporary tumult of the Broadwater Farm

Attie Kubyane (on crate) and Ewen Cummins in Temba Theatre Company's production of *Woza Albert* by Percy Mtwa, Mbongeni Ngema and Barney Simon, directed by Alby James in 1986

riots in north London and the Haitian revolution, and Benjamin Zephaniah's dub and rap plays *Job Rocking* and *Streetwise*, indicates plenty of creative energy still on tap. Others, like Carib Theatre's Anton Phillips, now concentrate on the vital but often unsung Theatre in Education work in schools. Many hopes now rest on Brewster's Talawa company, charged, as recipients of a substantial Arts Council grant and a building, the Jeannetta Cochrane Theatre in London, with the responsibility of more or less establishing a multicultural home for black theatre in Britain. The enormous and justifiable success, of Clarke Peters's musical, *Five Guys Named Moe*, based on the music of American jazz songwriter Louis Jordan, simply underlines the difficulties 'straight' Black Theatre is up against in the face of the huge popular appeal of musicals such as *Bubbling Brown Sugar* and *Ain't Misbehavin'*.

Try these:
For other black writers see ▷James Baldwin, ▷Amiri Baraka, ▷August Wilson and ▷African-American Theatre; White South African Susan Pam's multi-racial *Curl Up and Die*, Michele Celeste's *Hang the President*, Andrew Buckland's surreal one-man fable *The Ugly Noo Noo* were all critical responses to the effects of apartheid; ▷Asian theatre and Tara Arts for other British theatre companies.

BLEASDALE, Alan   [1946–]
British dramatist

Plays include:
The Party's Over (1975), *Down the Dock Road* (1976), *It's a Madhouse* (1976), *Should Old Acquaintance . . .* (1976), *No More Sitting on the Old School Bench* (1977), *Pimples* (1978), *Crackers* (1978), *Having a Ball* (1981), *Are You Lonesome Tonight?* (1985), *Love is a Many-Splendoured Thing* (1986)

A Merseyside writer who – up until 1985 – had developed a strong reputation without ever having been seen in the West End, Alan Bleasdale is a gritty comic satirist who has reached his widest theatre audience with what is, paradoxically, his most earnest work: *Are You Lonesome Tonight?*, an overtly hagiographic musical about Elvis Presley that aims to set the record straight about a musical legend Bleasdale thinks has been vilified. Set

on the last day of the King's life before drugs and booze did him in at forty-two in 1977, the musical is an unabashedly sentimental picture of a bloated talent looking back sardonically on his younger self, before he allowed himself to be mercilessly corrupted by managers, promoters and the press. Earlier stage plays of note include *It's a Madhouse*, set in a psychiatric hospital in the northwest of England, and *Having a Ball*, about four men awaiting surgery in a vasectomy clinic. In addition, Bleasdale has written memorably for other media: Peter Smith's 1985 film *No Surrender* had a strong Bleasdale script about rival factions in a Liverpool nightclub where the tensions mirror those in Northern Ireland. His TV writing has also tapped the psychic pulse of Britain in *Boys From the Blackstuff* (a 1983 howl of rage against unemployment, set in Liverpool, that nonetheless caught a national feeling) and *The Monocled Mutineer* (a 1986 parable of powerlessness in Thatcher's Britain) and *GBH* (1991) which wickedly satirised the battle for ascendency in Liverpool between the Labour Party and the Trotskyist Militant Tendency.

Try these:
▷Willy Russell as the other pre-eminent Liverpudlian writer, and Jim Hitchmough as a promising newcomer; ▷Hanif Kureishi as an urban realist with a comparable sense of humour; ▷Joe Orton for black comedy.

BLESSING, Lee   [1949–]
American dramatist

Plays include:
Independence (1983); *Riches* (formerly War of the Roses, 1984); *Eleemosynary* (1985), *A Walk in the Woods* (1987), *Two Rooms* (1988); *Down the Road* (1989), *Cobb* (1989); *Fortinbras* (1991)

Minnesota playwright Lee Blessing's early works were often read at the Eugene O'Neill Playwrights Center before being produced at Actors Theatre of Louisville, the company that premiered *Oldtimers Game*, *Nice People Dancing to Good Country Music*, *Independence*, and *War of the Roses*. Both *Independence* and his widely produced *Eleemosynary* feature all-female casts and concern relationships between mothers and daughters, strained by the mother's mental breakdown in the former and a grandmother's stroke in the latter.

More recently Blessing has shifted from family dynamics to political themes. His best-known play *A Walk in the Woods* (winner of the Best Play award from the American Theatre Critics Association) presents two statesmen negotiating in uncharacteristic poses of casualness and friendliness: we find them human. As potential annihilation hovers over the world, talks of disarmament are set in the context of hope – in the woods. We are reminded of the dangers of the artificial when placed in the harmonious milieu of the natural. A peculiar tension of pessimism and possibility dissolves into a nihilism that is inherent in survival games. The play was filmed for television and performed widely, including a command performance for members of Congress, and marked the beginning of a collaboration with the director Des McAnuff, head of LaJolla Playhouse, where *Two Rooms* and *Fortinbras* premiered under his direction.

The two rooms of his 1988 play's title are the windowless cubicle where a hostage is held in Beirut and the room, stripped of furniture, where the prisoner's wife hopes to share psychically her husband's ordeal. Some critics pointed to the obvious similarities to ▷Sartre's *No Exit*, but the play's lack of action or point of view distressed others.

Cobb, premiered at Yale Repertory Theatre under Lloyd Richard's hand, explores the myth surrounding the eponymous baseball-star legend portrayed at three stages of his life by three actors. Blessing sees Ty Cobb as a symbol of American greed (the player was an early investor in General Motors and Coca Cola), power (he frequently had violent encounters with strangers), and racism (the strangers were often black). Frank Rich wrote in the *New York Times* that the play was a 'retreat into nostalgic escapism' from the challenge of *A Walk in the Woods*. Nevertheless, the playwright's attempt to confront ugly American myths is a noble one.

Try these:
On the subject of negotiations, see John Adam's opera, *Nixon in China* where doubt over the efficacy of such manoeuvres resonats with the inadequacies of civilised human interactions. The aftermath of the nuclear accident at Chernobyl is dramatised by Vladimir Gubaryev's *Sarcophagus*; ▷Beckett's *Endgame* is perhaps the most memorable of all survival games, Stephen Sondheim's *Into the Woods*, a poignant musical treatment; for diplomacy see *Oh What a Lovely War* and ▷Hochhüth's *Soldiers*. Beth Henley's *Crimes of the Heart* for another Louisville play, that, like *Independence*, features three sisters dealing with the legacy of a mentally ill mother; Richard Nelson's *Principia Scriptoriae* and Allan Havis' *Morocco* for Americans held prisoner in foreign lands; Stoppard's *Rosencrantz and Guildenstern* for new takes on *Hamlet*.

BOGART, Anne [1951–]
American writer and director

Productions include:
Hauptstadt (1979), *Inhabitat* (1979), *Out of Sync* (1980), *Women and Men: A Big Dance* (1982), *History, An American Dream* (1983); *The Making of Americans* (adapted from Gertrude Stein, 1985); *'1951'* (with Mac Wellman, 1986); *No Plays No Poetry But Philosophical Reflections Practical Instructions Provocative Prescriptions Opinions and Pointers from a Noted Critic and Playwright* (1988)

Anne Bogart, one of the USA's most innovative and creative directors/writers, grew up a 'navy brat' in a military family. Although she creates theatre pieces that most would term 'experimental' she herself disavows such labels. She told Catherine Sheehy in a *Theatre* journal interview that 'I usually personally resent being called avant-garde because I spend most of my time thinking about history, tradition and culture.' She goes on to say in the same interview that her favorite playwright is Tennessee Williams 'bar none.' However, one wonders what the writer would have thought of her production of *Streetcar Named Desire*, retitled *Endstation Sehnsucht* because 'sehnsucht' also means 'addiction' in German. The play was performed in space set up as a nightclub into which the audience was led. The 23-member cast then performed a fantasy re-enactment of their own lives and included 10 Stanleys, some of whom impersonated Brando (Bogart's point of view; why not confront the mythic cloud Brando's performance has cast over the role instead of pretending it doesn't exist) and 12 Blanches (one of whom was played by a man).

Her use of a German title isn't surprising since she lived in that country at one time and lists 'Mnouchkine, Stein, Gruber, Bondi' as her main influences. Moreover, the pattern of replicate characters performing a play within a play in an environmental setting could be seen as one of Bogart's signature strokes. Her *South Pacific* at New York University was reconceived as a performance by patients in a psychiatric ward of a veterans' hospital; she made *On the Town* a performance by members of a battleship; and she produced her version of Marivaux's *The Dispute* in a shopping mall. *Inhabitant*, a play staged in a Brooklyn tenement, turns audience members into 'visitors' as they are transported by truck off a New York City street to the performance site. *Out of Sync* pursues this notion further as the audience moves in and out of the various real and familiar city settings of the characters' world to experience the nebulous 'truths' of a triangular relationship.

The violence of relationships moves to the public dimension in *History, An American Dream*, in which warmongering, the game of the world that constantly usurps prospects for peaceful coexistence, is played out personally and historically. Men and women enact the emotional chasms that place their lives into separate domains.

Her most widely acclaimed piece, however, may be *No Plays No Poetry*, described by a *New York Times* critic as 'an avant-garde carnival that carries the audience from scene to scene in a choreographed comic pageant that sends up the theoretical writings of Bertolt Brecht.' According to Bogart, 97 percent of the text came directly from Brecht's critical writing. As a sideshow barker spouted the history of the theatre according to Brecht, a tent opened and the audience could wander to any of nine scenes, including one where nine actors playing Brecht argued about acting or another where Tina Shepard played Brecht playing Charlie Chaplin playing Hitler.

This kind of work attracted the attention of Trinity Repertory Theatre's trustees who in an act of bravado hired Bogart to succeed Adrian Hall. She lasted one season, resigning after the board asked her at the last minute to slash 25 percent of her budget. Recently she followed in the footsteps of Lloyd Richards and Robert Falls when she was appointed President of Theatre Communications Group, the first independent artist to be so honored.

Try these:
▷ Linda Mussmann's *Civil War Chronicles* for similar questions as to how history is often perceived and conceived; ▷ Caryl Churchill, ▷ Strindberg for contrasting version of male – female relationships; Nancy Reilly for another American engaged in the re-arrangement of theatrical forms. ▷ Peter Sellars, especially for his radical interpretations of opera and musicals; ▷ Robert Wilson for another director prone to completely reconceptualizing classic drama; ▷ Brecht; ▷ Mac Wellman; Richard Schechner's environmental theatre work at the Performance Garage; Richard Foreman, the Wooster Group for a similar desire to disassociate language from physical movement; ▷ Mnouchkine; ▷ Performance Art.

BOGOSIAN, Eric   [1953–]
American writer and performer

Plays include:
Men Inside, Voices of America (1982), *FunHouse* (1983), *Talk Radio* (1987), *Drinking in America* (1988), *Sex, Drugs, Rock & Roll* (1990)

In *Talk Radio*, the late-night talk jockey, Barry Champlain (Bogosian), asserts, 'This decadent country needs a loud voice – and that's me.' (*Talk Radio* was subsequently made into a film by Oliver Stone.) This voice, one that characterises much of Bogosian's work, offers various versions of the macho male in a political comedy context that exploits their stereotypical fictions and makes them real. The characters embrace attributes of greed and fear that encumber America's ego – the boastful, the phoney, the hypocritical. As philistines of a decaying culture, Bogosian's characters are caught in addiction and victimisation. At the same time as monologuist Bogosian enacts the compulsive behavior of the white, American male, he strips bare this psyche. *Sex, Drugs, Rock & Roll* will also receive film treatment.

Try these:
Other monologuists, Karen Finley, ▷ Spalding Gray, John Leguizamo, John O'Keefe and ▷ Holly Hughes, in their different stylistic approaches communicate the same message: western civilisation is at its end; see also ▷ One-person shows, ▷ Performance Art; ▷ John Godber for British macho male.

BOLGER, Dermot   [1959–]
Irish poet, novelist and dramatist

Plays include:
The Lament for Arthur Cleary (1989),
Monologues (1990)

Dermot Bolger is one of Ireland's most prolific and best-known young writers. His initial
success came as a novelist, his second book,
The Woman's Daughter (1987) bringing him
the AE Memorial Award, The Macaulay
Fellowship and the Sunday Tribune Arts
Award. His first stage play, *The Lament for
Arthur Cleary* – based on his poem of the same
name – was premiered (to widespread critical
acclaim) at the Dublin Theatre Festival of
1989, picked up a Fringe First the following
summer in Edinburgh and subsequently won
the Samuel Beckett Award for Best First Play
of that year.

After fifteen years away – bumming round
Europe, putting down no roots – Arthur
Cleary comes home. He feels the need to belong again, but the Dublin he has carried in
his head and his heart is long gone. Not just
the streets of his boyhood, but the neighbourhood ways and hierarchies have been swept
aside by a new set of circumstances. Drug
traffic on the pavements where Cleary was
once cock o' the walk. Nowhere in his inner
being, not even in the soft corners of his heart
where he holds the love of a young girl he's
just met, can Cleary accommodate that
change. He meets his death – Celtic inevita-
bility. Was that not, after all, the reason for
his homecoming?

Bolger pinpoints the eternal baggage of the
migrant and the exile – a fixed vision of a time
and place when they themselves had rooted
identity. It's common to all races, but with the
Celts it's a particular shackle. At home or
abroad they cannot let go of the past, centuries
of it, albatross-like around their psyche.
Hence *The Lament* – wild with heady, poetic
imagery and yet tough with its spare, rapidly
shifting scenario, fond with its regard for
Arthur and sorrowing at the needless waste of
a bright spirit.

Try these:
Other Irish playwrights looking at the problems of change within tightly knit communities are Graham Reid (with his Billy plays,
set in modern Belfast) and Tom Murphy,
whose *Bailegangaire* uses language with
the same *nous* and love as the best traditional storytellers; ▷Brian Friel; Donal

O'Kelly, a professional actor/writer,
creates one-man plays that peruse the
landscape of Irish temperament and behaviour in a way that is Joycean and
Freudian – *Bat the Father, Rabbit the Son*
is one of his best: ▷O'Casey, ▷Synge,
▷Yeats also afford glimpses of Ireland
across decades of drama; ▷O'Neill's
Anna Christie has a nostalgia for the exiled
Irishman; ▷Bill Bryden for a Scottish
equivalent.

BOLT, Robert   [1924–]
British dramatist and screenwriter

Plays include:
The Critic and the Heart (1957), *Flowering
Cherry* (1957), *A Man for All Seasons* (radio
version 1954; staged 1960), *The Tiger and
the Horse* (1960), *Gentle Jack* (1963), *The
Thwarting of Baron Bolligrew* (for children;
1965), *Vivat! Vivat Regina!* (1970), *State of
Revolution* (1977)

A school teacher who began writing plays for
children and then for radio, Bolt modelled
The Critic and the Heart on ▷Maugham's *The
Circle*, while *Flowering Cherry*, his first popular success, was greeted as Chekhovian by
contemporary critics. Its picture of an insurance salesman living among his own illusions
has an edge of non-naturalism which contrasts
with its largely conventional structure; Ralph
Richardson's eccentric performance had
much to do with the play's original success.
Bolt has continued to essay a variety of styles.
Critics saw the influence of ▷Brecht in *A
Man for All Seasons* (it was staged four years
after the Berliner Ensemble's London season),
but the device of a chorus figure, the Common
Man, weaving in and out of the action, owes
much more to the techniques of radio, for
which it was originally written. However,
when interviewed in 1961, Bolt declared:
'Brecht is the writer I would most wish to
resemble.' *Gentle Jack* made a gesture towards
ritual theatre, drawing parallels between
pagan folklore and capitalist mores, and he
originally proposed that *Vivat! Vivat Regina!*
should be given an *Oh What a Lovely War!*,
pier-end-style presentation. *Vivat!* was
intended to provide a meaty role for his wife,
Sarah Miles, as Mary Queen of Scots, but he
overwrote the part and the more sparsely written Elizabeth I is dominant in performance.
State of Revolution, written for the ▷National
Theatre, is his most ambitious theatre work in

its attempt to present a political dialectic rather than a personal story but its hagiographic portrayal of Lenin against a complex revolutionary background does not come off as well as his Tudor portraits. His films have been more successful in handling epic themes.

Bolt's involvement in the Campaign for Nuclear Disarmament and membership of the Committee of 100 are reflected in *The Tiger and the Horse*, in which an academic wife has to decide whether to sign an anti-bomb petition although doing so will jeopardise her husband's elevation to Vice Chancellor of his university.

A Man for All Seasons

A Man for All Seasons presents the conflict between Sir Thomas More and Henry VIII, and the title role gave Paul Scofield a triumph in both play and film. Here most clearly is the thread that runs right through Bolt's work, of personal integrity, responsibility and the use of power. The human element holds the play together without need to explore religious or political polemics. As in *Vivat!* actors and director are offered chances to create striking theatre and the play has proved a durable favourite, on both sides of the Atlantic, *Vivat* and *A Man for All Seasons* both enjoying successful Broadway runs.

Try these:
▷Brecht, ▷Peter Shaffer ▷David Edgar, ▷David Hare and ▷Howard Brenton for historical epics; ▷Peter Barnes for debunking history; for plays on anti-nuclear issues, ▷Lee Blessing's *A Walk in the Woods*, ▷Steven Dietz's *Fooling Around with Infinity*; ▷Maria Irene Fornes' *The Danube*. ▷Nick Darke's *The Body*, ▷Brian Clarke's *The Petition*, and ▷Lanford Wilson's *Angels Fall*; and ▷Stephen Lowe for plays with an anti-war theme.

BOND, Edward   [1934–   ]
British dramatist

Plays include:
The Pope's Wedding (1962), *Saved* (1965), *Narrow Road to the Deep North* (1968), *Early Morning* (1968), *Black Mass* (1970), *Passion* (1971), *Lear* (1972), *The Sea* (1973), *Bingo: Scenes of Money and Death* (1973), *The Fool: Scenes of Bread and Love* (1975), *Stone* (1976), *The Bundle* (1978),

The Woman (1978), *The Worlds* (1979), *Restoration* (1981), *Summer* (1982), *The War Plays* (1985)

Bond, one of the most radical of playwrights, has been called 'the most important and controversial dramatist writing in Britain today'. Notorious for a scene in *Saved* in which a baby is stoned to death, he has consistently written from a Marxist perspective, and argues that the shock of such violent images is necessary to represent the violence that is done to people by capitalism.

Born in London, Bond left school at fourteen, worked in factories and offices, writing plays in his spare time, and sending them to the Royal Court. *Saved*, developed with the Writer's group at the Court, was instrumental in ridding British theatre of the censorship of the Lord Chamberlain. The theatre's attempt to stage the play under club conditions led to a prosecution which showed that such conditions did not offer any protection from censorship. In 1968, The Theatres Act abolished the powers of the Lord Chamberlain, and *Saved* and *Narrow Road to the Deep North* were toured throughout Europe under the auspices of the British Council.

A recent revival of his early work at the Royal Court, which gave *The Pope's Wedding* its first full production, confirmed Bond as a writer of savage power, with a command of language and poetic imagery that went beyond the shocking.

Bond refers to his drama as 'a Rational Theatre'. According to Bond: 'Theatre is an event about life and takes place in life. It is an experience about experience . . . The routes of communication between spectator and stage run both ways.'

Many of Bond's plays offer radical rereadings of historical events, texts and figures that are commonly held as a source of national pride: *Bingo* confronts the dying and unheroic ▷Shakespeare and ▷Ben Jonson, *The Fool* is about the 'peasant poet' John Clare. Bond has described his reworking of ▷Shakespeare's *King Lear* in *Lear* as 'an attack on Stalinism, as seen as a danger to Western revolution, and on bourgeois culture as expressed in Shakespeare's *Lear*'. He has consistently spoken out for political causes; *Black Mass* was written for the Anti-Apartheid movement; *Stone* for Gay Sweatshop; *Passion* was commissioned by the Campaign for Nuclear Disarmament.

In 1979 Bond cast his play *The Worlds* with

a non-professional cast of young people from the Court's Young People's Theatre Scheme; it was an early demonstration of his commitment to his principle that: 'New writing needs new acting, new directing and new audiences.' In recent years he has insisted on directing his own new work, with the perhaps predictable result that his uniquely trenchant voice has been less widely heard.

Saved

Saved is a difficult play to watch; dealing with a community of young people in South London it charts their desperate and violent lives. Its first performance at the Royal Court provoked extreme, and extremely polarised, reactions. The *Daily Telegraph* critic reported 'cold disgust' and horror at the scene in which a group of young men stone a baby to death (and was not alone in his reaction), while other critics and writers greeted the power of Bond's writing and imagery with acclaim. It is not only that scene which makes the play so harrowing; in one section, the baby wails unrelentingly while no one on stage responds to its cries, and the audience is made to physically experience the frustration and apathy of the play's characters.

Try these:

The Pope's Wedding was first staged on the set of ▷Beckett's *Happy Days*, and the pile of sand became a contributory factor to the final image of Scobey; ▷Ann Jellicoe, ▷Maureen Duffy, ▷John Arden and ▷Arnold Wesker were also members of the Writer's Group with Bond; Bond has cited ▷Joint Stock as 'the kind of theatre I want'; Artaud was an important influence on Bond; ▷Brecht is a strong influence and *The Narrow Road to the Deep North* and its companion play *The Bundle* use an oriental setting in ways reminiscent of *The Caucasian Chalk Circle* and *The Good Person of Sezchuan*; *The Woman* is a re-reading of the Trojan wars more familiar in ▷Euripides' *The Trojan Women*, ▷Shakespeare's *Troilus and Cressida* or ▷Giraudoux' *The Trojan War Will Not Take Place*; *Restoration* is a rereading of Restoration comedy. Bond himself has drawn attention to the Oedipal elements in *Saved* (see ▷Sophocles).

BOUCICAULT, Dionysus Larner   [1820–96]

Irish actor and dramatist

Plays include:

London Assurance (1841), *The Vampire* (1852), *The Corsican Brothers* (1852), *The Poor of New York* (1857), *The Octoroon* (1859), *The Colleen Bawn* (1860), *Arrah-na-Pogue* (1864) and *The Shaughraun* (1874)

Greatly admired as an actor in Britain and the USA, Boucicault was a wide-ranging and prolific dramatist who wrote nearly 150 original plays and adaptations, operettas, pantomimes and melodramas (including sixteen plays in one year). The flood was aided by reworking to suit new audiences: *The Streets of London* and *The Streets of Liverpool* are almost identical to *The Poor of New York*. Many of his plays offer opportunities for spectacle: the burning of a Mississippi steamer in *The Octoroon*, or, in *Arrah-na-Pogue*, the whole scene sinking slowly as the hero climbs an ivy-clad turret to seize the villain and hurl him to his death. Though melodramas like *The Vampire* follow the pattern for the genre, his work shows careful construction and keen observation. *The Octoroon* was one of the first plays in which an American black slave was treated seriously and the social themes which often attracted him prefigured later dramas about the common people. His Irish plays, such as *The Shaughraun*, provided fine vehicles for himself but, though he fought to establish copyright for dramatists in the USA and was the first to receive a royalty instead of a flat fee, he died an impoverished teacher of acting in New York.

His plays continue to be revived fairly regularly in Ireland and more occasionally elsewhere: in 1975 an ▷RSC production of *London Assurance*, with Judi Dench, found great success and restored the play to the modern repertory. A musical version of *The Streets of London*, transferred from Stratford East to Her Majesty's, was modestly successful in 1980; *The Shaughraun* more so, when it was revived at the ▷National Theatre in 1988.

London Assurance

London Assurance presents the courtship by a young gentleman, who is heavily in debt, of a cynical country beauty. She is at first happy at the idea of marriage to an old man who will provide her with a secure income, until she falls in love with his son. A witty piece which owes a great debt to earlier comedies of manners, its characters are sharply drawn, and a plot which turns upon a father not recognising his disguised son is acceptable within a structure that includes some farce-like devices. Donald Sinden, who played in the ▷RSC revival, considered this play the equal of ▷Wilde's *The Importance of Being Earnest*.

Try these:
Phantom of the Opera offers many of the attractions that delighted Boucicault's nineteenth-century audiences; *London Assurance* shows resemblances to the plays of ▷Goldsmith and ▷Sheridan (as well as another ▷RSC revival, John O'Keefe's *Wild Oats*), and through them to ▷Congreve and other Restoration comic dramatists; Boucicault's concern with Irish politics marks him out as an ancestor of ▷Sean O'Casey and ▷Brian Friel.

BRECHT, Bertolt   [1898–1956]
German dramatist, poet, theatrical innovator and theoretician

Plays include:
Baal (1918; performed 1923), *Drums in the Night* (1922), *In the Jungle of Cities* (1923), *Edward II* (1924; with Lion Feuchtwanger), *The Elephant Calf* (c 1924–5), *Man is Man* (1926), *The Threepenny Opera* (1928; with music by Kurt Weill, from ▷John Gay's *The Beggar's Opera*), *Happy End* (1929, with Elisabeth Hauptmann and music by Weill), *He who says Yes* and *He who says No* (1930), *The Measures Taken* (1930), *The Exception and the Rule* (1930), *The Rise and Fall of the City of Mahagonny* (1930; with music by Weill), *The Mother* (1932; from Gorki), *St Joan of the Stockyards* (1932), *The Seven Deadly Sins* (1933; with Weill, also known as *Anna Anna*), *Senora Carrar's Rifles* (1937; based on ▷Synge's *Riders to the Sea*), *Fear and Misery of the Third Reich* (1938; also known as *The Private Life of the Master Race*), *Mother Courage and Her Children* (1941), *The Resistible Rise of Arturo Ui* (1941), *The Life of Galileo* (1943), *The Good Person of Sezchuan* (1943), *Schweik in the Second World War* (1943), *The Caucasian Chalk Circle* (1945), *Mr Puntila and His Servant Matti* (1948), *The Days of the Commune* (1949), *The Tutor* (1950; from Jacob Lenz)

Brecht is one of the most influential (if often unacknowledged) figures in contemporary culture. His example has changed theatrical practice and affected a generation of socialist playwrights, his principles have informed contemporary film theory and a whole genre of 'agit-prop' theatre productions and companies, and his 'alienation effects' are now almost fashionable practice in stage, television and film.

Brecht's history is bound up in the rise of fascism in Germany. Working in 1918 at Augsburg military hospital gave him a lifelong commitment to pacifism. He became involved in the theatre through drama criticism and his first plays were very much influenced by ▷Expressionism. *Baal*, the life of a poet, prefigures his later work in its deliberately shocking effects. Brecht went on to become part of a group of radical intellectuals in the theatre and cultural life of Berlin, becoming increasingly involved with Marxist theory, and beginning to develop an aesthetic practice that integrated with his politics, and which was bound up with the social and economic conditions of the period. He became very much part of the European avant-garde, exchanging ideas with the Formalist group in Russia.

During the 1920s Brecht's collaboration with Kurt Weill gave rise to the musical productions *The Threepenny Opera*, *The Seven Deadly Sins* and *The Rise and Fall of the City of Mahagonny* (produced in the year of the German economic crash, and which presents a society in which *anything* can be had for money). These plays were much influenced by the Berlin cabaret of the 1920s and early 1930s, and Brecht argued that the theatre should be a place in which audiences could relax, smoke and drink, the better to take up the points of the play for discussion.

Brecht was on the Nazis' list of banned writers, and fled to Denmark the day after the Reichstag fire. The Danes refused to hand Brecht over to the German authorities, but when Germany invaded Denmark, Brecht escaped to Finland. The events of the rise of fascism are charted in the ironically allegorical *The Rise and Fall of Arturo Ui*, in which Brecht made an analogy between the rise of Nazism and Chicago gangsters. He spent the years of the war in exile in Hollywood, where he wrote the script for the film, *Hangmen Also Die*. In 1947, after an appearance before the House of Representatives' Committee of Un-American Activities, Brecht moved to Switzerland, and in 1949 he returned to East Germany, to take up an offer of his own theatre and extensive subsidy, founding the ▷Berliner Ensemble, on his own principles of political theatre. On his death it was taken over by his widow, Helene Weigel.

In his plays, Brecht often turned to fable and to history, to construct 'Parables' for the theatre, offering radical re-readings of familiar texts. When accused of plagiarism, Brecht's reply was ▷'Shakespeare was a thief', not an unreasonable analogy.

Brecht wrote forty plays altogether, which can roughly be divided into three groups (although there are elements of each phase in most of his plays): the early Expressionist plays and the musical pieces he devised with Weill; the Lehrstücke (or 'Learning pieces') and Parable plays; and his 'Epic theatre'.

In *The Messingkauf Dialogues* (one of his many writings on theatre) Brecht sets out his principles for a 'Theatre of Reason' (also known as epic theatre), in which acting, direction, set design, and all aspects of theatrical production were organised to produce a dramatic effect which challenged the audience and which implicated them in the dramatic events. Central to Brechtian theory is the 'Verfremdung' effect (often mistakenly translated as 'alienation effect', 'distancing' is closer) which refers to devices in staging, acting, music and direction which encourage the spectator to avoid cathartic identification. Songs which comment on the action of the play, placards which describe the context, direct address to the audience, open set changes all demonstrate the theatre as a place of work. Acting too becomes a means of distancing. Brecht was thoroughly opposed to Stanislavski's Method of acting the psychological 'truth' of a character.

Brecht's achievement was to demonstrate his principles in the theatricality of his plays: their politics become something which the audience experiences and is given space to think about and to debate. Few have achieved such a stimulating and actively engaging political theatrical practice since it is hard to produce work which combines dialectical toughness, humour and theatricality in the way that Brecht usually did. Brecht's politics are integral to the structure and form of his drama, his plays are structured around a dia-lectical principle, between scene and scene, between audience and stage, and between theatrical event and political practice. A Brechtian theatre practice should never be static, but respond to contemporary political events, and engage the audience in a challenge to 'common sense' modes of perception. For example, in *The Good Person of Sezchuan* and *The Caucasian Chalk Circle* the difficulties of behaving humanely are dramatised in, respectively, a woman who has to invent a male protector (actually herself in disguise) to fend off claims on her, and a woman who asserts the claims of nurture over biological motherhood.

Mother Courage and her Children

This play belongs to the 'epic' period of Brecht's work. Although it is often taken as a study of the struggle of a resilient woman and her family and her doughty survival in a period of war (The Thirty Years' War), the play is structured specifically not to be seen as the study of a single individual, but as parable and metaphor. Mother Courage is a small business woman, who struggles with her cart to scrimp a living for her daughter, the dumb Kattrin, and her sons. Over the course of the play she is confronted with decisions which become increasingly complex, and more overtly political. Mother Courage resolutely asserts that she is not interested in politics, only the survival and care of her family but the consequence is that she loses them all. Her fate is not a simple one; the play makes it quite clear that other decisions could have averted the events of Mother Courage's tragedy. Brecht once said: 'We must be able to lose ourselves in the agony and at the same time not to. Our actual emotion will come from recognising and feeling the double process.' This double process is at work in *Mother Courage*: while her situation is undoubtedly moving, the play constantly points to the events and system which have placed her there, and to her own collusion in that system. The play is intercut with songs at the moments at which Mother Courage is required to take action, which point to the far reaching implications of individual acts. The play has a stunning alienation effect at the moment when Kattrin, silent for the entire play, creates its most violent and loudest noise. In a moment in which she has to make a political choice between saving other lives or her own, by banging on a drum she alerts the villagers who are about to be destroyed.

Try these:

▷Edward Bond has called his own theatrical project 'Rational Theatre', in homage to Brecht's 'Theatre of Reason'; ▷Christopher Hampton's *Tales from Hollywood* ▷Günter Grass' *The Plebeians Rehearse the Uprising* and Nigel Gearing's *Berlin Days, Hollywood Nights* include Brecht among their characters; ▷Anne Bogart's *No Plays, No Poetry*, a theatricalisation of Brecht's theoretical work. ▷Shaw, ▷Pirandello, ▷Galsworthy, ▷O'Neill and ▷Strindberg were dramatists banned by the Nazis; ▷Howard Barker, ▷Howard Brenton, (whose *The Genius* is a response to *Galileo* which he adapted for the ▷National Theatre), ▷David Edgar, ▷Trevor Griffiths, and ▷John McGrath are dramatists who have inherited Brechtian principles of theatre; for child custody Gay Sweatshop's *Care and Control* and ▷Sarah Daniels' *Neaptide*; ▷Caryl Churchill's *Serious Money* has similarities to Brecht and Weill's analyses of capitalism in *Mahagonny* and *The Threepenny Opera*; *Edward II* is taken from ▷Marlowe and Brecht was generally impressed by ▷Shakespeare; *St Joan of the Stockyards* and *Simone Marchard* are treatments of a St Joan figure to be contrasted with ▷Shaw's *St Joan* and ▷Anouilh's *The Lark*; *Happy End* has remarkable similarities to the much later musical *Guys and Dolls*; the Glasgow Citizens' has been one of the most consistent champions of Brecht in the British theatre; Manfred Karge, whose *Man to Man* was presented at the Traverse (1987) and then The Royal Court (1988), worked with Brecht at the Berliner Ensemble.

BRENTON, Howard   [1942–]
British dramatist

Plays include:
Gum and Goo (1969), *Heads* (1969), *The Education of Skinny Spew* (1969), *Revenge* (1969), *Christie in Love* (1969), *Wesley* (1970), *Fruit* (1970), *Lay By* (1971; with ▷ Brian Clark, ▷Trevor Griffiths, ▷David Hare, ▷Stephen Poliakoff, Hugh Stoddart, ▷Snoo Wilson), *Scott of the Antarctic* (1971), *Hitler Dances* (1972), *England's Ireland* (1972; with Tony Bicât, ▷Brian Clark, ▷David Edgar, Francis Fuchs, ▷David Hare, ▷Snoo Wilson), *A Fart for Europe* (1973; with ▷David Edgar), *Magnificence* (1973), *Brassneck* (1973; with ▷David Hare), *The Churchill Play* (1974), *Weapons of Happiness* (1976), *Epsom Downs* (1977), *Deeds* (1978; with ▷Ken Campbell, ▷Trevor Griffiths, ▷David Hare), *Sore Throats* (1979), *A Short Sharp Shock* (1980; with Tony Howard), *The Romans in Britain* (1980), *Thirteenth Night* (1981), *The Genius* (1983), *Sleeping Policemen* (1983; with ▷Tunde Ikoli), *Bloody Poetry* (1984), *Pravda* (1985; with ▷David Hare), *Greenland* (1988), *Iranian Nights* (with Tariq Ali, 1989), *Moscow Gold* (with Tariq Ali, 1990)

Although he has achieved recognition as one of Britain's leading dramatists with plays produced by the ▷National Theatre, ▷RSC and even a Royal Court season in 1988 which included revivals of *Bloody Poetry* and *Sore Throats* as well as the premiere of *Greenland*, Brenton remains an independent figure willing to continue working on the fringe which first nourished him as much as within the established theatre. His is an uncomfortable talent, with a particular capacity for anatomising the unhealthy state of Britain today and exhuming the uncomfortable truths about the past that people would rather forget in ways that antagonise the Establishment, from his anti-Enoch Powell version of *Measure for Measure* at Exeter in 1972, through the presentation of the ghost of Airey Neave in *A Short Sharp Shock*, to the major row over *The Romans in Britain*, where moral uproar over the simulated anal rape of a Druid led to a prosecution which was ultimately abandoned. It was probably more than coincidental that *Romans* says some rather uncomfortable things about imperialism, including the present situation in Northern Ireland, since there was considerable resistance throughout the 1970s to theatrical treatments of the Irish question. A committed socialist, Brenton tackles his themes with a cartoon-like ferocity and humour which has not diminished since his early fringe days with the Combination and Portable Theatre. Brenton's work is consistently engaged with topical issues and immediate concerns, as in *Wesley*, written to be performed in a Methodist chapel, or *Scott of the Antarctic*, performed on an ice rink. But even in his most topical plays there is an abiding concern with making people aware of the underlying nature of their situation, what

repses them and what sustains them, and
encouraging them to change things for the
better. Brenton has written on the criminalisa-
tion and corruption of society, from his early
Revenge through to *Pravda*, and on the difficulties of effecting change, from the gesture
politics of *Magnificence* to the nuclear politics
of *The Genius*, in which two mathematicians
try to evade the forces that would turn their
discoveries to destructive use. In *Epsom
Downs* Brenton and the Joint Stock Theatre
Group take the temperature of Britain on
Derby Day 1977 in a kaleidoscopically inventive re-creation and interrogation of the contradictions of that event with the ghost of the
suffragette Emily Davison attempting to persuade a modern woman to try to slash the
picture as she did when she ran out in front of
the king's horse in the 1913 Derby. The play
is comically incisive in its presentation of contradictions and in its interweaving of threads
within the apparently haphazard events of
Derby Day.

Brenton's recent collaborations with Tariq
Ali have continued his engagement with contemporary political issues. *Iranian Nights*
arises from the Salman Rushdie affair, and
Moscow Gold offers a carnivalesque picture of
Gorbachev's rise to power and his attempts to
hold together the Soviet Union against the
forces of reaction and disintegration.

Bloody Poetry

Bloody Poetry, commissioned by the touring
company ▷Foco Novo of which Brenton was
a board member, grapples with sexual and
other politics, the role of the artist and the
need to make revolutions in the heart and
mind as much as in the body politic. Byron,
▷Shelley, Mary Shelley and Claire Claire-
mont reach out for a model of existence which
is beyond their grasp, at great cost to themselves and to their families. Brenton has described this as a utopian play, which has led
some critics to castigate him for his male
characters' sexism, but he is actually concerned with the forces, sexism included,
which militate against the creation of utopia.
Other forces also stand in the way: some
people refused to see the play because it had
'bloody' in the title, others because of the
presence of 'poetry'!

Try these:
▷Howard Barker, ▷David Edgar and
▷Trevor Griffiths are other leading British
socialist writers; ▷Ben Jonson's

Bartholomew Fair also takes the nation's
temperature on a holiday, ▷Peter Nichols'
The National Health does the same
through an institution; ▷Ann Jellicoe's
Shelley and Liz Lochhead's *Blood and Ice*
tackle the Shelleys, as does the women's
company, Tattycoram's *The Very Tragical
History of Mary Shelley* – a completely
biased and anti-Shelley piece; also
▷Doug Lucie's *Progress* for an attempt to
build a new society, flawed by old sexisms;
Howard Barker's *Scenes from an
Execution*, Nick Dear's *The Art of Success*
for the role of the artist and their relationship to the body politic.

BREUER, Lee   [1937–]
American avant-garde writer and director

Plays include:
The Red Horse Animation (1971), *The B-
Beaver Animation* (1974), *The Lost Ones*
(1975), *The Shaggy Dog Animation* (1977),
Prelude to Death in Venice (1980), *Sister
Suzie Cinema* (1980); *Red Beads* (1982);
Hajj (1983); *The Warrior Ant* (work in pro-
gress shown from 1986–1990), *Lear* (1990)

Although he has directed widely on his own,
Lee Breuer's work remains associated with the
avant-garde collective known as Mabou
Mines, which he founded in 1970 with David
Warrilow, JoAnne Akalaitis, Philip Glass, and
Breuer's sometime wife, actress Ruth
Maleczech. Long acclaimed as a leading
experimental theatre group, the company has
received awards and grants but little recognition among the larger American audience.
The company's work is intellectual in conception, drawing inspiration from various sources
and often blending mutli-media staging with
heavy use of linguistic play. Breuer travelled
through Europe during the 1960s, and much
of his early work reflects the alienating effects
of the European avant-garde.

In recent years, Breuer's work has drawn
heavily upon the intermingling of diverse cultures to shed new light on both traditional and
innovative material. His multi-cultural stagings have achieved mixed results ranging from
spectacular fusing of disparate elements to
what one critic has labelled 'grotesque
hybrids.' While few critics admired his 1981
Tempest for the New York Shakespeare
Festival, with its punk Caliban and mafioso
style villains, his 1982 collaboration with composer Bob Telson, *Gospel at Colonnus*, a sung

gospel version of the Greek tragedy, was a stunning illumination of the deepest spiritual elements in ▷Sophocles' text. His *Lear*, with all the sexual roles reversed, featured Ruth Maleczech as Queen Lear with her three sons. The play was set in the American South, a conceit arrived at when Breuer learned that the English of the South was closest to that spoken in the Elizabethan era. The Shakespearean lines scanned well on the southern cadence, but the tragedy was reduced to a ▷Tennessee Williams neurotic family drama. *The Warrior Ant*, Breuer's ongoing magnum opus with Telson, is to be seen in twelve parts performed over three evenings. This tale of a messianic ant is a collage of Japanese Bunraku puppetry, Afro-Caribbean rhythms, gospel singing and Disney plot. His post-modern gesamtkunstwerk is typical of Breuer's imaginative cultural cross-fertilization through which he seeks to create new art forms.

Prelude to Death in Venice

Images of Dracula and a Vampire bat are seen while the music of Bach plays on in a mixed-media experience that draws on such disparate sources as Thomas Mann, ▷Beckett, and the New York Police Department. A character, Bill, manipulates a dummy called John, who is suspended between two telephone poles; while tapes of various voices are heard, images appear and disappear in a fragmentary yet deliberate style that toys with form and meaning. For some, the absence of character and motivation in this sort of theatre dehumanises; for others, Breuer's brand of dramatic poetry excites through its embrace of a range of effects most theatres shut out.

Try these:
▷Samuel Beckett, Peter Handke and Ionesco for redefining the range of theatrical possibility; ▷Robert Wilson, San Franciso Mime Troupe, ▷The Wooster Group, ▷Ping Chong, Meredith Monk, ▷Richard Foreman, ▷Anne Bogart, ▷Peter Sellars for other pre-eminent figures in the American avant-garde; Impact Theatre, Jan Fabre for English and Continental comparisons; ▷Jean Genet for early inspiration; Robert Wilson and Peter Sellars for post-modern mise en scenes; Laurie Anderson for multi-media performance; Performance Art.

BRIDIE, James
(Osborne Henry Mavor)   [1888–1951]
British doctor and dramatist

Plays include:
The Sunlight Sonata (as Mary Henderson; 1928), *The Anatomist* (1930), *Tobias and the Angel* (1930), *Jonah and the Whale* (1932), *A Sleeping Clergyman* (1933), *Colonel Wotherspoon* (1934), *Mary Read* (1934), *The Black Eye* (1935), *Storm in a Teacup* (adapted from Bruno Frank; 1936), *Susannah and the Elders* (1937), *The King of Nowhere* (1938), *What They Say* (1941), *Mr Bolfry* (1943), *It Depends What You Know* (1944), *The Forrigan Reel* (1944), *Daphne Laureola* (1949), *Mr Gillie* (1950), *The Baikie Charivari* (1952), *Meeting at Night* (1954)

Born in Scotland, Bridie's plays range from biblical and hagiographic tales, to a play based on the Edinburgh body-snatchers Burke and Hare (*The Anatomist*), to the episodic history of an 18th-century woman pirate (*Mary Read*). His characters have occasioned many virtuoso performances and launched a number of actors into stardom. *Dr Bolfry*, one of his most successful plays, tells how the Devil visits a Scots minister in the shape of another clergyman. Together they form an alliance against non-believers, but when they meet later as antagonists the issue is undecided. The minister returns home thinking himself triumphant, only to see the Devil's umbrella rise and stalk slowly from his house. *A Sleeping Clergyman*, is a study of heredity through three generations, which shows that though 'evil' may persist through seduction, blackmail and murder, 'good' can reappear just when the world most needs it – in this case medical genius. Although it tends to be individual performances in Bridie's plays that people remember, rather than the plays themselves, they are still occasionally revived, particularly in Scotland, where Bridie was a co-founder of the Glasgow Citizen's Theatre, and instrumental in establishing the Royal Scottish Academy of Music (now the Academy of Music and Drama).

Try these:
▷Christopher Fry for similar treatments of religious themes; ▷Chekhov as another dramatist who brought his doctor's observation of character to his work; ▷Steve Gooch's *The Women-Pirates Ann Bonney and Mary Read*; ▷J. M. Barrie, as a

Scottish contemporary; ▷Lillian Hellman for discussions of moral values; ▷Mary O'Malley's *Talk of The Devil* and ▷Dekker, ▷Ford and ▷Rowley's *The Witch of Edmonton,* ▷Václav Havel's *Temptation* for devilish visitations; ▷Kaufman and Hart, ▷George Abbott for more American parallels.

BRIGHOUSE, Harold   [1882–1958]
British dramatist

Plays include:
Dealing in Futures (1910), *Lonesome Like* (one-act; 1911), *Graft* (originally entitled *The Polygon*; 1912), *Garside's Career* (1914), *Hobson's Choice* (1915), *Zack* (1916)

Part of the ▷'Manchester School' of playwrights, Brighouse wrote and produced some seventy plays, mostly realistic and set in Lancashire. The most well-known of these is *Hobson's Choice*, a play 'built like an iron girder' (Michael Billington), whose heroine, the strong-minded and down-to-earth Maggie Hobson, thirty years old and thought 'past the marrying age', marries the shy but talented boot-maker Willie Mossop, out of hand (he not having much say in the matter), and with him takes over the town's boot-making business from her heavy father. The play is still revived in Britain, and the comedy *Zack* has been played twice in ten years at the Royal Exchange, Manchester (1976 and 1986), with some success. Several of his one-act plays, such as *Lonesome Like*, would easily bear revival if anyone did one-act plays any more.

Try these:
▷Stanley Houghton for another 'Manchester School' playwright.

BRITISH THEATRES AND COMPANIES
The vast majority of the most interesting productions in British theatre originate within the subsidised theatre. Traditional West End theatres and their regional equivalents are now largely the preserve of transfers originating in subsidised theatres. Even large scale musicals can now often originate in the subsidised sector before West End and Broadway runs, often staged by companies in order to generate income for their other work (as in the case of the ▷Royal Shakespeare Company's

phenomenally successful *Les Miserables* and their equally unsuccessful *Carrie*). Subsidised theatres vary enormously in size and function, from the giant organizations of the RSC and the ▷National Theatre which operate on a large scale, both in permanent bases and in touring operations, to small touring companies like Gay Sweatshop and Red Shift, which tend to play smaller venues within an alternative or fringe circuit roughly equivalent to American Off- and Off-Off-Broadway. We cannot cover all the good work that goes on in theatres and companies throughout Britain, often in the face of great financial and material difficulties, but the following companies represent a range of the more established and more interesting groups in the British theatre.

At the top end of the market, Kenneth Branagh's Renaissance Company and the English Shakespeare Company offer a challenge to the RSC and the NT, while the success of Cheek by Jowl with lively small scale touring versions of the classics has been recognized by National Theatre commissions for its director and designer Declan Donnellan and Nick Ormerod. Mike Alfreds, the founder of Shared Experience, had rather less luck when he made the same transition but the company, now under the artistic directorship of Nancy Meckler, has continued to achieve considerable success, mainly with novel adaptations, such as Olwen Wymark's 1987 version of Zola's *Nana*.

Regional theatre centres offer considerable diversity of both theatre shape and policy. Most large towns have a repertory theatre, some housing internationally renowned companies such as the Glasgow Citizens' under Giles Havergal, Philip Prowse, and Robert David Macdonald. The Citizens' produces vibrant and often controversial reinterpretations of the classics in a proscenium arch theatre, while the Manchester Royal Exchange stages its classics in a challenging self-contained theatre that looks like a lunar module inserted into the echoing shell of the old Royal Exchange building. The Exchange is also home to the important Mobil sponsored New Playwriting Competition whose winners include ▷Robin Glendenning, ▷Iain Heggie, ▷Michael Wall, and ▷Lucy Gannon.

Many of the best British companies encourage new writing and also act as a nursery for new talents in directing, design and acting. The demise of Foco Novo, whose premieres included new plays by ▷Bernard Pomerance,

▷Howard Brenton, ▷Mustapha Matura, ▷Tunde Ikoli, and ▷C. P. Taylor, and of Joint Stock, whose unique method of co-operative collaboration between writers, actors, directors, and designers led to one of the great stagings of the 1970s, ▷David Hare's *Fanshen*, and who also produced successes from ▷Caryl Churchill, ▷Howard Brenton, ▷Howard Barker, ▷Karim Alrawi, ▷Stephen Lowe, and ▷Sue Townsend, as a result of removal of Arts Council funding is an indication of the precarious nature of this sector of the theatre.

However, some of the longer established companies with a commitment to new writing remain. Paines Plough established its reputation staging the works of its co-founder ▷David Pownall, but has continued to champion new writing by amongst others, ▷Stephen Jeffreys, ▷April de Angelis, ▷Louise Page, and ▷Doug Lucie. 7:84, which derived its name from an economic statistic that 7% of the population owned 84% of the capital wealth, continues, despite funding problems, to tour socially committed work with a strong emphasis on music and 'popular' forms. Its best known production is probably *The Cheviot, the Stag, and the Black, Black Oil*, but its longtime artistic director ▷John McGrath, which used the form of the traditional Scottish ceilidh to review critically the economic exploitation of the Scottish Highlands. Among new companies, Jonathan Holloway's Red Shift has established a reputation for bridging the gap between naturalistic narrative traditions and visually oriented work, staging plays by new talents ▷Neil Bartlett and April de Angelis.

Much of the best new work has arisen from the experiences of groups who were under- or mis-represented in traditional mainstream West End theatre. Work by or about women, black, Irish or Asian people, homosexuals, people with disabilities, and ex-prisoners has made a considerable impact on the fringe circuit, and, increasingly, beyond. Under its artistic director Jatinder Verma, Tara Arts, the first professional Asian company in Britain has developed from an early westernized agit-prop stance and exploration of contemporary Asian experience into a wider investigation of Asian cultural roots. The success of Tara's work has led to Verma being commissioned to direct ▷Moliere at the ▷National Theatre, a successful infusion of the previously marginalized into the mainstream.

Black Theatre Cooperative, founded by ▷Mustapha Matura and Charlie Hanson, has been one of the most dynamic black companies, staging works by ▷Edgar White, ▷Jacqueline Rudet, and Farrukh Dhondy, in a style that had a lot to do with exuberance, trust, risk-taking and some shrewd choices. Temba, another long established company founded by Oscar James and Alton Kumalo, has survived many vicissitudes to establish itself with a range of plays reflecting not only British but also black American and African life, including works by ▷Amiri Baraka, ▷Athol Fugard, Matura, White, and ▷Derek Walcott. Theatre of Black Women, founded by Bernardine Evaristo, Patricia Hilaire, and Paulette Randall, has shown a particular commitment to counteracting heterosexism, racism, and sexism in an exploration of what it feels like to be young, black, and female in modern Britain, often coupled with a search for cultural roots. Yvonne Brewster's Talawa company has, however, become the main repository of funding for black theatre in Britain with its own London theatre, the Jeanetta Cochrane, and ambitious plans for the future.

The Women's Playhouse Trust, which has plans for its own theatre devoted to women's work, has staged a number of significant revivals, but Monstrous Regiment and the Women's Theatre Group have played a leading part in establishing a greater presence for women's work. The Women's Theatre Group's productions span a wide range, from devised shows such as Tierl Thompson and Libby Mason's 1978 *Dear Girl*, a dramatization of letters and diaries, and Elaine Feinstein's 1987 reclamation of *Lear's Daughters*, to ▷Winsome Pinnock's *Picture Palace* (1988), though Deborah Levy's *Pax* (1984) was a surreal and intellectually stimulating highlight. Monstrous Regiment, founded in 1975 by a group of women as a means of gaining more control over their working lives, has always concentrated on challenging stereotypes of women, using work by writes including ▷Clair Luckham, ▷Caryl Churchill, ▷Bryony Lavery, ▷Franca Rame, ▷Susan Yankowitz, ▷Melissa Murray, and Debbie Shewell.

Clean Break, a women's collective, founded by ex-prisoners ▷Jacqueline Holborough and Jenny Hicks in 1978, has established a firm reputation for authentic drama about women and prison which challenges popular stereotypes. Their repertory has covered a wide range of subjects in a constant reminder that drama can have a socially constructive application rather than simply being a source of entertainment.

Field Day was co-founded by the dramatist ▷Brian Friel in Derry in 1980, as a theatre company and a forum for debate about current political and cultural issues in Ireland. They have staged plays by Friel himself, ▷Thomas Kilroy, ▷Stewart Parker, and Terry Eagleton, as well as adaptations of ▷Chekhov, ▷Sophocles, and ▷Moliere.

Gay Sweatshop, Britain's first and still only professional gay company has in the course of a precariously and intermittently funded existence produced many works of great merit and importance. Founded by ▷Dew Griffiths and Gerald Chapman in 1975, the company has consistently addressed gay issues in their wider social and political context, and has equally consistently attracted audiences from beyond the gay community. Among writers who have worked with the company are ▷Noel Greig, ▷Bryony Lavery, Philip Osment, ▷Michelene Wandor, and ▷Jackie Kay.

Graeae, Britain's major professional company of performers with disabilities, takes its name from the three mythological sisters who shared one eye and one tooth. Since its formation in 1980 by Nabil Shaban and Richard Tomlinson, the company has shaken up many preconceptions about physical disability being any kind of handicap to theatrical invention, humour, or enjoyment in such works as their adaptation of Mary Shelley's *Frankenstein*, which poignantly underlined the similarities between Frankenstein's feelings of isolation and general attitudes towards disabilities.

Try these:
▷Asian Theatre in Britain; ▷Black theatre in Britain; ▷Community Theatre in Britain; ▷Gay Theatre in Britain; ▷Gay Theatre in the USA; ▷Hispanic-American Theatre; ▷Lesbian Theatre in Britain; ▷Lesbian Theatre in the USA; ▷The National Theatre of Great Britain; ▷New Playwriting in Britain; ▷New Playwriting in the USA; ▷Off- and Off- Off Broadway; ▷Resident Theatre in the USA; ▷Royal Court Theatre; ▷Royal Shakespeare Company; ▷Theatre for Young People in Britain; ▷Theatre for Young People in the USA; ▷Women in Theatre in Britain; Women in Theatre in the USA; ▷Yiddish and Jewish-American Theatre.

BROOK, Peter   [1925–]
British director and theorist

Books include:
The Empty Space (1968), *The Shifting Point* (collected writings, 1988)

Peter Brook is probably the most influential director Britain has ever produced, though there was never a more international one, and much of his work has appeared outside his own country. Many of his productions have become legendary and his book *The Empty Space* rapidly became a set text for many theatre workers, with its crucial distinctions between 'rough' and 'holy' theatre. He has often been regarded as a theatrical guru, and by any standards he has been a key figure in exploring and developing the possibilities of drama. In 1968 he wrote 'I can take any empty space and call it a bare stage', and he has pursued his idea all over the world in a career which has spanned forty years of productions of theatre and opera, from the West End to Brooklyn to Persepolis to disused quarries in Australia to African villages that had never before seen a theatre company.

He was born in London of Russian parents, and directed his first (amateur) production (Marlowe's *Dr Faustus*) in 1942, before going to Oxford University. In 1946 he directed *Love's Labour's Lost* at Stratford, thus beginning a connection that lasted for more than twenty years. He also directed plays and operas in the West End, including Strauss' *Salomé* (with designs by Dali) for Covent Garden in 1949, and plays by ▷Sartre, ▷Anouilh, ▷Miller, and ▷Genet, in London and Paris. In 1962 he was appointed a co-director (with ▷Peter Hall and Michel Saint-Denis) of the newly named Royal Shakespeare Company, and there throughout the sixties he developed a range of experimental and innovative work, including the setting-up with ▷Charles Marowitz of a group to work on ▷Artaud's ideas. This culminated in the 'Theatre of Cruelty' season at LAMDA in 1964, where they staged Artaud's 'unstageable' play *Jet of Blood* and Marowitz's first *Hamlet* collage – in the process discovering the young Glenda Jackson – and prepared the way for the exciting production of ▷Peter Weiss's *Marat/Sade*. In 1966 Brook devised with the RSC the controversial *US*, a bitter attack on American involvement in Vietnam and British government support for it, and his only overtly 'political' work. Kenneth Tynan was probably right to say that Brook's political sense was naïve. However, his 1970 production of *A Midsummer Night's Dream* is still among the most celebrated and discussed of Shakespearean productions. Staged on a bare white box set, it used acrobatics, juggling and magic tricks in a joyous response to the play's challenges. The emphasis on visual spectacle was very much the direction that Brook's later work was to take.

In 1970 he left the British theatre and established an International Centre of Theatre Research in Paris to work out his ideas of a theatre laboratory along Grotowski's lines, 'to explore the source of theatrical expression – languge, movment, sound and space'. He extracted grants from the Ford, Anderson and Gulbenkian Foundations, gathered an international company of actors dedicated to his way of working, and proceeded to experiment with Kathakali dance techniques, circus skills, masks, and a general exploration of dramatic forms, in an attempt to work out an 'international theatre language' that would transcend Western theatrical conventions. In 1972 the company took a play, *Orghast*, written in an invented language by Ted Hughes, to Persepolis, subsidised by the Shah of Iran, and established a policy of international touring. They also toured parts of Africa, performing spontaneous improvisations to village audiences, and then developed a play based on a Persian story, *The Conference of the Birds*, which was performed to aboriginal audiences in Australia, to festival audiences in France, and across the Sahara desert. In 1974 the French Ministry of Culture took over the funding and the company moved to a long-disused and slightly ruinous operetta house in an immigrant quarter of Paris, the Bouffes du Nord, and began to put on plays for more conventional audiences – though not necessarily conventional plays. These have included *The Ik*, based on Colin Turnbull's account of an African tribe which had to change its lifestyle and thus lost most of its humanity, and a pared-down version of Bizet's *Carmen* with three separate casts.

The culmination of his work at the Centre so far has been the dramatisation, with Jean-Claude Carrière, of the Hindu epic *Mahabharata* in a cycle of three plays lasting nearly ten hours, using a multi-racial cast, many of them old Brook hands. It was played originally in a quarry near Avignon, the main features of which have now been reproduced (at considerable expense) from Australia to Glasgow. He used a cast of twenty-four to represent forty-five characters, omitted much of the theology, and was left with a great story superbly told with great economy of means (it not of money – the entire cast was sent to India for a month just before the opening). Although all the acting is fairly physical, there is no other attempt to impose a uniform style; instead, national differences are exploited. There are occasional unforgettable stage pictures, generally achieved very simply, with coloured floor mats and cloths, water, fire, and mime – two of the most powerful images are produced with nothing more than a bottle of petrol and a taper, producing a ring of fire within which Duryodhana can see what Arjuna is doing in the Himalayas, and a large jar full of red dye, as Drona pours bloods over his head and accepts death. By now it seems that Brook's mastery has reached the level of the truly great stylists – the man who makes it look easy.

Since reworking the *Mahabharata* for film and television, he has taken a revival of his production of ▷Chekhov's *The Cherry Orchard* to New York, made his third attempt on *The Tempest* at the Bouffes du Nord and in Glasgow (1990), and is rumoured to be working on *The Man who Mistook his Wife for a Hat*.

Try these:
▷Brecht and ▷Stanislavski were other major dramatic theorists of the twentieth century; ▷Robert Wilson and ▷Peter Sellars for equally electrifying and iconoclastic stagings and re-assessments.

BRYDEN, Bill   [1942–]
Scottish dramatist, director, film-maker

Plays include:
Willie Rough (1972), *Benny Lynch* (1974), *Old Movies* (1977), *Civilians* (1981), *The Ship* (1990).

Since the mid-sixties Bill Bryden has been assiduously involved in the making of drama either for stage or the screen, in Scotland and abroad. His expertise is considerable: often he will write and direct projects, or devise and produce them – as with ▷John Byrne's highly popular award-winning television series, *Tutti Frutti* (1988). His reputation, now international, was secured when he started working away from his native land. Increasingly, as his stature grew at the ▷National Theatre so his 'clout' grew in Scotland. His return visits, mostly to the Edinburgh Festival, with such celebrated National productions as his promenade *Mysteries*, roused sage acclaim from parties who (one suspects) had never really bothered to go along to Edinburgh's Lyceum while he was Associate Director there.

It was at the Lyceum (1971–4) that Bryden put his own plays into production. *Willie Rough* (1972), deriving from his grandfather's experience, looked at issues of working-class life against the backdrop of shipyard politics between the wars. *Benny Lynch* (1974) was again about the aspirations and daily drudge-and-grudge of the working classes, represented by this 'bonniest o' fechters' who rose to fêted world status only to end, exploited and discarded, in the gutter.

These productions represented a conscious drive on Bryden's part to stamp the Lyceum company with a 'national' identity and to encourage new Scots writers to create for *their* nation's stage. Unfortunately, it was not the right moment for his vision. And though he is based mostly in London – with forays Stateside for screenplays and the like – he returns North again and again with projects close to his own West of Scotland roots: in 1981, he wrote and directed *Civilians*, a fond, anecdotal glimpse of 1940s Greenock life, for the (short-lived) Scottish Theatre Company and in 1985 he took up the post of Head of Drama Television with BBC Scotland since when works by Peter MacDougall, Ian Heggie, John Byrne and others have seen the far-reaching light of transmission.

Perhaps the work that epitomises Bryden's entrepreneurial strengths and oft-criticised weaknesses as a dramatist is *The Ship* (1990), a spectacularly staged celebration of Clyde ship-building in its last years of greatness. Conceived as part of Glasgow's year-long thrash as European City of Culture in 1990, this mega-venture went directly to the city's erstwhile heartland and turned a disused riverside engine shed into an ad hoc theatre. Thanks to designer William Dudley, the performing space was encompassed by the inner decks and shell of a liner-in-progress. The action, such as it was (mostly short scenes of anecdotal exchange between workers interspersed with Jock-rock music), culminating in a cunning *coup de théâtre*, the apparent launching of the boat. The sheer, persuasive showmanship of all this did much to offset the saccharine banalities of the script which reduced the hard men and hard times of post-war Clydeside to a series of ciphers and clichés. Critical reaction was mixed, but *The Ship* proved one of the most popular events of Glasgow's 1990 programme and confirmed Bryden's charismatic image as a shaker and mover within theatre.

Try these:
▷Joe Corrie's *In Time o' Strife* (1927) portrays a Fife mining community during the last days of the General Strike; Ena Lamont Stewart's *Men Should Weep* and Benedict Scott's *Lambs of God* both show darker sides to tenement life in the 1930s and 1940s. Roddy McMillan's *The Bevellers* is a lively, shrewd depicition of men at work – the 'bevelling' is the finishing edge on mirrors; ▷Dermot Bolger's *The Lament for Arthur Cleary* as an Irish equivalent of the exile's nostalgia for home.

BÜCHNER, Georg   [1813–1837]
German dramatist

Plays:
Danton's Death (1835), *Leonce and Lena* (1836), *Woyzeck* (1836)

Although his plays were not performed until many years after his death, Büchner is one of the major influences in contemporary world drama. Somehow he managed to foreshadow many of the great theatrical movements of the twentieth century: epic theatre, Surrealism, Expressionism, and the Theatre of the Absurd. The sense of history as a major force dominates his work, as does society as the destroyer of the individual. His principal characters struggle unsuccessfully to communicate their feelings until they recognise their helplessness and incomprehension in the face of the forces that destroy them. The son of a doctor, Büchner studied medicine at the Universities of Strasburg and Giessen. Strongly influenced by the revolutionary 'Young Germany' movement, he developed his own political philosophy which turned its back on the educated classes, placing its hopes instead with the peasantry. After his involvement with an abortive attempt to overthrow the government of the state of Hesse in 1834, he withdrew from revolutionary politics. He wrote *Danton's Death* in 1835 and the following year became a lecturer in Anatomy at the University of Zürich. He worked on *Woyzeck* that year, drawing on the details of a controversial court-case, but died of typhoid fever in 1837, with *Woyzeck* still not complete.

Woyzeck

The central character, Woyzeck, is a repressed and oppressed soldier, crushed by his social superiors, goaded by his mistress, tormented by his own sense of guilt. Although the play was never put into a final form by Büchner, each of its scenes is remarkably powerful, and cumulatively they create an overpowering atmosphere of alienation and bleakness. Woyzeck ultimately perishes, but in highly ambiguous circumstances which deliberately confuse suicide and accident. Berg's operatic treatment, *Wozzeck*, owes its title to a misreading of the manuscript.

Try these:
Kafka's *Metamorphosis* and *The Trial* for a sense of the individual being crushed, ▷George Abbott's *Three Men on a Horse* for a more light-hearted treatment of the little man at the mercy of external forces; ▷Eugene O'Neill; ▷Arthur Miller's *Death of a Salesman* for individuals crushed by social forces; Büchner was much influenced by ▷Shakespeare; his plays in turn influenced such apparently opposed figures as ▷Artaud and ▷Brecht; ▷Mnouchkine's *1789* is *the* French Revolution play; also ▷Pam Gems' adaptation of Stanislawa Przybslewska's *The Danton Affair* which itself was highly influenced by *Danton's Death*; also ▷Peter Weiss' *Marat/Sade*.

BULGAKOV,
Mikhail Afanasievich   [1891–1940]
Russian novelist, journalist and dramatist

Plays include:
The Days of the Turbins (a dramatisation of his novel *The White Guard*; 1926), *The Crimson Island* (1927), *Dead Souls* (from Gogol; 1928), *Molière* (1936), *Don Quixote* (1940), *The Last Days of Pushkin* (published 1943)

Born in Kiev, Bulgakov qualified as a doctor, and became a professional writer in 1919. He wrote a novel *The White Guard* about the horrors of the civil war in Kiev, which was unusually sympathetic to the White side. He was asked by Pavel Markov, the Moscow Arts Theatre's dramaturg, to turn it into a play. At first delighted, Bulgakov was soon disconcerted by the cutting and reshaping required to suit the company, and the changing of the title and the ending to suit the censor (the

Bolsheviks are welcomed to the strains of the Internationale). However, he valued the experience for teaching him stagecraft, and he went on to write thirteen more plays and to become arguably the most important Soviet playwright of the period. His theatrical career was blighted by his *Molière*, in which the contemporary relevance of references to the frustrations of the artist controlled by the State were only too obvious. After four years in rehearsal, it was taken off after less than a week. But Bulgakov had his revenge in the very thinly disguised, very unkind, and very funny accounts of the Moscow Art Theatre and of ▷Stanislavski's system, in his novel *Black Snow* (written 1936–7, published 1965). The best section of the book is perhaps the instruction to the author to write in older roles (his play has no character over twenty-eight, but the company includes nobody under fifty). *The White Guard* is perhaps his best-known play in Britain; but *The Crimson Island*, an effective satire on both political censorship and the acting profession (and duly banned in 1927), appeared at London's enterprising Gate Theatre Club in 1981. Adaptations of his 1925 satirical novella *The Heart of a Dog* (banned in the USSR until 1987) have recently scored major successes in Britain, the USA and USSR. Keith Dewhurst's adaptation of *Black Snow* was staged by the National Theatre in 1991.

Try these:
▷Stanislavski for getting Bulgakov started as a playwright, and for his depiction in *Black Snow*; ▷Arbuzov, ▷Gorki, ▷Mayakovsky for other well known Soviet dramatists; ▷Molière for his own plays; Václav Havel's plays and ▷David Pownall's *Master Class*, for a musical variation, with Shostakovich and Prokofiev, on the theme of state control and artistic freedom, also tackled in ▷Tom Stoppard's *Every Good Boy Deserves Favour*.

BULLINS, Ed   [1935–]
American dramatist

Plays include:
The Theme of Blackness (1966). *The Electronic Nigger* (1968), *The Gentleman Caller* (1969), *The Duplex* (1970), *The Fabulous Miss Marie* (1970), *The Taking of Miss Janie* (1975), *Leavings* (1980).

Continual torment surrounds Bullins' drama as he presents a sceptical, and even cynical view of the dichotomy of black participation in a white, intellectual, middle-class community, and the exclusion from that life of the majority of blacks whose life in the inner-city slum plays out its own self-awareness. *The Electronic Nigger* dramatises the collective recognition of black artists and intellectuals of the 1960s – a rebellious voice that refuses the stamp of approval by the white, literary establishment. *Duplex* accomplishes Bullins' intent to write for a black audience, to expose the tragedy of the ghetto with a dramatic structure that is more about life than theatre. Scenes assault, conflicts abide, resolutions are sparse. As with the black ghetto, the play's end provokes frustration with no relief in sight. Bullins exposes the corruption of white values upon black culture that represses and denies any respectability for being black in America. Bullins' idiom clearly articulates the voice of black power that is resolute with future confrontation and promised change.

Try these:

▷Amiri Baraka traces a similar evolutionary black awareness. ▷Adrienne Kennedy's *Funnyhouse of a Negro* struggles with black identity. Lorraine Hansberry's *A Raisin in the Sun* places her black family in a middle-class district, struggling for acceptance; George C. Wolfe also shows the dichotomy of black participation in white society through astringent satire; ▷African-American theatre and ▷Black Theatre in Britain.

BUSCH, Charles   [1955–]
American writer and performer

Plays include:
Theodora, She-Bitch of Byzantium (1982), *Times Square Angel* (1985), *Vampire Lesbians of Sodom* (1985), *Gidget Goes Psychotic* (later changed to Psycho Beach Party, 1986), *Pardon My Inquisition,* or *Kiss the Blood Off My Castenets* (1986), *The Lady in Question* (1988), *Red Scare on Sunset* (1991)

Fresh out of Northwestern University, Busch started out in theatre by widely touring his own one-person revue entitled *Alone with a Cast of Thousands*. He eventually founded Theatre-in-Limbo, named after the now-defunct downtown New York nightclub called Limbo Lounge. All of Busch's camp comedies are filled with suspense, transformations and redemptions. The heroines, played by Busch in drag, range from vampire show-business queens, to the multiple personalities of Chicklet (a stand-in for Gidget), to Gertrude Garnet a concert pianist. Says Busch, 'I play her like Norma Shearer, with a little bit of Greer Garson thrown in for affection.' As the New York Times said about one performance, 'he flounces along the narrow line between too much and much too much, but manages not to burlesque the burlesque.' And while some may label Busch avant-garde he insists he's 'as avant-garde as Henny Youngman.'

Hollywood provides endless fascination for Busch. *Times Square Angel* sends up film noir as he plays Irish O'Flanagan, a 1940s torch singer. *The Lady in Question* spoofs World War II anti-Nazi films and enjoyed a lengthy off-Broadway run. In *Red Scare on Sunset*, perhaps his most ambitious work, Busch plays Mary Dale, a right-wing pro-McCarthy-ite who rats on her husband. The audience finds itself in the strange position of cheering on a heroine whose politics are repulsive, and critics largely seemed to feel this ambiguity gave the play a depth his previous work may have lacked.

All Busch's characters satirise Hollywood stereotypes, his dialogue is filled with the pungent humour of psychosexual cliches and the occasional hype of comic-book smut. Busch's women avoid the punch of cynicism and animosity that often accompany the convention of the drag show. Rather he allows the presentation of the woman as glamorous and heroic to be the liberation of a whole vocabulary of expression that is less political and more aesthetic.

Busch once stated: 'My great ambition is to have Lucy's [late comedian Lucille Ball] time slot Monday's at 8:00.' He almost had his wish when CBS hired him to write a pilot for a television sitcom; unfortunately they rejected it. He has also contributed new librettos to recent productions of *Ankles Aweigh* and *House of Flowers*.

Try these:

Camille, Charles Ludlam's Theater of the Ridiculous for camp that explores sexual ambiguity. The drag queen with pathos cacn be found in *La Cage aux Folles* and ▷Fierstein's *Torch Song Trilogy*, ▷Ethyl Eichelberger for a performance artist whose female impersonations combine a unique blend of camp with high art; also ▷Neil Bartlett's *Sarrasine* and *A Vision of Love Revealed in Sleep* along the same lines. Ronald Tavel's *Gorilla Queen*; Tom Eyen's *Women Behind Bars*, ▷Fierstein's *Cobra Jewels*; Charles Ludlam's *When Queens Collide* for outrageous melodrama coupled with equally excessive hammy acting; *The Rocky Horror Picture Show*; ▷Gay Theatre and ▷Lesbian Theatre.

BYRNE, John   [1940–]
British dramatist

Plays include:
Writer's Cramp (1977), *The Slab Boys* (1978; also known as *Paisley Patterns*), *Cuttin' a Rug* (1979; originally *The Loveliest Night of the Year*, also performed on radio as *The Staffie* and as *Threads*), *Normal Service* (1979), *Still Life* (1982)

Now widely known to British television audiences after the success of his series *Tutti Frutti* and *Your Cheatin' Heart*, Scottish-born John Byrne has been delighting theatre audiences in Scotland, England and the USA for years with his ironic observations on literary pretension (in *Writer's Cramp*) and everyday working life in *The Slab Boys* trilogy, which starts with adolescence in *The Slab Boys* itself, takes us through the staff dance in *Cuttin' a Rug*, and ends in the cemetery in *Still Life*. Byrne trained at the Glasgow School of Art and his work reveals in its different moods both a painter's eye for detailed observation and a cartoonist's gift for caricature; the interest tends to be less in plot and more in the presentation of memorable characters.

Try these:
▷Harold Pinter's *No Man's Land* and ▷Michael Hastings' *Tom and Viv* offer contrasting views of the literary world; ▷Doug Lucie's view of an advertising agency in *Fashion* makes an interesting comparison with the television station of *Normal Service*; ▷Arnold Wesker's *Trilogy* is one of the best known modern set of linked plays; ▷Iain Heggie, one of the newest Scottish voices for robust Glaswegian dialect.

 # C

CABARET IN BRITAIN

The origins of contemporary cabaret in Britain can be seen in ▷music hall in which audiences could drink while watching songs and sketches, and in the Weimar cabaret tradition of popular songs and political sketches which had a marked impact on ▷Brecht.

The appearance of the Cambridge Footlights team of Peter Cook, Jonathan Miller, Dudley Moore and Alan Bennett in the early 1960s marked the beginning of a new direction in British cabaret. Not only was their *Beyond the Fringe* an out-and-out theatre success, leading on to the weekly television series, *That Was The Week That Was* but the Establishment, a late night cabaret club, set up by amongst others, Cook and Ned Sherrin, placed satire back on the map and went on to spawn the Monty Python team (another set of Footlights alumni including Michael Palin, Terry Jones, John Cleese, Terry Gilliam, Eric Idle, and Graham Chapman), and The Goodies, (Graeme Garden, Bill Oddie and Tim Brooke-Taylor), as well as playing host to such American exponents of bitter satire as Lenny Bruce and Mort Sahl.

Cabaret in Britain is now more or less synonymous with 'alternative cabaret', a phenomenon that came up out of the 1970s with two Soho venues called the Comedy Store (based on a New York model) and The Comic Strip, which has produced its own stars such as Rik Mayall, Nigel Planer, Alexei Sayle, French and Saunders, Lenny Henry and Ben Elton, all of whom have subsequently moved into the mainstream via television. 'Alternative cabaret' started out like, the satire of the 1960s, as relentlessly anti-establishment, and as tasteless as possible. That remains, although there is a feeling that too many artists these days, with one eye on seduction into television, produce too much material that audiences/television researchers *want* to hear, rather than sharp, intrusive, intelligent criticism. Sexual politics, the Royal Family, and Margaret Thatcher (still!) are the current staples – topicality is the essence of good satire.

This ever-increasing 'alternative cabaret' circuit is mostly made up of pubs but also some clubs and the welcome restoration of the Hackney Empire which combines the best of variety, ▷music hall and alternative cabaret in its line-up. Today's cabaret stars – Simon Fanshawe, Jenny Lecoat, Arthur Brown, Jeremy Hardy, Kit Hollerbach, Hattie Hayridge, Jack Dee, Arthur Smith, John Hegley, Helen Lederer and Harry Enfield (another big television name whose 'loadsamoney' catchphrase entered the lexicon of everyday usage during the Thatcher era) like the best theatre, hold a jagged but truthful mirror up to nature – their weapons, irony, satire, exaggeration, and humour in various proportions of gentleness or brutality. Some cabaret performers like John Sessions, who specialises in impersonations, have gone on to fuller stage performances; his *Napoleon* was a superb, one-man tour-de-farce. And of course, there is the incomparable Victoria Wood who has raised cabaret/comedy sketches to the level of high, but extremely popular, art. Cabaret can also embrace the newer form of 'dub' poets, such as Benjamin Zephaniah whose rap poetry is a million miles away from the solemn discourses of traditional poetry recitals. The form has become very popular over the past four to five years and attracted a growing following of young supporters. Cabaret continues to be big business; the number of cabaret artists has steadily increased at the Edinburgh fringe, where one of the big awards is the Perrier Cabaret award. But cabaret performers, like today's pop stars have also acquired political and social consciences and are frequently to be seen lending their support to a variety of charity performances or benefits on issues ranging from the environment to the Third World, from Nicaragua to AIDS.

Try these:
▷Pub/cafe theatre; for other cabaret performers ▷Robyn Archer, ▷Women in Theatre; ▷Performance Art, ▷Lesbian theatre.

CALDERÓN DE LA BARCA, Pedro
Spanish dramatist   [1600–81]

Plays include:
La dama duende (*The Phantom Lady*; 1629), *El príncipe constante* (*The Constant Prince*; 1629), *La vida es sueño* (*Life is a Dream*; 1635), *El médico de su honra* (*The Physician of his Honour*; 1635), *El alcalde de Zalamea* (*The Mayor of Zalamea*; 1643), *El gran teatro del mundo* (*The Great Theatre of the World*; 1645)

Calderón is the most polished Spanish dramatist of the Golden Age; less prolific than ▷Lope de Vega, he borrowed freely from his predecessors, tightened up the plots and characterisation, and added a peculiarly intense line in passionate conflicts with often shocking outcomes. He studied for the priesthood, but soon took up duelling, women, and poetry; his first known play was staged at the Spanish Court when he was twenty-three, and he claimed to have written about 120 secular plays, eighty *autos sacramentales* (the Spanish form of morality play, performed on great church occasions) in his later and more pious years, and twenty minor pieces. He is also credited with the invention of the *zarzuela*, the classic Spanish musical form. His range covers cloak-and-sword plays, historical plays, honour-and-jealousy plays, comedies of manners, and the famous *Life is a Dream*, commonly thought his masterpiece. This is a complex and unusual play about the Polish Crown Prince Sigismondo, hidden away in a tower in a wood by his father because of a prophecy that he would grow up as a monster of cruelty, and his gradual education and emergence as a wise ruler. The plot incorporates philosophical discussion of reason versus natural impulses and free will defeating superstitious prophecy.

The Mayor of Zalamea
The Mayor of Zalamea, based on an earlier work attributed to ▷Lope de Vega, is the story of a Spanish peasant whose daughter is raped by an aristocratic captain, and who then becomes the Mayor and sentences the captain to a garrotting – all are agreed that the captain deserved it and that justice was done, but of course the girl still ends up in a nunnery. Nobody has recently tried *The Physician of his Honour*, his most notorious 'honour' play, in which a husband has his wife's blood drained on the mere suspicion of adultery, and the King not merely commends his action but offers our hero another bride.

Try these:
▷Lope de Vega, the earlier master playwright of the Spanish Golden Age, and source for some of Calderón's best known plays; von Hofmannsthal and Max Reinhardt for an updating of *The Great Theatre of the World*; Grotowski for his version of *The Constant Prince*; rape is handled very differently in Eve Lewis' *Ficky Stingers*; there is also an off-stage rape in *Last Summer in Chulimsk* by the modern Soviet playwright Alexander Vampilov; Peter Handke's *Kaspar*; ▷William Mastrosimone *Extremities*; ▷Richard Cameron *Strugglers*.

CAMERON, Richard   [1948–]
British dramatist and director

Plays include:
Handle with Care (1985), *The Moon's The Madonna* (1989), *Strugglers* (1988), *Can't Stand Up For Falling Down* (1990).

A sensitive chronicler of the joys and sorrows of adolescent experience with a sophisticated eye for structure, Richard Cameron won the Sunday Times Playwriting Award three times, but his concern for childish things and the unabashed kindness of spirit of his plays did not attract professional directors or adult audiences until *Can't Stand Up For Falling Down*. All his work up to and including this was devised with and for students at Scunthorpe Youth Theatre where he is a director and at the school where he was head of drama. His writing has a lightness and sureness of touch, an emotional honesty which is tender and lyrical but also encompasses cruelty and suffering, and does not shy away from difficult subjects. For the National Student Drama Company he wrote and directed *The Moon's The Madonna*, about child abuse, which was short-listed for the Independent Theatre Award, and *Strugglers*, set in a special school, which won the Sunday

Times Award. In *Strugglers*, a seemingly meandering plot portraying the day-to-day concerns of a group of teenagers just about to leave school, builds in complexity and momentum as the Real World encroaches bringing with it heartbreak, disillusionment, failure, and even rape. *Can't Stand Up For Falling Down*, selected as the National Student Theatre Company production for Edinburgh, won the Independent Theatre Award, transferred to the Hampstead Theatre, sold out, and was subsequently picked up by Hull Truck. At the time of writing, Cameron was completing his first adult play commissioned by the Hampstead Theatre, and a 15-minute television film.

Can't Stand Up For Falling Down

This is the story of the damage wrought on three women by one boorish, unthinking man, who never actually appears in the play. The women, played in the original production by three 17-year-old Scunthorpe school pupils, tell their tales in interweaving monologues: Jodie watches as the man bullies to death her simple-minded childhood friend; Ruby becomes pregnant and then is deserted by him, and Lynette is trapped in a violent marriage with him. The sentimentality of some of the earlier plays is avoided and the emotions explored, though seen through children's eyes, are thoroughly adult. A loose narrative which ranges widely over place and time dovetails to a thriller-like conclusion, is devastating and yet poignantly optimistic as the three women come together for mutual support.

Try these:

▷Nell Dunn's *Steaming*, Tony Roper's *The Steamie* and ▷Pam Gems' *Dusa, Fish, Stas and Vi* are some of the many British plays of the past decade to show women supporting each other under crisis; Monstrous Regiment for a company whose work very much endorsed that outlook; another contemporary play about sexual abuse is ▷David Spencer's *Killing the Cat*; for off-stage presences, ▷Beckett's *Waiting for Godot*; Helen Cooper's *Mrs Vershinin* gave flesh to the off-stage wife of ▷Chekhov's *Three Sisters*; Elaine Feinstein's *Lear's Daughters* reassessed *Lear* from his wife's and daughters' point of view, so too (perhaps) did ▷Howard Barker's *Seven Lears*; Breuer's gender-reversed adaptation of *Lear* featured Ruth Maleczech as the title character – a southern matriach.

CAMPBELL, Ken   [1941–   ]
British director, dramatist and actor

Plays include:
Old King Cole (1969), *Jack Shepherd* (1969; also known as *Anything You Say Will Be Twisted*), *Bendigo* (1974; with Dave Hill and Andy Andrews), *The Great Caper* (1974), *Walking Like Geoffrey* (1975; with Hill and Andrews), *Skungpoonery* (1975), *School For Clowns* (1975), *Illuminatus* (1977), *Deeds* (1978; with ▷Howard Brenton, ▷David Hare, ▷Trevor Griffiths), *The Hitch-hikers Guide To The Galaxy* (1979), *The Third Policeman* (1980), *War With The Newts* (1981), *The Furtive Nudist* (1990)

Campbell's directorial debut – organising the shallow end for the Summer Water Show at Bournemouth Baths – heralded a brilliant career as Britain's champion of anarchic fun. Ken Campbell's Roadshow toured to bars and theatres throughout Britain with a uniquely eccentric entertainment of staggering inventiveness coupled with red-noses and ferret-down-the-trousers interlude. Gleefully iconoclastic, Campbell recognised no boundaries, taking on the challenge of the *Illuminatus* books and triumphantly portraying Howard the talking dolphin as an operatic tenor. In *War With The Newts* the hilarity included a newt family called Olivia Newt, and John. In Michael Coveney's words, Campbell is 'a master of the ebulliently childish caper' who reaches for any and every theatrical device without regard to consistency or convention, demanding that the audience keep up with the crazed inventiveness on the stage.

Old King Cole

As it is almost impossible to do justice to the more anarchic of Campbell's scripts, it is perhaps best to look at this children's entertainment. It seems to spring directly from the imagination of an eight-year old. Hard-up, inventive genius Faz and his likeable but dim-witted assistant Twoo are approached by the weedy Baron Wadd, who asks Faz to ensure that Wadd wins the hand of Princess Daphne in a sporting competition against handsome, superbly fit, boring Cyril. Faz attempts to fix the events at the competition, but not even his outrageous trickery can defeat Wadd's weediness and incompetence. In a last-ditch effort to win the Princess, Cyril is put out of action by dropping a ton-weight on him and employing Faz's spectacular magic. All seems to be well, but Princess Daphne has other ideas, and runs off with Twoo. Wadd becomes Faz's new assistant, and they all live happily ever after. It is a minor masterpiece of cartoonery, mad invention and childlike glee.

Try these:
▷Snoo Wilson, ▷N.F. Simpson, ▷Jarry and ▷Ionesco share something of Campbell's anarchic surreal inventiveness; amongst other British writers for children are ▷Bryony Lavery, ▷Nona Shepphard, ▷David Wood, ▷Penny Casdagli, Stephen Wyatt, and preeminently ▷David Holman.

CAPEK, Karel   [1890–1938]
Czech novelist and dramatist

Plays include:
The Robber (1920), *R.U.R.* (1921), *The White Plague* (1937), *The Power and the Glory* (1937), *Mother* (1938); and with his brother Josef, *The Insect Play* (1922), *The Makropoulos Secret* (1922), *Adam with Creator* (1927)

A socialist and pacifist, Capek's second play *R.U.R.* (Rossum's Universal Robots) gave the world the word 'robot' and offered a protest against the dehumanising elements of mechanisation and industrial capitalism. Its final moments, when two advanced robots (androids as we would now call them) have emotions of love and sacrifice, with the suggestion that humans have a second chance in this new Adam and Eve, have been frequently copied, although Czechs consider Capek's last anti-fascist plays his best. *The Mother*, produced only months before Hitler marched into Czechoslovakia, shows a small nation invaded by a fascist state, provoking civil war. The mother, already a soldier's widow, has a pilot son killed in an aircrash, two other sons – one fascist, one communist – die in a feud, and she sees her last son, an antiviolence poet, go off to fight. Capek's love of freedom was in the end stronger than his pacifism but he died soon after, three months before his brother was taken off to Belsen by the Nazis. *The White Plague* was recently staged in the USA, a production at Northlight theater that clearly underlined the play's applicability to the current AIDS epidemic.

The Insect Play
John Gielgud who played the Chief Butterfly in the British premiere, declared this was a part almost certain to ruin the reputation of an actor, but Capek's expressionist vision of human greed, violence and self-interest presented through parallel behaviour in the insect world can still be disturbingly effective. When the insects' physical characteristics are used to highlight their human counterparts, (a myriad faceted mirror set, like an insect's eye, was used in the most recent London production by Miroslav Machacek) the play has the harsh reality of a Steve Bell cartoon. The presentation of this parallel world and its tramp observer – the only human character – has precursors in fabulists from Aesop to Swift but its bite is closer to that of ▷Brecht and less easy to sweeten.

Try these:
▷Brecht, particularly *Mother Courage, The Threepenny Opera*; ▷Galsworthy, ▷Edgar and ▷Shaw for presentations of industrial relations; adaptations of George Orwell's *Animal Farm*, ▷W. H. Auden's *On the Frontier*, ▷Tom McGrath's *Animal,* Terry Johnson's *Cries From the Mammal House* and ▷Steven Berkoff's adaptation of Kafka's *Metamorphosis*, Ron Tavel's *Gorilla Queen* Ping Chong's *Kind-Ness,* Breuer's *Shaggy Dog Animations* and more popularly *Harvey* by Mary Chase; for beast fables ▷Alan Bennett's *Kafka's Dick* for a similar use of disturbing and fabulous metaphor.

CARTWRIGHT, Jim   [1958–]
British dramatist

Plays include:
Road (1986), *Bed* (1989), *To* (1990)

Bolton-born Cartwright's first play, *Road*, was called the most exciting play of the decade in Britain. Its impact there could be compared to that of ▷John Osborne's *Look Back in*

Anger – but could also be said to have owed much to Simon Curtis's clever promenade production of its first performance at the ▷Royal Court Upstairs in 1986. It became a multiple award-winner, although Ros Asquith in *The Observer* noted that in this '*Under Milk Wood* for the Great Unemployed, men talk ideas, women only sex', whilst Jim Hiley in *The Listener* worried that there was barely a hint of dignity or sense of resistance in the characters. Constructed round a series of vignettes, Cartwright's raw, grim account of unemployment, seen through the eyes of its narrator Scully and the inhabitants of a Lancashire street, certainly signalled the arrival of an angry new voice, albeit one capable of capturing great tenderness. Revived twice within a year in the Court's main house (and the subject of a television production), it seems certain to be regarded as a seminal portrait of Thatcher's 'other Britain'.

If echoes of Dylan Thomas ran through his first play, his second, *Bed*, with its stream-of-consciousness monologues about sleep and dreams and surrealistic talking head found itself likened to Beckett (such references would presumably be denied by Cartwright who claimed at the time he'd only ever read four books in his life). *To*, his third play, has shown Cartwright reverting to a series of working-class cameos roughly congregated around a pub owner and his wife and the pub's guests. Less adventurous than *Bed*, it must be regarded as something of a vehicle for its two very popular stars, from the British television soap *Brookside*, Sue Johnston and John McArdle.

Try these:
▷J.M. Synge's *Playboy of the Western World* and ▷Iain Heggie's *A Wholly Healthy Glasgow* for boldness of dialect; ▷Thornton Wilder's *Our Town*, ▷Dylan Thomas's *Under Milk Wood* for a specific sense of place; ▷John Osborne's *Look Back in Anger* for a similar 1950s burst of national vitriol; for more views of Thatcher's Britain, try ▷Doug Lucie, ▷David Hare, ▷Karim Alrawi, ▷Jacqueline Holborough, ▷Caryl Churchill. Manfred Karge's *The Conquest of the South Pole* speaks of the same issue, unemployment; see also Promenade Performances.

CASDAGLI, Penny
(also known as Maro Green) [1948–]
British playwright

Plays for children include:
Wolfchildren (1980), *This Way or That?* (1982), *The Green Ginger Smuggler* (1984), *Thumbs Up!* (1985), *Pardon, Mr Punch!* (1987), *The Beggar in the Palace* (1989, with Caroline Griffin).

Adult plays (as Maro Green with Caroline Griffin) include:
More 1986, *The Memorial Gardens* (1988), *Mortal* (1990)

Penny Casdagli's pioneering work has demonstrated – sometimes to an initially sceptical world – ways both of increasing access to young people's theatre and of gaining from the diversity that entails. While at the Unicorn Theatre she first addressed the question of drama that could cater for deaf as well as hearing children, developing work that introduced sign language in a way that made it integral rather than a distracting extra. Her *Pardon, Mr Punch!*, applauded by the *Times Educational Supplement* as 'a marvellously jolly play', won the British Theatre Association's Drama Magazine award for young people's theatre in 1988. Subsequently Casdagli has drawn multilingualism into her plays, particularly those done under the aegis of the Neti-Neti Theatre Company, started by her and Caroline Griffin in 1987. At its best, the richly layered effect of this acts as a strong symbol for the imaginative potential of a multicultural society.

Her adult plays with Caroline Griffin have proved equally innovative – *More*, a highly physical piece of theatre, looked at the hidden disabilities of agrophobia and anorexia, *The Memorial Gardens* at child abuse.

Try these:
▷Nona Shepphard, ▷David Holman, ▷David Wood and ▷Ken Campbell are other playwrights who also write for children, see also Graeae; ▷Theatre for Young People; ▷Women in Theatre.

CHAMBERS, Jane [1937–1983]
American playwright

Plays include:
The Marvelous Metropolis (1957), *Christ in a Treehouse* (1971), *Random Violence* (1973), *A Late Snow* (1974), *Common*

Garden Variety (1976), *Late Summer at Bluefish Cove* (1980), *Kudzu* (1981), *My Blue Heaven* (1982), *The Quintessential Image* (1983)

Jane Chambers broke new ground in her frank writing about homosexual life. Nine months before her untimely death, she received the Fifth Annual Award of the Fund for Human Dignity, given as an acknowledgment of those who have made a major contribution to public understanding and acceptance of lesbians and gays. Chambers never concealed her homosexuality and created characters who dealt openly with the issues surrounding a gay lifestyle. Chambers was instrumental in founding the Women's Interart Center in New York, which continues to provide a forum for plays dealing with lesbianism and other feminist issues.

Chambers also wrote for the wider television audience. Her civil rights play – *Christ in a Treehouse* won the Connecticut Television award for best religious play, and she received a 1973 Writer's Guild of America Award for her work on the CBS-TV soap opera *Search for Tomorrow*. Chambers will be best remembered, however, for *A Late Snow* and *Bluefish Cove* among the many plays she wrote on homosexual themes.

Try these:
For pioneering work on gay themes, Mart Crowley, *The Boys in the Band*; for women's relationships, ▷Caryl Churchill, *Top Girls*; for homosexual lifestyles see ▷Harvey Fierstein, ▷Lanford Wilson's *Burn This*; ▷Gay Theatre; ▷Lesbian Theatre.

CHAPMAN, George   [c 1560–1634]
English Renaissance dramatist and poet

Plays include:
Monsieur D'Olive (1604), *Bussy D'Ambois* (1604), *Eastward Ho!* (with ▷Jonson and ▷Marston; 1605), *The Widow's Tears* (pre 1609), *The Revenge of Bussy D'Ambois* (c 1610), *The Wars of Caesar and Pompey* (c 1613)

A friend of and collaborator with ▷Ben Jonson, Chapman pursued the career of a professional writer with sufficient assiduity to serve a prison term for overstepping the mark in his criticism of the Scots and James VI and I in *Eastward Ho!* He is probably best known now for his poetry rather than his seldom performed plays, and his densely philosophical and erudite approach to writing may go some way to explain the discrepancy between his academic (traditionally high) and theatrical (virtually non-existent) reputations. Jonathan Miller's 1988 Old Vic production of *Bussy D'Ambois*, a revenge tragedy in the familiar Renaissance mode, is unlikely to herald a Chapman revival but it would be good to see its sequel *The Revenge of Bussy D'Ambois* (proof that the Renaissance theatre knew how to cash in on success as much as Hollywood does!). Chapman's comedies seem even less likely to be revived than his tragedies but *Monsieur D'Olive* with its weird mixture of elements, including a character who keeps his dead wife's body sitting in a chair because he hasn't come to terms with death, might be a good outside bet for an adventurous company.

Try these:
Most Renaissance dramatists used revenge plots and malcontent figures – ▷Shakespeare's *Hamlet* is the most famous example of both, but ▷Kyd's *The Spanish Tragedy* started the vogue for revenge and there are notable examples in ▷Ford, ▷Middleton, ▷Tourneur and ▷Webster; ▷Red Shift's *In the Image of the Beast*, a 'Science Fiction Revenge Tragedy', draws on *Bussy D'Ambois* to tell a chilling tale of a spaceman wreaking an awful revenge on those who abandoned him adrift in a spaceship.

CHEKHOV, Anton   [1860–1904]
Russian dramatist

Plays include:
On the High Road (1884), *Ivanov* (1887), *The Bear* (1888), *The Wood Demon* (1889), *The Wedding* (1890), *Platonov* (c1890; not produced until the 1920s), *The Seagull* (1896), *Uncle Vanya* (1899), *The Proposal* (1899), *Three Sisters* (1901), *The Cherry Orchard* (1904)

One of the greatest dramatists of the last century, Chekhov is a master at depicting groups, charting the nuances of dialogue and character with extraordinary sensitivity and subtlety. Many of his plays deal with temporary communities that are coming to an end; their elegiac qualities seem to foreshadow events in Russia with remarkable prescience.

Born the son of a grocer and the grandson

The Family Redgrave: Lynn, Jemma and Vanessa as Masha, Irena and Olga in Chekhov's *Three Sisters*, directed by Russian director, Robert Sturua, London 1990. Frank McGuiness's adaptation with the Cusack sisters – Sinead, Niamh, and Sorcha – also came to London in the same year in the Gate Theatre, Dublin's production, directed by Adrian Noble

of a serf, and brought up in a small port town on the Sea of Azov, he went to the University of Moscow to train as a doctor in 1879. On graduation, he practised medicine in Moscow and wrote for the *St Petersburg Gazette*. His first full-length plays, *Ivanov* and *The Wood Demon*, were unsuccessful. In 1890 Chekhov travelled through Russia and Siberia as a medical practioner, the first of many such journeys, in order to assist peasants. He then settled on a small estate outside Moscow, where he attempted to be an enlightened landlord and provided medical care and schooling for the peasants in the area, experience which is central to *Uncle Vanya* and *The Cherry Orchard*.

After the failure of the first production of *The Seagull* Chekhov swore that he would never have another play produced. However, ▷Stanislavski persuaded him to revive *The Seagull*. Stanislavski gave it a very careful production at his Moscow Arts Theatre, employing his methods of acting and direction, and the play was recognised as an important new drama. In a speech given to the writer Constantine in the play, Chekhov offers a damning critique of the contemporary conventions of theatre: 'I regard the stage of today as mere routine and prejudice . . . We must have new formulas. That's what we want.'

Uncle Vanya, a reworking of *The Wood Demon*, followed *The Seagull*, quite successfully, although *Three Sisters*, again produced at the Moscow Arts Theatre, was not well received. In 1904, after the first production of *The Cherry Orchard*, Chekhov suffered two heart attacks and died in the German spa town of Badenweiler, just as he was beginning to be recognised internationally as a major dramatist. In the notebooks of the period of the *Three Sisters* Chekhov wrote: 'We struggle to change life so that those who come after us might be happy, but those who come after us will say as usual, it was better before, life now is worse than it used to be.' Chekhov's plays stand as powerful statements which attest to the fact that things were *never* better, and that hope for the future matters more than anything.

Chekhov's plays appear regularly, if not exactly frequently, in the classic and regional repertories of the British and American theatre, though an over-reliance on Stanislavskian naturalism and the misguided perception of Chekhov as a uniformly melancholy writer unfortunately persist. Andrei Serban's controversial 1977 production of *The Cherry Orchard* (in ▷Jean-Claude van Itallie's translation) at New York's Lincoln Centre Theater provided a boldly humorous – at times farcical – reading of the play which went far in forcing a reassessment of traditional Chekhovian production. Other notable stagings in recent years include ▷Peter Brook's stunningly minimalist *Cherry Orchard* at the Brooklyn Academy of Music in 1988, and the Hungarian company Katona Jozsef's emotionally gripping *Three Sisters* (seen at the London International Festival of Theatre in 1989). The 1990–91 season in Britain boasted two productions of *Three Sisters* as vehicles for well-known acting families: Dublin's Gate Theatre mounted one with Cyril Cusack as Chebutykin and his daughters Sinead, Sorcha and Niamh as the siblings, while Vanessa and Lynn Redgrave (along with niece Jemma) played the title roles in London. An American *Three Sisters*, meanwhile, played fast and loose with convention in a deconstructed version of the play titled *Brace Up!*, conceived and performed by New York's Wooster Group.

Three Sisters

This is a study of three sisters, locked in a small military town, watching their lives drift past. The constant refrain of the play is the cry of the youngest sister Irina, 'Let us go to Moscow', but as the play progresses, even she, the youngest and therefore most hopeful, comes to realise that they will never leave, and that even if they *did* reach Moscow, they would bring themselves and all their frustrations with them. Each of the sisters suffers the frustration of her hopes: Olga, the eldest has given up all hope of children; the most sensual of the sisters, Masha, is trapped in a sterile marriage and loses the lover who promises her romance; Irina never achieves her ambition to see Moscow. The men who come within the orbit of the sisters also suffer from unfulfilled hopes and ambitions: the sisters' brother Andrey ends the play married to a vulgar woman; the Doctor has not sustained the commitment and conviction with which he entered medicine; Vershinin, the glamorous commander, has hopes for a 'beautiful life' in another two centuries. None of the characters can achieve contentment, with the exception of Andrey's wife, Natasha, whose dreams are only of material comforts. The play ends with the three sisters standing alone, their youth and romance leaving with the soldiers. Olga reaffirms the importance of their lives in a final and wistful speech: 'We shall be forgotten – our faces, our voices, even how many of us there were. But our sufferings will turn to joy for those who live after us.' The experience of the audience watching the play is such as to reaffirm its slender hopes, the act of watching the *Three Sisters* confirms that they have indeed not been forgotten.

Try these:
Chekhov said, '▷Ibsen is my favourite author', and claimed *The Wild Duck* as his favourite play; ▷Michael Frayn's *Wild Honey* is a version of *Platonov*; ▷Brian Friel has adapted *The Cherry Orchard* to an Irish setting, Michael Picardie's *The Cape Orchard* applied it to South Africa, and ▷Trevor Griffiths' version stressed its politics; his *Piano* is partly a reworking of *Platonov*; ▷Mustapha Matura has transferred *Three Sisters* to Trinidad in his *Trinidad Sisters*; ▷G.B. Shaw claimed *Heartbreak House* was Chekhovian; ▷N.C. Hunter was routinely compared to Chekhov; Helen Cooper's *Mrs Vershinin* tells the story of how she came to be the offstage neurotic in *Three Sisters*; ▷Michael Frayn, ▷Lanford Wilson and ▷David Mamet as recent translators/ adapters of Chekhov's major plays; ▷Beckett's *Waiting for Godot* for a play about longed-for transcendence.

CHONG, Ping   [1946–]
American writer, director and performer

Works include:
Fear and Loathing in Gotham (1975), *Humboldt's Current* (1977), *Nuit Blanche* (1981), *A.M./A.M. – The Articulated Man* (1982), *Anna into Nightlight* (1982), *The Games* (with Meredith Monk, 1983), *A Race* (1984), *The Angels of Swedenborg* (1985), *Nosferatu* (1985), *Kindness* (1986), *Noiresque: The Fallen Angel* (1989), *Maraya – Acts of Nature in Geological Time* (1989), *Skin – A State of Being* (1989) *4 a.m. America* (1990), *Deshima* (1990), *Elephant Memories* (1990)

Ping Chong, a one-time performer with Meredith Monk, formed his own Fiji Company in 1975 'to question the syntax of theatre.' In over 20 major pieces, his highly visual theatre mixes media and metaphor, while cultural traditions and paradigmatic experiences permeate the works. His characters, all explorers of one kind or another, grapple with geography, history and memory in the context of imperialism and the violence of the western world. Human experience is played out in haunting images composed of verbal, visual, gestural and sound texts that expose the oppression of 'the other'. *Kind Ness* makes the 'other' unmistakable, tracing the alienation of one 'student' (a gorilla) from his peers at a seemingly all-American high school. *A Race* also explores society's indoctrinating pressures; it takes place on graduation day in the year 2084 as android creatures prepare to enter the human race. The headmaster figure intones, 'You will learn to remember . . . and how to forget.'

Elephant Memories, whose sources include Orwell, Fritz Lang's *Metropolis*, and the cyberpunk function of William Gibson, presents the collective character of alienation in the context of a future in which its inhabitants participate in the obligatory rituals of an entropic universe. The characters scream 'memory' in a futile attempt to recuperate their lost selves.

Chong's work can be dense going. One critic called *Nuit Blance* the 'theatrical equivalent of archaeological digs.' Chong's rather cryptic use of time is evident in *Maraya . . .* a piece that begins in the 16th century and moves forward to the mid-20th century before jumping back to prehistoric times. *Maraya* echoes Chong's work with Monk in *The Games* (described by a critic as 'postnuclear holocaust science-fiction musical . . . as cautionary parable') as he mixes images, according to Mel Gussow, of 'the epochal and the ordinary (the creation of the atom bomb, the popularization of the waltz).'

Chong's work is not for all audiences; theatregoers have been known to stomp out of his performances infuriated by the ambiguities. While Chong's work is undeniably attractive in physical production, as critic Michael Feingold once questioned 'you never know what he might achieve if he put his mind to creating a work that communicated more than mere effects.'

Try these:
The Wooster Group's *L.S.D. (. . . Just the High Points . . .)* and Laurie Anderson's *Empty Places* use innovative language and techniques that include conventions of and subversions to theatricality; see also ▷expressionism, ▷Performance Art; Martha Clarke, Meredith Monk, Pina

Bausch as dancers whose work crosses boundaries; Richard Foreman for dense and abstract pieces dealing with alienation; Robert Wilson for emphasis on visual effects

CHRISTIE, Agatha (Mary Clarissa)   [1890–1976]
British author of detective stories and dramatist

Plays include:
Black Coffee (1930), *Ten Little Niggers* (also known as *Ten Little Indians*; 1943), *Appointment with Death* (1945), *Murder on the Nile* (1945), *The Hollow* (1951), *The Mousetrap* (1952), *Witness for the Prosecution* (1953), *The Spider's Web* (1954), *Towards Zero* (with Gerald Verner; 1956), *Verdict* (1958), *The Unexpected Guest* (1958), *Go Back for Murder* (1960), *The Rule of Three* (1962), *Fiddlers Three* (1971), *Akhnaton* (published 1973)

Writer of the longest-running play ever, *The Mousetrap* (now approaching its 40th year), Christie excels at telling a story. Though her characters verge upon the stereotypical, they have firm roots in the backgrounds of the middle-class audiences which have flocked to see her plays, giving them opportunities to identify with the characters and vicariously enjoy the excitement of involvement with murder and mayhem. However, her characters are not mere ciphers and she sometimes uses them to voice ideas that reveal a strong concern for the problems in relationships. As in many of her novels, the revelation of 'who-done-it' is often not signalled in the plot and comes as a surprise.

Several of Christie's detective stories have been adapted for the stage by other writers and they have been made into a number of feature films, though only recently adapted for television. Featuring her detectives, Miss Marple and the Belgian Hercule Poirot, they have been hugely successful.

The Mousetrap
In classic Christie fashion, *The Mousetrap* brings a number of characters together to a specific venue – in this case an old guest-house – where, cut off by bad weather, the members of the household are subjected to various trials by trauma before the culprit is revealed. Christie was very fond of introducing childhood elements into her stories (she had a particular sympathy for young people who had suffered in childhood and often wove their emotional distress in later life into her stories). As with *Ten Little Indians*, *The Mousetrap* takes its name and eerie leitmotif from a nursery rhyme, 'Three Blind Mice'. In comparison with modern thrillers, it's neither very shocking nor frightening and the stock characters over the years have become laughably dated. Nonetheless, the thriller's longevity says something about Christie's mastery of plot, and her psychological insights into the human state are as relevant and perceptive as ever.

Try these:
▷Alan Ayckbourn for similar plot manipulations; ▷J. B. Priestley's *An Inspector Calls* for the use of a detective plot to make a moral point; ▷Tom Stoppard's *The Real Inspector Hound* for a parody of the genre; ▷Anthony Shaffer's *Sleuth* is more psychologically oriented; Ariel Dorfman's *Death and the Maiden* for a superb psychological thriller concerned with the abuses of human rights; *The Woman in Black*, adapted from Susan Hill's novel, a more spine-tingling ghost story; Ira Levin's *Deathtrap* and Robert Holmes' *Accomplice* were recent Broadway Thrillers of varying success.

CHURCHILL, Caryl   [1938–]
British dramatist

Plays include:
Owners (1972), *Objections to Sex and Violence* (1975), *Light Shining in Buckinghamshire* (1976), *Vinegar Tom* (1976), *Cloud Nine* (1979), *Three More Sleepless Nights* (1980), *Top Girls* (1982), *Fen* (1983), *Softcops* (1984), *A Mouthful of Birds* (1986; with ▷David Lan, *Serious Money* (1987), *Ice Cream* (1989), *Hot Fudge* (1990), *Mad Forest* (1990), *Lives of the Great Poisoners* (1991)

Churchill has established herself as one of Britain's outstanding dramatists with a series of vibrant and inventive plays, almost all of which have been presented by ▷Joint Stock or the Royal Court, and she is now virtually as successful in New York as she is in Britain. In many ways she has been in an ideal position to chart the contradictions of the developing position of bourgeois women under the impact of feminism because of her own experience.

Sarah Lam (Lady Nijo), Deborah Findlay (Isabella Bird), Lesley Sharp (Dull Gret), Lesley Manville (Marlene) in the 1991 revival of Caryl Churchill's 1982 smash hit, *Top Girls*, directed by Max Stafford Clark, Royal Court, April 1991

After writing extensively for radio, which is traditionally more accommodating to female writers, and juggling the demands of her husband's career and of child care, Churchill moved into theatre in the early 1970s, writing initially as an individual but eventually learning different ways of working collectively as a result of her ventures with ▷Monstrous Regiment and particularly ▷Joint Stock. This move into collective creation reflects a significant challenge to traditional ways of organising theatre, which themselves reflect traditional divisions of labour in society.

Inevitably, Churchill has tackled many of the fashionable themes of British political and feminist theatre in the 1970s, including witches (*Vinegar Tom*), terrorism (*Objections . . .*), and seventeenth-century revolutionary sects (*Light Shining . . .*), as well as more unusual topics such as the nature of ideology and repression in the all male *Softcops*, inspired by a reading of the French theorist Michel Foucault. Her work has been particularly asociated with treatments of sexual politics, especially in *Cloud Nine* (in which the links between patriarchy and colonisation are mercilessly and wittily exposed) and *Top Girls*, a study of a 'successful' career woman. She has always been keenly aware of the socio-political dimension of oppression, which affects men as well as women, as in *Fen*, her study of the quiet horrors of rural life (notable for a stunning central performance from Jennie Stoller), and in the earlier urban landscape of *Owners*. Churchill uses time shifts, uneven ageing (the characters in *Cloud Nine* are twenty-five years older in part two than they were in part one, but one hundred years has passed), cross race and cross gender casting, doubling, pastiche Victorian light verse and also rhyming couplets, as part of a strategy of upsetting and destabilising conventional assumptions about both drama and life itself. Sometimes the sprightliness of her writing, the accuracy of her observation, and her unwillingness to be overly didactic can lead to reactions which call her effectiveness as a social critic into question: some people interpreted *Top Girls* as a hymn in praise of its central character and the runaway success in Britain of her exposé of the financial markets, *Serious Money*, owed much to its popularity with the very people it satirised, who flocked to see it both at the Royal Court and in the West End. *Ice Cream* and *Hot Fudge* are relatively minor pieces; *Mad Forest* is a fine treatment of Romania after the overthrow of Ceausescu, researched in Romania with a group of students from the Central School of Speech and Drama.

Top Girls

The play begins with a gathering of women from different periods and cultures to celebrate the promotion of Marlene, the central character, within the Top Girls employment agency. The choice ,f relatively unfamiliar historical characters reminds us of the way that women's histories have been submerged by traditional male-dominated approaches to history. It also brings us into a critical relationship with Marlene's story from the very beginning, forcing us to supply many of the connections between the first scene and the more 'normal' narrative that follows in which the women who played party guests reappear as contemporary women. In the first scene Marlene is apparently emancipated from the traps and entanglements of family and children that have constrained the others but much of the rest of the play is concerned with destabilising this privileged position by trapping audiences into semi-agreement with her and then encouraging them to see her putative success in a far wider context in which she is just as much a victim of the system. The play is both enormously funny and chilling in its brilliantly observed presentations of the everyday contradictions of life. Churchill, like ▷Brecht, suggests that what we need is a new way of seeing if we are to understand and confront the pressures the characters in *Top Girls* fail to grasp.

Try these:
▷Sarah Daniels' *Byrthrite* is another play about seventeenth-century women; ▷Edward Bond's mixture of 'historical' and invented characters in *Early Morning* ran into some of the same problems with critics as *Top Girls*; among the women dramatists to emerge in the UK since Churchill and ▷Pam Gems are ▷Timberlake Wertenbaker, ▷Daniels, ▷Bryony Lavery, ▷Debbie Horsfield, ▷Ayshe Raif, ▷Liz Lochhead, Clare McIntyre, Winsome Pinnock, and Sharman McDonald, ▷Charlotte Keatley; see also ▷New Playwriting and ▷Women in Theatre. One of the 'great poisoners' is Medea, also the subject of plays by ▷Euripides and ▷Seneca; Jerry Sterner's *Other People's Money* for a less successful attempt to show the naked thrust of capitalism.

CIXOUS, Hélène   [1937–]
French radical feminist and dramatist

Plays include:
Portrait de Dora (*Portrait of Dora*; 1976), *La Prise de l'École de Madhubaï* (*The Capture of the Madhubaï School*; 1983), *L'Histoire Terrible Mais Inachevée de Norodom Sihanouk, Roi du Cambodge* (*The Terrible But Unfinished Story of Norodom Sihanouk, King of Cambodia*; 1985), *L'Indiade* (*The Indiad*; 1987)

Born in Algeria, Hélène Cixous teaches at the University of Paris VIII where she runs the Research Centre for Women's Studies and publishes formidable theoretical works on feminism. Since 1967 she has also published novels, short stories, and essays, and made a tentative entry into playwriting in 1976, when Simone Benmussa produced her *Portrait de Dora* at the Théâtre d'Orsay. After an experiment with an opera libretto (*Le Nom d'Edipe*, Avignon Festival 1978) she had some success with *La Prise de l'École de Madhubaï* at the Petit Odéon in 1983, where most of the set in the tiny theatre was taken up with a banyan tree, and most of the play was a discussion on social responsibility and individual rights between a female bandit and a friendly prime minister with an umbrella. Since then, Cixous has been engaged in a rewarding partnership with ▷Ariane Mnouchkine and the Théâtre du Soleil, for whom and with whom she has researched and written two substantial and successful historical plays, one on the history of Cambodia and one on the partition of British India.

Try these:
▷Marguerite Duras, with whom she seems to have very little in common, but they were both born in French colonies and they have both written about what was formerly French Indo-China; ▷Spalding Gray's *Swimming to Cambodia* and ▷David Edgar's *Destiny* for other versions of Cambodia and India.

CLARK, Brian   [1932–]
British dramatist

Plays include:
Lay By (1971; with ▷Trevor Griffiths, ▷David Hare, ▷Stephen Poliakoff, Hugh Stoddart, ▷Snoo Wilson), *England's Ireland* (1972; with Tony Bicât, ▷David Edgar, Francis Fuchs, ▷David Hare, ▷Snoo Wilson), *Truth or Dare* (1972), *Campion's Interview* (1976), *Whose Life is it Anyway* (1978), *Post Mortem* (1978), *Can You Hear me at the Back* (1979), *Switching in the Afternoon; or, As the Screw Turns* (1980), *The Petition* (1986)

Originally a collaborator with younger left-wing dramatists such as ▷David Hare on plays for the anti-establishment Portable Theatre Company, Clark did not pursue consciously political theatre. The 1972 television version of his best-known play *Whose Life is it Anyway* was written in the same period and is more typical. In it an accident victim, paralysed from the neck down, fights for the right to die. It provides the opportunity for a virtuoso central performance, seized by Tom Conti on stage and in the subsequent film as a springboard to star status, but little opportunity for non-verbal theatre. Clark not only argues his case but writes elegantly and entertainingly, with an excellent feel for the mores and preoccupations of the English middle class. The problems of the mid-life male, professionally and domestically, are explored in *Can You Hear Me at the Back*, and especially in the 1979 British television series *Telford's Change*, both of which provide sensitive portraits that will assure the troubled professional that he (rather than she, although Mary Tyler Moore took the lead in *Whose Life?* on Broadway) is not alone – but do not look to Clark for the political critique his earliest work might seem to promise. In *The Petition* Clark is persuasive if predictable in his mainstream treatment of the anti-nuclear issue through discussions between a general and his quintessentially 'decent' middle-class wife, but the impact is fatally undermined by the melodramatic device of her political consciousness being made coincidental with the revelation that she is dying of cancer.

Try these:
For hospital, illness, and disability plays of various kinds see ▷Peter Nichols' *The National Health*, ▷Tom Kempinski's *Duet for One*, Michael Cristofer's *The Shadowbox*, ▷Louise Page's *Tissue*, ▷Phil Young's *Crystal Clear*, ▷Mark Medoff's *Children of a Lesser God*, ▷Bernard Pomerance's *The Elephant Man*, ▷Graeae Theatre Company; ▷Jean-Claude van Itallie's *The Traveller* creates a language to describe aphasia; ▷Beckett's

Happy Days offers another version of immobility; for anti-nuclear issues see ▷Nick Darke's *The Body*, ▷David Edgar's *Maydays*, ▷Sarah Daniels' *The Devil's Gateway*, ▷Edward Bond's *War Plays*, ▷Howard Barker's *The Passion*, ▷Howard Brenton's *The Genius*.

CLAUDEL, Paul   [1868–1955]
French dramatic poet and diplomat

Plays include:
Tête d'Or (*Golden Head*; published 1890, produced 1924), *Partage de Midi* (*Break of Noon;* published 1906, produced 1948), *L'Otage* (*The Hostage*; 1911), *L'Annonce Faite à Marie* (*The Tidings Brought to Mary*; 1912), *Le Soulier de Satin* (*The Satin Slipper*; published 1929, produced 1943), *Le Livre de Christophe Colomb* (*The Book of Christopher Columbus*; 1930)

Many of Claudel's plays, with their characteristic long psalm-like verse line, were not intended for production under the prevailing stage conditions in the first quarter of the century. They took on a new lease of life in the 1940s and 1950s when Jean-Louis Barrault persuaded the author to let him put on the painfully autobiographical *Break of Noon* and to turn the 'unplayable' six-hour-long *The Satin Slipper*, with its themes of sin and salvation and the destinies of civilisations, into a colourful piece of 'total theatre'. Although Edith Craig produced *The Tidings Brought to Mary* in 1916, and had a success with Sybil Thorndike in *The Hostage* in 1919, it would take a bold director to try *The Satin Slipper* in English.

Try these:
▷Jean Giraudoux for poetic French drama, though on less apocalyptic subjects; Charles Peguy's *Le Mystère de la Charité de Jeanne d'Arc* (*The Mystery of the Charity of Joan of Arc*) for similar treatments of Catholic themes; ▷Mary O'Malley's *Once a Catholic* for a very different view of Catholic upbringing.

CLIFFORD, John   [1950–]
English-born dramatist now working in Scotland

Plays include:
How Like an Angel (1983), *Losing Venice* (1985), *Lucy's Play* (1986), *Playing with Fire* (1987), *Ines de Castro* (1989)

Historical perspectives on present dilemmas and an abiding distaste for any meanness of human spirit, for cruelty and for indifference of the needs of others fill John Clifford's plays with a marvellous, concerned wisdom about what really matters in life. Clifford has a merry, questing imagination inspired, so he has said, by the child's play of his daughters where all things can happen on a mere say-so. But he also has a sophisticated academic background, a degree in Arabic and Spanish affording him the cadences and philosophies of two cultures strikingly different from our own.

His contribution to the British stage would be significant in terms of his stylish, vigorous translations alone – Calderón's *Schism in England* for the ▷National Theatre (1988) among them. And Hispanic influences – thematic and stylistic – permeate his original plays. For instance, the events used in *Ines de Castro* (1989) derive from Portuguese legends about the doomed love affair between Pedro, heir to the throne and a woman, Ines, who is from an enemy land. The plot is reminiscent of a Jacobean revenge tragedy. The writing melds the stateliness of Calderón, the poetic escape of Lorca, the gusto of medieval morality, and something which is Clifford's own, the heartfelt anger of the very gentle.

Clifford's association with the Edinburgh Traverse, started when Jenny Killick was artistic director in 1985 and constructively maintained when Ian Brown took over in 1988, has been a vital factor in his development as a playwright. The Traverse team encouraged him to give free rein to his ideas, offered guidance and provided a valuable platform by staging his works during the Edinburgh Fringe when they were most likely to be seen by major British critics and visiting agents.

Losing Venice
Since winning a Fringe First award in 1985 *Losing Venice* has been performed in London, Los Angeles, Australia, Hong Kong and has been broadcast on radio. It travels well because it depends on one simple, inspired notion: encourage adults to use their imagination with the same limitless scope enjoyed in childhood. And at one level, the games set in motion are not dissimilar – a Duke decides to go to war because that is what Dukes do, just as he gets married . . . because *that* is what Dukes do. And Dukes do these things because they are mimicking other Dukes, just like

children mimic grown-ups. So, off they go –
the Duke, his Poet, his Servant, to retrieve
Venice (which wasn't actually theirs, but
shouldn't be taken over by anyone else) and
they have adventures and catastrophes – without benefit of props, or fancy locations, but all
through conjuring with words and acting as if
such things are so – and eventually they come
home, heroes – by their own account anyway.
Meanwhile, home has crumbled away,
poverty and disorder reign. And the women-
folk who've struggled through these domestic
battles aren't all that impressed with this
macho bluster and hollow victory. It is a deli-
cious, sly, droll play which astutely deflates
national and male chauvinism, warmongering
(an exercise in cosmetic politicking usually),
scrutinises the actual usefulness of the Poet
within society, celebrates female common-
sense and loving, and does so with wit and
panache.

Try these:
For a play which explores escapism/
imagination and human relationships try
Kathy and the Hippopotamus by Mario
Vargas Llosa. For Spanish drama dip into
Cervantes, ▷Lope de Vega; ▷Calderón,
Echegaray and ▷Lorca; honour and
compromise are poignantly depicted in
C. P. Taylor's *Good*; Fyodor Abramov's
Brothers and Sisters for an epic Russian
and tragic equivalent of women keeping
the home front going during WWII; Howard
Barker is adept at using history to point up
cogent moral and social issues of our time;
Corneille's *Le Cid* in Cheek by Jowl's pun-
gently clear revival revealed it as a fascinating treatment of the corrosive effects of
honour and familial duty.

COCTEAU, Jean   [1889–1963]
French avant-garde poet, film-maker and
dramatist

Plays include:
Les Mariés de la Tour Eiffel (*The Wedding
on the Eiffel Tower*; 1924), *Orphée* (1927),
Antigone (1928), *La Voix Humaine* (*The
Human Voice*; 1930), *La Machine infernale*
(*The Infernal Machine*; 1934), *Les
Chevaliers de la Table Ronde* (*The Knights of
the Round Table*; 1937), *Les Parents
Terribles* (*The Terrible Parents*; 1938),
L'Aigle a Deux Têtes (*The Eagle Has Two
Heads*; 1946)

Cocteau was a permanent avant-gardist in the
1920s and 1930s (or, as his enemies put it, the
ultimate in trendy chic); his talents included
poetry, drawing, film- and playmaking, and
he had a considerable vogue in England after
the Second World War, but he has not been
popular with the next generation. However,
there are signs of a revival, which may grow as
the period flavour becomes sharper; since
1984 there have been London productions of
Orphée, *The Infernal Machine* (Cocteau's variations on the Oedipus story), and the short,
bravura piece for solo actress and telephone,
The Human Voice. In the USA, *The Human
Voice* has provided several talented actresses
with a vehicle for their virtuosity.

Try these:
▷Anouilh, ▷Gide, ▷Giraudoux, and
▷Sartre for using modernised Greek plays
and legends to comment on contemporary
French affairs.

COLLINS, Barry   [1941–]
British dramatist

Plays include:
And Was Jerusalem Builded Here (1972),
Beauty and the Beast (1973), *Judgement*
(1974), *The Strongest Man in the World*
(1978), *Toads* (1979), *The Ice Chimney*
(1980), *Atonement* (1987)

Halifax based writer, one-time provincial
journalist, and director of northern avant-
garde studio theatre, Collins writes of monumental themes – human beings at the extremes of experience, in the grip of personal
and social tragedy. Often, though not always,
his focus is a northern one; nineteenth-
century poverty and struggle in the Luddite
riots in West Yorkshire (*And Was Jerusalem
Builded Here*); Maurice Wilson the eccentric
Yorkshireman who tried to climb Everest (*The
Ice Chimney*), or the satirical swipe at Soviet
obsession with creating sporting champions,
The Strongest Man in the World (described by
Bernard Levin as 'a Great Passion Play'), written in a northern dialect.

Collins is, however, probably best known
for his dramatic monologue *Judgement* – a
horrific tale of cannibalism based on a real
war-time incident when seven Russian soldiers were left for sixty days without food,
recounted by one of the two remaining survivors. Described by critic Steve Grant as
having the 'hypnotic rhetoric of a John Donne

sermon, the moral intensity of a Conrad novel and finely observed lyric detail of a Louis MacNeice poem', Collins' two-and-a-half-hour tour de force has provoked magnificent performances from its interpreters, first Peter O'Toole (1974), then memorably Colin Blakely (1975, 1976), and Ben Kingsley (1977). By now a much travelled piece (it has been seen in over twenty countries), this cool, clinical investigation into the moral and philosophical laws of human degradation, survival and the nature of guilt and sanity conjures with themes Collins has continued to re-address though perhaps nowhere else with so much control. *Atonement*, his most recent stage play, grapples bravely with the nature of guilt and the symbiotic destructiveness of obsessive love but fails to draw us successfully into its world.

Try these:
For another monologue dealing with extremism, Alan Drury's *The Man Himself*; for three-handed images of destructive love, ▷Strindberg's *Creditors*; ▷Sam Shepard's *Fool for Love* depicts a similar scene between a brother and sister, ▷David Rudkin's *Ashes* for the sterility of a marriage; ▷Botho Strauss' *The Tourist Guide* for the obsessive destructiveness of sexual love (between an older man and younger woman); *K2* by Patrick Meyers for mountain climbing plays.

COMMUNITY THEATRE IN BRITAIN

In most cultures, all theatre is community theatre. Only in modern western cultures, where theatre aspires to the status of high art and its spectators are drawn from a cultural elite, does the idea of community theatre as a form distinct unto itself exist. In the Third World today, in the theatre of antiquity, and in Europe until at least the age of Shakespeare (and arguably up until the dawn of the present century) it is and was the function of theatre to inspire, inform and bring together entire communities.

Community theatre in Britain these days covers anything from performing in small community venues such as halls or old people's homes, to large-scale open-door spectaculars. If ▷David Edgar's definition of community theatre as something which addresses 'communities of ideas' means anything, then companies that particularly aim to address the gay, black or women's communi-

ties, or in times of industrial dispute striking communities, could all be said to be part of community theatre.

The 1960s saw the birth of modern community theatre as a movement and an idea that took many forms. Peter Schumann's Bread and Puppet Theatre (1961) in New York and R.G. Davis' San Francisco Mime Troupe (1959) on opposite sides of the States were creating highly visual performances that engaged the political issues of the moment in a popular style and were able to be staged anywhere there was an audience. The work of Welfare State (1968) in England was in a similar vein (though with whimsy in place of the politics), while elsewhere in England other groups were springing up to explore new ways of making theatre accessible to a population that had lost the habit of theatre-going. In Brighton, The Combination (1967) began work that was eventually to take it to London and the Albany Empire, while ▷John McGrath was touring his 7:84 companies (1971) around the working men's clubs of England and Scotland with polemical and politicising shows of the Left – a tradition that also spawned companies like Covent Garden Community Theatre, Foco Novo, Red Ladder, Roland Muldoon and CAST, North West Spanner, Belt & Braces and Portable Theatre.

The following decade saw a different type of community theatre – companies that played to communities defined by gender, sexuality and colour rather than class or geography. Jimmy Camicia's Hot Peaches (1972) were the camp trail-blazers of New York's gay theatre movement. In London, Gay Sweatshop (1975) grew out of Ed Berman's seasons at The Almost Free as did the Women's Theatre Group (1973) who, with Monstrous Regiment (1976), were soon establishing a rich tradition of work by and for women.

Many playwrights became involved with community theatre at one level or another in the 1960s and 1970s as part of the movement to take theatre out of theatre buildings and bring it to 'the people' – a time, too, when agitprop and 'street theatre' became the buzz words and popular mode of performance. ▷Margaretta D'Arcy with John Arden, for example, have been involved with community theatre since the early 1970s (particularly with the Galway Theatre Workshop), producing plays mostly on community or political themes. Peter Cheeseman at Stoke-on-Trent evolved a whole tradition of drama-documentaries based on the local community.

In the 1980s, ▷Ann Jellicoe's work with the Colway Trust sparked off yet another revival in the idea of the 'community play'. Her approach involved hundreds of local people in researching their local history and performing in the subsequent play, often scripted by a professional. In 1985 Jellicoe commissioned ▷David Edgar to write a play for performance by the townspeople of Dorchester in Dorset about their own history. The result was *Entertaining Strangers*, which eventually joined the ▷Royal National Theatre's repertoire (performed then by professional actors). ▷Nick Darke's *Ting Tang Mine*, set in Cornwall also started out life as a Colway Trust Project; under the title of *The Earth Turned Inside Out*. The method has spawned similar plays across the country notably Luke Dixon, working with designer Paul Dart in Deal in Kent to produce a series of large-scale, outdoor ▷Shakespeare productions and culminating in 1991 with *Age of Saints*, a community play that involves three towns in three different countries expressing their own shared sense of community on an epic scale through the Medieval mystery-play form.

For Dixon, Jellicoe, John Fox of Welfare State and others working in this form of community theatre, its essence is in participation, a shared sense of excitement between professional theatre workers and non-professionals alike in 'building a work of art in the community'. Community theatre and its aims remain diverse, embracing Young People's Theatre, Christmas shows, Reminiscence theatre (as in Age Exchange, a company created by Pam Schweitzer, focusing on the memories of older generations), and shows for those with special needs. Whatever their shape, the work of all these disparate groups re-unites individuals in a fragmented society with their place in a broader sense of community.

Try these:
▷Joan Littlewood; ▷Ann Jellicoe; Gay Sweatshop; Charabanc (see under ▷Marie Jones); Clean Break as examples of community theatre.

CONGREVE, William   [1670–1729]
English dramatist

Plays include:
The Old Bachelor (1693), *The Double-Dealer* (1693), *Love for Love* (1695), *The Mourning Bride* (1697), *The Way of the World* (1700)

English born and Irish educated, Congreve lived a fashionable life (his mistresses included the actress Anne Bracegirdle and the Duchess of Marlborough), indulged in some unsuccessful theatrical management, and wrote three comedies which are still staged. Although the satirical edge of Congreve's work is less sharp than ▷Wycherley's, public taste had changed sufficiently to make both *The Double-Dealer* and *The Way of the World* more successful with their later audiences than they were originally. *The Mourning Bride* is a tragedy but the other plays deal with the usual characters and issues of the period's comedy: arranged marriages and pretended marriages; the conflict between country and town values; lust and romance; rakes and fops and heiresses and mistresses; comic intrigues and revenges; age and youth and money and lack of it. Yet within this conventional material which is beautifully organised and wittily presented, the most interesting feature is Congreve's treatment of the romantic figures: in *The Double-Dealer*, *Love for Love*, and *The Way of the World* there are men and women who move towards a marriage based on mutual respect rather than money. The attitude to marriage is wary but ultimately positive, as in the so-called 'proviso scene' in *The Way of the World* where Millamant and Mirabelle lay down the ground rules of their marriage even as far as discussing how to bring up their children!

Try these:
Other Restoration comic writers, such as ▷Aphra Behn, ▷Etherege and ▷Wycherley; other writers of comedy of manners, such as ▷Goldsmith, ▷Molière, ▷Sheridan, ▷Oscar Wilde, ▷Philip Barry, ▷Noël Coward, and ▷Doug Lucie; ▷Edward Bond's *Restoration* uses conventions and themes derived from the practice of Restoration writers to make modern points.

COOKE, Trish   [1963–]
British dramatist

Plays include:
Shoppin People (1989), *Running Dream* (1989), *Back Street Mammy* (1989)

Trish Cooke was born in Bradford of Dominican parents. She later became an actress, and is now one of the newest of Britain's young black dramatists. She won a Thames TV Writers Bursary as writer-in-residence at Liverpool Playhouse, has published children's books (*Aisha's Brother* and *Mammy Sugar Falling Down*, the latter title being taken from a young West Indian child's first reaction to snow), and her *Running Dream*, about the interaction between three sisters after their mother leaves to go to England, was staged at London's Albany Theatre. However, *Back Street Mammy*, a play that audaciously weaves poetic and naturalistic forms in its exploration of the consequences of a young woman woman's finding herself pregnant after a one-night stand, may be a more important milestone in Cooke's career, even if some reviewers did dismiss her experimentation – nightmarish nursery rhymes, wordplay and dialogue – as 'pretentious'. Many others found the play perceptive, warm-hearted and joyous. Juggling with ideas about choices, independence, and generational conflicts, what could have been a routine drama of adolescence – and a stodgy enumeration of medical 'knowledge' for and against abortion – became in Cooke's hands a vigorous and imaginative expression of hope (appropriately, *Back Street Mammy* was presented by ▷Temba, the company whose Zulu name means 'hope'), profoundly on the side of life, if sceptical of marriage. The play has already been revived (by the new multi-million pound West Yorkshire Playhouse). It remains to be seen whether Cooke is gobbled up by television and film – she already writes for *EastEnders* (the BBC's flagship weekly 'soap') and has a film script in the pipeline.

Try these:
▷Winsome Pinnock is a young British dramatist writing about young black women and their experiences; ▷Liz Lochhead for a woman-centred Scottish writer; ▷Michael Ellis, Benjamin Zephaniah and ▷Nick Moffatt for contemporary black male writers; ▷Sharman Macdonald for plays on adolescent stirrings; the ▷Women's Theatre Group used an agit-prop form to put over information about contraception to young women in their 1974 play *My Mother Says*; see also ▷Black Theatre, ▷Women in Theatre.

COONEY, Ray [1932–]
British dramatist

Plays include:
One for the Pot (1963), *Chase Me Comrade* (1966), *My Giddy Aunt* (1970), *Bang Bang Beirut* (1971), *Not Now, Darling* (1971), *Charlie Girl* (1972), *Move Over, Mrs Markham* (1972), *Why Not Stay For Breakfast* (1974), *There Goes the Bride* (1975), *Run For Your Wife* (1984), *Two Into One* (1985), *Wife Begins at Forty* (1986), *It Runs in the Family* (1987), *Out of Order* (1990)

Cooney takes a perfectly mundane situation and swiftly transforms it by a series of misunderstandings into a collision of circumstances and the threat of ultimate disaster for our hero. In *Run for Your Wife*, for instance, a bigamous husband does his frantic best to keep his two wives from a catastrophic meeting. The improbabilities in Cooney's plots are made up for by a repeated, accelerating flurry of old jokes, and trousers choreographed to drop at just the right time. Cooney is a master of Whitehall, silly-ass ▷farce, a genre abhorred by theatre sophisticates but ever popular with audiences who want nothing more than to be entertained, their prejudices firmly intact.

Try these:
▷De Fillippo and ▷Feydeau for other masters of ▷farce; the 18th-century Irish playwright Arthur Murphy's *All in the Wrong* is a classic example of misunderstandings carried to the limit.

CORNEILLE, Pierre [1606–84]
French dramatist

Plays include:
Mélite (1629), *Clitandre* (1631), *L'Illusion Comique* (*The Illusion* or *The Comic Illusion*; 1636), *Le Cid* (*The Cid*; 1636–7), *Horace* (1640), *Cinna* (1640), *Polyeucte* (1641), *Rodugune* (1644–5), *Oedipe* (*Oedipus*; 1659), *Tite et Bérénice* (*Titus and Berenice*; 1670), *Suréna* (1674)

Corneille was a lawyer from Rouen; his early plays were comedies or tragi-comedies, but after the success of *The Cid* he settled down to write heroic tragedies, somewhat in the Spanish manner, with strong-willed heroes and heroines in impossible situations, with which they cope, at whatever cost. He suffered from being the first major French dramatist to try to keep the neo-Aristotelian rules, the three unities of time, place and action. Unlike Racine, he usually had too much plot for the requisite twenty-four hours,

J. Grant Albrecht in the Hartford Stage Company's production of Corneille's *The Illusion*, freely adapted by Tony Kushner, staged by its artistic director, Mark Lamos, January 1990

and was much discouraged by the resulting criticism.

Corneille's plays have not often been produced in English since they were translated in the seventeenth century by the Matchless Oridna. However, he has become more popular in recent years, especially since Giorgio Strehler's lively production of *The Illusion* in Paris in 1984. This play has a magician, a Spanish braggart called Metamore, a play within a play within a play, and characters who appear to die, and are then revealed as a company of actors sharing out the takings. It has also succeeded in London and in Hartford, Conn., and has led the way to London productions of *The Cid* (1987) and *The Liar* (1988).

The Cid

This is the archetypal 'Love against Honour' play. Rodrigue (the Cid) loves Chimène, but has to kill her father in a duel because the latter has insulted his (Rodrigue's) father; Chimène loves Rodrigue, but has to demand his life from the King because he has killed her father. Happily, the King needs to keep Rodrigue alive to beat the Moors, and persuades Chimène to avow her love by telling her Rodrigue is dead. The play is called a tragi-comedy, but no one seems quite sure whether this is a happy ending or not. The language is elevated and the sentiments of all concerned excessively noble; but the effect can be very powerful.

Try these:
▷Racine for seventeenth-century French drama and for keeping to the neo-Aristotelian rules better; ▷Calderón for the influence of Spanish ideas of family honour; Cheek by Jowl's production was an exemplary example of their approach to dusting off old classics and making them vividly alive and relevant.

CORRIE, Joe   [1894–1968]
British dramatist

Plays include:
In Time o' Strife (1927), *Martha* (1935), *Hewers of Coal* (1937)

Although Corrie was an admirer of Sean O'Casey and they were both self-educated former manual labourers (Corrie was a miner), unlike O'Casey Corrie remained in his native Scotland for most of his life. He wrote most successfully about Scottish mining–mainly one-act plays for groups within the Scottish Community Drama Association. Amongst his best plays are *Hewers of Coal*, the archetypal pit-disaster play, and *Martha*, which occupies similar territory to ▷J.M. Barrie's *Mary Rose*, in this case the ghostly return of a mother's lost son from World War I, in a more robust way. Corrie's greatest play, *In Time o'Strife*, chronicles the last days of the post-General Strike miners' lockout in a small Scottish village. The ▷7:84 Theatre Company's 1982 revival showed that the play's concentrated naturalistic virtues have stood the test of time, and the political issues remain as relevant now as in the 1920s. Although Corrie is sometimes sentimental, his sentiment is grounded in a genuine understanding and compassion for his characters and their predicaments, and it goes along with an unsentimental analysis of the responsibilities for those predicaments. The mine owners never appear in *In Time o'Strife* and many of its virtues stem from its willingness *not* to try to see both sides of the question.

Try these:
▷Sean O'Casey, particularly *The Plough and the Stars* for a play showing a working-class community under the strain of great political upheaval and *The Silver Tassie* for the impact of war on a community; Scottish playwright Ena Lamont Stewart's *Men Should Weep* for another example of a 1920s Scottish community under strain; ▷Synge's *The Riders to the Sea* for the impact of sons' deaths on a mother in a peasant community; 7:84 Scotland is a Scottish group touring socially-concerned plays in Scotland; ▷Galsworthy's *Strife* for a presentation of strikes from within a more established theatre; Peter Cox's *The Garden of England*, toured by 7:84 England, portrayed miners at bay during the 1984 miners' strike; Zola's *Germinal*, adapted by William Gaminara for Paines Plough, magnificently portrayed a French mining community of the late 19th century.

COWARD, Noël   [1899–1973]
British dramatist, actor, singer, screenwriter

Plays include:
The Young Idea (1921), *The Vortex* (1924), *Fallen Angels* (1925), *Hay Fever* (1925), *Easy Virtue* (1926), *Semi-Monde* (written

1926, performed 1977), *Bitter Sweet* (1929), *Private Lives* (1930), *Cavalcade* (1931), *Design For Living* (1933), *Tonight At 8.30* (1936), *Operette* (1938), *Blithe Spirit* (1941), *Present Laughter* (1943), *This Happy Breed* (1943), *Relative Values* (1951), *Quadrille* (1952), *Nude With Violin* (1956), *Waiting In the Wings* (1960), *Sail Away* (1961), *Suite In Three Keys* (1965)

Whether you see him as the doyen of bitchery or the ultimate connoisseur of camp, or if you find various moral tales peeking out from behind his characters' poor and pricelessly funny manners, Noël Coward remains this century's supreme wit, a playwright in a direct line from ▷Congreve through to ▷Sheridan, ▷Oscar Wilde and ▷Joe Orton (Millamant's 'I Love To Give Pain', from *The Way of the World*, could serve as the subtext for Coward creations). The consummate man of the theatre himself, theatrical folk figure heavily in Coward's plays, whether it's the matriarchal actress, Judith Bliss, in *Hay Fever* or the preening comedian Garry Essendine in *Present Laughter*, who admits, 'I'm always acting'. Non-actors in his plays act, too: the hypertheatrical Madam Arcati in *Blithe Spirit*, the polyglot houseboy Sebastien in *Nude With Violin*. For Coward, as for ▷Wilde, acting equals artifice equals disguise, and the tension in his work often comes from the effort required to sustain a pose without which his characters, and their egos, dry up. Coward's plays may come adorned with comic frills that continue to entice, but he is as serious and penetrating a dramatist as Britain has known this century. He was also an accomplished lyricist and cabaret performer.

Hay Fever

Last seen in the West End in 1983 (with Penelope Keith), and on Broadway in 1985 (with Rosemary Harris), *Hay Fever* is an anarchic precursor of 'get the guest' in ▷Edward Albee's *Who's Afraid of Virginia Woolf* – Coward's eccentric Bliss family invites guests to their home in Cookham only to drive them away again through their own accumulated eccentricities. The play both revels in, and comments on, the English fondness for ill-mannered artifice, and at its best – the visiting 'drearies' skulk away as the family carries obliviously on over breakfast – it can be a deliriously funny experience. As usual with Coward, a critique is implied: the Blisses may

be lethally exciting with their fondness for games and poses, but their mores also serve to isolate them; they are fundamentally alone.

Private Lives

Written by Coward for himself and Gertrude Lawrence to act, *Private Lives*, is one of the simplest, yet most subtle of comedies, and one can take pleasure in the perfect rhythms of its language: 'Don't quibble, Sybil' and 'very flat Norfolk' have both entered history books. Two divorcés, Amanda and Elyot, bump into one another on their second honeymoons only to end up ditching their new spouses, Victor and Sibyl, and absconding to Paris. Typically for Coward, elegant repartee hides hideous manners, and the characters are both aware of – and blind to – their own ruthlessness. It was last seen in 1982 on Broadway in a critically reviled but financially successful production co-starring Elizabeth Taylor and Richard Burton; recent London versions have paired Maggie Smith and Robert Stephens (in 1970) and Maria Aitken and Michael Jayston (in 1980).

Try these:
▷Oscar Wilde, especially *The Importance of Being Earnest*, for effortlessly funny repartee; ▷Joe Orton for epigrammatic similarities in tone, and ▷Philip Barry for the American equivalent; ▷Neil Simon for inferior variants on similar ideas; Lillian Hellman's *Little Foxes* for another ruthless family; ▷N.F. Simpson's *One Way Pendulum*, and ▷Alan Ayckbourn for more middle-class versions of the comic cruelties of English eccentrics; Charles Ludlam and Charles Busch for campier wit.

CRAZE, Tony   [1944–]
British dramatist

Plays include:
The Love You Take (1981); *Kaleidoscope* (1981); *Confrontations* (1981); *Shona* (1983); *Living with Your Enemies* (1985); *Angelus* (1987) *Going West* (1988), *Megabodies* (1989), *Flying Ashes*, (based on *Letters of Love* by Julia Voznesenskaya, 1990)

Craze, a former journalist and screen writer (he trained at the London Film School), was script and workshop adviser before becoming director of the Soho Poly which has staged three of his major plays. Craze's plays pack a powerful, emotional punch (though his dialogue can be irritatingly cryptic) showing individuals not only at loggerheads within the family but also victims of blighted dreams which reflect the way society has failed them. *Living with Your Enemies* relates a mother's lost opportunities, sacrificed in bringing up her children, back to her post-war youth and the promises offered by the creation of the Welfare State. The flawed but explosive *Angelus* is a three-hander in which the spectre of a Jimmy Porter figure is resurrected for the 1980s in Mick, bully-boy, drugs dealer and sinner seeking redemption. With its desperate spiritual yearnings, *Angelus* indicates Craze as something more than simply an adherent of the raw 'slice of life' school of drama. Though he has still to find a unified style, *Shona* (the first winner of the Verity Bargate new playwriting award and a terse, painful blast against modern psychiatric practices) and *Going West* (about a couple of hobos on the road from New York to LA) show Craze as a champion of the underdog–his is a voice of compassion, chronicling the area where frustrated dreams turn into anger and despair.

Try these:
Mick Mahoney's *When Your Bottle's Gone in SE1* and ▷Tony Marchant's *The Lucky Ones* for contemporary angst in the working class; for other images of insanity, Peter Weiss' *Marat/Sade*; Christopher Durang's *Beyond Therapy*; ▷Melissa Murray's *The Admission* and *Bodycell*, ▷David Edgar's *Mary Barnes*, ▷David Mercer's *In Two Minds*, ▷Alan Ayckbourn's *A Woman in Mind*; for rather different views, Gillian Plowman's seriously funny *Me and My Friend* about 'caring-in-the-community' and Joe Orton's gallows-humour treatment of madness in *What The Butler Saw*; for generational conflict between mothers and offspring, ▷Julia Kearsley, ▷Louise Page, ▷Ayshe Raif; ▷Caryl Phillip's *Strange Fruit* for generational differences in terms of the black community; ▷Stephen Lowe's *Touched* for more images of women's pleasures and pains in the 1940s; ▷John Osborne's *Look Back in Anger* for the original Jimmy Porter.

Carol Scanlan in the Belfast-based Charabanc company's production of *Somewhere Over The Balcony*, by Marie Jones, directed by Peter Sheridan at the Drill Hall Arts Centre, September 1987

CRIMP, Martin   [1956–]
British dramatist

Plays include:
Living Remains (1981), *Four Attempted Acts* (1984), *A Variety of Death Defying Acts* (1985), *Definitely the Bahamas* (1986), *Getting Attention* (1987), *Dealing with Clair* (1988), *Play With Repeats* (1989), *No One Sees the Video* (1990), *Getting Attention* (1991)

Martin Crimp, one of the brightest of Britain's new generation of playwrights, can rightly be claimed as a product of the small Orange Tree theatre at Richmond which, under Sam Walters, have presented no fewer than six of his plays. Born in Dartford, Kent, Crimp took a degree in English at Cambridge but has lived in Richmond for the past ten years where his association with the Orange Tree, through its writings workshops and one-act lunchtime slots has steadily borne fruit. Crimp's stock-in-trade is the creation of a tangible sense of unease. One of his early plays, *Four Attempted Acts* (the radio version, *Three Attempted Acts*, won the 1985 Giles Cooper award), built up a steady head of steam simply around a phone call. As *The Daily Telegraph*'s Charles Spencer has noted, 'he appears to deal with humdrum people in humdrum situations but nothing is as it seems.' Beneath the surface, Crimp implies worlds of darker meaning, thereby creating growing atmospheres of tension, even of menace. When you add to this his spiky, spare, apparently naturalistic but actually rigorously controlled and often very funny dialogue, it's little wonder he has been hailed, in some quarters, as a new ▷Pinter. Crimp's plays are certainly very much products of today, thinly disguised comedies of manners, expertly reproducing recognisable types and surface tics. Crimp likes to peel back the layers of social behaviour to reveal the horrors and void beneath the veneer of contemporary life. However, they also sometimes steer an uneasy course between the satirist and moralist vying: *No One Sees the Video*, a scathing attack on market research (based on his own experience), ended up as a series of short albeit brilliant sketches, ultimately lacking depth in characterisation, burdened with a heavy-handed plot development and an inconclusive ending. More successful perhaps was *Dealing with Clair*. A story set in very typical late 1980s territory, yuppie-land, it brought together Clair, a young, female estate agent, a sleekly upwardly mobile couple anxious to get the best possible price for their home, and a somewhat mysterious cash buyer (played originally by Tom Courtenay). Clair's possible murder at the end only coincidentally paralleled the mystery surrounding the real-life disappearance of Suzy Lamplugh, a young London estate agent. As in *No One Sees the Video*, Crimp's line is one of moral scruple – highlighting the greed and avarice behind smooth yuppie smiles, the emptiness and moral bankruptcy behind sleek market researchers rather than just denouncing unethical real estate practices or consumerism. In his latest play, *Getting Attention* (produced in 1991), a sense of tension around the possibility of knowing – and doing nothing – is perhaps really at issue, not the child abuse which is the ostensible subject. Certainly a writer to watch.

Try these:
▷Doug Lucie's *Fashion*, ▷Stephen Jeffreys' *Valued Friends*, ▷Howard Brenton's and David Hare's *Pravda* and Hare's *Secret Rapture* for other critiques of contemporary moral values; ▷Anouilh for another example of social satire digging away at the heart of moral darkness; ▷Arthur Miller's *The Price* for linkage with consumer spending and the nation's emotional state; ▷Ayckbourn for another British playwright fond of peeling away social exteriors to reveal the ooze beneath; ▷Marlane Meyer's *Etta Jenks* for an American equivalent of Liz in *No One Sees the Video*, reluctant beginner who takes on the traits of her original oppressors, with a vengeance; ▷Robert Holman's *Rafts and Dreams* also deals with child abuse, though in a somewhat surreal manner.

CROSS, Felix   [1953–]
Trinidad-born performer, writer and composer

Musical plays include:
Blues for Railton (1985), *Mass Carib* (1987), *Glory* (1988)

A former music teacher (at Goldsmiths College, London) actor and author, Felix Cross' contribution to black theatre over the past few years is hard to over-estimate. His major contribution lies in his cross-cultural pieces of musical theatre. *Blues for Railton* signalled the creation of a new form of black theatre in Britain – and one particular to Cross. Adapted with David Simon from Simon's original novel, it is a tragi-comedy about a black immigrant family's experiences in Britain whose sense of identity was underlined through musical leitmotifs and rituals recalling Afro-Caribbean rituals and rhythms. No other practitioner has come close to his achievement of fusing western and Afro-Caribbean musical idioms which in *Mass Carib* developed into a full-blown synthesis of the Roman Catholic mass absorbed into Afro-Caribbean musical forms. Incorporating elements of carnival, masks, drumming, it also told the story of the enforced conversion to Christianity of the slaves taken to the Caribbean, bringing them up to date as immigrants arriving in Britain brandishing British passports. Written and composed by Cross, *Mass Carib* was, by any standards, a tremendously impressive theatrical and musical achievement as well as a celebration of Afro-Caribbean cultural survival-by-adaptation (African Shango gods, for instance, being given Christian names). Certainly one of the theatrical landmarks of the past five years – ambitious, challenging yet fully realised by singers, dancers and actors alike.

Glory, following a similar theme, but with a more complex, anti-imperialist text by Cross, again combined a strong storyline with magnificent musicianship and theatrical spectacle, this time using calypso, alongside African Shango rituals and aspects of carnival. Cross's text ambitiously tries to interweave personal tragedy (a young woman abused by her father), with the story of Trinidad and Tobago's struggle for political independence from the British – a heavy mixture to sustain. Some critics carped about its over-simplicities (mostly of the white characters). Others accepted its shortcomings and still marvelled at its scope and Adjoa Andoh's stunning acting and rich-throated singing in the monumental role of Glory.

Try these:

Clarke Peter's *Five Guys Named Moe* for a black musical of a completely different temper, based on the music of American jazz songwriter, Louis Jordan; *King*, Richard Blackford's and Maya Angelou's ill-fated musical about Martin Luther King for one that certainly didn't work; *Once Upon This Island*, for another mainstream musical fashioned from Caribbean musical and narrative motifs; Lee Breuer's *The Warrior Ant* for a full-scale West Indian carnival; ▷Stephen Sondheim for *the* musical writer/composer par excellence; ▷Robert Lepage for theatre which extolls multiculturalism; ▷Penny Casdagli for a young British playwright who tries to do the same, albeit on a much smaller scale; see ▷Black Theatre for other contemporary black writers in Britain; also ▷Matura's *The Coup* for a contrasting, and almost farce-like view of post-colonial Trinidad.

 d

DANIELS, Sarah [1957–]
British dramatist

Plays include:
Ripen Our Darkness (1981), *Masterpieces*
(1983), *The Devil's Gateway* (1983),
Neaptide (1984), *Byrthrite* (1987), *The Gut
Girls* (1988), *Beside Herself* (1990)

A spirited, anarchically funny, angry young
writer, Daniels is also one of the most controversial British playwrights, and the only radical lesbian feminist to have made it into the
mainstream. She first came to prominence as
part of the 'new wave' of young women
writers in the early 1980s with *Ripen Our
Darkness* – a play famous for the line 'Dear
David, your dinner and my head are in the
oven' – premiered, like *Byrthrite*, at the Royal
Court Upstairs (which also presented
Masterpieces after its Royal Manchester
Exchange opening). Her attacks on patriarchy
involve the rebellion of mothers (*Ripen Our
Darkness* and *The Devil's Gateway*) and the
discussion of lesbian custody of children in
Neaptide (originally commissioned by Liverpool Playhouse). *Byrthrite* is a warning for
women about the possible consequences of
modern genetic engineering and reproductive
techniques and is linked to a familiar theme of
the persecution of the old 'wise women' of the
17th century (though by no means treated in
familiar fashion, and, in its high-camp, historical setting, a breakaway from Daniels'
usual quasi-naturalism). *The Gut Girls* continues the historical theme with its celebration
of Victorian working-class women, and *Beside
Herself* tackles childhood abuse in a mythological frame.

Needless to say, Daniels' plays and her expression of unpalatable truths (especially if
you are a man) have invoked, in their turn,
vitriolically hostile reviews from critics
(mostly but not exclusively male), particularly
over *Masterpieces* and *Byrthrite*. But Daniels'
early protagonists are recognisable suburban
wives and mothers rebelling – wittily – against

their roles as general moppers-up after men
and the male value system that has put them
there. In Daniels' world, the personal becomes graphically political. Despite the out-
cries, Daniels won the George Devine Award
in 1982 for *Neaptide*.

Masterpieces
This is an uncompromisingly didactic play
that makes a direct link between the seemingly innocuous dinner table misogynist joke
– 'a little harmless fun,' says one of the male
characters – and male violence against
women, as in *Ripen Our Darkness* and *The
Devil's Gateway*. It is a tale of growing awareness, focused on Rowena, a social worker (the
archetypal Daniels heroine), who gradually
moves from naivety to anger, from passivity to
action and wholesale rejection of the man-
made world in which she lives and to which
she has, in the past, given tacit acceptance.
The play has an irrefutable emotional force
about it and has deservedly come to be
regarded as a feminist classic, even if some
find its philosophical links questionable.

Try these:
For a contrasting male treatment of pornography, ▷Doug Lucie's *Progress*; ▷Gay
Sweatshop's *Care and Control* for an
earlier treatment of lesbian custody;
▷Caryl Churchill's *Vinegar Tom* and
▷Dekker, ▷Ford and ▷Rowley's *The
Witch of Edmonton* for witches; ▷Joe
Orton for a similarly anarchic approach to
wit (juxtaposing the surreal with the ordinary); ▷Bryony Lavery for a similar adven-
turer using wit to attack the bastions of
patriarchy; ▷Aphra Behn for a
seventeenth-century feminist equivalent;
see also ▷Lesbian Theatre; Alison
Lyssa's *Pinball* for an Australian lesbian
mother custody case; ▷Shakespeare's
The Winter's Tale uses the same Demeter
myth as *Neaptide*; Jane Chambers as an
American pioneer of lesbian drama. The

use of mythological figures in the first scene of *Beside Herself* parallels some of ▷Churchill's stylistic devices in *Top Girls*.

D'ARCY, Margaretta

Irish dramatist and long-time collaborator with ▷John Arden

Plays written in collaboration with John Arden include:
200 Years of Labour History (1971), *The Non-Stop Connolly Show* (1975), *The Little Gray Home in the West* (1978), *Vandaleur's Folly* (1978)

See ▷John Arden for his plays written in collaboration with D'Arcy.

D'Arcy started her career in Dublin in small experimental theatres. She then went to London where she acted in club theatres and at the Hornchurch Rep, one of the first regional companies to be local-authority funded. Her involvement with ▷community theatre stems from these early experiences, and much of her writing has been community-orientated. There are also several pieces written collectively, especially with Galway Theatre Workshop and with Galway Women's Voice Group, exploring a feminist interpretation of classical theatre. She has collaborated with Muswell Hill Street Theatre on *My Old Man's a Tory*, *Little Red Riding Hood and Granny Welfare* (1971); and with Corrandulla, Galway, *The Devil and the Parish Pump* (1974). Other pieces (some readings) include: *A Pinprick of History* (1977), *West of Ireland Women Speak* (1978), and *Trial and Prison Experience of the Countess Markievicz* (1979).

Try these:
For more voices of women in prison, Clean Break; for community theatre, ▷Ann Jellicoe; for women and Irish history, ▷Marie Jones and the young Irish women's company, Trouble and Strife, in *Now and at the Hour of Our Death*.

DARKE, Nick   [1949–]
British dramatist

Plays include:
Never Say Rabbit in a Boat (1978), *Landmarks* (1979), *A Tickle On the River's Back* (1979), *Say Your Prayers* (1980), *The Catch* (1980), *High Water* (1980), *The Body* (1983), *The Oven Glove Murders* (1986), *The Dead Monkey* (1986), *Ting Tang Mine* (1987), *Kissing the Pope* (1987)

An erstwhile actor, Cornish-born Darke is a prolific dramatist who has yet to write a play that can be endorsed without reservation. Some of his plays draw on the terrain of his upbringing, but his psychological grasp often falls short of his geographical one, and his writing becomes more earnest and pedantic the further it strays from his own roots. In *The Body*, an eccentric West Country community must contend with the presence of an American airforce base in one of those plays about the bomb that shows what poor art can come out of good politics. In *Ting Tang Mine*, orginally staged as a Cornish community play in 1984 under the title *The Earth Turned Inside Out*, the fate of two rival mining communities becomes an unconvincing parable of Thatcherite avarice. Greed's relationship to the screen gets the treatment in *The Oven Glove Murders*, set in the Soho offices of Absolutsky films, and Californian morality comes under the cudgel in *The Dead Monkey*, about a childless West Coast couple whose relationship has been kept alive for fifteen years by the now-dead simian of the title. Like many of Darke's plays, the topic is interesting but the style derivative. Even *Kissing the Pope*, inspired by a visit to Nicaragua, and an earnest attempt to confront that area's tragic ironies, failed to find general favour, being labelled as simplistic agit-prop and propaganda. However, his sensitive examination of the relationship between a young Contra and a young Sandinista 'growing up to be a man in a violent world; having to decide why to kill before you know why to live' was generally praised.

Try these:
David Manet's *Speed-the-plow*, George Kaufman and Moss Hart's *Once in a Lifetime*, Sam Shepard's *Angel City*, Arthur Kopit's *Road to Nirvana*, all deal with the machinations of the movie industry; ▷Charles Wood (especially *Has 'Washington' Legs?* and *Veterans*) for theatrical looks at film world life styles; ▷J.M. Synge (*Playboy of the Western World*) for *Ting Tang Mine* – like portraits of a community reacting to its errant son; ▷Sam Shepard, ▷Edward Albee, and ▷David Rabe for a kind of American absurdism which Darke seems to want to

In a supermarket hell, Lizzy McInnerny, June Watson, Dinah Stabb, and Marion Bailey in Sarah Daniels's *Beside Herself*, Royal Court, April 1990

capture for himself; ▷Brian Clarke's *The Petition,* ▷Sarah Daniels' *The Devil's Gateway,* ▷David Edgar's *Maydays* for other plays about American airforce bases (both Greenham) in Britain; see also ▷Ann Jellicoe, ▷Community Theatre.

DAVIES, Andrew   [1936–]
British dramatist

Plays include:
Filthy Fryer and the Woman of Maturer Years (1974), *Rose* (1980), *Prin* (1990)

A former teacher and university lecturer, Davies was a late starter. After some success with radio plays, he moved swiftly into television, films, stage plays and children's books (he won the 1978 Guardian Award and Boston Globe Horn Award for his children's book, *Conrad's War*). He is a dab hand at turning a good phrase, and has been in regular demand for television adaptations, creating en route a gallery of *monstres sacrées*, particularly in the series *A Very Peculiar Practice*, and in such dramatisations as *Mother Love* (with Diana Rigg) and *House of Cards*. The latter was screened during Mrs Thatcher's downfall, and was uncannily prescient as real-life mirrored fictional intrigues around the Palace of Westminster.

His recent play, *Prin* – staged on both sides of the Atlantic – introduces us to yet another 'sacred monster' (a type for whom Davies is said to have a soft spot) with a sharp line in repartee. Strictly within the well-made play formula (the action never stirs out of Prin's office), this sourly funny comedy focuses on the principal of an independent Teacher's Training College for Physical Education whose credo – excellence over mediocrity – marks her out immediately as one of that familiar breed, the English eccentric. Her admonishment to her charges is that everyone can be 'extraordinary' even whilst she herself divides them into 'job lots' or 'prima donnas'. Davies also covers his own bets: fighting a rearguard action against the grey drabness of modern educational policies, Prin is at once a symbol of the enlightened progressive in all its dangerous, thrilling glory (shades of Jean Brodie), and at the same time, more than faintly ludicrous in her refusal to move with the times. A bullying tyrant to friend, foe and young female lover alike, she is given all the best lines, but deprived at the play's end of happiness. With its sympathetic or abhorrent

character, *Prin* is accomplished if shallow fare which nonetheless offered opportunities for a star performer (Sheila Hancock in the West End, Eileen Atkins at the Manhattan Theatre Club). So did his earlier play, *Rose*, which ran with success with Glenda Jackson in the West End and subsequently on Broadway.

Try these:
Muriel Spark's *The Prime of Miss Jean Brodie,* and ▷Simon Gray's *Butley* for other articulate but fairly bilious educationalists; ▷Frank Marcus' *The Killing of Sister George* has obvious affinities with *Prin* in its depiction of lesbian life and loves; ▷Oscar Wilde for paradoxes in dialogue and character; ▷Peter Shaffer's *Equus* and *Amadeus* are other examples where flawed genius is pitted against mundane mediocrity; ▷Stephen Jeffreys' *The Clink,* like *House of Cards,* written many months before the fact, was uncannily accurate in its description of the sequence of events leading up to Mrs Thatcher's removal from office.

DE ANGELIS, April   [1960–]
British dramatist

Plays include:
Breathless (1986), *Wanderlust* (1988), *Women in Law* (1988), *Frankenstein* (1989), *Iron Mistress* (1989), *Crux* (1990), *Fanny Hill* (1991)

One-time actress, who has worked with ▷Monstrous Regiment, ReSisters and Lumiere and Son, April De Angelis is fast becoming the mistress of theatre noir. *Breathless,* an award winner in the 1987 Second Wave Young Women's writing festival at the Albany propelled her into prominence. A short, gothically atmospheric drama written with verve, wit and very contemporary consciousness about women and science, it rehashed the old Frankenstein myth and the stereotypical helpless Victorian heroine, with a contrasting pair of drooping mistress and obsessive maid, working away in the dungeons amongst the test tubes, frustrated at not being taken seriously as scientists. *Women in Law* carries on in something of the same vein. It uses a gothic setting, a thriller convention, unfortunately now becoming something of a cliché in women's theatre circles, and another, even more extravagant variant of *la châtelaine enchainé* (this one owes more than a little to a demented kind of Bette Davis/Miss Faversham) who is, again, a scientist manqué, pining for a lost career as a marine biologist. Commissioned by the ReSisters theatre company the play was ostensibly written to back up ideas about women and violence and the way they are treated in law, and though the polemic was laudable, the play suffered from its obvious brief. *Wanderlust*, created through the Oval House women writers' workshop is also set in the nineteenth century, and this time De Angelis' wilder shores and tongue-in-cheek imagination takes on the Great Man myth of David Livingstone, to make some serious points about colonialism in Africa. *Iron Mistress* continues to investigate the historical configurations of psychological confrontations between mothers and daughters. *Crux*, written for Paines Plough (with whom she is now writer-in-residence), uses the suppression of a medieval women's community's attempts to explore issues of power and desire.

Try these:
▷ Deborah Levy for a similar kind of verve and imaginative drive; Siren's *PULP* and Don Hale's *Every Black Day* for pulp thrillers à la Philip Marlowe; Brenton's *Bloody Poetry* for the Shelleys; ▷ Graeae for a version of Frankenstein; Annie Griffin directed the irreverent version of the story, *The Very Tragical History of Mary Shelley*, which gives an unflattering view of Shelley the husband; for other British plays on women, violence and the law, see Clean Break, ▷ Sarah Daniels; ▷ Kay Adshead; ▷ Julia Schofield and ▷ Sharman Macdonald are other new actress-dramatists; ▷ Howard Barker's *The Castle* for medieval communes of women.

DEAR, Nick   [1955–]
British dramatist

Plays include:
The Perfect Alibi (1980), *Temptation* (1984), *The Bed* (1986), *The Art of Success* (1986), *Food of Love* (1988), *In the Ruins* (1990)

The Portsmouth-born playwright Nick Dear came to attention in 1986–7 with his play *The Art of Success*, an ▷ RSC production that earned him an Olivier Award nomination for the Most Promising Newcomer in Theatre. Set during the eighteenth-century epoch of

William Hogarth, the satirical draughtsman, the play is purposefully revisionist and anachronistic in order to make a retroactive point about opportunism and lust, with Walpole as the Mrs Thatcher of his time facing off against the similarly Thatcherite entrepreneurial Hogarth. The play compresses ten years into one night and takes various liberties with personal and political history; still, there's no denying the Jonsonian vigour of Dear's scatology-laden language. His follow-up play *A Family Affair* (an ▷ Ostrovsky adaptation for Cheek By Jowl) has a similarly contemporary bent in its depiction of a society both goaded on, and paralysed, by matters financial. *In the Ruins* is a bravura, virtual monologue by King George III, which contrasts the image of the monarchy with the reality of the monarch. Dear's adaptation of Tirso de Molina's *The Last Days of Don Juan* was very successful for the ▷ RSC in 1990/1.

Try these:
▷ Edward Bond's *Bingo*, Constance Congdon's *Casanova* and Peter Shaffer's *Amadeus* for analogous debunkings of historical greats; ▷ Ben Jonson and, of Dear's contemporaries, ▷ Howard Barker for a similar robustness of language; ▷ Horváth and José Zorzilla for Don Juans.

DE FILIPPO, Eduardo   [1900–]
Italian actor, poet, dramatist

Plays include:
Oh These Ghosts! (1946), *Filumena* (1946), *Inner Voices* (translated by ▷ N.F. Simpson; 1948), *Fear Number One* (1950), *My Darling and My Love* (1955), *Saturday, Sunday, Monday* (translated by ▷ Keith Waterhouse and ▷ Willis Hall; 1959), *Ducking Out* (translated by Mike Stott; 1982); *Napoli Milionaria* (English version by Peter Tinniswood, 1991)

De Filippo has written more than fifty plays. Born into a family of actors (one of three illegitimate children), De Filippo began his career by touring with the famous Scarpetta acting company before founding a company with his brother Peppino and sister Titina.

Based on his experience as an actor, and his early days writing comedy and musical sketches, his later Neapolitan comedies are nothing if not supremely actable, distinguished by their craftsmanship and a Pirandellian involvement with the fine line between illusion and reality. However, three of the most recent productions in Britain have been more concrete examples of De Filippo's comedies in which the virtues of family life, in all their eccentric and extravagant glory, rule supreme. And, as in ▷Ayckbourn's plays (the British equivalent par excellence at chronicling the tragi-comedy of family life) the comic impetus comes from the recognisable ordinariness of domestic life, crashing up against the unexpected, the surreal, or the inappropriate emotional over-reaction.

Saturday, Sunday, Monday is the quintessential De Filippo, in which the warring factions of an extended family – squabbling off-spring, eccentric relatives, a paranoid husband, opportunistic friends, and lumbering maid – somehow live, love, fight, survive the heightened emotions of the rituals of Sunday lunch and become reconciled, presided over by the inevitable matriarch. Paternity and female subterfuge form the lynch-pins of *Filumena* in which the mistress for twenty-five years of a wealthy businessman hoodwinks him into marriage with her when he threatens to marry a younger woman, by refusing to disclose which of her three illegitimate sons is by him. *Filumena* tells us as much about male pride as it does about female deviousness. Once more, it is De Filippo's skill in creating characters of sympathy as well as pomposity that makes these Neapolitans so accessible. Mike Stott's relocation of the working-class Neapolitan family in *Ducking Out* to a council flat in west Lancashire was less successful and, some observers felt, sat oddly with the Christmas and Catholic rituals required. Nonetheless, most agreed that this grimmer than usual family portrait, with its kleptomaniac son, neurotic daughter, long-suffering mother, homosexual uncle, and presiding (if ultimately ineffective) paterfamilias, stroke-ridden and reduced to monosyllabic platitudes, once again showed De Filippo achieving a remarkable balance between laughter and pathos. Peter Tinniswood's Liverpudlian version of *Napoli Milionaria* for the National Theatre (1991) went down well and seemed an appropriately energetic cultural transplanting for this story of wartime wheeler-dealing and survival.

Try these:
▷Stephen Bill's *Curtains* and ▷Alan Ayckbourn for the joys (or otherwise) of families; ▷Pirandello, ▷Dario Fo and ▷Franca Rame are other regularly performed twentieth century Italian dramatists.

DEKKER, Thomas   [c 1572–1632]
English Renaissance dramatist and pamphleteer

Plays include:
The Shoemaker's Holiday (1599), *Sir Thomas Wyatt* (with ▷Heywood [?] and ▷Webster; pre-1607), *The Honest Whore* (with ▷Middleton; 1604), *The Roaring Girl* (with ▷Middleton; 1610), *The Virgin Martyr* (with Massinger; 1624), *The Witch of Edmonton* (with ▷Ford and ▷Rowley; 1621)

A rather shadowy figure who seems to have earned his living as a kind of house dramatist cum play doctor and pamphleteer, Dekker was imprisoned on more than one occasion for the debt that dogged him throughout his life. He seems to have spent much of his life producing collaborative work in whatever style was needed by the theatre manager Philip Henslowe. His work came back into theatrical fashion in Britain in the 1980s. This may reflect a more widespread awareness that co-authored works are not necessarily incoherent and inferior and may partly stem from the growth of collaboration elsewhere in the theatre at that time. Dekker's own dramatic work is generally genial, compassionate, London-centred and populist as in *The Shoemaker's Holiday* with its Dick Whittington-like tale of a cobbler who rises to become Lord Mayor of London while a disguised young nobleman woos and wins the daughter of the current Lord Mayor and receives the king's pardon for doing so. *The Roaring Girl* is particularly interesting since its portrait of a woman who scandalises contemporary society by wearing men's clothing and indulging in typical male pursuits like smoking and brawling is based on a real person, Mary Frith, who herself sat on stage to watch an early performance of the play. Dekker is also credited with the sympathetic portrayal of the witch in *The Witch of Edmonton*.

Try these:

▷Jonson satirised him in *The Poetaster*; Dekker's collaborators, ▷Ford, ▷Heywood, ▷Massinger, ▷Middleton, ▷Rowley and ▷Webster; ▷Auden and ▷Isherwood, ▷Brenton and ▷Hare, ▷Hecht and ▷MacArthur are examples of successful twentieth-century partnerships; among other contemporary writers who have also collaborated successfully are ▷Tunde Ikoli and Tariq Ali (with ▷Howard Brenton), ▷Caryl Churchill (with ▷David Lan), ▷David Edgar (with Susan Todd), ▷Trevor Griffiths (with ▷Brenton, ▷Clark, ▷Hare, ▷Poliakoff, Hugh Stoddart and ▷Snoo Wilson on *Lay By* and with ▷Brenton, ▷Ken Campbell and ▷Hare on *Deeds*); for another real-life portrait of a woman stepping outside traditional roles ▷Timberlake Wertenbaker's account of intrepid traveller, Isabelle Ebhardt, in *New Anatomies*; ▷Aphra Behn for other prototype feminists.

DELANEY, Shelagh   [1939–]
British dramatist

Plays include:
A Taste of Honey (1958), *The Lion in Love* (1960), *The House That Jack Built* (1978)

Delaney's main stage claim to fame is based on *A Taste of Honey*, the play she wrote at nineteen. Born in Salford, this one-time salesgirl, cinema usherette and photographer's lab assistant who left school at sixteen, wrote what has come to be regarded as one of the definitive plays of the 1950s. *A Taste of Honey*, her first play, was accepted by ▷Joan Littlewood's Theatre Workshop, was filmed (with Rita Tushingham as Jo), was hailed in New York (in 1961 and again twenty years later), and is constantly revived in the repertory in Britain. Delaney's second play, *The Lion in Love*, about a disturbed and unhappy family, again took a mother and daughter – Kit and Peg this time – as its focal point, but its more symbolic treatment found less favour, and some thought it was swamped by Littlewood's Theatre Workshop production. The play is seldom revived, although its style, themes, and sensitivities prefigure the work of such contemporary British dramatists as ▷Ayshe Raif and ▷Julia Kearsley. A revival giving us a chance to 'compare and contrast' would be fascinating.

Delaney has written many screenplays, notably *Charley Bubbles* (1968, starring Albert Finney) and the highly acclaimed *Dance With a Stranger* (1985) about the last woman to be hanged in Britain, Ruth Ellis.

A Taste of Honey
In many senses, this is a play that breaks with its time's conventions about motherhood and female sexuality in its portrait of Jo, the young working-class, reluctant mother-to-be and anti-heroine. In another sense it is very much of its time, the late 1950s, in that it celebrates a working-class approach, at once unsentimental and free of moral judgments in so far as illegitimacy, racial inter-marriage, or homosexuality are concerned. With its female-centred focus, and final opting for a life without men, it is a play that predates the concerns of later feminist writers – the optimism and the vulnerabilities, as well as the strengths of women – by well over a decade. However, despite its apparent affiliation to the realistic school of 'kitchen sink' drama, its original production by Littlewood made sure that audiences were not let off the hook as she confronted them with the challenges and the responsibilities raised by the play's sexual politics.

Try these:
See ▷Ann Jellicoe's *The Sport of My Mad Mother* for a bold, non-realistic treatment of the mother image; ▷Keith Waterhouse and ▷Willis Hall's *Billy Liar* for the theme of transposing grim reality into dreams; ▷Sharman Macdonald and ▷Louise Page for more recent images of mother/daughter in conflict; ▷John Osborne's *Look Back in Anger* for a contrasting treatment and male view of pregnancy; ▷Ibsen's *Hedda Gabler* for another image of reluctant pregnancy; for more warring families, ▷De Filippo's *Ducking Out*.

DE VEGA CARPIO, Lope Félix   [1562–1635]
Spanish dramatist

Plays include:
Fuenteovejuna (*The Sheep Well*; (1612), *The Simple Lady* (1613), *The King is the Best Judge* (c 1620), *Punishment without Revenge* (1631)

Lope de Vega claimed to have written an amazing total of 1500 plays, of which about 480 survive (mostly in manuscript). He also wrote (inter alia) three novels and 3000 sonnets, married twice, had some seven major love affairs, and sailed with the Spanish Armada. He fixed and developed the form of the Spanish *comedía*, attacking the pseudo-Aristotelian unities and freely mixing comedy and tragedy (and indeed pastoral and historical as well). His plays are well constructed, more inclined to entertaining action than subtle characterisation (most of his work was done at speed to satisfy the demands of theatre directors), and often deal with questions of family honour and paternal authority (of which he is in favour). The large remaining stock of his plays could well yield something revivable, though perhaps not many of the plays where private executions are condoned in the cause of restoring a wife's honour. The best of these is probably *The King is the Best Judge*, in which the king, disguised as a mayor, obliges a nobleman to marry a village girl he has abducted, has him beheaded and then grants her half of his estate and gives her back to her young lover – a satisfying solution on both a personal and a civic level. ▷John Osborne adapted *La Fianza Satisfecha* as *A Bond Honoured* for the ▷National Theatre in 1966, but the only play one is at all likely to see at present is some version of *Fuenteovejuna* (which was indeed very successfully revived by the National Theatre, directed by Declan Donnellan in 1989). This play is unusual in that the people of the village become a collective protagonist. The overlord snatches the mayor's daughter Laurencia from her wedding and imprisons the groom, but she escapes and incites the townspeople to behead him. The whole village, even under torture, declare that 'Fuenteovejuna did it', and finally King Ferdinand collectively pardons them for the justice of the act and reunites the lovers. The play is popular with progressive political groups, but some of the honour-and-revenge plays would give them more trouble.

McDonald, with music by Lindisfarne member Alan Hull, a piece of popular music-theatre inspired by the Jarrow March of 1936, Howard Goodall's *The Hired Man*, based on the book by Melvyn Bragg; and the *Larkrise to Candleford* trilogy, by Flora Thompson, adapted by Keith Dewhurst for the ▷National Theatre.

DEVLIN, Ann   [1951–]
Northern Irish dramatist

Play:
Ourselves Alone (1985)

Devlin's theatrical reputation rests on her only stage play to date, *Ourselves Alone*, which won both the George Devine and Susan Smith Blackburn awards (she had already won the Samuel Beckett award for her television plays, *A Woman Calling* and *The Long March* in 1984). She has also published short-stories.

Originally commissioned by the Liverpool Playhouse, *Ourselves Alone* opened as a co-production at the ▷Royal Court in 1985, and was soon revived. A warm, toughly plotted political thriller, set in the aftermath of the 1981 hunger strikes of Northern Ireland, it could now be regarded as something of a trailblazer, an early attempt to show the tragic consequences of entrenched views, from a female perspective. As such, its central focus was less concerned with the pros and cons of Republicanism than with showing the struggle of three sisters to escape stifling familial and political bonds. Argument has raged about whether the play reinforced certain stereotypes (chauvinism of Irish men), and whether the portrait of women was unduly pessimistic (one responds by escaping to England, the other, a former IRA supporter, settles down to blissful maternity). Whatever the verdict, this telling-it-how-it-is portrait has been produced in venues as far apart as Chicago and Hamburg's Schauspielhaus.

Try these:
▷Calderón, who borrowed plots from Lope de Vega and refined his plays; ▷Aeschylus' *The Persians*, for another collective protagonist; ▷Steve Gooch for an adaptation of *Fuenteovejuna*; Adrian Mitchell's adaptation of Robert Browning's *The Pied Piper* presents a town from which the children want to escape; other recent plays with a strong sense of community include *Heads Held High*, by Alan

Try these:
▷Christina Reid's *Tea in a China Cup* and Charabanc's *Marie Jones* for Belfast plays with a specifically women-centred focus; ▷Daniel Mornin's *Kate* and *Built on Sand* for showing the effects of the Troubles on women; ▷Seamus Finnegan for a more stylised, many-faceted exploration of Northern Ireland's religious and political loyalties; ▷Ron Hutchinson's *Rat in the Skull* for a different variant; ▷Sean

O'Casey's *Plough and the Stars* for similar concerns; and of course, for three sisters suffering in a very different but no less stifling environment, ▷Chekhov's *Three Sisters*.

DOWIE, Claire   [1950s–]
British dramatist and performer

Plays include:
Cat and Mouse (1986), *Adult Child/Dead Child* (1988), *Why Is John Lennon Wearing a Skirt* (1990)

Birmingham-born Dowie's work is distinguished by its uncompromising, hard-hitting quality. Formerly, a standup comic and performer of her own poems on the alternative cabaret circuit. Her dramatic monologues, couched somewhere between cabaret and theatre, have now made her an award-winning playwright/performer. Her three 'plays' have all been well received: epithets like 'raw' and 'honest' but also 'sensitive' and 'thought-provoking' regularly appear as descriptions of her work. *Adult Child/Dead Child* was the winner of the 1988 *Time Out–01 for London* Award; it has also been seen in Edinburgh, Dublin, Toronto and New York. With Dowie, performance and content are the two sides of a same coin. A galvanising, restless energy seems to invade this slight, androgynous figure whose latest piece, *Why Is John Lennon Wearing a Skirt* received one of its warmest welcomes in Honolulu (after touring Britain). It is a two-hour tour de force, part hilarious satire, part invective, against wearing a skirt and the whole teenage peer-pressure of becoming a woman (she just wants to be herself; the Beatles are her gang and John Lennon her model). Dowie is the quintessential outsider, never half so funny as when she is puncturing sacred cows, the women's movement included.

Cat and Mouse and *Adult Child/Dead Child* set a more sombre, indeed devastating tone, the first being 'about' child abuse, the second 'about' an unloved child teetering on the edge of schizophrenia. Dowie's jittery, gawky style as a cabaret performer is what gives her performances their particular intensity. She doesn't so much portray her roles as inhabit them, dragging the audience along with her on a journey that, in *Adult Child*, takes her from unwanted home environment to lonely bedsit and psychiatric treatment as she tries to come to terms with the rules of an adult world pressing her to conform. Dowie's monologues, often interlaced with poetry, are indeed nerveless exposures of the individual rebelling against social conformity.

Try these:
▷David Edgar, ▷Tony Craze, ▷Melissa Murray, for other British playwrights who have tackled the subject of schizophrenia; ▷John Sessions for a monologuist of equal persuasion but very different style; ▷Eric Bogosian, Karen Finley, John O'Keefe and ▷Spalding Gray for American equivalents; ▷One-Person Shows, ▷Cabaret and ▷Performance Art for other instances of solo shows; ▷Robert Holman's *Rafts and Dreams*, ▷Martin Crimp's *Getting Attention*, ▷Felix Cross's *Glory!* all touch on the issue of child abuse; new playwright Carl Miller's *Princess* also traces the development of a teenage girl through fantasy but treats it differently; ▷Sharman Macdonald, ▷Trish Cooke, ▷Winsome Pinnock for contrasting examples of young women and teenage development.

DREXLER, Rosalyn   [1926–]
American playwright, novelist, painter

Plays include:
Home Movies (1964), *Hot Buttered Roll* (1966), *The Line of Least Resistance* and *Skywriting* (1968), *Softly, and Consider the Nearness* (1973), *The Writer's Opera* (1979), *Graven Image* (1980), *Delicate Feelings* (1984), *Green River Murders* (1986), *The Heart that Eats Itself* (1988)

Rosalyn Drexler has distinguished herself as a playwright, novelist, screenwriter, painter, and sculptor: at the time her Obie Award-winning play *Home Movies* was produced in New York, her paintings were on exhibit at the Kornblee Gallery. A strong visual sense pervades her work, although she is as apt to get a laugh with elaborate puns as with sight gags. Related to Chico Marx by marriage, this Bronx-born multi-talented woman's work is marked by the influence of Marx Brothers humour. Absurdist situations and wordplay pervade her writing.

Early in her marriage, Drexler toured as a lady wrestler under the name of Rosa Carlo. Her semi-autobiographical novel *To Smithereen* (1972) recounts the story of a woman turned wrestler to please her art-critic lover who found female wrestlers a turn-on. This experience clearly inspired the peculiar angle on traditional male-female relationships evidenced in Drexler's early work, long before the women's movement got off the ground. In *Home Movies*, a resurrected husband challenges his wife to a wrestling match as sexual foreplay; in *Hot Buttered Roll*, a billionaire engages a crew of burly-girls to give him a kick that will break his sex-o-meter. As late as 1984, Drexler was still exploring these ideas in a musical play, *Delicate Feelings*, about two lady mud wrestlers. In 1979, she won her second Obie for *The Writer's Opera*, a comedy examining the role of women as artists and mothers inspired by the life of Suzanne Valadon and her son Maurice Utrillo.

A film about Drexler, *Who Does She Think She Is?* was presented at the Whitney Museum in New York in 1975. Her family life, fantasies, and artistry were recorded by filmmakers Gaby Rogers and Patricia Jaffe. Several of Drexler's plays have enjoyed London productions, and in the USA she has been associated with the Theater for the New City in New York.

Try these:
▷Caryl Churchill's *Cloud Nine* for sexual role reversal; ▷Eugene Ionesco for absurdism; ▷Jules Feiffer for comic book sketches; ▷Tina Howe for comic conceits; Megan Terry for early feminist playwriting; ▷Claire Luckham for wrestling as a metaphor; ▷Howard Sackler, ▷David Storey for other sporting metaphors.

DRURY, Alan   [1949–   ]
British dramatist

Plays include:
Asides (1974), *The Man Himself* (1975), *Sparrowfall* (1976), *Communion* (1976), *Change of Mind* (1977), *An Empty Desk* (1979), *An Honourable Man* (1980), *Nasty Stories* (1982), *The Dean's Tale* (1983), *Mr Hyde* (1984), *Little Brown Jug* (1985)

Drury has written some forty works for radio, television, stage and cinema, been a script editor for BBC television, resident dramatist at the York Theatre Royal and the Royal Court, and literary manager at the Hampstead Theatre. His work ranges from monologues to ▷pantomime, and his subjects have included many aspects of sexual politics, attitudes to the National Front (the monologue *The Man Himself*), the psychopathology of murderers, contemporary (*Sparrowfall*) and Victorian corruption (*Mr Hyde*), but he has yet to find a secure niche in the current repertory and his greatest success has been with his translation of Molière's *The Hypochondriac* (▷National Theatre, 1981).

Try these:
▷Peter Flannery's *Our Friends in the North* for contemporary corruption; ▷Christopher Hampton's *Treats* covers similar ground to *Asides*; ▷Lillian Hellman's *The Children's Hour*, like *An Honourable Man*, deals with accusations of sexual impropriety against a teacher; ▷Tony Marchant's *The Attractions* is a modern, gothic thriller about violence; see ▷Barry Collins' *Judgement* and *The Ice Chimney* for monologues of comparable intensity to *The Man Himself*.

DRYDEN, John   [1631–1700]
English dramatist, poet and critic

Plays include:
The Indian Queen (with Sir Robert Howard; 1664), *The Indian Emperor* (1665), *The Tempest* (with Sir William Davenant; 1667), *Tyrannic Love* (1669), *The Conquest of Granada* (in two parts; 1670 and 1671), *Marriage à la Mode* (1672), *Aureng-Zebe* (1675), *All for Love* (1677), *Oedipus* (with Nathaniel Lee; 1678), *Troilus and Cressida* (1678)

Dryden, one of the great literary figures of his age, wrote singly or in collaboration, nearly thirty plays but the only one of his plays to be staged regularly is *All for Love*. It is a treatment of the Antony and Cleopatra story, which is usually compared unfavourably with ▷Shakespeare's play by those who assume, wrongly, that because Dryden adapted *The Tempest* he did the same to *Antony and Cleopatra*. The fact that the very occasional productions of Dryden's *Tempest* demonstrate that it is a good acting play tend to be forgotten in routine denunciations of the depravity of even daring to adapt the Bard. Something similar happens with *All for Love*, which tends to get castigated for not achieving the epic grandeur and flexibility of ▷Shakespeare's play; in fact it is a far more concentrated and domestic work dealing with the theme in terms of a love/honour conflict of the kind beloved of Restoration tragedy.

Try these:
▷G.B. Shaw's *Caesar and Cleopatra* is another treatment of the Cleopatra story which, like *All for Love*, is sometimes staged in repertory with ▷Shakespeare's *Antony and Cleopatra*; ▷Otway's *Venice Preserv'd* is the only other tragedy from the period still staged regularly.

DUFFY, Maureen   [1933–]
British novelist, poet and dramatist

Plays include:
The Lay Off (1962), *The Silk Room* (1966), *Rites* (1969), *Solo* (1970), *Old Tyme* (1970), *A Nightingale in Bloomsbury Square* (1973)

Novelist, lesbian and feminist, whose dramatic output has been small but significant, Duffy is a writer of rich imagination and plunderer of classical mythologies, 'pitched between fantasy and realism' (Frank Marcus). Her main dramatic claim to fame resides in *Rites*, presented as part of a ▷National Theatre workshop evening. Set in a ladies public lavatory and loosely based on ▷Euripides' *The Bacchae*, *Rites*, with its collection of women, can be seen as a precursor to ▷Nell Dunn's *Steaming*. But it is considerably more audacious in its mix of classical and modern ritual (a latter-day chorus inveighing against daily frustrations) and violence (the murder of a transvestite lesbian). It is a brave and questioning play that prefigures many of the concerns of female playwrights of the past decade about language, territory, gender and making the personal public and political. *Solo* and *Old Tyme* are other studies based on the mythological characters of Narcissus and Uranus respectively. *A Nightingale in Bloomsbury Square*, by contrast, is more of a bio-drama-cum-monologue around the figure of Virginia Woolf, nudged on by Vita Sackville-West and Freud.

Try these:
▷Bryony Lavery's *Kitchen Matters* is also based on *The Bacchae*; ▷Sharman Macdonald's *When I Was a Girl I Used to Scream and Shout* for another example of female privacy made public; innumerable subsequent plays by writers like ▷Caryl Churchill, ▷Pam Gems, and ▷Sarah Daniels, and women's groups like Scarlet Harlets, working from a female perspective; Eileen Atkins performed Virginia Woolf's lecture *A Room of One's Own*, adapted by Patrick Garland, to great effect.

DUMAS, Alexandre (fils)   [1824–95]
French dramatist and novelist

Plays include:
La Dame aux Camélias (variously translated as *The Lady of the Camellias*, *Heartsease*, but most often as *Camille*; 1851), *Le Demi-Monde* (1855), *Le Fils Naturel* (*The Natural Son*; 1858), *Francillon* (1857)

In general, Dumas fils' worthy studies of contemporary problems of the bourgeois family have survived much less well on stage than have adaptations of the yarns of his reprobate father (*The Three Musketeers*, *The Count of Monte Cristo*, etc). However, his first play, *La Dame aux Camélias*, remains one of the most potent myths of the present day, and there is often a version running somewhere (even though it is generally the opera version *La Traviata*). Modern permutations of *La Dame aux Camélias* include ▷Terence Rattigan's *Variation on a Theme*, and references in ▷Tennessee Williams; and it is interesting that recent versions have been by women writers, who have re-assessed Camille in terms of her relationship to society and the values of the times. ▷Pam Gems' *Camille* made most of the characters a good deal less high-minded (especially Alfred's father, who becomes improbably wicked instead of improbably noble) and stressed the power of money as the driving force in society, while still giving Frances Barber the chance not to leave a dry eye in the house. Nancy Sweet's thrilling ▷Brechtian *Camille* (Old Red Lion, London 1987) turned the play into a rehearsal directed by a tyrannical Dumas, who made the real-life Alphonsine (Marguerite) and others re-enact his version of their lives; she tries and fails to escape by tearing down the blood-smeared curtains of the set. This version deserves a wider audience.

Try these:
▷Zola's *Nana* rings the changes on the courtesan theme; ▷Pinero for the 'woman with a past' in *The Second Mrs Tanqueray*; ▷G.B. Shaw for an attack on this kind of

play in *Mrs Warren's Profession*; ▷Tennessee Williams for echoes of the theme in *A Streetcar Named Desire* and *Camino Real*; Charles Ludlam's *Camille* for a comic take on this character; ▷Pam Gems for feminist re-assessments of other mythical/legendary figures such as Piaf, Queen Christina.

DUNBAR, Andrea   [1965–90]
British dramatist

Plays include:
The Arbor (1980), *Rita Sue and Bob Too* (1981), *Shirley* (1986)

Andrea Dunbar was brought up on a council estate on the outskirts of Bradford, and sent *The Arbor*, her first play, written at the age of fifteen, to the Royal Court Young Writer's Festival. Produced at the Theatre Upstairs in March 1980 and transferred to the main stage in an expanded version, it is a bleak study of life on a council estate in Bradford, of the violence and deprivation of family life in the midst of urban decay. Sex offers the only pleasure, and that is seen to lead to abuse and pregnancy. Dunbar was seen to mark a return to the Royal Court's heyday of finding and championing work by working-class writers.

The film *Rita Sue and Bob Too* was developed from the play of the same name and incorporated sections from *The Arbor*. It was filmed on the council estate where Dunbar lived, and provoked the same kind of critical controversy as her plays: does Dunbar offer a patronising and unnecessarily bleak account of working-class life, or is that how it is? Dunbar remained unimpressed and continued to live in Bradford with her children until her tragically early death. Her plays present a stark account of the frustrations and impoverishment of economic deprivation, and she wrote with a remarkable ear for nuances of language.

Try these:
▷Shelagh Delaney's *A Taste of Honey* for obvious echoes (*Shirley* is like *A Taste of Honey* for the eighties); ▷Arnold Wesker for affinities with the gritty social realism of family life; ▷Jim Cartwright's *Road*, ▷Christina Reid's *Joyriders*, ▷Julia Kearsley and ▷Ayshe Raif are other likeminded contemporaries.

DUNN, Nell   [1936–]
British novelist and dramatist

Plays include:
I Want (with Adrian Henri, 1972; staged 1982), *Steaming* (1981), *The Little Heroine* (1988)

London-born Dunn made her name in 1963 with the award-winning television play *Up the Junction*, a gritty tale of down-and-out urban life that summed up a whole era.

Dunn has continued to explore the female situation with sympathy. Her most famous stage play, *Steaming* (which started out at the Theatre Royal, Stratford before transferring with great success to the West End, and to Broadway with less, and being filmed), was hailed on both sides of the sexual politics divide as a popular breakthrough. However, directed by Roger Smith with an eye on the satirical, this apparent celebration of female solidarity, set in a public Turkish bath threatened with closure, posed more problems about voyeurism and the male gaze than it answered, and could be seen as a more populist successor to ▷Maureen Duffy's *Rites* without the moral clout. *The Little Heroine*, staged by the Southampton Nuffield Theatre, is another variation on exploring the vulnerabilities – and strengths – of women, this time through the example of a young heroin junkie and her successful kicking of the habit.

Try these:
▷Maureen Duffy's *Rites*; ▷Maria Irene Fornes' *Fefu and her Friends* and ▷Sharman Macdonald's *When I Was a Girl I Used to Scream and Shout* for other pictures of female intimacies unveiled; ▷Pam Gems' *Dusa, Fish, Stas and Vi*; and Wendy Wasserstein's *Uncommon Women* for women under pressure finding support in each other; Clean Break's *The River That Ran Away* is a powerful prison-based portrait of a heroin addict's rehabilitation through therapy; ▷C.P. Taylor's *Withdrawal Symptoms* takes withdrawal from heroin and from Empire together, in a fine study of the personal and the political.

DURANG, Christopher   [1949–]
American dramatist and actor

Plays include:
I Don't Generally Like Poetry But Have You Read 'Trees' (with ▷Albert Innaurato; 1972), *The Mitzi Gaynor Story, or Gyp*

(1973), *The Idiots Karamazov* (1974), *Death Comes to Us All, Mary Agnes* (1975), *When Dinah Shore Ruled the Earth* (with ▷Wendy Wasserstein; 1975), *Das Lusitania Songspiel* (with Sigourney Weaver; 1976), *The Vietnamization of New Jersey* (1977), *A History of the American Film* (1978), *'Dentity Crisis* (1978), *The Nature and Purpose of the Universe* (1979), *Sister Mary Ignatius Explains It All For You/The Actor's Nightmare* (1979), *Beyond Therapy* (1981), *Titanic* (1983), *The Baby and the Bathwater* (1983), *The Marriage of Bette and Boo* (1985), *Laughing Wild* (1987)

Some critics damn Durang for self-absorption – Benedict Nightingale called him a 'diaper dramatist' – and others find fault with his glibness – *The New York Times* once termed his humour merely 'collegiate' – but even when not at the top of his form, Durang far outranks most other American satirists with his bracing irreverence and impatience with convention. His most notably plays take on the destructive pieties of Catholicism, the ideals of family life and seductive cultural fashions, always with the deceptively bright-eyed high energy that has become his trade-mark. Early works were primarily parodies and often written in collaboration with fellow Yale Drama School graduates ▷Wendy Wasserstein, ▷Albert Innaurato and the actress Sigourney Weaver. On his own, he wrote the zany comic circus, *A History of the American Film*, in which a variety of actors play screen icons from Cagney to Bogie to – most memorably – Anthony Perkins in *Psycho*. More recently the tone has darkened. In *Sister Mary Ignatius Explains It All For You*, his best-known play, four former students of an authoritarian nun return to her classroom to exact revenge for her wrong-headed instruction. *The Baby and the Bathwater*, *The Nature and Purpose of the Universe* and *The Marriage of Bette and Boo* are blackly and anarchically funny depictions of households in crisis. *Bette and Boo* in particular wreaks wonderful havoc with traditional ideas of 'family drama' – Durang finds the right balance between the madcap and the mordant; the sweet questioning spirit of Matt (played by Durang himself when the play was first produced at the Public Theater) keeps the absurdity from spinning out of control.

Whether you regard him as the quintessential American 'diaper dramatist' – Benedict Nightingale's term for what he sees as the terminal self-absorption of Durang and his literary peers – or as a tough-minded satirist lashing out at his Catholic upbringing, the sweet-faced Durang is an idiosyncratic absurdist who writes deceptively fast, bright-eyed plays about dark and furious subjects. His earlier works were primarily parodies and often written in collaboration with fellow Yale Drama School graduates ▷Wendy Wasserstein, ▷Albert Innaurato, and the actress Sigourney Weaver (who starred in *Alien*). On his own, he wrote the zany comic circus *A History of the American Film*, in which a variety of actors play screen icons from Cagney and Bogie to – most memorably – Tony Perkins in *Psycho*. More recently, the tone has darkened. In *Sister Mary Ignatius Explains It All For You*, his best-known, longest-running play, four former students of an authoritarian nun return to her classroom to exact revenge for her wrong-headed instruction. *The Baby and the Bathwater* and *The Marriage of Bette and Boo* (a son's episodic narration of his parents' horrific marriage) are blackly and anarchically humorous depictions of families in crisis.

As an actor, Durang has appeared in several of his plays including the two most recent ones.

Try these:
▷Mary O'Malley's *Once A Catholic* for contrasting take-offs of Catholic dogma; ▷Wendy Wasserstein, ▷Ted Tally, ▷Albert Innaurato for other Playwrights' Horizons-schooled authors fuelled by familial disorder; ▷Jules Feiffer's *Grown Ups* for that domestic intersection where home and hatred meet, also ▷Tony Craze's *Atonement*; ▷De Filippo's *Ducking Out*; ▷Alan Ayckbourn for recent anatomies of families. *Nunsense*, Dan Goggin's satiric cabaret-style revue; ▷John Guare's *House of Blue Leaves* for antic comedy featuring nuns and an impending visit from the Pope.

DURAS, Marguerite [1904–]
French novelist, dramatist and writer of screenplays

Plays include:
Le Square (*The Square*; 1965), *La Musica* (1965), *Les Eaux et les Forêts* (*The Waters and the Forests*; 1965), *Le Shaga* (1967), *L'Amante anglaise* (*A Place Without Doors*,

or *The Lovers of Viorne*; (1968), *Suzanna Adler* (1971), *India Song* (1973; commissioned by the ▷National Theatre but not performed), *L'Eden-Cinéma* (*Eden Cinema*; 1977), *Savannah Bay* (1984)

Marguerite Duras, born near Saigon in what was then French Indo-China, used her recollections of these childhood years for her novel *Le Barrage Contre le Pacifique* (*The Sea Wall*; 1950), her play *Eden Cinema*, and her autobiographical novel *L'Amant* (*The Lover*; 1984). It is characteristic of her methods to rework material into different forms and to try to break down the boundaries between media; her first play, *The Square*, was taken from her novel of the same name; *A Place Without Doors* is the second version of a play about a horrifying real-life murder, and she turned it into a novel as well, treating the story from a different point of view each time. Most of her characters are women, and they suffer; they are often in love, about to take leave of their lovers, or abandoned by them. The plays are not linear, but unfold gradually like petals and the dialogue is full of hesitations, pauses, fragments of memory, ellipses, and the sudden recollection of violent or painful events. The story is not explained, sometimes there is only a stream of discourse, with questions left about motives or ideas or even identity. Duras is concerned with the processes of the artist's own mind rather than those of society, and with problems of language, rather than ideas or a story line.

Savannah Bay

This ninety-minute two-handed Proustian play was written for Madeleine Renaud, who played an ageing actress visited each day by a girl who may be her grandchild, and with whom she reconstructs the story of her daughter Savannah, who met a lover, gave birth, and later drowned in Savannah Bay in Siam. Both characters obsessively relive this story and gradually unfold it in a dream-like and elliptical text, with recurring images of two lovers on a white rock; it has strong resemblances to *Eden Cinema*, where again there is a piecing together of memories by an old and a young woman. It was beautifully produced in Britain in what turned out to be Foco Novo's swansong in 1988, with the main theme echoed by the black mirror-glass floor, rocks, and white gauzy curtains.

Try these:
▷Hélène Cixous, who was also born in a French colony, and who writes about what was formerly French Indo-China, but with quite different intent; ▷Beckett for the recurring theme of the nature of memory; Alain Robbe-Grillet and Nathalie Sarraute for moving freely between novel, play and film; ▷Coward's *Private Lives* for an aftermath to divorce to contrast with *La Musica*; performance artist Annie Griffin's *Ariadne*, very loosely based on Strauss' opera, also had a rock as a central image.

DÜRRENMATT, Friedrich   [1921–90]
Swiss dramatist

Plays include:
It Is Written (1947), *The Blind Man* (1948), *Romulus the Great* (1949), *The Marriage of Mr Mississippi* (1952), *An Angel Comes To Babylon* (1953), *The Visit* (1956), *The Physicists* (1962), *The Meteor* (1966), *King John* (1968), *Play Strindberg* (1969)

Son of a Protestant clergyman, Dürrenmatt was brought up amidst a highly educated, family and their friends. After studying at the Universities of Bern and Zurich, he decided to commit himself full-time to writing, becoming one of the leading dramatists in the German language and achieving worldwide fame as a dramatic theorist. Clearly influenced by the pre-war German Expressionists and by ▷Brecht, Dürrenmatt's sense of theatricality is allied to an acute perception of the moral dilemmas of the contemporary world. But unlike Brecht, Dürrenmatt's ability to chill in the midst of grotesque comedy, the clarity with which he raises great issues of personal and public morality, lead not towards an argument for hopeful political change, but towards despair. And although his characters frequently achieve a transcending dignity and even heroism, they do so in a world which renders individual action and sacrifice irrelevant. Although much of his work is built on the form of classical Greek tragedy, this sense of individual irrelevance denies the possibility of catharsis. To Dürrenmatt, the human condition is unchangeable and meaningless, and best examined through sardonic humour. He is best known for *The Visit* which was the subject of a famous production by the Lunts on Broadway in the 1950s, subsequently brought to London in 1960, and *The*

Kathryn Hunter as Clara Zachanassian, Marcello Magni as her butler in the mime based Théâtre de Complicité's highly idiosyncratic version of Dürrenmatt's *The Visit* (Royal National Theatre, 1991 but premiered at the Almeida Theatre, 1989)

Physicists, revived by The RSC at the Aldwych also in the early 1960s. *The Visit* has recently been revived by Théâtre de Complicité in a radical and gloriously eccentric adaptation in England, and in the USA in Adrian Hall's version, staged in an abandoned terminal in Providence, RI.

The Visit

A bitter fable of greed and human weakness, its highly convoluted plot revolving round the return of an ageing millionairess Claire Zachanassian to her economically depressed home town, raising local expectations of a substantial act of charity. However, the millionairess is bent on vengeance on the man who wronged her many years before, the town's most honoured citizen, Alfred III. Finding that she was pregnant by him, he denied that the child was his and bribed two men to assert that she was no better than a prostitute, with the result that she left the town destitute and in disgrace. Since that time she has diligently whored and married her way to a fortune, and the price she demands for the town to share her wealth is the death of Alfred III. At first the townspeople refuse, but money eventually talks and Alfred is strangled by the townspeople during a celebration of the town's new wealth. The old woman gives her money to the town, and is cheered on her departure.

Try these:

For Expressionist influences on his style, ▷Wedekind, Toller and Kaiser; for political themes and epic theatre see ▷Brecht; for a comparison with other German contemporary writing, see ▷Franz Xaver Kroetz; ▷Heiner Müller, ▷Max Frisch; ▷Ibsen's *An Enemy of the People* is another play highlighting the dubious motivations of townspeople. *Etta Jenks* by Marlane Meyer also features a heroine who wreaks a terrible revenge on her original oppressors; Shaw's *Mrs Warren's Profession* for another successful prostitute.

DYER, Charles (Raymond)   [1928–   ]
British dramtist, actor and director

Plays include:
Clubs Are Sometimes Trumps 1948) *Rattle of a Simple Man* (1962), *Staircase* (1966)

Dyer's first play, *Clubs Are Sometimes Trumps*, was followed by nine more (all as C. Raymond Dyer) before *Rattle of a Simple Man* brought critical and commercial acclaim. His practical experience in the theatre shows in efficient, well-constructed plays that are commercially viable with small casts and simple sets, but his quality lies in the sensitivity with which he presents his characters and subjects. His major plays, *Rattle of a Simple Man* (about a prostitute and a football fan) and *Staircase*, handled subjects and characters then rarely treated in theatre – *Staircase*, was extensively cut by the Lord Chamberlain's Office – and centre on dependence and our attempt to escape loneliness. This is not a theatre of action but of need. In his characters Dyer shows the audience their own inadequacies and fears; but while stripping away self-illusion he also offers hope and a lot of laughs.

Staircase

This two-hander set in a Brixton barber's shop presents the mutual dependence of two middle-aged homosexuals: Harry, a totally bald barber, and Charlie, the ex-actor he picked up in a tea-shop years before and who faces a summons after being caught cross-dressing by police raiding a club. Charlie Dyer (the character carries the author's name) has created a more successful fantasy life, peopled by characters who are all anagrams of his own name, to cover a period he spent in jail on a sex charge and clings to the fact that he was once married and fathered a child. Harry is self-disgusted by his baldness and the physical side of life. The characters fascinate and repel at the same time, totally convincing yet offering a parallel of the struggle in any relationship. Dyer's work is totally unsentimental. At the end of the published text Dyer suggests that Harry, perhaps even the summons, perhaps all we have seen exist only in Charlie's imagination.

Try these:
▷Genet, ▷Harvey Fierstein, ▷Larry Kramer, and ▷Martin Sherman for treatments of male homosexual relationships; for two-handed relationships, ▷Manuel Puig and Tom Kempinski; ▷Pam Gems's transvestite farce *Aunt Mary* and the work of Charles Ludlam and Charles Busch for images of the seemingly outrageous, expressing questions about society's conventional images of gender; ▷Joe Orton for a heightened sense of shock to overturn conventional attitudes; Gay Sweatshop.

e

EDGAR, David [1948–]
British dramatist

Plays include:
A Fart for Europe (with ▷Howard Brenton; 1973), *Excuses, Excuses* (1973), *Dick Deterred* (1974), *Saigon Rose* (1976), *Blood Sports* (1976), *Destiny* (1976), *Wreckers* (1977), *Our Own People* (1977), *Mary Barnes* (1979), *The Jail Diary of Albie Sachs* (1979), *Teendreams* (with Susan Todd; 1979), *The Life and Adventures of Nicholas Nickleby* (adaptation; 1980), *Maydays* (1983), *Entertaining Strangers* (1985; revised version 1987), *That Summer* (1987), *The Shape of the Table* (1990)

One of Britain's major dramatists, Edgar has written for both radical touring companies and theatres of the ▷National Theatre and the ▷RSC. He is active in socialist debates on theatre and culture, and has written regularly for a number of journals. He has been particularly active in anti-racist politics (both *Our Own People* and *Destiny* are studies in the racism of British life), and he has written essays for the Institute of Race Relations and for the anti-fascist journal, *Searchlight*.

Edgar was born in Birmingham, of a theatrical family, and much of his early work was written for political theatre groups (*Wreckers* was written for 7:84, *Teendreams* for Monstrous Regiment) or in response to political events (*Dick Deterred* followed Nixon's part in Watergate, *A Fart for Europe* was written as an anti-EEC polemic at the time of Britain's entry into the EEC).

As a socialist dramatist Edgar has chosen to base his intervention in the theatre, believing that television is an isolating experience, while theatre has to be experienced in a collective audience. *Maydays*, an epic account of Britain from 1956 to the present, was produced by the ▷RSC as one of the first new plays to be produced on the main stage at the Barbican, and established an important precedent. Edgar has said that the complicated set, which

includes a moving train and a gate at Greenham Common was written in as a strategy, so that the play technically had to be put on at the main stage at the Barbican and could not be relegated to the small Pit Theatre, where new writing invariably ended up.

Edgar's greatest success, *The Life and Adventures of Nicholas Nickleby* (for which, with *Mary Barnes*, he is best known in the States) was developed over a long period with the cast, who thoroughly researched and devised the play with Edgar. The result was a collaborative project and a conviction in the performances and production that is rarely seen in mainstream theatre. Edgar was later invited by ▷Ann Jellicoe to collaborate in a theatre community project in Dorset: *Entertaining Strangers* was based on research into the history of Dorchester, and devised by and for the local community. It was then given a production in revised form at the ▷National Theatre with professional actors. His two most recent plays *That Summer* and *The Shape of the Table* have continued his readiness to engage with recent political events. *That Summer*, an unusually small-scale work for Edgar, written in the form of a domestic comedy, examines culture clashes and left-wing reactions to the miners' strike of 1984. *The Shape of the Table* by contrast, although considered a static, talking-head piece by some (most of the action takes place around a large conference table), is still a fascinating attempt to analyse the *realpolitik* behind momentous changes in Eastern Europe at the end of 1989, in an imagined capital not a million miles away from Prague.

Destiny

Destiny was the play which established Edgar as a major dramatist. The first of his plays to be produced by the ▷RSC, at The Other Place, it was so well received that it transferred to their then home, the Aldwych. An analysis of fascism and racism in British culture through its links with the imperialist past, and the wave of immigration in the 1970s, it juxtaposes a politician at the moment of a by-election with soldiers of 1947 discussing the independence of India. In the contemporary scenes, *Destiny* explores the relation of parliamentary politics to fascist groups, and also the way in which immigration becomes a scapegoat for the problems of British society. Written as a response to the rise in National Front activity in the mid-1970s, a period in which the Anti-Nazi League (which Edgar was involved with) was a central campaign for the Left, the play acts as a warning about the conditions that give rise to totalitarianism, and draws an analogy with the position of the Jews in Germany; Adolf Hitler appears at the end, to give a warning.

Try these:
▷Caryl Churchill employs a similar juxtaposition of past and present to that of *Destiny* in *Cloud Nine*; ▷Brecht is the effective originator of the dialectical theatre practised by ▷Howard Brenton, Edgar, ▷Edward Bond, ▷Trevor Griffiths and ▷John McGrath; ▷Adaptations; *That Summer* is about the 1984 miners' strike as is Peter Cox's *Garden of England* and Cordelia Ditton and Maggie Ford's *About Face*; *Saigon Rose's* treatment of venereal disease anticipates AIDS plays such as ▷Larry Kramer's *The Normal Heart*; *Mary Barnes'* treatment of schizophrenia links it with ▷Tom Stoppard's *Every Good Boy Deserves Favour*; ▷Tony Craze's *Shona* and ▷Heathcote Williams' *AC/DC* though their approaches are very different are other studies of schizophrenia; ▷David Mercer's *In Two Minds*, and Charlotte Perkins Gilman's *The Yellow Wallpaper* are two further studies of women and madness; ▷Karim Alrawi's *A Child in the Heart* is a contemporary exploration of British racism and National Front allegiances in London's East End; ▷Howard Brenton's and Tariq Ali's *Moscow Gold* and ▷Caryl Churchill's *Mad Forest* for plays emerging from *glasnost*; Mikhail Shatrov's table-talk *The Peace of Brest* for a contemporary Russian equivalent, reviewing events around 1917; Christopher Hein's *The Round Table* for an allegorical comment on East Germany in 1987, set in Camelot; ▷Sarah Daniels's *The Devil's Gateway*

and ▷Christina Reid's *My Name Shall I Tell You My Name* both use Greenham Common but in different ways.

EICHELBERGER, Ethyl   [1945–1990]
American actor, dramatist, director

Plays/Performance Adaptations include: *Phèdre* (1977), *Neferti-ti* (1978), *Medea* (1980), *Minne the Maid* (1981; Villager Award), *Elizabeth I and Mary Stuart* (1982), *Marie Antoinette* (1982), *Hamlette* (1984), *Medusa* (1985), *Leer* (1985), *Casanova* (1985), *Rip Van Winkle* (1986), *The Lincolns* (1988; Serious Fun Commission), *Ariadne Obnoxious* (1988), *Herd of Buffalo* (1989), *Das Vedanya Mama* (1990)

Born James Roy Eichelberger in Pekin, Illinois, performance artist Ethyl Eichelberger delighted avant-garde audiences with his outrageous adaptations of the classics of world literature. Getting his start at La Mama – one of the first homes of the off-Broadway movement – in the mid-1960s, Eichelberger wrote and directed his comic tour de forces and typically portrayed the 'flamboyant femme fatale'.

Eichelberger's move to New York in 1975 and his immediate involvement with Charles Ludlam's Ridiculous Theatrical Company proved to be the most direct influence on his own work. He acted in Ludlam's *Camille*, *Caprice*, *Salammbo*, *Der Ring Gott Farblonjet*, *Stage Blood*, and *The Artificial Jungle* and became convinced of the power of cross-dressing on stage to make a political statement, to force audiences to re-examine their notions of sexual stereotypes. Eichelberger utilized the conventions of such great comics as Bert Lahr and Laurel and Hardy, and furthermore followed in the tradition of great American actors like Joseph Jefferson who wrote and starred in their own adaptations of classic tales.

The name 'Ethyl', adopted legally in the late 1970s, came to symbolize the 'high-octane', combustible nature of his thirty-odd classic roles. His plays are dense, filled with obscure facts, puns, double entendres, and flexibility for ad-libs; the pace was dizzying, displaying a frenetic style with echoes of vaudeville, burlesque, and the Yiddish stage.

Taking the genre a step further from the still-legitimate structure of Ludlam's adaptations, Eichelberger continued to break down conventional forms: He juxtaposed dancing on pointe with acrobatics and cartwheels, added accordian-accompanied songs to nearly all performances, and incorporated fire-eating into his last plays. The effect he sought was large, evidenced in his heavy, mask-like use of makeup and wigs and the effective use of music, much of which he came to compose himself.

Eichelberger's plays/performances also evolved beyond Ludlam's in his portrayal of male and female roles, often simultaneously. In *Ariadne Obnoxious* (his re-working of the Strauss opera *Ariadne auf Naxos*), Eichelberger played Theseus, Dionysus, and a mermaid. In *Leer* seen at Lincoln Center's Serious Fun Festival among other venues, he played all three roles – Lear, Cordelia, and the Fool. *Hamlette* found him playing three roles in the closet scene to actress Black-eyed Susan's protagonist. Eichelberger starred as both Abraham and Mary Todd Lincoln in *The Lincolns*. At the time of his death, Eichelberger was appearing in the HBO Children's Television Workshop series *Encyclopedia*, playing historic characters ranging from Sigmund Freud to Hammarabi, King of Babylon.

His plays remain unpublished, as it is widely felt that their impact on the printed page could not approach the dynamic and uniqueness of their on-stage incarnations.

Try these:
Charles Busch's *Theodora, She-Bitch of Byzantium* (1984), *Vampire Lesbians of Sodom* (1984), and *Pardon My Inquisition* (1986), where Eichelberger uses cross-dressing to adapt classical genres, Busch uses his toward a more conventional, legitimate theatrical structure spoofing popular genres of melodrama and film. Eric Bogosian (*Talk Radio*) and Jeffrey Essmann (*Triplets in Uniform*), while not necessarily utilizing drag, illustrate a similar use of long monologue in the camp tradition; Annie Griffin's *Ariadne* was also 'inspired' by Strauss' opera; Drew Griffiths for a British, less extravagant, equivalent; ▷Gay theatre, ▷Lesbian theatre.

ELDER, Lonne   [1931–]
American playwright

Plays include:
A Hysterical Turtle in a Rabbit Race (1961), *Kissing Rattlesnakes Can Be Fun* (1966), *Seven Comes Up, Seven Comes Down* (1966), *Charades on East Fourth Street* (1967), *Ceremonies in Dark Old Men* (1969), *Splendid Mummer* (1988)

An African-American playwright who refuses 'to bend from the truth' in his plays, Elder achieved celebrity in the 1960s when black playwrights were finally making their voices heard. Through his political activities for the NAACP (National Association for the Advancement of Colored People), Elder met such notables as ▷Langston Hughes, ▷Lorraine Hansberry, and Douglas Turner Ward, whose poetic realism was to shape his work. Elder worked as an actor before making his mark as a writer, performing as Bobo in the landmark, 1959 Broadway production of *A Raisin in the Sun*, and as Clem in Ward's *Day of Absence*. From 1965–67, Elder attended the Yale School of Drama on a scholarship for filmmaking and playwriting. He joined the Negro Ensemble Company in 1967, as head of the Playwrights Unit. Shortly after his successful play, *Ceremonies in Dark Old Men*, Elder moved to California to forge a career as a screenwriter. With several Hollywood films to his credit, Elder organized a symposium, in 1972, to address his concerns over the portrayal of African-Americans on film and television.

Although Elder has returned to writing for the theatre, his reputation as a playwright is largely based on the award-winning *Ceremonies in Dark Old Men*. Set in a Harlem barbershop, the play chronicles the struggles of the Parker family in their efforts to overcome the debilitating effects of ghetto life. The family patriarch, who let his wife work herself to death to support the family, must now face the legacy he has left to his children, as his unemployed sons and bread-winning daughter choose divergent, and sometimes fatal paths to their dreams.

Try these:
The Negro Ensemble Company for early African-American theatre, Douglas Turner Ward, ▷Lorraine Hansberry, and ▷Langston Hughes for stylistic influences; ▷Charles Fuller's *Zooman and the Sign* for an examination of the brutalization of

the ghetto; James Baldwin's *The Amen Corner* has a Harlem setting, as does *Story in Harlem Slang*, one of three Zora Neale Hurston short stories adapted by George C. Wolfe in *'Spunk'*; ▷African-American theatre, ▷Black theatre in Britain.

ELIOT, T.S.
(Thomas Stearns)   [1888–1965]
Anglo-American poet and dramatist

Plays include:
Sweeney Agonistes (1926), *The Rock* (1934), *Murder in the Cathedral* (1935), *The Family Reunion* (1939), *The Cocktail Party* (1949), *The Confidential Clerk* (1953), *The Elder Statesman* (1958)

One of the great poets of the twentieth century, Eliot led a mid-century revival of verse drama, which ultimately failed because it assumed that the 'poetic' in the theatre was a function of the text rather than the whole theatrical process. The most innovative of his plays is *Sweeney Agonistes*, an unfinished piece which has proved very effective in performance, with its jazz rhythms and dialogue which anticipates the early ▷Pinter. *Murder in the Cathedral* is probably the most successful of the plays because the historical subject sanctions the use of non-naturalistic dialogue, but the verse of *The Family Reunion* is probably the most flexible of the completed plays. *The Cocktail Party* tends to be given star productions from time to time but it already shows the pernicious effect on his work of Eliot's decision to adapt contemporary theatrical forms: there is an uneasy match between the poetic impulse and the drawing-room form which becomes more pronounced in his last two plays, which are (justly) seldom revived. The success of the musical *Cats*, based on his *Old Possum's Book of Practical Cats*, indicates another route which might have led Eliot, an admirer of the ▷music-hall, to find the popular audience he craved.

Try these:
▷Aeschylus, ▷Euripides, ▷Sophocles, who provided models for Eliot's plays, generally in terms of the use of the chorus, and specifically in respect of particular plots; ▷medieval drama, particularly *Everyman*, for the inspiration for *Murder in the Cathedral*; ▷Harold Pinter for an approach to dialogue similar to *Sweeney Agonistes*;

▷Community Theatre for plays in similar form to *The Rock*; ▷Christopher Fry for contemporary verse dramas.

ELLIS, Michael J.   [mid-1950s–]
British dramatist

Plays include:
A Temporary Rupture (1983), *Starliner 2001, a Soap Odyssey* (1984), *Chameleon* (1985), *Sticky Fingers* (1989)

An East-ender of Jamaican parents, Ellis picked up various writing awards whilst still at school. *Chameleon*, the play with which he is most associated at present, was toured for a year by Temba to enthusiastic houses, despite a lukewarm reception from reviewers. It is easy to see why there was the discrepancy, however: Ellis' office-bound two-hander is not especially sophisticated, but it is unusually satirical about its leading character, the awful, social-climbing Benjamin, and it is a brave and cautionary tale against buying into the system and against ignorance. *A Temporary Rupture* carries on in like vein as a sprightly dig at the macho insensitivity of young black males, with a jilted girlfriend getting her own back on the returning former lover and father of her child. Both plays would certainly repay further viewing. In the meantime and now a full-time student, Ellis has turned to writing for television (*Eastenders* and *The South of the Border* series) – the only way, he says, to stay solvent.

Try these:
▷Tony Marchant's *The Lucky Ones* is also an office-based saga of contrasting attitudes to 'making it'; Earl Lovelace's *The Hardware Store* is another cautionary tale connecting capitalism and the black community; Nigel Moffatt, ▷Winsome Pinnock, Trish Cooke, Benjamin Zephaniah and Gabriel Gbadamosi are other young contemporary black British voices; for contrasting styles see ▷Edgar White and ▷Derek Walcott; for other black dramatists writing about being black in Britain, ▷Mustapha Matura, ▷Caryl Phillips, ▷Tunde Ikoli, ▷Barry Reckord, ▷Jacqueline Rudet, and ▷Jackie Kay.

ELTON, Ben   [1959–]
British comedian, author, dramatist

Plays include:
Gasping (1990), *Silly Cow* (1991)

Born in Catford, Elton studied drama at
Manchester University, where he wrote and
directed several plays, some of which were
taken to the Edinburgh Festival. On leaving
university, he quickly carved out a successful
career as a comedy scriptwriter and standup
comedian, co-writing the hugley successful
television series *The Young Ones* (with Rik
Mayall and Lise Mayer) and the three series of
Blackadder (with Richard Curtis). The blend
of social comment and prurient humour both
in his routines, which he performed live and
on television, and in his scripts, brought him a
huge, young audience. Elton's commitment to
social and Enviromental issues – explored in
his first novel, *Stark* – were evident in his first
West End play, *Gasping*. This was a sharp,
bitterly funny comedy about a vast multi-
national company introducing the concept of
purified 'designer air', and ending up privatis-
ing oxygen. Despite a tendency to indulge
himself with gags at the expense of plot, Elton
acquitted himself well in his debut, although
some critics thought it would work better on
television. The savaging meted out to *Silly
Cow*, which followed *Gasping* was altogether
easier to justify. Depicting the deserved
downfall of a gutter-tabloid critic. *Silly Cow*
was overwritten, full of improbable holes, and
suffered from the dilution of its main theme
with some indulgent, affectionate broadsides
at the pretensions of actors. Although it had
its moments, the production (which Elton
chose to direct himself) was vastly inferior to
Gasping. Nevertheless, he remains a sharp,
popular writer who is able to command large
audiences for overtly, if not subtly, political,
comic plays.

Try these:
▷Caryl Churchill's radio play *Not . . . Not
. . . Not . . . Not . . . Not Enough Oxygen*
anticipates *Gasping* by nearly 20 years;
Churchill's *Serious Money*, Doug Lucie's
Fashion, Howard Brenton and David
Havel's *Pravda*, Stephen Jeffreys' *Valued
Friends* for other political satires of 1980s
values; *Pravda* was also a fairly vitriolic
swipe at tabloid journalism.

ENGLISH, Rose   [1950–]
British dramatist and performer

Plays include:
Plato's Chair (1983), *The Beloved* (1985),
Thee Thy Thou Thine (1986), *Moses* (1987);
Walking on Water (1990); *The Double
Wedding* (1991)

Rose English, ex-art student and solo performer extraordinaire, has been described as
'the doyenne of the subtle, the ambiguous and
the comic' (Naseem Khan), and as a performer directed as if 'by a choreographer specialising in ballets performed by pelicans'
(Ros Asquith). Rose English has the mischief
of a child let loose in a circus, and the same
wonder; she is the spirit of Bloomsbury translated to the 1980s, a philosophical butterfly,
with the curiosity of Isadora Duncan and the
grace of Anna Pavlova. Playing with the
notions of the infinite, the nature of reality,
the wonder of theatre illusion, hopefulness,
and the quirky uneasy relationship between
audience and performer, her 'plays' or performances have been forays into the unknown
waters of deconstruction that have left her
audiences either outraged (claiming to have
had more entertainment from a bus ticket) or
demented with delight. Rose English is a pure
original, an English eccentric not afraid to
disarm and disorientate. Prior to her theatre
career, she was a luminary of the Performance
Art circuit, performing in places as diverse as
Swiss Cottage's Adelaide Pool, Sherwood
Forest, the Serpentine Gallery in London, and
the Southampton Horse Show, often with
avant-gardist Jacky Lansley and Sally Potter
director (of *The Gold Diggers*).

Try these:
For solo performers, see ▷Cabaret; Barry
Humphries for audience engagement; Ken
Campbell and The People Show for their
own brands of sustained anarchy and mix
of circus, music hall and pantomime conventions; Théâtre de Complicité for
another intensely physical/mime-oriented
group; ▷Amlin Gray; Annie Griffin for a
solo performer with Performance Art ante-
cedents, who also writes and devises her
own shows, and brings a similar, though
different, iconoclasm to her work; also Ben
Keaton, another minimalist; see also
▷Performance Art.

ETHEREGE, George [1634–91]
English Restoration dramatist

Plays include:
The Comical Revenge: or, Love in a Tub (1664), *She Would If She Could* (1668), *The Man of Mode* (1676)

Etherege has some claims to have invented what we now call Restoration Comedy in his plays, which present fashionable, witty, amoral characters engaged in a round of sexual intrigues in a recognisable version of contemporary London society. His own life could have been a model for one of his characters: his actress mistress, Elizabeth Barry, also had a liaison with the Earl of Rochester (identified as the original of Dorimant in *The Man of Mode*); his outrageous behaviour as ambassador in Regensburg scandalised the inhabitants and he ended his career by joining James II in exile in Paris where he died.

The contemporary canvas is broadest in *The Comical Revenge*, where the humiliation of a venereally diseased French valet at the hands of English female servants gives the play its title, and contrasts with three other plots, including a rather more 'heroic' one largely conducted in rhyming couplets. Etherege, like other Restoration dramatists, is much more open about women's sexuality than dramatists of many other periods, though his view can be inferred, not unfairly, from the title of his second play, *She Would If She Could*. As with ▷William Wycherley, the difficulty is knowing where celebration of a society ends and criticism of it begins. Particularly in *The Man of Mode*, the only one of his plays to appear regularly in the modern repertory, the absence of an obvious authorial point of view and explicit moral judgments leads to contradictory evaluations of the characters and of the play. Clearly Sir Flopling Flutter, the man of mode of the title, is a comic butt because of his ridiculous pretensions to be fashionable but the energetic protagonist Dorimant's dealings with various potential and actual mistresses and wives are much more open to scrutiny. This can be regarded either as masterly ambiguity or as poor dramatic technique.

Try these:
Other Restoration comic writers such as ▷Aphra Behn, ▷William Congreve and ▷William Wycherley; other writers of comedy of manners, such as ▷Goldsmith, ▷Sheridan, ▷Oscar Wilde, ▷Noël Coward, ▷Doug Lucie; ▷Edward Bond's *Restoration* uses conventions and themes derived from the practice of Restoration writers to make modern points.

EURIPIDES [484–406/7 BC]
Greek tragic dramatist

Surviving plays include:
Alcestis (438 BC), *Medea* (431 BC), *The Children of Heracles* (c 429 BC), *Hippolytus* (428 BC), *Hecuba* (c 425 BC), *The Suppliant Women* (c 420 BC), *Andromache* (c 419 BC), *Heracles* (c 416 BC), *The Trojan Women* (415 BC), *Electra* (413 BC), *Helen* (412 BC), *Iphigenia in Tauris* (c 411 BC), *Ion* (c 411 BC), *Orestes* (408 BC), *The Phoenician Women* (c 408 BC), *The Bacchae* (produced c 405 BC), *Iphigenia in Aulis* (405 BC), *Cyclops* (date unknown); *Rhesus* is also attributed to Euripides

Euripides wrote over ninety plays during a long career but was less immediately popular than his contemporary, ▷Sophocles. His subjects are those of the other Athenian tragic dramatists – stories of the gods and heroes, particularly those relating to the Trojan wars – but his treatment of them is more domestic and more sceptical, almost realistic and sociological rather than religious and philosophical. It was probably this aspect of his work, together with his penchant for experiments in form, that made him a controversial figure. His subsequent reputation was high, but his plays are still as elusive on the modern stage as those of the other Greek dramatists. *The Bacchae*, a very powerful treatment of the relationship between the Apollonian and the Dionysiac impulses, has been influential on various experimental theatres in the twentieth century (eg the Performance Group's *Dionysus in 69*) but the most recent large-scale staging in Britain was John Barton and Kenneth Cavander's ▷RSC production, *The Greeks*, which used seven of Euripides' plays in its marathon cycle of the Trojan wars. This kind of approach, in which the audience is immersed in the subject matter for a large part of a day, appears to be the best hope for Greek drama in the contemporary theatre, and the popularity of marathon stagings of ▷medieval drama, Dickens, ▷Shakespeare's history plays and *The Mahabarata* (by ▷Peter Brook) could encourage a revival of Greek drama.

Try these:

▷Aeschylus and ▷Sophocles wrote the other surviving Greek tragedies; see ▷Artaud for a theory of theatre with close connections to *The Bacchae*; ▷T.S. Eliot, ▷Giraudoux, ▷Tony Harrison ▷O'Neill and ▷Soyinka (*The Bacchae of Euripides*) are among modern playwrights who have tackled themes drawn from Greek drama; ▷Caryl Churchill and ▷David Lan's *Mouthful of Birds*; ▷Bryony Lavery and ▷Maureen Duffy have both adapted *The Bacchae* from a lesbian feminist perspective; Nancy Meckler took a less radical line for Shared Experience.

EXPRESSIONISM

Expressionism as a historical phenomenon is mainly associated with Germany and the first quarter of the twentieth century, but Expressionist influence is widespread in twentieth-century drama and theatre, in terms of both production style and subject matter. Although it is notoriously hard to pin down exactly what people mean by Expressionism, its most common feature is a reaction against current versions of realism. There tends to be a concentration on the individual standing out against the dehumanising tendencies of modern civilisation, especially in relation to the horrors of World War I. This can lead both to a stress on the importance of fighting capitalism (as the prime example of dehumanisation) and to a cult of the individual (which in turn leads to worship of the super hero), although (curiously) the characters in Expressionist plays tend to be types rather than individuals. Expressionist staging is characteristically symbolic, dealing more with the landscapes of the unconscious, dreams and nightmares, than with the everyday. ▷Büchner, whose works were 'discovered' in the late nineteenth century, ▷Wedekind in (*Spring Awakening* and *The Lulu Plays*), and the ▷Strindberg of such plays as *The Road to Damascus* and *Easter* are often regarded as major precursors of Expressionism.

Relatively few German Expressionist plays are now staged professionally, although there is the occasional oddity such as the ▷Glasgow Citizens' staging of Karl Kraus's mammoth *The Last Days of Mankind*, ▷C.P. Taylor's adaptation of Carl Sternheim's *Schippel* (which surfaced in the West End with Harry Secombe, under the title of *Plumber's Progress*), ▷Michelene Wandor's reworking of Ernst Toller's *The Blind Goddess*, or Ballet Rambert's adaptation of Oscar Kokoschka's *Murderer Hope of Womankind*. Expressionist influence is much more widespread, particularly in terms of approaches to staging and playwriting, often mediated through ▷Brecht's epic theatre, in a general refusal to be confined to reproducing surface realities of everyday life and a willingness to search for theatrical means of showing underlying causes.

The major German dramatists associated with the movement are George Kaiser (1878–1945) and Ernst Toller (1893–1939). Kaiser's plays include *From Morning to Midnight* (1912) and *The Burghers of Calais* (1914); the *Gas* trilogy (1917–1920), has fared less well in recent British productions than has Toller. Kaiser's *Flight to Venice*, about Georges Sand and Alfred De Musset (Gate, 1986), and Sue Dunderdale's production of *From Morning to Midnight* (Soho Poly, 1987), were both received politely as mildly interesting historical curiosities but there was little sense of excitement. Toller's plays, which include *Transfiguration* (1918), *Masses and Men* (1920), *The Machine Wreckers* (1922), *Hinkemann* (1923), *Hoppla! We're Alive* (1927), manifest both his pacifism (a result of his experiences at the front during World War I) and his hatred of the effects of industrial capitalism on the workers. Their very heightened language can be emotionally bludgeoning, and the tone can be virtually hysterical, but there are compensations. *Hinkemann*, staged at the Old Red Lion by The Group in 1988, shows the unemployment, moral degradation and impotence of the working class in 1920s Germany through the story of Hinkemann who, castrated by a battle wound, joins a circus to find work biting the heads off rats, while his wife is seduced by his best friend. Peter Stein's Schaubühne production of O'Neill's *The Hairy Ape* was well received when it was brought to The National in 1987.

Try these:

Adaptations of Franz Kafka's novels usually stress their Expressionist elements; among the many dramatists influenced by Expressionism are ▷Eugene O'Neill, Elmer Rice, ▷Tennessee Williams, ▷Sean O'Casey, the ▷Capek brothers and ▷Mayakovsky; for contemporary Expressionistic approaches see Red Shift and ▷Steven Berkoff.

f

FAGON, Alfred [1937–86]

Plays include:
11 Josephine House (1972), *Death of a Black Man* (1975), *Four Hundred Pounds* (1983), *Lonely Cowboy* (1985)

Jamaican born Fagon went to Britain in 1955, worked on the railways and served in the army before emerging as a professional actor and dramatist in the 1970s. He died while out jogging and, before any of his friends found out, was buried anonymously because the police believed he was a vagrant. As his subsequent *Times* obituary put it, 'his plays take as their theme the relationship between the cultures of the English and Caribbean peoples, their friendships and conflicts'. This theme is characteristically treated in the form of a comedy of manners with an underlying seriousness as in *11 Josephine House* with its black family trying to adjust to the temptations of English life, particularly in the form of the white woman who causes the black preacher's fall from grace. In *Four Hundred Pounds* TeeCee's sudden refusal to pot the black in a snooker game on ideological grounds loses him and his more pragmatic gambling partner that sum of money, and in *Lonely Cowboy* a couple's attempt to start a café leads first to comedy and then tragedy as the values of a world they try to ban from their café reassert themselves.

Try these:
11 Josephine House has affinities with ▷Molière's *Tartuffe* and ▷Baldwin's *The Amen Corner*; Fagon's work offers interesting points of comparison with that of other British black writers such as ▷Michael Ellis, ▷Mustapha Matura, ▷Tunde Ikoli, and ▷Caryl Phillips; ▷Michael Abbensetts and ▷Trevor Rhone also handle racial conflicts through humour.

FAIRBANKS, Tasha [1948–]
British dramatist

Plays include:
Wedlocked (1978), *Lucy and the Steel Queen* (1978), *Mama's Gone a-Hunting* (1980), *Curfew* (1981), *From the Divine* (1982), *Now Wash Your Hands, Please* (1984), *Ties* (1984), *PULP* (1985), *Fixed Deal* (1986), *Up For Demolition* (1987), *Hotel Destiny* (1987), *A Private View* (for Graeae; 1987), *Swamp* (1989), *Two Cities* (1989), *A Foreign Correspondence* (1989)

One of the busiest playwrights on the circuit, writer/director Fairbanks' output ranges from a television film on sexual fantasy to community plays, texts for dance-based companies and devising a musical, as well as being co-founder of Siren, the radical lesbian feminist theatre company, for whom she wrote several plays. At her worst, Fairbanks' scripts can be over-dense and heavy-handed (*A Private View*, on the subject of disability, is a case in point) and in need of firm editing, perhaps because, as with much work on the fringe, they are often the result of a collaborative process of workshops and improvisations with the companies concerned. At her best, Fairbanks' scripts are imaginative Molotov cocktails, launched into the arena of sexual politics with energy and humour. *From the Divine* used the hysteria of the Falklands War to explore ideas about war, machismo, power, and female stereotypes through the use of a 1940s concert party, with a Master of Ceremonies, a ventriloquist's dummy and a 'bolshie angel in a plastic mac'. *PULP*, a lesbian thriller on the theme of double identities combined glamour with sleaze in its parody of the femme fatale images of 1950s Hollywood, alongside issues of betrayal, deceit, McCarthyism and espionage. *Up for Demolition*, on the other hand, set in a derelict house which a local women's group are trying to turn into a knitting co-op, was more in line with predictable radical feminist agit-prop, but took an interesting approach to the way oppression gets passed on, and how the past can teach us lessons for the future. *Hotel Destiny*, though uneven, had fun at the expense of macho images and the western.

Try these:
▷Bryony Lavery's *Calamity* and Peter Parnell's *Romance Language* for a different kind of reassessment of the Western myth, and *Her Aching Heart* for further pastiche; Split Britches for more entertaining radical departures; ▷lesbian theatre; for other post-Falklands explorations, ▷Tony Marchant's *Coming Home*; ▷Noël Greig's *Poppies* for another gay perspective on militarism; for double identity, ▷Tom Stoppard generally, ▷Alan Bennett's *The Old Country*, ▷Thomas Kilroy's *Double Cross*; ▷David Lan's *Desire* focused on expiation of the past, in an African setting.

FARABOUGH, Laura   [1949–]
American writer, director and performer

Performances include:
Surface Tension (1980), *Femme Fatale: The Invention of Personality* (1981), *Obedience School* (1982), *Beauty Science* (1985), *bodily concessions* (1987)

'Danced-out painting' is the expression Laura Farabough used to describe the style she envisioned for her newly formed Nightfire Theater in 1980. Farabough seeks to discover a theatrical language that places the facts of our experiences in a variety of contexts that imbue them with new and different meanings. Using the languages of painting and sculpture, gestural dance, music, and words, expression is more than verbal; it is iconographic and somatic. The stage environments are inhabited by human beings whose physical, personal and social behaviours, in one way or another, are enigmatic (actions arise from culturally-determined circumstances). *Femme Fatale: The Invention of Personality* targets one aspect of patriarchy's moral code in its exploration of the role of women as *femme fatales*, adoption of this role invented by the male psyche is a fatal act. The pursuit of the ideal of perfection in American culture is explored in *Obedience School*, a multi-media work in which formal devices convey the vacuous lives of the perfect couple. *bodily concessions*, a one-woman work performed by Farabough, explores the dimen-

sions of live performance and video in which the philosophical notion of mind/body split is tested in action.

Try these:
Snake Theater's *Somewhere in the Pacific* and *24th Hour Cafe*, for earlier attempts to create sparse dialogue and psychology of character with visual imagery that evokes moods and feelings; ▷Performance Art.

FARCE/LIGHT COMEDY IN BRITAIN
Farce is both the more popular and the more intellectually respectable of these two forms, at least since Eric Bentley and the other theorists got at it. It is also, with musicals and ▷thrillers, one of the current mainstays of the commercial theatre. The reasons for its popularity may throw a disturbing light on the modern world, especially if one believes the theorists about its subversive qualities and its role in satisfying our unspoken urges. However, what is certainly true is that farce is the most technically difficult of all dramatic forms. Even Ben Travers needed the ferocious criticism of Tom Walls to produce his classics, and the history of the stage is littered with the ruins of those who ignored Garrick's aphorism that, 'Comedy, sir, is a serious business'.

The most successful school of postwar British farce began at the Whitehall Theatre in 1950, where Brian Rix put on a series of long-running 'Whitehall farces', including Colin Morris' *Reluctant Heroes* (1950) and John Chapman's *Dry Rot* (1954) and *Simple Spymen* (1958). Rix played leading roles in most of these plays with amiable gusto, and many of them became widely known through being televised. He is a trustee of Ray Cooney's 'Theatre of Comedy' Company. Ray Cooney appeared at the Whitehall in *Dry Rot* and *Simple Spymen*, and then wrote for them (with Tony Hilton) his first play, *One for the Pot* (1961), a classic farce with Brian Rix playing four brothers, and later *Chase Me, Comrade!* (1964). After other successful farces (all in the genteel British line of cheerful suggestive sex rather than the manic and more explicit style of ▷Feydeau or ▷Orton, and guaranteed to please the coach parties) he formed the 'Theatre of Comedy' Company in 1983, put on his own *Run For Your Wife!*, which is still running (1991), and has since managed to attract a very wide public to efficient, slick and very funny farces with reliable actors of the quality of Maureen Lipman, Richard Briers and Paul Eddington.

Try these:
For theatrical writing using elements of farce ▷Peter Barnes, ▷Alan Bennett, ▷John Bishop, ▷Chris Durang, ▷de Filippo, ▷Feydeau, ▷Dario Fo, ▷Michael Frayn, ▷W.S. Gilbert, ▷Goldoni, John Guare, ▷Ronald Harwood, ▷Hecht and McArthur, ▷N.C. Hunter, ▷Ionesco, ▷Jarry, ▷Jonson, ▷Kaufman and Hart, ▷Labiche, ▷Larry Larson, ▷Levi Lee and Rebecca Wackler's *Tent Meeting*, ▷Mike Leigh, ▷Doug Lucie, Charles Ludlam, ▷Nestroy, ▷Ostrovsky, ▷Pinero, ▷Terence Rattigan, ▷Peter Shaffer, and ▷Tom Stoppard, and ▷Oscar Wilde.

FARQUHAR, George   [1678–1707]
Irish dramatist

Plays include:
Love and a Bottle (1698), *The Constant Couple, or A Trip to the Jubilee* (1699), *Sir Harry Wildair, being a sequel to The Constant Couple* (1701), *The Inconstant, or The Way to Win Him* (1702), *The Twin Rivals* (1702), *The Stage Coach* (1704), *The Recruiting Officer* (1706), *The Beaux' Stratagem* (1707)

Farquhar left Trinity College, Dublin, to become an actor but gave up the boards when he injured his opponent in the duel at the end of ▷Dryden's *The Indian Emperor* and took to writing. He married a woman he mistakenly believed to be an heiress and died in poverty aged only 29.

His writing is witty and stylish, and rather warmer than that of ▷Congreve and ▷Wycherley who precede him. The later plays are more closely drawn from life with a very positive attitude to the situation of women in his society. In *The Constant Couple* he created the role of Harry Wildair, a kind-hearted rake, which became a celebrated breeches part for Peg Woffington and other actresses for many years, but he is now best known for his two last plays.

The Recruiting Officer is set in Shropshire, where Sgt Kite is recruiting. Silvia, the daughter of a local Justice, enlists, disguised as a man, so that she can be near her lover. An outstanding production by Bill Gaskill, in the ▷National Theatre's opening season at the Old Vic in 1963 (partly influenced by ▷Brecht's adaptation *Trumpets and Drums*), emphasised the clarity of Farquhar's presentation of his divided society and its power structures so that the affected mannerisms which had previously tended to suffice for 'Restoration style' began to lose their foothold in contemporary productions. Set in Lichfield *The Beaux' Stratagem* shows two London beaux seeking country marriages to restore their fortunes, one posing as his own elder brother, the other as his servant. It makes a case for divorce on the grounds of incompatability and, in introducing Lady Bountiful, added an expression to the English language.

Try these:
▷Aphra Behn, ▷Congreve, ▷Etherege, ▷Vanbrugh and ▷Wycherley for other 'Restoration' dramatists; ▷Goldsmith (who refers to *Beaux' Stratagem* in *She Stoops to Conquer*) and ▷Sheridan wrote within broadly similar conventions; ▷Philip Barry, ▷Neil Simon, ▷Noël Coward, ▷Oscar Wilde, ▷Doug Lucie, ▷Mike Leigh and ▷Alan Ayckbourn for more contemporary comedy of manners; ▷Timberlake Wertenbaker's *Our Country's Good* centres on the staging of *The Recruiting Officer* as the first production in Australia, performed by convicts.

FEIFFER, Jules   [1929–]
American dramatist and cartoonist

Plays include:
The Explainers (1961), *Crawling Arnold* (1961), *The World of Jules Feiffer* (1962), *Little Murders* (1967), *The Unexpurgated Memories of Bernard Mergendelier* (1968), *God Bless* (1968), *The White House Murder Case* (1970), *Munro* (1971), *Watergate Classics* (1973), *Knock, Knock* (1976), *Hold Me* (1977), *Grown-Ups* (1981), *A Think Piece* (1982), *Jules Feiffer's America* (adapted by Russell Vandenbroucke; 1987), *Anthony Rose*, (1989), *Eliot's Love* (1990)

Most prolific in the 1960s, Feiffer was an important figure in the off-, off-off-Broadway and regional theatre movements. *Little Murders*, *Knock, Knock* and *Grown Ups* are his most frequently revived plays, and have several US productions each year. *Little Murders*, the first American work ever produced by the ▷RSC (1969), won the London Drama Critics award for Best Foreign Play. Feiffer's is a psychic landscape, full of domestic and social violence. *Little Murders*, in which a family shoots at passersby through their nice, middle-class windows, may best illustrate the author's vision of intermarried urban and domestic blight. Feiffer's plays, like the cartoons for which he is famous, are typified by mordant, often self-mocking, existential humour. But Feiffer is adept at farce too, as evidenced by *Watergate Classics*, a spoof of the Nixon presidency. *Feiffer's People* and *Hold Me*, which the author has dubbed 'sketch plays', have the quick, direct punch of a good drawing. *Grown-Ups*, about an affluent New York family spiralling into emotional chaos, invites comparisons with no less a dramatist than Strindberg. In the USA Feiffer is considered something of a classic. His best plays capture the confused searching, the crises of courage and failed political vision of a particular segment of the middle and upper-middle class during the turbulent 1960s, mixed-up 1970s and ruthless 1980s.

Feiffer's latest play is *Elliot's Love*, which centres on the mid-life crisis of an urban male. It was premiered in 1990 under the direction of Mike Nichols at New York's Promenade Theatre. The same season saw the off-Broadway revival of *Carnal Knowledge*, a play that most have come to associate with the film version (directed by Mike Nichols). Feiffer is an accomplished screenwriter. His other credits include *Little Murders* (adapted from his play), *Popeye* and *I Want to Go Home*, which won the 1989 Venice Film Festival award for best screenplay.

Try these:
▷Strindberg and ▷Edward Albee for households in dire distress; Murray Schisgal's *An American Millionaire* for a Feifferesque black farce about violence and affluence; John Guare's *House of Blue Leaves* and *Six Degrees of Separation* for their incisively comic look at two very different New York families; ▷Herb Gardner's work also imbued with the frustrations of New Yorkers' lives; and ▷David Mamet's *Edmond* for perhaps the darkest look at urban life; ▷Lynda Barry, another *Voice* cartoonist had a hit with her first play *The Good Times Are Killing Me*; ▷Neil Simon for more sanitised version of New York angst; ▷Christopher Durang and early ▷Arthur Kopit (especially *Oh Dad Poor Dad*) for comparably deranged families.

FEYDEAU, Georges   [1862–1921]
French dramatist

Plays include:
Tailleur pour Dames (The Ladies' Tailor; 1886), *Champignol Malgré Lui (Champignol in Spite of Himself*; 1892), *L'Hôtel du Libre-Echange (Hotel Paradiso* or *A Little Hotel on the Side*; 1894), *Un Fil à la Patte (Cat Among the Pigeons* or *Get Out of my Hair*; 1894), *Le Dindon (Ruling the Roost* or *Sauce for the Goose*; 1896), *La Dame de chez Maxim (The Lady from Maxim's*; 1899), *La Puce à L'Oreille (A Flea in Her Ear*; 1907), *Occupe-toi d'Amelie (Look After Lulu*; 1908), *Feu la Mère de Madame (My Late Mother-in-law*; 1908), *Léonie est en Avance (Any Minute Now*; 1911), *Hortense a dit: 'Je m'en fous' (Hortense said 'Stuff it'*; 1916), *A Journey to London* (unfin and finished by Saunders 1985)

Feydeau's middle-period plays are the archetype of French farce. The principal characters are Parisian bourgeois, their major driving force is extra-connubial lust, and the basic source of the humour is their ever more desperate attempts to avoid being found out. Although no respectable married woman is ever seduced by her husband's best friend, it is not for want of trying on either side. The plots seem to have been constructed by a mad watchmaker, but the status quo is always restored at the end. His later one-act plays (after he left his wife) are more misanthropic, more loosely constructed, and need more careful production; but the full-length plays come up as fresh as ever.

A Little Hotel on the Side
It would be a waste of time to detail the whole plot of this farce, but in Act Two (set in the eponymous hotel) the attempt of M Pinglet (a building contractor) to spend the night with Mme Paillardin is frustrated by the presence in the hotel of their friend M Mathieu and his four daughters, M Paillardin (an architect, there as an officer of the court, who quite reasonably believes M Mathieu's daughters to be ghosts), M Pinglet's nephew and the maid Victoire (who alone get what they came for),

the hotel manager's habit of drilling holes in the wall to admire what is going on, and a final visit from the Vice Squad.

Try these:
▷Labiche for nineteenth-century French farce; ▷Joe Orton for the occasional casual cruelty of the humour (eg the man with no roof to his mouth, the character with bad breath, the comic foreigners); perhaps the contemporary English equivalent is ▷Ray Cooney's farces, also invariably focused on extra-marital lust.

FIERSTEIN, Harvey   [1954–]
American actor and dramatist

Plays include:
In Search of the Cobra Jewels (1973), *Forget Him* (1982), *Freaky Pussy* (1982), *Flatbush Tosca* (1982), *Torch Song Trilogy* (1982), libretto for *La Cage aux Folles* (1983), *Spookhouse* (1984, *Safe Sex* (1987)

Fierstein made his acting debut in 1971 with Andy Warhol, but did not come to general prominence for another decade. *Torch Song Trilogy* was a landmark in ▷gay theatre, winning two Tony and Drama Desk Awards (Best Play and Best Actor) and catapulting the author to mainstream fame. The moving mother and son scenes that close the work may be Fierstein's best writing. Don Shewey, in the Introduction to *Out Front: Contemporary Gay and Lesbian Plays*, wrote that the trilogy (*International Stud*, *Fugue in a Nursery* and *Widows and Children First*) is 'superbly theatrical in the way each play's interior structure tells part of the story itself. . . . What's finally remarkable about *Torch Song Trilogy* is that it portrays gay life not as an isolated phenomenon but in constant relation to the society at large. And the society it exposes is one whose sexual values have undergone an enormous upheaval, a contemporary revolution that has left gays and straights alike struggling to learn new rules.'

Fierstein's plays since then have not had equal commercial success. *Spookhouse*, seen off-Broadway (1984) and at Hampstead (1987), a Paul Zindel-like tale of a harridan mother living in Coney Island, was not totally convincing, although Fierstein again showed his talent for creating sensitive, intimate scenes. *Safe Sex*, also a trilogy, was one of the first overtly post-AIDS dramas. Though extremely important in terms of its subject matter, it closed after only two weeks.

Try these:
▷Larry Kramer (*The Normal Heart*) and William M. Hoffman (*As Is*) are two other contemporary gay American writers whose works have reached a broad audience; ▷Terrence McNally and ▷Craig Lucas as playwrights have written about AIDS and gay life; also Neil Bell, ▷Robert Chesley, ▷Martin Sherman as dramatists who write frankly about gay life and issues; for British equivalents, see ▷Gay Sweatshop, ▷Noël Greig, ▷Drew Griffiths and newcomer Robin Hooper.

FINNEGAN, Seamus   [1949–]
Northern Irish dramatist

Plays include:
Laws of God (1978), *Paddy and Britannia* (1979), *I Am a Bomb* (1979), *Victims* (1979), *Act of Union* (1980), *Herself Alone* (1981), *Soldiers* (1981), *James Joyce and the Israelites* (1982), *Loyal Willy* (1982), *The Little People* (1982), *Tout* (1984), *North* (1984), *Beyond a Joke* (1984), *Mary's Men* (1984), *Bringing It Home* (1984), *Gombeen* (1985), *The Spanish Play* (1986), *The German Connection* (1986), *Ghetto* (1987), *The Murphy Girls* (1988), *1916* (1989), *Mary Maginn* (1990)

Belfast-born, Catholic-bred former teacher (at the Jewish Free School in London) and one-time political activist (for the now almost moribund socialist Civil Rights movement), Finnegan has become one of the most prolific commentators on Northern Ireland – his output in the past decade (all directed by Julia Pascal, and mostly for her own company on the fringe circuit) amount to a magnum opus. Ambitiously wide-ranging in his themes, Finnegan has moved from the early monologues of outrage through the complexities of the situation (*Act of Union*, *Soldiers* and *North*) to exploration of loyalties and principles on a wider scale in *The War Trilogy* which spans the Spanish Civil War (*The Spanish Play*), the Holocaust in Europe (*The German Connection*) and Israel (the radio play *The Cemetery of Europe*). Eschewing nationalism, Finnegan's plays have been notable for their non-sectarian, even ironical detachment, and for their concern, like James Joyce, with exploring Jewish links (*James Joyce and the Israelites*, *The War Trilogy*). Finnegan is equally capable of providing dramatic cameos on a smaller, more domestic canvas such as in *Mary's Men*, a poignant portrait of lost dreams among Belfast's down-and-outers. But history, language and the ironies of fate continue to be at the centre of his work.

Resident in London since 1974, Finnegan has yet to see any of his plays performed anywhere in Ireland, North or South (although a radio play, *Wild Grass*, is to be broadcast by BBC Radio Belfast). Some enterprising producer would do well to organise a major revival, particularly of *The War Trilogy* – something which may be prompted once his film version of *The German Connection* (*Shadows of Time*) opens.

Try these:
▷Marie Jones' *Somewhere over the Balcony* for Charabanc and ▷Daniel Mornin's *Kate* for another view of the madness of living under constant army surveillance; for soldiers and barrack room scenes of British squaddies, ▷Tony Marchant's *Coming Home*, Greg Cullen's *Taken Out*; for a view of black British squaddies, *Black Poppies* (compiled from interviews) and Fred D'Agivar's *A Jamaican Airman Forsees his Death*; for contrast, other contemporary Northern Irish playwrights: ▷Christina Reid, ▷Ann Devlin, ▷Thomas Kilroy, Martin Lynch, ▷Frank McGuinness, ▷Stewart Parker.

FLANNERY, Peter [1951–]
British dramatist

Plays include:
Heartbreak Hotel (1975), *Last Resort* (1976), *Savage Amusement* (1978), *The Boy's Own Story* (1978), *The Adventures of Awful Knawful* (1979), *Jungle Music* (1979), *Our Friends in the North* (1982), *Heavy Days* (1982), *Silence on My Radio* (1983), *Singer* (1989)

Flannery, a Manchester University drama graduate, has had most of his work staged by the Manchester based Contact Theatre Company or the ▷RSC, for whom he was resident dramatist in 1979–80. Much of his work includes songs, often by fellow Manchester student Mick Ford, and he has been particularly concerned with problems of despair and urban decay in *Savage Amusement* and *Jungle Music*. *Our Friends in the North*

won the John Whiting Award for its vivid and trenchant recreation of some of the interlocking strands of corruption in British life between 1964 and 1979, from faulty high rise blocks and corrupt policemen to Rhodesian sanctions-busting. It has all the virtues of a thriller and reserves its anger for the Labour politicians who wasted their golden opportunity. Perhaps it seemed a little long in performance, but then there was a lot of material to be considered; an updated version would be far more chilling and would presumably be even longer. *Singer*, staged by the ▷RSC at the Barbican, is another epic recreation of corruption in Britain, centring on concentration-camp survivors who react in chillingly different ways to their experiences. It's partly a panoramic history of post-War Britain, partly a meditation on the meaning of the Holocaust, partly a modern version of Renaissance tragi-comedy, complete with chorus out of *Henry V*.

Try these:
▷Howard Brenton and ▷David Hare's *Brassneck* and *Pravda*, ▷Peter Barnes' *The Ruling Class*, ▷Howard Barker's *A Passion in Six Days* and *Stripwell* are among the many contemporary British plays that deal with politics, corruption and the establishment; ▷Thomas Otway's *Venice Preserv'd*, ▷John Gay's *The Beggar's Opera*, ▷Shaw's *Widower's Houses*, ▷Granville Barker's *Waste* are examples from the seventeenth, eighteenth, nineteenth and early twentieth centuries; for 'bent' policeman see ▷G.F. Newman's *Operation Bad Apple*, ▷Nigel Williams' *WCPC*, ▷Joe Orton's *Loot*; ▷Caryl Churchill's *Serious Money* offers a satirical view of some aspects of current City scandals; ▷C. P. Taylor's *Good* and ▷Martin Sherman's *Bent* for concentration-camp experiences; ▷Harwaint Bains' *Blood* for the brutalisation process in terms of the partition of India in 1947.

FLETCHER, John [1579–1625]
English Renaissance dramatist, collaborator with ▷Francis Beaumont, ▷Philip Massinger and ▷William Shakespeare

Plays include:
The Woman's Prize (with ▷Beaumont; after 1604), *Philaster* (with ▷Beaumont; pre 1610), *The Maid's Tragedy* (with

▷Beaumont; pre 1611), *A King and No King* (with ▷Beaumont; 1611), *Henry VIII* (with ▷Shakespeare; 1613), *The Two Noble Kinsmen* (with ▷Shakespeare; 1613), *The Custom of the Country* (with ▷Massinger; c 1619)

Son of a clergyman who eventually died in poverty despite having been Bishop of London, Fletcher was a prolific and popular dramatist who succeeded ▷Shakespeare as resident dramatist with the King's Men. His current theatrical reputation rests almost entirely on his collaborations with Shakespeare and *The Maid's Tragedy*, though he wrote many comedies of manners which might repay attention as precursors of Restoration comedy and he also wrote *The Woman's Prize; or The Tamer Tamed*, a revivable sequel to *Taming of the Shrew*, in which Petruchio gets his just deserts at the hands of his second wife. *Henry VIII* is a celebratory epic of the birth of Protestant England in which Henry is presented rather more favourably and seriously than he tends to be in our contemporary picture of him. It uses non-naturalistic dramatic devices in a way that ▷Brecht would have admired. The two gentlemen who meet at major events throughout the play and remind each other and the audience of the historical context are particularly endearing if you like that kind of approach to dramatic writing (and particularly irritating if you like tightly controlled causality and plausability).

The Two Noble Kinsmen
The Two Noble Kinsmen is a fascinating study of conflict between honour and love, derived from Chaucer, in which Palamon and Arcite, the kinsmen of the title, imprisoned by Theseus, vie for the love of Hippolyta's sister Emilia. In the subplot the gaoler's daughter, who loves Palamon, goes mad for love and is subsequently cured by the attentions of her former suitor disguised as Palamon. The whole effect is truly tragi-comic with many possibilities of death and disaster but virtually everything turns out well for everybody in the end, except for Arcite who wins the contest for Emilia but is killed accidentally, thus leaving the way clear for Palamon to marry Emilia. Quite what Emilia makes of this last minute substitution is not clear. The 1986 ▷RSC revival showed that the play can hold its own; what it needs now is regular revivals so that we can gauge its true strengths.

Try these:
Theseus figures in ▷Euripides' *The Suppliant Women* and *Hippolytus* (which deals with the Phaedra story later dramatised by ▷Racine, in which Hippolytus dies in a similar way to Arcite); ▷Shakespeare uses Theseus and Hippolyta in *A Midsummer Night's Dream*; the substitution of one beloved for another which figures in *The Two Noble Kinsmen*, ▷Shakespeare's *Two Gentlemen of Verona, Measure for Measure* and *All's Well that Ends Well*, has sinister parallels in the substitution of one woman for another in a man's bed in ▷Middleton's *The Changeling*; ▷Bolt's *A Man for All Seasons* offers a different interpretation of Henry VIII to that of ▷Fletcher and ▷Shakespeare; ▷Shakespeare's other history plays cover the period from *King John* to *Richard III*.

FO, Dario   [1926–]
Italian political performer, dramatist and manager

Plays include:
Stealing a Foot Makes you Lucky in Love (1961), *Mistero Buffo* (1969), *Accidental Death of an Anarchist* (1970), *Can't Pay? Won't Pay!* (1974), *Female Parts* (with Franca Rame; 1977), *Trumpets and Raspberries* (1981), *Elizabeth* (1984) *The Open Couple* (with Franca Rame; 1986–7)

Dario Fo is one of the funniest performers alive, especially in his solo piece, *Mistero Buffo*, which he has performed all over the world. His peculiar strutting walk, leaning backwards as he goes, and his expressive features and shark-like smile, are inimitable. He has also written forty or so plays – some of which have upset successive Italian governments considerably – which have made him in recent years one of the most widely performed dramatists in the world. His combination of popular farce and savage political comment is unique and very effective.

Fo's father was a socialist railway worker and amateur actor. He started in the Italian theatre in Milan in the 1950s, with revue sketches, radio comedy and songs, and some early farces with the Fo-Rame Company (founded with his wife ▷Franca Rame) from 1959 to 1968. They are very competent but have no great political content except for a general dislike of authority. He had a good deal of commercial success in Italy in the 1960s, but in 1968 he and his wife left the bourgeois theatre to set up a co-operative group called the Compagnia Nuova Scena, where he first performed his bravura solo act *Mistero Buffo*. A free-wheeling act, it is partly written in *grammelot*, an invented language which he declares was made up by medieval strolling players to avoid political censorship, and in which he satirises the Catholic Church, politicians, big business, repressive laws, and generally presents the irrepressible underdog, improvising freely as he goes. (Fo miming the Pope kissing babies is the sort of thing that makes you laugh until your ribs hurt.) He has been developing and changing this act for the last twenty years.

In 1970 he founded a new company, La Comune, a theatrical collective, which worked as a ▷community theatre in a working-class suburb of Milan where his work became overtly political and revolutionary. In December of the same year the company put on 'a grotesque farce about a tragic farce', *Accidental Death of an Anarchist*.

Later Fo plays include *Can't Pay? Won't Pay!*, a well structured farce about civil disobedience in the face of high prices; *Trumpets and Raspberries*, which makes hilarious use of the 'double' joke, as the Fiat boss, Agnelli, is saved in an attempted assassination by a Fiat worker, but is given the worker's features by mistake in plastic surgery; the misconceived *Elizabeth* (which showed that Fo should stay with his own cultural and historical assumptions) and *The Open Couple*.

Accidental Death of an Anarchist

This play was based on the death of Giuseppe Pinelli, an anarchist railway worker who had 'accidentally' fallen from a Milan police station window during interrogation about planting bombs. Fo himself played the part of the 'Maniac' who infiltrates police headquarters and shows the unlikeliness of the police story; the mode is farcical, but the content profoundly disturbing. (The show was changed nightly through its run, as more facts about the Pinelli affair emerged.) It was produced in London by the fringe group Belt and Braces in 1979, and had a great commercial success; such was not the case for Richard Nelson's adaptation on Broadway starring Jonathan Pryce, it closed after a handful of performances.

Try these:
▷Franca Rame, Fo's wife and long-time collaborator; ▷John McGrath for the mixture of comedy and politics, and also ▷John Arden's *Non-Stop Connolly Show*; Plautus, ▷Goldoni and ▷Shakespeare for plays about doubles.

FOOTE, Horton   [1916–]
American playwright, screenwriter, actor

Plays include:
Wharton Dance (1940), *Texas Town* (1941), *Only the Heart* (1942), *Celebration* (1948), *The Chase* (1952), *The Trip to Bountiful* (1953), *The Traveling Lady* (1954), *A Young Lady of Property* (1955), *Gone with the Wind* (musical adaptation of the novel, 1972), *The Roads to Home* (1982), *Courtship* (1984), *The Road to the Graveyard* (1985), *Blind Date* (1986), *Lily Dale* (1986), *The Widow Claire* (1986)

Hailing from Wharton, Texas, Horton Foote arrived in New York in 1940 with aspirations of becoming an actor. Together with such notables as Agnes de Mille, Mildred Dunnock, and Jerome Robbins, he created the American Actor's Company, devoted to the production of American drama. Here he tried his hand at playwrighting and his early work, *Texas Town*, drew a favorable review by Brooks Atkinson launching his writing career. Although he still maintains a home in Wharton, Texas, Foote spends the majority of his time up north; his work, however, is marked by his southern roots, and all his plays are set in Texas. With a style that is starkly realistic and marks the slow passage of time in the heat-baked South, his work is Chekhovian in tone and Faulkneresque in sensibility.

During the 1950s, hardly a season went by without a Horton Foote play on Broadway, and his work attracted such stars as Kim Stanley and Geraldine Page. His themes centre on family relationships and characters in search of the roots that give meaning to their lives. A stoic acceptance of life's travails is seen as passive heroism. During the fifties and sixties he adapted many of his stage plays, as well as stories by William Faulkner, for television. Foote's plays, conservative in theme and style, found a shrinking audience during the 1960s, when the changing American theatre scene was reflected in a burgeoning avant-garde and a decline in

Broadway productions. Despite his Academy Award winning screenplay for *To Kill a Mockingbird* in 1962, Foote was little in demand. He never stopped writing, and eventually his time came again in the more conservative eighties. Several of his plays have enjoyed recent Off-Broadway productions, while his film *Tender Mercies* received an Academy Award for best screenplay in 1984, and the screen adaptation of *The Trip to Bountiful* earned him an Academy Award nomination and an Oscar for its star, Geraldine Page in 1985.

Try these:
▷Chekhov for realistic writing and passive characters; ▷Neil Simon and ▷Arthur Miller for plays that explore family relationships, ▷Tennessee Williams and ▷Beth Henley for plays that reflect the values of the American South.

FORD, John   [1586–c 1640]
English Renaissance dramatist

Plays include:
The Witch of Edmonton (1621, with Dekker and Rowley), *Perkin Warbeck* (c 1622–32), *The Broken Heart* (c 1629), *'Tis Pity She's a Whore* (c 1632)

Ford had a legal training at the Middle Temple but may not have practised law. He made his theatrical debut with *The Witch of Edmonton*, collaborated in five plays and wrote another eight by himself. Because *'Tis Pity She's a Whore* deals sensitively and not unsympathetically with incest, Ford has been subject to high moral condemnation and treated as the prime representative of the alleged decadence of the drama during the reign of Charles I. He, ▷Middleton and ▷Massinger are, in fact, the latest of the pre-Civil War dramatists to be staged on anything like a regular basis in the contemporary theatre, and there can be no denying the sensational quality of *'Tis Pity* in view of such moments as Giovanni's entrance with the heart of his sister Annabella on the point of his dagger. Nevertheless, it is a play well within the Renaissance tradition of scrutinising limits and defying convention which still attracts modern audiences. *Perkin Warbeck*, a very late example of the chronicle play fashionable in the Elizabethan period, is a fascinating study of role-playing with its protagonist, who

claims to be the son of Edward IV, choosing to be executed rather than admit his imposture.

Try these:
Ford was clearly heavily influenced by ▷Shakespeare in both *'Tis Pity She's a Whore* (aspects of *Romeo and Juliet*) and *Perkin Warbeck* (particularly the *Henry VI* plays and *Richard III*, which deal with the historical events preceding the action of Ford's play); ▷Middleton's *Women Beware Women* has an incest plot which is thought to have influenced Ford's treatment; incest is also a main theme in ▷Shelley's, and ▷Artaud's, *The Cenci*; ▷Barry Reckord's *X* also uses incest as a main theme; ▷Tom Stoppard's *The Real Thing* uses *'Tis Pity* as one of its intertexts; ▷Pirandello's *Henry IV* (which is not about the English king) is a significant modern play about the construction of identity.

FOREMAN, Richard   [1937–]
American dramatist, director, scene designer

Plays include:
Elephant Steps (music by Stanley Silverman, 1968), *Real Magic in New York* (music by Stephen DIckman, 1969), *Total Recall: Sophia = (Wisdom) Part 2* (1970), *Sophia = (Wisdom) Part 3: The Cliffs* (1972), *Classical Therapy: or, A Week Under the Influence* (1973), *Vertical Mobility: Sophia (Wisdom) Part 4* (1974), *RA-D-IO (Wisdom) Part 1* (music by David Tice 1974), *Rhoda in Potatoland (Her Fall starts* (1975), *Livre de Splendeurs (Part II): Book of Levers: Action at a Distance* (1977), *Blvd. de Paris (I've Got the Shakes)* (1978), *Madame Adare* (music by Stanley Silverman, 1980), *Egyptology: My Head Was a Sledgehammer* (1983), *George Bataille's Bathrobe* (1984), *Miss Universal Happiness* (1985), *Africanus Instructus* (music by Stanley Silverman, 1986), *The Cure* (1986), *Film is Evil: Radio is Good* (1987), *Love and Science* (1987), *Symphony of Rats* (1988), *Eddie Goes to Poetry City* (1991)

Richard Foreman has established himself in the forefront of the American avant-garde as both a playwright and director. His plays relegate linear plot, emotion, character development, and narrative to the expression of the workings of the human consciousness. The

Adale O'Brien and Pamela Stewart in the Actors Theatre of Louisville's production of Horton Foote's *The Trip to Bountiful*, autumn/fall 1990

overall design resulting from a series of often-incomprehensible incidents aspires not to logic, but to psychological truth. The viewer is made aware that the on-stage action aims to illustrate Foreman's mind at work, resulting in an aesthetic distance like that inherent in the drama of ▷Bertolt Brecht.

Born in Scarsdale, NY, Foreman was raised on the popular commercial theatre in nearby New York City. After he received his B.A. from Brown and an M.F.A. in playwrighting from Yale, Foreman moved to Manhattan, where he soon founded the Ontological-Hysteric Theatre and his unique blend of lyric poetry with theatre of the absurd. These early plays care not about the psychological peculiarities of their characters, but rather stress the states of perception, understanding, and expression. Foreman uses aggressive techniques such as shining lights in spectators' eyes or sounding loud buzzers to disorient the audience, leading them to see the familiar as strange and the unexpected as inevitable. From 1968 to 1975, Foreman was most influenced by the alienation of Brecht and the poet Gertrude Stein's lyric use of language; in addition, like both, he has explored the genre of musical plays in six critically-acclaimed musical collaborations with Stanley Silverman.

In 1975, Foreman's work moved into a second phase, one which presents the play as a series of fragmented thoughts, capturing the 'buzz of consciousness'. Even though more frenzied, plays such as *The Cure* and *Film is Evil; Radio is Good* are less fatalistic, funnier, more playful. Although he originally directed productions of his own plays because no one else would take on the challenge, by 1980, Foreman had earned a reputation as an astute director for the New York stage and various American regional theatres. As a director, Foreman has developed techniques that allow him to supplement the effects sought by his plays. He sometimes uses untrained actors who speak flatly and without emotion as part of the visual/aural environment. Backdrops, small stages, strings, ropes, and other props divide the stage instantaneously, isolating specific words or incidents; sounds, lights, and other effects serve as similar framing devices; he has served as the designer for all of his own plays. Foreman stresses the importance of the visual unity in his productions, asserting that a particular strength of his work 'is the spacial manipulation of actors, scenery, and decor, and all the elements of the theatre choreographed in a given space'.

Try these:
Gertrude Stein's 1934 opera (with music by Virgil Thompson), *Four Saints in Three Acts* and the Brecht/Kurt Weill collaborations, *The Threepenny Opera* (1928), *Happy End* (1929), and *The Rise and Fall of Mahaganny* (1930).   ▷Heathcote Williams, ▷N.F. Simpson, ▷Snoo Wilson, ▷Beckett for other versions of fragmented consciousness; Peter Brook and Peter Stein for other singular, spatially-oriented directors.

FORNES, Maria Irene   [1930–]
American playwright, director and adaptor

Plays include:
The Widow (1961), *Tango Palace* (as *There! You Died*; 1963), *The Successful Life of Three: A Skit for Vaudeville* (1965), *Promenade* (1965), *A Vietnamese Wedding* (1967), *Dr. Kheal* (1968), *Molly's Dream* (1968), *Aurora* (1974), *Fefu and Her Friends* (1977), *Blood Wedding* (adapted from ▷Lorca; 1980), *The Danube* (1982), *Mud* (1983), *Sarita* (1984), *The Conduct of Life* (1985), *Cold Air* (adapted from Virgilio Pinera; 1985), *The Trial of Joan of Arc on a Matter of Faith* (1986), *The Mothers* (1986), *Abingdon Square* (1987), *And What of the Night?* (1990)

Fornes was born in Havana, Cuba, then emigrated to the United States and became an American citizen. An artist by training, she began writing plays while living with Susan Sontag in the early 1960s. She has become one of the most consistently innovative American playwrights, eager to work in a range of styles, and unintentionally has been viewed as part of the feminist theatre movement in the United States. During the 1960s, Fornes generally wrote one-act plays and music-theatre pieces that were farcical, solidly in the Absurdist tradition of Ionesco and Mrozek, yet expressed an ironic attitude about such American myths as economic success and true love. During the 1970s, and notably with *Fefu and Her Friends*, Fornes moved away from her comparatively light-hearted style and began to write plays that were often minimalist in their language and often conveyed what she perceives as the isolation and anguish experienced by women through the centuries. Fornes works in an elliptical style, structuring her plays in short, haunting scenes whose images often burn in the darkness long after each blackout. She actively seeks to inject the spontaneous into her creative process: her first play was composed of scenes each of whose first line came from a different page of a cookbook. *Fefu and Her Friends*, whose second act action takes place simultaneously in three different locations, was partly inspired by the loft-like theatre in which she workshopped the piece. The idea for *The Danube*, a romance between an English-language teacher and his pupil that takes place in post-World War II Hungary before moving into an unnamed post-apocalyptic future (it was commissioned as an anti-nuclear-weapons play by Theater for the New City), came from Fornes' discovery of a recording of Hungarian language lessons in a second-hand record store. And *Mud*, a dark, domestic triangle at whose centre is an entrapped and abused woman whose quest for freedom and escape is met with a bullet from her lover/husband, was completed after she came across a broom in a rummage store, and proceeded to make it a central prop (this play stirred many feminists to question Fornes' loyalties to the women's movement). One of her most terrifying plays, *The Conduct of Life*, is a brutal look at the moral, spiritual, and physical corruption attending the lives of a Latin American colonel (whose job is torturing prisoners) and his wife, who at first wilfully ignores her husband's occupation – as well as the young woman he's brought home as a concubine – although by the end of the play she knows enough to kill him (with a gun, of course, a prop Fornes frequently uses). She has won many Obie Awards for her work, including one for sustained achievement. She frequently directs and designs the first productions of her plays. She has been working on an opera *Terra Incognita*, a commission for the quincentenary of Columbus' arrival in North America.

Fefu and Her Friends

Fefu and Her Friends is a mood play that captures both the insecurities and the aggressions of a group of eight women. Set in America during the 1930s, it is nonetheless rooted emotionally in the 1970s, for it explores the position of women on the edge of self-definition. The economy of the language lends the script both a lyricism and a sense of mystery. The women in the play seem to communicate with each other through nuance and implication, as though operating in a private world that only they comprehend. Fornes

tries to bring the audience into that world by requiring spectators to walk into the spaces that the characters inhabit, while scenes are being performed (the audience is to be divided into groups, and scenes are to be repeated until each group has participated). This breaking of theatrical convention, as well as the poetic nature of the script, drew praise for the play and for Fornes, who directed it.

Try these:
▷Caryl Churchill, ▷Susan Glaspell, ▷Deborah Levy for innovative work centred on women; ▷Frank Xaver Kroetz for dark, somber plays written in short blackout scenes; ▷Arthur Miller for questioning the American dream; ▷Hispanic-American Theatre; *Hedda Gabler* for a famous character with a gun; ▷Women in theatre; Marguerite Duras for a dramatist who shares something of Fornes' concerns with language, mystery and a poetic lyricism describing women's experience, if not her minimalism.

FRAYN, Michael   [1933–]

British dramatist, novelist, journalist and translator

Plays include:
The Two of Us (comprising *Black and Silver*, *The New Quixote*, *Mr Foot*, *Chinamen*; 1970), *The Sandboy* (1971), *Alphabetical Order* (1975), *Donkey's Years* (1976), *Clouds* (1976), *Balmoral* (1978; retitled *Liberty Hall*), *Make and Break* (1980), *Noises Off* (1982), *Benefactors* (1984), *Look Look* (1990)

Born in the London suburbs, Frayn co-scripted the 1957 Cambridge University Footlights revue 'Zounds', on graduating worked for *The Guardian*, and *The Observer* until 1968, a period during which he wrote four of his novels. He also wrote award-winning articles on Cuba. *Clouds* is about the experience of journalists in Cuba.

Frayn's plays are often comic, but the comedy is very edgy and sometimes even, as in *Noises Off*, manic. Many of them explore behaviour within the constraints and frames of institutions; *Alphabetical Order* is set in the library of a provincial newspaper, *Donkey's Years* at an Oxford college reunion, *Make and Break* is about a businessman's experience of an international trade fair. His film script for *Clockwise* (1986) is about the host of trials and tribulations that thwart the journey of a headmaster (played by John Cleese) to a conference.

In a television interview, Frayn acknowledged that the tragi-comedy of his plays was something that he associated with ▷Chekhov, and in recent years, he has proved himself a sensitive and intelligent translator of Chekhov. Of *Three Sisters* he has said: 'It is about the irony of hopes . . . the way life mocks them', a sentiment that applies to his own work too, particularly perhaps to *Look Look* (1990), an attempt to revisit the territory of *Noises Off* which simply didn't work.

Noises Off

Of all Frayn's work, *Noises Off* has been the most successful. It is at one level an extraordinarily well-crafted farce, at another, a play about the hopes and frustrations of a group of actors as they tour the provinces with the farce, 'Nothing On'. 'Nothing On' is a play-within-a-play, complete with a programme that lists the cast biographies of the characters. The first act opens on a traditional farce set, inhabited by the stock character of a cleaning woman, although this is soon interrupted by the interventions of a director, and the cleaning lady emerges as an actress rehearsing for the first night of the farce. The second act turns the set around, and the audience is confronted with the backstage events during a performance of 'Nothing On'. In the third act, the backstage relationships between the actors, stage management and director, after long months of touring, invade the performance of the play to chaotic effect. *Noises Off* is a brilliant parody of a particular kind of farce, of certain kinds of actors, and of theatrical conventions.

Try these:

▷Ray Cooney and Brian Rix, whose farces provide the bones of the play-within-the-play of *Noises Off*; ▷Chekhov and ▷Anouilh, whom Frayn has adapted and translated, and with whom he clearly feels an affinity; ▷Feydeau is *the* classic French farceur; ▷Tom Stoppard and ▷Alan Ayckbourn, like Frayn, use the conventions of farce innovatively.

FREISTADT, Berta   [1942–   ]
British dramatist

Plays include:
Chicken Licken (1981), *Keely's Mother* (1981), *Poor Silly Bad* (1982), *The Burning Time* (1983), *Woman with a Shovel* (1983), *A Fine Undertaking* (1984), *The Life and Death of Laura Normill* (1986)

Writing since the age of ten, Freistadt has worked in the theatre as an actor, teacher, director as well as playwright. Her plays take up where many leave off and challenge the most comfortable and established ideas from a feminist, often lesbian feminist, perspective, with a dark, surreal sense of humour that frequently mixes absurdism with realism and is not afraid of the grotesque make her point.

Her targets have ranged from the domestic to the grave: chauvinist fathers who stick their daughters into hen coops because they want sons (*Chicken Licken*); possessive mothers who brandish six foot knives and forks over their daughters because they want to eat them (*Keely's Mother*); echoes of Evelyn Waugh's *The Loved One* in a lesbian farce set in a funeral parlour in *A Fine Undertaking*. If male domination and independence from mothers are key themes in her earlier plays, they crop up again in two of her most provocative pieces. *Woman with a Shovel* is a highly dramatic monologue that culminates in a woman turning her pent-up wrath on men with unusual violence. As performed by Maggie Ford its spine-chilling ending is all the more shocking for its slow, unassuming build-up. *Poor Silly Bad*, on the other hand, is a funny, sensitive portrayal of three women, and particularly of an old woman, Dot, living alone and trying to preserve some degree of dignity and choice in her own death. Set alongside her growing relationship with a young woman rebel, it is one of the few plays in recent years to try to make a generational bridge between young and old.

Freistadt has also looked beyond the present: in the post-Holocaust *The Burning Time* she renews the domestic theme (quoting Engels about the modern family being based on slavery) and makes a plea to change the old systems of domination, a stance given a rather more humorous twist in *The Life and Death of Laura Normill*, where a lesbian is waiting at the Pearly Gates to see whether Himself or Satan (a woman of course) will claim her for their own!

Try these:

▷Franca Rame's collection of monologues, *Female Parts*, also details female domestic and sexual oppressions; ▷Tasha Fairbank's *Curfew*, like *The Burning Time* engages with a separatist culture; Americans ▷Susan Yankowitz ▷Roslyn Drexler and Adrienne Kennedy have also used grotesque and sometimes violent images to put over feminist ideas; ▷Joe Orton for similar macabre and outrageous humour; Peggy Shaw's and Lois Weaver's Split Britches' *Dress Suits To Hire* is an equally provocative treatment of male domination; for contrasting images of a woman wreaking revenge, Marlane Meyer's *Etta Jenks* and ▷Durrenmatt's *The Visit*; ▷Wendy Kesselman's *I Love You, I Love You Not*, ▷Charlotte Keatley's *My Mother Said I Never Should*, ▷Sharman MacDonald's *All Things Nice* all explore young and old through a grandmother/granddaughter relationship; ▷Barrie Keefe's *Not Fade Away* has an independent-minded old pensioner at its centre.

FRIEL, Brian   [1929–   ]
Northern Irish dramatist

Plays include:
This Doubtful Paradise (1959), *The Enemy Within* (1962), *Philadelphia, Here I Come!* (1965), *The Loves of Cass McGuire* (1967), *Lovers* (1968), *Crystal and Fox* (1970), *The Gentle Island* (1971), *Freedom of the City* (1973), *Volunteers* (1975), *Living Quarters* (1977), *Aristocrats* (1979), *Faith Healer* (1979), *Translations* (1981), *Three Sisters* (from ▷Chekhov; 1981), *The Communication Cord* (1982), *Fathers and Sons* (from ▷Turgenev; 1987), *Making History* (1988), *Dancing at Lughansa* (1990)

Friel, born in Derry, is probably both the best-known and the best contemporary Irish dramatist. His work is naturally much preoccupied with the current political situation in Ireland in the broadest terms, particularly with the pressures that contribute to the intractability of that situation, the difficulty of rational responses to the legacy of hundreds of years of hostility and mistrust, communities divided by religion and language and the search for a way out of the impasse. There is a strong emphasis on the theme of exile which reflects one traditional escape route from the economic and political ills of Ireland; in *Philadelphia, Here I Come!* the escape is to America, in *The Gentle Island* it is to Glasgow. The renewed violence and gradual breakdown of the political situation after 1968 is reflected in such plays as *The Freedom of the City* and *The Volunteers* which deal directly with aspects of 'the Troubles', but Friel is also concerned with the wider problems of communication and identity. He may not be a particularly daring dramatist in terms of formal experimentation but he makes effective use of splitting a character into public and private selves in *Philadelphia* and of the contrast between the judicial inquiry which 'establishes' that the civil rights marchers were terrorists in *The Freedom of the City* and their innocent behaviour in the flashbacks that show what led up to their deaths. In *The Faith Healer* three characters speak four forty-minute monologues in a hauntingly written multi-viewpoint drama which again draws on the themes of exile and return and the pains of both.

Translations

Translations, the first play staged by ▷Field Day, the company Friel co-founded with the actor Stephen Rea, is a very fine parable of the current situation in Northern Ireland which also teases out some of its cultural roots. The play is set in 1830s Donegal, in a world where tramps can read Homer in the original but not ▷Shakespeare, a world doomed to vanish under the assault of state education (in English) and the Royal Engineers' Survey of Ireland. Earnest English subalterns and unhappy Irishmen try to produce English equivalents of Irish placenames in an act of cultural appropriation which remakes Ireland in the image of England. The English Lieutenant Yolland and the Irish woman Maire (who have no common language at all) fall in love, but the barriers of others' suspicion are too great for them to surmount and the play ends in muddle, confusion and destruction. Although the issues are serious and the allegorical applications clear, Friel handles events with a light touch and there is much gentle comedy at the expense of the two lovers failing to communicate – they both actually speak English in the play but neither understands the other – and at the expense of linguistic failures in general.

Try these:

For images of rural Irish life see Synge, particularly *Playboy of the Western World* for parallels with *The Gentle Island*; ▷Sean O'Casey is the great dramatist of an earlier period of political strife in Ireland; among contemporary dramatists writing about Ireland are ▷Christina Reid, ▷Seamus Finnegan, ▷Stewart Parker, ▷Bill Morrison; ▷Marie Jones; Seamus Heaney; Allan Cubitt's *Winter Darkness* also has language as one of its main concerns; other notable plays with tribunal settings are ▷Brecht's *The Measures Taken*, ▷John Osborne's *Inadmissable Evidence* and ▷David Edgar's *Our Own People*; Robert Patrick's *Kennedy's Children* intercuts monologues in a powerful re-creation of the mood of 1960s USA; ▷Harold Pinter's *Old Times* deals with differing recollections of events in ways reminiscent of *The Faith Healer*; ▷Peter Nichols' *Passion Play* is a memorable example of the use of two actors to play the public and personal faces of one character; for another variation on the theme of colonialism, ▷Derek Walcott's *Pantomime*.

FRISCH, Max   [1911–1991]
Swiss dramatist and novelist

Plays include:
Now You Can Sing (1946), *Santa Cruz* (1947), *The Great Wall of China* (1947; revised 1955), *When the War was Over* (1949), *Oederland* (1951; revised 1961), *The Fire Raisers* (USA, *The Firebugs*; 1958), *The Fury of Philip Hotz* (1958), *Andorra* (1961), *Don Juan, or The Love of Geometry* (1962)

Born in Zurich, Frisch did not complete his doctoral studies in philosophy because of lack of money, and took up journalism. He went back to university to study as an architect, and produced his first building and his first novel in 1943. He worked simultaneously as a writer and an architect for ten years but then went to live in Rome as a full-time writer. Frisch was an influential figure in bringing new European drama and its ideas to a British theatre that was dominated by the social realism of 'The Angry Young Men'. Edna O'Brien has described him as a 'European brain that is as witty as it is adult'.

The Fire Raisers

This is a key text for the Theatre of the Absurd, and the most 'absurdist' of Frisch's plays. Its performance at the Royal Court in 1961 was central to the British awareness of new forms of European and non-realist drama. A dark comedy and a cautionary tale, the play is subtitled (with a nod at ▷Brecht) 'A didactic play without a moral'. Throughout the play a chorus of firefighters acts to extend the individual history of Biedermann to a wider political allegory. Biedermann, the central figure of the play is a Bourgeois (the translation of his German name), who constantly protests his status as 'a good citizen'. Two strangers appear in his house and lodge in the attic, without any protest from Biedermann, where they prepare to raise a fire. The play has an afterpiece in which the devil appears; Biedermann is still protesting his innocence and good citizenship in the face of hell fire. It becomes clear that the fire, and Biedermann's lack of resistance, is a parable for the way in which 'good citizens' can collude with the forces of tyranny. It thus refers to the position of those intellectuals in Germany who did nothing to resist the rise of fascism, but also to any political context in which 'good citizens' refuse to question.

Try these:

Sartre's *The Condemned of Altona*, ▷Genet's *The Blacks*, and *The Fire Raisers* all had their first London productions in 1961, and were significant in bringing an awareness of European theatre to Britain; ▷Ionesco and ▷Beckett were the other main figures in the so-called 'theatre of the absurd'; C.P. Taylor's *Good* is another treatment of the contribution of 'good citizens' to the rise of fascism; Adrian Mitchell's deservedly much-acclaimed adaptation of *The Pied Piper*, a highly effective utopian allegory, poses more fascinating questions about 'good citizenry'.

FRY, Christopher   [1907–]
British dramatist and director

Plays include:
The Boy with a Cart: Cushman, Saint of Sussex (1938), *A Phoenix Too Frequent* (1946), *The Firstborn* (1948), *The Lady's Not for Burning* (1948), *Thor, With Angels*

Bríd Brennan and Robert Gwilym in the award-winning production of Brian Friel's *Dancing at Lughnasa* (Royal National Theatre and West End 1990/91)

(1948), *Venus Observed* (1950), *A Sleep of Prisoners* (1951), *The Dark Is Light Enough: A Winter Comedy* (1954), *Curtmantle* (1961), *A Yard of Sun: A Summer Comedy* (1970)

Fry's early writing included revue material, lyrics and pageants. He is a Quaker, whose compassion is reflected in all his work – several plays use biblical material or religious and ethical conflicts and he wrote the screenplays for a number of movie bible-epics. He uses words like a skater giving dazzling displays of speed and balance, and his witty verbal dexterity is something you either love or loathe. His plotting is not very strong, but neither is it important. He has written that 'progress is the growth of vision: the increased perception of what makes for life and what makes for death. I have tried, not always successfully, to find a way for comedy to say something of this, since comedy is an essential part of man's understanding.'

Fry's first success came with the one-act play *A Phoenix too Frequent*, a retelling of Petronius' story of the widow of Ephesus, with the addition of the idea that being useful after death is a kind of resurrection. Fame came with *The Lady's Not for Burning*, especially its second production with John Gielgud (1949), although few people, including the director, seemed to respond to the dark undercurrent of bitterness and war-weary disenchantment that permeates the play below its springtime charm. The later seasonal pieces more clearly show their sombre colours through the surface glitter. His most direct statement is *A Sleep of Prisoners* in which four soldiers, prisoners in a church, each dream the others into enactments of Old Testament conflicts.

Try these:
▷John Whiting for the same combination of verbal skill and comedy with a deep undercurrent; ▷T. S. Eliot and ▷Anouilh are among other dramatists handling the Becket-Henry II theme of *Curtmantle*; Ronald Duncan (who shared the Mercury season), Maxwell Anderson, ▷W.H. Auden for other verse drama; ▷James Bridie for religious drama; ▷Barry Collins' *Judgement* for contrasting prison setting with soldiers; ▷Adaptations and Adapters.

FUGARD, Athol   [1932–]
South African dramatist

Plays include:
No Good Friday (1959), *Nongogo* (1960), *Blood Knot* (1961), *People Are Living There* (1968), *Hello and Goodbye* (1965), *Boesman and Lena* (1969), *Statements After an Arrest Under the Immorality Act* (1972), *Sizwe Bansi is Dead* and *The Island* (with John Kani and Winston Ntshona, 1973), *Dimetos* (1975), *A Lesson from Aloes* (1978), 'Master Harold' . . . and the Boys (1982), *The Road to Mecca* (1984), *A Place with the Pigs* (1987), *My Children! My Africa* (1989)

The leading South African playwright of his generation, Athol Fugard has been a major influence in creating an understanding of the black and the 'coloured' person's situations in South Africa. He is to drama what writers like Alan Paton and Nadine Gordimer are to fiction and essays – clear-eyed white chroniclers of apartheid and its ills, who remain bound in what is, to co-opt the title of a Fugard play, a tortured and complex 'blood knot' with a homeland they both love and hate.

Born to an Irish father and a Dutch mother, Fugard began his reputation with the 1961 play *Blood Knot*, which was first performed secretly in a Johannesburg attic because of its mixed-race cast, and which was staged twenty-five years later much more publicly in an acclaimed 'anniversary revival' on Broadway, with Fugard and his original co-star, Zakes Mokae. Interested in dramatically distilled situations, often with very few characters, Fugard has been linked with a writer he expressly admires – ▷Samuel Beckett – particularly because of *Boesman and Lena*, a play about two coloured outcasts inhabiting a plaintive Beckettian void. After collaborations with the black actors John Kani and Winston Ntshona, Fugard reached into his childhood to write the piercingly autobiographical 'Master Harold' . . . and the Boys, and into real-life situations, either experienced first-hand or read about in the newspapers, to write *The Road to Mecca* and *A Place with the Pigs* (suggested by a report of a Red Army deserter who hid in a pigsty for over forty years). If his writing is marred by anything it is an excessive fondness for metaphors which are sometimes used gracefully – the ballroom dancing in 'Master Harold', the detritus in *Hello and Goodbye* – and often overemphatically – the resilient aloes plant in *A Lesson from Aloes*, the 'pigsty' of Pavel's soul in *A Place with the Pigs*. Still, at his best, Fugard's overwhelming humanity redeems everything. You may quarrel with individual moments from his plays, indeed with individual plays, but the strength of the playwright's searching and generous vision ultimately silences all argument.

Boesman and Lena

The most Beckettian of Fugard's plays and – like most of his works, few of which have more than three characters – an intimate, small-scale piece on vast themes. Two abject castaway 'coloureds' make their way across the mud flats of South Africa's River Swartkops, in what the playwright calls in his notebooks 'a poem of destruction'. They are a comical and pitiable pair – the talkative fidget, Lena, chattering into the void in an effort to stave off madness, and her brutalising Boesman. An elderly, near-mute black, Outa, appears at the campsite, but the emphasis is on the title characters – two living embodiments of 'white man's rubbish', who like ▷Beckett's tramps, are bound ever more closely through their mutual teasing and torment.

'Master Harold' . . . and the Boys

In a Port Elizabeth tea room one rainy afternoon, a young boy commits a reprehensible act which will haunt him the rest of his life. Such is the bare-bones background to Fugard's most intensely autobiographical play, whose 1982 world premiere at New Haven's Yale Repertory Theater remains the high point of a fruitful and happy relationship between Fugard and the venue. Fugard wrote the play to honour his childhood servant, Sam Semela, whom the young Fugard once cruelly humiliated as Hally does in the play; as an act of atonement, it's a piercingly magnanimous gesture. As an act of playwriting, the work has a devastating simplicity and force which pull you through its ninety minutes (without interval) from a beginning steeped in good cheer and high spirits to a conclusion that leaves you stunned. As Hally turns on the two black servants, Sam and Willie, whom he has loved as surrogates for the alcoholic father he loathes, Fugard shows the sources of racism in self-loathing, in an inward despair so profound it can only lash out and wound. A shapely and graceful piece of writing, the play makes a restorative theatrical experience out of spiritual depletion.

Try these:
Market Theatre of Johannesburg and Barney Simon as the initiators of multiracial and anti-apartheid plays; for other treatments of apartheid by South Africans ▷Nicholas Wright ▷Ronald Harwood, ▷David Lan, Michael Picardie, Yana Stajno's *Salt River*, and Peter Speyer's *Old Year's Eve*; ▷David Edgar's *The Jail Diary of Albie Sachs*; ▷Michael Abbensetts, ▷Mustapha Matura, ▷Edgar White and ▷Derek Walcott for treatments of racism in Britain; *Poppie Nongena* (from the Market Theatre), Vusisizwe Players' *You Strike the Woman You Strike the Rock*, Upstairs Theatre Company, Durban's *You Can't Stop The Revolution*; ▷Tina Howe, ▷Neil Simon and ▷Hugh Leonard for the formation of the artist; ▷Tennessee Williams for a similar use of metaphor; Mfundi Vundla's *A Visitor to the Veldt* and ▷August Wilson's *Joe Turner's Come and Gone* for forging a link between black America and black South Africa.

FULLER, Charles   [1939–   ]
American playwright

Plays include:
The Village: A Party (1968; 1969, as *The Perfect Party*), *In My Many Names and Days* (1972), *Candidate* (1974), *In the Deepest Part of Sleep* (1974), *The Lay Out Letter* (1975), *The Brownsville Raid* (1976), *Sparrow in Flight* (1978), *Zooman and the Sign* (1980), *A Soldier's Play* (1981), *Sally* (1988), *Burner's Frolic* (1990)

Fuller confronts the nature of a society that he perceives as basically rascist, and he explores the experience of black people struggling to survive in that climate. The world of Fuller's plays is inevitably violent, since its figures often gravitate toward destructiveness in order to claim their rightful place in America. Frequently, as in *Zooman and the Sign* and *A Soldier's Play*, this racist-engendered violence ends up pitting black people against each other, in what Fuller dramatizes as the tragic outcome of a morally chaotic world.

A Soldier's Play
A Soldier's Play is a forceful indictment of America's racist attitudes and social structures. As in many of Fuller's dramas, white America is the fundamental cause of this

racism, but it is the black's self-hatred, learned at the hands of whites, that ultimately poisons the black person's existence. One of the more complex of Fuller's scripts structurally, it is also one of his most sophisticated in terms of the many points of view that he dramatizes. His central character, the black sergeant Waters who heads one of the few all-Negro units waiting to ship out during World War II, is both hateful and pitiable. Filled with contempt for his own blackness, he loses any sense of moral balance, and in the process destroys what he set out to preserve. *A Soldier's Play* won the 1982 Pulitzer Prize for Drama.

Try these:
▷African-American Theatre; ▷Black Theatre in Britain; ▷Hanif Kureishi.

g

GALATI, Frank [1943–]
American director and adaptor

Plays include:
Winnebago (1974), *Heart of a Dog* (1985, from Bulgakov), *She Always Said No, Pablo* (1987, conceived by Galati, with words by Gertrude Stein), *A Flea in Her Ear* (1988, from Feydeau), *The Grapes of Wrath* (1988, from Steinbeck)

Galati has combined an academic career with a career as director and playwright in the professional theatre. A professor of performance studies at Northwestern University in Evanston, Illinois, he has also directed at such local regional theatres as Body Politic, Wisdom Bridge, Steppenwolf, where he became a member in 1985, and the Goodman, where he is an associate director. His academic background leads him to classics of world literature, into which he is able to infuse new theatrical life. He is particularly adept at shaping novels into performable scripts, as with *Heart of a Dog* and *The Grapes of Wrath*, both of which retain the philosophical and emotional essences of the original.

The Grapes of Wrath
The Grapes of Wrath conveys the scope of the Steinbeck novel, largely because Galati preserves the book's episodic structure and forward-moving action, its many characters and incidents. In addition, Galati constructs his script so that, as in the novel, Ma Joad is the emotional centre of the story, a choice that not only lends unity to Galati's play but also communicates Steinbeck's vision of Ma Joad as a symbol of never-ending struggle for existence. Practically all the lines in *The Grapes of Wrath* are taken from the novel, although, in Brechtian fashion, Galati incorporates songs which the characters swing to the audience from time to time. The original production was designed for a large proscenium stage; the one prop or set piece was the Joads' overburdened truck, which could be moved around the stage and gradually took on an emotional resonance of its own, much like Courage's wagon in *Mother Courage and Her Children*. *The Grapes of Wrath* won the 1990 Tony Award for Best Play.

Try these:
▷Brecht for parallels; ▷Adaptations and adapters; ▷David Edgar.

GALLAGHER, Mary [1947–]
American playwright

Plays include:
Little Bird (1977), *Father Dreams* (1978), *Chocolate Cake* (1980), *Dog Eat Dog* (1983), *How To Say Goodbye* (1986), *Love Minus* (1988), *De Donde?* (1990)

Gallagher chronicles the initimate relationships of unhappy people who see themselves as outcasts from society. Her characters are usually middle-class and well educated, yet for reasons they cannot understand, they are unable to acquire even the basic accoutrements of the 'good life': a lover, marriage, a job, children. In the end, however, the characters usually attain some degree of knowledge about themselves and often find a measure of happiness. Although Gallagher often adopts an episodic structure in her plays, her style tends to be realistic, her characters recognisable, and their conversation that of day-to-day living. On occasion, she has diverged from this style to write plays such as *Dog Eat Dog*, a satire in which the American capitalist system disintegrates, or *De Donde?*, an agitprop dramatisation of illegal Mexican immigration into the United States.

How To Say Goodbye

Although *How To Say Goodbye* often lapses into sentimentality, it is a carefully detailed picture of a marriage that falls apart when the couple's only child becomes terminally ill. Once again, Gallagher portrays characters who believe that there is no place for them in the American mainstream, although, as so often in Gallagher's scripts, she rewards these characters by giving them more moral courage than their superficially successful counterparts. *How To Say Goodbye* was co-winner of the 1987 Susan Smith Blackburn Prize.

Try these:

▷Tom Kempinski's *Duet For One* for the impact of illness; ▷David Hare for anatomies of discontent; ▷Peter Nichols' *A Day in the Death of Joe Egg* and Lucy Gannon's *Keeping Tom Nice* for families with children with disabilities.

The old Chairman of the Board and the strike leader both suffer from the long strike, and are both repudiated when agreement is reached on the same terms as were offered at the start. Galsworthy meant the play not to take sides, and the cases for capital and labour are both strongly made, but his anti-extremist conclusions are too obviously underlined.

Try these:

▷Ibsen for well-crafted plays with a 'social message'; ▷Shaw and ▷Granville Barker for similar concerns, but more experimental approaches with character-drawing; for other plays about strikes, Peter Cox's *The Garden of England*, *About Face* by Cordelia Dutton and Maggie Ford, Stephen Wakelam's *Deadlines* and ▷David Edgar's *That Summer*, all responses to the miners' strike of 1984; ▷Clifford Odet's *Waiting for Lefty*.

GALSWORTHY, John   [1867–1933]
British novelist and dramatist

Plays include:
The Silver Box (1906), *Strife* (1909), *Justice* (1910), *The Skin Game* (1920), *Loyalties* (1922), *Escape* (1926), *Exiled* (1929)

Galsworthy practised for a time as a barrister, but then set out methodically to learn to write fiction; after ten years' hard work he hit the jackpot with *A Man of Property* (1906). By contrast his first play *The Silver Box*, written for the Court Theatre, was an immediate success, though it now seems an over-schematic treatment of the theme of 'one law for the rich and another for the poor'. He wrote twenty-six more plays, many of which did well; they tend to be well-made sub-Ibsen problem plays, with mild social criticism, not-too-stereotypical characters, a strong narrative line, a touch of melodrama, and upper-middle class settings; but only a few now hold the stage.

Justice, which Galsworthy meant as a demonstration that society tends to destroy its weaker members, is unusual in having had a direct effect on the law – the silent scene with the prisoner in solitary confinement seems to have persuaded Winston Churchill that the practice should be reformed forthwith. *Strife* is an over-symmetrical but well crafted strike play that carries a powerful punch on stage.

GANNON, Lucy   [1948–]

Plays include:
Keeping Tom Nice (1987), *Janet and John* (1988), *Wicked Old Nellie* (1987), *Raping the Gold* (1988), *A Dog Barking* (1988), *Dancing Attendance* (1990)

Lucy Gannon only began to write seriously in her late thirties, having worked as a residential social worker. In five years she achieved almost whirlwind success and established herself as one of the major voices in womens' playwriting with awards being heaped upon her for almost every play written. Her plays often reflect her former occupation, concerned as they are with the elderly, the handicapped and the socially disadvantaged. *Keeping Tom Nice*, her first play, about a family's attitude towards their severely handicapped son, won the Richard Burton Award and was presented by the RSC at the Almeida Theatre, establishing her as a new talent. The play went on to win two further prestigious awards: the Susan Smith Blackburn Prize and the John Whiting Award. Her play, *Wicked Old Nellie*, had a production at the Derby Playhouse but generally her work has been embraced by the London Fringe, most notably The Bush Theatre, where she was writer-in-residence. Accusations levelled against Lucy Gannon are that she is too simplistic in

The Steppenwolf Theatre production of Steinbeck's *The Grapes of Wrath*, adapted by Frank Galati, 1988

her attitudes, that she wears her left-wing, anti-Thatcherite politics on her sleeve which in consequence gives her plays a one-note quality. However, they are popular with audiences and prize-giving bodies alike and represent a powerful voice of the late 1980s. She has also written two plays for television: *Testimony of a Child* (1989) and *Soldier, Soldier* (1991).

Try these:
▷Peter Nichols' *A Day in the life of Joe Egg* for an earlier play about bringing up a handicapped child, also ▷Julia Kearsley's *Wednesday*; Kearsley's *Under the Web* dealt like Gannon's *Raping the Gold* with some of the strains of looking after an aged parent; ▷Marie Jones *The Hamster Wheel* for Charabanc, and ▷Jean-Claude van Itallie's *The Traveller* dealt with post-stroke traumas; ▷Gregory Motton, ▷David Spencer for contemporary chronicles of the disadvantaged; ▷Robin Glendinning's *Danny Boy* also deals with the relationship between a mother and her brain-damaged son, in the context of Northern Ireland.

Father, premiered at Seattle Rep., traces a New York Jewish immigrant family from 1930s to 1970s, exploring the tensions caused by the father's desire to be assimilated into American society.

I'm Not Rappaport

I'm Not Rappaport is a moving, if sometimes sentimental, comedy that depicts both the desperation and the fesitiness of two elderly men, one black and one white, who become friends after meeting on a park bench. The cliché of this premise was overcome in the original production through sensitive performances of Cleavon Little as the nearly blind building superintendent, and Judd Hirsch as the former Jewish waiter with the soul of a political agitator. *I'm Not Rappaport* won the 1986 Tony Award for Best Play.

Try these:
▷Neil Simon for New York humour; ▷Alfred Uhry's *Driving Miss Daisy* for ageing across the racial divide; ▷Edward Albee's *Zoo Story* for a different use of a park bench.

GARDNER, Herb   [1934–   ]
American playwright

Plays include:
A Thousand Clowns (1962), *The Goodbye People* (1968), *Thieves* (1974), *Love and/or Death* (1979), *I'm Not Rappaport* (1984), *Conversations with My Father* (1991)

Gardner has acquired a reputation for writing commercially successful comedies that at the same time reveal the potential for sadness in contemporary life. Gardner's characters are usually social misfits, rejected by the mainstream either because they rebel against middle-class conventions or because, as in the case of the elderly men in *The Goodbye People* and *I'm Not Rappaport*, the world appears to have no use for them anymore. Inevitably however, these characters overcome the disapproval of the world around them, usually by finding other nonconformists with whom they can share a belief in the joy of living. Stylistically, Gardner employs both the long monologue and the one-liner, and his plays are flavoured with a particularly New York brand of humour. *Conversations with My*

GARRICK, David   [1717–1779]
British actor-manager and dramatist

Plays include:
Miss in her Teens (1747), *The Clandestine Marriage* (with George Colman the Elder; 1766), *The Irish Widow* (1772), *Bon Ton; or, High Lift Above Stairs* (1775)

Garrick may have been the greatest actor-manager in the history of the British stage, but as a dramatist he was no more than a very competent hack. Beside a number of farces, he collaborated with George Colman the Elder on *The Clandestine Marriage*, which is revived from time to time. It is an amiable farcical comedy with a reliably well-worn plot, involving a new-rich bourgeois trying to buy his two daughters into marriages with the minor aristocracy. The fun arises because the younger daughter is already secretly married to her father's clerk and is also fancied by both the aged and lecherous Lord Ogleby (the best part in the play) and his son; the satirical possibilities of this marriage market are on the whole fudged, and of course all are reconciled at the end.

Try these:
▷Sheridan, ▷Goldsmith for more original eighteenth-century comedies; ▷Aphra Behn, ▷Congreve, ▷Etherege, ▷Jonson, ▷Wycherley for earlier treatments of this theme.

GATTI, Armand   [1924–]
Italian director, dramatist and film-maker

Plays include:
La Deuxième Existence du Camp de Tatenberg (*The Second Existence of the Tatenberg Camp*; 1962), *La Vie Imaginaire de l'Eboueur Auguste Geai* (*The Imaginary Life of the Streetsweeper August Geai*; 1962), *Chant Public Devant Deux Chaises Electriques* (*Public Song in Front of Two Electric Chairs*; 1966), *V as in Vietnam*; 1967), *La Passion du Général Franco* (*The Passion of General Franco*; banned until 1976)

Gatti was born into a poor immigrant family in Monaco, and spent part of World War II in a German labour camp. The concentration-camp theme recurs in several of his plays. He is an engagingly optimistic and energetic character, who believes that theatre can truly change the world. He wrote a number of plays on political themes during the 1960s, influenced by ▷Adamov and ▷Planchon (and of course ▷Brecht), but often showing a fragmentation of character and of reality. For example, his semi-autobiographical play, *La Vie Imaginaire de l'Eboueur Auguste Geai*, shows his father at five different ages, played by five different actors (sometimes all on stage at once), and in seven possible different spaces on stage. These 1960s plays, on subjects such as the Chinese Civil War, the execution of Sacco and Vanzetti, and the Vietnam War, had considerable success all over France. However, Gatti gradually came to believe that the audience should participate in the production rather than merely consume it, and since the mid-seventies he and a troupe of faithful followers have devoted themselves to the production of community plays and films on politically sensitive themes and often in politically sensitive areas. He was invited to Londonderry by ▷John Arden in 1984, and his film *The Writing On the Wall* (*Nous Etions*

Tous des Noms d'Arbres; 1985) used Catholic teenagers to play Protestant characters and vice versa. Unlike ▷Ann Jellicoe, he deals with contemporary events, and aims to stir up the community rather than to reconcile it. His results are less artistically finished than hers, and he provokes more local hostility, but his activities seem to have no less of a liberating effect on the participants.

Try these:
▷Ann Jellicoe and, in the USA, Cornerstone Theatre for plays involving the community; ▷Brecht for his views on the ability of plays and role-playing to change lives (though Gatti styles himself an anarchist rather than a Marxist); see also ▷Community Theatre in Britain.

GAY, John   [1685–1732]
English poet and dramatist

Plays include:
The Beggar's Opera (1728), *Polly* (published; 1729)

A friend of Jonathan Swift and Alexander Pope, Gay wrote a number of comedies and the libretto to Handel's *Acis and Galatea* but is remembered largely for *The Beggar's Opera*, a send up of the eighteenth-century fashion for Italian opera and a satire on the Prime Minister Sir Robert Walpole and his administration. It takes a great number of popular songs and folk tunes, provides them with new words and sets them in a tale of thieves, whores and highwaymen, which, in turn, mirrors the corruption of contemporary society. Its first production achieved the then longest run on the London stage. The play's popularity continues but its satire is less personal now and it survives more for its lively action and memorable tunes. *Polly*, a sequel which carries heroine Polly Peachum to the West Indies, failed to pass the censorship imposed by Walpole and it was seven years before it could be staged. Gay lost most of his profits in South Sea Bubble speculation and died only four years after his great success.

Try these:
▷Brecht's *Threepenny Opera* reworked the story of *The Beggar's Opera*, adding a more consciously political polemic and re-

placing the songs with new biting lyrics to music by Kurt Weill; Sue Frumin's *Beggar's Opry* (1990) is a lesbian revision of Gay's play; ▷Nick Dear's *The Art of Success* presents Walpole's Licensing Act as an allegory for modern censorship; Frank Loesser's *Guys and Dolls* for a more sentimental musical approach to thieves and rascals; for satires on political corruption, see ▷Barrie Keeffe, ▷Mrozek, and for a blander attempt, John Wells' *Anyone for Dennis*.

GAY THEATRE IN BRITAIN

Openly gay theatre is perhaps a phenomenon of the last twenty years. Certainly, in the UK there have always been areas of theatre given to a degree of cross-sexual adventure, from ▷Shakespeare's female roles played by boys, to the uniquely British pantomime traditions of thigh-slapping Principal Boys played by women, and Ugly Sisters played by men, but it is only since the beginning of Gay Sweatshop in 1975 that homosexual love has been openly presented on the professional stage in Britain. Since then, there has been a steady increase that has shown gay theatre moving out from the underground circuit into the mainstream – at least in so far as gay *male* plays are concerned. Gay is here used in the generic sense, though strictly speaking these days, gay is usually taken to mean a reference to men, gay women nearly always being referred to as lesbian; for more on specifically ▷lesbian theatre, see separate entry.

Gay theatre has steadily grown since the decriminalisation of male homosexuality in 1967, and the influence of the Women's and Gay Liberation Movements. However, Gay Sweatshop's *Mister X* in 1975 could be said to have played a fairly influential role with a line that can be traced from the success of its first tour to the West End successes of ▷Harvey Fierstein's *Torch Song Trilogy*, ▷Larry Kramer's *The Normal Heart* etc. From the success of *Mister X* came a season of gay plays the following year at the ICA (see under ▷Noël Greig), followed by *As Time Goes By*, co-written by Griffiths and Greig – a seminal play which spawned *The Dear Love of Comrades*, and ▷Martin Sherman's *Bent*, which by its success in Britain, and on Broadway showed the audience demand for plays on gay subjects.

But whilst such plays about male homosexuals became acceptable (even as television fodder, both the soap-operas *Brookside* and *Eastenders* have seen fit to introduce credible homosexual characters), lesbians are notable by their absence on the main stage and television soaps, with one or two rare exceptions (▷Sarah Daniels' *Neaptide* is one of them; ▷Andrew Davies' *Prin*, from a very different political perspective, another).

There have been as many different styles and directions as there have been individuals, for one thing gay theatre has tried to show is that there is no one stereotype of a gay man or lesbian; nor any one mode of expressing it, be it agitprop, or 'coming out' exercises, examinations of social and political forces in the creation of sexual identity, investigations into lesbian custody, off-the-wall comedy, cultural debunking à la Donna & Kebab, stand-up comics such as Simon Fanshawe or the wilder shores of drag epitomised by Bloolips and in a different sense by ▷Neil Bartlett's glittering exposés. With the onset of AIDS, that too has obviously become a main focus of gay playwrights, though in the UK not exclusively so. Much of gay theatre takes place in the smaller fringe theatres, pub, club and college circuits, and the few lesbian and gay centres around the country. London's Lesbian and Gay Centre for the past couple of years has also played host to a fair range of entertainers and plays in its basement theatre. However, such activity and steady liberalisation of attitudes seems increasingly in jeopardy now, following. Section 28 of the Local Government Bill prohibiting local authorities from giving any financial aid to any activity seen to be promoting homosexuality. As the onus is all on the 'intention' of the local authority, and how that can be interpreted in law, the effect of the legislation has been to create widespread uncertainty. Gay Sweatshop has been in imminent danger of suspension from withdrawal of financial support (GS tour in many venues directly or indirectly funded by local authorities) as are YPT (Young People's Theatre) whose work may often deal with topics of sexuality. GS have, however, recently won recognition from The Arts Council in terms of a three-year grant award. The biggest danger, as voiced by many performers, playwrights and directors remains the more insidious self-censorship that has inevitably begun to creep in.

Try these:
▷Harvey Fierstein; ▷Noël Greig; ▷Lesbian Theatre; ▷Cabaret; ▷Larry Kramer, ▷Terence McNally, Robert Patrick ▷Martin Sherman, ▷Tony Kushner for American playwrights writing on gay issues; ▷Neil Bartlett, Philip Osment for British equivalents; ▷Michael Wilcox, ▷Peter Gill, ▷Michel Tremblay and ▷Lanford Wilson also write from a gay perspective, as do the 'comedy of manners' writers ▷Oscar Wilde, ▷Noël Coward, ▷Christopher Durang and ▷Joe Orton; see also ▷Genet and ▷Lindsay Kemp for elements of 'camp'.

GAY THEATRE IN THE USA

Gay theatre in the United States (that is, theatre that in some way depicts the lives of gay men; ▷lesbian theatre is dealt with in its own entry) is, with good reason, customarily dated from Mart Crowley's 1968 play *The Boys in the Band*. This sentimental and melodramatic comedy has its questionable aspects, particularly its association of homosexuality and self-hatred, but its vivid characters with their exuberant argot clearly brought a new kind of life to American dramatic writing. Its big commercial success permitted other writers to feature gay characters in mainstream plays. Ten years earlier, however, Joe Cino had launched his Caffe Cino, which soon became a real (if tiny) theatre, and an almost wholly gay one. Short plays by writers such as ▷Oscar Wilde, ▷Jean Genet and ▷Tennessee Williams (whom we now think of as the American theatre's greatest homosexual playwright) were put on, along with new work by young writers, including William M. Hoffman, H.M. Koutoukas, Robert Patrick, Doric Wilson and Lanford Wilson. Other important centres of the off-off-Broadway movement which galvanised the American theatre in the 1960s – Judson Poets' Theater, La Mama – also produced the work of these and many other gay artists.

In 1966 Ronald Tavel and John Vaccaro launched their Play-House of the Ridiculous. Charles Ludlam, a young actor who was in the first production, split off to form his own Ridiculous Theatrical Company in 1967. For the next twenty years his writing, directing and acting would sustain a theatre that was the quintessence of camp, a comic theatre some say without peer since the days of ▷Molière. Strong enough to survive Ludlam's death from AIDS in 1987, the Ridiculous is now headed by his long-time companion and fellow actor Everett Quinton. Ludlam's renowned, deeply moving performance as Camille was a superb example of drag theatre. Other drag artist–creators of the first rank include the late Ethyl (né James) Eichelberger, tall, gaunt, hilarious and fiercely affirmative, Charles Busch who has created a bevy of Hollywood-type harridans, and John Kelly, whose sweet face and beutiful falsetto enable him to present images of great purity.

The gay liberation movement, inspired by the Stonewall rebellion of 1969 – when patrons of a Greenwich Village gay bar reacted to an all-too-familiar police raid by taking to the streets in protest – has led to the formation of gay theatres in cities across the country. The Glines in New York (now defunct, though founder John Glines is still active) and San Francisco's Theatre Rhinoceros are perhaps the best known, but each plays a crucial social and political role in its community, whatever the merits of any given script generated by the group.

When *The Torch Song Trilogy* was named Broadway's best play in 1983, and its creator and star, ▷Harvey Fierstein, won the Tony for best actor, the universal appeal of some of the plays written by and for the gay community was confirmed. Made up of three one-acts originally staged at La Mama between 1978 and 1982, the 4½-hour piece, produced by The Glines, told the story of a drag queen (very like the author) who is determined to create his own family. The play overflows with wit, good spirits and sentiment, and the sultry-voiced Fierstein is a larger-than-life performer who radiates charisma and charm. Most found the trilogy irresistible. Fierstein went on to write the book of the long-running Broadway musical *La Cage aux Folles*, whose affirmation of the union of two aging homosexuals is most strongly expressed in co-creator Jerry Herman's already-classic pop anthem *I Am What I Am*.

While Harvey Fierstein's embodiments of gay pride and hope were running on Broadway, the shadow of AIDS was beginning to darken the work of other gay playwrights, and by the mid-eighties one could not talk about gay theatre without discussing AIDS plays. William M. Hoffman's *As Is* and ▷Larry Kramer's *The Normal Heart* both opened in New York in 1985, and are still the best-known plays on the subject. The touching central story of *As Is* – a man with AIDS and the ex-lover who takes care of him – is surrounded with vignettes of the cheerfully promiscuous life now gone forever, and scenes showing the difficulties everyone from family members to health professionals has in dealing with those who have the disease. The main character in *The Normal Heart* is a thinly disguised portrait of the author, one of the country's leading AIDS activists, who in the play depicts the founding of the Gay Men's Health Crisis and the organisation's struggle to make known what the rest of the world preferred not to see. Kramer is famous for his rage; in *The Normal Heart* his targets include *The New York Times*, then New York City Mayor Ed Koch, promiscuity and cowardice within the gay community. In this polemical context the scenes that reveal the love between the Kramer surrogate and his AIDS-stricken lover are especially powerful.

As Is and *The Normal Heart*, both staged around the world, are best seen as the very visible tip of a substantial iceberg. Several writers of significant AIDS plays are already dead, notably Alan Bowne and Robert Chesley. Other writers are known, at least within the theatre community, to have the disease, and many more are obviously writing out of grief at the death of loved ones. This often means that feeling overwhelms clear-sighted dramaturgy; it also means that even the most inept plays are likely to contain moments of emotional power and truth. Such well-known American playwrights as ▷Lanford Wilson, ▷Terrence McNally, ▷Jean-Claude van Itallie, ▷Harvey Fierstein, ▷Christopher Durang, ▷Harry Kondoleon and ▷A.R. Gurney have written plays with AIDS at the centre; the disease is a presence in everything from Broadway comedies (Richard Greenberg's *Eastern Standard*, ▷Wendy Wasserstein's *The Heidi Chronicles*) to the performance art of ▷Spalding Gray and ▷Karen Finley.

In his 1979 anthology *Gay Plays: The First Collection*, editor William M. Hoffman explained: 'I define a 'gay play' as one whose central figure or figures are homosexual, or one in which homosexuality is a main theme. A gay play is not necessarily written by a homosexual or for homosexuals.' It is increasingly true that many of the plays being written in the USA fit this definition, and that they are being staged in mainstream theatres. One reason for this is that virtually everyone in the theatre has been profoundly affected by AIDS; all sorts of playwrights and producers are driven to memorialise colleagues they have loved, and to confront homophobia in their society. Another is that a substantial number of America's most gifted younger playwrights are openly gay. Having experienced a degree of freedom and acceptance unknown to their predecessors, such writers as ▷Craig Lucas, ▷Tony Kushner and ▷David Greenspan are not part of a gay fringe, but rather are steadily making their way into the heart of their country's theatre. The expression of their sensibility is not always confined to 'gay plays'; their work is not often considered in a separate category. They simply write some of the most important dramatic literature of our time and place.

Try these:
▷Martin Sherman; ▷Gay theatre in Britain; ▷Lesbian theatre in Britain; ▷Lesbian theatre in the USA; ▷Noel Greig; ▷Drew Griffiths; ▷Joe Orton; ▷Oscar Wilde. Don Shewey's anthology *Out Front: Contemporary Gay & Lesbian Plays* (Grove Press, 1988); the theatrically sophisticated demonstrations of ACT-UP (AIDS Coalition To Unleash Power) are perhaps the most important gay theatre of our time in the USA.

GELBART, Larry   [1928–]
American playwright/lyricist/screenwriter

Plays include:
The Conquering Hero (1961), *A Funny Thing Happened on the Way to the Forum* (book with Burt Shevelove; 1962), *The Frogs* (book of musical adapted from Aristophanes; 1974); *Sly Fox* (adapted from ▷Ben Jonson; 1976), *Mastergate* (1989), *City of Angels* (book of the musical; 1989), *Power Failure* (1991)

Gelbart has garnered a reputation as one of the most consistently clever writers of comedy in theatre, film and television. (He has worked in television since 1952, notably as the originator, chief writer and co-producer of the award-winning series *M.A.S.H.*) His films and plays reveal a comic imagination that is at ease with a range of forms, from the satire of *Sly Fox*, an adaptation of ▷Ben Jonson's *Volpone* set in San Francisco during the 1800s, to the farce of *A Funny Thing Happened on the Way to the Forum*. He is as adept at creating oddball characters, as in the film *Tootsie*, as he is at writing the repartee for *City of Angels*. His last two plays, both produced originally at American Repertory Theater, are scathing satires of government ineptitude. *Mastergate* sends up the 'investigation' into the Iran-Contra Affair, while *Power Failure*, structured similarly to Schnitzler's *La Ronde*, satirises the abuse of power in the USA. Gelbart brings to his comedies both a realistic appreciation for the dark side of human nature and an ever-hopeful expectation that situations will resolve themselves happily.

City of Angels

The musical *City Angels* functions on several levels, for it is simultaneously a parody of the contemporary Hollywood film industry, a love letter to the Philip Marlowe/Sam Spade style of movie in the 1940s, and a writer's examination of his commitment to art. Structurally, *City of Angels* is a play within a play, and scenes alternate between the film script on which the central character, a writer, is working, and the real-life scenes involving the writer, his wife and the moguls of Hollywood (in the Broadway production, the film sequences were designed in 'black and white', the rest in 'colour'). The musical succeeds most creatively in the imagined film sequences, and Gelbart's sharp dialogue infuses the other half of the book with life. The script lapses into sentimentality, however, as the writer makes his choice between commercialism and high art. The highly theatrical Broadway production defused any problems in the script, which was praised as a hilarious lampoon of Hollywood and received the 1990 Tony Award for Best Musical.

Try these:
▷Kaufman's and Hart's *Once in a Lifetime*; Charles Wood's *Veterans*; ▷Christopher Hampton's *Tales From Hollywood* for plays about film-making.

GELBER, Jack   [1932–]
American dramatist

Plays include:
The Connection (1959), *The Apple* (1961), *Square in the Eye* (1965), *The Cuban Thing* (1968), *Sleep* (1972), *Barbary Shore* (1974), *Farmyard* (1975), *Jack Gelber's New Play: Rehearsal* (1976)

'I have no theory of the theatre to proclaim,' Jack Gelber once announced, but the Chicago-born playwright nonetheless remains associated with the breakdown of the fourth wall and a freer, looser theatrical style in keeping with the improvisatory off-Broadway climate in which he was spawned. Gelber got his start with New York's Living Theatre, who performed what remains his best-known work, *The Connection*, a piece about drug addiction featuring its own play-within-a-play. Celebrated both for its bold realism and its seeming formlessness, *The Connection* opened to general pans ('oh man! what junk!' cried one critic), but time has bolstered its reputation as a frontrunner of the drama of the dispossessed that ▷Miguel Pinero, ▷Sam Shepard and ▷Lanford Wilson (in *Balm in Gilead*) would go on to write. None of his later plays has garnered equal attention, although their subjects range from scientists in a sleep lab (*Sleep*) to an overtly theatrical piece about the nature of the theatre (*Jack Gelber's New Play: Rehearsal*) in which a play is cast, developed, and then cancelled. Since 1972, Gelber has been devoting the bulk of his energies to teaching as a Professor of English at Brooklyn College in New York City.

Try these:
▷Pirandello, ▷Sam Shepard for theatrical gamesmanship and plays about theatricality; ▷Lanford Wilson's *Balm in Gilead* for loose, improvisatory and powerful treatments of New York low-lifers in an all-night coffee shop; ▷Miguel Pinero's *Short Eyes*, ▷Nell Dunn's *The Little Heroine* and the documentary-like *The Concept* for plays about addicts, also Clean Break's *The River That Ran Away* by Rena Owen; ▷José Triana, ▷Howard Sackler's *Goodbye, Fidel* for Cuba-related works.

GEMS, Pam   [1925–   ]
British dramatist

Plays include:
Betty's Wonderful Christmas (1972), *My Warren & After Birthday* (1973), *The Amiable Courtship of Miz Venus & Wild Bill* (1973), *Sarah B Divine* (1973), *Piaf* (1973; not produced till 1978), *Go West Young Woman* (1974), *Dusa, Fish, Stas and Vi* (1975, originally called *Dead Fish*), *The Project* (1976; expanded and re-titled *Loving Women*; 1984), *Guinevere* (1976), *The Rivers and Forests* (1976; from Marguerite Duras), *My Name is Rosa Luxemburg* (1976), *Franz in April* (1977), *Queen Christina* (1977), *Ladybird, Ladybird* (1979), *Sandra* (1979), *Uncle Vanya* (1979; from ▷Chekhov), *A Doll's House* (1980; from Ibsen), *The Treat* (1982), *Aunt Mary* (1982), *Camille* (1984), *The Danton Affair* (1986; from Stanisława Przybyszewska)

Socialist realist, mother of four, Gems is one of the few women playwrights to span two generations. Rooted in a working-class consciousness with a racy, pungent turn of phrase, she did not, in fact, take up writing full-time till after forty, though she had written scripts for radio and television whilst also bringing up her children and had been involved with the early feminism of the 1970s. More than any other writer, she consistently explores the dilemmas and specificity of what it is to be female in a world still largely dominated by men. Her best known play *Piaf* (written in 1973, but not staged until 1978), which started out at the ▷RSC's studio theatre and ended up triumphant on Broadway, was a typically earthy – some called it rude – debunking of the myth surrounding the Little Sparrow. Piaf's battle to overcome the pressures of fame, alcohol and drugs is also the story, warts and all, of a gritty, working-class woman searching for economic and sexual independence – a treatment Gems served up also on *Camille*, which stripped Dumas's original of its sentimentality to show the high price of love in a money-regulated market. *Dusa, Fish, Stas and Vi*, the play that put Gems on the map, is a reiteration of these pressures, worked out through four young women of the 'post-pill' generation, a theme which consistently intrigued Gems, a pre- and war-time young mother. It is a pioneering work in its depiction of women struggling towards self-fulfilment, confronted with problems of sexuality, (anorexia, rejected love), child-rearing (the children have been taken by a former husband) and survival (one character, a physiotherapist by day is a high-earning prostitute by night), yet still supportive of each other. Deservedly, it remains a favourite staple of regional repertory. Gender too is at the heart of the epic *Queen Christina*, (the first play by a woman to be staged at the ▷RSC's Other Place), which juggles with the contradictions of gender stereotyping and choices (Queen Christina was brought up as a man but longs in the end to give birth; Gems calls it her 'uterine' play), and the less successful transvestite farce, *Aunt Mary*. *The Danton Affair*, another epic, but based on the manuscript of Stanisława Przybyszewska, unusually for Gems centres on two male protagonists, and stands rather as an implicit homage by Gems to the almost forgotten creativity of the young Polish woman writer.

Try these:
For a comparison of women as stereotypically bitchy, see Clare Booth Luce's *The Women*; for contemporary women, see ▷Caryl Churchill's *Top Girls*, ▷Jacqueline Holborough's *Dreams of San Francisco*; for male characters being bitchy and unsupportive see ▷Harold Pinter's *No Man's Land*; Nancy Sweet's excellent free adaptation of *Camille* for the fringe group, London Actor's Workshop, directed by Catherine Carnie; ▷Charles Ludlam's *Camille* for a quite different debunking of Dumas. ▷Robyn Archer for more 'alternative' images of female stars as victims; Gems has described her playwright son Jonathan as encapsulating 'the nihilism, the anarchic humour of his group' in *The Tax Exile* (1979), *The Paranormalist* (1981), *Naked Robots* (1983), *Susan's Breasts* (1985).

GENET, Jean   [1910–1986]
French novelist, poet and dramatist

Plays include:
Les Bonnes (*The Maids*; 1946), *Haute Surveillance* (*Deathwatch*; 1949), *Le Balcon* (*The Balcony*; 1956), *Les Nègres* (*The Blacks*; 1959), *Les Paravents* (*The Screens*; 1961)

A delinquent and thief who spent much of his first thirty years in reformatory or jail, where he began to write, Genet was released from a life-sentence on the plea of ▷ Jean-Paul Sartre and other French existentialist luminaries who recognised his prodigious talent. Even those repelled by the subject matter of his books, in which he presents the violence and vice of criminals and prostitutes as a mixture of luminous beauty and masturbatory fantasy, can be reached by his plays which act as a mirror to the 'normal' world in which he sees true vice and corruption. The tough dream objects and fantasising homosexuals of his novels and his romantic obsession with homosexuality give place to more accessible portraits of men outside society in the prisoner relationships of *Deathwatch* and to more abstract studies of private and public exploitation and interdependence in *The Balcony* and *The Blacks*. His theatre is often ritualistic and abstract, its form sometimes echoing Catholic liturgy. Cross-casting, both sexual and racial is intended in *The Maids* and *The Blacks*. *The Screens* echoes the Algerian struggle for independence but the other plays offer a more general criticism of society, playing on the prejudices of the audience to intensify their effect. As well as fiction and autobiographical works, Genet also wrote three screenplays and a ballet scenario.

The Balcony

Set in a brothel where representatives of establishment power groups – church, police, etc – act out their fantasies while a revolution brews outside, *The Balcony* turns a mirror on society which it sees as a whorehouse. Its images, drawn from the conventional repertoire of the pornographer, are not used to titillate but to show how people wilfully preserve the sham of conventional society and power structures. It offers a challenge to directors and to audiences to convey and comprehend the twists and turns of its ideas and provides an opportunity for an Artaudian theatricality.

Try these:

▷ Peter Weiss, whose *Marat/Sade* uses a madhouse for its charades and demands similar virtuoso staging; John Herbert's *Fortune and Men's Eyes* and ▷ Manuel Puig's *Kiss of the Spider Woman* for homosexuals in prison; ▷ Lindsay Kemp for his work based on Genet; Joint Stock

and ▷ Caryl Churchill for the use of cross-casting; ▷ Brendan Behan for alternative treatments of prison life and the brothel setting; ▷ Wendy Kesselman's *My Sister in This House* for feminist treatment of the real-life incident at Le Mans that gave rise to *The Maids*; Michele Celeste's *Hanging the President* for a controversial South African prison setting.

GILBERT, (Sir) William Schwenck   [1836–1911]
English librettist, dramatist and director

Plays include:
The Palace of Truth (1870), *Pygmalion and Galatea* (1871), *Dan'l Druce, Blacksmith* (1876), *Engaged* (1877), *Rosencrantz and Guildenstern* (1891)

Savoy Operas (with music by Sir Arthur Sullivan) include:
Thespis (1871), *Trial by Jury* (1875), *HMS Pinafore* (1878), *The Pirates of Penzance* (1879), *Patience* (1881), *Iolanthe* (1882), *Princess Ida* (1884), *The Mikado* (1885), *Ruddigore* (1887), *The Yeoman of the Guard* (1888), *The Gondoliers* (1889), *Utopia Limited* (1893), *The Grand Duke* (1896)

Although Gilbert's real claim to fame must be as the librettist half of Gilbert and Sullivan, he was also a considerable (and at times rather sour) dramatist in his own right, ranging from burlesque-extravaganza to comedy to straight melodrama. *Engaged* shows to a high degree the fundamental Gilbertian discrepancy between the characters' noble speeches and their actual intentions; the humble but warm-hearted Scottish peasants whom we find exchanging highly moral platitudes as the curtain rises rapidly prove to be an updated version of Cornish wreckers – they derail trains so that they can rob the passengers; and under the many romantic protestations of true love (Cheviot Hill, the hero, manages to become engaged to three women at once) lies simple fiscal arithmetic. It reads very well, but never seems to work as well on stage as it does on the page and is revived with reasonable frequency.

In the operas too, things are seldom what they seem; the highest principles are applied in a way which somehow produces the most material benefit, as with Pooh-Bah's readiness to humble his family pride for the smallest of bribes; this combines happily with the Carrollian logic of a world in which (for example) all problems are resolved by the mere insertion of a 'not' in a royal decree (*Iolanthe*). It is probably significant that, though Strauss and Lehar and even Offenbach travel well, Gilbert and Sullivan opera is put on only by the English-speaking.

Since the operas came out of copyright, and left the dead hand of D'Oyly Carte historicism, there have been some interesting productions: for instance the *Black Mikado* (1975), Joe Papp's exuberant production of *The Pirates of Penzance* and Ned Sherrin's sharply satirical updates during the last stand of the Greater London Council against abolition by central government, *The Ratepayer's Iolanthe* (1984) and *The Metropolitan Mikado* (1985).

Try these:
▷Oscar Wilde for similarities to *Engaged* in *The Importance of Being Earnest*; ▷Tom Stoppard for variations on the adventures of Rosencrantz and Guildenstern; ▷Joe Orton for the deadpan delivery of preposterous sentiments.

GILL, Peter   [1939–]
British actor, director and dramatist

Plays include:
The Sleeper's Den (1966), *A Provincial Life* (from ▷Chekhov; 1966), *Over Gardens Out* (1969), *Small Change* (1976), *Kick for Touch* (1983), *As I Lay Dying* (after William Faulkner; 1985) *In the Blue* (1985), *Mean Tears* (1987)

Welshman Gill began his theatrical career as an actor, but has been largely known as a director since he attracted attention with a sensitive and very naturalistic production of D.H. Lawrence's *A Collier's Saturday Night* (1965) at the Royal Court. An associate director at the Royal Court (1970–72) and Director of Riverside Studios (1976–80) he joined the ▷National Theatre where, from 1984 to 1990 he was director of the Studio, running experimental workshops for performers and developing new work with writers, as well as directing for the main auditoria.

Of his own plays, *The Sleeper's Den* is a naturalistic study of a poverty-stricken housewife pressured into breakdown by the indifference and demands of her family. Later plays have been more abstract – indeed often highly elliptical – but focus as relentlessly on what would seem to be semi-autobiographical memories taken from Gill's Welsh background: scars left by an adolescent sexual relationship in *Small Change*; the triangular relationship of two brothers and a wife in *Kick for Touch*; in both, the damage done by obsessive rugby-playing male bonding. *Over Gardens Out* with its two misunderstood boys driven by violence is also an impressionistic emotional battle in both past and present.

Mean Tears
This is an episodic presentation of a hopelessly ill-balanced affair between a vaguely academic or literary figure and his younger bisexual love object, shown in terms of anguish and emotion. Gill's own production (he has directed all his own plays), set on a steep rake with no furniture or scenic indication of locations, was the antithesis of his detailed recreations of working-class life in the Lawrence plays. But anyone who has found themselves trapped in a relationship where the love object seems totally egocentric bad news will confirm its emotional truth; frustration and confusion blocking out the rest of life. Like a sonnet, the play is seemingly slight but resonant.

Try these:
▷Caryl Churchill's *Fen*, ▷Nick Ward's *Apart from George* for imprisoned emotions (in rural East Anglian communities); for the painful distance between speech and silence in personal relationships, see ▷Harold Pinter, ▷Marguerite Duras, ▷Sam Shepard, ▷David Mamet, also, of course, ▷Chekhov and ▷Beckett; other contemporaries charting the parameters of personal pain in relationships are ▷Julia Kearsley, ▷Ayshe Raif, ▷Barry Collins, ▷Alan Ayckbourn, David Spencer; ▷Michael Wilcox's *Accounts* also dealt with a rugby-playing environ-

ment. ▷Lanford Wilson's *Burn This* for an American view of a destructive egocentric; Paul Godfrey for a National Theatre protegé, under Gill, whose style approximates to his minimalism.

GIRAUDOUX, Jean   [1882–1944]
French dramatist

Plays include:
Siegfried (1928), *Amphitryon 38* (1929), *Intermezzo* (1933), *La Guerre de Troie N'aura Pas Lieu* (*Tiger at the Gates* or *The Trojan War Will Not Take Place*; 1935), *Electre* (*Electra*; 1937), *Ondine* (1939), *Sodome et Gomorrhe* (*Sodom and Gomorrah*; 1943), *La Folle de Chaillot* (*The Madwoman of Chaillot*; 1945), *Pour Lucrèce* (*Duel of Angels*; 1953)

Giraudoux, a diplomat until 1940, was forty-six when the actor/director Louis Jouvet urged him to try adapting his novel *Siegried et le Limousin*, the story of a Frenchman brought up as a German who has to choose between his nationalities. The great success of his plays in the 1930s was largely due to the continued partnership with Jouvet, whose inventive staging and superb acting combined with Giraudoux's verbal glitter to cover any deficiencies in the dramatic action. Several of the plays show the fashionable 1930s French interest in updating Greek myth; the most successful of these was *La Guerre de Troie N'aura Pas Lieu*, into which he put all his strong conviction that the French and the Germans were not natural enemies. World War II came as a particular catastrophe to Giraudoux; it is poignant that on the outbreak of war he was set to run French propaganda, as an unlikely rival to Dr Goebbels.

In 1955 Kenneth Tynan called *The Trojan War Will Not Take Place* the 'highest peak in the mountain-range of modern French theatre', but either the fashion has moved against Giraudoux (as against ▷Christopher Fry, who translated it as *Tiger at the Gates*), or else one just needs the right production, since it seemed wordy, precious and static in the 1985 ▷Royal National Theatre revival. *The Madwoman of Chaillot* is occasionally revived as a star vehicle for actresses such as Geraldine Page or Eleanor Bron.

Try these:
▷Claudel for poetic rhetoric; ▷Anouilh, Gide, ▷Cocteau, and later Sartre for relating classical legends or Greek play themes to contemporary French concerns; ▷Caryl Churchill and ▷David Lan's *A Mouthful of Birds*, is based on ▷Euripides' Greek classic, *The Bacchae*, as is ▷Maureen Duffy's *Rites*.

GLASPELL, Susan   [1882–1948]
American dramatist

Plays include:
Suppressed Desires (1915, with George Cram Cook), *Trifles* (1916), *The Outside* (1917), *Bernice* (1919), *Inheritors* (1921), *The Verge* (1921), *Alison's House* (1930)

Glaspell, a founder of the influential Provincetown Players with her husband George Cram Cook and ▷Eugene O'Neill, played an important part in establishing the serious American theatre but the majority of her plays are now neglected. *Trifles*, a murder mystery which presents an acute account of different understandings of the nature of events and motivations on the basis of gender, is finely observed but too short to be frequently revived professionally. *Inheritors*, a well crafted longer play which examines the corruption of the pioneering spirit and the American Dream, sheds light on the historic roots of many contemporary American attitudes. *The Verge*, with its heroine on the point of a breakthrough into either madness or understanding anticipates the hothouse atmosphere of ▷Tennessee Williams. *Bernice* and *Alison's House* (based on Emily Dickinson's life) share the device of an off-stage female protagonist with *Trifles*; an economical way of suggesting the absences which can constitute the notion of 'woman'.

Try these:
Glaspell's work links with many strands of American playwriting, particularly the work of ▷Eugene O'Neill and ▷Tennessee Williams; there is also a ▷Strindbergian quality in her analysis of the ways marriage can work, although her conclusions unsurprisingly differ from his; for another view of women from the same period try Sophie

Treadwell's *Machina*. The contrast between a desire for immolation and a desire for life in *The Outside* anticipates ▷ Beckett; Noël Greig takes up similar themes in *Poppies*, as does Megan Terry in *Approaching Simone*.

Heggie and ▷ Michael Wall for other Mobil Playwriting Award winners; ▷ Lucy Gannon's *Keeping Tom Nice* and ▷ Peter Nichols' *A Day in the Death of Joe Egg* for plays about caring for children with disabilities; ▷ O'Casey for earlier Irish troubles.

GLENDINNING, Robin   [1938–]
Northern Ireland dramatist

Plays include:
Jennifer's Vacation (also known as *Stuffing It*; 1982), *Mumbo Jumbo* (1986), *Culture Vultures* (1988), *Donny Boy* (1990)

Glendinning was raised on a farm in County Armagh and educated at Trinity College, Dublin where he read Modern History and Political Science. He taught for eleven years before co-founding the moderate Alliance Party of Northern Ireland in 1970. He worked as its full-time organiser for five years and stood unsuccessfully for election on two occasions. He combined a return to teaching with a new career as a radio dramatist and quickly established a firm reputation. His first work for the stage was *Jennifer's Vacation*, an adaptation of one of his own radio plays, produced at the Dublin Festival. He was joint winner of the Manchester Royal Exchange's 1986 Mobil Playwriting Competition for *Mumbo Jumbo*. *Donny Boy* was produced by the Royal Exchange in November 1990. The Northern Irish troubles form an inevitable backdrop to Glendinning's work which is concerned more broadly with questions of community and individual identity.

Donny Boy
Donny, who is mentally impaired, is left holding the gun that killed an RUC officer, and his Catholic mother has to cope with her own complex and wildly confused loyalties. In this harrowing thriller, set in the Belfast battlefield, the terror for everyday life is tempered by much laughter. Nonetheless, Glendinning's play is essentially a sorrowful look, free of polemics, at the troubles in Northern Ireland.

Try these:
▷ Daniel Mornin, ▷ Marie Jones, ▷ Christina Reid for writers whose plays, rooted in Belfast, are also concerned with community and the effects of violence; ▷ Iain

GLOWACKI, Janusz   [1938–]
Polish-born playwright

Plays include:
Cinders (1981), *Tea with Milk* (radio play; 1982), *A Walk Before Dawn* (radio play; 1982), *Hunting Cockroaches* (1985), *Fortinbras Gets Drunk* (1990)

Glowacki was in London in December 1981 when martial law was declared in Poland; he chose not to return to his country and emigrated with his family to New York City. His plays generally focus on the experience of political repression, which his characters live with even in the most supposedly free society, America. The mood of Glowacki's plays tends to be tragicomic, for the world that Glowacki depicts mingles horror with irony, the potential for imminent death with man's apparently uncontrollable urge to persist. Like other post-war Polish playwrights, such as Rozewicz and ▷ Mrozek, Glowacki's style is grounded in absurdist theatre, yet he also brings to his writing a humanism and compassion that make his plays particularly accessible to western audiences.

Hunting Cockroaches
Hunting Cockroaches presents as its central metaphor the image of two emigrés, a married couple, isolated and in effect imprisoned in their roach-infested Manhattan tenement. Like the two men in ▷ Beckett's *Waiting for Godot*, the man and woman, 'He' and 'She', talk with each other obsessively in order to keep their desperation at bay and retain some semblance of existence. The habit of living with political repression has made them fearful even in their new environment, and they experience the economic and social pressures of their new country as yet another form of tyranny, which renders them impotent. The New York production in 1987 under the direction of Arthur Penn emphasised the humour and was so naturalistic in style that the play's dark edge was lost.

Try these:
▷Hanif Kureishi (who adapted *Cinders*),
▷Beckett, ▷Pinter for obsessive talking
on the edge of disaster.

GODBER, John   [1956–]
British playwright and director

Plays include:
Up 'N' Under, (1984), *Bouncers* (1985),
Shakers (1986; with Jane Thornton, *Blood
Sweat and Tears* (1986), *Cramp* (1986),
Putting on the Ritz (1987), *Teechers* (1987),
Salt of the Earth (1988), *On the Piste* (1990)

The son of a miner, Godber began writing
short stories for Radio Sheffield at the age of
sixteen, trained as a teacher and taught for five
years, while doing postgraduate work in
drama at the University of Leeds. At twenty-
two he co-wrote *Toys of Age* with Richard
Lewis, which was filmed for television, and
then began to contribute to the television
series *Crown Court*, *Grange Hill* and
Brookside. He has continued to move between
theatre and television – *Blood Sweat and Tears*
was televised in 1986, *Putting on The Ritz* was
adapted from his six-part television series *The
Ritz* (1987) and in 1991 the BBC commissioned both a new series and a film from him –
but he is most closely associated with the Hull
Truck Theatre Co, of which he has been artistic director since 1984. Godber has said: 'I
think the theatre should be exciting. It should
involve action. His involvement with Hull
Truck is an expression of his commitment to a
'genuinely serious popular theatre' and also to
a theatre outside London, as opposition to the
enshrining of 'theatre' at the ▷National
Theatre and the ▷RSC. Most of his plays are
social comedies which take place in public
arenas and are generally concerned with what
Godber has called 'working class leisure
activities'; *Up 'N' Under* and *Cramp* (which is
about a body-builder, and has music by Tom
Robinson) both take a sport as their central
device. Intensely physical pieces of theatre,
they draw heavily on caricature for effect as do
Bouncers and *Putting on the Ritz*, both of
which are set in discos. *Up 'N' Under*, which
won the Laurence Olivier Comedy of the Year
award for 1984, is about rugby league
(Godber is himself a rugby player) which becomes a means of exploring the contradictions

of machismo and the energy and resources
devoted to the game, and also becomes a
powerful image of resources that have gone to
waste in contemporary Britain (body building
is used similarly in *Cramp*). *Bouncers*, similarly, adopts a fairly ambivalent stance
towards its macho, working-class characters –
celebratory, but there's also something dis-
tinctly distasteful about this lot. Nonetheless,
it has been something of a success, produced
on both the east and west coasts of the USA,
as well as in Australia, Germany, Belgium and
Israel.

Try these:
▷David Storey's *The Changing Room*,
▷David Williamson's *The Club*, ▷Louise
Page's *Golden Girls*, ▷Claire Luckham's
Trafford Tanzi, ▷Howard Sackler's *The
Great White Hope* for plays with sport as a
central element; ▷Willy Russell's *Stags
and Hens* is *the* disco play; ▷Steven
Berkoff for another form of highly physical
theatre; ▷Nigel Williams' *Class Enemy* for
a classroom play; ▷Mike Leigh and
Théâtre de Complicité for more theatre of
caricature.

GODFREY, Paul   [1960–]
British dramatist

Plays include:
Inventing a New Colour (1986), *Once in a
While a Funny Thing Happens* (1990)

Godfrey trained and worked as a director in
Scotland before turning to writing. Whilst
there he intended to mount a production of
Benjamin Britten's *Noyes Fludde*, as a result of
which he met Peter Pears just before he died –
a fact which clearly inspired further enquiry
into the nature of artistic creativity and
resulted eventually in *Once In a While*.
As a product of the National's studio wing
(which, under Peter Gill, gave both *Inventing
a Colour* and *Once in a While* workshop productions) Godfrey's style – spare, elliptical,
fragmented – bears a certain comparison with
Gill's own work. *Inventing a New Colour*, even
has similar protagonists to those in Gill's
Small Change. However, whereas Gill's
youngsters and mothers reflected the pain of
growing up in rugby-dominated Wales,
Godfrey, who comes from Exeter, locates his
lads in Devon during WWII. And his tale of

Peter, the young 17 year old, London eva-
cuee, billeted on a middle-class couple and
their own son, Francis, suggested – though
perhaps not as clearly as some would have
liked – a sense of lives destroyed beyond re-
pair, 'a poetic elegy for the world before the
war' as one critic put it.

Godfrey's concern with mood and atmosphere seemed further distilled in the tone
poem-like *Once in a While*. Far from sensatio-
nalising the possible intimacies of the Auden/
Britten, Britten/Pears relationships, Godfrey
opted instead for an understatement of expression that drew harsh criticism from some
as 'precious' and 'lean, bloodless realism' but
moved Helen Rose of *Time Out* to describe
the play's images as lingering 'in the mind
with the pleasing insistence of a beautiful
melody'.

***

Try these:
▷Sharman Macdonald for Britain in the
Blitz; ▷David Hare for sense of Britain pre-
WWII; ▷Martin Crimp for another British
contemporary with a tendency to write
scenes in a short, televisual mode;
▷David Pownall's *Master Class* for a con-
trasting treatment of musical composition.

***

GOETHE,
Johann Wolfgang von   [1749–1832]
German dramatist and poet

Plays include:
Götz von Berlichingen (1773), *Clavigo*
(1774), *Stella* (1775), *Egmont* (1788, produced 1796), *Iphigenia in Tauris* (1779,
second (verse) version 1787), *Torquato
Tasso* (1789, produced 1807), *Faust* Part I
(published 1808), *Faust* Part II (published
posthumously 1833)

Goethe studied in Leipzig, like the young
Faust, and like him studied alchemy and forbidden subjects. His first play, *Götz von
Berlichingen*, was written in what he hoped
was a Shakespearean manner, under the eager
influence of Herder; the result is the story of
an honourable robber knight in revolt against
tyrannical rulers, and a very untidy construction. *Clavigo* is a curiosity, presenting a heightened version of ▷Beaumarchais' real-life

journey to Spain to avenge his sister's seduction and abandonment by a Spaniard; the
subject of *Egmont* is the revolt of the
Netherlands against Spain, and again the
hero is shown as a noble and honourable
humanist who goes to his death as a fighter
against tyranny. Goethe began the play just
before accepting an invitation to Weimar,
where he inadvertently stayed for the rest of
his life, becoming Finance Minister and Lord
High everything else. He managed the Court
Theatre from 1791 until 1817, when he was
displaced by an actress who had the advantage of being the Grand Duke's mistress.
From a literary point of view, his reign was a
golden age – besides his own plays, he put on
most of ▷Schiller's – but as a director he was
less successful, finding it difficult to get on
with the less intelligent actors, and tending to
drill them. In a two-year absence in Italy he
wrote *Iphigenia in Tauris* (from ▷Euripides)
and *Torquato Tasso*, a study of a poetic hero
with emotional difficulties which were not
unlike his own.

Faust (I and II)
His last play, the two parts of *Faust*, was
written over a long period, and is usually
regarded as unactable, though from time to
time somebody is rash enough to try to scale
its dizzying heights. The story of the scholar
tempted by the devil to barter his soul for the
things of this world was already well-known,
but Goethe turned it into a vast poem on the
destiny of man, and his Faust is redeemed at
the end (which led George Steiner to call it
'sublime melodrama'). The style of the play
shifts from broad farce to high tragedy and
most stages in between without warning,
changing verse forms as it goes. There have
been many attempts to put it on in English,
usually making much of the Gretchen episode. Robert David Macdonald's fine 1988
version at the Lyric, Hammersmith, with
Simon Callow outstanding as Faust, is the
most complete so far.

***

Try these:
▷Schiller for eighteenth-century German
drama; ▷Marlowe for *Dr Faustus*, ▷Havel
for *Temptation*, ▷Wertenbaker for
Faustian bargains; Berlioz and Gounod
are among opera composers who used the
Faust theme; ▷Ibsen's *Peer Gynt* has

Faustian redemptive overtones; ▷David Hare and ▷Howard Brenton's *Pravda* and *Brassneck*; Helen of Troy, who figures in both Goethe's and ▷Marlowe's treatments of the Faust story also figures in ▷Shakespeare's *Troilus and Cressida*, ▷Euripides' *Trojan Women*, *Helen*, *Orestes* and ▷Giraudoux's *The Trojan War Will Not Take Place*; *Iphigenia in Tauris* is a reworking of ▷Euripides' play of the same name; ▷Edward Bond's *The Fool* (about John Clare) and ▷Howard Brenton's *Bloody Poetry* (about the Shelleys and Byron) are other plays about poets to contrast with Goethe's treatment of Tasso.

GOGOL, Nikolai Vasilevich   [1809–52]
Russian novelist and dramatist

Plays include:
The Government Inspector (1836), *Marriage* (1842), *The Gamblers* (1842)

Gogol worked as a civil servant, took a course in painting, tried to become an actor and lectured on medieval history – failing at them all – before he achieved success with two volumes of Ukrainian tales in 1831–32. He is best known for his novel *Dead Souls* (of which he destroyed a second volume shortly before his death) and the comedy *The Government Inspector* of which he wrote: 'I decided to collect everything that was evil in Russia, all the injustices committed in places where justice is most of all expected of man – and laugh it off.' The play is a satire on official corruption in a small provincial town where an impecunious imposter is mistaken for a government official making an inspection, *The Government Inspector* introduced a grotesque farcical realism to the Russian theatre. Its humour found an instant response and aroused considerable anger which for a time drove Gogol from Russia. Its frequent revivals show how little the basic satire dates and the name part has provided a vehicle for some outstanding interpretations. In Britain Jatinder Verma's 1988 transposition of the play to post-colonial, small-town India has been particularly successful. *Dead Souls* was dramatised by ▷Bulgakov.

Try these:
▷Dario Fo and ▷Larry Gelbart's plays, for similar broad satire of petty officials; ▷Peter Flannery's *Our Friends In The North* for local government corruption; ▷Barry Collins' *The Strongest Man in the World* as a modern equivalent; ▷Barrie Keeffe's many social satires; ▷Ibsen's *Pillars of Society* for Norwegian hypocrisy and corruption in high places.

GOLDONI, Carlo   [1707–93]
Italian dramatist

Plays include:
Belisario (1734), *The Servant of Two Masters* (1746), *Mine Hostess* (also known as *Mirandolina*; 1753), *Il Campiello* (1756), *The Mania for the Country*, *The Adventure in the Country* and *The Return from the Country* (a trilogy; 1761), *The Fan* (1763)

Goldoni wrote his first play at eleven and ran away with some travelling players at fourteen. He practised law for a short time before a tragi-comedy, *Belisario*, was accepted for performance in 1734 and he became the playwright of the Teatro San Samuele in Venice. For thirty years he tried to change the pattern of Venetian theatre before accepting the post of director of the Comédie Italienne in Paris. He remained in Paris until his death. He wrote about 200 plays in Italian or French, the majority of them comedies.

Productions of Goldoni's plays have too often been conceived in *commedia dell'arte* style when, in fact, Goldoni's intention was to replace the improvised and now debased *commedia* with scripted plays which would reflect and comment on contemporary society. But he did not want to lose his audience – he had to wean them gradually. He considered that, 'the secret of the art of writing comedy is to cling to nature and never leave her' and, because his comedy is rooted in the way people behave rather than political satire, much of it is as relevant today. His comedies are mainly of middle-class life and they become increasingly sharp and critical. There is no 'typical' Goldoni play. *The Servant of Two Masters* comes early in his campaign of reform and still retains much of the structure of *commedia* with its fast moving farce. The development to a new form is gradual, reaching a peak with the last plays written in Venice.

Try these:
▷Beaumarchais' *Marriage of Figaro* for its treatment of servant and master relationships; ▷Molière, writing in a more formal style, is more savage in exposing bourgeois and aristocratic hypocrisies; for dramatists in the Goldoni tradition, ▷Eduardo De Filippo and ▷Dario Fo.

GOLDSMITH, Oliver   [1730–74]
Irish dramatist and man of letters

Plays include:
The Good-Natured Man (1768), *She Stoops to Conquer* (1773)

Goldsmith appears to have been an attractively indigent figure in fashionable London society who, as well as earning the friendship of Dr Johnson, amongst other notables, wrote one play, one poem and one novel that have stood the test of time (*She Stoops to Conquer*, 'The Deserted Village' and *The Vicar of Wakefield*). Few eighteenth-century dramatists find a regular place in the twentieth-century repertory but *She Stoops to Conquer*, a genial comedy of manners, owes much of its continuing popularity to its combination of the sentimental and the satirical. The central character, Kate Hardcastle, uses great skill to expose the contemporary double standard of sexual morality and force the otherwise eligible Charles Marlow to come to terms with his own sexism. These characters are surrounded by foils, each with a prevailing character trait which allows actors considerable scope for comic invention.

Try these:
▷Sheridan is the only other late eighteenth-century British dramatist whose work is regularly performed; the Restoration dramatists ▷Aphra Behn, ▷William Congreve, ▷George Etherege, ▷William Wycherley offer more robust treatments of similar themes; Kate herself refers to similarities between ▷Farquhar's *Beaux' Stratagem* and the play she exists in, and her name points to *The Taming of the Shrew*, in which the situation is reversed.

GOOCH, Steve   [1945–   ]
British dramatist and translator

Plays include:
Will Wat, If Not, Wat Will? (1972), *Female Transport* (1973), *The Motor Show* (1974; with Paul Thompson), *Strike '26* (1975), *Back-Street Romeo* (1977), *The Woman Pirates Ann Bonney and Mary Read* (1978), *Future Perfect* (1980), *Landmark* (1980, revised version of *Our Land, Our Lives*, 1976), *Fast One* (1982), *What Brothers Are For* (1983), *Taking Liberties* (1984), *Star Turns* (1987)

Keenly interested in ▷community theatre, Gooch has pursued an interest in the labour movement, class and gender issues which has not brought him great recognition, despite his capacity to find genuinely interesting subjects such as the Peasants' Revolt of 1381 in *Will Wat*, nineteenth-century transportation of women convicts from Britain to Australia in *Female Transport* or late eighteenth-century mock elections involving Samuel Foote and John Wilkes in *Taking Liberties*. Even his treatment of the potentially fascinating story of Ann Bonney and Mary Read in *The Woman Pirates* failed to convince in an ill-received and short-lived ▷RSC production. His translations have been more consistently successful than his own original work: his version of ▷Brecht's *The Mother* is the standard one in the British theatre and he has also translated Harald Mueller (*Big Wolf*, 1972, *Rosie*, 1977, *Flotsam*, 1982), Fassbinder (*Cock-Artist*, 1974), Martin Walser (*Säntis*, 1980) and ▷Franz Xaver Kroetz's (*Home Work*, 1982). His 1982 version of ▷Lope de Vega's *Fuente Ovejuna*, in which a village defeats a local tyrant through collective action, was an apt combination of Gooch's own political interests and his talent for adaptation, and *What Brothers Are For* was based on the Roman dramatist Terence's *The Brothers*.

Try these:
▷Arnold Wesker's *Caritas* is also set at the time of the Peasants' Revolt; ▷James Bridie also wrote on *Mary Read*; see ▷Ann Jellicoe and ▷community theatre; see also ▷Howard Barker, ▷Howard Brenton, ▷David Edgar, ▷Trevor Griffiths, ▷David Hare for other, more successful, contemporary British socialist dramatists; ▷Ted Whitehead's *Old Flames*

for another party where the male guest is outnumbered; ▷Caryl Churchill, ▷Pam Gems, and Timberlake Wertenbaker, for women's treatments of gender issues in both contemporary and historical contexts; ▷Bryony Lavery for *Calamity*, re-examining pioneer women of the Wild West.

GORKI, Maxim
(Alexei Maximovitch Peshkov)
[1868–1936]
Russian dramatist

Plays include:
The Philistines (1901), *The Lower Depths* (1902), *Summer Folk* (1904), *Children of the Sun* (1905), *Barbarians* (1906), *Enemies* (1906), *Vassa Shelesnova* (1910)

One of the great Russian dramatists, despite writing only a few major plays, Gorki's importance stems from his success as a dramatist both under the Czar and after the Revolution. His obvious feeling for the down-trodden underclass of Czarist Russia and his enormous status after the Revolution – he was the first president of the Soviet Writers' Union – won him at least the outward approval of Stalin, and he used his position to champion literary culture and to protect other writers from the censor and the secret police.

An orphan at the age of eleven, he worked through his adolescence and youth at every kind of ill-paid, temporary work. He learned to read while employed on a river steamer, turned to writing, and found literary success in 1895 with his story *Chalkash*. He became active in politics, befriended Tolstoy, was befriended by ▷Chekhov, and left the country after the failure of the 1905 Revolution. He returned to Russia in 1913, and became a champion of the Bolshevik Revolution. He developed the theory of 'Socialist Realism' which was soon distorted by Stalin's requirement for exclusively positive images of Soviet life. He died of TB in 1936, a death later laid at the door of a supposed Trotskyist plot 'uncovered' during the show-trials of Stalin's enemies.

An implacable enemy of the wealthy and the intellectual in pre-revolutionary society, his sympathy for the poor and the oppressed is powerful and sincere and found its most powerful expression in *The Lower Depths*,

probably his best-known and most-often-performed play. Set in a squalid slum in Moscow, the play portrays with unflinching candour the miserable lives of the misfits and failures who live there. Although in his time the realism of his portrayals of poverty was unprecedented – and even today the unremitting pessimism and gloom of his vision is hard to take – it is transcended by Gorki's obvious compassion for suffering and by his anger at its causes. The plays are weakened sometimes by his tendency to moralise and preach – a flaw of which he himself despaired. Perhaps too, as some reviewers have commented, the violent mood-swings in his plays are not easily accepted by British audiences (though Chekhov and Gogol equally, are not without their sudden switches from tragedy to farce). But as recent British revivals of his other plays have confirmed (notably David Jones' for the ▷RSC and *Vassa Shelesnova* revived both at Greenwich and at the tiny Gate Theatre), Gorki's panoramic view of a society tottering before the fall can still make a powerful impact. Though there are insistent – and often disparaging – comparisons made with Chekhov (like ▷Granville Barker by ▷Shaw, Gorki has been consistently overshadowed), his political grasp and rigorous examination of bourgeois values can be regarded as a complement to the Chekhovian canvas, not inferior to it. Where *Summer Folk*, for example, focuses on the idle, nouveau riche *dacha* class, *Barbarians*, set in a small provincial town, pits the old peasant and petit-bourgeois Russia of crude greed and corruption against the emotional violence of the new in the shape of two visiting railway engineers. *Enemies* tells us in no uncertain terms about class conflict and why the overthrow of the old order in 1917 was so inevitable; the same goes for *Vassa Shelesnova*, Gorki's last play, which, set ten years before the Revolution, ends on a note of plangent despair.

Try these:
Gorki is a character in Dusty Hughes' *Futurists*; ▷Tunde Ikoli produced a memorable adaptation of *The Lower Depths*; ▷David Pownall's *Master Class* investigates the whole issue of socialist realism in the context of music; ▷Chekhov and ▷Mayakovsky were Russian contemporaries of Gorki; the visionary who briefly

transforms lives is a notable figure in ▷Eugene O'Neill's *The Iceman Cometh* and ▷Ibsen's *The Wild Duck*. ▷Gregory Motton is a young, contemporary playwright who has certain affinities with Gorki in his compassion for down-and-outers in the 1980s; ▷Trevor Griffiths' *Piano* recalls Gorki as well as ▷Chekhov; Isaac Babel's *Marya* also concerns itself with the underclasses during the Revolution.

GOTANDA, Philip Kan   [1949–]
American playwright

Plays include:
The Avocado Kid or Zen in the Art of Guacamole (1979), *A Song for a Nisei Fisherman* (1981), *The Dream of Kitamura* (1982), *The Wash* (1985), *Yankee Dawg You Die* (1989)

Gotanda is increasingly being recognized as one of the foremost Asian-American playwrights in the United States. A Sansei, or third-generation Japanese American, Gotanda writes scripts that often are of two worlds. *The Dream of Kitamura*, for instance, is a stylized tale of murder in the time of the Samurai, while *The Wash* is a realistic drama about the marriage of two second-generation Japanese Americans. Gotanda is concerned about the place of Japanese Americans in American society, and on occasion, as with *Yankee Dawg You Die*, he explores this situation in a polemical manner that undermines the truth and lyricism of his writing.

The Wash
The Wash is a sensitive, unmannered exploration of the varying emotions experienced by an elderly married couple who are on the verge of divorce. The play dramatizes both the estrangement of two people and the limitations of a male-dominated Japanese-American marriage in the context of American society. In contrast to *Yankee Dawg You Die*, Gotanda creates characters with several dimensions, and delicately presents a situation that can be understood from more than one point of view.

Try these:
▷Hanif Kureishi, ▷David Henry Hwang, ▷Arnold Wesker for questions of assimilation and marginality.

GRANVILLE BARKER, Harley   [1877–1946]
British director, dramatist, actor and theorist

Plays include:
The Marrying of Anne Leete (written 1899; produced 1902), *The Voysey Inheritance* (1905), *Waste* (1907), *The Madras House* (1910), *The Secret Life* (written 1919–22; published 1923; produced 1988), *His Majesty* (written 1928; not produced)

After ▷Shaw, Granville Barker is perhaps the most important figure in the renaissance of English drama in the 1900s. He was also an excellent actor who played ▷Ibsen and ▷Shaw parts for the Stage Society. Sometimes regarded as the father of Britain's National Theatre movement, from 1904 to 1907 he directed and managed the Court Theatre (now the ▷Royal Court) with John E. Vedrenne. With an ensemble company he produced contemporary European drama, translations of ▷Euripides, and new British plays, above all those of Shaw. They lost money, but their influence was seminal.

As a dramatist, he is most often bracketed with ▷Galsworthy (and both are generally cross-referenced to Shaw), but his plays are livelier and less well-made than Galsworthy's, and he is better at putting argument on stage than Shaw. Barker's reputation has been eclipsed by Shaw's but he is a considerable dramatist whose status has been confirmed by recent revivals of his plays in Britain. All his major plays except *The Voysey Inheritance* have been produced by the ▷RSC or the ▷Royal National Theatre in recent years, and one of his final unperformed plays, *The Secret Life*, dealing with the perhaps autobiographical theme of public versus private life, was resurrected at the Orange Tree, Richmond in 1988. His early play *The Marrying of Anne Leete* was found unconventional, elliptical, and somewhat ambiguous in 1902, and the ▷RSC production in 1975 produced much the same reactions. *The Madras House* (Royal National Theatre, 1977) was revealed as a very rich play: its structure seems loose at first – Barker is capable of creating the six carefully differentiated unmarried Huxtable girls in Act I and then abandoning them altogether – but the theme of the role of women in society holds it together. *The Voysey Inheritance* is a good, well-crafted play, which generates considerable suspense, and the dreadful Voysey family are a fine collection of well-rounded upper-middle class characters, all visibly related. *Waste*, about the ruin of a politician through a casual affair which leads to abortion and death was written in 1907, banned by the censor, rewritten in 1926, and then almost unperformed until its quality was shown by the ▷RSC revival in 1985. It is very well constructed, with a modern resonance to the abortion arguments and some fine long suspenseful scenes of political and personal argument.

Try these:
▷Ibsen for problem plays and ▷Shaw for argument plays – Granville Barker often seems a cross between the two; ▷Gorki was an equally strong examiner of bourgeois values; ▷Chekhov too, though in a different vein; for more well-crafted, family dramas with moral intent; ▷Lillian Hellman, much of ▷Terence Rattigan and, perhaps surprisingly, some of ▷Noël Coward; see also ▷John Galsworthy.

GRASS, Günter   [1927–]
German novelist and dramatist

Plays include:
Onkel, Onkel (*Mister, Mister*; 1958), *Die Bösen Köche* (*The Wicked Cooks*; 1961), *Die Plebejer proben den Aufstand* (*The Plebeians Rehearse the Uprising*; 1965, produced 1966), *Davor* (*Beforehand*; 1969)

Socialist writer Grass was born in Danzig, and spent some time after the war in Paris, but now lives in Berlin; he experimented with short Absurdist plays, stage design, poetry, and sculpture before making a hit with his novel *Die Blechtrommel* (*The Tin Drum*) in 1959. His most successful play internationally has been *The Plebeians Rehearse the Uprising*, an interesting metatheatrical piece. It is set in the Berliner Ensemble on 17 June 1953, when the East German workers demonstrated against demands for higher productivity; the boss is (unhistorically) rehearsing the plebeians' uprising against Coriolanus, when a group of construction workers breaks in to ask for a statement of his support. He refuses to give it, seeing the senselessness of this unplanned action, but he also refuses to denounce the uprising when asked by the authorities; and he continues the rehearsal, making the real workers participate, record-

ing their voices and studying their reactions to improve his play. The situation is not treated naturalistically – parts are in verse – and there are touches of Expressionism; and it is far from being a simple attack on ▷Brecht.

Try these:
▷Brecht; ▷Hochhüth for German 1960s 'documentary' drama, but Grass has fewer pretensions and a sense of humour; ▷Trevor Griffiths' *The Party* for the relationship between rhetoric and political involvement, similarly ▷Bulgakov's *Molière*.

GRAY, Amlin   [1946–]
American playwright and adapter

Plays include:
Villainous Company (1978, adapted from *Henry IV* and other plays of Shakespeare), *How I Got That Story* (1979), *The Fantod* (1979), *Kingdom Come* (1983, adapted from *Giants in the Earth*), *Zones of the Spirit* (1984, includes *Outlanders* and *Wormwood*, suggested by material from Strindberg), *A Christmas Carol* (1984, adapted from Dickens)

Gray first received significant recognition as a playwright with his surreal, hard-hitting satire about the Vietnam War, *How I Got That Story*. Since then, Gray's work has tended to be more realistic in style, and he has frequently chosen to write or adapt plays that are set in historical periods. He is especially interested in creating central figures who have artistic or moral strengths that set them apart from the average person, such as the writer in *Wormwood*, or the minister Harstad in *Kingdom Come*.

How I Got That Story
How I Got That Story is a scathingly satiric portrait of the Vietnam War, experienced from the point of view of an American reporter. North and South Vietnamese and Americans come under Gray's fire, as he demonstrates all factions to be both dishonest and unintelligent. The reporter's eventual physical and emotional disintegration come to symbolize the War's destructiveness, and the final image of the play is of death. The imaginative script requires that a character called 'The Historical Event' transform into 20 other characters who make up parts of the Event, an

approach that was handled skilfully in the New York production by director Carole Rothman, and by actor Bob Gunton.

Try these:
▷Spalding Gray, ▷David Rabe, ▷Charles Wood, ▷Nicholas Wright for images of war; ▷Howard Brenton's *Epsom Downs* for imaginative transformations of actors.

GRAY, Simon   [1936–   ]
British dramatist and novelist

Plays include:
Wise Child (1967), *Dutch Uncle* (1969), *Butley* (1971), *Spoiled* (1971), *Otherwise Engaged* (1975), *The Rear Column* (1978), *Close of Play* (1979), *Stagestruck* (1979), *Quartermaine's Terms* (1981), *The Common Pursuit* (1984; revised version 1988), *Melon* (1987), *Hidden Laughter* (1990)

Gray is a university lecturer; a prolific writer (for stage, television and film, as well as of adaptations, novels and even autobiography) whose plays have often involved academics and people in publishing. His usually articulate characters are witty and often outrageous, so that audiences react to even his more macabre themes as comedies and have given him greater popular success than his rough handling by critics would suggest. Most of his plays present at least one homosexual character, though only in *Butley* and *Spoiled* (in which a schoolteacher with a pregnant wife teaches a pupil at home and becomes increasingly involved with him) is a homosexual relationship central to the play. Leading characters are often egocentric, sharp-tongued misfits, badly in need of a psychiatrist (*Melon* is a study of one such character's breakdown). Many of Gray's plays deal with sexual fetishism: *Wise Child* features transvestism, though the cross-dresser in fact turns out to be a crook in disguise; *Dutch Uncle* has a masochist seeking the attentions of a policeman by trying to murder his own wife; and in several plays characters indulge in sado-masochistic games. Such situations are usually exploited for laughs, though in *The Rear Column*, set in the Victorian Congo, sadism and cannibalism are used more seriously to show the degradation of the whites.

Several of Gray's plays have become award-winning adaptations on television, including *Quartermaine's Terms*, *Butley* and *The Common Pursuit*. His screenplays for television include *After Pilkington* (1987) and *Old Flames* (1990), and for the cinema, *A Month in the Country* (1987) which won the Grand Prix award at the Brussels Film Fair. It is a gentle and understated script, quite different from the 'cleverness' of his stage plays. *Hidden Laughter* is his most English play to date. Taking its title from ▷T.S. Eliot's *Four Quartets* and set in a quintessential English garden, its semi-elegiac tone, tragi-comic vicar and disintegrating family unit amount to an uneasy attempt to delineate current moral and spiritual crises in the English middle-class. Its underlying axiom that the collapse of the nuclear family can somehow be put at the door of selfish women who choose to concentrate on their own artistic creativity, thereby neglecting their family, seems pretty questionable.

Butley
Butley has a typical Gray protagonist, a bitchy university lecturer with a marriage in collapse, who drives away not only his wife but her replacement, the ex-student, now colleague, with whom he shares office and home. The savage tongue which makes him so offensive is also what provides much of the audience's fun. But if they enjoy seeing his selfishness get its come-uppance there is also a release for some of their own frustrations in seeing the characters find such vitriolic language for all those rows that happen in any highly stressed relationship. Gray is often too busy scoring points for the serious content of his plays to show but his exposure of our own selfishness and failure can be caustic and accessible to those prepared to think while they laugh.

Try these:
▷Alan Bennett for wit with more compassion; ▷Tom Stoppard for wordplay with more intellect; ▷Christopher Hampton's *Philanthropist* offers a different view of an academic; ▷Mike Leigh and ▷Alan Ayckbourn are as vituperative about middle-class mores, ▷Doug Lucie as vicious about contemporary media men; ▷Martin Crimp's *No-one Sees the Video* is an equally jaundiced swipe at women, work and contemporary mores.

GRAY, Spalding   [1941–   ]
American playwright, monologist, actor

Plays and Monologues include:
Three Places in Rhode Island (1977), *Sex and Death to the Age 14* (1979), *Booze, Cars, and College Girls* (1979), *A Personal History of the American Theatre* (1980), *Points of Interest* (1980), *In Search of the Monkey Girl* (1981), *India and After* (1982), *Interviewing the Audience* (1982), *Swimming to Cambodia* (1984), *Terrors of Pleasure* (1986), *Rivkala's Ring* (adaptation of ▷Chekhov's *The Witch* 1986), *Our Town* (actor, 1988), *Monster in a Box* (1990)

An integral part of the Off-Off Broadway theatre since the 1960s, Spalding Gray launched his career with the Performance Group's production of ▷Sam Shepard's *Tooth of Crime*. He later co-founded the Wooster Group with Elizabeth LeCompte, where he launched his successful solo career as a monologist. A self-described 'poetic journalist', Gray transmutes his daily life into theatrical pieces in which any event – from his nervous breakdown in India to his purchase of a country house in upstate New York – is material for comic, often acidic investigation. Actual people figure prominently in his monologues: ▷Athol Fugard and Roland Joffe – his colleagues in the 1985 film *The Killing Fields* pop up in *Swimming to Cambodia*, and his long time girlfriend Renee Shafransky is well known to those who regularly attend Gray's performances. Between monologues, Gray works as a stage and screen actor, only to return to his favorite material – himself. Gray has elevated narcissistic story-telling to high art with his amazingly compelling low-key delivery. Some see Gray as a self-obsessed exhibitionist, while others claim he is a profound commentator on our age. In either case, his work reflects the obsession with self-analysis that pervades American life.

Swimming to Cambodia
Told in two parts, Gray's monologue (filmed by Jonathan Demme in 1987), was inspired by his experience playing the aide to the American ambassador in *The Killing Fields*. With no props except a microphone, a glass of water, and several maps of Cambodia behind him, Gray charts a terrifyingly funny journey to the human heart of darkness in which the making of a film about genocide acts as a catalyst for ruminations on sex, death, human compassion and destruction. One remarkable section recounts that LA extras had to be flown to Asia to play Cambodia refugees, since Pol Pot had killed off all the real ones. In a voice capable of sustaining hypnotic waves of discourse, Gray's monologue combines keeneyed analysis with irony.

Try these:
▷David Rabe for explorations of the Vietnam experience; monologists ▷Eric Bogosian,   ▷Karen Finley,   John Leguizano, Lily Tomlin, John O'Keefe, Laurie Anderson and Sandra Bernhart for use of Self as central performance subject.

GREEN, Paul   [1894–1981]
American dramatist, screenwriter and novelist

Plays include:
The Last of the Lowries (1920), *White Dresses* (1923), *The No 'Count Boy* (1924), *In Abraham's Bosom* (1926), *The Field God* (1927), *The House of Connelly* (1928), *Tread the Green Grass* (1932), *Roll, Sweet Chariot* (1934), *Shroud My Body Down* (1934), *Johnny Johnson* (1936), *Native Son* (adaptation from Richard Wright; 1941)

Symphonics dramas include:
The Lost Colony (1937), *The Nighland Call* (1939), *The Common Glory* (1947), *Wilderness Road* (1955), *The Confederacy* (1958), *The Stephen Foster Story* (1959), *Cross and Sword* (1965), *Texas* (1966), *Trumpet in the Land* (1970), *The Lone Star* (1977)

Green was the son of a North Carolina farmer, and his lifelong subject was the American South – its land, history and people. A poet, novelist and screenwriter as well as playwright, he filled his plays with all the South's dramatic riches, including tragedy, comedy, burlesque, poetry, music, songs, processionals and mass chants. In his work as in his region, bitter realities often confront the most soaring imagination.

His first plays were one-act dramas concerning strained race relations, conflicting religious values and the disintegration of old, wealthy families. Some of these were produced (with limited commercial success) by progressive New York theatre groups including the Provincetown Playhouse and the Theatre Guild. Despite uneven reviews, Green was awarded the Pulitzer Prize for *In Abraham's Bosom*, a tragedy of an educated mulatto killed by a white mob when he attempts to open a school for black children.

In 1931 *The House of Connelly*, a drama of the decay of an old southern family, was chosen for the first major production by the Group Theatre. The production was very successful, though Green later complained that the Group convinced him to change the original tragic ending to a happy one for reasons of left-wing political correctness. The Group also produced the satire *Johnny Johnson*, with music by Kurt Weill: the plot revolves round an anti-war folk hero who ends up in an insane asylum.

In the late 1930s, after a decade of favourable critical notices but mixed box-office success, Green turned away from Broadway and put his energies into what he called 'symphonic dramas'. These monumental outdoor historical spectacles – modern secular equivalents of medieval religious pageants – depicted various episodes of exploration, settlement, government and culture in specific southern localities. The best-known symphonic drama was the first, *The Lost Colony*, which has been performed at Roanoke, Virginia, every summer (except during World War II) since 1937.

Try these:
▷Langston Hughes' *Mulatto*, a black perspective on interracial families. Jack Kirkland's *Tobacco Road* for another perspective on poor white southern families; ▷Brecht for epic theatre and political drama; ▷O'Casey's *The Silver Tassle* as an anti-war play; ▷Ann Jellicoe ▷Community Theatre and ▷Performance Art for British equivalents of 'symphonic dramas'; ▷Athol Fugard's *My Children! My Africa!* for a tragic meditation on education and race; ▷Lilian Hellman for families in decay.

GREENBERG, Richard   [1958–]
American playwright

Plays include:
The Bloodletters (1984), *Life Under Water* (1985), *Vanishing Act* (1986), *The Author's Voice* (1987), *The Maderati* (1987), *Eastern Standard* (1988), *The American Plan* (1990)

Greenberg has begun to make a reputation in regional theatre and on and off Broadway as a dramatist with a flair for capturing the manners of the selfish, urban, American middle class. His canvas is small, yet he paints the world of his characters with a fine eye for the isolation that lies beneath the clever surfaces, whether he is dramatising a young man's adolescent troubles, as in the one-act *Life Under Water*, or taking aim at upwardly mobile New Yorkers, as in *Eastern Standard*.

Eastern Standard
Eastern Standard is a witty and uncompromising portrayal of the carelessness and self-absorption of the 'yuppies' of the 1980s. The characters are well educated, sexually sophisticated and generally successful in their careers, yet they have little ability to sustain intimate relationships and have only the most superfical concern for those less fortunate than themselves. Their one act of social consciousness, which involves 'adopting' a homeless woman for the summer, is self-congratulatory, and they cannot understand why the woman turns on them when they abandon her at the summer's end. The original production under the direction of Michael Engler realised both the charming surfaces and the casual selfishness of the world of Greenberg's comedy.

Try these:
▷Doug Lucie, ▷Noël Coward and ▷Joe Orton for witty amorality; ▷Martin Crimp for a new British voice peeling away the layers of casual selfishness; ▷Christopher Durang for another American dramatist presenting a full-frontal assault on the middle classes; ▷Chekhov's *The Seagull* for an older example of casual selfishness.

GREGORY, (Lady) Isabella Augusta   [1852–1932]
Irish theatre manager and dramatist

Plays include:
Twenty-Five (1903), *Spreading the News* (1904), *The White Cockade* (1905), *The Rising of the Moon* (1907), *The Workhouse Ward* (1908)

Lady Gregory was an energetic Protestant landowner from Galway, who took to the theatre in middle age; after three years of experiment in Dublin with the Irish Literary Theatre (1899–1901), in the company of ▷W.B. Yeats, Edward Martyn, and George Moore, and then with the Fay brothers' company, she helped to found the Abbey Theatre in 1904, and was involved in its management almost until her death in 1932. She did not start writing plays until she was fifty, but thereafter wrote around forty, mostly one-act farces, but also more pretentious (and thus less revivable) plays about Irish history, and such ventures as translations of ▷Molière into the Galway dialect. She is probably more important for her management role than for her workmanlike plays; however her farcical comedies, such as *Spreading the News*, make a lively attempt to render Irish peasant speech patterns, and the plots crack along.

Try these:
▷Yeats and ▷Synge for serious attempts to use Irish dialect in the theatre; ▷Brian Friel's *Translations* bemoans the destruction of native Gaelic by imposed English.

GREIG, Noël   [1944–]
British dramatist

Plays include:
Men (1976), *As Time Goes By* (1977), *The Dear Love of Comrades* (1979), *Angels Descend on Paris* (1980), *Poppies* (1983), *Rainbow's Ending* (1984), *Spinning a Yarn* (1984), *Do We Ever See Grace?* (1985), *Best of Friends* (1985), *Working Hearts* (1986), *Laughter from the Other Side* (1986), *Whispers in the Dark* (1987), *Plague of Innocence* (1988), *Familiar Feelings* (1989), *The Death of Christopher Marlowe* (1989), *Paradise Now and Then* (1990), *The Good Sisters* (translation from ▷Michel Tremblay; 1991)

A prolific playwright whose work has covered an amazingly wide range, his associations as writer/director with various groups reflects many of the major theatrical trends of the past two decades. He was co-founder of The Combination, one of the first fringe groups to emphasise group work, improvisation and flexible working spaces; director at the Almost Free, scene of the first gay season of plays put on by Ed Berman; writer/director with the Bradford community based company The

General Will; director with Gay Sweatshop from 1977–87 and writer-in-residence with Theatre Centre, the theatre-in-education group.

A writer who consistently explores the points at which sexuality and social and political forces touch, his early work shows an interest in historical roots, making connections with the present, and linking the personal with the public. *Men*, for example, deals with socialism's inability to extend its ideology into personal, gay politics. Probably Greig's best-known play is *Poppies* which was presented by Gay Sweatshop and has also been produced in Germany and Australia. His earlier plays for Gay Sweatshop, *As Time Goes By*, tracing gay repression through three different time periods (co-written with ▷Drew Griffiths), and *The Dear Love of Comrades*, have also been highly influential and performed in the USA and Australia. Another important, highly complex exploration of repression and its responses was *Angels Descend on Paris*. Presented in the form of an operetta, this six-character epic, threading its way from Nazi Berlin to Paris drew on Jacobean tragedy and the story of Bluebeard to explore the responses of people under pressure, sexual identity, role playing, and opportunism.

Many of Greig's most recent plays have however been aimed specifically at young people, TIE (theatre in education) and YPT (Young People's Theatre) groups, although *Working Hearts* was written for ▷Graeae, the company of performers with disabilities. *Best of Friends*, (an adaptation of Dickens' *Hard Times*) *Dusty Dreamtime* and *Plague of Innocence* are all plays commissioned and written for YPT's, the latter dealing with AIDS. *Laughter from the Other Side*, and *Whispers in the Dark* are both plays written for Theatre Centre (which works in schools). Rattling good yarns on one level, these modern myths also deal with contemporary issues such as cultural suppression, imperialism, sexuality, Thatcherism and Greenham Common.

Poppies
Poppies is an anti-militaristic and anti-nuclear play. Set on Hampstead's Parliament Hill where two middle-aged men, Sammy and Snow, are having a picnic, it utilises a favourite Greig technique, mixing past with present and poetry with polemics. A symbolic piece, it was inspired by images of mothers sticking

photos of their own children on the wire fencing at Greenham Common air force base which Greig admitted had captured his imagination: 'I've always been preoccupied with the idea we shouldn't divorce our lives from history'. Nicholas de Jongh in the *Guardian* accused the play of being an incompatible mixture of styles, but Jim Hiley in *City Limits* hailed its arrival as 'unflashy, intricately thoughtful and often elliptical . . . very much the product of gay consciousness', contradicting common criticism of gay theatre 'by looking out from the ghetto and addressing itself with wit and sometimes brilliance to the biggest questions of the day'.

Try these:
▷Louise Page's *Salonika*, ▷Stephen Lowe's *Seachange*, ▷Greg Cullen's *Taken Out* all introduce corpses into plays which have a common war theme; ▷Jacqui Shapiro's *Winter in the Morning* shows the responses of a group of young Jews to Nazism and the Warsaw Ghetto; see also ▷Community Theatre; Gay Sweatshop; ▷Gay Theatre.

GRIFFITHS, Drew   [1947–84]
British dramatist

Plays include:
Mister X (with Roger Baker; 1975), *Indiscreet* (with Roger Baker; 1976), *The Jingle Ball* (1976), *As Time Goes By* (with ▷Noël Greig; 1977)

Director, playwright and founder member with Gerald Chapman of ▷Gay Sweatshop in 1975, Griffiths is a seminal figure in the history of gay political theatre in Britain. Remembered also as a devastating performer, and raised in the tradition of northern vaudeville and music hall, his final entrance in *Mister X* as a T-shirt and jeans drag queen (complete with feather boa) is said to have turned laughter to frozen chill. The first British gay play to challenge internalised self-oppression and assert gay pride, by implication, *Mister X's* style set a precedent whose influence can be traced along a line of gay plays from *La Cage aux folles* on Broadway to Neil Bartlett. Equally influential and innovating was *As Time Goes By* co-authored with ▷Noël Greig. An exploration of gay repression, it drew on three periods in history –

Victorian England (▷Oscar Wilde's trial and after), Nazi Germany in the 1930s and America 1969 with the beginning of the Gay Liberation Movement in the Stonewall Riots of that year. Again a pivotal play because of the way it draws together personal and political strands, it subsequently spawned a number of plays, including ▷Martin Sherman's *Bent*. *The Jingle Ball* was a spoof pantomime on Cinderella, with the usual male Ugly Sisters, but a female Principal Boy whose love for Cinders was unequivocally lesbian.

Griffiths went on to write further plays for television and radio about gay relationships: *The Only One South of the River*, a comedy set in a gay disco over a straight pub. What they all had in common was a basic love and concern to show gay people with dignity and not a little humour.

Mister X
Based on a pamphlet, *With Downcast Gays* by David Hutter and Andrew Hodges this is a cathartic 'coming out' play that made an enormous impact on audiences, gay and straight, wherever it went. Written in revue form – as though a personalised biography of the cast, with six sections telling different experiences and a gradually changing consciousness about being gay – the production used minimal props (chairs, a table and a tape recorder) in order to tour anywhere. It did, for over a year, (along with ▷Gay Sweatshop's other 'coming out' play, Jill Posener's *Any Woman Can*) in pubs, clubs, the Mickery Theatre in Amsterdam, even Dublin. Times may have changed and so too some of the targets of homophobia, but its radical use of laughter in breaking down stereotypes and over-riding humanitarianism make it a seminal work.

Try these:
▷Noël Greig; Philip Osment; Gay Sweatshop; ▷Lesbian Theatre; see also Jackie Kay's *Twice Over* as another gay play dealing with honesty in all relationships; for laughter with a sting in the tail, see ▷Trevor Griffiths' *The Comedians*, ▷John Osborne's *The Entertainer*, all of ▷Joe Orton, ▷Mike Leigh's *Abigail's Party* and a good deal of ▷Alan Ayckbourn particularly *Absent Friends*; see also American comedians such as Lenny Bruce, Eric Bogosian; Cheryl Moch's *The Real True Story of Cinderella*

is a spoof, all lesbian Cinderella; see also ▷Cabaret; ▷Ethyl Eichberger for a charismatic performer using 'drag' for political purposes; similarly ▷Neil Bartlett's *Sarrasine* and *A Vision of Love Revealed in Sleep*.

GRIFFITHS, Trevor   [1935–]
British dramatist

Plays include:
The Wages of Thin (1969), *Occupations* (1970), *Apricots* (1971), *Thermidor* (1971), *Lay By* (with Howard Brenton, ▷Brian Clark, ▷David Hare, ▷Stephen Poliakoff, Hugh Stoddart, ▷Snoo Wilson; 1971), *Sam, Sam* (1972), *The Party* (1973), *Comedians* (1975), *Deeds* (1978; with ▷Howard Brenton, ▷Ken Campbell and ▷David Hare), *Oi for England* (1982), *Real Dreams* (1986), *Piano* (1990)

Griffiths is among the most important of contemporary socialist writers, and a central figure in the debate about the role of the dramatist in a capitalist culture. An unequivocal revolutionary Marxist, his work constantly questions which forms and which media are most appropriate to a socialist theatre practice.

Born in Manchester Trevor Griffiths was of the first generation to reap the consequences of the 1944 Education Act and was the first of his family to go to university. His first play *Sam, Sam* is a semi-autobiographical tale about two brothers, one of whom moves socially upward while the other is trapped by the class position of the family. Griffiths' first full length play *Occupations* (a study of Gramsci) was taken up by the ▷RSC, while his one-act plays *Apricots* and *Thermidor* were produced by the socialist company ▷7:84. *The Party* takes the form of a political debate among representatives from left-wing groups at the moment of May 1968.

Griffiths very much sees his role as a writer as interventionist; he says 'my sort of writing is about impact and penetration' and the productions of *Occupations* and *The Party* on the stages of the Establishment theatres of the ▷National and ▷RSC were very much part of this. Griffiths' concern is to make socialist ideas accessible, and to make cultural forms part of a broader political struggle.

Griffiths has often chosen to work in tele-vision rather than the theatre in order to achieve the widest possible audience; he has adapted many of his plays for television, has contributed episodes to popular series, and adapted novels for television. His television series *Bill Brand* took the form of a socialist soap-opera, in its account of a Labour MP, whose career encompassed a range of socialist debates. His film work includes major contributions to the script of Warren Beatty's *Reds*, and *Fatherland* (1986). Griffiths has said: 'I chose to work in those modes because I have to work with the popular imagination . . . I am not interested in talking to thirty-eight university graduates in a cellar in Soho.'

Comedians
A study of the nature of comedy, it works both as a scabrous attack on the racist and sexist humour which passes for comedy in British popular culture, and as an exploration of the radical potential of comedy. The play begins in the classroom where an old comedian (originally, and appropriately, played by Jimmy Jewel) is training a group of stand-up comics. The group is made up of a docker, a milkman, an insurance agent, a labourer, a night club owner and a van-driver; for them all, success as a comedian is an escape route from the tediousness of their work; in the second act, the group perform for an agent who may supply the means. While desperate ambition fires most of the group to come out with a spate of cracks against the blacks, Pakistanis, Jews and women, the youngest member dumps his prepared act and in a stunning alienation effect, turns directly to the audience with a coruscating speech of class hatred. The final act of the play returns to the classroom, where pupil and teacher debate the private and public possibilities of comedy. The play's theatrical practice of challenging the basis of what it is possible to laugh at can be very unsettling for an audience.

Try these:
▷David Hare, ▷Howard Brenton and ▷Howard Barker are among the 'political' dramatists of Griffiths' generation; ▷Tony Marchant's *Lazy Days Ltd*, ▷Caryl Phillips' *Strange Fruit* and ▷Tunde Ikoli's *Scrape Off the Black* all contrasts brothers' opposing attitudes to life; Drew Griffiths and Roger Baker's *Mister X* uses comedy to subvert homophobic attitudes and was

directly influenced by *Comedians*; ▷David Edgar like Griffiths, engaged in the debate about the best form for socialist drama throughout his writing career; ▷Margaretta D'Arcy and ▷John Arden have also engaged in the debate but have turned instead to community-based theatre; ▷John McGrath has remained with ▷7:84; ▷Cabaret. *Piano* draws on ▷Chekhovian themes and *Piantonov* in particular.

GUARE, John   [1938–]

Plays include:
The Loveliest Afternoon of the Year (1966), *Something I'll Tell You Tuesday* (1966), *Muzeeka* (1967), *Cop-Out* (1968), *Kissing Sweet* (1969), *A Day of Surprises* (1970), *The House of Blue Leaves* (1971), *Two Gentlemen of Verona* (musical adaptation and lyrics; 1971), *Rich and Famous* (1974), *Marco Polo Sings a Solo* (1976), *Landscape of the Body* (1977), *Bosoms and Neglect* (1979), *Lydie Breeze* (1982), *Gardenia* (1982), *Women and Water* (1984), *The Talking Dog* (1985), *Six Degrees of Separation* (1990)

John Guare's work brims with inventiveness – bizarre situations, eccentric characters and unimaginable plots haunt his plays. Although his conceits seem implausible, his writing touches the heart with an inner truth that surpasses surface realism. It is the truth of human aspiration and disillusionment.

After completing an MFA in Playwriting at Yale School of Drama in 1963, Guare achieved immediate success off-off-Broadway with his early one-act plays. At the ▷Eugene O'Neill Memorial Theatre Playwrights' Conference (of which he was a founding member), he began work on *The House of Blue Leaves* whose 1971 off-Broadway production earned Guare his second Obie and a New York Drama Critics' Circle Award for best American play of the season. A scathing farce set in the Queens apartment of an Irish Catholic family on the day of the Pope's visit to New York, the play is rooted in Guare's own Queens childhood. The central character, a zoo keeper with aspirations of 'making it' as a songwriter, longs to commit his mentally ill wife Bananas so he can pursue fame and fortune in Hollywood with his ambitious girlfriend. Plot complications abound including a scheme hatched by his son to blow up the Pope. Each character pursues his own empty dreams until they explode in their faces literally and figuratively. While uproariously funny, the play ends in the despair and anguish of broken dreams. Guare proved himself an inventive lyricist in 1971. The New York Shakespeare Festival's musical adaptation of *Two Gentlemen of Verona* transposed the drama to modern day Puerto Rico and New York. When the play moved to Broadway, it collected two Tony Awards in addition to the Drama Desk and New York Drama Critics' Circle awards.

Guare's next few plays, although intriguing and imaginative, received little critical acclaim. Reviewers seemed uncomfortable with his neurotically obsessive characters, disorganised plots, and quick shifts from farce to tragedy. His poetic language failed to assuage the unease his writing provoked. However, his haunting and touching screenplay for *Atlantic City* (1981), was universally acclaimed, and nominated for an Academy Award for best original screenplay. The film proved that Guare could construct a tightly woven story around his complex characters and still hold on to his unique blend of absurdism and realism.

Guare then turned his hand to a series of historical plays exploring the collapse of the American dream. Set in the nineteenth century, and written in a more serene and subdued style that highlighted his poetic prowess, the plays failed to please the critics.

The 1990 New York theatre season witnessed the fulfilment of his promise with *Six Degrees of Separation* at Lincoln Center. Here his old themes of unfulfilled dreams, emotional alienation and escape from introspection converge in a whirligig plot. 'Successful' Manhattanites are duped by a conman posing as the son of Sidney Poitier. He works his way into their homes, claiming to be a friend of their children (all away at Ivy League colleges). These sophisticated urbanites are one step removed from Guare's working-class characters in Queens who dreamed of getting to Manhattan. Even on Park Avenue, empty lives illuminate empty dreams. 'Imagination,' Guare tells us, 'is God's gift to make the act of self-examination bearable.' Without self-knowledge one can't know anyone else, and the result is the isolation of contemporary life.

Jonathan Pryce as Gethin Price performing his act, in Richard Eyre's original Nottingham Playhouse production of Trevor Griffiths' brilliant dissection of comedy and politics *Comedians*, later seen at the Old Vic

Try these:
▷Eugene Ionesco for absurdism; ▷Joe Orton for farce; ▷Anton Chekhov for the theme of unfulfilled dreams; ▷August Strindberg for characters with internal angst; ▷Georges Feydeau for farcical plots; ▷George S. Kaufman and Moss Hart for the American dream as farce; Wallace Shawn for a bitter edge; ▷Christopher Durang for farcical treatment of troubled families; ▷Jean Genet for plays revolving around the nature of authentic identity.

GURNEY, A.R.
A(lbert) R(amsdell), Jr   [1930–]
American dramatist and novelist

Plays include:
Three People (1956), *Turn of the Century* (1958), *The Golden Fleece* (1968), *The Open Meeting* (1969), *The Love Course* (1970), *Scenes from American Life* (1970), *The Old One-Two* (1973), *Children* (1974), *Who Killed Richard Cory?* (1976), *The Golden Age* (1981), *What I Did Last Summer* (1981), *The Dining Room* (1982), *Another Antigone* (1986), *The Perfect Party* (1986), *Sweet Sue* 1987), *The Cocktail Hour* (1988), *Love Letters* (1988), *The Snow Ball* (1991), *The Old Boy* (1991)

A.R. ('Pete') Gurney's main subject is the decline of White Anglo-Saxon Protestant (WASP) mores in contemporary America. To him, WASP culture – by turns sincere and pretentious, principled and inflexible – is built upon rituals that have lost much of their meaning. His plays show a society in flux, torn between old and new, age and youth, wisdom and naïvete, tradition and rebellion.

Gurney, born to an established Buffalo, New York family, and educated at the Yale School of Drama, began teaching literature at the Massachusetts Institute of Technology in 1960, becoming a full professor in 1970. He started writing plays in the late 1950s, and quickly decided to concentrate on his own WASP community. In the 1960s and 1970s, when WASP culture was out of fashion, his work was rarely produced except in New England. Then in the 1980s, the return to more traditional values suddenly gave Gurney an audience, and *The Dining Room*, *The Cocktail Hour* and *Love Letters* all had good runs on and off Broadway.

Although he lists as his influences ▷Arthur Miller, ▷Tennessee Williams, Rogers and Hammerstein, and Cole Porter, Gurney often draws his characters from academia, and his subjects from the classics. *Another Antigone* depicts a young woman's Antigone-like stand against a male professor when she tries to update ▷Sophocles' play; *The Old One-Two* is a Plautine farce on university life; and *The Golden Fleece* and *Children* are dominated, as were many classical plays, by god-like offstage characters. Gurney has also written several chronicles covering the period from the 1930s to the present. *Scenes from American Life* and *The Dining Room* are montages influenced by Thornton Wilder, and *Love Letters* is the story of a long romance carried on by mail.

Try these:
For classical influences, ▷Sophocles' *Antigone*, Plautus' *The Captives*, ▷Seneca's *Medea*; for chronicle plays, see ▷Thornton Wilder's *The Long Christmas Dinner* and *Our Town*; for the original of *Children*, see John Cheever's story *Goodbye, Mr Brother*, and for the original of *The Golden Age*, see Henry James' novel *The Aspern Papers*; Richard Nelson's *Some Americans Abroad* and ▷Edward Albee's *Who's Afraid of Virigina Woolf?* for American academics; ▷Keith Waterhouse and Hugh Whitemore for epistolary drama.

 h

HALL, Willis

see WATERHOUSE, Keith

HAMPTON, Christopher [1946–]
British dramatist

Plays include:
When Did You Last See My Mother?
(1964), *Total Eclipse* (1968), *The Philanthropist* (1970), *Savages* (1973), *Treats*
(1976), *After Mercer* (1980), *Tales from
Hollywood* (1982), *White Chameleon* (1991)

Adaptations include:
The Portage to San Cristobal of A. H. (from
the novel by George Steiner; 1982), *Les
Liaisons Dangereuses* (from the novel by
Choderlos de Laclos; 1985)

The Oxford University Dramatic Society put
on Hampton's first play (written when he was
eighteen) *When Did You Last See My Mother?*,
about two school leavers. It was taken up by
the ▷Royal Court and produced there as a
Sunday night performance when Hampton
was still an undergraduate. In 1966 it transferred to the West End and Hampton was the
youngest dramatist in living memory to have a
West End production.

On leaving Oxford, Hampton became the
first Resident Dramatist at the Court which
produced *Total Eclipse*, a play about Verlaine
which Hampton had written as a student and
then *The Philanthropist*, written while
Hampton was Resident Dramatist. This became, as Hampton puts it, 'disgracefully successful, so much so that I've always felt I left
under something of a cloud'.

In the early 1970s Hampton translated and
adapted a number of ▷Ibsen's most important plays. He was much affected by *The Doll's
House*, and became preoccupied with questions of feminism and gender which he
explored in *Treats*, and which have continued

to inform his writing. His adaptation of *Les
Liaisons Dangereuses* is not only a skilled dramatisation of a great French novel, but also a
very contemporary study of sexual power
struggles and exploitation, written with a controlled and witty elegance which made it a
great success in London and, as *Dangerous
Liaisons*, as a film, though it was less completely successful on Broadway.

The Philanthropist
The Philanthropist was the play which made
Hampton a truly 'commercial' playwright.
Subtitled 'a bourgeois comedy' the play
focuses on the ironically named philanthropist, an academic, whose most apt line is: 'I'm
a man of conviction – I think'. The title is a
sideways nod at Molière's *Le Misanthrope*, of
which it is something of an inversion. The
play initially appears as an apparently conventional comedy, with wit and wisecracks flying
in a bourgeois intellectual setting. But, in the
first scene, an undergraduate (playwright)
shoots himself, and introduces a dark edge to
the comedy. The literary jokes and wit trans-
mute into a bleak desperation. Over the
course of the play, Philip, the philanthropist,
demonstrates his ineffectuality, and thereby
the sterility of the conventions by which he
(and, by implication, the conventional form of
this kind of play) work. In attempting not to
do any harm, he actually wreaks havoc.

Try these:
▷Brecht is a character in *Tales from
Hollywood*; the treatment of sexual politics
in *Les Liaisons Dangereuses* and *Treats*
makes an interesting comparison – to
▷Ted Whitehead and ▷Strindberg; the
eighteenth century setting of *Liaisons* is
reminiscent of the world of Restoration
comedy; ▷adaptations; ▷Terry Johnson
and ▷Stephen Lowe as male playwrights

whose work is informed by feminism; ▷Tony Marchant is a contemporary male playwright who came to prominence while still in his early twenties; ▷Louise Page is an equivalent female dramatist; ▷Timberlake Wertenbaker for a female adapter with some success with another elegant French stylist, Marivaux.

HANDKE, Peter   [1942–]
Austrian dramatist

Plays include:
Offending the Audience (1966), *Prophecy and Self-Accusation* (1966), *Cries For Help* (1967), *Kaspar* (1969), *My Foot My Tutor* (1969), *Quodlibet* (1970), *The Ride Across Lake Constance* (1971), *They Are Dying Out* (1974), *A Sorrow Beyond Dreams* (1977)

Obsessed with the problems of language and communication, Handke constantly challenges preconceptions of theatrical form, style and content. *Offending the Audience* – the title seems all too accurate a description of the piece – conspicuously lacks conventional plot or character. This 'Sprechstuck' or 'speech-piece' presents four speakers of any age or sex who take an hour to work up to a climax of insults to the audience, deploying elaborate, structured sequences, often contradicting themselves, subverting all possible responses. In *Kaspar* Handke takes the story of Kaspar Hauser, who lived without speech in total isolation until he was a full-grown adult, to illustrate his thesis that language defines personality and locks each of us within its patterns of cliché and custom. His later work continues to explore this theme of the 'crisis of language'.

Try these:
▷Ionesco, ▷Eric Overmyer and ▷Mac Wellman for word-games and the attempt to construct the world by the use of language; ▷Samuel Beckett for a similar theatrical nihilism; ▷Tom Stoppard for different kinds of word games; ▷Kroetz for a similar obsession with speech and communication; ▷Brian Friel's *Translations* for language as the symbol of cultural freedom.

HANNAN, Chris   [1958–]
Scottish playwright

Plays include:
Klimkov (1984), *Elizabeth Gordon Quinn* (1985), *Orphan's Comedy* (1986), *Gamblers* (1987), *Evil Doers* (1990), *The Baby* (1990)

The individual's right to be just that – individual, non-conformist, apparently wayward and even destructive of self, is a recurring theme in Chris Hannan's work. Even when the play deals in social issues of class, power, the abuse of privilege and the exploitation of the poor and weak, at or near the centre of the action is an individual likely to go against the accepted or expected grain. Such characters are perforce often a blight on the lives of others, who carry the can for their ideals. One such vehement individual is Elizabeth Gordon Quinn, the full-blooded main character in one of Hannan's earliest and strongest plays. Though circumstance has firmly rooted her and her family in a poor Glasgow tenement, Elizabeth holds herself better than her hand-to-mouth, working-class neighbours. And the visible symbol of this superiority is her piano – which she can't play. . . . The year is 1919, there is a rent strike. Women are banding together, defying the authorities, refusing to pay. But even though it causes schism within her own family, Elizabeth will not be one of the herd if it doesn't suit her. Hannan treats the ensuing scenes of domestic conflict with touches of wise humour (that have elicited comparisons with ▷O'Casey and a fine understanding of the mixed emotions – from admiration to resentment – such free spirits can unleash in us.

Yet another headstrong woman, Macu, is at the centre of his most recent work, *The Baby*. Set in ancient Rome, this is a sprawling play that deals with the different faces of love, the different forms of tyranny. Macu, in challenging political forces she doesn't agree with, precipitates a new form of personal oppression, an all-consuming grief that taints not only her own life but that of her friends, her enemies and especially that of her gentle, devoted lover. Hannan attempts a broad canvas – historical fact extended by his complex fiction – and the essential drama of Macu's journey through loss, self-loathing and madness to her inevitable death is jeoparidsed as a result. Nonetheless, it is a significant development in the career of a young writer who was voted *Plays and Players* Most Promising

Lindsay Duncan in Christopher Hampton's stunning adaptation of Laclos' epistolary novel *Les Liaisons Dangereuses*, directed for the RSC by Howard Davies in 1985

Playwright of 1990 and who had just completed a new adaptation of Ibsen's *The Pretenders* for the RSC.

Try these:
Another young Scottish-based playwright concerned with individuals and their rights within society is Peter Arnott – his plays include *Thomas Muir* (1986) and *Salvation* (1990). ▷John Clifford for plays that make cogent points about modern society through a historical perspective; for tub-thumping politics of a Socialist persuasion see ▷John McGrath and 7.84 Scotland in the 1970s and mid-1980s, and Dave MacLennan and Dave Anderson of Wildcat whose style of music-theatre offers a different kind of reproach.

HANSBERRY, Lorraine   [1930–1965]
American dramatist

Plays include:
A Raisin in the Sun (1959), *The Sign in Sidney Brustein's Window* (1964); and finished posthumously by her former husband, Robert Nemiroff, *To Be Young, Gifted and Black* (1969), *Les Blancs* (1970)

Like ▷O'Casey and ▷Delaney, Hansberry transformed the grim world around her into something touched with gold dust. Both *The Sign in Sidney Brustein's Window* and *A Raisin in the Sun* are idealistic works, in which the protagonists manage to rise above adversity. The latter play is considered a cornerstone in the development of black theatre – a powerful, poignant protest against racial injustice and white bigotry still valid today despite its solid naturalism and contradictory values (a black family striving for white middle-class values). The warm-hearted characterisations of the downside Chicago family – chauffeur Walter Lee and his dreams of a liquor store and his battle for self-respect, his put-upon wife Ruth, young son, sister-in-law and above all the dominating figure of Momma – still draw audiences into their world. Far more than any agitprop theatre, *A Raisin in the Sun* is to this day inspirational theatre, focusing as it does on a family struggling to maintain their dignity in the face of racism, sexism and a culture whose ethos increasingly is tied to the fast buck. In many ways ahead of its time, the play ran for two years on Broadway (winning the coveted New York Critics' Circle Award for 1959). To celebrate the 25th anniversary of

Raisin's premiere, Lloyd Richards directed the work again at Yale Repertory Theatre. That production was taken to the Roundabout Theatre in New York in 1986 where again it had a highly successful run. In Britain, there was a notable recent revival of *Raisin* at the Tricycle. In the USA in recent years *Les Blancs* has been Hansberry's most frequently revived play, with two regional theatre productions in 1987–8. Hansberry died of cancer at the age of 34. It was she who inspired the song Nina Simone took from the post-humously completed *To Be Young, Gifted and Black*.

Try these:
▷James Baldwin's *Amen Corner* for comparable style but more bitter analysis of his black community; ▷Robert Ardrey's *Jeb* for a white liberal approach to American racism; ▷Tennessee Williams and ▷Arthur Miller for contemporary white American treatments of the family; Zora Neale Hurston's and ▷Langston Hughes' *Mule Bone* for contrasting representation of black life and language; ▷Caryl Phillips' *Strange Fruit* for a more pessimistic black British view; ▷Ntozake Shange for contrast with black women's writing, thirty years later; ▷Adrienne Kennedy, whose surreal, even grotesque, imagery contrasts with that of Hansberry.

HARE, David   [1947–]
British dramatist and director

Plays include:
Slag (1970, *Lay By* (with ▷Howard Brenton, ▷Brian Clark, ▷Trevor Griffiths, ▷Stephen Poliakoff, Hugh Stoddart, ▷Snoo Wilson; 1971), *England's Ireland* (with Tony Bicât, ▷Brenton, ▷Clark, ▷David Edgar, Francis Fuchs, ▷Wilson; 1972), *The Great Exhibition* (1972), *Brassneck* (with ▷Brenton; 1973), *Knuckle* (1974), *Teeth'n'Smiles* (1975), *Fanshen* (1976), *Plenty* (1978), *A Map of the World* (1983), *Pravda* (with Brenton; 1985) *The Bay at Nice* (1986), *Wrecked Eggs* (1986), *The Secret Rapture* (1988), *Racing Demon* (1990)

Hare came to prominence in the 1970s as one of a breed of committed socialist writers who included ▷Howard Barker, ▷Howard Brenton, ▷David Edgar, ▷Snoo Wilson and

▷Trevor Griffiths. He founded Portable Theatre with the dramatist Tony Bicât in 1968 and the still vibrant ▷Joint Stock company with William Gaskill and Max Stafford-Clark in 1974. He has also been literary manager and resident dramatist at the Royal Court Theatre and currently runs one of the companies at the ▷National Theatre. Hare has also carved out a singular niche in television with his television films, *Licking Hitler* (1978), *Dreams of Leaving* (1980) and *Saigon – Year of the Cat* (1983), which subtly modified traditional television techniques.

Hare has described himself in recent years as a 'commentator' on the ills of contemporary capitalism. *Fanshen*, a documentary play about the Chinese revolution, was a seminal play of the 1970s, popularising the Joint Stock rehearsal method. Unusually for Hare, the play concentrates on the processes of revolution rather than individual characters. His plays still reflect a highly charged political consciousness but recent work – such as *The Bay at Nice*, *Wrecked Eggs* and the films *Wetherby*, *Paris by Night* and *Strapless* – marks a return to a predominant interest in the topography of personal relationships. *The Secret Rapture* concentrates on the contrasting attitudes of two sisters to questions of morality and caring; *Racing Demon* pursues similar spiritual themes in the context of modern attitudes to religious faith.

Pravda

Pravda, probably Hare's most popular play to date, was written, like *Brassneck*, in collaboration with ▷Howard Brenton (an intermittent partnership that began in the days of Portable Theatre). Both are exuberantly comic political satires on an epic scale. Much of *Pravda*'s popularity in performance in Britain was due to its coincidental topicality with real-life press dealings involving Rupert Murdoch and Robert Maxwell, as well as a lethally comic central performance from Anthony Hopkins as Lambert Le Roux, the energetically ruthless, reptilian newspaper magnate. Despite its popularity, *Pravda* confirmed a general unease among female critics about Hare's handling of female characterisation. As in *Plenty*, the leading female character carries the play's moral force, but remains an unreal, one-dimensional figure, on the periphery of the main action – more of a cipher than a fully rounded character.

Plenty

Plenty attempts to use the story of the mental disintegration of its heroine, a former Resistance worker, to reflect the collapse of British post-war ideals, part of Hare's continuing preoccupation with wartime and immediate post-war England. The use of 'flashback' techniques is characteristic, giving historical depth and context to Hare's analysis of what he sees as decay in contemporary Western society particularly amongst the middle classes. In *Plenty* audiences have tended to focus on the heroine's neuroticism but Hare insists on the importance of the social context to which she responds. The film version, starring Meryl Streep, released in 1986, abandons some of the narrative complexity and specifically British detail of the play.

Try these:

▷Bertolt Brecht and ▷Edward Bond, like *Fanshen*, use epic style and geographical or spatially distanced settings; for plays about World War II see ▷Terence Rattigan's *The Deep Blue Sea*, Ian McEwan's *The Imitation Game*, ▷Stephen Lowe's *Touched*; ▷Ben Jonson, particularly *Bartholomew Fair* and *The Devil is an Ass*, for his violently entertaining attacks on capitalism; ▷Marlowe's *Dr Faustus* for the interplay between a dupe and a satanic figure which parallels the relationship between the ineffectual editor Andrew May and Le Roux in *Pravda*; ▷Michael Frayn and ▷Hecht and McArthur for newspaper plays; ▷Peter Nichols' *The National Health*, ▷Brenton's *Epsom Downs*, ▷Trevor Griffiths' *Comedians* for plays which treat the state of Britain through a national institution; for rock musicals taking the temperature of a nation in similar fashion to *Teeth'n'Smiles* see ▷Barrie Keeffe's *Bastard Angel*.

HARRIS, Richard   [1934–]
British dramatist

Plays include:
Albert and Virginia (1972), *Outside Edge* (1979), *The Business of Murder* (1981), *Stepping Out* (1984), *The Maintenance Man* (1986), *Visiting Hour* (1990), *Party Piece* (revised, 1991), *Mixed Blessings* (with Keith Strachan, 1991)

Although predominantly a television writer (Shoestring, The Darling Buds of May to name but two), Harris has achieved great commercial success with his stage plays. *The Business of Murder* played for over seven years in the West End before touring for well over a year. *Outside Edge*, an Ayckbourn-esque farce set in a cricket pavilion, won the Evening Standard Comedy Award for 1979 and has been a repertory stalwart of the circuit ever since. *Stepping Out* is his best known play to date, a comedy set in an adult education tap dancing class. It follows the fortunes of nine women and one man as they transform from awkward dancers to a final *Chorus Line* troupe of tappers. A gentle, unchallenging play, it played for over a year in the West End before touring. It has since been performed up and down Britain and is an acknowledged 'sure thing' in terms of programming. *Stepping Out* was peformed on Broadway in 1987 and is also being made into a film starring Liza Minnelli. Richard Harris's work is also beloved by amateurs, *Outside Edge* being one of the most widely performed plays in Amateur Dramatic Societies in the 1980s.

Try these:
▷Nell Dunn's *Steaming*, set in a Turkish bath, Richard Harling's *Street Magnolias* set in an American hair parlour, Tony Roper's *The Steamie*, set in a Scottish bath-house, and Susan Pam's *Curl Up and Dye*, set in a South African hair-dressing salon, for other women-congregated plays; ▷Ayckbourn, ▷Michael Frayn, ▷Alan Bennett, for other forms of English comedy; ▷Anthony Shaffer for thrillers.

HARRISON, Tony   [1937–]
British poet and dramatist

Plays (originals and translations) include:
Lysistrata (from ▷Aristophanes; 1965), *The Misanthrope* (from ▷Molière; 1973), *Phaedra Britannica* (from ▷Racine; 1975), *The Oresteia* (from ▷Aeschylus; 1981), *The Mysteries* (*The Nativity*, *The Passion*, *Doomsday*; 1985), *The Trackers of Oxyrhynchus* (from ▷Sophocles; 1988, revised 1990)

A poet and translator, Harrison made his theatre debut in 1965, collaborating with James Simmons on an adaptation of Aristophanes in a Nigerian setting. Harrison had spent four years in Nigeria after reading Classics at the University of Leeds. His reputation as a poet of international standing was secured by the time he turned his attention to

the theatre again in the mid-1970s with much-praised translations of Molière and Racine. He has also collaborated with the composer Harrison Birtwistle on an opera, *Yan Tan Tethera*, and has translated Smetana's *The Bartered Bride*. His version of *The Oresteia* was great theatre and marvellous writing. The complete cycle of his medieval mystery plays was presented at the ▷Royal National Theatre's Cottesloe auditorium and subsequently at the Lyceum in 1986. The juxtaposition of an austere classical tradition and proletarian irreverence is sometimes startling, often entertaining and controversial, as in the extended poem *v*.

The Trackers of Oxyrhynchus
Two Oxford dons travel to Egypt in 1907 on the trail of a lost manuscript. The rediscovery of a fragment of a satyr play by ▷Sophocles and the situation of the homeless in present-day 'cardboard city' are used to demonstrate comically the spurious divisions between high and low culture. The effect is brilliantly enhanced by Harrison's imaginative use of language and physical action, and his playing with convention – you don't often find yourself singing along in ancient Greek at the National (and enjoying it!).

Try these:
▷Neil Bartlett who also translated *The Misanthrope*, is also an exponent of mixing high and low culture together; see ▷Medieval Drama, ▷Euripides, ▷Aeschylus, ▷Lee Breuer.

HART, Moss

see KAUFMAN, George S.

HARWOOD, Ronald   [1934–]
South African-born novelist and dramatist

Plays include:
Country Matters (1969), *A Family* (1978), *The Dresser* (1980), *After the Lions* (1982), *Tramway Road* (1984), *Interpreters* (1985), *The Deliberate Death of a Polish Priest* (1985), *J.J. Farr* (1987), *Another Time* (1989)

Born in South Africa, Harwood joined Sir Donald Wolfit's Shakespeare Company as actor and dresser to this last of the old-style actor-managers (an experience which later

Barrie Rutter as Silenus in Tony Harrison's *The Trackers of Oxyrhnchus*, Royal National Theatre, 1990

spawned a biography and the play *The Dresser*). He continued as an actor until 1959, but in 1960 he had a play produced on television and published his first novel in 1961. As a screenwriter his subjects have been varied and his work is difficult to categorise in any medium, though you can expect well characterised parts for actors and a strong sense of theatre. *J.J. Farr*, about the loss of religious faith, offers acting opportunities, but found little favour with critics. Up to *Another Time*, *The Dresser* was probably his most successful play. Inspired by, though not a portrait of, Wolfit and his company, *The Dresser* set on tour in the provinces in the middle of World War II, as the actor-manager gets through his last performance of *King Lear*. Anyone with memories of that kind of theatre will recognise the authenticity with which Harwood has captured it. *Another Time*, also drawing on Harwood's own experience – this time, a South African childhood (the setting, too, of *Tramway Road*) – was a theatrical tour de force. Elijah Moshinsky's humorous and clever production with its simulated recording studio was a constant source of quiet amusement. Ostensibly dealing with the nature of musical genius, the heart and soul of the play lay in Harwood's uncovering of the sinews of an embattled lower middle class Jewish marriage and the process of ageing. A cast which included Albert Finney, Janet Suzman, Sara Kestelman and David de Keyser ensured it a long run in London before transferring to Broadway.

Try these:
▷John Osborne's *The Entertainer* for a study of life on the variety circuit; ▷J.B. Priestley's *The Good Companions* and ▷Noël Coward's *Hay Fever* for other portraits of a life in theatre; ▷Trevor Griffiths' *Comedians* for a more barbed view; *42nd Street*, *Chorus Line*, *Mame* and a whole bandwagon of American musicals for the tears and bliss of showbiz; Graham Greene for plays about loss of faith; ▷Peter Shaffer's *Amadeus* deals with musical genius very differently.

HASTINGS, Michael   [1938–]
British dramatist

Plays include:
Don't Destroy Me (1956), *Yes – and After* (1957), *The World's Baby* (1964), *Lee Harvey Oswald* (1966), *The Cutting of the Cloth* (1973), *For the West* (1977), *Gloo Joo* (1978), *Full Frontal* (1979), *Carnival War a Go Hot* (1979), *Midnite at the Starlite* (1980), *Tom and Viv* (1984), *The Emperor* (1986), *A Dream of People* (1990)

Hastings began his theatrical career as a trainee actor and writer at the ▷Royal Court. Born in London, his first play, *Don't Destroy Me*, an exploration of a Jewish household in Brixton, was produced when he was only eighteen and working as a tailor's apprentice. *The World's Baby*, a Sunday night performance with Vanessa Redgrave as the central character, a woman whom the play follows over twenty years, was never given a full-scale production. *Lee Harvey Oswald*, produced at the Hampstead Theatre Club, is an example of what was known at the time as 'Theatre of Fact', a sort of documentary account of Oswald's life up to the point of Kennedy's assassination. *Gloo Joo*, a study of a West Indian's experience of London, was produced at the Hampstead Theatre Club and went on to transfer to the West End. *The Emperor*, a controversial account of Emperor Haile Selassie (there were protests outside from Ethiopians and Rastafarians), was a subtle if quirky study of power and its acolyte tendencies. *A Dream of People* is a complex and compelling examination of the resonant relationships between past, present and future, personal and public morality, morality and expediency, all focused through the issue of pensions.

Tom and Viv
Probably Hastings' most successful play, *Tom and Viv* pursues his concern with the theatrical possibilities of biography in a study of the fraught marriage between ▷T.S. Eliot and his first wife, Vivienne Haigh-Wood. Vivienne ended her life in a mental hospital, and the play explores her mental fragility, her tortuous relationship with Eliot, and the contemporary British upper-class culture which produced Vivienne. The play is ultimately quite unsympathetic to Eliot and his role in their relationship. *Tom and Viv* was produced in America after a successful Royal Court run under the auspices of Joe Papp, and has been one of the most successful of the exchanges between the Royal Court and The Public Theater in New York.

Try these:
▷Derek Walcott's *O Babylon* for other views of Haile Selassie; Emily Mann for 'Theater of Testimony' documentary style.

▷Edgar White, ▷Michael Abbensetts, ▷Mustapha Matura and ▷Caryl Phillips for contrasting views of West Indians in London; ▷Barrie Keeffe's *King of England*; for other plays about poets and their domestic lives, ▷Howard Brenton's *Bloody Poetry*, Liz Lochhead's *Fire and Ice*, ▷Hugh Whitemore's portrait of the poet Stevie Smith, *Stevie*, ▷Susan Glaspell's *Alison's House* based on Emily Dickinson, and ▷Bond's *Bingo*.

HAVEL, Václav   [1936–]

Czech dramatist, dissident and latterly President

Plays include:
The Garden Party (1963), *The Memorandum* (1965), *The Increased Difficulty of Concentration* (1968), *Audience, Private View* and *Protest* (three short plays, 1975), *Largo Desolato* (1984), *Temptation* (1985), *Redevelopment* (1990)

Havel did not like the term 'dissident', but from 1969 until the extraordinary run of events in November 1989 which brought down the Czech communist government and soon after installed him as his country's President, he was known in the West as Czechoslovakia's leading dissident playwright. Havel preferred to see it in terms of 'living in truth'; his plays from that period (notably the three that are known as the Vanek plays, *Audience*, *Private View* and *Protest*) bear witness to that 'living in truth' as a stubborn, unflinching morality. The plays themselves are far from being perfect dramatic models, being short on conflict and little more than talking-head pieces. But the delineations of the characters and their relationship to society are fascinatingly created, and what they have to say about personal integrity, individual responsibility and 'accommodation' to the system have as much resonance for audiences in the West as for those for whom the plays were then intended. In fact, Havel had not been able to see any of his own plays after 1969 (except for a video of *Temptation* smuggled in by the ▷RSC). They were not published openly in Czechoslovakia, though they had been widely performed in the West. Havel had wanted to study drama at university, but because of his 'bourgeois' family background he was forced to start as a stagehand; he then worked as a lighting technician and later became dramaturg at the avant-

garde Prague Theatre on the Balustrade, for which he began to write plays in the 1960s. Havel's early plays were classified as absurdist, and *The Memorandum* showed one of his recurring themes: life in an organisation where mechanical clichés and deformation of language conceal the fact that nothing actually gets done, and employees are always watching their backs. In 1968 he left the Theatre on the Balustrade, and he was effectively excluded from live theatre after the Soviet invasion of that year. He continued to work for human rights and in 1977 was a founder member of Charter 77. He was imprisoned in 1979 for his involvement in VONS (the Committee for the Defence of the Unjustly Prosecuted). ▷Samuel Beckett dedicated *Catastrophe* to him during this imprisonment. When released in 1983 Havel wrote the short play *Mistake* as a response; both were shown at the Barbican as *Thoughtcrimes* in 1984. *Largo Desolato* shows a dissident scholar reduced to near-nervous breakdown by the impossibility of living up to his reputation as a symbol of resistance and is an allegory of the artist's relationship to society; ▷Tom Stoppard translated it for the New Vic, Bristol, in 1986, and it played in London at the small Orange Tree in Richmond in 1987.

Temptation

This is another satire on organisational hierarchies and yesmen, but based on the Faust story. It has a broader satirical sweep than his earlier plays, showing multiple layers of fear, disloyalty and double-cross. Dr Foustka, who wishes to study forbidden knowledge, is tempted to ever meaner betrayals by a Mephistophelean figure with smelly feet, who turns out to be a spy for the Director of his Institute; all is revealed at a wild Walpurgisnacht fancy dress party. The play was produced, to some acclaim, at the ▷RSC's Other Place in 1987 and the Barbican in 1988; the RSC had to book a special call to Havel to give him news of its success.

Try these:
▷Beckett, for *Catastrophe*, possibly the nearest he ever went to making a political statement; ▷Mrozek, for Eastern European plays using 'absurdist' techniques to show political desperation; Soviet playwright Alexsandr Gelman's *We, the Undersigned* and *A Man with Connections* for more barbed revelations

of bureaucratic bungling under communism; ▷David Edgar's *The Shape of the Table* features Havel in its fictionalised account of events in Prague in November 1989. ▷Tom Stoppard (Ken Tynan was the first to link these two Czechs and to see Stoppard's potential political streak); ▷Arthur Miller's *The Archbishop's Ceiling* for East European dissidents; ▷Goethe and ▷Marlowe for the Faust story; ▷Timberlake Wertenbaker's *The Grace of Mary Traverse* has Faustian resonances.

HAVIS, Allan   [1951–   ]
American dramatist

Plays include:
Mink Sonata (1986), *Haut Gout* (1987), *Hospitality* (1988), *Morocco* (1988), *A Daring Bride* (1990), *Lilith* (1990), *Ladies of Fisher Cove* (1991), *Albert the Astronomer* (1991)

▷Strindberg, ▷Pinter, ▷Albee, ▷Hare, ▷Shepard, and ▷Churchill are among the writers whose brooding, ironic, and even cynical works have influenced Allan Havis. A native New Yorker, Havis received graduate degrees in drama from Hunter College and Yale. Though he started writing in the mid-1970s, his work began to be performed only in the late 1980s, largely at off-off-Broadway and regional theatres.

Many of Havis' plays are intrigues dealing with political and metaphysical evil. In *Haut Gout*, an American doctor is caught up in the Haitian revolution; *Hospitality* covers two political detainees in an American immigration service detention center; and in *Morocco*, an American architect tries to free his wife from a Moroccan prison where she is held on charges of prostitution.

Havis has also written a number of fables concerned with sex, myth and magic. For example, *Lilith*, based on Jewish folklore, tells of Adam's divorce from his first wife, and of her ensuing competition with Eve. Other plays in this vein include *Mink Sonata* and *A Daring Bride*.

Havis now teaches theatre in southern California.

Try these:
For a late 19th-century look at sex roles, ▷August Strindberg's *Miss Julie*; for dark perspectives on modern family life, ▷Edward Albee's *Who's Afraid of Virginia Woolf?*, ▷Jules Feiffer's *Little Murders*, and ▷Sam Shepard's *True West*; for political plays, ▷Richard Nelson's *Principiae Scriptoriae* ▷Douglas Turner Ward's *Day of Absence*, ▷Peter Weiss' *The Investigation*, ▷Arthur Kopit's *Indians* and ▷David Rabe's *Streamers*; ▷Sarah Daniels' *Beside Herself* also features Lilith.

HAYES, Catherine   [1949–   ]
British dramatist

Plays include:
Little Sandra (1976), *Not Waving* (1983), *Skirmishes* (1982), *Long Time Gone* (1986)

When she was younger, Catherine Hayes wanted to be a detective. Instead she became a French teacher, and it was only when she saw ▷Alan Bleasdale's advertisement for new writers for the Liverpool Playhouse that she decided to turn her hand to plays rather than novel writing. *Skirmishes* is the play that brought her to public attention. Essentially a two-hander (it won *Drama* magazine's Most Promising Playwright award for 1982), it has been performed all over the world, from Manhattan's Theatre Club in New York, to Australia, Japan and Germany. It cast an unsentimental eye on the subject of mother/daughter and sibling relationships. Round a dying mother's bed, a bitter, if witty, war of verbal and emotional attrition is let loose as two sisters give vent to long-stored-up resentments and misunderstandings. Hayes' drama is a searing, yet compassionate analysis, confronting painful truths about death, love, and the awful taboos to do with duty. Further revelations of female self-doubt and vulnerability were also behind *Not Waving*, about the crumbling fortunes of a female cabaret comic, brought on by ill-health, failing confidence (she can't get the audience to laugh any more) and a break-up with her manager. Variations on both subjects turned up again in Hayes' latest play, *Long Time Gone* – another delve into sibling rivalries, and love/hate relationships, this time around the Cain and Abel myth of brothers. Hayes took the 1960s pop stars the Everly Brothers as her model but freely embroidered it in facts and chronology – an approach which some reviewers accepted, but to which others, surprisingly, took a certain exception.

Try these:

▷Marsha Norman's *'night Mother* takes an equally painful view of the symbiotic mother/daughter relationship; ▷Sharman Macdonald, ▷Julia Kearsley, ▷Ayshe Raif and ▷Louise Page are other contemporary playwrights who have dealt with equal realism about mothers and daughters; ▷Shelagh Delaney's *A Taste of Honey* and ▷Ann Jellicoe's *The Sport of My Mad Mother* for more extended treatments, one realistic, the other surreal; ▷Stephen Bill's *Curtains* also dealt with family pressures around a dying mother; Honor Moore's *Mourning Pictures* is a free verse treatment of a dying mother and her daughter; ▷Michel Tremblay's *Johnny Mangano and His Astonishing Dogs* has a cabaret club setting for its two downward spiralling performers; ▷John Osborne's *The Entertainer* and ▷Trevor Griffiths' *Comedians* are more extended explorations into the nature of comedy as prop and social weapon; ▷Peter Nichols' *A Day in the Death of Joe Egg* for comparable humour; ▷Alan Bleasdale's *Are You Lonesome Tonight?* plays freely with the Presley legend.

HECHT, Ben   [1894–1964]
MacARTHUR, Charles   [1895–1956]
American dramatists

Plays include:
The Front Page (1928), *Twentieth Century* (1932), *Jumbo* (1935; book for the musical), *Ladies and Gentlemen* (1939), *Swan Song* (1946)

A team who found success together writing screenplays, and also on their own, Hecht and MacArthur helped define a style of boisterous, cheerfully anarchic comedy which is definably American in its determined avoidance of anything genteel or refined. The duo are best known for two plays, *The Front Page* and *Twentieth Century*, both of which became films – or, in the case of the former, several films. Each is a kind of courtship comedy. In *Front Page*, an editor tries to lure his star reporter away from his fiancée by extolling the passion of journalism over that of romance. In *Twentieth Century*, which became a hit Broadway and West End musical in the late 1970s, an egomaniacal Broadway producer

makes a young shopgirl a star, and when she makes moves to leave him, he spends a lengthy train journey trying to win her back. (Howard Hawks' 1934 movie version, with Carole Lombard and John Barrymore, is a comedy classic.) *Ladies and Gentlemen*, a romantic thriller set during a trial, was MacArthur's attempt to concoct a vehicle for his wife, Helen Hayes. The two found less success as collaborators in later plays.

The Front Page
A perennial favourite for revivals (most recently in London at the Old Vic in 1972 and in New York at the Lincoln Center Theater in 1986), this gregarious tale of Chicago newspapermen in the 1920s has spawned three films, one musical (the 1982 *Windy City*) and any number of spiritual children, from ▷Thomas Babe's *Buried Inside Extra* to, in their own more politicised way, British works like ▷Hare and ▷Brenton's *Pravda* and Stephen Wakelam's *Deadlines*. Politics were not upmost in Hecht and MacArthur's minds as they spun a rapid-fire yarn about a scheming editor's attempts to keep his star reporter, Hildy Johnson, from succumbing to the enticements of love; but in its subplots about corruption in the sheriff's office and its often blistering portrait of male camaraderie, the play can seem surprisingly biting and contemporary.

Try these:
▷Thomas Babe's *Buried Inside Extra*, ▷Hare and Brenton's *Pravda*, Stephen Wakelam's *Deadlines*; ▷George Abbott's *Broadway* and ▷Kaufman and Hart for similarly large-scale, rumbustious American works; and ▷David Mamet (especially *Glengarry Glen Ross*) for capturing both the brio and the venality that go with careerism.

HEDDEN, Roger   [1960–]
American dramatist

Plays include:
Been Taken (1985), *Terry Neal's Future* (1986), *Bodies, Rest, and Motion* (1986), *The Artistic Direction* (1990), *As Sure as You Live* (1991)

The central preoccupation of Hedden's work is the quest for self-fulfilment in American life. He observes a society on the run, searching for some greater meaning in life, and yet never standing still long enough to find it. 'People don't take the time to see what's around them or inside of them,' comments Hedden. In *Bodies, Rest, and Motion*, produced at the Mitzi Newhouse Theatre at Lincoln Center, we follow the desperate wanderings of the principal character who along the way loses his parents (who moved without leaving a forwarding address), his girlfriend (whom he abandons), and the job he thought he wanted in the 'city of the future' – Canton, Ohio. *Been Taken* traces the changing expectations of young college students over a five-year period from their campus antics through life in the workaday world. Hedden finds his message best expressed in comedy, and his deft language explores the power of dramatic irony. A 1984 graduate of Columbia University, Hedden received a National Endowment for the Arts Playwriting Fellowship in 1985.

Try these:
For characters who develop from their college days see ▷Wendy Wasserstein's *Uncommon Women and Others*; for characters in search of meaning try ▷Tennessee Williams' *Camino Real*, ▷John Guare's *House of Blue Leaves*, ▷Michael Weller's *Moonchildren*, and ▷Anton Chekhov's *The Seagull*.

HEGGIE, Iain   [1953–]
British dramatist

Plays include:
Politics in the Park (1986), *A Wholly Healthy Glasgow* (1987), *American Bagpipes* (1988), *Clyde Nouveau* (1990)

One-time PT instructor, drama teacher, and member of the ▷Royal Court's writing group, Glasgow-born Heggie took the theatre world by storm with his first full-length play *A Wholly Healthy Glasgow*. Awarded a special prize in the first Mobil Playwriting competition in 1985, it was taken up by Manchester's Royal Exchange, toured the Edinburgh Festival and came down to the Royal Court in February 1988 (being televised at about the same time). Hailed as Glasgow's answer to ▷David Mamet, Heggie's dialogue, steeped in Glaswegian, is the driving force of his work, with its febrile energy and oddball syntax. Set in a health club, the play has been seen by some as a metaphor of modern-day survival; nearly all have agreed that, in the

words of *The Observer*'s critic, Michael Ratcliffe, it is 'one of the funniest plays of the last few years'. However, in a post-AIDS climate, it is also fair to say that its libidinous gay character, with eyes set on 'a bit of nookie every fifteen seconds', now seems like a limp-wristed throwback to another era. *American Bagpipes*, a suburban comedy about family disintegration, was commissioned and produced whilst he was writer-in-residence at the Royal Exchange. *Clyde Nouveau*, his latest, sees Heggie continuing to draw comparison to Mamet in its examination of the world of small-time thieves and big-time property speculators.

Try these:
▷Jim Cartwright's *Road* for a similarly dynamic use of language; ▷John Byrne's *The Slab Boys Trilogy* for a similarly volatile if more socialist view of Glasgow working life; ▷David Mamet's *Glengarry Glen Ross* for an American equivalent of small-time capitalism.

HELLMAN, Lillian   [1905–1984]
American dramatist, screenwriter, journalist

Plays include:
The Children's Hour (1934), *Days to Come* (1936), *The Little Foxes* (1939), *Watch on the Rhine* (1941), *The Searching Wind* (1944), *Another Part of the Forest* (1946), *Montserrat* (1949), *Regina* (1949), *The Autumn Garden* (1951), *The Lark* (1955; adapted from Anouilh), *Candide* (musical; 1956), *Toys in the Attic* (1960), *My Mother, My Father and Me* (1963; adapted from Burt Blechman's novel, *How Much?*)

Screenplays include:
The Dark Angel with Mordaunt Shairp (1935), *These Three* (1936), *Dead End* (1937), *The Little Foxes*, with others (1941), *Watch on the Rhine* with Dashiell Hammett (1943), *The North Star* (1943), *The Searching Wind* (1946), *The Children's Hour*, with John Michael Hayes (1961), *The Chase* (1966)

Playwright and long-time companion of thriller writer Dashiell Hammett, Hellman's wit is typical of the Dorothy Parker period (she was a close personal friend). To audiences now, however, Hellman is probably less associated with the theatre than with the writing of such classic films as *The Little Foxes*, which starred Bette Davis. Her volumes of autobiography, *Scoundrel Time*, *Pentimento* and *An Unfinished Woman*, were the subject of a huge literary controversy regarding their historical reliability and truthfulness. Her plays have not been seen much in England since the 1950s, the most recent being the ▷National Theatre's 1980 production of *Watch on the Rhine*, directed by Mike Okrent.

By modern standards, her plays are shamelessly melodramatic, though they do also have a moral centre, ruthlessly exposing money as the most corrosive of agents, particularly in the family. Hellman's malign protagonists often have the best of the fray (and afford golden opportunities for actresses to play a 'bitch'), but she uses them to show human perversity and the destructive power of evil on human relationships. Her world of decaying aristocrats and the upwardly mobile middle-classes is frequently a world of moral bankruptcy. Throughout her plays there is, too, a consistent concern to voice uncomfortable emotional truths as well as socio-political issues (her stand against the House Un-American Activities Committee of Senator McCarthy in 1952 is legendary if still disputed): in *Toys in the Attic*, her Southern portrait of a man dominated by two sisters, it is the injuries people inflict on each other in the name of security and love; in *Watch on the Rhine*, it is American non-interventionism, the spectre of fascism and the Holocaust. Several of her plays have women in central roles, but by contemporary feminist standards they lack any radical re-assessment – rather, reinforcing certain female stereotypes. In *The Little Foxes*, the women are hard and narcissistic; in *The Children's Hour*, unhappily lesbian, or emotionally dependent on men in *Toys in the Attic*. William Luce's biographical play based on Hellman, *Lillian*, produced in New York with Zoe Caldwell and in London (1985) with Frances de la Tour proved that, posthumously, Hellman remains as controversial a figure as ever.

The Children's Hour

First produced in 1934, this is probably one of her best known and certainly most successful plays. Audaciously, for its time, it tackles the taboo subject of lesbianism, although the real subject of the play is considered to be the destructiveness of innuendo and rumour. Predictably, the tale is a tragic one: one of the teachers is accused by a revengeful pupil of having an 'unnatural' relationship with a

colleague and commits suicide. Hellman's achievement is to show the consequences of the pupil's 'little lie' and, perhaps inadvertently, the consequences of society's intolerance towards lesbianism.

Try these:

▷Jonson for characters as embodiments of moral evil; ▷Tennessee Williams for many of the plays' Southern setting (especially *Toys in the Attic*); for other female 'villains', ▷Ibsen's *Hedda Gabler*, ▷Racine's *Phèdre*, and ▷Euripides' *Medea*; for dramas of family life, ▷Alan Ayckbourn; ▷Arthur Miller's *The Crucible* for the consequences of spiteful rumour; for a contrasting contemporary treatment of plays on an anti-fascist theme, Maxwell Anderson; ▷Chekhov for family sagas of tight narrative, leisurely discussion and high moral intent.

HENLEY, Beth   [1952–]
American dramatist

Plays include:
Am I Blue (1973), *Parade* (book for a musical, 1975), *Crimes of the Heart* (1979), *The Miss Firecracker Contest* (1980), *The Wake of Jamey Foster* (1982), *The Debutante Ball* (1985), *The Lucky Spot* (1987), *Abundance* (1990)

Born in Jackson, Mississippi, Beth Henley epitomises the Southern Gothic voice in the American playwriting industry dominated either by urban East Coast angst or mimetic pieces about LA blankness. *Crimes of the Heart*, her Pulitzer Prize-winning play (first performed at Actors' Theatre of Louisville, and immediately picked up by Manhattan Theater Club before its highly successful Broadway run) introduced Henley's cheerfully eccentric tone and lunatic domestic tangles. Set five years after Hurricane Camille, *Crimes of the Heart* (later made into a film with Diane Keaton, Jessica Lange and Sissy Spacek) generates a comic tempest of its own as the three McGrath sisters struggle to make their peace with a world that never quite matches their perceptions of it. Her later plays extended Henley's gallery of Southern eccentrics who counter the world's cruelties with daffy strategies for survival, though none has been as well received as *Crimes of the Heart*. *Abundance* tackles a different and more ambitious topic: the fortunes of two mail-order brides in the Old West as they angle for adventure and self-fulfilment.

Henley has been criticised for 'Dixie whimsy-and-water' superficiality, but others have noted the desperation under the surface of the 'molasses meandering', suggesting that Henley is a more serious writer than her productions generally acknowledge.

Try these:
▷Chekhov's *Three Sisters* for another family of grown sisters clinging to a vision of a world elsewhere; ▷Marsha Norman, Jane Martin, Deborah Pryor, ▷Larry Larson, ▷Levi Lee and other Actors' Theatre of Louisville playwrights with a similar Southern sensibility; Robert Harling's *Steel Magnolias*; ▷Kaufman and Hart for families bound by their own peculiar logic (and fireworks!); Clare Booth Luce.

HEYWOOD, Thomas   [1574–1641]
English Renaissance dramatist

Plays include:
A Woman Killed with Kindness (1603), *The Fair Maid of the West* (pre 1610; published 1630), *The English Traveller* (published 1633)

Heywood's current theatrical status depends largely on the ▷RSC's romping 1986 conflation of his two-part *The Fair Maid of the West*, treated by Trevor Nunn as 'a comical/tragical adventure entertainment celebrating the birth of a nation', and on memories of a 1971 ▷National Theatre production of *A Woman Killed with Kindness*. Heywood was a prolific writer and sometime actor who claimed to have contributed to over 200 plays, of which some 20 survive. He wrote in just about every genre and style available to him but, despite the success of the RSC's *The Fair Maid of the West*, *A Woman Killed with Kindness*, with its realistic treatment of domestic strife in a bourgeois context, is more likely to be revived. It is particularly interesting for its husband who forgives his adulterous wife and her lover rather than pursuing revenge.

Try these:
Heywood's treatment of adultery in *A Woman Killed with Kindness*, with its realistic treatment of domestic strife, contrasts strikingly with ▷Shakespeare's in *Othello*;

The Fair Maid of the West is one of many Renaissance plays to use the so-called substitute bed mate trick which occurs most notably in ▷Middleton's *The Changeling* as well as ▷Shakespeare's *All's Well That Ends Well* and *Measure for Measure*.

HIGHWAY, Tomson   [1951–]
Canadian dramatist

Plays include:
The Rez Sisters (1987), *Dry Lips Ought To Move To Kapuskasing* (1989)

Tomson Highway is one of the major forces in Native People's theatre in Canada. For many years, the native people or 'indians' of North America have felt their culture was something both used and abused by the white people. In Canada, in recent years, native people have started to claim back theatre for themselves, producing work which is performed on reservations and in urban community centres for the indigenous population. Often the plays are written in indigenous languages as well as English and feature familiar 'spirits' from native culture. Tomson Highway is at the forefront of young native people artists. He is the Artistic Director of Native Earth Performing Inc., Toronto's only Native professional theatre company. *The Rez Sisters*, reminiscent of Michel Tremblay's *Les Belles Soeurs*, follows the adventures (and misadventures) of seven Native women who leave their reservation to go to Toronto in order to take part in The Biggest Bingo Game in the World. Both funny and tragic, it portrays their lives with affection and sympathy, showing both the spirituality and the difficulty of life for contemporary Native people. Both this play, and its companion piece 'Dry Lips' (about seven Native men and hockey) won the Dora Mavor Moore Award for Best New Play of the Year, one of the most prestigious awards in Canada.

Try these:
▷Robert Lepage for another Canadian artist dealing with cross-cultures, particularly in *The Dragons Trilogy* and *Tectonic Plates*, ▷Wole Soyinka for a Nigerian playwright combining African and western cultures; Jatinder Verma for one who synthesises Asian with western culture; ▷Debbie Horsfield's *Red Devils Trilogy* for 'leaving the reservation'.

Amanda Plummer and Tess Harper in Beth Henley's *Abundance* at the Manhattan Theatre Club, directed by Ron Lagomarsino, 1990

HILL, Errol   [1921–]
Trinidadian dramatist and academic

Plays include:
Brittle and the City Fathers (1948; later known as *Oily Portraits*), *Square Peg* (1949), *The Ping-Pong* (radio 1950; staged 1953), *Dilemma* (1953), *Broken Melody* (1954), *Wey-Wey* (1957), *Strictly Matrimony* (1959), *Man Better Man* (1960; originally 1957), *Dimanche Gras Carnival Show* (1963), *Whistling Charlie and the Monster* (1964), *Dance Bongo* (1965)

Hill is a major figure in the creation of a West Indian theatre through his work as writer, director, actor, editor of play anthologies, author of the standard work *The Trinidad Carnival* and academic (he has held posts in the West Indies, Nigeria and the USA). His aim, in his own words, has been 'to treat aspects of Caribbean folk life, drawing on speech idioms and rhythms, music and dance, and to evolve a form of drama and theatre most nearly representative of Caribbean life and art'. He draws on folklore associated with the calypso and carnival traditions in *Man Better Man*, which he selected to represent him in his own edition of three Caribbean plays (*Plays for Today*, Longman, 1985), with its obeah man brought in to help a young lover to win his bride in a duel with the village stick-fighting ('calinda') champion. The original version was written in prose and had no music, but in its current form it uses calypso verse and music in a comic form which celebrates aspects of folk culture that have survived despite colonial rule.

Try these:
▷Mustapha Matura is a Trinadadian-born dramatist who shares many of Hill's interests, particularly in carnival in *Play Mas* and in folk culture in *Meetings*; ▷Synge's *Playboy of the Western World* (and Matura's reworking of it as *Playboy of the West Indies*) for one of the classic celebrations and interrogations of folk culture in drama; ▷Derek Walcott as the pre-eminent Caribbean dramatist who also shows Hill's concern for a rich theatrical language expressing Caribbean culture as fully as possible; John Constable's *Black Mas* and ▷Lee Breuer's *The Warrior Ant* for a white writer's treatment of carnival; Felix Cross' musicals *Blues for Railton* and *Mass Carib* also celebrate pre-colonial, pre-Christian Caribbean cultures in music.

HISPANIC-AMERICAN THEATRE

The history of Hispanic theatre in the United States, which begins with performances by Spanish colonisers in the sixteenth century (more than a hundred years before the first theatre in English), is complicated by the wide variety of cultures it must subsume. Hispanic-Americans come from Spanish-speaking countries throughout the Americas. The theatre of Mexican-Americans in the Southwest has been entirely separate from that of Cuban exiles in Manhattan, or Puerto Ricans in the South Bronx. Still, because the heritage of these artists is Catholic as well as Spanish-speaking, and because Hispanics are a minority in North America, one can find common ground in the art they make. Today, with the world becoming an ever-smaller global village and with ever-increasing communication among theatre people throughout the United States, the consideration of Hispanic-American theatre as an entity makes a new kind of sense.

The 1920s were the golden age of Spanish-speaking theatre in the United States. Melodramas and *zarzuelas* (operettas) from Spain, plays created locally, and variety shows filled the stages of more than twenty theatres in San Antonio and Los Angeles. Touring Mexican companies played New York, Philadelphia, Cleveland and Chicago, as well as throughout the Southwest. *Carpa* (tent) theatres traveled rural circuits in the region with shows, derived from circus and clowning, filled with humour, music and satire. New York City and Tampa, Florida, the eastern centres of Spanish-language theatre, saw performances by resident professionals as well as by touring companies from Spain, Cuba and Argentina.

Many factors, from the Depression, the Spanish Civil War and World War II to the advent of movies and television, contributed to the decline of Spanish-language theatre. It was the 1960s before Hispanic theatre flourished again in the United States. In the West, the seminal figure was Luis Valdez, who founded his El Teatro Campesino in 1965 as part of the struggle for California farmworkers' rights. By the early 1970s there were nearly one hundred Chicano theatre groups spread through the region, bringing political, often improvisational pieces to their communities, usually in a mixture of Spanish and English.

All three of New York City's current leading Hispanic theatres were created in the sixties. Miriam Colon's Puerto Rican Travelling Theatre, now handsomely housed in midtown Manhattan, stages contemporary plays in both English and Spanish during the theatre season, while maintaining its summer touring programme through the city's parks. Under the direction of Cuban émigrés Rene Buch and Gilberto Zaldivar, Repertorio Español has grown into the country's leading Spanish-speaking theatre. The company presents a wide range of classic and modern works – the latter including plays originally written in English by contemporary Hispanic-American dramatists – as well as dance and music theatre. INTAR Hispanic American Arts Center, still led by one of its founders, Max Ferra, is an English-speaking theatre whose focus is new work (which may include new translations of older Spanish-language plays).

On the West Coast the 1970s saw the first Chicano theatre festival, the formation of the coalition of Chicano *teatros* known as TENAZ, and ultimately the disappearance of most of these collectives. The strongest of them, however, created two notable pieces during this period, *La Victim* and *Zoot Suit* (both 1976). The former, an ensemble creation by California's El Teatro de la Esperanza, dealing with the immigration and deportation of Mexicans has been produced by community groups all over the United States. Luis Valdez' *Zoot Suit*, which was premiered at the Mark Taper Forum in Los Angeles, went on to a long commercial run in LA and then lasted a disappointingly short time on Broadway, was inspired by local history – the race riots between Mexican-American gangs and US servicemen which inflamed the southern California city in 1943. This hit show proved to be a model of successful integration of Hispanic-American work into mainstream theatres.

Landmark Hispanic-American plays were also being written in New York. *Short Eyes*, a powerful recreation of prison life by the late Puerto Rican writer Miguel Piñero, was staged off-off-Broadway by The Family, a company of mostly black and Hispanic ex-inmates. The production wound up on the main stage at Lincoln Center, and the New York critics voted *Short Eyes* best play of the 1973–4 season. Another off-off-Broadway production to transfer – this one to the off-Broadway American Place Theatre – was ▷Maria Irene Fornes' poetic and inherently feminist *Fefu and Her Friends* (1977), a breakthrough play she wrote after a long fallow period. This Havana-born writer and director had already established herself off-off-Broadway in the sixties; from now on her work would be marked by a new gravity.

Through the early years of her career Irene Fornes was rarely thought of as a Hispanic artist; when many knowledgeable theatre people place her with the very best of American playwrights, there is no ethnic qualifier. But when in 1981 the Ford Foundation helped launch INTAR's Hispanic Playwrights-in-Residence Laboratory, which Fornes has conducted for a decade, her importance to Hispanic-American theatre soon became clear. Evidence suggests that she may be the best playwrighting teacher in America: ▷Eduardo Machado and Milcha Sanchez-Scott are just two of the gifted writers to emerge from her workshops. For years she also worked with playwrights in California every summer, and has taught in many other states as well. Her workshops have served to bring many kinds of Hispanic writers together, and are a major force behind the current flowering of Hispanic-American drama.

New York Shakespeare Festival producer Joseph Papp's long record of support for Hispanic theatre is now exhibited in an annual Festival Latino that features work from many countries. South Coast Repertory's annual Hispanic Playwrights Project brings a group of writers to the southern California theatre for a series of workshops and readings. Hispanic-American theatre is thriving. What it needs is a wider audience.

Try these:
Lynne Alvarez, Migdala Cruz, ▷John Jesurun, John Leguizamo, Carlos Morton, Reinaldo Povod, Jose Rivera, Bernardo Solano, Ana Maria Simo are among the most gifted Hispanic-American theatre writers. *On New Ground: Contemporary Hispanic-American Plays* (Theatre Communications Group, 1987) is a pioneering anthology; Arte Publico Press (Houston, Texas) is a major publisher of Hispanic-American plays. ▷African-American theatre, ▷Asian theatre in Britain, ▷Black theatre in Britain, ▷Yiddish and Jewish-American theatre for parallels and contrast.

HOCHHÜTH, Rolf   [1931–]
German dramatist

Plays include:
The Representative (1963), *Soldiers* (1967), *Guerillas* (1970), *The Midwife* (1972)

Hochhüth spent some years as a reader with a publishing firm, potentially a useful training for writing 'documentary' dramas. He has had some international success as a dramatist, largely because of the controversial nature of his best known plays. *The Representative* was his first play, in five acts and in free verse; Piscator used it to open the new Freie Volksbühne in 1963, to immediate international controversy. It showed Pope Pius XII as failing to do anything to prevent the Holocaust because he was more concerned about the spread of Communism and the state of the Church's finances. Hochhüth suffers from being unable to make up his mind whether the great moments of history are caused by individual decisions or by economic and social forces; and the verse did not help the documentary side of the play either. It was put on by the ▷RSC at the Aldwych in 1963, in Robert David Macdonald's translation, and revived by the Glasgow Citizens' in 1986, when it was given a respectful reception, though found to look its age.

Soldiers
In *Soldiers*, matters were somewhat improved by the use of 'rhythmic prose' for the play-within-the-play, but the subject caused as much controversy; it deals with Churchill's 1943 decision on saturation bombing of Dresden and other German cities, and he is also accused of conniving at the assassination of the Polish leader, Sikorski. The picture of Churchill is more sympathetic than that of the Pope, but the attempt to put on *Soldiers* at the ▷National Theatre in 1967 led to a burst of patriotic objection that did nothing for the positions of either Olivier or Ken Tynan. It was produced at the New Theatre in 1968, after the Lord Chamberlain's powers had been removed, but did not run for long (partly because the pilot of Sikorski's plane successfully sued for libel). Hochhüth has never really repeated the *succès de scandale* of these two plays, though in *Guerillas* he still seems to think that American society could be changed by disposing of a small number of industrialists.

Try these:
Piscator, for documentary theatre in the 1920s; Heinar Kipphardt's *In the Matter of J. Robert Oppenheimer* (1964), ▷Peter Weiss's *The Investigation* (1965), and ▷Peter Brook's *US*, for documentary theatre in the 1960s; ▷John Arden and Peter Cheeseman at Stoke-on-Trent, for other British equivalents; in the USA, the ▷Wooster Group, for a more experimental, highly charged mode of documentary; ▷Brenton's *The Churchill Play* for an equally controversial portrait of the statesman.

HOLBOROUGH, Jacqueline
                                    [1949–]
British playwright

Plays include:
A Question of Habit (1979), *Killers* (1980), *Avenues* (1981–2), *Fallacies* (1983), *Decade* (1984), *The Sin Eaters* (1986), *The Garden Girls* (1985), *Dreams of San Francisco* (1987), *The Way South* (1989)

Holborough was an actress before before she started writing out of her own experience – a short stay in Durham high-security prison, the result of placing an ad in the paper and subsequently being charged for conspiracy. Her early plays, mostly naturalistic in style, were devised with Jenny Hicks and members of the women prisoners company, Clean Break, which they co-founded. Their concerns, in *Question of Habit*, *Killers* and *The Sin Eaters*, were such subjects as lesbianism, mother and daughter relationships, terrorism and maximum-security wings. Holborough has a very specific 'tone' – partly humorous, partly realistic with a real capacity for creating recognisably sympathetic, three-dimensional characters. Her earlier plays were decidely anti-establishment, though 'screws' and prisoners were seen as equal victims of institutional violence. *The Garden Girls*, Holborough's first full-length play, if too long, was a rare and interesting depiction of the roots of conflict in prison showing the inter-relationship between institution, class and peer group. Its images also challenged the idea of women criminals as hysterics and neurotics showing their imprisonment to be the penalty for retaliating to ill-treatment from men or because they had infringed some social code of the way women ought to behave. Her most recent play, *The Way South* (a ▷Royal National Theatre commission; there is another pending) is a return to the subject of *The Sin Eaters* about IRA bomb-suspect Judith Ward and her treatment in Durham's H-block and has been broadcast by the BBC.

Holborough's sharp wit, prominent in *Dreams of San Francisco*) – a ferociously satiric comment on late 1980s' feminism's capitulation to 'Thatcherite' market forces – also indicates her potential as a television sit-com writer. (She has indeed gone on to write for British television's weekly hospital soap, *Casualty* and a new upcoming cop series *Rookies*.

Try these:
▷Brendan Behan, ▷Tom McGrath; Jimmy Boyle's *The Hard Man*, Michele Celeste's *Hang the President*, and *In the Belly of the Beast*, for other expressions of penal life; for the relationship between women, mental illness and custodial treatments see ▷Melissa Murray's *Bodycell*, ▷Tony Craze's *Shona*, ▷David Edgar's *Mary Barnes*; ▷Caryl Churchill's *Top Girls*, *Serious Money* for other images of opportunism in the Thatcher decade; ▷Pam Gems' *Dusa, Fish, Stas and Vi* for another treatment of women interacting; ▷Fo/Franca Rame's *Ulrike Meinhof* for an extraordinary portrait of woman as terrorist.

HOLMAN, David
British dramatist

Plays include:
Drink the Mercury (1972), *Adventure in the Deep* (1973), *No Pasaran* (1976), *Big Cat, Big Coat* (1980), *Peacemaker* (1983), *Susummu's Story* (1983), *1983* (1983), *No Worries* (1984), *Small Poppies* (1986), *Solomon and the Big Cat* (1987), *Whale* (1989), also an adaptation of Dickens' *A Christmas Carol*

David Holman has written more than 70 works for stage, radio, film and opera which have been performed for or by children of all ages. His sympathy with children goes back to his rather bleak childhood in Harringay, north London. Bullied at primary school, he says, as 'a weed in glasses', he drew his main consolation from books and awe-struck visits to museums. His plays are consequently per-

ceptive about loners, such as the Australian country-girl, moved to a city life that renders her powerless in *No Worries*. But they're more than that. Set against a refreshingly broad sweep of concerns, they are wider-ranging, energetic pieces put over with a stinging outrage at incidences of injustice. Holman is not afraid to place moral issues before his young audiences. Many explore environmental questions with great feeling. ('Children of five sit spellbound,' marvelled the *Sunday Times*, 'and forget their packets of crisps, and strong men find tears welling in their eyes.') These include his most-performed play, *Drink the Mercury*, about the effects of heavy-metal pollution on the fishermen of Minamanta in Japan; *Adventure in the Deep*, whose subject is the despoliation of the ocean, *Big Cat, Big Coat* and *Solomon and the Big Cat*, which concern endangered species in Africa. *Whale*, at the ▷Royal National Theatre, was based on the real-life race by Americans and Russians in 1988 to free whales trapped under the ice in the Arctic, interwoven with an ancient Inuit (eskimo) myth.

Other widely performed plays include *No Pasaran*, about a Jewish boxer in Nazi Germany, *The Disappeared*, about victims of repression in Argentina, and three 'peace' plays, *Peacemaker*, *Susummu's Story* (about Hiroshima and the atom bomb) and *1983* (written for various age ranges and all presented by Theatre Centre) – which were attacked by certain members of the British Tory government, for their pacifism. Despite this, he remains much admired, particularly in Australia. As he says: 'I'm very big in Australia, very small in Hackney'.

Try these:
Tomson Highway's *The Rez Sisters*, which follows the journey of some Native Canadians to the Big City; *The Ancient Mariner. Hiawatha, Sir Gawain and the Green Knight*, and *The Pied Piper* are all plays for children done at the RNT, adapted from major literary texts; ▷Alan Ayckbourn's *Invisible Friends* is a play for children; ▷Wendy Kesselman's *Becca*, about a young girl who is shut up in a cupboard, uses fantasy and music to push the boundaries of children's theatre; ▷Penny Casdagli, ▷Nona Shepphard and ▷David Wood are other British writers for children; see also ▷Theatre for Young Audiences.

HOLMAN, Robert   [1952–]
British dramatist

Plays include:
Coal (1973), *The Natural Cause* (1974), *Outside the Whale* (1976), *German Skerries* (1977), *Mucking Out* (1978), *Other Worlds* (1983), *Today* (1984), *The Overgrown Path* (1985), *Making Noise Quietly* (1986), *Across Oka* (1988), *Rafts and Dreams* (1990)

At a time when too many playwrights seem content to score ideological points off their characters, Holman is to be commended for his droll, compassionate voice in a series of plays that movingly examine both the stresses and the bliss of intimacy amongst people of varying backgrounds and nationalities and at different times (*Other Worlds* is set during the Napoleonic era). Born in North Yorkshire, the son of a farm manager and a teacher, Holman moved to London at nineteen and spent two-and-a-half years working in the newsagent's on Paddington Station; perhaps his immersion in the world gives his plays their peculiar realism, but few writers chart human truths so perceptively, particularly the truths that accompany sudden intimacy. 'I always think you can hear silence,' a character comments in his play *The Overgrown Path*, and that's what Holman does, he keeps time with the human dialogues that go unspoken but are, nonetheless, felt. A resident playwright at the ▷Royal National Theatre from 1977–9, Holman regularly crops up in London's subsidised fringe – memorably, in 1986, in *Making Noise Quietly*, a trio of plays about relationships that flourish and flail under the strains of gender and class. Written in a temperate, considered mode, its title summed up what Holman had been doing: making noise quietly – and invaluably. The scope of his two most recent plays, however, has baffled some and distanced others. *Rafts and Dreams* tackled the long-term damage of child abuse through surreal fantasy, and *Across Oka* is concerned with global conservation.

Today
A probing treatment of English idealism between the wars, this episodic play tells of Victor Ellison, the musically-gifted son of a Yorkshire joiner, who flirts with men during his days at Cambridge, with Socialism in the anti-fascist crusade of the Spanish Civil War, and with religious conversion in his Barcelona-based courtship of a British nun

who ends up becoming his wife. Set alongside this spiritual development is an array of characters written with the deft, swift insight and immediate empathy one associates with the best British mini-series. This is that rare play where one admires the leading figure yet wants to know as much as possible about the supporting characters (whether it's a Marxist ventriloquist or a German male prostitute) as soon as they are introduced.

Try these:
▷Michael Frayn's *Benefactors* for discussions of English idealism; ▷Louise Page (especially *Salonika*) for often elliptical domestic conflict; ▷Tina Howe and ▷Lanford Wilson for clear, non-judgmental views of character; ▷Sarah Daniels' *Beside Herself* also tackles the long term effects of child abuse, ▷Nick Ward's *Apart from George* confronts it indirectly; ▷Terry Johnson for ecological and global worries.

HOME, William Douglas   [1912–]
British actor and dramatist

Plays include:
Now Barabbas . . . (1947), *The Chiltern Hundreds* (*Yes M'Lord* in USA; 1947), *The Thistle and the Rose* (1949), *The Reluctant Debutante* (1955), *Betzi* (1964), *The Queen's Highland Servant* (1967), *The Kingfisher* (1977), *After the Ball is Over* (1985)

An actor who appeared in many of his own plays, and whose experience shows in their careful construction, Home was rejected by the 'angries' of the late 1950s as an irrelevant writer of upper-class and well-made plays. Many of his more than forty plays are set in the world of lords and debutantes but the plots are often developed from real life. *The Chiltern Hundreds*, for example, was suggested by the political activities of his father's butler, and *The Reluctant Peer* was linked to his Prime Minister brother's resignation of his title. Subjects range from a chronicle play of events leading to the Battle of Flodden Field (*The Thistle and the Rose*) to Napoleon's last love affair (*Betzi*), and marriage in *Lloyd George Knew My Father* and *The Secretary Bird*. His early play *Now Barabbas . . .*, a study of life in a prison, from the arrival of a condemned murderer to his execution, plumbed much greater depths than his later work, including what was then a very daring treatment of a homosexual friendship.

Home writes about the people he knows but he is not a Tory propagandist – their behaviour, prejudices and eccentricities are the butt of his humorous observation which relies more upon elegant construction and skilful timing than dazzling wit.

Try these:
▷Sheridan for similar comedies of an earlier time; ▷Genet, John Herbert's *Fortune and Men's Eyes* and ▷Brendan Behan's *The Quare Fellow* for death-cell dramas; ▷Alan Ayckbourn for Home-like treatment of the middle and lower-middle classes; ▷Noël Coward for more bitter observation of the British 'country house' set; ▷Ray Cooney and ▷Ben Travers for blander versions.

HOOD, Kevin   [1949–]
British dramatist

Plays include:
Beached (1987), *The Astronomer's Garden* (1988), *Sugar Hill Blues* (1990)

A chemistry graduate and sometime research biochemist, born and raised in Spennymoor, County Durham, Kevin Hood devised *The Fence* (about the experiences of the Greenham Common peace campaigners) with a teacher colleague and a group of pupils. It was performed at the Albany Empire and on the Edinburgh Fringe. In 1988, the Croydon Warehouse premiered the play which first brought Hood serious attention: *The Astronomers Garden*. Charting rivalries both professional and sexual amongst the scientific community at the Greenwich Observatory in the 18th century, the play was likened to the film work of Peter Greenaway. Working as the Warehouse's writer-in-residence under the Thames TV Playwriting Award, in 1990 Hood produced *Sugar Hill Blues*, an intricate tale, partly set on board ship, of two couples, divided by class and race and brought together by jazz in the 1950s. The experiences of prejudice and class among the four are explored with an ironic commentary from a fifth, chorus-like character, Norman. Although at times overflowing with ideas and themes, Hood's depiction of the power relations between his characters is fascinating. Moments such as a gutsy, unaccompanied

blues solo, and a spontaneous scat-sung version of Charlie Parker's 'Ornithology' by all four main characters display a shrewd instinct for the use of music on stage and for dramatically riveting *coups de theatre*. Although charges of over-complexity and deliberate cleverness have been levelled at Hood, his work continues to impress in its linking of wide socio-political themes to believable characters in unusual but very effective situations.

Try these:
August Wilson's *Ma Rainey's Bottom*, Ben Caldwell/Clarice Taylor's *Moms and Her Ladies* about 'Moms Mabley' for other plays with jazz as a major component; ▷Tom Stoppard for over-cleverness; ▷James Baldwin's *The Amen Corner* for religious obsession; ▷Sarah Daniels' *The Devil's Gateway* for Greenham. The subject of race and ships is treated rather differently in Heidi Thomas' *Indigo*, and Gabriel Gbadamosi's *Abolition*, both of which involve slave-ship scenes; ▷Timberlake Wertenbaker's *Our Country's Good* for ships, class and prejudice.

HOPKINS, John   [1931–]
British dramatist

Plays include:
This Story of Yours (1968), *Find Your Way Home* (1970), *Economic Necessity* (1973), *Next of Kin* (1974), *Losing Time* (1979)

Hopkins is best known for the creation of BBC-TV's *Z-Cars* (of which he wrote fifty-three episodes), a police series which changed the way in which the force was presented. His stage plays have been as strong as his television work. In *This Story of Yours*, a self-loathing detective in a bad marriage, with a job that both repels and fascinates him, beats a suspected child rapist to death. *Find Your Way Home* shows the relationship between a young occasional male prostitute and a married man who leaves his wife to live with him. Hopkins paints a bleak picture of the homosexual scene and of the difficulties they face, uncompromising and unsentimental, but it is as much about the difficulties of making any relationship as about homosexuality. Hopkins' dramas are strong meat, firmly rooted in contemporary experience, and confronting both private and public problems.

Try these:
▷Michael Wilcox (*Rents*), ▷Peter Gill (*Mean Tears*), ▷Martin Sherman (*Bent*), and ▷Hugh Whitemore's *Breaking the Code* for other plays about the difficulty of homosexual relationships; G. F. Newman's *Operation Bad Apple*, Vince Foxall's *Pork Pies* for plays on 'bent' police; ▷Howard Brenton's *Sore Throats* for a graphic portrait of domestic violence and the difficulty of heterosexual relationships; Gay Sweatshop.

HOROVITZ, Israel   [1939–]
American playwright, screenwriter and producer

Plays include:
The Comeback (1957), *Rats* (1963), *The Line* (1967) *The Indian Wants the Bronx* (1968), *It's Called the Sugar Plum* (1968), *Morning* (1969), *Spared* (1973), *The Primary English Class* (1976), *The Wakefield Plays* (1979), *The Alfred Trilogy* (1979), *The Good Parts* (1983), *Today I Am a Fountain Pen* (1985), *A Rosen By Any Other Name* (1986), *North Shore Fish* (1987), *The Chopin Playoffs* (1987), *Park Your Car in Harvard Yard* (1987), *Sunday Runners in the Rain* (1987), *Firebird at Dogtown* (1987), *Year of the Duck* (1989), *Widow's Blind Date* (1989)

This prolific New England playwright, who now boasts authorship of more than forty plays, has yet to see a commercial success on the Broadway stage, although he has enjoyed long runs off- and off-off-Broadway. *The Line*, at Cafe La Mama, marked Horovitz's New York debut as both author and actor in 1967. The play has had a continuous run since 1976 at the 13th Street Theatre. *The Indian Wants the Bronx*, in which Al Pacino made his New York stage debut, gave Horovitz his first Obie award in 1968.

Horovitz' early plays are slick, witty sketches that explore the thirst for power in the human dynamic. Five people vie for first place in line in *The Line*, demonstrating the fiercely competitive nature of the human condition. *The Indian Wants the Bronx* is a study in the evolution of terrorism as two streetwise toughs confront a passive East Indian at a bus stop. The later *The Primary English Class* is about the breakdown of communication, as a teacher becomes frustrated and hostile as she explains basic English skills to a class where no one speaks the same language. What binds these plays together is that just below the surface lurks a menace that erupts in psychic violence.

The Widow's Blind Date, which had its New York premiere at Circle in the Square downtown in 1989, makes Horovitz' strongest statement about human aggression. Here a young widow returns to her hometown with the sole purpose of exacting justice on two of her high-school classmates who gang-raped her twenty years earlier. This is Horovitz' Grand Guignol revenge play, where frustration, isolation and anger coalesce into a climax fraught with mental, verbal and physical violence. The play's bloody finale signals not the ending, but the beginning of revenge.

Horovitz has experimented with adaptations of the classics, notably *Year of the Duck*, a contemporary view of ▷Ibsen's *The Wild Duck*. His autobiographical film *Author! Author!* was produced in 1982, starring Al Pacino. Horovitz is a founding member of the ▷Eugene O'Neill Memorial Playwrights' Conference, the New York Playwrights' Lab, and the Gloucester Stage Company, where he currently directs his own new works. His many awards include a second Obie, an Emmy, the French Critics Prize, the Elliot Norton Award, The Vernon Rice Award and a Pulizer Prize nomination.

Try these:
For psychological and physical violence see ▷Edward Albee's *Who's Afraid of Virginia Woolf*, ▷Mark Medoff's *When Ya Comin' Back Red Ryder*, ▷Harold Pinter's *The Birthday Party* and ▷Christopher Durang's *Sister Mary Ignatius Explains It All for You*. For revenge plays see ▷Friedrich Dürrenmatt's *The Visit*, and ▷William Mastrosimone's *Extremities*; ▷Sue Townsend's *Groping for Words* and ▷Terence Rattigan's *French Without Tears* for other versions of language classes.

HORSFIELD, Debbie   [1955–]
British dramatist

Plays include:
Out on the Floor (1981), *Away From it All* (1982), *All You Deserve* (1983); trilogy comprising *Red Devils*, *True Dare Kiss* and *Command or Promise* (1983); *Touch and Go* (1984; now known as *Revelations*)

One of the 'second wave' of young women writers who emerged in the early 1980s, Manchester-born Horsfield came to prominence with *Red Devils*, the saga of four female Manchester United supporters. She has written plays on computer dating (*Touch and Go*), northern discos (*Out on the Floor*), and more youthful dilemmas (*All You Deserve*), but the football trilogy remains her *pièce de resistance* at present. Like ▷Alan Bleasdale's television winner *The Boys from the Black Stuff*, the three plays have a compulsive drive (like good soap-opera) as they follow the progress of four friends, through early adulthood, work and personal crises, often conflict-ridden but held together by loyalty and a shared obsession for Manchester United football team – Horsfield's own particular passion. *Red Devils* was reworked from an earlier play, *In the Blood*, which was written in just two weeks and staged at the Edinburgh Festival whilst she was still at Newcastle University. Two plays from the trilogy were performed as part of the ▷National Theatre's short season of new plays in 1985, when some critics found them repetitious, soap-operaish (in the bad sense) and sentimental, and one male reviewer even commented that it was unfair to men. Most agreed her great strength was her ear for dialogue – like a sort of Julie Walters on speed. Michael Billington has even dubbed her the funniest woman dramatist since ▷Shelagh Delaney. Certainly, there is the same youthful energy, gritty turn of phrase and spiky humour, but Horsfield also reflects a quarter of a century in which feminism, unemployment, the increasing north/south divide, television and the consumerist society have changed perceptions.

Red Devils

Red Devils is the story of four teenagers, Alice, Nita, Beth and Phil, their ambition to get to Wembley to see their team in the Cup Final, and the outcome when they actually achieve it. But the other half of the equation is the exploration of the idea of friendship, what binds four such disparate young women together, and the development of each – nascent punk Beth's incipient racism towards Nita and her better-heeled, Asian background (her father is a doctor), Alice who is going with Kev and wants to settle down; and Phil, whose ultimate return to her roots, as a fledgling journalist in the final part of the third play forms the real heart of the trilogy. There is plenty of aggro (these women are not exempt

from showing the same sort of feelings as male football supporters), but throughout it all runs a solid thread of kinship, and the play is enormous fun. As Horsfield has said in reply to criticisms: 'It was never my intention to turn [my characters] into political mouthpieces or agitprop caricatures; I am aware only of recording what it was like for four young women growing up in the Manchester of the early 1980s.' She has subsequently turned her hand to TV writing with considerable success – *Making Out* her series about factory girls and the larks they get up to was extremely popular.

Try these:
▷Sarah Daniels and ▷Ayshe Raif are other writers to emerge in the early 1980s; Victoria Wood's humour springs from the same northern roots; ▷Sharman Macdonald for female adolescent badinage; ▷Willy Russell's *Educating Rita* seems like a forerunner to *Touch and Go* and his *Stags and Hens* exploits a disco setting, as does ▷John Godber's *The Ritz*; ▷Louise Page's *Golden Girls* is a different look at young women, individually and in a group, at the competitive end of sport; ▷Pam Gems' *Dusa, Fish, Stas and Vi* for another young quartet coming to terms with womanhood; ▷Charles Dyer's *Rattle of a Simple Man* deals with a soccer fan from the North hitting the Big City; ▷Peter Terson's *Zigger-Zagger* is the definitive football supporters play; for an equivalent male trilogy, ▷John Byrne's *The Slab Boys*.

HORVÁTH, Ödön Joseph von   [1901–1938]
German dramatist

Plays include:
Italienische Nacht (*Italian Night*; 1931), *Geschichten aus dem Wiener Wald* (*Tales from the Vienna Woods*; 1931), *Kasimir und Karoline* (*Casimir and Caroline*; 1932), *Figaro Lässt sich Schieden* (*Figaro Gets a Divorce*; 1937), *Don Juan Kommt aus dem Krieg* (*Don Juan Comes Back from the War*; produced 1952)

Horváth, like ▷Aeschylus and ▷Molière, tends to be anecdotally remembered for the way he died; he was killed in the Champs Elysées when a tree struck by lightning fell on him, leaving several plays, novels and film scenarios unfinished. His plays were banned when the Nazis came to power, then neglected in Germany until the 1950s. He has been increasingly recognised as an important dramatist in Britain and the USA since the 1970s. His peculiar mixture of disdainful criticism of bourgeois capitalist greed and hypocrisy, sharp ironic observation of lower-middle-class stupidity, and melancholy resignation may stem partly from his background. He was born in Fiume (now Rijeka in Yugoslavia, but then a part of the Austro-Hungarian Empire) of an aristocratic Hungarian-speaking family and spent much of his life on the move – first because his father was a diplomat, then in search of artistic success, and finally in exile from the Nazis. *Tales from the Vienna Woods* is a hard and cynical picture of the lower middle classes, with a strong story-line; *Figaro Gets a Divorce* is set some years after *The Marriage of Figaro* and gets its effects by unexpectedly putting ▷Beaumarchais' characters into a detailed social context; *Don Juan Comes Back from the War* is a very sardonic play, showing Don Juan as a modern disillusioned war veteran.

▷Christopher Hampton, who translated *Tales from the Vienna Woods* and *Don Juan* for National Theatre productions in 1977 and 1978, also anachronistically included him in *Tales from Hollywood* (1983) as part of the German community in exile; Horváth did in fact mean to join them towards the end of his life.

Try these:
▷Franz Xaver Kroetz for the further development of the 'Volksstück', or plays dealing with working class life; ▷Brecht for contemporary attacks on the capitalist system, though Horváth tends to despair rather than recommending positive action; ▷Chekhov's *Platonov*, re-worked and re-titled *Wild Honey* in ▷Michael Frayn's adaptation, was also known as *Don Juan in the Russian Manner*.

HOUGHTON, Stanley   [1881–1913]
British dramatist

Plays include:
The Dear Departed (1908), *Independent Means* (1909), *The Younger Generation* (1910), *Hindle Wakes* (1912)

Part of the ▷'Manchester School' of playwrights, Houghton wrote all his successful plays for the Gaiety Theatre in Manchester, before dying untimely young. *Hindle Wakes*, the most controversial at the time and the most frequently revived, is the story of the independent-minded mill-hand Fanny Hawthorn, who is unrepentant after spending a weekend in Llandudno with the mill-owner's son, and turns down his offer of marriage. It is an effective mixture of the comic and the serious, with strong feminist overtones and a *Doll's House*-type ending that nowadays leaves us asking a number of awkward questions about contraception and her possibilities of future employment.

Try these:
▷Manchester School; see also ▷Harold Brighouse for another 'Manchester School' playwright; ▷Ibsen's *A Doll's House*.

HOWE, Tina   [1937–]
American dramatist

Plays include:
The Nest (1969), *Birth and Afterbirth* (1973), *Museum* (1976), *The Art of Dining* (1979), *Painting Churches* (1983), *Coastal Disturbances* (1986), *Approaching Zanzibar* (1987)

Although she has written comparatively few plays, Howe is a leading American dramatist. 'God help me if I ever write a realistic play,' she once said in an interview, 'I take a familiar reality and lift it about six feet off the ground.' *Birth and Afterbirth*, which enraged feminists even more than men and non-feminists, is a hallucinatory, absurdist look at the ways in which a new birth affects a family. *Museum*, which the author still dreams of seeing produced in such a place, has an art exhibit as its set. Praised for its wit, humour and wry view of modern art, the play has been described both as a medieval *theatrum mundi* and a contemporary comedy of manners. It is concerned with the artist's hunger to make art, and the viewer's hunger to consume art – literally, here, for the exhibit is destroyed by the museum goers. *The Art of Dining* is a more classic comedy of manners, without the menace of *Museum*. The work, which grew out of the author's abhorrence of food and eating in public, is an hilarious send-up of *haute-cuisine* and the rituals attached to its contemplation, preparation and delectation. *Painting Churches* is generally considered the author's deepest, most touching work. It won the 1983 Obie Award for Distinguished Playwriting. Although Howe insists that the play is not realistic but 'very off-centre', it was her tidiest, most conventional structure to date. It concerns Mags, a painter with a deep need for her staid, intimidating parents to recognise her talent. As she paints their portrait, Mags is forced to confront her artistic and psychological insecurities. The writing is distinguished for close attention to the small but telling character detail, and for its Chekhov-like sympathies. *Painting Churches* was the first of the author's plays to enjoy a healthy commercial run in New York. *Coastal Disturbances* is a valentine about three generations of lovers on a beach in Nantucket. Tame, even simplistic, in comparison with earlier work, it nonetheless had a very successful run on Broadway at Circle in the Square after its debut twenty blocks north at Second Stage.

Try these:
Absurdists like ▷Ionesco and ▷Pirandello; ▷Chekhov, for his compassion, irony and sympathy for people's capacity for self-dramatisation; ▷Lanford Wilson, ▷August Wilson and ▷Athol Fugard (see his *Road to Mecca*, another play about the formation of an artist) for their breadth of emotional generosity; ▷Hugh Leonard for treatments of the formation of an artist. ▷Philip Barry and, later, A.R. Gurney Jr, for ruefully comic views of the American upper class; ▷David Hare's *Wrecked Eggs* for an Englishman's view of East Coast sensibilities and its companion piece *The Bay at Nice* for the uses of art; Nancy Reilly's *Assume the Position*, and ▷Timberlake Wertenbaker's *Three Birds Alighting in a Field* for more and contrasting views on art as commodity; ▷Nick Dear's *The Art of Success* and ▷Howard Barker's *Scenes from an Execution* for the nexus between art and politics.

HUGHES, Dusty   [1947–]
British dramatist

Plays include:
Commitments (1980), *Heaven and Hell* (1981), *Molière* (adapted from ▷Bulgakov; 1982), *Bad Language* (1983), *Philistines* (adapted from Gorki; 1985), *Futurists* (1986), *Jenkins' Ear* (1987), *Life with Mr Gopal* (1990), *The Angelic Avengers* (adapted from the Karen Blixen novel; 1990), *A Slip of the Tongue* (1991)

Born in Lincolnshire and educated at Cambridge, Hughes has shown an impressive ability to leap between various periods and styles in his first four plays and two ▷RSC adaptations from Russian. At one point the theatre editor of the London listings magazine *Time Out* and then the artistic director of the Bush Theatre, Hughes came to attention with his play about English Trotskyites, *Commitments*, and consolidated his somewhat wry, acidic point-of-view with the bitterly funny *Bad Language*, about university disaffection amongst the Cambridge ranks. *Futurists*, galvanically staged by Richard Eyre at the ▷National Theatre, remains his major achievement to date. Set in a Petrograd café in 1921, the play charts, with exhilarating theatricality, a literary movement whose fate was contrastingly bleak. In the process, Hughes explores the paradox of twentieth-century Russia; the century ushered in by ▷Chekhov and ▷Gorki (a passage from *The Cherry Orchard* begins the play) gave way to the Cheka and Stalin despite the belief of one futurist poet, Osip Mandelstam, that 'poetry is a plough [that] turns time upside down'. After this risk-taking, Hughes' *Jenkins' Ear*, set in a 'small central American country north of Nicaragua', was all too prosaic and jumbled, the best of political intentions notwithstanding. *Metropolis*, the musical for which he co-wrote the libretto and lyrics with American song-writer Joseph Brooks, unfortunately fared no better. There are two more plays and films (*In Hiding* and *Torn Apart*) currently in the pipeline.

Try these:
▷Doug Lucie, ▷Simon Gray for *Bad Language*-like depictions of Oxbridge; ▷Bernard Pomerance's *Foco Novo*, Donald Freed's *The Quartered Man*, ▷Manuel Puig's *Kiss of the Spider Woman*, Richard Nelson's *Principia Scriptoriae* for plays about Latin America; ▷C.P. Taylor's *Allergy* and ▷Christopher Hampton's *Philanthropist* are other contemporary university plays; ▷Howard Brenton's and Tariq Ali's *Moscow Gold* for a recent exploration of Russian history.

HUGHES, Holly [1956–]
American playwright and actress

Plays include:
The Well of Horniness (1984), *The Lady Dick* (1986), *Dress Suits to Hire* (1987), *World Without End* (1989)

This pre-eminent lesbian playwright and theatre personality made the headlines in 1990 along with three other controversial artists, when she was denied a National Endowment for the Arts grant. Hailing from Saginaw, Michigan, this daughter of a General Motors executive rebelled against the Republican respectability of her upper-middle-class upbringing by publicising her 'coming out'. Armed with an art degree from Kalamazoo College and planning to be a feminist painter and visual artist, she moved to New York in 1979 to attend the Feminist Art Institute. A protege of the WOW Cafe, a lesbian-feminist theatre collective in the East Village, she became a playwright by accident, writing her first campy, and overtly sexual romp, *The Well of Horniness*, as a challenge.

She found her voice in *Dress Suits to Hire*, commissioned by lesbian actresses Peggy Shaw and Lois Weaver who performed the piece at the Veselka Festival in 1987, winning an Obie in 1988. The work is quintessential 'Dyke Noir', exploring the darker side of the women's gay movement. A memory play, loosely based on the story of two sisters living in a costume shop on the lower East Side, it is a brash and overt portrayal of lesbian seduction. One sister locks herself in the shop following the murder of the other, and relives their lives together in an orgiastic fantasy of past, present and future. Using the inventory of the shop they dress up, strip down and change identity to heighten and prolong foreplay, seduction and fulfilment.

Hughes wants to be known as a good playwright, who speaks from a lesbian perspective and not just as a gay, female writer. Self-defined as a 'queer' and an 'outsider', she often antagonises other lesbians and feminists because she refuses to present lesbian fairy tales where women come out, get it on and live happily ever after. She makes her women brash and sometimes trashy, lesbian sex-objects, and glories in reclaiming words like 'pussy', 'slut' and 'whore' that were thrown out with women's liberation.

Her most recent work, *World Without End*, an autobiographical monologue exploring her own gayness and semi-incestuous relationship with her mother, has neither the cohesiveness nor impact of her earlier work. Although Hughes, who now performs her own work, aims for comedy, she never quite seems at home with her own material. Her performing style, often criticised as awkward and stiff, undercuts her comic aims.

Try these:
For homosexual erotic plays see ▷Jean Genet's *The Maids* and ▷Wendy Kesselman's *My Sister in This House*; Charles Ludlam's Ridiculous Theatrical Company and The WOW Cafe; for plays on lesbian themes see ▷Frank Marcus' *The Killing of Sister George*, and Jane Chambers' *Last Summer at Blue Fish Cove*; for personal monologues see the work of ▷Spalding Gray; see also ▷Lesbian theatre.

HUGHES, Langston [1902–67]
American dramatist, poet and novelist

Plays include:
Mulatto (1928), *Mule Bone* (with Zora Neale Hurston; 1930), *Scottsboro Limited* (1932), *Don't You Want to be Free* (1936), *The Sun Do Move* (1942), *Street Scene* (lyrics for musical; 1947), *The Barrier* (opera, 1949), *Simply Heavenly* (musical, 1957), *Soul Gone Home* (1959), *Black Nativity: A Gospel Song-Play* (1961)

One of the guiding lights of the Harlem renaissance, Langston Hughes was in the vanguard of modern black American literature. Although known primarily for his poetry, he worked with theatres throughout his career and wrote or collaborated on several successful plays and musicals.

Hughes himself credited Paul Laurence Dunbar, Walt Whitman and Carl Sandburg as his literary models, but his writing was also clearly influenced by black folklore, dialect and music. He treated contemporary subjects in a timeless way, and the language of both his poetry and his plays is bluesy and melodic. His strengths were in characterisation – both of individuals and of societies – and in his glorious use of language. His plots, however, often tend to wander.

Hughes' first and best-known play, *Mulatto*, tells of a mulatto son's rejection by his white father, a Georgia plantation owner. In a violent confrontation, the son kills the father and then commits suicide. While the racial subject is important to the play, Hughes concentrates on the more universal issue of a father's denial of love for his son.

In the 1930s, Hughes became politically radicalised. He served for two years as a reporter in Moscow, and was the only black American correspondent in the Spanish Civil War. During this period he wrote political-activist plays, *Scottsboro Limited*, exploring the racial issues surrounding the rape trial of the 'Scottsboro Boys', and the agitprop piece *Don't You Want to be Free*.

Hughes often collaborated with other writers and composers. He and Zora Neale Hurston created *Mule Bone*, a vernacular folk drama which received a controversial first production at Lincoln Center in 1991. He also worked with Kurt Weill on a musical version of ▷Elmer Rice's *Street Scene*, and with composer Jan Meyerowitz on the opera *The Barrier* (based on *Mulatto*). In 1957 he created his financially successful romantic musical comedy, *Simply Heavenly*, based on the humble, folksy character Jesse B. Semple. *Black Nativity*, among his last works, is still often produced as a Christmas show.

Try these:
The first Broadway play written by a black American was *The Chipwoman's Fortune*, by Willis Richardson; for a mainstream black musical of the 1930s, Hall Johnson's *Run, Little Children*; for a white southern perspective on interracial relations, Paul Green's *In Abraham's Bosom*; Amiri Baraka's *Dutchman* and *Slave Ship* for bitter plays by a jazz-influenced poet; compare black women's perspectives, such as ▷Lorraine Hansberry's *A Raisin in the Sun* and ▷Ntozake Shange's *for coloured girls who have considered suicide when the rainbow is enuf*; ▷Dion Boucicault's *The Octoroon* for an early treatment of race issues in the USA; ▷George C. Wolfe's *Spunk* is an adaptation of three short stories by Zora Neale Hurston.

HUNTER, N. C.
(Norman Charles)   [1908–71]
British dramatist

Plays include:
All Rights Reserved (1935), *A Party for Christmas* (1938), *Waters of the Moon* (1951), *A Day by the Sea* (1953), *A Touch of the Sun* (1958), *The Tulip Tree* (1962)

Beginning as a writer of light comedies, Hunter turned to plays of atmosphere and character, such as *Waters of the Moon* and *A Day by the Sea*, which the H.M. Tennent management presented with star casts at the Theatre Royal, Haymarket. Hailed by some critics of the time as 'English Chekhov', they do not seem quite so impressive today, although a recent revival at Chichester of *Waters of the Moon* still found it according to one critic, 'a play of gentle melancholy, rich in humour'.

Try these:
▷Chekhov, with whom Hunter was routinely compared (to his disadvantage); ▷Enid Bagnold as another dramatist of the period; ▷Eugene O'Neill's *The Iceman Cometh* and *Long Day's Journey into Night* and ▷Agatha Christie's *Ten Little Indians* for plays in which isolated groups learn home truths as in *Waters of the Moon*.

HUTCHINSON, Ron   [1946–]
Irish dramatist

Plays include:
Says I, Says He (1978), *Eejits* (1978), *Anchorman* (1978), *Christmas of a Nobody* (1979), *The Irish Play* (1980), *Risky City* (1981), *Into Europe* (1981), *The Dillen* (1983), *Rat in the Skull* (1984), *Babbit: a Marriage* (1987; a musical adaptation of Sinclair Lewis' novel)

The fact that Hutchinson, writer in residence with the ▷RSC in 1978–9, is now writing film scripts in Los Angeles might surprise those for whom he is best known as the author of two plays about Britain and Ireland (*The Irish Play* and *Rat in the Skull*) but might seem logical to those who know him as the writer of the television series *Bird of Prey* and *Connie*. Although Hutchinson's work also encompasses the highly successful Stratford-set promenade production *The Dillen*, which used both. The Other Place and locations within Stratford, *Rat in the Skull* is probably the best of his plays. It's a fine study of the convoluted, almost incestuous, relationship between a Protestant RUC police officer and a Catholic terrorist suspect played out in a London police station populated with English policemen who want to keep their noses clean. Deceptively simple in its style, with many virtual monologues to the audience, the play never settles for an easy answer in its analysis of the interplay of personal and political motives and perspectives that lead to the intractability of the situation.

Try these:
Promenade Performances and ▷Community Theatre for analogues of *The Dillen*; Hector MacMillan's *The Sash* for Orangemen in Glasgow; ▷Brian Friel, ▷Stewart Parker, Peter Sheridan, ▷Margaretta D'Arcy and ▷John Arden, Martin Lynch, ▷Seamus Finnegan, ▷Bill Morrison, ▷Daniel Mornin, Frank McGuinness; ▷Marie Jones, ▷Seamus Heaney and ▷Christina Reid are among the contemporary Irish writers who have dramatised the situation in Northern Ireland; ▷Brendan Behan and ▷Sean O'Casey did the same for earlier periods; ▷Howard Barker, ▷Howard Brenton and ▷David Rudkin offer perspectives from the mainland; G. F. Newman's *Operation Bad Apple*, Vince Foxall's *Pork Pies* and ▷Nigel Williams' *WCPC* are contemporary studies of the police.

HWANG, David Henry   [1957–]
Asian-American dramatist

Plays include:
F.O.B. (1980), *Dance and the Railrod* (1981), *Family Devotions* (1981), *The House of Sleeping Beauties* (1983), *The Sound of a Voice* (1983), *Rich Relations* (1986), *M. Butterfly* (1987)

A first generation Asian-American from a white, suburban California neighbourhood, Hwang is the son of Shanghai-born businessman and a Philippine-born pianist. Brought up in a home that did not reinforce his Chinese heritage, he is nevertheless one of the strongest voices speaking out on Asian-American themes today and is the first to break into the mainstream of American theatre, creating a place for himself and Asian performers. Hwang is fascinated by the cross-cutting of Asian and American stereotypes and the conflicts that arise from assimilation into the mainstream.

Hwang's play *F.O.B.*, an abbreviation of 'Fresh Off the Boat', confronts the assimilation question head-on. Written while an undergraduate at Stanford, developed at the ▷O'Neill Playwrights' Conference, and brought by Joseph Papp to the New York Shakespeare Festival in 1980, it won an Obie award in 1981. Set in a restaurant in Chinatown, *F.O.B.*'s characters are all Chinese college-age immigrants, who must deal with the problems of being a minority in America. Hwang exposes a ruthless caste sytem within the Chinese-American subculture, where social climbing means abandoning one's roots.

M. Butterfly, Hwang's most powerful and moving play to date, marks his Broadway debut. Loosely based on a true story of a French diplomat who falls in love with a Chinese actress, only to discover she is really a man, it explores and explodes culturally biased stereotypes and their use to justify political and sexual exploitation. The play is set against backdrops of the Peking Opera and Puccini's *Madame Butterfly*. Directed by John Dexter, it captured the 1988 Tony for best play, as well as the Outer Critics' Award, the John Gassner Award for best American Play and the Drama Desk Award. It is Hwang's first work using both Asians and Americans.

Hwang has earned a Cine Golden Eagle Award, a Guggenheim, both Rockefeller and NYSCA fellowships, and two fellowships from the National Endowment for the Arts.

Try these:
For exploding and mocking sexual stereotypes see ▷Caryl Chuchill's *Cloud Nine* and ▷Joe Orton's *What the Butler Saw*; ▷Philip Kan Gotanda's *Yankee Dawg You Die* for an examination of American stereotyping of Asians; for problems of different ethnic groups from within and without try, ▷Joshua Sobol's *The Ghetto*, ▷August Wilson's *Ma Rainey's Black Bottom*, George L. Aiken's *Uncle Tom's Cabin*, George Wolfe's *The Colored Museum*, and ▷Hanif Kureishi's *Borderline*.

i

IBSEN, Henrik [1828–1906]
Norwegian dramatist

Plays include:
Catalina (1850), *Lady Inger of Østraat* (1854), *The Feast at Solhaug* (1856), *The Vikings at Helgeland* (1858), *Love's Comedy* (1862), *The Pretenders* (1863), *Brand* (1866), *Peer Gynt* (1867), *Emperor and Galilean* (1873), *Pillars of Society* (1877), *A Doll's House* (1879), *Ghosts* (1881), *An Enemy of the People* (1882), *The Wild Duck* (1884), *Rosmersholm* (1886), *The Lady from the Sea* (1888), *Hedda Gabler* (1890), *The Master Builder* (1892), *Little Eyolf* (1894), *John Gabriel Borkman* (1896), *When We Dead Awaken* (1899)

Ibsen's influence on European and American drama has been enormous; he has been described as 'the father of modern theatre'. According to Rebecca West (who took her name from the heroine of *Rosmersholm*), expressing the feelings of many who felt the impact of the first productions of Ibsen in London: 'Ibsen converted me to the belief that it is ideas which make the world go round.'

Most of his early plays were traditional historical dramas, very much influenced by the German theatre of Hebbel and ▷Schiller. They were unsuccessfully produced at the theatre in Bergen, where Ibsen worked as an assistant to the director, Ole Bull. After the theatre went bankrupt, Ibsen moved to Oslo where his satirical verse drama *Love's Comedy* was produced successfully. He travelled to Italy and Germany, living for two years in Rome where he wrote *Brand*. Never really intended for stage production it is often performed in an abridged version because of staging problems. However, *Brand* established Ibsen's reputation in Norway and across Europe and led to the awarding of a state pension, which left him free from financial worry and able to devote himself to writing. He spent most of the rest of his life in Italy and Germany. *Peer Gynt*, the last of Ibsen's

verse dramas, is a fairy-tale fantasy which challenged traditional dramatic forms. It uses fantasy to explore fantasy and dream, and to investigate motivation and will through a young man's quest. From this point on Ibsen's plays were written in prose, and attempted, as Ibsen wrote to his publisher 'the very much more difficult art of writing the genuine, plain language spoken in real life'.

The plays which follow *Peer Gynt* are the beginnings of Ibsen's development of a naturalist drama and a refusal of traditional forms of theatre. Of his play *Emperor and Galilean* Ibsen wrote: 'The illusion I wished to produce was that of reality.' *Pillars of Society*, *A Doll's House* and *Ghosts* mark a decision to write about contemporary life: they are claustrophobic studies of small town parochial life, and of the conflicts, hypocrisies and destruction that families and small groups inflict on one another. These begin to develop a form of characterisation and action in which the emphasis is not on action, but on psychological complexity.

In Ibsen's later plays these dramatic techniques move close to symbolism. *The Wild Duck* and *Hedda Gabler* extend the symbolic elements that are already apparent in *A Doll's House* and *Ghosts*, and in *Rosmersholm* he moved to a thoroughly psychological drama.

While Ibsen is seen as the great Naturalist dramatist, Ibsen himself was careful to distinguish his work from Zola's naturalism, and once said: Zola 'descends into the sewer to bathe in it; I to cleanse it.'

A Doll's House
A Doll's House is the study of the marriage of Nora and Torvald. In the first act, Nora is childlike, singing and taking pleasure in domesticity and her child. Her husband refers to her as a 'skylark', a 'squirrel', but the charm of their relationship takes on an uneasy edge as Nora has to beg for money from him, and her economic dependency becomes brutally clear. Nora attempts to enter into an

economic transaction on her own, as she confides to her friend, the dying Dr Rank. But the money-lender blackmails her, and she comes to recognise her own dependence and gullibility. She dances an impassioned tarantella, an expression of her as yet unspoken rage and frustration. In the final scene of the play, Nora confronts Torvald with her own realisation that she has moved from her father's doll's house into yet another, and that she must leave both him and her child to find her own independence. The play ends with the door slamming behind her. The play was greeted with shock on its first production; both its style and subject matter were seen as radical and subversive. The play's form was technically innovative, in its use of contemporary and simple language and dress, and it became a topic of international debate. Pamphlets and books were written about it, sermons and public debates held about it, and the text sold out within a month of its first printing. Feminism was a central issue in Norway at the time, and for Ibsen himself; his wife, Susannah, was an outspoken feminist, and the Norwegian novelist Camilla Collett had taken him to task about the representation of woman in his earlier plays. The play was based on an actual incident, but unlike Nora who boldly leaves the 'doll's house', the real woman ended her life in an insane asylum. In the notes for the play Ibsen writes: 'There are two kinds of moral laws, two kinds of conscience; one for men and one quite different for women. In practical life, woman is judged by masculine law, as though she weren't a woman but a man. A woman cannot be herself in modern society. It is an exclusively male society, with laws made by men.'According to one critic: 'With the slamming of the door behind Nora, the theatres of Europe woke up.'

Try these:
Ibsen powerfully influenced ▷Shaw, who wrote a defence of him in *The Quintessence of Ibsenism*; ▷Strindberg, although he would have denied it, was much influenced by Ibsen; ▷Christopher Hampton was inspired by Ibsen's studies of gender relations to write *Treats*; ▷John Osborne's *Look Back in Anger* could be regarded as a reworking of *A Doll's House*; ▷Sarah Daniels' *Ripen Our Darkness* is a modern-day version of the rebellious wife, striking out for independence; ▷Trevor Rhone's *Two Can Play* goes two-thirds of the way down the line only to cop out at the

end; ▷Franca Rame's *A Woman Alone* and ▷Berta Freistadt's *Woman with a Shovel* as studies of a woman pushed to extremes; images of women striving for independence run deep in much of women's writing, from ▷Shelagh Delaney to ▷Sarah Daniels.

IKOLI, Tunde   [1955–]
British dramatist

Plays include:
Short Sleeves in Summer (1974), *On the Out* (1977), *Scrape off the Black* (1977), *Sink or Swim* (1981), *Wall of Blue* (1982, part of *Breach of the Peace*), *Sleeping Policemen* (with ▷Howard Brenton; 1983), *Duckin'n'Divin'* (1984), *Week In Week Out* (1985), *Soul Night* (1985), *The Lower Depths* (from ▷Gorki; 1986), *Please and Thank You* (1986; as a double bill with *Soul Night* under the title *Banged Up*)

One of Britain's leading black dramatists, Ikoli had a long and fruitful relationship with Foco Novo, whose artistic director Roland Rees directed many of his works. Ikoli, born in the East End to a Nigerian father and a Cornish mother, was encouraged to involve himself in drama by a social worker, wrote and co-directed *Tunde's Film* at the age of eighteen, and became a professional writer. His non-Caribbean background may help Ikoli to look beyond the stereotypes of black writing in Britain, to investigate the realities of survival in a world which is increasingly hostile to those who have been identified as losers, be they black or white. Perhaps this comes over most clearly in *Please and Thank You* where a nervous, newly appointed, black, well-educated social worker finds his first client, a white, poorly-educated woman, about to put her head in the oven, and in *The Lower Depths* where his long admiration of Gorki is put to use to show the persistence of the attitudes and situations of the original in the new/old world of Thatcherism. Ikoli's collaboration with ▷Brenton on *Sleeping Policemen* was highly unusual since, after a workshop period, each wrote his own play and they were then intercut to form what Michael Billington called 'a radicalised, phantasmagoric *Under Milk Wood*'.

Try these:
The brothers' reunion in *Scrape Off the Black* has been compared to ▷Eugene O'Neill's *Long Day's Journey Into Night*;

▷Caryl Phillips' *Strange Fruit* and Tony Marchant's *Lazy Days Ltd* also fiercely centres on two brothers; ▷Mustapha Matura is another black dramatist to rework the classics; ▷Jacqueline Rudet and ▷Jackie Kay and ▷Winsome Pinnock are among the new generation of black women dramatists; ▷Jim Cartwright's *Road* has also been compared to *Under Milk Wood* for the 1980s.

INGE, William   [1913–73]
American dramatist

Plays include:
Come Back Little Sheba (1950), *Picnic* (1953), *Bus Stop* (1955), *The Dark at the Top of the Stairs* (1957), *A Loss of Roses* (1959), *Natural Affection* (1962), *Where's Daddy?* (1966), *Summer Brave* (1973)

The son of a travelling salesman, Inge had his heyday in the 1950s when he wrote four Broadway hits back-to-back, several of which were made into well-known films, particularly *Bus Stop*, with Marilyn Monroe. Chronicles of small-town America, Inge's plays can seem dated today in their rather obvious symbolism and bald Freudian psychology, but he can paint a poignant image of desolation – as in *Come Back Little Sheba*, in which the lost dog Sheba functions as an image of the child the central couple, Doc and Lola Delaney, will never have. A homosexual, Inge wrote often about sexual magnetism, comically, in *Bus Stop*, between a Montana braggart and a nightclub singer, and, more seriously, in *Picnic*, in which the sexually attractive drifter Hal galvanises a Kansas community. The film *Splendor in the Grass* (1961) features Inge in a bit part as a minister

Try these:
▷Tennessee Williams, a friend of Inge's, for small-town despair and dashed hopes; ▷Mark Medoff, Ed Graczyk, Sally Nemeth for more recent plays set off the beaten American track.

INNAURATO, Albert   [1948–]
American dramatist

Plays include:
Urlicht (1971), *The Transfiguration of Benno Blimpie* (1973), *Gemini* (1976), *Earth Worms* (1977), *Ulysses in Traction* (1977),

Passione (1980), *Coming of Age in SoHo* (1985), *Magda and Callas* (1988), *Gus and Al* (1988), *Herself as Lust* (1991), and, in collaboration with Christopher Durang, *I Don't Generally Like Poetry But Have You Read 'Trees'* (1972), *The Mitzi Gaynore Story, or Gyp* (1973), *The Idiots Karamazov* (1974)

Is he a South Philadelphian ▷Shaw, as one New York critic once suggested, or a voyeur with a gleeful interest in the grotesque? Whatever one's individual slant, opinions on Innaurato are unlikely to be neutral, since his emotional, Italianate writing – Christopher Durang meets Lina Wertmuller – tends to elicit equally emotional responses. At his best, his plays, and their images, are frighteningly immediate and powerful, as in his early *The Transfiguration of Benno Blimpie*, in which the obese, unattractive Benno gorges himself to death. Food is also central to his greatest success, *Gemini*, which lasted four years on Broadway. Set on the twenty-first birthday of a sexually and socially confused Harvard undergraduate, the comedy is loud, rude and psychologically insightful, in Innaurato's typical blend. His follow-up Broadway show, *Passione*, was better on character than on overall concept (a circus fat lady's diatribe against the grapefruit diet still reverberates), a problem that also beset *Coming of Age in SoHo*. *Magda and Callas* had much of the histrionic loopiness of *Gemini* (as would befit a play about a declining diva), but many critics found it paled in comparison with most of Innaurato's other work. Innaurato took on those same reviewers in *Gus and Al* and judging by the positive response, he may have won this round. Al is Innaurato himself, pained by bad notices, who travels back to *fin-de-siècle* Vienna to meet and commiserate with another troubled artist, Gustav Mahler. The play is quieter than anything else Innaurato has written, its comedy more subtle, and despite the passages that one critic found 'treacly', it marks an exciting new direction for a restless writer not afraid to be passionate.

Try these:
▷Christopher Durang, his erstwhile collaborator, for writing with an often manic tilt; ▷Kaufman and Hart for great scenes of familial hurlyburly; ▷Harvey Fierstein for gay dilemmas treated with an absence of hand-wringing; ▷De Filippo's *Saturday,*

Sunday, Monday and ▷Howe's *The Art of Dining* for other scenes of gastronomic mayhem.

IONESCO, Eugène   [1912–90]
French dramatist, born in Rumania

Plays include:
La cantatrice chauve (*The Bald Prima Donna* or *The Bald Soprano*; 1950), *La Leçon* (*The Lesson*; 1951), *Les Chaises* (*The Chairs*; 1952), *Victimes du devoir* (*Victims of Duty*; 1953), *Amédée ou comment s'en débarasser* (*Amédée or How to Get Rid of It*; 1954), *L'Impromptu de l'Alma ou Le caméléon du berger* (*Improvisation or The Shepherd's Chameleon*; 1956), *Le nouveau locataire* (*The New Tenant*; 1957), *Tueur sans gages* (*The Killer*; 1959), *Rhinocéros* (*Rhinoceros*; 1960), *Le roi se meurt* (*Exit the King*; 1962), *La soif et la faim* (*Hunger and Thirst*; 1966), *Macbeth* (1966), *Voyages chez les morts* (*Journey Among the Dead*; 1982)

Ionesco was born in Rumania, spent his childhood in France and his student days in Bucharest, and then settled in Paris in his twenties; this may have led to some of his questioning of identity. His short (and probably best) plays, *The Bald Prima Donna*, *The Lesson*, and *The Chairs*, became popular all over the world in the 1950s, but as he became more acceptable to the establishment his plays grew longer and lost some of their power to please and shock. His combination of inexhaustible and often hilarious linguistic invention with brooding despair in the face of death and contingency still has a good deal of force. What remains in the memory is a number of highly theatrical images; the rhinoceros, typifying the thick-skinned man of immovable conviction; the vast dead body in the next room haunting the pair in *Amédée*, that may or may not symbolise their former love; the girl killed by the word 'knife' in *The Lesson*; the stage filled with expectant empty chairs, addressed in vain by a dumb orator, in *The Chairs*; and the man in a bare room in *The New Tenant*, gradually engulfed by furniture, and the final turning off of the light – a simple but nightmarish metaphor for life.

Ionesco wrote a certain amount of dramatic theory, besides two plays about the act of playwriting (*Improvisation* and *Victims of Duty*) and in 1958 he engaged in a lively controversy with Kenneth Tynan, about the necessity for plays to be rooted in reality and to engage with society. Ionesco declared himself against (and free from) any political ideology: 'No political system can deliver us from the pain of living, from our fear of death, our thirst for the absolute.'

There were many Ionesco productions in Britain in the great days when Olivier and Barrault both played Berenger in *Rhinoceros* – and Zero Mostel has played it off-Broadway. But in recent years he has largely been confined to amateur and student groups. However in 1983 Christopher Fettes directed *Exit the King* at the Lyric Studio; and *The Bald Prima Donna* did well at the Almeida in 1985. His last play, *Journeys among the Dead*, was performed at Riverside Studios in 1987, but this semi-autobiographical Freudian dream journey among dead friends and relatives was on the whole found to be self-indulgent and badly shaped. Wilma, meanwhile, revived *Macbeth* with success in Philadelphia.

Ionesco himself was last seen in London at Riverside Studios in 1983 in one of the strangest productions ever put on the London stage – Simone Benmussa's production (in French) of Virginia Woolf's *Freshwater*, a private but quite funny Bloomsbury joke, in which he played Alfred Lord Tennyson, his wife was the maid, Nathalie Sarraute the butler, and ▷Snoo Wilson a porpoise.

The Bald Prima Donna (The Bald Soprano)
This short 'anti-play' epitomises the 'Theatre of the Absurd' in that it tries to reject all established theatrical conventions: it has no linear plot, proceeding instead by a series of disparate 'ten-minute takes'; its characters are interchangeable (indeed at the end of the play the Martins begin it again with the Smiths' dialogue); and the attempts at communication gradually disintegrate from cliché to reworded proverb to meaningless syllables. It is less nightmarish than *The Lesson* or *The Chairs*, but it has considerable staying power; it played at the Théâtre de la Huchette in Paris for longer than *The Mousetrap*.

Try these:
▷Tom Stoppard, who borrowed the device of the clock that struck at random from *The Bald Prima Donna*, and used it in *Travesties*; ▷N.F. Simpson for verbal invention and logical paradoxes, though

without the desperation; ▷Cocteau's film *Le Testament d'Orphée* (*The Testament of Orphée*) for a similar retrospective to *Journey among the Dead*; French playwrights ▷Alfred Jarry and Boris Vian for further adventures into the 'Theatre of the Absurd'.

ISHERWOOD, Christopher

see AUDEN, W.H.

j

JARRY, Alfred [1873–1907]
French dramatist

Plays include:
Ubu Roi (*King Ubu*; 1896), *Ubu Enchaîné* (*Ubu in Chains*; 1900), *Ubu sur le Butte* (*Ubu on the Butte*; published 1906), *Ubu Cocu* (*Ubu the Cuckold*; published 1944)

For a play that ran for only two nights when it first appeared, and could barely be heard at the first of these performances, *King Ubu* has had a considerable after-life. Jarry's first version was written with other schoolfriends as a puppet play when he was fifteen, satirising an unpopular physics master, who then became a caricature of the greedy and cowardly French bourgeoisie. It shows a schoolboy's cruelty, love of lavatory jokes, and parody of ▷Shakespeare, French Romantic drama, and Rabelais, besides a joyous taste for inventing words. When staged at the Théâtre de l'Oeuvre in 1896, it almost caused a riot, and it has been popular ever since – the Surrealists loved it, Apollinaire and ▷Ionesco acknowledged its influence, and someone is always putting it on again, with varying emphases. The nearest to an establishment production has been ▷Peter Brook's minimalist version at the Bouffes du Nord in 1977 which replaced the traditional fat figure of Ubu by the very tall Andreas Katsoulas and used very simple props – bricks, cable drums, silvered rubber balls, a bearskin rug – in a highly imaginative way. The play is clearly not yet so familiar as to be felt entirely safe.

Try these:
Apollinaire, for the Surrealist *Breasts of Tiresias*; ▷Ionesco, for wordplay and subversive invention. ▷Ken Campbell, ▷Joe Orton, ▷Tom Stoppard, ▷N.F. Simpson for subversive intention in the British theatre; ▷Arthur Kopit for something similar in America.

JEFFREYS, Stephen [1950–]
British dramatist

Plays include:
Like Dolls or Angels (1977), *Mobile 4* (1978), *Year of the Open Fist* (1979), *The Vigilante Trail* (1979), *Jubilee Too* (1980), *Imagine* (1981), *Peer Gynt* (1981), *Clearing House* (1982), *Hard Times* (1982), *Carmen* (1984), *Futures* (1984), *Returning Fire* (1985), *Valued Friends* (1989), *The Clink* (1990)

Jeffreys first came to prominence when *Like Dolls or Angels* won the Best New Play award at the *Sunday Times* National Student Drama Festival in 1977. An apprenticeship with Pocket Theatre, Cumbria, and ▷Paines Plough paid off with the Hampstead Theatre hit, *Valued Friends*, which won him the *Evening Standard*'s Most Promising Playwright award. It was successfully revived in the following year at Hampstead but plans for a West End transfer did not materialise. A subsequent play, *The Clink*, an ambitious political satire ostensibly set in the economic gloom of 16th-century Merrie England, was produced jointly by Paines Plough and Plymouth's Theatre Royal. Though the plot follows the skulduggery in the corridors of power surrounding the dynastic succession to the Virgin Queen, *The Clink* took on an amazing topicality when presented in London during the week of Mrs Thatcher's downfall. Though written two years before, it hit the mark with uncanny accuracy.

Valued Friends
In this subtle comedy, set during the London property boom of the 1980s, four friends who have been renting a flat together since student days succumb to the temptation to buy it at a knock-down price. In the process, the chums trade their caring 1970s values for Thatcherite greed, and their communal harmony for individualist division. Jeffreys does not, however,

withdraw sympathy from his characters, who emerge regenerated from their collision with changing times.

Try these:
▷Doug Lucie's *Fashion*, ▷David Hare's *Secret Rapture* for 1980s state-of-the-nation plays; Stephen Fagan's *The Hard Shoulder* and Martin Crimp's *Dealing with Clair* for more property-related issues; ▷Richard Greenberg for an American equivalent.

JELLICOE, (Patricia) Ann   [1927–]
British dramatist, director and teacher

Plays include:
The Sport of My Mad Mother (1958), *The Knack* (1961), *Shelley; or, The Idealist* (1965), *The Rising Generation* (1967), *The Giveaway* (1968), *You'll Never Guess* (1973), *The Reckoning* (1978), *The Tide* (1980)

Jellicoe's second play, *The Sport of My Mad Mother*, which won joint third prize in *The Observer* Play Competition in 1956, is a fantasy about a group of teddy-boys led by a sort of earth-mother. Based on action, not text, and exploiting the medium of theatre as her work has continued to do, it baffled audiences who had recently found *Look Back in Anger* revolutionary. Perhaps the most extreme example of this tendency is *The Rising Generation*, written in 1960 as a commission for the Girl Guides which, prefiguring her later work, needed a cast of thousands. In it a great mother-figure urges the girls to reject men, but the youngsters finally opt for co-operation and boys and girls set off together to colonise outer space. Unsurprisingly, the Girl Guides did not put it on, although a truncated version was eventually staged in 1967. *The Knack*, about the relationships and shifting power balances between a woman and three men sharing a house, could seem flat and confusing on the page but sparkles in performance and was a major success. *Shelley*, a documentary of the poet's life from university to his death, showed a more conventional approach.

From 1979, Jellicoe became involved in putting on plays with the people of Lyme Regis, Dorset, and channelled her energies into community theatre with casts of up to 150 in promenade performances and many more in support activities. Jellicoe has been the catalyst for their development, often as director and dramatist, through the Colway Theatre Trust which she helped found. Her style of working has been widely copied and she is now consulted internationally on such projects.

Try these:
▷Royal Court Theatre which encouraged her earlier work; ▷Howard Barker, ▷David Edgar, ▷Charles Wood for dramatists commissioned by Jellicoe to write community plays; ▷John Osborne's *Look Back in Anger*, ▷Arnold Wesker's *Trilogy*, ▷John Arden's *Serjeant Musgrave's Dance* for contrasting contemporary treatments of women with men by male writers; ▷Harold Pinter and ▷Samuel Beckett for break-up of form; the non-linear approach of many women's groups such as Monstrous Regiment (which takes its name from one of the major concepts of *The Rising Generation*), the Women's Theatre Group, Cunning Stunts, Scarlet Harlets; Welfare State, IOU for open-space spectacles; ▷community theatre, ▷women-in-theatre.

JENKIN, Len   [1941–]
American dramatist

Plays include:
Limbo Tales (1980), *Dark Ride* (1981), *My Uncle Sam* (1983), *Five of Us* (1983), *A Country Doctor* (1986), *Soldier's Tale* (with Paul Magid 1986); *American Notes* (1988)

Len Jenkin is not a playwright who caters to the interests of matinee audiences of senior citizens or those evening performances for tired businessmen. There are critics, in fact, who find his style so esoteric and self-indulgent as to declare that he toys only with is own emotions for some personal satisfaction. If so, he presents a challenging form of theatre. With few exceptions (Obie-Award-winner *Five of Us*, for example) Jenkin's vision of life is surrealistic and flowery. Consistency in plotting or character development has little interest for him, and his plays are frequently disorienting. Aristotelian logic is replaced with hallucinatory observations by strange people who are involved in opaque adventures where surprises are frequent – for them as well as the audience. Without a line of hesitation or preparation, Jenkin can digress as flippantly as a wren on a limb – for a joke, a haunting aside or a purposeful wild goose chase. His use of language shows his love of American idiom. *My Uncle Sam* is a 'pulp fiction parody' in the words of one reviewer; 'a loony detective story' in the words of another. Given to expressing his feelings and aspirations through nocturnal journeys into mythic environments, Jenkin has created a following which enjoys discovering the shrewd observations he implants in his abstract approach to theatre. He is currently a professor of playwriting at New York University.

American Notes
As one who chose to dramatise a Franz Kafka's story *A Country Doctor* as well as Stravinsky's *The Soldier's Tale*, Jenkin can be expected to present an American landscape that may appear normal but most assuredly turns out to be something quite different. The scene is a motel, of which six rooms on two floors are exposed to the audience. It happens at night when all characters, except for the desk clerk, are mysterious and enigmatic, ranging from the mayor to a pimp and his whores. By definition the play is episodic, while the character and their stories may be defined by the motto of the motel: 'We are easy to get to, but hard to leave'. There is, however, a haunting fascination to it all, and one feels somewhat like the central character who wanders around trying to piece together the fragments of the narrative.

Try these:
▷Susan Glaspell's *Trifles* for piecing together a narrative, ▷Pinter for elliptical treatment of experience,▷Ionesco for opacity and surprise.

JESURUN, John   [1951–]
American   playwright,   director   and screenwriter

Plays include:
Chang in a Void Moon (1982), *Red House* (1984), *Number Minus One* (1984), *Dog's Eye View* (1984), *Changes in a Void* (1985), *Deep Sleep* (1986), *White Water* (1986), *Black Maria* (1987), *Sunspot* (1989)

This Hispanic-American playwright, raised in Puerto Rico and Germany, came of age in the United States and is one of the emerging voices in the new wave of the American avant garde. A   sculptor,   educated   at   the Philadelphia College of Art and the Yale School of Fine Arts, it was at the latter that he

was first seduced by the world of film. Fascinated by the scope, power and manipulative potential of the film and video media, Jesurun tries to capture and replicate the essence of film on stage, bringing the resonant multiplicity of cinematic angles and images to his plays.

Jesurun directs his own works, several of which had New York premieres at experimental theatres including La Mama, the Kitchen, the Performing Garage and the Pyramid. Multi-media events, with non-linear plot structures, telescopic wordplay and rapidly kaleidoscoping images, his works always include film and video segments, and are designed to reach out to the 'television generation'. His multi-focus performance style both seduces and disorients with its multiple moving arenas of simultaneous action. Knowing it is impossible to take in the whole theatre piece, Jesurun wants the audience members to participate in the play by selecting their own points of focus. His shifting and aberrant perspective has its roots in surrealism.

Jesurun worked as a production assistant on the 'Dick Cavett Show' and, draws on his own television experience in *Chang in a Void Moon* and *White Water*, which parody the form, content, and technology of popular programming. In *Red House* the influence of ▷Samuel Beckett is apparent in the minimalist dialogue, set and action. *Deep Sleep*, which is at least half film, captures the essence of his love-hate relationship with the electronic media and earned him an Obie in 1986. Here Jesurun constructs a dialectic between live actors and their images on video monitors, each group insisting that it has a stronger claim on reality. Jesurun explores the powerful hold of electronic images on our minds and asserts our right to resist.

Try these:
For the effect of film on our self image ▷Sam Shepard's *Angel City*; for minimalist structure see ▷Samuel Beckett's *Play* and *Not I*; for multi-focused performance see Richard Schechner, ▷Anne Bogart and Martha Clarke's *Endangered Species*; for use of electronic images in live performance see the work of Laurie Anderson and SQUAT Theatre, also the Wooster Group; ▷Howard Brenton's *Hess is Dead* for onstage televisions; ▷Pirandello's *Six Characters* for argument between 'actors' and 'characters'.

JOHN, Errol   [1924–88]
Trinidadian actor and dramatist

Plays include:
Moon on a Rainbow Shawl (1956)

John's acting roles include Othello at the Old Vic in 1962, but he is best known for his play *Moon on a Rainbow Shawl*. Winner of the 1956 *Observer* Play Competition, this was produced at the Royal Court in 1958 and was revived at London's Almeida theatre in 1988, directed by Maya Angelou. The play shows a trolley-bus driver abandoning the girl he has made pregnant in his determination to escape from the realistically presented back-yard life surrounded by prostitution, petty thieving and poverty. Other scripts and the television play *The Exiles* have shown black middle-class and intellectuals exiled in a white world, while *The Dawn* has a white protagonist and attempts to show the effect of his exposure to anti-black violence in Africa.

Try these:
▷Shelagh Delaney's *A Taste of Honey* for a play of the same period dealing with similar issues to *Moon on a Rainbow Shawl*; ▷Willis Hall and ▷Keith Waterhouse's *Billy Liar* for contemporary escapism; for a 1980s view of the East End ▷Karim Alrawi's *A Colder Climate*; for other treatments of strain put onto personal relationships through poverty and racism, ▷Michael Abbensetts, ▷Caryl Phillips, ▷Mustapha Matura, ▷Tunde Ikoli, ▷Barry Reckord; ▷Black Theatre Forum, ▷Temba.

JOHNSON, Terry   [1955–]
British dramatist and director

Plays include:
Days Here So Dark (1981), *Insignificance* (1982), *Unsuitable for Adults* (1984), *Cries from the Mammal House* (1984), *Tuesday's Child* (1986; with Kate Lock), *Imagine Drowning* (1991)

Johnson, who has worked in ▷community theatre and with the Science Fiction Theatre of Liverpool, is best known for *Insignificance* (which was filmed in 1985) and, increasingly for his work as a director (he directed the superb 1988 television adaptation of ▷Ayckbourn's *Way Upstream*). His other work includes the somewhat portentous Viking/Scottish *Days Here So Dark*, and

Tuesday's Child which deals with the complications that arise following the discovery of an Irish virgin's apparently immaculate pregnancy. *Cries from the Mammal House* is a dramatically powerful meditation on themes of conservation, religious and political enlightenment, family life and child abuse which deserves to be more widely staged. On the other hand, *Insignificance* is a heady mix of issues and characters as Marilyn Monroe and Einstein demonstrate the theory of relativity with interruptions from Dimaggio and McCarthy. Witty, imaginatively concerned with important questions about natural and personal power and responsibility, the creation of myth and the gap between public and private personas, Johnson's plays are impressively willing to address the big themes, and even if he occasionally loses his way (as in *Tuesday's Child*), his readiness to tackle the wider canvas makes his a refreshing talent in a climate increasingly dominated by miniaturists. The brave, tender, awkward *Imagine Drowning*, his latest play, has found him, true to the form of *Cries from the Mammal House*, engaged in making new-age and global warnings – and meditating again on personal violence, 'the dark nugget' within, and the challenge of disability – among other things – in the acerbic personality of Nabil Shaban – Needless to say, it split the critics, but deservedly won the John Whiting Award for 1991.

Try these:
▷Brecht's *Galileo* and ▷Howard Brenton's *The Genius* also deal with the responsibilities of scientists; Quincy Long's *Virgin Molly* for an immaculate conception, but experienced by a marine private; ▷Dürrenmatt's *The Physicists* takes a surreal look at scientists; ▷Caryl Churchill's *Top Girls* brings together a wide group of disparate characters out of historical time; ▷Tom Stoppard's *Hapgood* juggles with theories of physics, espionage and the nature of responsibility; ▷Arthur Miller's *After the Fall* has echoes of Marilyn Monroe; ▷Deborah Levy's *Pax* and *Clam* also give global warnings.

JONES, Marie   [1949–]
Northern Irish dramatist

Plays include:
Lay Up Your Ends (1984), *Oul Delf and False Teeth* (1984), *Now You're Talkin* (1985), *Gold in the Streets* (1986), *The Girls*

in the Big Picture (1986), Somewhere Over The Balcony (1987), Weddings, Wee'ins and Wakes (1989), The Hamster Wheel (1990), The Blind Fiddler of Glenadaugh (1990)

Belfast born, Marie Jones has been writer-in-residence for Charabanc, the Belfast touring company since it started in 1983, and has devised all its shows. She and four other actresses founded the company to provide themselves with employment after months of being unemployed, and to give themselves more challenging and interesting work than they were being offered when jobs did come their way. Charabanc's success has stemmed partly from the verve, versatility and energy the performers have brought to the work but also partly from the kind of material they have chosen to do and the way they have created it.

Charabanc shows, drawing on the history of the province, have involved intensive research and hours of interviews which Jones has then turned into scripts. As a touring company (often to community centres) and minimally funded, the company has made a virtue out of necessity, using the barest of props. However, Jones and Charabanc's particular skill has been to create such vivid detail and characterisation that you seldom come out of a Charabanc show without having experienced an emotional identification with its protagonists. Where Jones' skill as a writer and the performers stop and start however is hard to differentiate, so much of each other have they become. Most productions have been naturalistic in form, though Somewhere Over The Balcony experimented with a more surrealistic treatment. Subjects have ranged from the 1911 Belfast mill girls' strike through the disillusionment with Labour politics since the war, the complexities of reconciliation between Protestant and Catholic, emigration, rural social patterns and pressures, and the effects of the British Army presence and institutionalised violence on Catholic residents in a Belfast high-rise block. The Hamster Wheel, by contrast, took a look at the more general but no less tortuous problems involved in the aftercare of stroke victims in the home.

As a strictly non-sectarian company (the company employs both Catholics and Protestants, men and women), the strength of Charabanc's productions and Jones' plays has lain in its ability to reveal social networks and loyalties even if, as some commentators complain, it has sometimes lacked a deeper sense of political analysis. But it is one of the most

entertaining companies to emerge from Northern Ireland, and one whose flair and warmth have made it as popular throughout Ireland as in London, the US and the USSR. The plays have opened eyes to the resilience and spirit of the Belfast people alongside the sufferings they have endured over the past twenty years.

Now a freelance writer, Marie Jones also writes for Belfast Theatre-in-Education companies and for television. In 1991, she won the John Hewitt Memorial Award in recognition of her writing and Charabanc's contribution to Northern Ireland.

Try these:
Many companies use oral history and researched interviews for the basis of their work, including the Reminiscence group aimed at pensioners, Age Exchange; also ▷Ann Jellicoe and Robert Leparge's Quebec-based Theatre Repere company; for the vernacular and exploration of a Catholic rural community, J.M. Synge's Playboy of the Western World, ▷Brian Friel's Translations and Dancing at Lughnasa; Nell McCafferty's The Worm in the Heart followed a particularly female-oriented view culminating in the Kerry Babies trial, a subject also treated by Polly Teale's Fallen; for other playwrights writing on the subject of Northern Ireland, see ▷Ann Devlin, ▷Seamus Finnegan, ▷Ron Hutchinson, ▷Thomas Kilroy, ▷Frank McGuinness, ▷Christina Reid, ▷Daniel Mornin; see also Rona Munro's Bold Girls.

JONSON, Ben   [1572–1637]
English dramatist, poet and actor

Plays include:
Every Man in His Humour (1598), Every Man Out of His Humour (1599), Poetaster (1601), Sejanus His Fall (1601), Eastward Ho (1605; with ▷George Chapman and ▷John Marston), Volpone (1605), Epicene or The Silent Woman (1609), The Alchemist (1610), Catiline (1611), Bartholomew Fair (1614), The Devil is an Ass (1616), The Staple of News (1625), The New Inn (1629), The Magnetic Lady (1633)

Jonson worked as a bricklayer, served as a soldier, became an actor, escaped hanging after killing another actor in a duel by virtue of his ability to read Latin which meant he could claim what was called benefit of clergy, and became a highly successful dramatist in his own day, although his subsequent reputation has been eclipsed by that of his contemporary and fellow actor ▷William Shakespeare. As well as being a successful dramatist, Jonson also wrote many of the Court entertainments known as Masques, working with architect and stage designer Inigo Jones until they quarrelled over the respective importance of their own contributions to the shows. Jonson was an energetic and somewhat turbulent figure who engaged in the theatrical controversies of his time in *Poetaster*, which attacked ▷Marston and ▷Dekker. He then collaborated with ▷Marston on *Eastward Ho* which landed them and their co-author ▷Chapman in prison for offending powerful Scots at the Court. His tragedies, *Sejanus* and *Catiline*, both on Roman subjects, are very seldom performed and his current theatrical fortunes tend to depend on *Volpone* and *The Alchemist* with occasional forays into other comedies. The ▷RSC's Swan theatre, designed for staging the works of ▷Shakespeare's contempories, has so far seen revivals of *Every Man in His Humour* (an imbroglio of jealous husband, braggart soldier, knowing servants and would-be gallants) and *The New Inn* (a saturnalian feast of role reversals with a spice of clothes fetishism). *The Devil is an Ass* (in which a trainee devil coming to London is mercilessly outplayed by the human devils) and *Bartholomew Fair* (which takes place in and around the famous annual fair as a wide cross section of society join in its pleasures and pitfalls) were fairly widely seen in the 1970s, particularly in versions adapted and directed by ▷Peter Barnes. Perhaps surprisingly, *Epicene*, with its man who marries a woman who is supposed to be completely silent only to discover that she is not silent and eventually that she is not a woman, has not attracted recent theatrical interest.

The Alchemist

Jonson's galaxy of would-be street-wise dupes, get-rich-quick speculators, religious hypocrites, sexual opportunists and overreaching con men (and woman) remains a devastating and delightful critique of the unacceptable faces of capitalism. There is a kind of manic farcical drudgery in running this London dream factory with the partners reacting increasingly frenetically as new markets open up for their corporate strategy of marketing and planning consultancy, brothel-keeping and speculation in human and other currencies of all kinds. The alchemical jargon can be a problem if you read the play, but treat it as the equivalent of someone trying to sell you insurance or convert you to the beauties of the latest model computer (or car) and you won't go far wrong.

Volpone

Another satire on the acquisitive society, set in a Venice that reflects contemporary London, *Volpone* uses the beast fable to characterise its stereotypes: Volpone (the fox) and Mosca (the fly) prey on the carrion birds (Voltore, Corbaccio and Corvino, the vulture, the crow and the raven) who come to prey on the apparently dying Volpone. There is the same delight in trickery as in *The Alchemist* and we tend to admire the comic verve of the protagonists as they outsmart those who are trying to outsmart them. The whole play ends more sourly than most comedies with Volpone and Mosca overreaching themselves and an outbreak of near poetic justice that leaves you questioning the right of the venal judges to administer justice.

Try these:
▷Marlowe's *Tamburlaine* and *Doctor Faustus* and ▷Massinger's *A New Way to Pay Old Debts* for portrayals of characters overreaching themselves; for satirical comedies about the acquisitive society, ▷Middleton, the Restoration dramatists ▷Aphra Behn, ▷Wycherley and ▷Congreve, ▷John Gay's *The Beggar's Opera* and ▷Brecht's *The Threepenny Opera*, ▷Caryl Churchill's *Serious Money*; for Venetian capitalism, ▷Shakespeare's *Merchant of Venice* and John Clifford's *Losing Venice*; Shakespeare and Jonson are characters in Edward Bond's *Bingo*. Michael Coveney described *The New Inn* as 'The Winter's Tale meets Nicholas Nickleby'.

k

KANIN, Garson [1912–]
American dramatist, director and actor

Plays include:
Born Yesterday (1946), *The Smile of the World* (1949), *The Rat Race* (1949), *The Live Wire* (1950), *Do Re Mi* (musical; 1960), *Peccadillo* (1985), *Happy Ending* (1988)

Kanin graduated from the American Academy of Dramatic Arts and began his career as an actor in *Little Ol' Boy* (1933), before becoming an assistant director to the legendary ▷George Abbott. Kanin's own directorial credits include *Hitch Your Wagon* (1937), *The Diary of Anne Frank* (1955), *Funny Girl* (1964), and *Idiot's Delight* (1970). He made the transition to Hollywood and with his wife, Ruth Gordon, wrote the screenplays for *Adam's Rib* (1949), *Woman of the Year* (1942), *Pat and Mike* (1952), *The Girl Can't Help It* (1957) and many more. His films became the vehicles for such stars as Judy Holiday, Katherine Hepburn and Spencer Tracy. Thematically, his dramatic material deals with a witty battle of the sexes. His two recent plays are also romantic screwball comedies. Unfortunately, both lacked the verve and star-power sparring to make it to New York.

Born Yesterday
Billie Dawn, a dumb blonde, accompanies tough Harry Brock, the scrap-iron millionaire, to Washington, DC. Harry is in the capital to buy Congressional support for favourable business legislation. Finding Billie a social liability, he engages reporter Paul Verrall to give her 'class'. Paul makes Billie into a socially responsible citizen and in the process the two fall in love. Together they outmanoeuvre and defeat Harry relieving him of millions of dollars. Revived in New York 1989, with star performances by Madeline Kahn as Billie and Ed Asner as Brock, *Born Yesterday* lacked the punch to achieve a long run (the original production ran for 1,643

performances). Critics felt that the flag-waving finale in which Billie and Paul intone democratic sentiments was no longer convincing.

Try these:
▷Shaw's *Pygmalion* is *the* social engineering play, ▷Kaufman and Hart, ▷Philip Barry, ▷Thornton Wilder ▷Neil Simon, ▷A.R. Gurney, ▷Tina Howe for chronicles of class in the USA.

KAUFMAN, George S. [1889–1961]

HART, Moss [1904–61]
American dramatic collaborators

Plays include:
Once In a Lifetime (1930), *Merrily We Roll Along* (1934), *You Can't Take It With You* (1936), *I'd Rather Be Right* (book for the Richard Rodgers musical; 1937), *The Fabulous Invalid* (1938), *The Man Who Came To Dinner* (1939), *The American Way* (1939), *George Washington Slept Here* (1940)

For period pieces of Americana in towns both small and large and told with affection and wit, few playwrights could match this duo who, although they had other collaborators throughout their careers (Kaufman worked with Edna Ferber and Marc Connelly, among many others; Hart with Irving Berlin and Cole Porter), had their finest moments together. While their terrain shifted from Hollywood during the talkies (*Once In A Lifetime*, memorably revived by the ▷RSC in 1980) to a remote Ohio town (*The Man Who Came To Dinner*), the two took pleasure in parody but remained sentimentalists at heart, particularly – as in *The Fabulous Invalid* – when the subject involved the stage. ('We mustn't let that die,' the idealistic young

Ed Asner (as Harry Brock) and Madeline Kahn (as Billie Dawn) in The Cleveland Play House production of *Born yesterday* by Garson Kanin, September 1988

director remarks stirringly of the theatre at the close of the play.) Even the potentially astringent *Merrily We Roll Along*, a story of lost ideals told in flashbacks, has gone on to exert an emotive pull that can be seen not only in Stephen Sondheim's ill-fated musical version of it but in such similar-themed pieces as ▷Simon Gray's *The Common Pursuit* and films like *The Big Chill*. In their plays, emotional decency wins out over rules and regulations; they are foes of the reactionary, friends of the eccentric.

You Can't Take It With You

Set in New York in 1936, this three-act Pulitzer Prize winner is one of the most cheerfully anarchic of American plays and, unsurprisingly, one of the most often revived works in regional theatres throughout the USA. (Frank Capra's 1938 film adaptation won Oscars for Best Picture and Best Director.) A celebration of innocence and relaxation as well as personal eccentricity, it pitches the idiosyncratically zany Vanderhof clan against the boring money-minded conformists in the world around them. The part of Grandpa Vanderhof, a man who opted not to become rich 'because it took too much time', is one of the most delightful on the American stage, and Jason Robards performed it memorably on Broadway in 1982. The play sets off small comic explosions of fireworks, much like those being lit on stage, and Kaufman and Hart aren't beyond bringing in a Russian countess, Olga, at the eleventh hour to raise spirits again.

Try these:
▷Noël Coward's *Hay Fever* for a more lethal hymn to family eccentrics; ▷Eugene O'Neill's *Ah, Wilderness!* and William Saroyan's *The Time of Your Life* for complementary comic Americana; ▷Philip Barry for deflations of pomposity; ▷Christopher Durang ▷Beth Henley, Harry Kondoleon, A. R. Gurney for contemporary comic shenanigans; ▷Charles Wood's *Veterans* and ▷Christopher Hampton's *Tales from Hollywood* for film-making; ▷George Abbott and John Cecil Holm's *Three Men on a Horse* for more warm-hearted live-and-let-live moralities.

KAY, Jackie   [1961–   ]
British dramatist and poet

Plays include:
Chiaroscuro (1986), *Twice Over* (1988)

Kay was brought up in Scotland and is a graduate of Stirling University. *Chiaroscuro* commissioned by Theatre of Black Women, is a delicate but potentially powerful piece written in a mixture of forms (dreams, songs, poetry, naturalism) in which cultural histories, friendship, 'coming out' as a lesbian and the difficulties of communication in a largely white-dominated and heterosexual world are confronted and overcome. For each of the four women it is a journey, their reunion and acknowledgement at the end a measure of how far they have travelled and how far they still have to go. *Chiaroscuro*, as the word itself implies, is about light and shade, variation and change and requires a subtle balancing act in performance. But there is little doubt that time will prove the play to have been a turning point in black women's theatre in Britain.

Kay's second play, *Twice Over*, given a rehearsed reading at Gay Sweatshop's 1987 workshop festival, confirmed her promise as a developing playwright whose black and lesbian perspective is only a starting point to further explorations. *Twice Over* elaborates, with great good humour and not a little pathos, some of the issues introduced in *Chiaroscuro* – 'coming out' (this time the revelations turn on a recently deceased grandmother), race, class and an implied plea for honesty in all relationships, whatever their inclination.

Try these:
▷Ntozake Shange's *for colored girls who have considered suicide when the rainbow is enuf* for influence and transformatory theatre; ▷Jacqueline Rudet's *Basin* for another treatment of black women's friendship, labelling and lesbianism; ▷Lesbian Theatre; ▷Black Theatre.

KEARSLEY, Julia   [1947–   ]
British dramatist

Plays include:
Wednesday (1979), *Baby* (1980), *Waiting* (1982), *Leaving Home* (1986), *Under the Web* (1987)

A Northern dramatist who lives in Blackpool, Kearsley is highly regarded as an observer in the naturalistic, 'slice of life' mould, who uses

Mark Zeisler, Robert Stanton and Candy Buckley in the American Repertory Theatre's production of George S. Kaufman and Moss Hart's *Once in A Lifetime*, directed by Anne Bogart

irony as a leavening counterweight to the darker schisms revealed in the modern nuclear family. *Wednesday*, first produced at the Bush Theatre and later on Broadway, earned her the Susan Smith Blackburn Prize runner-up award for Best New Female Playwright. Whilst some critics have commented on her somewhat shaky plotting techniques, others find her work overly televisual (*Leaving Home* actually did transfer to the small screen). Nearly all, however, agree on the emotional authenticity of her characters and her capacity to reveal hidden tensions and truths beneath the surface of family life, in looking after a retarded son (*Wednesday*) or an aged mother (*Under the Web*), or coping with the consequences of a father leaving home (*Leaving Home*). *Waiting*, written in response to the Yorkshire Ripper murders, divided critics, some of whom saw it as an outright feminist tract. Kearsley does not see herself as 'a feminist writer'. Nonetheless, Kearsley's plays certainly reflect contemporary disharmonies – the self-delusional defences, the aggressions – of women in the home, with faithful accuracy and affection.

Try these:
▷Alan Ayckbourn and ▷Mike Leigh for other scenes from family life; ▷Stephen Bill's *Curtains*, ▷Ayshe Raif's *Fail/Safe* and ▷Sharman Macdonald for mother/daughter relationships under stress; ▷Rona Munro's *Bold Girls*, ▷Darrah Cloud's *The Stick Wife* for more female self-delusion; ▷De Filippo's *Ducking Out* and ▷Lee Blessing's *Eleemosynary* for another portrait of post-stroke gallows humour; ▷Peter Nichols' *A Day in The Death of Joe Egg* for a surreally bitter view of caring for a mentally handicapped child; Lucy Gannon's *Keeping Tom Nice* is on a similar theme; Graeae for alternative views of disabilities.

KEATLEY, Charlotte   [1960–]
British dramatist

Plays include:
Underneath the Arndale (1982), *Dressing for Dinner* (1983), *The Iron Serpent* (1984), *Waiting for Martin* (1987), *My Mother Said I Never Should* (1987)

London-born Keatley has worked as a theatre critic, actress and radio scriptwriter, but her national reputation rests on her astonishing

1987 tour de force *My Mother Said I Never Should*, a brilliantly assured treatment of four generations of women as they struggle with the everyday traumas of domestic life. A complex and moving play, it moves effortlessly across time and place using repeated motifs and properties to convey the textures of everyday life and to bring out the underlying significance of the apparently trivial and humdrum.

Try these:
▷Catherine   Hayes,   ▷Sharman Macdonald, ▷Marsha Norman and ▷Neil Simon's *Lost in Yonkers* for mothers and daughters; ▷Priestley's *Time and the Conways*, ▷Maugham's *For Services Rendered*, ▷Granville Barker's *The Voysey Inheritance* for families over time.

KEEFFE, Barrie   [1945–]
British dramatist

Plays include:
Only A Game (1973), *Scribes* (1975), *A Mad World My Masters* (1977), *Gimme Shelter* (1977), *Barbarians* (1977), *Frozen Assets* (1978), *Sus* (1979), *Bastard Angel* (1980), *Black Lear* (1981; revised as *King of England*, 1987), *Chorus Girls* (1982), *Better Times* (1985), *My Girl* (1989), *Not Fade Away* (1990)

An East Londoner who began his career as an actor and journalist, Keeffe has established a career as a gritty, hard-driving writer whose affiliation with the East End is maintained via his sustained relationship with the Theatre Royal, Stratford East, where his last five plays have been premiered. He is known for his topicality and the controversy it can cause, his television play *Gotcha*, for example, was the subject of a BBC ban, but nevertheless received premieres in San Francisco and Moscow. Keeffe paints an unromanticised portrait of contemporary England, occasionally using past events, as in *Better Times*, about the 1921 imprisonment of 30 East End labour councillors who refuse to levy an unfair government rate, to illuminate local government problems over rate-capping in the mid-1980s. His *A Mad World My Masters*, written in 1977 and revised in 1984, placed a Margaret Thatcher look-alike amidst an updated response to ▷Thomas Middleton's similarly titled 1608 comedy. In *King of England*, a revision of his earlier *Black Lear*

for Temba, a widower decides to return to the West Indies after thirty-five years in England, only to find that one of his daughters doesn't share his feelings of gratitude towards the UK. *Sus*, written in the year of Thatcher's election is a prophetic view of relations between young blacks and the police. *My Girl* is about a young East End couple struggling to retain their marriage in impoverished circumstances. A playwright with a vigorous sense both of comedy and of social responsibility, as witness his latest play, *Not Fade Away*, about a spry pensioner's bid for independence, Keeffe is best known for his debut film script in 1980 for John MacKenzie's gangster drama *The Long Good Friday*.

Try these:
▷Hanif Kureishi, ▷Karim Alrawi, ▷David Hare, ▷David Edgar, ▷Howard Brenton and ▷Howard Barker for committed topical writing (though, like Hare, Keeffe claims he does not 'set out to write political plays'); ▷Sam Shepard's *Tooth of Crime* and Thomas Babe's *Kid Champion* for Bastard Angel-like rock stars on the skids; ▷Shakespeare's *King Lear*; ▷Edward Bond's *Lear* for another modern version of Shakespeare's play.

KEMP, Lindsay   [1939–   ]
British mime artist, choreographer, director and painter

Key performances include:
Flowers (1974), *The Parade's Gone By* (1975), *Salomé* (1977), *Cruel Garden* (1977), *Onnagata* (1990)

Born in Scotland, Kemp studied painting at Bradford before attending the Rambert School of Ballet and went on to study mime with Marcel Marceau. He mounted events ranging from Soho strip shows to 1960s 'happenings', first forming a company in 1962. In 1974 he attracted popular attention with the Ziggy Stardust concerts staged for David Bowie, a former company member. *Flowers*, a fantasy based on ▷Jean Genet's *Notre Dame des Fleurs*, brought cries of both outrage and acclaim. This was followed by a production of ▷Oscar Wilde's *Salomé*, and two ballets for Ballet Rambert: *The Parade's Gone By* and *Cruel Garden*, with choreography by Christopher Bruce, before Kemp decided to base his company in Spain. His own version of *A Midsummer Night's Dream* and *Nijinsky*

and *The Big Parade* have continued to divide critics. In *Cruel Garden*, based on the life of ▷Federico García Lorca and using many bullfight themes, Kemp and Bruce created a vital and magnificent ballet. Certainly an innovator with a touch of genius, Kemp's own performances have been characterised by slow movement and flickering gesture. Their power is illustrated by the way in which his grotesque impersonation of Salomé, instead of a whirling sinuous dance of the seven veils, offered a slow motion mixture of the coy and the lascivious. His is a theatre of erotic sensuality, abandoned yet highly controlled. He plays with gender, often adopting a female role. But he is in no way a drag artiste, he does not impersonate but seems to embody the femininity he seeks to present, and he can generate a feeling at odds to the physical appearance. In *Flowers* for instance, he was able to show the beauty and sensitivity that can grow from apparent brutality and pornography. Often Kemp seems to be trying to shock but then caps that with moments of great theatrical beauty that outweigh his lapses into the banal.

Try these:
▷Performance Art; ▷Neil Bartlett for another high-definition performer, particularly his *A Vision of Love Revealed in Sleep*; ▷Steven Berkoff as another iconoclastic performer/writer/director; Karen Finley.

KEMPINSKI, Tom   [1938–   ]
British Dramatist

Plays include:
Duet for One (1980), *Self-Inflicted Wounds* (1985), *Separation* (1987); *Sex Please, We're Italian!* (1991)

A sometime actor, London-born Kempinski is best known for his two studies of relationships between women with life-threatening illnesses and their male confidants. *Duet for One* traces the gradual unmasking by a paternal psychologist of the problems of the concert violinist who will never play again, and *Separation* tells a story of a mainly telephonic relationship between a London-based reclusive one-hit writer (widely regarded if mistakenly as a self-portrait) and a New York actress with a potentially fatal disease. Both plays offer very strong parts for their protagonists, both verge on the sentimental and the melodramatic (but don't cross the line). *Self-Inflicted Wounds* is about a Nazi hunter who finds himself unable to publish his findings, and Kempinski has also adapted Jean-Claude Grumberg's *The Workshop* (known in the US as *The Workroom*) and *Dreyfus*. His attempt to write a farce, *Sex Please, We're Italian!* proved markedly unsuccessful.

Try these:
▷Keith Waterhouse's *Bookends*; *84 Charing Cross Road*; *Love Letters* and *Same Time Next Year* for long-distance relationships; ▷Robert Chesley's *Jerker* for a very different telephone relationship; ▷Brian Clark and ▷Phil Young for people with disabilities; ▷Nicholas Wright and ▷Peter Shaffer for psychiatrists; ▷Christopher Hampton's *Portage to San Cristobal* and ▷Peter Weiss for Nazi hunters.

KENNEDY, Adrienne   [1931–]
American dramatist

Plays include:
Funnyhouse of a Negro (1964), *A Rat's Mass* (1966), *In His Own Write* (1967), *The Owl Answers* (1969), *A Lancashire Lad* (1980)

One of the most innovative and subjective American playwrights to appear during the 1960s, Adrienne Kennedy blends symbols, historical figures, racial images and myths in highly surreal plays. Avoiding linear plots, Kennedy creates theatrical nightmares, fragmented mental states of characters who sometimes change costumes to show changing personalities or separating aspects of themselves. Generally, her plays are set in the mind of the central character where horrifying images clash with cryptic and static conversations or monologues to reveal memories and enliven imaginations. Nearly everything occurs within a person's mind. Conventional dramatic conflict and dialogue do not exist, as Kennedy's characters show themselves to be torn mentally and emotionally within that obsessive contrast between the imagined elegance of White European royalty and the vulgar existence of Black Americans in the Rural South or the Northern ghettos. Much of the dramatised confusion within her characters rests upon issues of prejudice, racial heritage and sexual identity.

Funnyhouse of a Negro

Typical of her best work in both style and concept, this play dramatises the last moments on earth of a mulatto woman, Sarah, about to commit suicide after being unable to reconcile herself to her racially mixed heritage. An English major at a city college in New York, Sarah has traditional female fears and fantasies, yet her education only intensifies her internal conflict. She attempts to deny it with her adoration of Queen Victoria, but she experiences the White prejudice, the feeling of Black as evil and the sexual oppression bound to both traditions. In carefully worded yet fragmented monologues, Sarah the Negro and She Who is Clara Passmore are created in Sarah. The only characters external to Sarah are her boyfriend, the funnyhouse man, and her landlady, the funnyhouse lady, who mock Sarah throughout the play with their insane laughter.

Try these:
▷Timberlake Wertenbaker and ▷Caryl Churchill for inventive, non-linear tendencies and fragmentation; ▷David Pownall's *Motorcar* for confused states of mind and racism; ▷Alan Ayckbourn's *Woman in Mind* and Sarah Daniels' *Beside Herself* for sexual identity and mental turmoil; ▷George C. Wolfe, ▷Derek Walcott, ▷Winsome Pinnock, ▷Lorraine Hansberry and ▷Ntozake Shange for other views of black experience; ▷Snoo Wilson for inventive dramaturgy.

KESSELMAN, Wendy   [1940–]
American dramatist, adaptor, translator

Plays include:
Becca (1977), *My Sister in This House* (1981), *The Juniper Tree: A Tragic Household Tale* (1982), *Maggie Magalita* (1985), *Merry-Go-Round* (1987), *I Love You, I Love You Not* (1987), *The Griffin and the Minor Canon* (1988), *Olympe and the Executioner* (1990)

Originally a songwriter and author of children's books, New Yorker Kesselman is known in Britain through Nancy Meckler's 1986 ▷Monstrous Regiment – Leicester Haymarket co-production of *My Sister in This House*, which won the Susan Smith Blackburn Prize. The story of the play – two sisters who murdered their mistress in Le Mans, France – is perhaps best known through ▷Genet's *The*

Maids. Kesselman's original source, however, was Janet Flanner's account of the incident in *Paris Was Yesterday*. Kesselman's version, which places the sisters in a realistic social context – a claustrophobic female household, petty obsessions, oppressions and stifled emotions – is an indictment of French bourgeois values rife with piercing psychological insights. In style it contrasts with Genet's extravagant hallucinatory treatment, which has the two sisters played by male actors in drag.

Maggie Magalita, a bi-lingual work inspired by Kesselman's work with young Hispanics in a New York hospital, is concerned with assimilation. The title character only feels at ease after anglicising her name. *Becca*, a Coppelia-like children's musical, has dark psychological undertones and hauntingly lyrical songs written and recorded by Kesselman. *I Love You, I Love You Not*, delicately traces the relationship between a Jewish grandmother and granddaughter against a backdrop of German wartime memories.

Kesselman's most recent work, *Olympe and the Executioner*, was a finalist for both the Susan Smith Blackburn Prize and the Beverley Hills Theatre Guild – Julie Harris Playwright Award. She is currently at work on an adaptation of Dickens' *A Tale of Two Cities*, commissioned by Stage One: The Louisville Children's Theatre in Kentucky.

Kesselman is an extremely intelligent and lucid writer whose style has a darkly lyrical grace reminiscent of fairy tales. She deserves wider recognition.

Try these:
▷Genet for a contrasting treatment of *The Maids*; ▷Blood Group's *Barricade of Flowers* takes *The Maids* as its starting point for a female imagistic treatment; Sartre for a different kind of claustrophobic household in *Huis Clos*; ▷Pam Gems' *Dusa, Fish, Stas and Vi* and *Piaf*, ▷Caryl Churchill's *Top Girls* and *Fen* for other treatments of women and class; ▷Catherine Hayes' *Skirmishes* for a contrasting treatment of sisters; ▷Jacqui Shapiro's *Winter in the Morning* for an extended image of the Holocaust in the Warsaw Ghetto; ▷Joshua Sobol; ▷Barbara Lebow's *A Shayna Maid* and ▷Emily Mann's *Annulla: An Autobiography* for further female perspectives on the Holocaust.

KESSLER, Lyle   [1940–]
American dramatist

Plays include:
Watering Place (1969), *Possessions* (1978), *Orphans* (1985), *Robbers* (1990)

Born in Philadelphia, Kessler now works as playwright, director, actor and teacher in Santa Monica, California. With his wife, he is co-founder of Imagination Workshop which uses drama to work with hospitalized schizophrenics. He is presently moderator of the Playwrights and Directors Unit of the Actors Studio in Los Angeles. As a playwright, he has had limited success. His first full-length play, *Watering Place*, about a Vietnam vet's angst-ridden encounter with the family of a dead buddy, opened and closed on Broadway at the Music Box Theatre on March 12, 1969. It was nine years before Kessler offered another play, and not until 1985, with *Orphans*, that he achieved any success. Critics have founds his plays derivative of ▷Sam Shepard and ▷Harold Pinter – almost a pastiche, in fact – but have also noted the strength of his characters as acting vehicles, and the passion of their dialogue. There has, however, been little interest shown in any intellectual or imaginative quality within Kessler's plays.

Orphans
As reviewed by Frank Rich, *Orphans* was theatre for the senses and the emotions, not for the mind. The scene is the trashy living-room of a North Philadelphia home which two brothers share after the death of their parents. The younger brother has been mentally defective since childhood, the other is a petty thief who has imprisoned his brother in their home. One night the thief brings home a drunk, whom he gags and ties in a chair. But the drunk, a natty Chicago mobster, soon frees himself and assumes a control through which the three men, in their various idiosyncratic manners, expose both literally and metaphorically, through role-reversals and power struggles, the horrors of their orphaned lives. The younger brother dramatises a life of staring through closed windows; the mobster becomes a crying and pitiable figure revealing his Chicago orphanage experiences. *Orphans* won the Drama League Award, was produced in the West End with Albert Finney, and was made into a movie with Kessler writing the screenplay.

Try these:
▷Emily Mann's *Still Life*; ▷David Rabe's *Streamers* for Vietnam plays; Shepard's *True West* for battling brothers.

KILROY, Thomas   [1934–]
Irish dramatist

Plays include:
The Death and Resurrection of Mr Roche (1968), *The O'Neill* (1969), *Tea and Sex and Shakespeare* (1976), *Talbot's Box* (1977), *Double Cross* (1985)

Born in Callan, County Kilkenny, in southeast Ireland, Tom Kilroy combines playwriting with teaching, and was a lecturer in the English department at University College, Dublin, before becoming Professor of English at University College, Galway. One of Ireland's leading playwrights, Kilroy draws on different theatrical genres and moments of history, and he unapologetically requires a commitment from his audience in an effort to elicit 'an intellectual response to what's happening on-stage'. Like many of his colleagues, Kilroy casts a sceptical glance at his country, and *The Death and Resurrection of Mr Roche* takes place at a celebratory party for an Ireland described, somewhat ironically, as 'on the move . . . up and up'. In *Talbot's Box*, Kilroy uses the story of a real-life Dublin labourer, Matt Talbot, to address the nature of modern-day sainthood. *Double Cross*, written for the Derry-based touring company Field Day, applies the psychology of dissimulation to two Irishmen who were roughly contemporary: Brendan Bracken, Churchill's Minister of Information, and William Joyce (Lord Haw-Haw), the Nazi sympathiser and fascist who was hanged in 1946, to explore, with unfashionable non-partisanship, the nature of 'treason', national identity and racism.

Try these:
▷Tom Stoppard for overtly intellectual theatre which often plays fictional games with fact (see *Travesties* and particularly *Hapgood* for dealing in, amongst other things, the philosophical similarities of 'double agents' and physics); ▷Hugh Leonard ▷Brian Friel for Irish contemporaries, both of whom write in more immediately recognisable modes; ▷Pirandello,

▷Brecht,   ▷Ariane   Mnouchkine's *Mephisto* for plays that link theatrics with power.

KLEIST, Heinrich von   [1777–1811]
German dramatist

Plays include:
Der zerbrochene Krug (*The Broken Jug*; 1808), *Penthesilea* (1808; produced 1878), *Käthchen von Heilbronn* (1810), *Die Hermannschlacht* (*The Battle of Arminius*; 1810, produced 1860), *Prinz Friedrich von Homburg* (*The Prince of Homburg*; 1811, produced 1821)

Kleist never really recovered from leaving the Prussian army and taking up the study of Kantian metaphysics; he was given to asking his friends of both sexes to join him in a suicide pact, and eventually a faithful female friend agreed. Most of his plays (except *The Broken Jug*, which is a good broad comedy using the structure of ▷Sophocles' *Oedipus Rex*), display a neurotic emotional power, with verse to match; several were not performed until well after his death. Henry Livings' *Jug* is a version of *Der zerbrochene Krug*. A fine attempt to stage the epic mythological *Penthesilea* at London's Gate at Latchmere in 1983 featured Susannah York as the Amazon queen sinking her teeth into Achilles' bleeding heart and then killing herself in a frenzy of erotic violence. (Kleist changed the story from the usual versions in which Achilles kills Penthesilea.) *The Prince of Homburg* is a play that has been variously described as both fascist and subversive, in which the hero is sentenced to death for disobeying an order, even though his action won the battle, and comes to agree with the verdict (and be pardoned). One Kleist play that has yet to appear in English is *The Battle of Arminius*, a patriotic play (aimed at Napoleon) dealing with the German defeat of the Roman army; it includes a German maiden called Thusnelda who sets a bear on her faithless Roman lover (surely a natural for the ▷Glasgow Citizens').

Try these:
▷Schiller's *William Tell* for a historical play proclaiming national freedom; Grillparzer for plays in German dealing with mythology and with strong parts for women;

▷Sarah Daniels' *Byrthrite*, ▷Shakespeare's *The Winter's Tale* and ▷Jarry's *King Ubu* for plays in which bears appear on stage.

KONDOLEON, Harry   [1955–]
American dramatist

Plays include:
The Cote D'Azur Triangle (1980), *The Brides* (1980), *Rococo* (1981), *Andrea Rescued* (1982), *The Fairy Garden* (1982), *Self-Torture and Strenuous Exercise* (1982), *Slacks and Tops* (1983), *The Vampires* (1984), *Linda Her* (1984), *Anteroom* (1985), *Zero Positive* (1988)

During the first half of the 1980s Kondoleon was considered a very promising playwright. He received several awards, including an Obie in 1983 for Most Promising Young Playwright, and was given tremendous opportunity by the New York theatre community. Presently, however, most critics feel that he has not fulfilled that promise. It was an asset in his early stages that he seemed full of surprises. In an absurdist fashion he tackled many aspects of modern life and mocked both the life he presented and the theatrical forms which he felt obligated to use. He has the reputation for writing well-paced dialogue, for having a tart tongue given to expressing tasteless jokes and one-sentence messages, and for boasting a strange set of sensibilities. Overall, he has an interesting style of writing – imitative of ▷Joe Orton and ▷Christopher Durang – and he can be very funny, but he has not been able to avoid cliché writing and build upon his talents to create an effective and well structured play. *Zero Positive*, a play about AIDS, emphasises the nonsensical with fantasy sketches, and eschews coherent plotting or concept.

Christmas on Mars
In this absurdist fantasy which opens in New York apartment as an actor closes the window to block out all sounds of humanity, Kondoleon collects a number of odd characters: a male model, a casting director who is pregnant with his child, a homosexual who is a former flight attendant, and a mother who has returned to make amends with the daughter she abandoned twenty years earlier. For two acts this odd combination of mankind talk, fight, cry, tell a few jokes, and reveal the chaos and violence of their respective lives.

All want, and even demand from God, help in their searches for contentment, and the play ends on Christmas Day with the approaching birth and an assumption of sainthood on the part of the homosexual who is overwhelmed with his apparent wisdom.

Try these:
▷Simon Gray's *Otherwise Engaged* and ▷Beckett's *Endgame* for attempts to black out humanity; ▷Harvey Fierstein and ▷Larry Kramer for AIDS plays.

KOPIT, Arthur   [1937–]
American dramatist

Plays include:
The Questioning of Nick (1957), *On the Runway of Life, You Never Know What's Coming Off Next* (1958), *Across the River and Into the Jungle* (1958), *Sing To Me Through Open Windows* (1959), *Aubade* (1959), *Oh Dad Poor Dad Mama's Hung You In the Closet And I'm Feelin' So Sad* (1960), *Asylum, or What the Gentlemen Are Up To, Not To Mention the Ladies* (1963), *The Conquest of Everest* (1964), *The Hero* (1964), *The Day the Whores Came Out To Play Tennis* (1965), *Indians* (1968), *Wings* (1978), *Nine* (book of the musical; 1980), *End of the World (with Symposium to Follow)* (1984); *Road to Nirvana* (formerly Bone-the-Fish) (1991)

Born in New York the son of a jeweller, Arthur Kopit has been writing some of the most intriguing American drama for more than three decades, in a career that stretches from Ionesco-like comic absurdism (the celebrated *Oh Dad Poor Dad*, written while Kopit was still a Harvard undergraduate) to the Swiftian sting of *Road to Nirvana* (a scathing indictment of Hollywood first produced at Kentucky's Actors' Theatre of Louisville under the title *Bone-the-Fish* – a deliberate send-up of ▷Mamet's *Speed-the-Plow*). In between are some lengthily titled black comedies and two acclaimed dramas diametrically opposed in style and scope: *Indians*, which had its world premiere at the ▷RSC, a Pirandellian piece about cultural imperialism, with Buffalo Bill Cody as an early white liberal confronted by the ghosts of Indians who resented being put on display at his Wild West show; and *Wings* (a radio drama later staged at the Yale Repertory Theater), an intimate, impressionistic play about an aviatrix who suffers a stroke. Kopit's recent work includes the books of two musicals (the Tony award-winning *Nine*, inspired by Federico Fellini's *8½*, and *Phantom of the Opera*; both with music composed by Maury Yeston) and *End of the World*, another Pirandellian experiment, this time on the subject of nuclear destruction.

Oh Dad Poor Dad Mama's Hung You In the Closet and I'm Feelin' So Sad

The man-eating and violent matriarch Madame Rosepettle arrives in Cuba on holiday with a silver piranha and two belligerent flowers, as well as her stammering 26 year-old son, in this crazed and noisy comedy, a deliberate pastiche of ▷Ionesco and ▷Tennessee Williams that made Kopit's international name. The son begins to discover women, but his efforts at seduction are continually thwarted – ▷Joe Orton-style – by the tumbling corpse of his embalmed father. In between, his mother is pinioning him under blankets in order to keep him under control, and the domestic comedy spirals into a kind of chaotic disorder that suggests ▷Kaufman and Hart on speed.

Try these:
▷Pirandello, ▷Tom Stoppard for theatrical self-consciousness; ▷Jack Gelber and ▷Murray Schisgal for similar 1960s iconoclasm, America-style; ▷Bernard Pomerance for analogously liberal looks at American history; ▷Brian Clark's *The Petition*, ▷Lanford Wilson's *Angels Fall*, ▷Nick Darke's *The Body* ▷Sarah Daniels' *The Devil's Gateway*, ▷David Edgar's *Maydays* for other contemporary plays about the Bomb along the lines of *End of the World*; ▷Jean-Claude van Itallie's *The Traveller* and Susan Kantowitz's *Night Sky* for another recent play about a stroke victim (namely Joseph Chaikin); ▷De Filippo's *Ducking Out* for a play on a similar theme; ▷Mamet's *Speed-the-Plow* and ▷Rabe's *Hurlyburly* for other vituperative Hollywood satires.

KOPS, Bernard   [1926–]
British poet, novelist and dramatist

Plays include:
The Hamlet of Stepney Green (1957), *The Dream of Peter Mann* (1960), *Enter Solly Gold* (1962), *Ezra* (1981), *Simon at Midnight* (1985)

First produced at about the same time as ▷Arnold Wesker, and from the same East End Jewish background (the privations and vigour of which are both reflected in his work), Kops declared in 1962 that he and his contemporaries ▷John Arden, Alun Owen, ▷Robert Bolt, ▷Willis Hall and ▷Wesker would ensure that theatre would never again be a 'precious inner-sanctum for the precious few'. He believed then that by tackling issues of immediate social concern they could change the way the world works. However, his issues are the rather broad ones of the poor quality of working-class life, the futility of riches and the need for love and joy rather than hard political polemic. In *The Hamlet of Stepney Green* his Hamlet seeks revenge, but not against an actual murderer, and he ends the play optimistically, the ghost satisfied by the reconciled characters' promise to always carry a little revolution in their hearts. All his work is not so optimistic, though the con-man 'rabbi' in *Enter Solly Gold*, posing as the long awaited Messiah, brings a sense of real values and a new joy to the materialistic family he cons. The title character of *The Dream of Peter Mann*, like his namesake ▷Ibsen's Gynt, sets out on a quest for riches, while in the dream which forms the second part of the play he finds himself in a world preparing for nuclear war, waking when the bomb explodes, and ending reconciled to home. Kops' plays are always lively, though sometimes dramatically overstated and given to over-sentimentality.

Try these:
▷Arnold Wesker and ▷Harold Pinter write from the same background; ▷Tom Stoppard's *Rosencrantz and Guildenstern are Dead* and ▷Lee Blessing's *Fortinbras* for one of many dramatic responses to Shakespeare's plays; ▷De Filippo, ▷David Storey, ▷Alan Ayckbourn, ▷David Lan's *Flight* and ▷Neil Simon's *Brighton Beach Memoirs* for plays of family drama; ▷Ronald Harwood's *Another Time* for a South African version; Jean-Claude Grumberg and Joshua Sobol for more

Edward Seamon, Barry Sherman, Lynn Cohen in Circle Repertory Company's production of *Love Diatribe* by Harry Kondoleon, 1990

specifically Jewish-oriented theatre; see also ▷Yiddish and Jewish-American theatre.

KORDER, Howard   [1958–]
American dramatist

Plays include:
Life on Earth (1985), *Episode 26* (1985), *Fun* (1987), *Nobody* (1987), *Boy's Life* (1988), *Lip Service* (1986; television play, 1989), *Search and Destroy* (1990)

Since 1985 Korder has been closely associated with the Manhattan Punch Line and its twice annual 'One-Act Comedy Festival' where several of his one-act plays – *Life on Earth*, *Middle Kingdom*, *Lip Service* and *Night Manuevers* – have been presented. His sketches and plays have been produced mainly in New York. Korder has received an award from the Louisville Actors' Theatre One-Act Festival (1988) and an HBO Writer's Award at the summer Eugene O'Neill Festival (1989). He also acts occasionally in TV situation comedies. His latest play, *Love's Diatribe*, a comedy about two adult children who return home to live with their parents, opened in New York in December 1990. Frank Rich has written that Korder has a 'pungent voice'. Perhaps so; perhaps even modelled on ▷David Mamet, who might claim Korder as a protégé, but it is also a voice of youthful humour – good humour from a male point of view, and satiric humour throughout – as Korder perceptively toys with the real-life situations of the persistently young. On the other hand, *Search and Destroy* is a dark, comic fable about the moral bankruptcy of America as a businessman-cum-film producer deals drugs and commits murder in order to produce a film version of a questionable self-help book. It is scheduled to appear on Broadway in 1992.

Boy's Life
In a chain of related blackout sketches Korder follows his three young protagonists through their continuing search for easy women. Belligerently heterosexual, the three freely admit their cynical approach to their adventures. Insensitive, rude, thoroughly manipulative in their associations with women, the 'boys' candidly confess their pessimistic views of mankind while trying to find something admirable in their boyish fun. Perhaps in contrast to the potentially offensive atmosphere for the more staid members of an audience, Korder creates a lightness and a sense of self-amusement in which the women characters insist on presenting their views, and the evening's entertainment slides unevenly away from moral judgements toward a position of boyish misanthropy which reveals both charm and a cutting edge.

Try these:
▷Wedekind's *Spring Awakening*; ▷Sharman Macdonald; ▷Mary O'Malley's *Once a Catholic*; ▷Mamet's *Sexual Perversity in Chicago* for immature males on the prowl; ▷Neil Simon's *Brighton Beach Memoirs* for other versions of adolescence.

KRAMER, Larry   [1936–]
American author and dramatist

Plays include:
Sissies' Scrapbook (1972), *The Normal Heart* (1985), *Just Say No: A Play About a Farce* (1989), *Reports from the Holocaust: The Making of an AIDS Activist* (1989)

A graduate of Yale, Larry Kramer began his career in London in the 1960s working as a story editor for Columbia Pictures. As a playwright, he is best known for *The Normal Heart*, a semi-autobiographical drama which made such an impact that its author merits an entry for sociological and historical reasons as much as anything else. Set in Manhattan over a three-year period from 1981 to 1984, the play is a howl of rage from a writer incensed at his city's sluggish response to the alarms of AIDS. A founding member of Gay Men's Health Crisis, Kramer casts as his on-stage alter ego one Ned Weeks, a consciousness-raising writer who refuses to rest until such disparate institutions as *The New York Times*, the Mayor's office, and the national government have given the fatal disease the attention it deserves. Wildly polemical and issue-obsessed – Kramer claims he was emboldened to write the play after seeing ▷David Hare's *A Map of the World* at the ▷Royal National Theatre – the play is basically a harangue written at white heat, and it ends with a deathbed scene that recapitulates dozens of 1930s movies, this time from a gay vantage-point. Other playwrights on both sides of the Atlantic – William M. Hoffman (*As Is*), ▷Harvey Fierstein (*Safe Sex*), ▷Harry Kondoleon's *Zero Positive*, Andy Kirby (*Compromised Immunity*) – have addressed the ill-

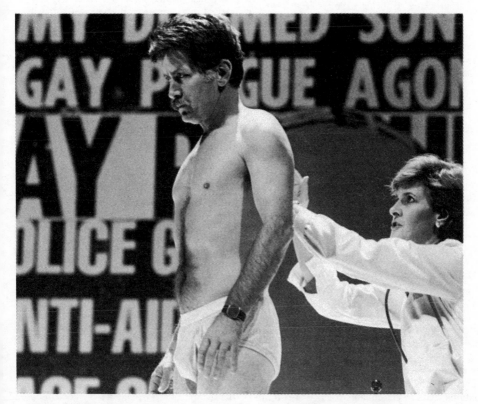

Martin Sheen and Frances Tomelty in Larry Kramer's *The Normal Heart*, Royal Court, 1986, which subsequently transferred to the West End

ness on-stage, but Kramer's play, if not the best, is certainly the most well-travelled. Productions have been seen in eighteen countries, including in Britain at the Royal Court and then at the Albery, and Barbra Streisand plans to produce and direct a film version, possibly starring her *Nuts* colleague, Richard Dreyfuss.

Try these:
▷Ibsen's *An Enemy of the People* as a play of ideas centred on illness; ▷Clifford Odets for social arousal; also ▷Sherman's *Passing By*, for a pre-AIDS treatment of illness; Gay Sweatshop for other gay plays dealing with social issues; ▷Noël Greig and ▷Tony Kushner for further AIDs-related plays.

KROETZ, Franz Xaver   [1946–]
German dramatist

Plays include:
Wild Game Crossing (1969), *Homeworker* (1971), *Staller Farm* (GB) *Farmyard* (US) 1972, *Ghost Train* (1972), *Request Concert* (1972), *Upper Austria* (1972), *Maria Magdalena* (1973, from Hebbel), *Wider Prospects* (1974), *The Nest* (1975), *Agnes Bernauer* (1976, from Hebbel), *Through the Leaves* (1978), *Mensch Meier* (1979), *Neither Fish Nor Fowl* (1981), *Fear and Hope in the German Federal Republic* (1984), *Dying Farmer* (1985), *Help Wanted* (1986)

Franz Xaver Kroetz is a German dramatist rooted in the 'Volksstück' (Folk Play) tradition. His subject matter is the contemporary industrial lower class, who he sees as caged animals reacting with long-repressed violence. Owing much to the influence of Oden von Horváth, whose *Tales of the Vienna Woods* (1930) and *Kasimir and Karoline* (1931) depicted the terror that lay beneath the surface of the proletariat's life, Kroetz stresses the terrible living conditions, moral repression, and linguistic deprivation of the lower classes. His naturalistic attention to detail and precise use of Bavarian dialect call to mind Gerhart Hauptmann; his characters grope for words to describe their dispair and outrage. Their inability to fully articulate their frustrations leads to passionate violence also reminiscent of ▷George Büchner's *Woyzeck*. Kroetz uses dialect to fully express the limi-

tations thrust on the lower classes: 'Dialect is connected with work, with nature and landscape, with money even. Dialect is man's dirty underpants. The figures in my early parts have been dispossessed of their language, of their ability to articulate.' Naturalistic detail is also seen in the often-shocking action: *Homework* portrays an unsuccessful abortion and the murder of a deformed child; *Staller Farm/Farmyard* vivifies the seduction of a mentally-defective girl and masturbation on a toilet. By the mid-1980s, Kroetz had lost his belief in the theatre's potential to correct society's wrongs, and his subsequent plays are lower-keyed and their political themes clearer.

Several of his plays have been successfully mounted in Britain and the United States: *The Nest*, at the Orange Tree in 1981 and at the Bush in 1985, shows in short simple scenes the clichéed conversation and domestic detail of the lives of a lorry-driver and his wife, including a long silent sequence in which he dumps barrels of industrial waste in a bathing pool; theatricality takes over when the baby is burned by the waste; and he is thus driven to join the union. *Through the Leaves*, at New York's Public Theatre in 1984 and at London's Bush in 1985, almost eschews plot in showing the relationship between a lonely middleaged pair, a female offal-seller and a construction worker, finally destroyed by the conditioned inadequacies of their language and sexual assumptions. *Staller Farm/Farmyard*, at London's Bush in 1984, Manchester Library Theatre in 1986 and 1987, and New York's Theatre Workshop in 1986, presents us with a young girl, Beppi, doubly hindered by both her class's lack of linguistic skills and her own mental retardation, which lead her to seduction, pregnancy, and further isolation. Its successor, *Ghost Train*, seen in the Bush in 1976 and at the Manchester Library Theatre in 1987, shows the naive country girl Beppi taking her baby to the city and encountering the violence and repression of the urban lower classes.

Despite Kroetz's prolific output of over forty plays in the past twenty years, less than ten have been translated and performed on English-speaking stages. He has recently written a new play about a family's failure in coping with AIDS, but he has lost his belief in the theatre's power to alter society, noting that 'the theatre doesn't make a very good fist; it's essentially a peaceable force, it's honeycomb, papier-mâché in the face of a society which is riddled with horrific violence.' In early 1991, he published four volumes of journalism, essays, and poetry.

Try these:
Gerhart Hauptmann's naturalistic dramas *Before Sunrise* (*Vor Sonnenaufgang*, 1889) and *The Weavers* (*Die Weber*, 1992) written in precise Silesian dialect juxtaposed with High German; Friedrich Hebbel's *Maria Magdalena* (1844), *Agnes Bernauer* (1852); ▷Edward Bond's *Saved* influenced many German dramatists of the 1970s with its violence and inarticulacy in speaking out against oppression. Kroetz's thematic contemporaries ▷Peter Handke, Rainer Werner Fassbinder, and ▷Heiner Müller.

KUREISHI, Hanif   [1954–]
British dramatist and screenwriter

Plays include:
Soaking the Heat (1976), *The King and Me* (1979), *The Mother Country* (1980), *Tomorrow-Today!* (1980), *Outskirts* (1981), *Borderline* (1981), *Cinders* (adaptation, from Christina Paul's translation, of a play by Janusz Glowacki; 1981), *Artists and Admirers* (with David Leveaux, from ▷Ostrovsky; 1982), *Birds of Passage* (1983)

Kureishi is probably best known now for his scripts to Stephen Frears' two films *My Beautiful Laundrette* and *Sammy and Rosie Get Laid*. But both his theatre and film work share the same preoccupation with the difficulties of making and establishing meaningful personal contacts in the face of major cultural obstacles, particularly those deriving from prejudice. Kureishi evokes brilliantly the wastelands of the inner cities and the casualties of endemic poverty of vision and racism, both white and non-white. *The King and Me* is a study of a young couple on a housing estate who are at once sustained and trapped by adherence to the Elvis Presley cult, but who eventually make a new start; *Cinders*, incidentally, shares the same concern with the role of media mythologies in shaping people's lives and responses. In *Tomorrow-Today!* urban blight is given added poignancy and urgency by the young characters' inability to believe in the future because of the nuclear threat. In *Outskirts* scenes from the past and present of two South London white men who once

joined in a violent racial attack are intercut in a landscape of despair from which one has escaped to become a liberal teacher while the other has become involved with a fascist organisation. *Borderline*, which caused some controversy in the Asian community because white actors doubled both white and Asian parts in the ▷Joint Stock production, is a fine evocation of the strains of living on the borderlines of different cultures and different conventions which shows a complex picture of class, racial and gender expectations across Asian and white communities. *Birds of Passage*, a Sydenham *Cherry Orchard*, shows the erosion of old loyalties to neighbourhood, class and family in the face of socio-economic changes made concrete in the shape of the Pakistani former lodger who buys the house he lodged in. In the past few years, disillusioned by the theatre, Kureishi has stopped writing stage plays, confining himself to film scripts and his first, highly successful novel *The Buddha of Suburbia*.

Try these:
▷Karim Alrawi's *A Colder Climate* charts racism in the East End; ▷Harwant Bains is a new British Asian writer; ▷Farrukh Dhondy's *Vigilantes* explores cultural clashes in the British Bangladeshi community; ▷Mustapha Matura's *Playboy of the West Indies* and *Trinidad Sisters* are reworkings of classics to West Indian settings; ▷Peter Flannery's *Savage Amusement*, ▷Trevor Griffiths' *Oi for England* and ▷Nigel Williams' *Class Enemy* tackle themes of urban deprivation as do Mick Mahoney, ▷Gregory Motton, ▷Jim Cartwright and certain plays of ▷Tony Marchant and ▷Barrie Keeffe; ▷Alan Bleasdale's *Are You Lonesome Tonight?*, a musical portrait of the 'King'.

KUSHNER, Tony   [1956–]
American dramatist

Plays include:
A Bright Room Called Day (1986), *L'Illusion* (adapted from Pierre Corneille; 1988), *Angels in America* (1989), *Millennium Approaches* (1991)

Tong Kushner's plays have been performed mainly outside New York, sometimes only in workshop productions. In New York he has been associated with the New York Theater Workshop, New Directors Project, as associate artistic director in 1987 for Lynn Siefert's *Coyote Ugly*. He also served as Director of Literary Services for the Theatre Communications Group, the national organisation for professional not-for-profit theatres. In that capacity he wrote a very brief essay, 'A Simple Working Guide for Playwrights', designed to help playwrights submit their plays to theatres (published in *The Dramatist's Sourcebook*, 1989). *L'Illusion*, his free adaptation of Corneille's *L'Illusion Comique* was presented by the Hartford Stage Company (and was subsequently bought by Columbia Pictures). Although Kushner wrote in prose and omitted many scenes as well as some characters, he was very successful in capturing both the soul of Corneille's wit and merriment as well as the imagination of his audience. Now Kushner's plays are being performed Off-Broadway. At the Public Theater Joseph Papp produced *A Bright Room Called Day*: 'Germany in the '30s, America into the '90s. The only people sleeping soundly are the guys who are giving the rest of us bad dreams.' *Millennium Approaches*, commissioned by the Eureka Theater in San Francisco, was staged there in May 1991. The first half of this play, which Kushner has been writing for years, entitled *Angels in America*, has been given a workshop production at the Mark Taper in Los Angeles. The entire piece, *Millennium Approaches*, deals with the position of gay men in America and has a performance time of about 6½ hours.

Try these:
Ranjit Bolt for a successful British adaptation of *L'Illusion Comique*; ▷Martin Sherman's *Bent*, Gay Sweatshop's *As Time Goes By* for parallels to *A Bright Room Called Day*; see also ▷Gay Theatre.

KYD, Thomas   [1558–94]
English Renaissance dramatist

Plays include:
The Spanish Tragedy (c 1589)

Kyd's *The Spanish Tragedy* is, for all practical purposes, the play that started the vogue for revenge tragedy in the Elizabethan theatre but unlike many trendsetters it still bears comparison with its successors. The details of Kyd's life and career are somewhat obscure: London born, he may well have followed his father's profession of scrivener and he was working in the theatre by 1585. The main biographical information we have about him comes from 1593 when he was arrested and charged with blasphemy. After ▷Marlowe's suspicious death Kyd claimed that the 'blasphemous' material found in his home had belonged to Marlowe since they had shared a room at one point. Whatever the truth of the matter, Kyd's death just over a year after he was released may well have been related to his sufferings in prison. Kyd is thought to have been the author of an earlier version of *Hamlet* as well as other works, most of which have not survived. All the ingredients of the later revenge plays are to be found in *The Spanish Tragedy*, some derived from ▷Seneca, some indebted to the Elizabethan picture of ▷Machiavelli: the search for justice thwarted by corruption, ingenious murders, the masque that converts pretend deaths into real ones, the ghost, the play within the play, madness, the dumb show, and the Machiavellian villain. But there is more to it than sensationalism: the theme of revenge serves as a way of dramatising and heightening everyday conflict, thus opening up revenge tragedy as a medium for presenting major issues in a dramatically effective way.

Try these:
Most Renaissance tragic dramatists used revenge plots and malcontent figures – ▷Shakespeare's *Hamlet* is the most famous example of both, and there are notable examples in ▷Tourneur, ▷Webster and ▷Middleton; Bernard Kops' *The Hamlet of Stepney Green* for a contemporary, Jewish variation.

1

LABICHE, Eugène [1815–88]
French dramatist

Plays include:
Un Chapeau de Paille d'Italie (*An Italian Straw Hat*; 1851), *Le Voyage de M Perrichon* (*M Perrichon Takes a Trip*; 1860), *La Poudre aux Yeux* (*Dust in Your Eyes*; 1861), *Célimare le Bien-Aimé* (*Beloved Célimare*; 1863), *La Cagnotte* (*The Piggy-Bank*; 1864)

The most successful writer of French farce, and certainly the most prolific, Labiche published fifty-seven plays, but had a hand in perhaps a hundred more. Given this vast output, it is not surprising that he is distinguished less for originality than for the professionalism with which he reworks all the oldest and most reliable jokes. His satire of the bourgeois is often sharp but his plays are more genial and less manic than ▷Feydeau's. He had a sunny temperament, helped no doubt by the success that brought him the money for a chateau in Sologne and eventually a seat in the French Academy. Many of the plays would bear revival. *An Italian Straw Hat* has an unequalled chase theme, as a hapless bridegroom, followed by his entire wedding party, rushes around Paris in search of a replica straw hat for one that has been eaten by his horse in circumstances of maximum embarrassment to the owner. This play is usually reliable, and René Clair's 1927 film version still has great charm; but the 1986 Ray Cooney production fell flat on its face, as did one by Orson Welles in 1936, retitled *Horse Eats Hat*.

Try these:
▷Feydeau for nineteenth-century French farce; ▷Pinero, ▷Ben Travers; ▷Joe Orton and ▷Alan Ayckbourn for English variations; ▷Michael Frayn's *Noises Off* for the best theatrical exposure of the mechanisms of farce; ▷Neil Simon.

LAN, David [1952–]
South African-born dramatist

Plays include:
Painting a Wall (1974), *Bird Child* (1974), *Paradise* (1975), *Homage to Bean Soup* (1975), *Winter Dancers* (1977), *Red Earth* (1978), *Sergeant Ola and his Followers* (1979), *Flight* (1986), *A Mouthful of Birds* (with Caryl Churchill; 1986), *Desire* (1990)

Born in Cape Town, where he was a teenage magician and puppeteer, Lan went to Britain in 1972 to study social anthropology and lived in Zimbabwe from 1980 to 1982. Considerations of racism and anthropology are central to his plays which concern themselves with the search for both political and personal freedoms. *Paradise*, set during the Peninsular War, lacks the basis of personal experience or research which gives substance to his other work, whether the Canadian Indian culture of *The Winter Dancers*, the cargo cult of *Sergeant Ola and his Followers* or the African background of his other plays. *A Mouthful of Birds*, developed with ▷Caryl Churchill for ▷Joint Stock from the cast's improvisations, is a collage of variations growing from the Dionysus story. Exploring sexism, racism and other forms of exploitation through ritual, dance, and strong visual theatre rather than any verbal dialectic, it is a totally different experience to its predecessor *Flight*. *Flight* is a Jewish family chronicle demonstrating the compromising effects of political, personal and religious standards and of refusing to do so and of refusal to recognise one's tacit acceptance of such compromise. A long and demanding play which would benefit from cuts, it nevertheless totally held the attention in the 1986 ▷RSC Other Place production.

Try these:
South African born playwrights John Robin Baitz ▷Athol Fugard, ▷Ronald Harwood; ▷Deborah Levy, and ▷Nicholas Wright;

▷Stephen Poliakoff's *Breaking the Silence* for another family chronicle of Jewish origins; and ▷Joshua Sobol, whose *Ghetto* Lan translated.

LAPINE, James Elliot   [1949–]
American dramatist

Plays include:
Photograph (1977), *Table Settings* (1979), *Twelve Dreams* (1981), *Sunday in the Park With George* (1984), *Into the Woods* (1986), *Falsettoland* (1990)

Lapine was a photographer and graphic designer before he became interested in the theatre. His work has won him an Obie, a New York Drama Critics' Circle Award and a Pulitzer Prize. From his earliest work Lapine has shown great skill in combing wit and good sense to produce effective stage entertainment. His humour can be zany or absurdist, but it is overlaid with a kind of wisdom that appeals even if it is ordinary. Lapine's interest in psychology is apparent in *Twelve Dreams*, an exploration of the theories of Freud and Jung as revealed in the dreams of a twelve-year-old girl. His serious approach to life which surfaces throughout is well illustrated in his retelling of some of Grimm's fairy tales in *Into the Woods* where he wants his audience to avoid repeating the mistakes of history. The basis of his dramaturgy, the sketch, is also evident in his most successful work with ▷Stephen Sondheim, *Sunday in the Park With George*, which Lapine also directed, a second facet of his theatrical career which demands attention.

Sunday in the Park With George
Lapine wrote the book of this appealing musical and directed its Broadway premiere; Sondheim composed the music and the lyrics. Lapine also devised the concept: the conflict between an artist who devoutly follows his principles and his critics who fail to appreciate his creativity. Act One shows the 19th-century French painter Georges Seurat thinking about and creating his best known *pointilliste* work *A Sunday Afternoon on the Island of La Grand Jatte*. Act Two, set in 1980, dramatises the creative struggle of a fictional American descendant of Seurat. Seurat ignores his pregnant mistress, Dot, who marries another painter and goes to America. Later, Seurat's great-grandson, who practises his art with a laser beam and photo projections, is mesmer-ised by his great-grandmother's diary, and returns to the island to meet the original Dot. A number of critics thought that Sondheim and Lapine trivialised their subject matter; others found their vision of love and art in a high-tech world sufficient and lauded it as an ambitious innovative in American musical theatre.

Try these:
▷David Pownall's *An Audience Called Edouard* for a Manet – based parallel with *Sunday in the Park*; ▷Nicholas Wright's *Mrs Klein* for psychiatrists; Timberlake Wertenbaker's *Three Birds Alighting in a Field* for a new art-based play (about today's record prices).

LARSON, Larry   [1948–]
American dramatist and actor

Plays include:
Far From the Peaceful Shores (1987), *Christmas at the Palace* (1987), *Tent Meeting* (with ▷Rebecca Wackler and ▷Levi Lee; 1983), *The Blood Orgy Series* (*Mirandolina Unchained*, *The Grubb Chronicles* and *Tales of Rat Alley*; with Levi Lee; 1983–7), *Some Things You need to Know Before the World Ends: A Final Evening With the Illuminati* (with Levi Lee; 1986)

After joining Rebecca Wackler and Levi Lee in the Southern Theatre Conspiracy, Larry Larson gained a reputation along with his fellow playwrights and actors. Although the three act and work independently, they have a small but devoted following in Atlanta where their most successful work has been collaborative. Satire, fast-paced humour, and a mocking of thoughtlessly accepted conventions mark Larson's plays which have mainly been produced in Atlanta theatres. As an actor, Larson has performed more than fifty roles in such theatres as the Academy Theatre, the Southern Theatre Conspiracy, the Atlanta New Play Project and the Alliance Theatre Company. He has also toured as an actor with the Academy Theatre Southern Arts Federation and written as well as acted for television.

Some Things You Need to Know Before the World Ends: A Final Evening With the Illuminati

This play has been described as a two man (Lee and Larson) knockabout, blackout comedy about sermons and sacrilege. It is clearly a spin-off from *Tent Meeting*. Lee dresses in long johns to recreate the blasphemous minister while Larson acts as his faithful hunchback and second banana. Indeed, the show is partially spontaneous, in the style of Penn and Teller, as Larson and Lee encourage audience participation. In Louisville at the Humana Festival, they played upon the basketball-mania that controls much of the population there by declaring that 'Life is a basketball game', and replacing the cross above the pulpit with a hoop. In essence, the pair of actors ridicule every creed – political, economic, religious – that perverse minds can manipulate and sheep-like man can follow with stubborn and thoughtless persistence.

Try these:
▷Levi Lee and ▷Rebecca Wackler; ▷Ken Campbell and ▷Snoo Wilson for anarchic humour.

LAVERY, Bryony   [1947–]
British dramatist

Plays include:
I Was Too Young at the Time to Understand Why My Mother was Crying (1976), *Sharing* (1976), *Grandmother's Footsteps* (1976), *The Catering Service* (1977), *Helen and her Friends* (1978), *Bag* (1979), *The Wild Bunch* (1979), *Gentlemen Prefer Blondes* (from the Anita Loos novel; 1979), *Family Album* (1980), *Missing* (1981), *Zulu* (1981), *The Black Hole of Calcutta* (1982), *Götterdämmerung* (1982), *For Maggie, Betty and Ida* (1982), *Hot Time* (1984), *Calamity* (1984), *Origin of the Species* (1984), *Witchcraze* (1985), *The Mummy* (1987), *The Headless Body* (1987), *Her Aching Heart* (1990), *Kitchen Matters* (1990)

Author of over 30 plays, Lavery has been prodigious in her output: satire, sketches, plays for children, cabaret, television and radio. At one end, she is scriptwriter for the highly original National Theatre of Brent (anarchic interpreters of grand myths and legends, usually played by two or at most three performers); at the other, frequent provider of, in *The Guardian*'s words, 'wistful satire, ingenious fantasy'. She also wrote the words for the wonderfully off-beam Wandsworth Warmers (to be a Warmer, you had to live in Wandsworth, have little sleeps in the afternoon and tie bits of wool round your wrist to keep your arms warm). But behind the satire Lavery has also sought to question and challenge a whole range of assumptions. An open lesbian feminist writer, 'I am passionately dedicated to the rediscovery of women's strength through positive theatrical presentation,' her problem has been to find the right balance between content and style, a difficulty perhaps exacerbated by the collaborative process of many of the fringe companies she has worked with – Women's Theatre Group, Monstrous Regiment, Gay Sweatshop, Theatre Centre, Clean Break – which can leave a writer with a lot of demands to fulfill. *Calamity* (a spoof on the Wild West), *Witchcraze* (about connections between witches in the 17th century and Greenham women), *Mummy* (about death, mothers and daughters) and *Origin of the Species* (Darwinism revisited), were all criticised for being 'ill-organised' – a flaw not detected in the earlier plays, *Helen and Her Friends*, *Bag*, *Family Album* and *Catering Service* (an allegory on paramilitarism). (These were produced by *Les Oeufs Malades*, the company Lavery set up with friends, Gerard Bell and Jessica Higgs.) However, she seems to have hit the button with her two latest productions – *Her Aching Heart*, a shameless pastiche of romantic fiction given a lesbian twist, carried off with brilliant ease; and *Kitchen Matters* for Gay Sweatshop. Loosely based on ▷Euripides' *The Bacchae*, it is typical Lavery, witty and wacky, ransacking a number of theatrical conventions with glee but with a serious intent – to attack homophobia and, in passing, to warn against allowing theatre to wither on the vine from lack of funds. In short, a play of good heart and great warmth.

Try these:
▷Maureen Duffy's *Rites* is also based on *The Bacchae*, ▷Sarah Daniels' *Byrth Rite* for witches, and *The Devil's Gateway* for Greenham scenes; ▷David Edgar's *May Days* takes us to Greenham too; for a lesbian version of the Wild West, ▷Tasha Fairbanks; ▷Cabaret in Britain, ▷Women in Theatre.

LEBOW, Barbara   [1936–]
American dramatist

Plays include:
I Can'd Help It (1965), *Little Joe Monaghan* (1981), *A Shayna Maidel* (1984), *The Adventures of Homer McGundy* (1985), *Cyparis* (1987), *The Keepers* (1988), *Trains* (1991)

Barbara Lebow is best known for her play, *A Shayna Maidel*, yiddish for 'A Pretty Girl', which played off-Broadway in 1987 to sold-out houses for over a year. It continues to be performed in regional theatres throughout the United States, where it first started. This haunting play about the reunion between a concentration-camp survivor and her sister who came to America before World War II won accolades from critics and audience alike. The play explores the guilt of those who were spared the horror of the Holocaust. Lebow examines the pesonal emotional context rather than the historical or political issues surrounding the Holocaust. The play includes dream sequences and memory scenes, although the action takes place in the present.

Lebow wants to reflect the way the mind works in all its complexity. She often uses 'memory scenes', subjective retellings of the past, as opposed to flashbacks, which she sees as objective narration. Similarly, her fantasy scenes project what her characters wish to happen. Her play *The Keepers* uses these devices to reveal the blend of present and fantasy in the mind of the mother, Olivia. Lebow is playwright-in-residence at Atlanta's Academy Theatre where she directs, teaches playwriting and is director of human service programmes. She has also written and directed several plays with homeless people, addicts, prisoners and the elderly.

Try these:
▷David Hare's *Plenty* for flashback scenes and the effect of war on the psyche; ▷David Rabe, who deals with the aftermath of another war, Vietnam; ▷Arthur Miller's *Death of a Salesman* and ▷Peter Shaffer's *Equus* for similar uses of flashback technique. ▷Martin Sherman's *Bent*, Jean Claude Grumberg and ▷Peter Flannery for drama of the Holocaust; Age Exchange is a British company working for and with the elderly; Clean Break with former prisoners; Los Angeles Poverty Department work with the homeless.

LEE, Leslie   [1937–]
American dramatist

Plays include:
Elegy to a Down Queen (1970), *First Breeze of Summer* (1975), *Colored People's Time* (1982), *Hannah Davis* (1987), *The Rabbit Foot* (1988), *Golden Boy* (musical; 1989), *Ground People* (1990), *Black Eagles* (1991)

Lee grew up in a small town in eastern Pennsylvania. His plays depict black American middle-class life and family values. In *First Breeze of Summer*, his best-known work, Lee contrasts the confused and restless younger generation with the stability of the older generation. In Lee's plays, the family matriarchs and patriarchs recount their personal experiences which serve as the backdrop to the family's present-day predicament. In *Hannah Davis*, Lee explores the lives of a highly successful suburban black Philadelphia family. The founding patriarch recalls his affair with the play's title character, the town trollop, much to the amazement of his children, and opera singer, a TV celebrity and a mayor. *The Rabbit Foot* tells two stories about impoverished blacks in rural Mississippi just after World War I. The stories reflect conflicting drives – an urge to head north for better opportunities against a reluctance to leave cherished people, places and customs. In *Colored People's Time* Lee deals with the emergence of black pride during the Harlem Renaissance. In the musical *Golden Boy* (a black version of ▷Clifford Odets's 1930s' drama), Lee chronicles the life of a Harlem boxer Joe Wellington. *Black Eagles* explores the racism confronted by the USA's first squadron of black fighter pilots in WWII.

The First Breeze of Summer
A lyrical reflection on three generations of a black family from the period following the Civil War to the civil rights movement. Set against the background of impatient quarrels of the younger members of the family, a lovable but indomitable grandmother recalls some of the sacrifices and heartaches she had to endure in her struggle to bring the family to its current middle-class status. Following a highly successful run at the Negro Ensemble Company, the play was moved to Broadway's largest houses, a theatrical environment ill-suited to this intimate drama.

Try these:
▷Eugene O'Neill's *Long Day's Journey Into Night*, ▷J.B. Priestley's *Time and the Conways*; ▷Maugham's *For Services Rendered* for contrasting family sagas; Lorraine Hansberry, James Baldwin for earlier black family sagas; August Wilson for later ones; Zora Neale Hurston and Langston Hughes for writers who were part of the Harlem Renaissance.

LEE, Levi   [1940–]
American dramatist

Plays include:
Tent Meeting (with ▷Rebecca Wackler and ▷Larry Larson; 1983), *The Blood Orgy Series* (*Mirandolina Unchained*, *The Grubb Chronicles*, and *Tales of Rat Alley*; (with Larry Larson; 1983–7), *Nicholas de Beaubien's The Hunchback of Notre Dame* (with Rebecca Wackler; 1984), *Some Things You Need to Know Before the World Ends: A Final Evening with the Illuminati* (with Larry Larson; 1986)

With Rebecca Wackler, Lee co-founded the Southern Theatre Conspiracy in 1979. A few years later Lee, Wackler and Larry Larson launched their humorously blasphemous *Tent Meeting*, a comedy about a deformed infant names Jesus O. Tarbox. Taking aim at religious fundamentalism in the South, Lee and his associates shattered conventions with their boisterous irreverence in *Tent Meeting* just as they had satirised some of the most sacred shibboleths of Southern life and culture in previous works produced in Atlanta theatres. As playwright and actor, Lee is a master of comic control. Reviewers invariably comment on the hilarious tone of the entire production. As the Reverend Ed Tarbox, Levi Lee is a mean-spirited and supremely arrogant preacher who crushes his family as he tramps across the continent in a never-ending search for souls to save. Lee's superior expression of comic exaggeration and his acute sense of timing suggest the potential of this talented and witty actor–dramatist.

Tent Meeting
Admitedly designed to appeal to a special taste among audiences, *Tent Meeting* may actually be no more astonishing or entertaining than the currently reported hypocrisy of some Bible preachers. Most of the play takes place in a trailer on the road, as the preacher, having kidnapped his daughter's deformed baby from a scientific laboratory, decides that he is Jesus in disguise and heads for a tent meeting in Canada with his son, daughter and her baby. The journey is enlivened by divine intervention in the form of mysterious messages, while each of the three actors has at least one moment of comic histrionics – the son as a World War II veteran questioning the baby, the daughter singing 'Raped by God'. The tent meeting lasts only ten minutes, but each act manages an ingenious climax, the second somehow blending with exemplary comic effect the simultaneous baptism and the drowning of an eggplant.

Try these:
▷Dennis Potter's *Brimstone and Treacle*, ▷Lucy Gannon's *Keeping Tom Nice* for God and disability; ▷Beckett's *Waiting for Godot* for mysterious messages and divine non-intervention; ▷Brian Friel's *The Faith Healer*.

LEIGH, Mike   [1943–]
British dramatist, director

Plays include:
The Box Play (1966), *Bleak Moments* (1970), *Wholesome Glory* (1973), *The Jaws of Death* (1973), *Babies Grow Old* (1974), *The Silent Majority* (1974), *Abigail's Party* (1977), *Ecstasy* (1979), *Goose Pimples* (1981), *Smelling a Rat* (1988), *Greek Tragedy* (1989)

Salford born Leigh trained as an actor at the Royal Academy of Dramatic Art, moved to the Camberwell and Central Schools of Art and the London Film School, before becoming Associate Director of the Midlands Arts Centre, Birmingham. His first original play, *The Box Play* evolved from improvisation work in Birmingham.

Leigh has developed a form of theatre which can best be described as structured improvisation; as he has said: 'It's necessary that the improvisations serve a particular theme or idea. I discover the substance of the play during rehearsals . . .' Working closely with actors, his plays develop out of a long process of workshops and improvisation from which Leigh devises a final script. Actors work in great detail with their characterisation, often beginning by developing their character alone with Leigh, and then moving towards meeting other characters gradually over the rehearsal period. For example, Anthony Sher has described his experience of preparing for his role as an Arab in *Goose Pimples* by dressing the part, exploring the West End of London in character and taking great pride in being treated in character by a London taxi driver. The process has the effect of constructing a very intense and stylised form of naturalistic theatre, which can border on caricature. Nonetheless it often works very well for television, for which Leigh has devised over twenty plays. *Bleak Moments*, Leigh's tenth improvised play, which explores the relationship between two painfully lonely people, transferred beautifully into a feature film, which won prizes at the Chicago and Locarno Film Festivals. *High Hopes*, his 1988 feature film, and the recent stage play *Greek Tragedy* – about an Australian Greek community – demonstrate Leigh at his best: acute, bitter observation tempered by compassion, his latest film is *Life is Sweet*.

Abigail's Party

Abigail's Party is structured around a group of neighbours who meet for drinks while one couple's teenage daughter is holding a party. The play is set in the living room of the fearsome hostess, Beverley. Alison Steadman, Leigh's wife, won the *Plays and Players* and *Evening Standard* best actress awards for her performance. The play charts the tensions of the relationships as they move over the course of the evening to a final dramatic conclusion. The experience of the play is something like spending an evening among a group who become increasingly embarrassing and painful to watch. A wickedly sharp satire on lower-middle-class social pretensions, it can be overplayed to the point of parody.

Try these:
Mike Bradwell's early work with Hull Truck is similar in approach to Leigh's; ▷Alan Ayckbourn and ▷Joe Orton for fierce demolition of middle-class pretensions; ▷Edward Albee's *Who's Afraid of Virginia Woolf* for an American equivalent of fierce satire; ▷Neil Simon; ▷Keith Reddin, ▷de Filippo for domestic satires of a gentler nature; ▷Alan Bennett for another form of satire on a whole range of middle-class mores.

LEONARD, Hugh   [1926–   ]
Irish dramatist

Plays include:
The Big Birthday (1956), *A Leap in the Dark* (1957), *Madigan's Lock* (1958), *Walk On the Water* (1960), *The Poker Session* (1964), *The Family Way* (1964), *Mick and Mick* (1966), *The Au Pair Man* (1968), *The Patrick Pearse Motel* (1971), *Da* (1973), *Summer* (1974), *Irishmen* (1974), *Time Was* (1976), *A Life* (1978), *The Mask of Moriarty* (1986), *Pizzazz* (three short plays: *Pizzazz, A View From the Obelisk*, and *Roman Fever*; 1986)

Born John Keyes Byrne, Leonard is one of Ireland's most popular contemporary playwrights, and his success has led to the same sorts of misconceptions that plague ▷Alan Ayckbourn in England. Indeed, like Ayckbourn, Leonard frequently indicts the same moneyed bourgeois audience who flock to see his plays, and even his crowd-pleasers (such as *The Patrick Pearse Motel*, which uses the conventions of French farce to comment on the development of modern-day Ireland) have their moments of bile as well. The link between the present and the past, and between people and their country, are twin themes Leonard explores repeatedly. In *A Walk on the Water*, the exiled protagonist comes home to Ireland for his father's funeral, only to encounter his erstwhile companions, from an era which now seems lost both to them and to their city. *Mick and Mick* refracts the same sentiment through the eyes of an Irishwoman working in Britain who returns to Ireland and who sees with the clarity of an outsider. One of his recent works – a trilogy of short plays collectively called *Pizzazz* – delves even further into questions of rootedness: each is about 'travellers apart from their natural environment', says Leonard, 'trying to retain their memories of a lost time and place while also enjoying the special challenges of their new homes'. (Leonard extends his examination of this balancing act in his two memoirs, *Out After Dark* and *Home Before Night*.)

Leonard has also written fiction and many adaptations (his *Stephen D.*, taken from Joyce, remains a model of its kind) and pastiche (*The Mask of Moriarty*, about Sherlock Holmes's sidekick), but he's best known for *Da* and *A Life*, two plays opposed both in tone and subject matter – the first finds life in death, the other death in life.

Da

The middle-aged Charlie comes to terms with his dead foster-father, the 'da' of the title, in Leonard's quasi-autobiographical comedy/ drama, which was a Tony-winning Broadway smash, abetted by superb leading performances from Brian Murray and Bernard Hughes as Charlie and his crusty old 'da'. A gardener who has made a lifetime career out of exasperating his son, 'da' is a ghost who just won't lie down, and the play is a comic exorcism with darker shades, as well. The man who gave Charlie his first job, the civil servant Desmond Drumm, has the floor in *A Life*, in which he is diagnosed as having cancer.

Try these:
▷Brian Friel, ▷Thomas Kilroy and ▷Tom Murphy for Leonard's pre-eminent contemporaries, who examine the Irishman's relationship to his country; also newcomer Dermot Bolger; ▷Eugene O'Neill, ▷John Mortimer's *A Voyage Round My Father* and J.M. Barrie's *Mary Rose* for familial ghosts, both literal and figurative; ▷Lanford Wilson's *Lemon Sky* and ▷Tina Howe's *Painting Churches* for analogous contemporary American plays about adult children and their parents.

LEPAGE, Robert   [1958–   ]
Canadian dramatist, director and performer

Plays include:
In the Meantime (1982); *Circulations,* (1984); *Vinci,* 1986; *(The Dragon's Trilogy)* 1985–87; *Polygraph,* (1988–89); *Tectonic Plates,* (1989–92).

Robert Lepage, has established himself at the forefront of new theatre in Quebec. A multi-talented performer, Lepage was only 31 years old when he was appointed the director of French theatre at the National Arts Centre, Ottawa. From 1980 he worked with Théâtre Repère in Quebec city, all work in the Company being characterized by its work process, the Repère cycle known as RSVP, which means Resource: Search: Value (Evaluate): and Presentation. Lepage's work very much reflects this process. Lepage will often take, as his starting point, some pre-determined form. From these established parameters the work evolves through research and improvisation involving the entire company. His best known pieces are: *Polygraph*, a murder story in which all the characters are in different ways linked to a murder that took place six years earlier ('Polygraph' means different stories/writings and is also the technical name for the lie detector which the police use); *The Dragon's Trilogy,* a play about three different generations of Chinese immigrants and three different towns, Quebec City, Toronto and Vancouver where at different times in this century the Chinese community has flourished; and finally, *Tectonic Plates,* a highly romantic piece which took as its resource the geological movement of the earths crust, known as continental drift. Into this show are woven several layers, all interlinked: Chopin and the Nineteenth century, the century of revolution, linked to the 1960s, the revolution of love (both Jim Morrison and Chopin are buried in the same cemetery in Paris); people drifting around the world; sexuality and transsexuality. In Britain this was done in collaboration with Scottish celtic actors, and in Barcelona, in 1992, the collaboration will be with Catalan actors – a political statement in itself as these ethnic groups, like French-Canadians, are often marginalised by a more dominant ethnic group; a statement too, of the way productions are perceived as an on-going process of development.

Try these:
▷Peter Brook, ▷Mike Alfreds, ▷Joan Littlewood; ▷Performance Art, ▷Claire McDonald for collaborative, multi-media theatre; ▷Lindsay Kemp, ▷Neil Bartlett for comparable theatricality and Bartlett's *A Vision of Love, Revealed in Sleep* which like Lepage's work, went through a continuous process of development with four different incarnations; J. B. Priestley's *An Inspector Calls* for a very different approach linking characters to death.

LESBIAN THEATRE IN BRITAIN

Lesbian theatre, it seems, has always had a hard struggle to exist. Indeed the attempted suppression of lesbian writing goes back to Sappho. Plays showing women together such as ▷Nell Dunn's *Steaming* or ▷Sharman Macdonald's *When I Was a Girl I Used to Scream and Shout* seem fair game for mainstream runs providing the female interaction stays within heterosexual bounds. Although gay male theatre was beginning to make inroads into the West End, with for example ▷Larry Kramer's *The Normal Heart* and

▷Harvey Fierstein's *Torch Song Trilogy* before the AIDS scare, lesbian theatre has remained on the fringe. Much of the credit for the creation of lesbian theatre in Britain goes back to Gay Sweatshop who presented Jill Poesner's 'coming out' play *Any Woman Can* in their first season. GS's women's company, including Kate Crutchley, Nancy Diuguid, Kate Phelps and ▷Tasha Fairbanks also created *Care and Control* about lesbian mothers and custody (scripted by ▷Michelene Wandor. Diuguid, Crutchley and Fairbanks have been instrumental in the creation and support of feminist and lesbian feminist work in Britain. Crutchley's tenure at the Oval House in London guaranteed a steady stream of gay, lesbian and feminist work; the radical lesbian and gay American groups Spiderwoman, Hot Peaches and Split Britches made their British debuts there. Split Britches returned in 1987, in the guise of Peggy Shaw and Lois Weaver with *Dress Suits To Hire*, and, at the Drill Hall, with *Little Women: The Tragedy* and *Anniversary Waltz* – object lessons in the art of how to gender-bend with dash, flair and adventurousness.

Tasha Fairbanks set up the theatre group Siren, whilst Diuguid, in a varied career, directed *Patterns* by Barbara Burford, an ambitious multi-racial mythic treatment of women's history at the Drill Hall. The Drill Hall, under the encouragement of ex-Gay Sweatshopper, Julie Parker, has been another haven for radical feminist and gay and lesbian work (though Parker's catholic tastes have included small-scale opera and cabaret from the Berliner Ensemble alongside Split Britches, Hot Peaches and ▷Neil Bartlett). In particular, the all-women Drill Hall pantomimes, most of them written by ▷Nona Shepphard have become a seasonal feature of London life for many at Christmas with New Yorker Cheryl Moch's *The Real True Story of Cinderella* being one of the first to turn the tables and give Cinders her dyke heart's desire.

Lesbian theatre nonetheless has yet to break into the mainstream with any force. There are no television soap lesbian characters (though they have, from time to time, crept into film, such as *Desert Hearts* and *I've Heard The Mermaids Singing*). Since Frank Marcus's *The Killing of Sister George*, which, unintentionally since it was intended as farce, set up irrevocable lesbian stereotypes, only Andrew Davies' 1990s' London and Broadway hit *Prin*, which again presented its central lesbian figure as a monstrous, ego-sapping dyke, has made it to the West End. Win Wells' *Gertrude Stein and Companion* with Miriam Margoyles and Natasha Morgan, did transfer respectably from the Edinburgh Festival fringe to the Bush for a sell-out run. But on the whole British mainstream theatre seems determined to view lesbians and their life experiences one-dimensionally, as generally doomed and unhappy.

Sarah Daniels' *Neaptide* about lesbian mothers and child custody, which surfaced briefly at the National's Cottesloe in the 1980s is the notable exception to this rule, and still the only play to even dare to present a lesbian character sympathetically on the National's stage. Maureen Duffy's *Rites*, based like Bryony Lavery's recent *Kitchen Matters* for Gay Sweatshop, on *The Bacchae*, was also part of a short season of experimental plays at the National in 1969.

The counter-balance to all this negativity is most visibly struck on the fringe, where, despite lack of funds and the small scale, lesbian theatre has flourished. For example, three-dimensional lesbian characters appeared regularly in the plays of the ex-prisoners group, Clean Break. A lesbian feminist consciousness, too, can be traced and informs the work of many women's companies (Scarlet Harlets, the ▷Women's Theatre Group, Re-Sisters when it started, and the Black Theatre of Women from time to time).

British Lesbian theatre, for all its shortcomings (it can tend to be over-self-conscious and self-limitingly personal), reflects the diversity of its community. Lesbian theatre can be celebratory (as in the wild, gothic spoof, *The Fires of Bride*, adapted by Red Rag from Ellen Galford's novel) or gently probing as with Caron Pascoe's *The Seduction of Ms Sarah Hart* contrasting a lesbian love affair in the 1930s with the present; or it can be naturalistic as in Sue Frumin's comedies of life, love and women's friendship (*Rabbit in a Trap* and *Home Sweet Home*), Sandra Freeman's (*Supporting Roles*), or, as in *Patience and Sarah* by Isobel Miller, a simple tale of two women who loved each other. It can explore racial and cultural roots and homophobia as in ▷Jackie Kay's *Chiaroscuro* or ▷Jacqueline Rudet's *Basin*, or it can be abstract, stylistic and almost epic as in *Madonna in Slag City* by Sadista's founder Jude Alderson. It can also be experimental as in Maro Green's and Caroline Griffin's *More* about hidden disabilities and *The Memorial Gardens* about abuse and self-insemination; or as in *Ophelia*, the now defunct Hormone Imbalance's blank-verse parody of Shakespeare. Lesbian plays can, as in the work of Siren, take the form of a re-examination of the value system within which we live – patriarchy (with its overtones of militarism), masculinity, femininity and the female images most popularly transmitted in society. Much lesbian theatre has absorbed the tenets of feminism into its work – though not all lesbians are feminists or vice versa! It does not follow that it must be (though it may be) man-hating, shrill or strident, as male critics often accuse women's theatre of being. It may be didactic, and will almost certainly be subversive. The plays may be about abuse or a sense of grievance, but lesbian theatre also shows a remarkable capacity for imaginative leaps (see the brilliance of ▷Bryony Lavery's pastiches, Berta Freistadt's surrealism or the Ortonesque farces of Jill Fleming). Lesbian theatre at its best is about rediscovery, re-examination, honesty, laughter, compassion, imagination, and a positive response to the mistrusts, mistakes and misunderstandings of society around us – a good place to be, and to stay, at any time.

Try these:
▷Lesbian Theatre in the USA; ▷Sarah Daniels;   ▷Jacqueline   Holborough; ▷Maureen Duffy; and ▷Women in Theatre; ▷Cabaret in Britain; and ▷Performance Art.

LESBIAN THEATRE IN THE USA

Lesbian theatre, as a movement, is inextricably linked to ▷women's theatre of feminist theatre, all of which flowered from the 1960s' radical fringe-theatre movement in American. Because lesbian theatre began as an explicitly political movement, its form was agitprop at the beginning, when it was explicitly involved in defusing steroptypes about lesbians. Today, however, lesbian theatre is such a broad genre that it encompasses womens' issues like rape and misogyny, coming-out plays, or performance pieces about wacky sexualities. Lesbian theatre sometimes tries to heal, as in Karen Malpede's dreamy *Sappho and Aphrodite* (1983), the story of five different women and the ebbs and flows of their love affairs; or her *The End of the War Making Peace: A Fantasy* (1981), which eschews violence and focuses on the power of love. Other

times, it can screech, as in Roberta Sklar's *Elektra Series*, angry-woman dramas produced by the Women's Experimental Theater.

Lesbian theatre often tried to offer alternative, non-hierarchical ways of working. Thus many of the early lesbian theatre groups were collectives The Lavender Cellar Theater (1973–5), for example, saw itself as a vehicle for revealing lesbian oppression. LCT produced *Prisons* by Pat SunCircle, which dealt with the consequences of defying sexual roles, and *Cory*, a traditional, coming-out narrative. Other collectives included The Rhode Island Women's Theater and At the Foot of the Mountain ((Minneapolis) which dealt with women's issues as well as lesbian ones, Medusa's Revenge, a New York-hased group founded in 1976, and the Red Dyke Theater, founded in Atlanta in 1974, which produced satirical skits. Few of these collectives lasted longer than a few years. One notable woman-run theater is ▷Megan Terry's and Joanne Schidman's Omaha Magic Theater, although the issues its programming explores are extremely diversified.

Initially lesbian theatre was split into two camps about how to acknowledge straights: some used theatre as a way to explain their sexuality and others explicitly refused to use their theatre as a lesbian primer. But with the 1980s, economics and formalism changed the way lesbians viewed their audiences: the radical theatre Alice B. in Seattle, for example, strives for an audience divided into thirds of gay women, gay men and straights. In their cabaret-revue *The 7.95 Club*, Alice B. used layers of cross-dressing to confound any conventional ideas of sexual identity. This is a fortunate far cry from the militant dogmatism of the 1970s.

Lesbianism, however, appeared on the American stage long before then. *Sappho*, a play by Alphonse Daudet and Adolph Belot was first performed in the USA in 1895. It caused a scandal and was banned. The 1926 play *The Captive* by Edouard Bourdet was described by critic Brooks Atkinson as 'the tragedy of a young woman who falls into a twisted relationship with another woman.' In the 1950s, ▷Lillian Hellman's *The Children's Hour* presented lesbianism as a painful, defeating experience, which could occur only within a heterosexual relationship.

The proof that lesbian theatre has acquired recognition, if not legitimacy, is that the Annual Gay Theater Conference, which began as a weekend affair, now lasts 18 days.

Mainstream theatres now find lesbianism an acceptable topic; Kathleen Tolan's *A Weekend Near Madison* was premiered in 1982 at the Actors' Theatre of Louisville to critical acclaim. Perhaps two books contributed to the acceptance of lesbian theatre: Helen Krich Chinoy's and Linda Jenkin's *Women in American Theater*, published in the early 1980s, and *Places Please*, an anthology of lesbian plays, which includes *Dos Lesbos* by Terry Baum and Carolyn Myers and *8 $M 10 Glossy* by Sarah Dreher. The Baum/Meyers play captures 'bar dyke' culture in San Francisco while Dreher's work is a realistic coming-out play. The heir to these alternative soap operas is the work of Jane Chambers, whose *Last Summer at Blue Fish Cove* (1982) dramatises collisions between the regulars in a lesbian summer resort community and a heterosexual woman who unknowingly rents one of the cabins. Chambers' one-act *Quintessential Image* (1983) dramatises a conflict between the reality of lesbian experience and the social perception of the lesbian.

These plays are less interesting than some of the less naturalistic cabaret work by Split Britches, formed by Lois Weaver (formerly of the woman-run WOW Cafe), Peggy Shaw and Deborah Margolin. Spiderwomen and Hot Peaches also perform out of the Lower East Side in New York. ▷Holly Hughes, whose 'dyke noir' series (*The Well of Horniness, The Lady Dick* and *Dress Suits to Hire*) were produced at the WOW Cafe in the early eighties, has been the subject of controversy recently when the chairman of the National Endowment for the Arts vetoed her grant. (The backlash against the NEA seems successful since Hughes has recently been awarded another grant.)

Most recently, feminist critics like Jill Dolan have begun to propose alternative drama structures because traditional drama is based on conflict and difference. Doland asks whether this aesthetic is suitable to a single-gender experience and wonders what kind of theatre would occur distanced from a culture based on conflict and opposition. The implications for lesbian theatre are interesting: What kind of theatrical form would arise from a dramatic focus on similarity?

Try these:
▷Lesbian Theatre in Britain; Gay Sweatshop; ▷Women in Theatre; ▷Performance Art; ▷Michelene Wandor; ▷Sarah Daniels.

LESSING, Gotthold Ephraim
[1729–81]
German dramatist and critic

Plays include:
Miss Sara Sampson (1755), *Minna von Barnhelm* (1767), *Emilia Galotti* (1772), *Nathan the Wise* (1779)

Lessing combined the theory and practice of drama in much the same way as ▷Granville Barker and ▷Shaw; his witty and influential theatre criticism, collected as the *Hamburgische Dramaturgie* (1769), includes both reviews of live performances at the National Theatre in Hamburg and general thoughts on the way German drama should develop. The direction he advocated was away from the previous influence of French Classical tragedy and towards ▷Shakespeare and Diderot as models for the writing of plays about everyday bourgeois life (though not with everyday incidents). He wrote several plays following his own precepts: *Miss Sara Sampson* is a domestic tragedy owing much to Richardson's *Pamela*, but too sententious and violent in its end. *Emilia Galotti*, though equally emotional, works much better, as the story of the father killing his daughter (at her request) to save her from dishonour; the narrative line is strong, and the political protest at the princely abuse of power is striking, though it is carefully distanced by an Italian Renaissance setting. *Minna von Barnhelm* is an enjoyable romantic comedy of a penniless officer discharged under a cloud at the end of the Seven Years' War, and scrupulously refusing to marry his betrothed because she is an heiress. She gets him in the end, of course. Someone should try an English version of *Nathan the Wise*, Lessing's great plea for religious tolerance.

Try these:
▷Goethe and ▷Schiller for 18th-century German drama and the influence of ▷Shakespeare; *Minna von Barhelm* is not dissimilar in tone to ▷Sheridan and ▷Goldsmith; ▷Corneille's *Le Cid* brings the issues of women's honour related to man-made social codes firmly to the fore.

LEVY, Deborah
[1959–]
South African-born dramatist, poet

Plays include:
Eva and Moses (1983), *Pax* (1984), *Dream Mama* (1985), *Clam* (1985), *Ophelia and the Great Idea* (1985), *The Naked Cake*

(1986), *Our Lady* (1986), *Heresies* (1986), *Silver Herrings* (1989), *Judith and Holofernes* (with ▷Howard Barker; 1990), *Swallowing Geography* (1991), *Nights at the Circus* (adapted from Angela Carter's novel; 1991)

South African-born Levy is one of the most exciting new writers to have emerged in the 1980s. A self-confessed avant-gardist, with a prodigious intellectual and political curiosity she made her mark quite suddenly in 1984 with *Pax*, for the Women's Theatre Group, following it up with another five plays in two years, culminating in *Heresies*, commissioned for the short-lived ▷RSC Women's Group. Created through workshop improvisations, this distillation of contemporary modes around sexual and other politics, seen through the eyes of different archetypes (Cholla, the Displaced Person; Leah, the Composer etc) seemed unusually short on plausibility, but long on emotional power. Even when not sparking on all plugs, the power and intelligence of Levy's writing and the breadth of her vision about such recurrent themes as grief, displacement, the nuclear threat, resistance, the importance of female values, and survival make hers a singular and uncompromising talent. She has published poetry, novels and short stories, and has also been a performance artist, her love of words being matched by a desire to give visual images equal weight – a balance, which Levy herself agrees, makes considerable imaginative demands on a director. Levy has recently completed a libretto from ▷Lorca's *Blood Wedding*, commissioned by the Women's Playhouse Trust.

Pax

As time goes on, this play has taken on something of the lustre of a legend. Complex, densely worded, and a play so rich in allusion and ideas as to feel like a hallucinatory journey into the contemporary female psyche, this rummage through female archetypes, with its confrontations with past, present and warnings of a precarious future in a nuclear age, remains a landmark in mid-1980s feminism with its exploration of mothers and daughters, philosophical meditations on death, patriarchy, the Holocaust and survival. It was directed by Sue Todd (who also directed *Heresies*) and Anna Furse, in a production that matched Levy's adventurousness with equal visual audacity.

Try these:
Hilary Westlake and Lumiere and Son's *Panic* for women exploring external and inner realities; Burnt Bridges' *Deals* was a stylised feminist encounter with the Big Bang and 1986 City psyche, pre-dating ▷Caryl Churchill's *Serious Money* by several months; ▷Susan Yankowitz's *Alarms* for a heightened Cassandra treatment of the nuclear future; ▷Bryony Lavery's *Origin of the Species* for a feminist reassessment of history; ▷Berta Freistadt's *The Celebration of Kokura* and ▷Stephen Lowe's *Keeping Body and Soul Together* for more plays on peace themes; ▷April de Angelis for a similarly allusive use of language; ▷Red Shift for a parallel aspiration to visual/verbal theatre.

LINNEY, Romulus   [1930–]
American dramatist

Plays include:
The Sorrows of Frederick (1967), *Holy Ghosts* (1971), *The Love Suicide at Schofield Barracks* (1972), *Esther* (1973), *Autopsie* (1973), *Childe Byron* (1977), *Tennessee* (1979), *The Captivity of Pixie Shedman* (1981), *The Death of King Philip* (1984), *Why the Lord Came to Sand Mountain* (1984), *A Woman Without a Name* (1986), *Unchanging Love* (1989), *2* (1990), *Miss Julie* (1991)

Romulus Linney has been called (by Martin Gottfried, of *The New York Post*) 'one of the best-kept secrets of the American theatre, a playwright of true literacy, a writer in the grand tradition'. In spite of numerous productions, publications and honours, Linney is not well known to the general public. His work generally is produced off- and off-off-Broadway and in the regional theatres and festivals. Raised in Tennessee and North Carolina and educated at the elite Oberlin College and Yale Drama School, Linney is concerned with big themes – history, religion and the meaning of art in the light of history and religion. In an interview with Craig Gholson in *Bomb*, Linney said, 'I believe Katharine Anne Porter somewhere says that the only interesting things are art and religion, because you have to go to extremes in order to be successful in them. I certainly still find that relevant today.' Linney's plays, many of which are set in the rural American South, are often referred to as 'gothic'. Partly this is due to the subject matter, which often derives from folklore and myth: snake handlers (*Holy Ghosts*), illusion (*Tennessee*), ghosts (*Childe Byron*, *The Captivity of Pixie Shedman*). The gothic label stems also from Linney's language, in which characters' day-to-day speech may be heightened and lyrical. The playwright emphasises that his use of language has its roots in the King James version of the Bible. As he told Gholson, 'it's gorgeous. It's loquacious. People talk like that . . . Southerners love to sit out on the porch in the evening and just talk over family history. And they do it in this loquacious, colorful style.'

Linney's first major play, *The Sorrows of Frederick*, about Frederick II of Prussia, is often revived. Mel Gussow, writing in *The New York Times* of the work's New York premiere, noted that the play is 'not primarily an epic about wars and power plays, but an interior psycho-drama about what goes on in the crumbling mind of a philosopher-king'.

The Love Suicide at Schofield Barracks is presented as a court investigation into the death of an army general and his wife. Each witness adds his or her testimony until the completed mosaic reveals that the couple committed a ritual double suicide to protest against the Vietnam War. A recent revival prompted critic Michael Feingold to call it the best American Vietnam War play.

2, a portrait of Hermann Goering, Hitler's second-in-command, won the Best Play Award at the 1990 Humana Festival of New American Plays at Actors Theatre of Louisville. *Unchanging Love*, based on the ▷Chekhov story *In the Ravine*, is Linney's most recently produced play. Set in the 1920s, in the foothills of Appalachia, the work features more independent female characters than in the original tale as well as an impending environmental disaster. Writing in *The New York Times*, Mel Gussow affirmed, 'In this adaptation, Mr. Linney continues to be a poet of America's heartland'.

Try these:
▷Christopher Hampton's *Total Eclipse*, ▷Howard Brenton's *Bloody Poetry* for plays about nineteenth-century poets; ▷Sam Shepard for an alternative mode of American Gothic; James Duff's *The War Back Home*; ▷Lanford Wilson's *Fifth of July* and Stephen Metcalfe's *Strange Snow* as anti-Vietnam plays with a dom-estic setting; ▷Chekhov; Deborah Pryor for lyrical, mystical portraits of Appalachian life; ▷Pirandello's *Henry IV*.

LITTLEWOOD, Joan   [1914–   ]
English actress and director

Largely unacknowledged by British critics, though invited to perform abroad with great success, Littlewood overcame conditions of continuous financial crisis to create productions of great energy and power with Theatre Workshop from negligible resources. One of the first British directors to make extensive use of improvisation, she had remarkable skills in developing performances. She was sometimes accused of working best with second-rate material but a great many fine actors – not to mention designer John Bury – look back on their days with Theatre Workshop as a key period in their careers.

Best known as founder-director of Theatre Workshop Littlewood was born in Stockwell, London, and went to RADA but left without completing the course, reacting against the teaching and against West End theatre in general. In Manchester she became involved with Ewan McColl's Theatre of Action, a left-wing group inspired by the theories of Adolphe Appia and described by one critic as 'the nearest thing any British theatre has got to Meyerhold.' Reconstituted after a wartime gap as Theatre Workshop, the company toured throughout the country – often with one-night-stands, in new plays created by the company and occasional classics, until finding a permanent home at the Theatre Royal, Stratford, in East London.

Littlewood was trusted by ▷Brecht with the first British production of *Mother Courage* (Barnstable 1955), which she directed as well as playing the title role, and should be remembered as much for the anti-nuclear war *Uranium 235*, a pro-peace *Lysistrata* and classic productions of *Volpone* and *Richard II* as for the plays by ▷Behan, ▷Delaney and Lionel Bart which gained wide audiences when Theatre Workshop productions transferred to the West End. These transfers meant that each time a new company had to be built at Stratford.

Then in 1963 came another smash hit *Oh What a Lovely War*, a fiercely satirical anti-war World War I documentary built around popular songs and presented as a pierrot show. But the long-running transfer again removed the company.

In 1967 *Mrs Wilson's Diary*, a satire on life at 10 Downing Street developed in improvisations from material supplied by John Wells and Richard Ingrams, was Littlewood's last Workshop success to transfer to the West End. The demolition of the district around the theatre and failure of funding eventually led to the end of Theatre Workshop. Since the early death of Gerry Raffles, her partner in life and work, Littlewood has not worked in theatre.

Try these:
For Littlewood's style of collective script techniques, Joint Stock, and much of the early work of companies such as Monstrous Regiment, Women's Theatre Group and socialist companies like 7:84, Belt and Braces; for community oriented companies, Ann Jellicoe and Community Theatre; for British companies committed to new writing, Foco Novo, Paines Plough, Theatre of Black Women; for a vision, though unacceptably middle-class, of Joan's 'fun palace', see, ironically, the ▷National Theatre; for smaller theatres round Britain see Peter Cheeseman at Stoke-on-Trent, Sheffield's Crucible, Leicester Haymarket, Solent People's Theatre, Theatre Foundry, and in London, The Albany in Deptford and Battersea Arts Centre.

LOCHHEAD, Liz   [1947–]
Scottish poet, playwright and performer

Plays include:
Blood and Ice (1982), *Shanghaied* (1983), *Dracula* (1985), *Mary Queen of Scots Got her Head Chopped Off* (1987), *The Big Picture* (1988), *Patter Merchants* (1989), *Jock Tamson's Bairns* (1990)

Liz Lochhead has a brilliant way with words, both as a writer and performer. She can have them carry several messages at once, ordering them adeptly so that they pun on one level, offer serious revelation on another and still sound just like your granny's favourite long-in-the-tooth wisdom all the same! Her early poetry, with its wry observations on awry love affairs, street life and everyday folk, was full of playful, exact phrases. She has a painter's eye for local colour and situation, a wordsmith's ability to shape that perception into vital language, and underpinning all this a strong sense of how female sexuality influences actions and reactions within past history and modern society. *Blood and Ice* Lochhead's first serious attempt at playwriting, has undergone several changes since its first production but the main thrust of the piece is unchanged: the nature of female creativity. The plot concerns the hectic, febrile relationship between Byron and the Shellys and the circumstances which led to Mary Shelley's penning *Frankenstein*. Mary's 'natural' creations were, of course, her children, but they died. Enter that most unnatural of creations, the monster which Frankenstein, defying the laws of flesh and blood, brings to life and which Mary, so conscious of mortalities around her, makes immortal in print. Why? asks Lochhead. And supplies a fascinating, shrewd scenario of how an impressionable girl takes on not just womanhood and its periodic burdens, but begins to question society's perception of womankind. With speeches heightened with vigorous, poetic language, *Blood and Ice* is seen incresingly as a landmark play in Scottish women's writing.

'We bleed. Even when you don't prick us.' could be the byword of many of Lochhead's women, whether they be out of history or off the Byres Road in Glasgow. Lochhead doesn't ignore or sanitise the human mess of sex, menstruation or birth any more than she avoids the mess and confusion of human relationships. She will poke marvellous, well-judged fun at pretension – female or male – but she has compassion and insight when it comes to analysing how and why men and women so often get it wrong about themselves and about each other

Jock Tamson's Bairns (1990), a performance piece with Lochhead created with Communicado (it involved music, dance and mime as well as spoken text) revealed just how closely she scans the Scottish psyche as well as her fellow man and woman. Subtitled 'The Last Burnt Supper', the project took the patriotic and macho myths surrounding Scotland's national hero-bard, Robert Burns, and used them to point up the underlying sadness and inadequacy of a race that celebrates the poet's drunkenness and womanising as much, if not more than, his poems and his politics. Here Lochhead was on some of her best territory, the Scotsman's apparent inability to express emotion, except when drunk, or at a football match, or when no-one's looking. Love women? Course they do. Don't *understand* them, mind you. But love them? Goes without saying, doesn't it? Doesn't it?

She has translated ▷Molière into nippy, colloquial Scots, penned monologues and adapted Bram Stoker's *Dracula* for the stage; a dramatisation that understands the bone marrow issues of sex, possession, surrender and redemptive love which are the (almost subconscious) subtext of the novel. And, being Lochhead there are rich female resonances to Renfield's litany of 'The blood is the life'.

Try these:

Scotland currently rejoices in a wealth of new, bright, female writers: Marcella Evaristi (*Eve Set the Balls of Corruption Rolling*, *The Offski Variations*) has an almost cabaret-spark of hilarious one-liners to her portraits of knees together Catholic girlhood and 'the times they are liberated' womanhood; but her humours are well-rooted, observant and engaging; look out for Anne-Marie de Mambro, Paula McGee, Rona Munro, Aileen Ritchie too; ▷Sharman Macdonald's *When I was a girl I used to scream and shout* is strong on love and conflict between mothers and daughters; Alan Spence's *Sailmaker* evokes images of a Glasgow childhood even as it explores the sad way that a widowed father and teenage son can't express their love for each other; ▷Howard Brenton's *Bloody Poetry* also grapples with sexism and the Shelley's; Tattycoram's *The Very Tragical History of Mary Shelley* was an all-female, performance-art piece that effectively took an anti-Shelley stance; for more indicators of women at work, see ▷Women in Theatre.

LORCA, Federico García [1898–1935]
Spanish dramatist, poet, artist

Plays include:
The Butterfly's Evil Spell (1920), *Mariana Pineda* (1927), *In Five Years' Time* (1930), *The Public* (1930), *Blood Wedding* (1932), *Yerma* (1934), *Dona Rosita la Soltera* (1935), *The House of Bernarda Alba* (1935)

Lorca was brought up on the family farm near Granada and always said that he was unable to speak and walk until the age of four because of illness as a baby. As a student he forged close friendships with Salvador Dali and Luis Buñuel. Surrealism was something that sat easily with Lorca – *The Public* and *In Five Years' Time* are Surrealistic fantasies – but he was mistrustful of intellectual and literary élites, and his plays are rooted in Spanish folk lore and traditions. His second play, *Mariana Pineda*, told the story of a heroine of the revolution of the 1830s. Lorca thought of himself as a playwright for the Spanish people; he became involved in 1931 with a travelling theatre group, La Baracca, which toured classic Spanish drama throughout the regions of Spain. Many of his texts employ farce, folk tale and poetry, popular and traditional forms, to make them accessible.

His most important works are those which bring together Lorca's passionate feeling for the history and traditions of Andalusia with his poetic power. The 'trilogy of the Spanish Earth'; *Blood Wedding*, *Yerma* and *The House of Bernarda Alba*, are firmly rooted within Spanish communities, and are all concerned with marriage, sexuality and the constraints and commitments of the community. *Blood Wedding* is based on an actual story Lorca came across in a newspaper fragment which told of a family vendetta and a bride who ran away with the son of the enemy family. In his play the first act is relatively naturalistic, but in the second, the moon and death appear in an extraordinarily powerful image to oversee the fleeing lovers. *The House of Bernarda Alba* is a play exclusively of women, in which the destructive power of the matriarch Bernarda Alba becomes a metaphor for sexual repression and constraints on liberty.

On August 19, 1936 Lorca was shot by the fascist paramilitary Black Squad in the early days of the Spanish Civil War. His body lies in an unmarked grave, but he remains Spain's most celebrated playwright.

Yerma
Yerma means 'the barren one'. The play is a powerful study of a peasant woman, obsessed with the desire for a child. But childlessness in Lorca's hands becomes a metaphor for other kinds of barrenness: Yerma's marriage is not only sterile because it has not produced children, her racking pain is quite clearly a desire for another way of being. Yerma and her marriage are firmly located in a community of traditional wisdoms and attitudes to marriage. She is offered the commandments of marriage: 'You must obey your husband who is your owner and master'; and while keeping to her own code of honour, recognises that she is

alone in her integrity. In a final act of revenge she strangles her husband, with the recognition that he can never satisfy her and that she has been denied the one positive outcome of her marriage, a child. The play is a powerful study of sexual hypocrisies, of the constraints on women of traditional 'femininity', and of the 'macho' on men. Yerma was given a magnificent and legendary production by Victor Garcia (later revived by Nuria Espert) in which the play was performed on a huge trampoline and billowing drapes.

Try these:
▷Joe Orton and Lorca write with a bitter awareness of sexual hypocrisies; ▷Lindsay Kemp has mounted a dance version of *Blood Wedding* and with Christopher Bruce of Ballet Rambert a dance/drama portrait of Lorca, called *The Cruel Garden*; Lorca shared with ▷Brecht, 7:84, ▷Trevor Griffiths, ▷John McGrath and David Edgar a commitment to bringing the theatre to the people; ▷Wendy Kesselman's *My Sister in This House* is another claustrophobic household of sexual repression; ▷Bryony Lavery's *Mummy* (now made into an opera by Jessica Higgs) naughtily satirises a typically claustrophobic Lorca household.

LOWE, Stephen   [1947–]
British dramatist

Plays include:
Cards (1971), *Stars* (1976), *Touched* (1977), *Shooting Fishing and Riding* (1977), *Sally Ann Hallelujah Band* (1977), *The Ragged Trousered Philanthropists* (1978; from the book by Robert Tressell, *Glasshouses* (1981; retitled as *Moving Pictures*), *Tibetan Inroads* (1981), *Strive* (1982), *Trial of Frankenstein* (1984), *Seachange* (1984), *Keeping Body and Soul Together* (1984), *Desire* (1986), *Demon Lovers* (1987), *The Storm* (1987; from Ostrovsky), *Divine Gossip* (1988), *Paradise* (a musical; 1990); adaptation of ▷Schiller's *William Tell* (1989)

Nottingham-born Lowe worked as an actor at the Stephen Joseph Theatre at Scarborough under ▷Alan Ayckbourn before becoming Resident Playwright at Dartington and at the Riverside Studios. His work has tended to centre on socialist and feminist themes which he has tackled from a wide variety of angles: in *Cards* the idea is that Donald McGill-style

seaside postcards are actually photographs of real people who we see discussing their work as they wait for their photographs to be taken; *Stars* shows two couples acting out film fantasies during World War II; *Shooting Fishing and Riding* is a play about rape, based on Susan Brownmiller's *Act of Will*. Lowe has written about the Falklands in *Strive* and, allegorically, in *Seachange* and about the Chinese annexation of Tibet in *Tibetan Inroads*. He is always a challenging playwright with a strong concern for human dignity and a firm commitment to the idea of 'a decent, equal, peaceful future', which comes over strongly in his two best known works, *Touched* and *The Ragged Trousered Philanthropists* (which received a respectable production off-Broadway at the SoHo Rep). *Touched*, set in Nottingham in the period between the end of Word War II in Europe and the surrender of Japan, explores the relationship between a group of working-class women as they hope and fear for the future, set against the background of the discovery of Belsen, the election of the Labour government and the dropping of the first atomic bombs. Lowe's version of the socialist classic *The Ragged Trousered Philanthropists*, first developed in workshops with ▷Joint Stock, is a moving account of the struggle of working men to come to an understanding of their oppression and carry the fight back to the capitalists.

Try these:
▷David Hare's *Fanshen*, another Joint Stock play, shows the Chinese working-classes reaching an understanding of the roots of their situation; ▷Arthur Miller, ▷Marc Blitzstein's *The Cradle Will Rock* and ▷Clifford Odets's *Waiting for Lefty* for comparable American examples; ▷Howard Brenton and David Hare, separately and together, have written plays which, like *Touched*, take Angus Calder's *The People's War* as their inspiration; other writers who have taken the Falklands war as their theme are ▷Louise Page in *Falkland Sound/Voces de Malvinas*, ▷Tony Marchant in *Coming Home*, and Greg Cullen in *Taken Out*; ▷Noël Greig's *Poppies* takes a look at pacifism from a gay perspective; Tony Roper's *The Steamie* for a Scottish working-class community of women; ▷Nell Dunn's *Steaming* for another English version.

LUCAS, Craig   [1951]
American dramatist

Plays include:
Missing Persons (1980), *Marry Me a Little*
(with Norman Rene; 1980), *Reckless*
(1983), *Blue Window* (1984), *Three
Postcards* (1987), *Longtime Companion*
(screenplay; 1989), *Prelude to a Kiss* (1990)

Craig Lucas' plays are distinguished by unusual dramatic techniques: simultaneous dialogue in *Blue Windows*, a homicidal husband
in *Reckless* and spiritual possession in *Prelude
to a Kiss*. Lucas explores issues of love and
devotion with these devices; a logical development for a playwright who was orphaned and
wrestled with his sexuality until after he graduated from Boston University where he was
advised by the poet Anne Sexton to make his
writing 'strange'. In his address to the First
National Gay and Lesbian Theatre
Conference in July 1990, Lucas attributed his
dramatic development and style to his homosexuality, his study with Sexton and, later in
his career, the AIDS epidemic. Neither the
crisis, nor his homosexuality, is obvious in his
plays. Lucas examines the commitment between people who have professed love and
devotion, especially within sanctified institutions; his techniques are ingenious. In
Reckless a wife leaves home on Christmas Eve
to escape her husband's plan to have her killed
for an insurance settlement; an ironic and
humorous convolution of American family
ideology. He uses separate scenes presented
simultaneously in *Blue Window* to highlight
the coincidence and frailty of human relationships. His combination of unusual theatrical
devices, deceptively real characters and paradoxical themes sets Lucas apart from his
peers.

Prelude to a Kiss
Prelude to a Kiss, a song recorded by Ella
Fitzgerald in 1938, is a tender ballad about
one's yearning for another, a fitting metaphor
for Lucas' plot that surrounds two newlyweds
who become spiritually separated and have
their fidelity tested in an odd way. The young
wife's body is overtaken by a dying man's
soul, a strange and oblique reference to love
and devotion in the era of AIDS. Specifically,
can, or how will, the young husband remain
faithful when his wife's soul has been overtaken by the spectre of death? His conundrum
does not compromise the plot's romantic tone,
it elevates the sense of the play to one of
universality.

Try these:
▷Arthur Miller's *Death of a Salesman* for
another version of dying to collect the
insurance; S. Ansky's *The Dybbuk* for possession; ▷Harry Kondoleon, ▷Larry
Kramer, ▷Tony Kushner, ▷Harvey
Fierstein for AIDS plays.

LUCIE, Doug   [1953–]
British dramatist

Plays include:
John Clare's Mad Nuncle (1975), *Rough
Trade* (1977), *We Love You* (1978), *Oh
Well* (1978), *The New Garbo* (1978), *Heroes*
(1979), *Poison* (1980), *Strangers in the
Night* (1981), *Progress* (1984), *Key to the
World* (1984), *Force and Hypocrisy* (1986),
Fashion (1987)

Lucie has made a reputation as the satirical
chronicler of the underside of the bright new
world of style, be it that of the liberated new
man in *Progress* or the marketing of politicians
in *Fashion*, which, as the decade grew to a
close, turned out to be ever more prescient.
Lucie reserves his attacks for those who use
current trends for their own egocentric ends,
but since that is almost everyone in his plays
they achieve major heights of misanthropy in
their depiction of a hard, uncaring, manipulative lifestyle. Lucie can be very funny in his
presentation of the mannerisms and jargon of
his characters but there is no compensating
warmth and little hope in a world in which
cynicism is the norm and where the plots
ensure that what little progress is made is
ignored by the other characters.

Progress
Progress is an uncomfortably accurate presentation of right-on people attempting to grapple
with all the hazards and pitfalls of negotiating
the contradictions of patriarchy and capitalism
while using a working-class battered wife as a
medium for their own antagonisms. Many of
the characters are homo- or bi-sexual and
there are important points about the manipulation of trendy ideas to give people sexual
credibility, particularly the Men's Group's
attempt to discuss pornography. Under the
brilliantly vitriolic comedy of surface manners, there is a genuine sense of the waste of
human potential as relationships collapse and
sexual politics becomes sexual warfare.

Try these:
▷Noël Coward, ▷Wycherley, ▷Keith Reddin, ▷Ben Jonson, ▷Congreve, ▷Aphra Behn, ▷Joe Orton for manipulative societies where wit is at a premium; ▷Sarah Daniels' *Masterpieces* for a contemporary feminist approach to the question of pornography; ▷Caryl Churchill's *Cloud Nine* for polymorphous sexuality; ▷Deborah Levy's *Heresies* for another contemporary view of sexual politics; ▷Christopher Hampton's adaptation of Laclos' *Les Liaisons Dangereuses* as *the* portrait of cunning and viperish manipulation; ▷Caryl Churchill's *Serious Money*, Stephen Jeffreys's *Valued Friends,* Martin Crimp for further brittle barometers of the age; also Jeffreys' *The Clink* for political skulduggery.

LUCKHAM, Claire   [1944–   ]
British dramatist

Plays include:
Scum (with Chris Bond; 1976), *Yatsy and the Whale* (1977), *Tuebrook Tanzi the Venus Fly Trap* (1978, later known as *Tugby Tanzi* and then *Trafford Tanzi*; 1980), *Aladdin* (1978), *Fish Riding Bikes* (1979), *Finishing School* (1982), *The Girls in the Pool* (1982; later known as *Gwen*), *Walking on Water* (1983), *Moll Flanders* (1986 from Defoe's novel), *Imber* (1986), *Alice in Wartime* (1986), *Mary Stuart* (1988; adapted from ▷Schiller)

Nairobi-born Luckham stands somewhere between the 'older generation' of female playwrights who won success in the 1970s such as ▷Pam Gems, ▷Caryl Churchill, ▷Mary O'Malley, and ▷Nell Dunn and the next generation of ▷Sarah Daniels, ▷Louise Page, and ▷Sharman Macdonald in the mid-1980s. With her husband, director Chris Bond, she was initially associated with Liverpool's Everyman and is best known for *Trafford Tanzi* which has been performed all round the world (often with a different place name to reflect local geography) and translated into more than a dozen languages. Her other plays have also explored female issues, particularly relationships between women, to each other and to work, with the series of monologues (*Fish Riding Bikes, Finishing School*) about women's friendship, a typists' strike at Liverpool Council (*The Girls in the Pool*), and

the adaptations of Defoe's *Moll Flanders* and ▷Schiller's *Mary Stuart*. But there have also been a couple of ▷community plays including one about the whaling industry and the army occupation of Salisbury Plain (*Imber*). *Scum*, commissioned by Monstrous Regiment and directed by Sue Todd, set in a laundry during the Paris Commune of 1871, an early exploration of sexual and socialist politics entwined in women's relationships to work and society, was co-written by Luckham and Bond.

Trafford Tanzi
Trafford Tanzi, a storming visual and physical metaphor of female liberation (as it was then seen) enacted through an actual wrestling match between Tanzi and the various characters in her life, first started out doing the rounds of the pubs of Liverpool. Taken up and toured by various companies, it finally settled into a long and successful run at the Mermaid. No doubt about it, *Trafford Tanzi*, with its direct appeal to audience participation, gives value for money as a theatrical experience as Tanzi changes from socially conditioned, feminine little girl to renegade and ultimate wrestler, meeting her husband on equal terms and literally throwing him. The play operates within both sporting and agitprop conventions, eliciting gender-based responses from its audiences. However, from a current point of view, some of its sexual politics leave a good deal to be desired, particularly if you are no great lover of the right-by-might or blood sports lobby.

Try these:
For taking men on in their own sphere, ▷Timberlake Wertenbaker's *The Grace of Mary Traverse*; for an earlier counterpart, ▷Middleton and ▷Dekker's *The Roaring Girl*; Robert David McDonald has also adapted ▷Schiller's *Mary Stuart*; for early feminist work, Monstrous Regiment and Women's Theatre Group; ▷Arnold Wesker's *The Kitchen* is another industrially based piece, also ▷John Byrne's *The Slab Boys Trilogy*, Kevin Heelan's *Distant Fires* Robert Tressell's *The Ragged Trousered Philanthropists*, adapted both by ▷Stephen Lowe and 7:84 (re-titled *The Reign of Terror and the Great Money Trick*); for other realistic sporting images, Johnny Quarrel's *The Wednesday Night Action,* ▷Howard Sackler's *The Great White Hope,* ▷John

Godber's *Up 'n' Under*, ▷Louise Page's *Golden Girls*; ▷Caryl Churchill's *Top Girls* and *Serious Money* are perhaps two of the most commercially successful variants of women making it on male terms; Dion Boucicault for titles adapted to local situations.

LUDLAM, Charles   [1940–87]
American dramatist and performer

Plays include:
Big Hotel (1966), *Conquest of the Universe or When Queens Collide* (1967), *Turds in Hell* (with Bill Vehr; 1969), *The Grand Tarot* (1969), *Bluebeard* (1970), *Eunuchs of the Forbidden City* (1971), *Corn* (music and lyrics by Virgil Young; 1972), *Camille* (1973), *Hot Ice* (1974), *Stage Blood* (1975), *Jack and the Beanstalk* (1975), *Isle of the Hermaphrodites or The Murdered Minion* (1976), *Caprice or Fashion Bound* (1976), *Der Ring Gott Farblonjet* (1977), *The Ventriloquist's Wife* (1978), *Utopia, Incorporated* (1978), *The Enchanted Pig* (1979), *A Christmas Carol* (1979), *Reverse Psychology* (1980), *Love's Tangled Web* (1981), *Secret Lives of the Sixties* (1982), *Exquisite Torture* (1982), *Le Bourgeois Avant-Garde* (1983), *Galas* (1983), *The Mystery of Irma Vep* (1984), *Medea* (1984), *How to Write a Play* (1984), *Salammbo* (1985), *The Artificial Jungle* (1986)

Playwright, actor, producer and director, Charles Ludlam is best known for his work with The Ridiculous Theatrical Company, which he founded in 1969. After graduating from Hofstra University in 1965, where he first developed his style of whimsical high camp and farce (though he felt the term 'camp' was homophobic), his work was sprinkled with puns, satire, reversals of logic and literary allusions. Bizarre alterations of classic plays, novels and films prevail in productions that alternate between homage and camp, a revisionist strategy to tear down the walls of the 'silent war waged against anyone who's different'.

If homosexual stereotypes are an issue in Ludlam's art, more so is liberation from preconceived notions of happiness and morality. Ludlam gave us an endearing, lovable and sometimes laughable portrait of the homosexual community without ever losing a biting satirical edge. *Hot Ice*, for example, is a mad anarchic comedy where dead bodies are put on ice for renewed life in some more peacable era than the present. *Camille*, one of his most widely acclaimed works, starred Ludlam in the title role dressed as a beautiful woman, save for the exposed hair on his chest. The theme of forbidden love is ridiculed; the concept of undying love mocked. In *Bluebeard*, the plot hinges on Bluebeard's infatuation with creating a third gender by inventing a new genital.

At the time of his death from AIDS in 1987, Ludlam was one of the busiest people in show business, acting in feature films while continuing work on new plays for the theatre. A skilful actor, he gained fame first in the downtown gay community and then with the wider New York audience. As a female impersonator he was unrivalled and reached his peak as Hedda Gabler at the American ▷Ibsen Theatre in Pittsburgh.

Awards include a 1969 Obie for the founding of the Ridiculous Theatrical Company, a Guggenhem Fellowship in playwriting in 1979 and Obies for acting in 1972 for *Corn* and 1973 for *Camille*. In 1987 he received an Obie for sustained life achievement. His work continues to be revived by The Ridiculous Theatrical Company, now run by his longtime lover and friend Everett Quinton, who continues Ludlam's model of 'Theater without the stink of art'.

Try these:
▷Caryl Churchill's *Cloud Nine* and ▷Joe Orton's *What the Butler Saw* for transvestism; ▷Christopher Durang for sexual spoofs; Hasty Puddings for drag; ▷Peter Brook, ▷Tom Stoppard's *Rosencrantz and Guildenstern Are Dead* for new takes on the classics; ▷Alfred Jarry's *Ubu Roi* for profaning theatrical traditions; Neil Bartlett for mould-breaking.

LUKE, Peter   [1919–]
British dramatist

Plays include:
Hadrian the Seventh (1967), *Bloomsbury* (1974), *Married Love* (1985)

Peter Luke has written relatively few plays in the course of a varied career (wine trade, Head of Scripts for ABC Television, farming in Andalucia, director of the Abbey Theatre, etc), but his version of Frederick Rolfe/Baron Corvo's novel *Hadrian VII* reproduced much of the neurotic fascination of that amazing piece of wish-fulfilment, and became an international hit. Hadrian VII, like Rolfe, was a failed priest but, unlike Rolfe, he was made Pope, forgave all his enemies at great and self-righteous length, and revolutionised the Church and the world before being assassinated by a crazed Irishman. Luke's play uses details from Rolfe's life and his other books as an effective frame for the story – at the end we see Rolfe standing on stage, clutching his manuscript, as he watches Hadrian's funeral. Later plays, such as *Bloomsbury*, about Virginia Woolf, and *Married Love*, about Marie Stopes, have had only moderate success.

Try these:

Actress Pauline Devancy's *To Marie with Love* is another, one-woman version of the contradictory personality of Marie Stopes; ▷adaptations; for other popes see ▷Brecht's *Galileo* and ▷Hochhüth's *The Representative*; Patrick Gonland's adaptation of Virginia Woolf's *A Room of One's Own* with Eileen Atkins turned her essay into riveting drama.

m

MacARTHUR, Charles

see HECHT, Ben

MacDONALD, Claire [1954–]
British performance artist/director/writer

Plays include:
The Undersea World of Erik Satie (1980),
Dammerungstrasse 55 (1981), *Useful Vices*
(1982), *No Weapons for Mourning* (1983), *A
Place in Europe* (1983) with composer,
Jeremy Petyon Jones; *The Song of the Clay
People* with composer, Andrew Poppy
(1984); *Carrier Frequency* (1984) with
Russell Hoban; *The Price of Meat* (1985),
with composer/writer Andrew Poppy;
Dark Water Closing (1986), *The Sleep*
(1987), *An Imitation of Life* (1987) with
Pete Brooks; *Dream of a New Machine*
(1987), *The Menaced Assassin* (libretto)
(1989); *Storm from Paradise* (1989), *The
Fall of Lucas Fortune* (1990)

As a founder member of Impact Theatre Co-
operative with Pete Brooks, Tyrone Huggins,
Graeme Miller and Lesley Stiles, Claire
MacDonald has been at the forefront of ▷Per-
formance Art in Britain for over a decade as a
performer, deviser and director.

During the years 1979–1986, Impact
became one of Britain's most important performance art companies. Impact's essence was
in working collaboratively, its performers and
style of performance – enactment of real
events in real time – one of the key developments. With Heather Ackroyd, Richard
Hawley, Niki Johnson, Steve Shill, later
members of the group, Impact's work developed a voice distinctive in its creation of
atmosphere, in the forceful, sometimes
aggressive, physicality of its performance style
and in its determination to work against narrative and the literary tradition of British
theatre. In a seminal work, *Carrier Frequency*,
Simon Vincenzi, another long-term collabora-

tor, created a swimming pool into which the
performers plunged with increasing ritualistic
frenzy. Impact pieces became increasingly
choreographic (layered sound-tracks were also
an essential component), though some pieces
did start by taking their cue from existing
stories and myths; in *Carrier Frequency*,
Conrad's *The Heart of Darkness* and the
Orpheus and Eurydice legend; in *No Weapons
for Mourning*, the Dashiell Hammett 'film
noir' genre. The influence of Impact continues to be widely felt despite the group's
split in 1986. Impact's former members continue their own developments, whilst also collaborating together.

MacDonald has devised texts for Steve Shill
(the claustrophobic and resonant *Dark Water
Closing*, with Shill nightmarishly trapped in
an urban apartment) and collaborated with
Pete Brooks in work reflecting ongoing
Impact concerns in her use of isolated
strangers in nameless, post-apocalyptic settings (in *The Fall of Lucas Fortune* it is after a
flood), and male/female tensions (*An Imitation
of Life*).

MacDonald's new company, Insomniac
Productions, and the idea its title conjures up
to do with the hallucinatory sums up the quality both of her work and that of Impact: 'my
work is not about representing a shared tangible world but about dreaming something up.'

Try these:
Hilary Westlake's Lumiere & Son,
Geraldine Pilgrim's Hesitate and Demonstrate and Forced Entertainment for
British Performance Art groups; Robert
Lepage for a comparative use of immersion in water in *Tectonic Plates* and *film
noir* allusions in *Polygraph*; Terry Johnson
uses it in *Imagine Drowning* as a symbol
of rebirth; Wooster Group for an American equivalent; Anna O for a group of
Dartington students (where MacDonald
and has been Head of Theatre) whose *The*

Mourning After also mirrors Impact influences; ▷Sally Nemeth's *Mill Fire* for a quite different treatment of the psychology of disaster dealt with in *The Fall of Lucas Fortune;* Annie Griffin's *Ariadne* (with Neil Bartlett's Gloria group) was a contemporary Performance Art piece based on the Strauss opera; ▷Performance Art; ▷J. M. Barrie for *Peter Pan*.

MacDONALD, Sharman   [1951–]
British dramatist

Plays include:
When I Was a Girl I Used to Scream and Shout (1984), *The Brave* (1988), *When We Were Women* (1988), *All Things Nice* (1991)

With her wit and razor-sharp observation, Glasgow-born actress-turned-writer Macdonald has made a speciality out of revealing the growing pains of young Scottish girls' rites of passage to womanhood. She is particularly strong on the conflict of emotions inherent in burgeoning sexual awareness, but it was hard to know whether the huge success of her first play, *When I Was A Girl I Used to Scream and Shout* – a painful, bitterly funny study of a Scottish childhood and adolescence for which she won the *Evening Standard*'s Most Promising Playwright award for 1984 – was due more to its voyeuristic pleasures than its intrinsic artistic merit. Although much of its popularity did indeed come from its wonderfully caustic humour about adolescent sexual curiosity, and sex remains a staple ingredient of Macdonald plays to date, she also has a remarkable skill in deciphering and uncovering the emotional terrain of young women, as subsequent plays have shown. *When I Was A Girl* was a remarkably honest study in stunted womanhood – of compromised choices, mother/daughter warfare, the dead hand of Presbyterianism and the pull of the past in the present. In her most recent play, *All Things Nice*, the variations on some of those themes are wittily and delicately worked out in a young Scottish schoolgirl's ambivalent relationships with her immediate circle: her best friend, her mother (absent in the Middle East), her grandmother and her grandmother's 'friend', her boyfriend and an off-stage 'flasher'. Macdonald's plays, along with those of Clare McIntyre and ▷Charlotte Keatley, have become worthy successors to ▷Shelagh Delany's *A Taste of Honey* in working out the parameters of female development.

Try these:
▷Clare McIntyre, for comparison; Nell Dunn's *Steaming*; for a Catholic variation on sexual repression, ▷Mary O'Malley; for mother and daughter relationships, ▷Julia Kearsley, ▷Louise Page, ▷Shelagh Delaney; ▷Neil Simon's *Brighton Beach Memoirs*, for a male equivalent; for Scottish adolescence see Muriel Spark's *The Prime of Miss Jean Brodie* and ▷John Byrne's *The Slab Boys Trilogy;* Daniel Mornin's *Kate* describes a young girl's growing up in Belfast; likewise ▷Christina Reid; Wendy Wasserstein's *The Heidi Chronicles* for an American equivalent of female coming-of-age.

McGRATH, John   [1935–]
British dramatist and director

Plays include:
A Man Has Two Fathers (1958), *Events While Guarding the Bofors Gun* (1966), *Random Happenings in the Hebrides* (1970), *Trees in the Wind* (1971), *Soft or a Girl* (1971; revised as *My Pal and Me*), *Fish in the Sea* (1972), *The Cheviot, the Stag and the Black, Black Oil* (1973), *The Game's a Bogey* (1974), *Little Red Hen* (1975), *Yobbo Nowt* (1975; also known as *Mum's the Word* and *Left Out Lady*), *Joe's Drum* (1979), *Bitter Apples* (1979), *Swings and Roundabouts* (1980), *Blood Red Roses* (1980), *Nightclass* (1981), *Rejoice!* (1982), *The Women of the Dunes* (1983), *The Baby and the Bathwater* (1984), *Behold the Sun* (1985; opera libretto with Alexander Goewr), *Mhàri Mhór* (1987)

McGrath is among the most inventive and prolific of contemporary socialist dramatists. He was a co-founder of *Z Cars* (an innovation in television police series), and directed arts shows, documentaries, and new plays until 1965 when he left full-time television work to concentrate on writing his own plays. In 1971 he founded 7:84 Theatre company. Much of his theatre work as a writer and director since then has been based with them, but he has continued to write and direct for television and film, and remains an insistent and important voice in socialist debates around drama, theatre and cultural forms, both in his theory and his practice.

Besides his own plays, much of McGrath's writing has been a reinterpretation of classic theatre texts. His version of *The Seagull* sets ▷Chekhov's play in the contemporary Scottish Highlands; *The Caucasian Chalk Circle* is set in a building site and McGrath has added a prologue spoken by Liverpool workers (a reworking which ▷Brecht would surely have approved).

The Cheviot, the Stag and the Black, Black Oil

The Cheviot, the Stag and the Black, Black Oil is a musical, which takes the form of a traditional Highland ceilidh, exemplifying the 7:84 principle of political theatre which is also a 'good night out'. It was developed with the 7:84 Scotland Company, who researched the text, and devised the music and performance in rehearsal with McGrath. The play is a chronicle of the economic exploitation of the Highlands, from the nineteenth-century 'clearances', which cleared land for profits from the Cheviot sheep, through the migration of Highlanders to Canada, to the appropriation of land for grouse-shooting, the development of North Sea Oil and tourism. The play also celebrates working-class struggle, from the refusal to enlist for the Crimean War to organised resistance against landlords. The television version, filmed in performance to a Highlands audience, in 1977, uses Brechtian alienation effects to demonstrate the mythologising of Scottish history.

Try these:
▷Brecht (*Caucasian Chalk Circle*; 1972), ▷Peter Terson (*Prisoners of the War*; 1972), ▷John Arden (*Serjeant Musgrave Dances On*; 1972), and ▷Aristophanes (*Women in Power; or Up the Acropolis*; 1983) are among the dramatists McGrath has reworked; ▷Brecht is a central influence; ▷John Arden and ▷Margaretta D'Arcy, ▷David Edgar, ▷Trevor Griffiths and ▷Howard Brenton are contemporary 'political' dramatists who have differing views of the most effective ways of reaching audiences; *Swings and Roundabouts* is a reworking of ▷Noël Coward's *Private Lives*.

McGRATH, Tom   [1940–]
British dramatist

Plays include:
The Great Northern Welly Boot Show (1972), *Laurel and Hardy* (1976), *The Hard Man* (1977), *The Android Circuit* (1978),

Sisters (1978), *The Innocent* (1979), *Animal* (1979), *123* (1981), *The Nuclear Family* (1982), *The Gambler* (1984), *End of the Line* (1984), *Pals* (1984), *Kora* (1986), *Thanksgiving* (1986), *Trivial Pursuits* (1988)

Already known as a musician and the creator of *International Times*, McGrath joined with Billy Connolly to celebrate the Upper Clyde Shipbuilders' work-in with *The Great Northern Welly Boot Show*, and since then has built a solid reputation as a playwright. To date his work has taken most of its impetus from autobiographical incident or from real events: *The Hard Man* is closely based on the life of Jimmy Boyle, Scotland's best-known ex-convict; *The Innocent* stems from his own involvement with drugs and the 'alternative society' of the 1960s; *123* clearly drew on personal experience of attempts to shake off society's demands with the aid of Buddhism and mythology. *Animal* is probably his most exotic piece, presenting a colony of apes under scrutiny from zoologists, with delightful and frequently comically surreal visions of ape movement and relationships before tragedy results from contact with the humans.

The Hard Man

A startling impressionistic account of a life of violence, based on the life of Jimmy Boyle. A clever use of non-naturalistic devices and direct address to the audience establishes a terrifying underworld of unthinking brutality and exposes the conditions which breed it, only to uncover an equally appalling world in the violence of prison life as authority tries to contain and break the spirit of dangerous inmates. It is a measure of McGrath's honesty that he does not turn his central figure into a stereotyped 'victim of society', but that having established him as a truly terrifying figure wedded to uncontrollable violence – telling his own version of the events depicted – he then finds in him a symbol for the enduring human spirit, at a point when he crouches naked in a cage smeared with excrement to protect himself from the attacks of prison officers. The play is a stimulating exercise in sustained anti-naturalism and theatricality in the service of serious thought.

Try these:
▷Eugene O'Neill's *The Hairy Ape*, Terry Johnsons' *Cries from the Mammal House* are zoological allegories; for more prisoner

portraits, ▷Genet's *Deathwatch*, various adaptations of *In the Belly of the Beast* by Jack Henry Abbott, Miguel Pinero's *Short Eyes* and John Herbert's *Fortune and Men's Eyes*.

McGUINNESS, Frank   [1953–]
Irish playwright

Plays include:
The Factory Girls (1982), *Baglady/Ladybag* (1985), *Observe The Sons of Ulster Marching Towards The Somme* (1985), *Innocence* (1986), *Carthaginians* (1988), *Mary and Lizzie* (1989), *Breadman* (1990)

McGuinness was born into a Catholic family in Buncrana, County Donegal where his mother worked in a local shirt factory and his father was a breadman. He went to University College Dublin and took a Masters degree in English and Medieval Studies, taught linguistics and drama at the University of Ulster, Coleraine, then returned to UCD to teach Old and Middle English, and now lectures in English at St Patrick's College Maynooth. He began writing at the age of 30 during a spell of unemployment, when he wrote *Factory Girls*. It is a funny, racily written tale of a group of women in a Donegal shirt factory who, faced with cuts and closure and advised to accept redundancies, decide to occupy the building. Its form is conventional and its tone naturalistic, and although well received it did nothing to prepare public or critics for the towering poetic language and the expressionistic forms, the passion and compassion combined with high moral and intellectual seriousness of his later work. His inspiration seems to be the need to give a voice to those who are oppressed or ignored, whether that is a group of factory workers, Protestant soldiers killed at the Somme, a victim of incest (*Baglady*), or two Irish sisters who lived with and influenced Engels yet who have been written out of history (*Mary and Lizzie*). He has an enviable ability to understand the other person's point of view (many mistakenly took him for a Protestant after *Observe The Sons*), and this gives him the rare distinction of being able to write excellent parts for women. His preoccupations are classically Irish as he himself admits (oppressed people, mother figures, father figures, religion, Irishness), but although he is a political writer, there are no easy answers to be found in his work. His translations and adaptations of the classics –

▷Lorca's *Yerma*, and ▷Ibsen's *Rosmersholm* and *Peer Gynt* – have broadened the scope of his own work. As translations, they are wirtten with exacting precision to produce a refreshingly spirited and effortless result (notably *Three Sisters* for the Abbey Theatre, Dublin, starring the Cusack family, Cyril, Sinead, Sorcha and Niamh). His stage plays are intensely theatrical, using objects in a very precise and symbolic way, but his television play *Henhouse* (starring Sinead Cusack) was a *tour de force* of television writing, the haunting story of a community closing in on a strange and silent woman who keeps her child locked up in a henhouse.

Observe the Sons of Ulster Marching Towards the Somme
Inspired by a visit to two war memorials and telling of the Protestant experience in World War I, McGuinness had to 'confront my own bigotry' to write it. It takes the form of an old man's reminiscences, which take tangible shape when the ghosts of his comrades in arms rise up to meet him. It is both a criticism and a celebration of the Irish obsession with the dead – the past must be understood, but bitterness and regret must not prevent progress. We see Pyper, the old man, in his youth as a mercurial, provocative, cynical middle-class sculptor who claims to have joined up to die. We see eight men the night they join up, on leave after several months at the front, and finally on the eve of the Battle of the Somme. Pyper eventually earns the respect of the others and the love of one in particular, and is the only one to survive the war. Unable to rebuild the world as he had hoped, he is left behind to speak for the dead. The play was first presented at the Abbey Theatre, directed by Patrick Mason and then at the Hampstead Theatre, London directed by Michael Attenborough. It won almost every prize available: the London *Evening Standard's* Most Promising Playwright award, the Rooney Prize for Irish Literature, the 1985 Harvey's Best Play Award, the Cheltenham Literary Prize, the *Plays and Players* Award and the London Fringe Award for Best Playwright and Best Play.

Try these:
▷Christine Reid's *My Name, Shall I Tell You My Name* also confronts an Orangeman's memories of World War I; ▷Seamus Finnegan's *The Spanish Play*

explores Irish Protestants and Catholics in Spain during the Civil War; other contemporary Irish playwrights include ▷Brian Friel and ▷Thomas Kilroy; ▷Sarah Daniels' *Beside Herself* also looks at the after-effects of incest; Charabanc's *Lay Up Your Ends* was another account of working-class women on strike.

MACHADO, Eduardo [1953–]
Cuban/American dramatist

Plays include:
The Modern Ladies of Guanabacoa (1983), *Fabiola* (1984), *Broken Eggs* (1984), *Stevie Wants to Play the Blues* (1990)

Machado was born to a wealthy family which was forced to flee Castro's Cuba. He arrived in the United States when he was eight years old without being able to speak English. The Machado family settled in Los Angeles where Eduardo was raised. These circumstances help to set the background for Machado's major work, the autobiographical 'Floating Islands' trilogy: *The Modern Ladies*, *Fabiola* and *Broken Eggs*. *The Modern Ladies* takes up the family story in 1930s' Cuba and explores the complex caste system. This play lays the foundation for subsequent family history which includes a final episode, *Broken Eggs*, set in Los Angeles. In *Stevie Wants to Play the Blues*, Machado breaks away from Cuba and the family to explore the life of 'Stevie', based on the real-life story of a young woman who can only realise her desire to become a jazz pianist by becoming a man.

Broken Eggs
Broken Eggs, although it is the final episode of the Guanabacoa trilogy, stands entirely on its own as a play. The central event of the play is a wedding which requires the attendance of the brides' divorced father. The dynamics of the family structure are set in high relief when the father insists on bringing his second wife to the party. The presence of this woman poses a threat not only to the primacy of the first wife but to the family myth that nothing has changed since Guanabacoa. Clearly, accepting the father's remarriage also means accepting the reality of lost dreams and exile in Los Angeles. Machado proves his dexterity as a writer by moving easily between hilarious satire and compelling drama. He displays a respect for Cuban tradition while maintaining the freedom to laugh at some of its absurdities. As the title indicates, to make an omelette you need to break eggs.

Try these:
▷DeFilippo for Italian family sagas; ▷Timberlake Wertenbaker's *New Anatomies*; most of ▷Shakespeare's comedies; ▷pantomime; Manfred Karge's *Man to Man* for cross-dressing; José Triana as another well-known Cuban dramatist; ▷David Hare's *Wrecked Eggs* for use of a similar metaphor.

MACHIAVELLI, Niccolo di Bernardo dei [1469–1527]
Italian political theorist and occasional dramatist

Plays include:
La Mandragola (1518), *Clizia* (1525)

Machiavelli was a civil servant in Florence under the republican government that succeeded the rule of Savonarola. He wrote his plays, and also *The Prince* (1513), in compulsory retirement in the country after the restoration of the Medici. *The Prince* was inspired by the expedient political methods of Cesare Borgia, rather than vice versa, but it led to his reputation in England and elsewhere for advocating the ruthless and amoral pursuit of power. Although *La Mandragola* is one of the best of Italian Renaissance comedies, it is probably Machiavelli's reputation as the Demon King (see for example ▷Marlowe's prologue to *The Jew of Malta*) which leads to its occasional appearance on the modern stage (as against plays by, say, Bembo or Ruzzante). It is a classical example of academic wish-fulfillment; the rich old lawyer Nicia is cuckolded by the dashing young scholar Callimaco, with the assistance of the parasite Ligurio and a pretended potion made from the mandrake root. Surprisingly, all live happily ever after.

Try these:
▷Marlowe for using 'Machiavel' as a prologue; Shared Experience for adapting Ruzzante as *Comedy Without a Title*; Giordano Bruno's *Il Candelaio* is another Italian Renaissance comedy that surfaces in the modern repertory.

McINTYRE, Clare   [1953–]
British dramatist

Plays include:
I've Been Running (1986), *Low Level Panic*
(*Don't Worry, It Might Not Happen*; 1988),
My Heart's a Suitcase (1990)

McIntyre turned to writing plays after spending some years acting on stage and in television and films. *I've Been Running*,
McIntyre's first play, a sharp two-hander,
delved into the murky waters of contemporary
sexual politics to take a look at the division
between the young modern woman (a bit of a
health freak, but questioning and curious
about life) and her sluggish, complacent boyfriend who can't understand what she is on
about at all. *Low Level Panic* has made the
biggest splash. Opening with a bathroom
scene, it is about three young women sharing
a flat together, with some sharp and revealing
writing (naturalistic dialogue and monologues
of internalised thoughts) on images, commer-
cialisation, female sexual fantasies, and the
more frightening realities as women experience them on the street. The action seldom
extends beyond the bathroom (except for a
monologue scene recounting a street attack on
one of the women and a fantasised revenge
sequence to do with an advertising hoarding),
and lacks overall development. Nonetheless,
Low Level Panic accurately articulates the current thoughts, fears and feelings of many
young women. *My Heart's a Suitcase* deals
with the emotional baggage with which we
surround ourselves and, like *Low Level Panic*,
succeeds in conveying the textures of quiet
desperation in everyday life, rather than gripping you with a strong plot line.

Try these:
▷Winsome Pinnock draws attention to
similar issues in *Picture Palace*; ▷Jacqui
Shapiro's *Dead Romantic* is another contemporary look into the sexual politics
scrum; ▷Ted Whitehead's *Alpha Beta* is
an older, male though equally pessimistic
view of coupledom; Lumiere and Son have
dealt with street and other female anxieties
in *Panic*; ▷Nell Dunn's *Steaming* is set in
a larger, public, bath; ▷Michel Tremblay's
Albertine in Five Times for an even more
extended application of the monologue
technique to express internal thoughts and
feelings; ▷Kay Adshead; ▷Sharman
Macdonald and ▷Julia Schofield are other
actress/writers.

McINTYRE, Dennis   [1943–90]
American dramatist

Plays include:
Modigliani (1978), *Split Second* (1986),
National Anthems (1986), *Established Price*
(1987)

Dennis McIntyre's first produced play,
Modigliani, was a poignant testament to his
struggle as a playwright, following the
painter's artistic achievement and commercial
failure. It was a cruel twist on McIntyre's
artistic creation imitating his life, since the
play was written in 1966 but not produced
until 1978, a predicament McIntyre faced repeatedly as he tried to have his plays presented in New York. Notice only came after
Modigliani and the successful presentations of
other pieces in regional venues. His early
death by cancer suspended hopes for additional plays that would demonstrate
McIntyre's ability to address global issues
through personalised situations. His second
play, *Split Second*, was an uncompromising
examination of personal integrity in a racially
charged confrontation, and his last work,
Established Price, was a timely scrutiny of corporate takeovers. Mel Gussow eulogises
McIntyre as 'a fine playwright with the potential to be a major one'.

National Anthems
The acquisition and materialism of 1980s'
America serves as the thematic core of
National Anthems. An archetypal young
couple have relocated to an affluent suburb.
Their vacuous identity is sharply defined by a
neighbour who happens in following their
housewarming. His cynical cracks and condescending questions serve as McIntyre's
thinly guised contempt for the 'me' generation
of the 1980s. *National Anthems* crackles with
pointed dialogue and clearly defined characters but sometimes descends to transparent
social righteousness. McIntyre does not move
the plot just by the psycho-therapeutic needs
of the characters, he punctuates the drama
with theatrical tricks. In one scene, the neighbour intentionally spills vodka on an expensive carpet. In another, McIntyre pits the
competitive homeowner against the aggressive
neighbour in a physical match: football in
the living room. The dramatic structure of
National Anthems combined with McIntyre's
stage knowhow, moves the play toward a resolution that echoes with questions long after
the final curtain.

Try these:
▷Albee's *Who's Afraid of Virginia Woolf?*, ▷Mike Leigh's *Abigail's Party*, ▷Pinter's *The Birthday Party* for celebrations that go wrong; ▷Doug Lucie for a British chronicler of the 'me' generation; ▷Caryl Churchill, *Serious Money* for takeovers; ▷David Pownall for artists of various kinds.

McLAUGHLIN, Ellen   [1957–   ]
American dramatist and actress

Plays include:
Days and Nights Within (1987), *A Narrow Bed* (1987), *Infinity's House* (1988)

Ellen McLaughlin has said her three plays demonstrate an interest in the 'potency of thought in dramatic action'. *Days and Nights Within*, based upon the imprisonment of Erica Wallach, depicts one woman's struggle to maintain personal integrity while undergoing extreme physical and psychological strain. *Infinity's House*, the structural opposite of *Days and Nights Within*, includes 37 characters and is set in the American west during three very different time periods. A sweeping work compared to its predecessor, *Infinity's House* remains rooted in the interpersonal relationships of people bound together by coincidence. Since *Infinity's House* McLaughlin has devoted more time to her acting career. She has also been working on a television script entitled *Hat Tricks*, based upon a friend's life in and out of the circus.

A Narrow Bed
Ellen McLaughlin's reputation as a playwright rests mostly upon *A Narrow Bed*, co-winner of the 1987 Susan Smith Blackburn Prize for women playwrights. The plot moves between past and present circumstances stemming from the Vietnam War. It shows individuals pressured to change ideals that were shaped by whether they decided to fight or to protest against that conflict. The thread of the play lies in personal stories from members of a farm commune. One woman's husband remains missing in action, a tragic and unexplained reversal of his earlier activism against the war. Another woman's husband lies dying of alcoholism, the last man of the farm and another mockery of the ideals that founded the commune. The women's steadfast friend-

ship serves as a challenge to the Vietnam generation, and others, about the solidity of their values.

Try these:
▷Melissa Murray's *Body-Cell* for a woman imprisoned; ▷Arnold Wesker's *Caritas* for a more voluntary confinement; ▷Arthur Kopit's *Indians* for the American West; ▷Emily Mann, ▷David Rabe for Vietnam plays.

McLURE, James   [1951–   ]
American dramatist

Play include:
Lone Star (1979), *Pvt. Wars* (1979), *Laundry and Bourbon* (1980), *The Day They Shot John Lennon* (1983), *Thanksgiving* (1983), *Wild Oats* (1984), *Max and Maxie* (1984), *The Very Last Lover of the River Cane* (1985), *Lahr and Mercedes* (1985), *Fran and Brian* (1988), *Napoleon Nightdreams* (1987), *The Agent* (1989), *The Hair Cut* (1990)

Born in Louisiana and educated in Texas, McLure first pursued a career as an actor. He made his mark as a playwright in New York with plays about Texas. His tough-talking bar-room brawlers spoke Texan, a hyperbolic language frequently punctuated with hilarious backwoods expressions. McLure made a significant contribution to the well-developed macho mystique of the Southwest. Several of his plays were premiered at regional theatres such as the Actors' Theatre of Louisville, Denvier Theatre Centre, and the McCarter Theatre. Lately, McLure has turned his attention to the urban romantic landscape emerging as a sensitive and witty observer of the post-Woodstock generation, a generation suffering from loss of innocence and idealism while being over burdened by materialism. His current work although more complex and mature is less striking than his earlier work indicating that McLure has yet to find his niche with this new material.

Lone Star
Lone Star takes its name from the long-necked bottled beer made in Texas that is consumed in great quantities in this one act play. Roy, the only 'Vit Nam Vet' in Maynard, Texas, is the play's hero. Although he has been home from the war for two years, he does nothing but drink and tell stories about his wartime

prowess and his sexaul conquests. Roy is both worshipped and feared by Ray, his kid brother, and Cletis, an appliance-store salesman. During the course of the play, Cletis steals Roy's 1959 pink Thunderbird and smashes it to pieces. Ray who fears being thought of as Cletis' accomplice decides to distract Roy by revealing that he slept with Roy's wife, Elizabeth, while Roy was away at war. Although the play contains the seeds of a violent and tragic confrontation, McLure converts the tension into an uproarious folk farce. *Lone Star* and *Laundry and Bourbon* have met with success throughout the United States, Canada and Britain. They are frequently revived.

Try these:
▷Emily CMann's *Still Life*, ▷Romulus Linney's *Love Suicide at Schofield Barracks*, James Duff's *The War Back Home* for Vietnam plays; ▷Stephen Lowe's *Touched* and Terence Rattigan's *Flarepath* for British wartime domestic dramas.

McNALLY, Terrence   [1939–]
American dramatist

Plays include:
Things That Go Bump in the Night (1965), *Botticelli* (1968), *Next* (1969), *Noon* (1968), *Sweet Eros* (1968), *Where Has Tommy Flowers Gone?* (1971), *Whiskey* (1973), *Bad Habits* (1974), *The Ritz* (1975), *Broadway, Broadway* (1978), *It's Only A Play* (1982), *The Rink* (musical; 1984), *Frankie and Johnny in the Clair De Lune* (1987), *The Lisbon Traviata* (1989), *Up In Saratoga* (1989), *Hope* (1989), *Kiss of the Spider Woman* (musical; 1990), *Lips Together Teeth Apart* (1991)

McNally began his career as a writer of sharp-edge black comedy and satire, developing his craft in the off-Broadway movement of the late sixties and seventies. A mordant social critic, his characters were eccentric, displaced victims of society desperately seeking refuge. In his early works, McNally's craft is rooted in finding contemporary situations and embellishing them with a prickling display of verbal humour. Few are more adept with bitchy one-liners than McNally, earning him a reputation as a master of the comedy of insult. Unlike many of his contemporaries, he continues to

work closely with a collaborative group of actors and directors. He has never been afraid to rewrite his plays two or three times even after openings. The results of McNally's persistence are now apparent. His most recent plays continue to crackle wittily yet they have moved closer to reality showing a compassionate understanding of character and relationships.

Frankie and Johnny in The Clair de Lune
Frankie and Johnny chronicles the developing relationship between two ordinary middle-aged people who work at the same restaurant. Frankie is an embittered, self-protective waitress fearing commitment while Johnny, a short-order cook, is ready to serve up heaping measures of marriage and family. We discover them after a passionate, 'get-acquainted' session of lovemaking discussing all the reasons why their relationship can't succeed. Obviously, their level of physical intimacy belies deeper feelings of alienation and distrust. In this play, McNally has managed to connect humour with character allowing Frankie and Johnny to reveal themselves through repartee that is both funny and painful. The play moves from night towards a rosy dawn suggesting that intimacy is possible even in an age when everything seems to militate against it.

Try these:
▷Noël Coward's *Private Lives* for an oddly parallel view of human relationships; Doug Lucie, Alan Ayckbourn, Neil Simon for variations on comedy of manners.

MAMET, David   [1947–]
American dramatist

Plays include:
American Buffalo (1975), *Sexual Perversity in Chicago* (1976), *Duck Variations* (1976), *Reunion* (1977), *The Woods* (1977), *The Water Engine* (1977), *A Life In the Theatre* (1978), *Lakeboat* (1981), *Edmond* (1982), *Glengarry Glen Ross* (1983), *Vermont Sketches* (1984), *Prairie du Chien* (1985), *The Shawl* (1985), *The Frog Prince* (1985), *Speed-the-Plow* (1988), *Sketches of War* (1988), *Bobby Gould in Hell* (1989), Adaptation of Chekhov's *Uncle Vanya* (1991), *Where Were You When It Went Down* (1991)

The Chicago-born playwright David Mamet is that unique American dramatist whose work seems simultaneously absolutely indigenous to the USA and peculiarly European. While his expletive-laden language and volatile situations seem part of an innately American idiom, his understanding of linguistic wordplay and of silence recalls such English and European forebears as ▷Beckett and ▷Pinter, and Mamet's British acclaim both at the ▷National Theatre (where *Glengarry Glen Ross* had its world premiere) and the Royal Court is not surprising. Still, as the co-founder of Chicago's St Nicholas Theatre Company, where he functioned as both playwright-in-residence and artistic director, he writes with that city's street-wise, colloquial rhythm, whether on subjects as dense as the underside of American capitalism (*American Buffalo, Glengarry Glen Ross*) or as relatively benign as the intertwined lives and careers of two actors (*A Life In the Theatre*). His plays rarely have more than two or three characters (*Speed-the-Plow*, his three-character Broadway hit of 1988, marked the Broadway debut of Madonna), and works like *Edmond* – an impressionistic tableau about one man's descent into Sodom and Gomorrah in New York – are unusual. More typical is a piece like *The Shawl*, a three-character play about a charlatan seer, which further dissects a topic – the psychology of the con game – that Mamet returns to time and again (it's the raison d'être of *House of Games*, the 1987 film on which he made his directorial debut). His plays, of course, speak of another kind of shawl: the cloak of language beneath which lies a multiplicity of human instincts too few playwrights address with Mamet's courage.

American Buffalo

Three small-time crooks bungle a coin robbery, and out of their comedy of frustration Mamet weaves an exhilaratingly telling and poignant account of avarice and ambition in which the promise of monetary gain makes everyone both victor and victim. (The title refers to an American coin, an old nickle that Bobby, the young addict, finds in Act Two.) At once edgy and elegiac in tone, the play is also a rending treatment of friendship under stress, and its three roles – the mastermind Teach; the older shop-owner Donny; and his side-kick, Bobby – are so superbly written that it's small wonder the play pops up on the London fringe and in regional theatre, perhaps more than any other American drama.

'Fuckin' business' reads the last line of Act One, and a few plays have summed up the price of the capitalist ethic with such terse and moving irony.

Bobby Gould in Hell

This comprises a one-act coupled with another one-act by Shel Silverstein and produced under the title *In Hell* at Lincoln Center Theater in 1989. The title character is one of the movie producers in *Speed-the-Plow*.

> **Try these:**
> ▷Arthur Miller (especially *Death of A Salesman*) and ▷Clifford Odets for socially conscious writing, often about the limits of American capitalism; other recent serio-comic satires on American business include Jerry Steiner's *Other People's Money*, ▷Keith Reddin's *Life During Wartime*, Matthew Witten's *The Deal*, and Richard Fire and June Shellene's *Dealing*; ▷Georg Büchner's *Woyzeck* for *Edmond*-like descents into a psychological hell; ▷Kaufman and Hart, and Terrence McNally's *It's Only A Play*, ▷Richard Nelson's *Two Shakespearean Actors* and ▷Bulgakov's *Black Snow* for works about the theatre; ▷Sam Shepard, ▷Harold Pinter, ▷Samuel Beckett for charting that elusive terrain midway between speech and silence. ▷David Rabe for raw examination of male relationships; ▷Sam Shepard for American archetypes.

MANCHESTER SCHOOL

This is the name commonly given to a small school of regional playwrights who flourished at the Gaiety Theatre in Manchester from 1908. Annie Horniman, who also co-founded the Abbey Theatre in Dublin, managed the Gaiety as a repertory theatre until 1917, specialising in naturalistic productions of local plays, many of them with 'strong' parts for women (often played by Sybil Thorndike). The two playwrights whose work still appears most often, ▷Harold Brighouse and ▷Stanley Houghton, were both from Manchester.

The 'Manchester School' did not survive World War I, but other plays produced at the Gaiety would be worth reviving, eg Allan Monkhouse's *Mary Broome* (1911), not a Lancashire play, but in the same vein of careful naturalism and social questioning (a middle-class man makes an unsatisfactory marriage to a parlourmaid when the girl becomes pregnant; again the girl has the strongest part, showing qualities of survival); or Elizabeth Baker's *Chains* (1911), a fresh, understated, non-didactic play whose characters come to question their reasons for either staying in boring jobs or marrying to get free of them.

Try these:

Other repertory theatres past and present – the Court Theatre under Granville Barker provided the pattern for the Gaiety's seasons; the Glasgow Citizens' Theatre; and Lilian Baylis whose efforts at the Old Vic predated the ▷National Theatre by a good half century, and were a precursor to ▷Joan Littlewood's still unfulfilled dream of a 'fun palace' for the people; see also ▷Harold Brighouse and ▷Stanley Houghton.

MANN, Emily   [1952–]
American playwright and director

Plays include:
Annulla Allen: Autobiography of a Survivor (1974), *Still Life* (1980), *Execution of Justice* (1983), *Nights and Days* (1985), *Betsey Brown* (in collaboration with ▷Ntozake Shange; 1989)

Emily Mann launched her career as a director and playwright with incursions into traditionally male theatre bastions. A Harvard graduate who apprenticed at the Guthrie while earning an MFA at the University of Minnesota, she was the first woman to direct on the Guthrie's main stage. Her directing work has since taken her to prestigious repertory theatres such as the Actors' Theatre of Louisville, The Goodman, La Jolla Playhouse, the Mark Taper Forum, Hartford Stage and BAM Theatre Company. All of Mann's plays use outside source material: interviews (*Annulla*, *Still Life*) and court transcripts (*Execution of Justice*), for example. Her theatre harks back to the Federal Theatre's Living Newspapers and has been called 'Theatre of Testimony'.

Execution of Justice
Execution of Justice, which opened at New York's Virginia Theatre in January 1986, marked Mann's Broadway debut as both author and director and was the first time a woman had ever directed her own play for the Broadway stage. Based on the court transcripts of the trial of Dan White, the drama

retells the events surrounding the killings of San Francisco mayor, George Moscone, and city supervisor, Harvey Milk, and directly confronts homosexual issues and homophobia. The production failed to capture critical acclaim. However, she has directed some of her other own works with great success in New York, notably *Still Life* in 1981 at the American Place Theatre where it won six Obies. A Vietnam War play, it is based on actual taped interviews with a veteran, his wife and his mistress, and shows how war can transform a gentle man into an eager and willing killer. Presented as a clever cross-cutting of three monologues, it is her strongest and most successful stage work to date, and won a First Fringe Award at the Edinburgh Festival in 1982.

Selected in December 1989 for a three-year appointment as Artistic Director of the prestigious McCarter Theatre of Princeton, Mann launched her reign there with a production of *The Glass Menagerie*. Among her many awards are a Guggenheim and NEA Playwrights Fellowship, a CAPS Grant, a McKnight Fellowship in Theatre.

Try these:

For treatment of the Vietnam War see ▷David Rabe's *Streamers* and *The Basic Training of Pavlo Hummel*; for courtroom dramas about actual events see Abe Polsky's *Devour the Snow*, Saul Levitt's *The Andersonville Trial*, ▷Peter Weiss' *The Investigation* and Tom Topor's *Nuts*.

MARCHANT, Tony   [1959–]
British dramatist

Plays include:
Remember Me? (1980), *London Calling* (1981), *Thick as Thieves* (comprising *London Calling* and *Dealt;* 1981), *Stiff* (1982), *Raspberry* (1982), *The Lucky Ones* (1982), *Welcome Home* (1983), *Lazy Days Ltd* (1984), *The Attractions* (1987), *The Speculators* (1987)

A grammar-school-educated, working-class East Ender of Catholic parents, Tony Marchant has become one of Britain's major young playwrights, but alas for the stage, now writes more often for television. He came to prominence, along with Mick Mahoney, ▷Barry Keeffe, and Andy Armitage as one of the 'Angry Young Cockney', 'Yobbo' playwrights – something of a misnomer for

Marchant himself, who is immensely likeable and very far from being a 'yobbo'. But certainly his early plays showed a remarkable capacity to articulate the problems and feelings of East End youngsters, often unemployed, with sensitivity and compassion. A Marchant world was a jungle where the scavenging law of economics was never very far away.

Remember Me? is a young, unemployed school-leaver's cry of outrage against an educational system he felt failed him. *The Lucky Ones* (those who have jobs), is an equally passionate yet witty riposte to the argument of a 'job at any price' as a group of young East Enders battle for advancement in the bowels of a large stockbroking firm opposed by an emblematic working-class rebel anti-hero who refuses to bend the knee to the system. In contrast, *Raspberry* is a short study about the social stigmas surrounding abortion and infertility, treated with great skill, shown through the growing friendship between two women who find themselves in hospital in adjoining beds.

His two most recent stage plays, *The Attractions* and *The Speculators* were perhaps different sides of the Thatcher coin. *The Attractions* is a fascinating study about violence, juxtaposing examples from the past (it is set in a museum of horrors on Britain's south coast) with present-day manifestations, and triggered once again by one of those not enjoying the fruits of Thatcherism. *The Speculators*, on the other hand, dug into a seam that was mined by other writers (such as ▷Caryl Churchill and also the women's group Burnt Bridges with *Deals*), focusing on the City and financial greed, but unlike Churchill's *Serious Money*'s stock-exchange activities, it concentrated on the foreign exchange market where, said Marchant, the jumping pound was more synonymous with national identity.

Welcome Home

Commissioned by Paines Plough, this was one of the first plays to take a look at the Falklands. Characteristically, Marchant spent time with an army unit before sitting down to write, and his beautifully constructed play, centred round a group of paratroopers assembled to bury one of their number with full military honours, constantly mirrors that authenticity: in its refusal to present its soldiers as ciphers, and in its understanding of the army mentality and its disadvantages (in

the shape of an over-zealous corporal whose belligerence and neo-fascism are barely under control). Equally in its awareness of the emotional and psychological price paid in that South Atlantic exercise, Marchant's play makes a tangible plea for a new kind of masculinity, based on an acknowledgement of weakness as much as forced machismo.

Try these:

▷R.C. Sherriff's *Journey's End* makes similar points about the psychological traumas of war; ▷Noël Greig's *Poppies* for Gay Sweatshop explored a pacifist ethic; ▷Robert Holman, ▷Louise Page, and Greg Cullen have dealt with aspects of the Falklands; for comparison with post-Vietnam responses see Emily Mann's *Still Life*, ▷David Rabe's *Streamers* and Stephen Metcalfe's *Strange Snow*, filmed as *Jackknife* starring Robert DeNiro. ▷Doug Lucie's *Fashion* for a jaundiced study of go-getting comparable with *Speculators*; ▷Michael Ellis' *Chameleon* looks at being on the make from a black perspective; Bill Cain's *Stand-Up Tragedy* and Shirley Lauro's *Open Admissions* for indictments of the US educational system's neglect of the underprivileged. Robin Glendenning's *Donny Boy*, ▷Terry Johnson's *Imagine Drowning*, and Heinar Kipphardt's *Brother Eichmann* are other investigations into the roots of violence. ▷Tony Craze's *Angelus* and Billy Roche's *A Handful of Stars* are examples of contemporary protest expressed through anti-heroes, (Roche's is an Irish counterpart of the young James Dean's *Rebel Without a Cause*); ▷Jim Cartwright's *Road* is an outcry against unemployment.

MARCUS, Frank   [1928–   ]
British dramatist and critic

Plays include:
The Formation Dancers (1964), *The Killing of Sister George* (1966), *Notes on a Love Affair* (1972)

Born in Germany, but arriving in Britain in 1939, Marcus acted, directed and ran an antiques business as well as writing. With well over a score of plays produced, he is best known for *The Killing of Sister George*, a study of a disintegrating lesbian partnership in which the butch half is a radio soap lead about to be killed off in the programme. A serious study of caring, need and dominance, its sadness is heightened by its hilarity. Unfortunately, due to the paucity of mainstream plays with lesbian characters, *The Killing of Sister George* has become the stereotypical image of lesbians and their relationships and despite many variants on the fringe to the contrary, *George* maintains a fierce hold on the public imagination. Marcus' earlier success, *The Formation Dancers*, a much lighter four-hander, presents feigned infidelity as a method of regaining an unfaithful husband, but the treatment of women and love is a recurrent theme in much of his later work.

Marcus' work has some echoes of ▷Molnar and ▷Schnitzler whose work he has adapted. He has also adapted Kaiser and Hauptmann.

Try these:
▷Charles Dyer's *Staircase* for a comparable treatment of male homosexuality; ▷Maureen Duffy's *Rites*, ▷Lillian Hellman's *The Children's Hour* for earlier examples of lesbian themes; ▷Lesbian Theatre and ▷Sarah Daniels; ▷Andrew Davies' *Prin*; ▷Bryony Lavery's *Her Aching Heart* for a very different treatment of lesbian love.

MARGULIES, Donald   [1954–]
American dramatist

Plays include:
Resting Place (1982), *Gifted Children* (1983), *Found a Peanut* (1984), *The Model Apartment* (1988), *The Loman Family Picnic* (1989), *What's Wrong with This Picture* (1990)

Donald Margulies' Jewish heritage is his dramatic foundation and is demonstrated by his ability to capture Jewish humour and values in believable characters and caricatures. This strength may be a limitation since he has been criticised for not extending the characterisations into plots of more universal implication; *Gifted Children* is indicative of this problem. Margulies' more recent effort, *What's Wrong with this Picture*, which was premiered at the Jewish Repertory Theatre while he was playwright in residence, demonstrates a potential for overcoming this critique. It surrounds with humour the death of a Brooklyn housewife, and demonstrates Margulies' sensitive insight into how the woman's surviving husband and son reconcile their familial relationship. Primarily a playwright (Margulies is a member of New Dramatists and The Dramatists Guild), he also has written screenplays and a number of television scripts.

The Loman Family Picnic
The boy's bar mitzvah, one of the most celebrated rituals among Jewish families, is often stereotyped as an exaggerated event of lavish presents and big cheques. *The Loman Family Picnic* takes license with this stereotype as a family reveals some of their less admirable traits prior to the eldest son's bar mitzvah. The mother relishes the social importance of the event and the father transforms into a green eyed avaricious monster. The play has unusual, if not unworkable, dramatic effects including the ghostly appearance of an aunt who died in the Holocaust plus four separate endings. *The Loman Family Picnic* gets its title from the youngest son's efforts to write a musical version of ▷Arthur Miller's *Death of A Salesman*. Unfortunately, Margulies' attempts to convey a family's anguish and disconnection does not compare with Miller's classic.

Try these:
▷Neil Simon, ▷Wendy Wasserstein, and ▷Arnold Wesker for Jewish upbringings; Bernard Kops for a British equivalent; ▷Rolf Hochhuth, ▷C.P. Taylor's *Good* for Holocaust plays; ▷Catherine Hayes, ▷Charlotte Keatley, ▷Eugene O'Neill for families.

MARIVAUX, Pierre Carlet de Chamblain de   [1688–1763]
French dramatist and novelist

Plays include:
Arlequin Poli par L'Amour (*Harlequin Polished by Love*; 1720), *La Double Inconstance* (*The Double Inconstancy*; 1723), *Le Jeu de L'Amour et du Hasard* (*The Game of Love and Chance*; 1723), *Le Triomphe de l'Amour* (*The Triumph of Love*; 1732), *L'Heureux Stratagème* (*Successful Strategies*; 1733), *Les Fausses Confidences* (*False Admissions*; 1737), *L'Epreuve* (*The Test*; 1740), *La Dispute* (*The Dispute*; 1744)

Marivaux was born of a nouveau riche family (his father started as Carlet and added the 'de Chamblain' and 'de Marivaux' as he moved up the pecking order), but lost his money in the Mississippi scheme (the French equivalent of Britain's South Sea Bubble), and so was forced to make his living by writing plays, novels and journalism, and by relying on the generosity of various noble ladies who welcomed his wit in their salons; he made it to the Academy in 1742. His long association with the Comédie-Italienne and their lively acting helped to make his plays successful; indeed it was noticeable that those of his plays put on by the Comédie Française worked much less well. His best known plays deal with the beginnings of love, often unrecognised and sometimes unwelcome, through subtle dialogue rather than complicated plots. This delicate dialogue was found affected by some of his contemporaries, who called it 'marivaudage', but in fact it wears (and acts) very well. Out of fashion in English for most of the twentieth century, he now seems to be doing rather better, particularly in ▷Timberlake Wertenbaker's translations of *False Admissions* and *Successful Strategies* which successfully bring out the complexity and ambiguity of these delightful plays. Clearly Marivaux is not as difficult to translate as people have long said. There are some thirty other plays that have never been produced in English.

Try these:
▷Beaumarchais for eighteenth-century French comedy, though with much broader brushstrokes and a larger canvas; ▷Turgenev's *A Month in the Country* for a comparable game of love and chance, but without a happy ending; ▷Noël Coward's *Private Lives* for a set of mixed doubles like *The Double Inconstancy*.

MARLOWE, Christopher [1564–1593]
English Renaissance dramatist

Plays include:
Tamburlaine the Great, I and II (1587), *Doctor Faustus* (c 1588), *The Jew of Malta* (c 1589), *Edward II* (c 1592), *The Massacre at Paris* (c 1592), *Dido, Queen of Carthage* (c 1593)

Marlowe led a brief and turbulent life in which he was involved in espionage, accused of heretical opinions and killed in a pub brawl before the case was tried in circumstances which suggest that he may have been eliminated to avoid political embarrassment. He also managed to write plays which gave a new impetus to Renaissance theatre writing. Unfortunately, some of them have only been preserved in mangled form but, with the exception of the two last plays, they are still staged fairly regularly and even *The Massacre at Paris* has been staged by the ▷Glasgow Citizens' Theatre. *Tamburlaine* is interesting because of Marlowe's use of what ▷Ben Jonson called the 'mighty line' to display the superhuman characteristics of its hero, who starts off a shepherd in Part I, conquers the world, and then dies in Part II. The play presents a full circle of Fortune's Wheel but there is little dramatic conflict and no particular tension within the presentation of Tamburlaine himself – his tragedy arises simply from the fact that, in the end, he is not superhuman. *The Jew of Malta*, a savage farce, also has a larger than life protagonist, the comic villain Barabbas, who indulges in wholesale Machiavellian slaughter until he, literally, falls into one of his own traps. *Edward II* has a more developed set of conflicts between characters and, although the verse is less obviously memorable than in some of Marlowe's other plays, there is a satisfying movement in the play as Edward's fortunes decline and Mortimer's rise only to fall again.

Doctor Faustus
Faustus sells his soul to Mephistopheles in return for twenty-four years of magic power but those years are spent mainly in comic conjuring exercises and slapstick. So, although there is powerful verse and a real tragic situation at the beginning and at the end, the play can tend to sag in the middle since many directors find it hard to reconcile the clowning with the sense of Faustus' tragic situation. The best productions are those which try to bring out the way in which these scenes show Faustus frittering away the possibilities open to him thus emphasising the tragedy of his bargain.

Try these:
Other plays which use the Faust legend are ▷Goethe's *Faust*, ▷Howard Brenton and ▷David Hare's *Pravda*, and ▷Vaclav Havel's *Temptation*; ▷Shakespeare's *Merchant of Venice* offers an interesting comparison with Marlowe's treatment of the Jews; ▷Brecht adapted *Edward II* and the English version of his play is sometimes staged; ▷Kyd, ▷Middleton, ▷Webster and other English Renaissance dramatists

MAROWITZ, Charles   [1934–]
American-born director, dramatist, editor and critic, long resident in London

Plays include:
Artaud at Rodez (1975), *Shakespeare: Adaptations and Collages of Hamlet, Macbeth, The Taming of the Shrew, Measure for Measure, The Merchant of Venice* (published 1978), *Clever Dick, Sex Wars: Free Adaptations of Ibsen and Strindberg* (published 1983), *Sherlock's Last Case* (1987), *Disciples* (published 1987), *Wilde West* (1989)

Marowitz, born in New York, went to Britain in the 1950s to act and direct; he worked with ▷Peter Brook on *King Lear* in 1962, and on the experimental Theatre of Cruelty season at LAMDA in 1963. ▷Brook and ▷Artaud have been continuing influences on his work. He was founding Artistic Director of the Open Space Theatre from 1968 to 1979, with his indispensable colleague Thelma Holt as administrator and actress. They put on a wide range of plays, including new or previously unproduced work by ▷Howard Brenton, ▷Peter Barnes, ▷David Edgar, ▷Howard Barker, ▷Trevor Griffiths, and ▷Sam Shepard; they also staged a number of Marowitz's own 'collage' or cut-up versions of ▷Shakespeare. *Hamlet* (1966) is probably the most successful of these, perhaps because the play is so familiar to most audiences, but the Black Power *Othello* (1972) and the feminist *Shrew* (1973) are also effective, and are still put on by student and experimental groups. All his work, both as author and director, displays and enjoys great power to shock. In his collage works he used film-like techniques to switch rapidly from one image to another, dream or nightmare sequences, verbal and visual shock tactics, simple sets, and aggressive lighting. In other productions he used 'environmental' staging – for example in the opening production, John Herbert's *Fortune and Men's Eyes* (1968), he transformed the theatre into a prison; in *Palach* he used multiple stages; and in his production of Picasso's *Four Little Girls* the audience entered through a tiny door into a colourful Alice in Wonderland fantasy world, which cost more than the Open Space's total grant for a year.

Marowitz has written lively accounts of his work with Brook and his ideas on acting, and he is a fine bruising critic of other people's theatre – see for instance *Confessions of a Counterfeit Critic* (1973) and *The Method as Means* (1981); and some of his Open Space productions would be interesting to revive. Though few of the Open Space productions reached the West End, one of his 'potboilers' (*Sherlock's Last Case*) did quite well on Broadway in 1987–8. Since then the play has had several notable American revivals. Recent directing work includes ▷Orton's *What the Butler Saw* and ▷Chekhov's *The Seagull*, both at Los Angeles Theatre Centre and *A Macbeth*, which he also wrote, at Odyssey Theatre Ensemble in Los Angeles. His translation of ▷Ionesco's *Macbett* was done in 1987 at the Wilma Theater in Philadelphia and the following season at Playhouse on the Square, Memphis, Tennessee.

Try these:
▷Peter Brook, for collaboration on Artaud-influenced work; ▷Genet's *Deathwatch* for prison and homosexual themes; see also the Wooster Group for a company of collage makers; ▷Tom Stoppard's *Rosencrantz and Guildenstern are Dead* and ▷Lee Blessing's *Fortinbras* draw on *Hamlet*, as does W.S. Gilbert's *Rosencrantz and Guildenstern*; Chris Hardman's Antenna Theater, much of ▷Ann Bogart's work, the Yugoslav radical theatre group Red Pilot, and Germany's Peter Stein also transform their spaces into part of the theatrical experience.

MARSTON, John   [1576–1634]
English Renaissance dramatist

Plays include:
Antonio and Mellida (1599), *Antonio's Revenge* (1600), *The Dutch Courtesan* (1604), *The Malcontent* (1604), *The Fawn* (1605; also known as *Parasitaster*)

Marston, like John Donne, eventually became an Anglican clergyman but before that he had a fairly successful career as a satirical poet and dramatist, being heavily involved in the so-called 'War of the Theatres' in which a number of dramatists, including ▷Jonson, attacked one another in a succession of plays. He often wrote within the popular revenge conventions of his day but both *Antonio and Mellida* and *The Malcontent*, despite the sordidness and corruption of their court worlds and their apparently tragic dynamic, have 'happy' endings. *The Dutch Courtesan* also operates on the fringes of tragi-comedy. *Antonio's Revenge*, the second part of *Antonio and Mellida*, is, however, a fully fledged revenge tragedy in the traditional Elizabethan mode. Although his tendency to dwell on excretion and sexuality is probably more acceptable than it might once have been, Marston tends to be an occasional rather than a regular feature of the contemporary repertory, perhaps because so many of his characters, situations and plots are to be found elsewhere in Renaissance drama, handled in ways that have proved more acceptable to modern audiences.

Try these:
Most Renaissance dramatists used revenge plots and malcontent figures – ▷Shakespeare's *Hamlet* is the most famous example of both, but ▷Kyd's *The Spanish Tragedy* started the vogue for revenge and there are notable examples in ▷Tourneur, ▷Webster and ▷Middleton; there are disguised Dukes (like Malevole in *The Malcontent*) in many Renaissance plays, notably *Measure for Measure* and *The Tempest*; Malevole has also been compared to the protagonist of ▷Brecht's *The Good Person of Szechwan*.

MASSINGER, Philip   [1583–1640]
English Renaissance dramatist

Plays include:
A New Way to Pay Old Debts (1625), *The Roman Actor* (1626), *The City Madam* (1632)

Massinger eventually succeeded ▷Fletcher as resident dramatist with the King's Men, writing jointly or singly some fifty-five plays. The manuscripts of eight of them were used to line pie dishes in the eighteenth century and others have also failed to survive. Only *A New Way to Pay Old Debts*, a satirical comedy of contemporary manners, which uses such stock elements as young lovers outwitting parental marriage plans, a young man reduced to poverty who is still a gentleman at heart, and a wily servant outwitting his master, survives in the contemporary repertory. Much of its success has been due to the popularity of its apparently larger than life protagonist Sir Giles Overreach, whose extravagant extortions and ultimate madness have long been a favourite with actors and audiences. In fact, Overreach is based on the historical Sir Giles Mompesson, a particularly outrageous figure of the period who was eventually tried and convicted for his corrupt practices. *The City*

Madam (also a citizen comedy but its prodigal turns out to be corrupt when given a second chance) was revived in the 1960s and is probably due for another production but *The Roman Actor*, despite its use of three plays within plays and a speech defending the profession of actor which should make it appeal to the post-modernist sensibility, has not yet had a large scale contemporary revival.

Try these:
▷Marlowe's Tamburlaine and Faustus are probably the most famous Renaissance over-reachers, though ▷Shakespeare's *Twelfth Night* contains another fine comic example in Malvolio; ▷Dekker, ▷Heywood, ▷Middleton and ▷Jonson wrote comedies of contemporary London life; many Restoration comedies tackle similar themes, as does ▷Caryl Churchill's *Serious Money*; ▷Howard Brenton and ▷David Hare's *Pravda* offers a contemporary portrait of the megalomaniac businessman; for plays about the theatre ▷Michael Frayn's *Noises Off*, ▷Pirandello's *Six Characters in Search of an Author*, ▷Bulgakov's *Molière*.

MASTROSIMONE, William   [1947–]
American dramatist

Plays include:
The Woolgatherer (1980), *Extremities* (1981), *A Tantalizing* (1982), *Shivaree* (1983), *The Undoing* (1984), *Nanawatai* (1985), *Cat's Paw* (1986), *Tamer of Horses* (1986), *The Understanding* (1987), *A Stone Carver* (1988), *Sunshine* (1989)

Acclaimed for his play and film versions of *Extremitites*, (it won the Outer Critics' Circle Award for Best off-Broadway play in 1983), Mastrosimone has fearlessly taken on the tough themes of our day: rape, pornography, vengeance, power and guilt. His plays present unbalanced characters thrown into intense and dangerous situations that threaten their survival. In *Extremitites*, a woman fights off an attempted rape and traps her attacker. In her rage, her dilemma is whether to destroy him or let him go – a choice which she cannot make. Controversial because of its difficult subject matter, the play was lauded by some and criticised by others for its overly happy conclusion that we are all bound by a common humanity.

This idea was examined earlier in *The*

Woolgatherer, where a disturbed girl obsessed with images of death and violence and collecting men's sweaters, projects her fears onto a mythical friend and brings home a trucker looking for a sexual encounter. Mastrosimone shows us the pain and humour involved in two desperate people's struggle to reach out and trust.

Mastrosimone is currently the playwright-in residence at Seattle Repertory Theatre.

Try these:
▷Shakespeare's *Titus Andronicus* for treatment of rape; ▷Amiri Baraka's *The Dutchman* and ▷Marsha Norman's *Getting Out* for women committing violence; ▷Shepard's *True West* and ▷Pinter's *The Birthday Party* for power struggle in relationships; Ariel Dorfman's *Death and the Maiden* for the ethics of revenge after rape and torture.

MATURA, Mustapha   [1939–]
Trinidadian dramatist

Plays include:
Black Pieces (1970), *As Time Goes By* (1971), *Bakerloo Line* (1972), *Nice* (1973), *Play Mas* (1974), *Black Slaves, White Chains* (1975), *Rum an' Coca Cola* (1976), *Bread* (1976), *Another Tuesday* (1978), *More More* (1978), *Independence* (1979), *Welcome Home Jacko* (1979), *A Dying Business* (1980), *One Rule* (1981), *Meetings* (1981), *The Playboy of the West Indies* (1984), *Trinidad Sisters* (1988), *The Coup: A Play of Revolutionary Dreams* (1991)

Trinidad-born Matura settled in England in the 1960s, and eventually established himself as one of Britain's major (not to mention most prolific) black dramatists and co-founded the Black Theatre Cooperative with Charlie Hanson. Matura's early works were given exposure at the Royal Court and a variety of fringe venues; his writing for television – particularly the series *No Problem* and *Black Silk* – helped widen his audience in the 1980s (though he remains underappreciated in the US). His work has concentrated both on the black experience in Britain and on Trinidadian issues, with a recent development into versions of classics adapted to his own interests. The common thread that links both the Trinidadian and the British-set plays is Matura's interest in the contradictions that arise when people drawn from different social and racial groups interact. This stems partly from Trinidad's rich mixture of people of African, East Indian, Chinese, Spanish, British, Portuguese and French descent, as a result of its colonial past. Like many contemporary writers Matura is particularly interested in colonialism as a state of mind as well as a physical institution. Thus in *Play Mas* people of Indian and African descent work out power relations against the background of Carnival and of independence; in *Independence* different versions of independence are mobilised in contradiction; and in *Meetings* we see the tensions between old and new focused in a wealthy couple, one nostalgic for traditional cooking (and, by extension, a life rooted in the old values), the other enslaved to the values of American economic colonialism. Matura has a great gift for witty and revealing dialogue which he puts to particularly good use in his adaptations of the classics; *The Playboy of the West Indies* is an adaptation of ▷J.M. Synge's *Playboy of the Western World*. *Trinidad Sisters* is a particularly poignant relocation of ▷Chekhov's *Three Sisters*, as a statement of 'mother country' and its mental stranglehold.

Try these:
▷Tunde Ikoli, another black dramatist whose early career was also fostered by the director Roland Rees, successfully adapted ▷Gorki's *The Lower Depths* for a mainly black cast; ▷Caryl Churchill's *Cloud Nine* looks at the relationship between the patriarchal and the colonial impulses; ▷Brian Friel's *Translations* offers an Irish dimension; ▷Barrie Keeffe is a white writer who has used a theme drawn from the classics to underpin his portrayal of black British experience, in *Black Lear* (revised as *King of England*); ▷Derek Walcott, ▷Trevor Rhone, ▷Barry Reckord, ▷Errol Hill, ▷Errol John, ▷Edgar White, ▷Caryl Phillips are other Afro-Caribbean writers; ▷Winsome Pinnock, ▷Jacqueline Rudet and Theatre of Black Women.

MAUGHAM, William Somerset
English novelist and dramatist   [1874–1965]

Plays include:
A Man of Honour (1903), *Penelope* (1909), *Our Betters* (1917), *Caesar's Wife* (1919), *Home and Beauty* (1919), *The Circle* (1921),

East of Suez (1922), *The Constant Wife* (1926), *The Letter* (1927), *The Sacred Flame* (1928), *The Bread Winner* (1930), *For Services Rendered* (1932), *Sheppey* (1933)

His twenty-two plays, mainly neatly constructed comedies, are entertaining and witty. They often tend to moralise, but, though set in the fashionable middle class to whom he was seeking to appeal, he by no means toes the establishment line. Although his closet homosexuality does not figure in his plays, his unsatisfactory marriage may have influenced the criticism of the divorce laws found in *Home and Beauty* and the debate on economic and social sexism in *The Constant Wife*.

In *For Services Rendered* his cynical wit is put aside to show the caustic effect of war on family life and in *Sheppey* he shows hostile public reaction to a barber who, on winning a lottery, attempts to use his winnings according to Christ's teaching. *The Sacred Flame*, probably the best of his serious dramas, shows his greatest depth of feeling in a study of unrequited love, part of a murder story that offers a defence of euthanasia.

The Circle

Maugham's finest comedy, *The Circle* was booed at its premiere. An MP and his wife await the arrival of his mother, whom he has not seen since childhood, when she ran away with a married man. When she and her lover arrive, no longer a romantic couple but she a middle-aged, over made-up, scatterbrain and he an elderly balding man, who was forced out of a brilliant political career, they bicker over the 'sacrifices' each made to be with the other. When the young wife then falls for a house guest the parallels between wife and mother become clear. Though others try to dissuade her from throwing away her marriage, she is eventually won by her lover's realistic, if romantic, declaration, 'I don't offer you peace and quietness. I offer you unrest and anxiety. I don't offer you happiness. I'm offering you love.'

Try these:
▷J.M. Synge's *In the Shadow of the Glen* for a lover offering unrest and anxiety; ▷Noël Coward for similar cynical wit with flashes of social comment; Shaw's *The Marriage* for discusssion of the institution. ▷Terence Rattigan for comparable neat

construction and subversive tackling of socially unacceptable themes; ▷Doug Lucie, ▷Keith Reddin for modern equivalents.

MAYAKOVSKY, Vladimir Vladimirovich   [1893–1930]
Russian poet and dramatist

Plays include:
Vladimir Mayakovsky (1913), *Mystery-Bouffe* (1918), *A Comedy Of Murder* (1927), *The Bedbug* (1929), *The Bathhouse* (1930)

Born in Georgia, Mayakovsky espoused the Bolshevik cause at an early stage, and became a champion of Futurism. After the 1917 Revolution he was a leading activist in the new art forms, but with the rise of Stalinism he was subjected to increasingly severe criticism from the Communist Party bureaucracy for individualism and Formalism. In the early 1920s he was a great experimenter with form, writing many fragments and one-act pieces, drawing on a great variety of sources, but he is best known for his two last plays – brilliantly inventive satires on the Soviet Bureaucracy of the late 1920s. These attacks hardly endeared him to his opponents, and in he committed suicide in a fit of depression, convinced that the Revolution had been subverted.

The Bathhouse

A deeply corrupt official, Pobedonosikov, is informed that a man called Kranov has invented a time-machine, with the intention of employing it in the service of the Peoples' Revolution. Pobedonosikov refuses to listen to the inventor, finding the present power he wields entirely satisfactory and unwilling to risk any change, initiative or responsibility. However, when a miraculous Woman from the Future appears from 2030 AD to assist the Soviet people, Pobedonosikov claims the time-machine as his own. He is left behind when the Woman transports the ordinary people off to the glorious future, leaving only his fellow bureaucrats to console him.

Try these:
Dusty Hughes' *The Futurists* is a political satire featuring Mayakovsky as a character; Meyerhold directed the plays of Mayakovsky; ▷David Pownall's *Master Class* is a vivid evocation of Stalinist pressure on artists; ▷Mrozek, and ▷Havel are

modern East European dramatists who have clashed with their states; ▷Gogol's *The Government Inspector* is the classic Russian bureaucracy play.

MEDIEVAL DRAMA

The most commonly produced medieval plays are the so-called mystery plays drawn from the cycles staged in the open air once a year by the craft guilds (also called mysteries, hence the name) in many English towns. They take biblical stories as their subject matter and a complete cycle could run from the Creation to the Last Judgement, with each individual play staged by an appropriate guild – at York the plasterers were responsible for the Creation, the shipwrights, fishmongers and sailors took charge of the Noah story and the Crucifixion was done by the nail makers! This division of responsibility was related to the enormous community effort that went into the stagings and to the didactic purpose of the plays, which was to give readily understandable religious instruction to a largely illiterate population. This does not mean that the plays are solemn: they include such figures as the hen-pecking Mrs Noah, and the sheep-stealing Mak in the Wakefield Master's *Second Shepherd's Play*. The cycles continued to be staged, despite official disapproval after the Reformation, until late in the sixteenth century, even after the erection of the first purpose-built professional theatre in London in 1576. They had a considerable influence on Renaissance playwriting and theatrical practice, and they have found a new popularity both in Bill Bryden's highly successful promenade staging for the ▷National Theatre and in the regular stagings now offered at Chester, Coventry and York.

Also from the late medieval period are the Moralities which use personification and allegory to make their didactic points. The most famous are probably *The Castle of Perseverance* (from the early fifteenth century), *Mankind* (from the 1460s) and *Everyman* (from the 1490s). They make effective theatre, particularly in such scenes as Everyman's descent into the grave deserted by all his companions (Beauty, Strength, Goods and so on) except Good Deeds. *A Satire of the Three Estates* (1540) by Sir David Lindsay (1468–1555), a Scottish Morality, is noteworthy as the surprise hit of the 1948 Edinburgh Festival in Tyrone Guthrie's inspired staging which res-

cued it from four hundred years of oblivion, and it is revived fairly regularly.

The earliest medieval writer who is likely to be produced is the tenth-century nun Hroswitha (also known as Roswitha) who wrote six Latin plays dealing with Christian subjects, modelled on the Roman comic dramatist Terence. Apart from their historical significance as the first known plays by a woman and as an outcrop of literary dramatic activity in an otherwise barren period, they deserve professional revival.

Try these:
▷John Arden's and ▷Margaretta D'Arcy's *The Business of Good Government*, and *The Non-Stop Connolly Show*, ▷Ann Jellicoe, Promenade Performances and ▷Community Theatre for modern approximations to the dynamic behind the Mysteries; ▷Brecht for didactic theatre; ▷Women Dramatists for other neglected female playwrights; ▷Marlowe's *Doctor Faustus* for the influence of the medieval tradition on Renaissance dramatists; ▷T.S. Eliot's *Murder in the Cathedral* for medieval influence. The Medieval Players is a British professional touring company that produces medieval and pre-Shakespearian drama.

MEDOFF, Mark   [1940–]
American dramatist

Plays include:
The Kramer (1973), *The Wager* (1973), *When You Comin' Back Red Ryder?* (1974), *Doing a Good One for The Red Man* (1974), *The War on Tatem* (1974), *The Conversion of Aaron Weiss* (1977), *Children of a Lesser God* (1979), *The Hands of Its Enemy* (1986), *The Heart Outright* (1986), *The Majestic Kid* (1986), *The Homage That Follows* (1987)

The Illinois-born son of a doctor and a psychologist, Medoff teaches English at New Mexico State University where he premieres many of his plays. His reputation has been built on three works: *The Wager*, a study of two university graduate students who make a bet about seducing a woman called Honor; *When You Comin' Back, Red Ryder?*, a play about blighted lives set in a third-rate Southwest diner at the end of the 1960s; and *Children of a Lesser God*, a love story between a hearing therapist for the deaf, James Leeds, and his stubborn and proud non-hearing student, Sarah Norman. A substantial success on Broadway, in London, and as a film, the play prompted the predictable backlash that Medoff was simply milking the tear-jerking potential inherent in any disability drama; still, the play is more worthy than that, and the role of Sarah has given long-overdue exposure to several deaf actresses including Phyllis Frelich, Jean St Clair, Marlee Matlin, and Elizabeth Quinn. Medoff's follow-up play, *The Hands of its Enemy*, proved harder to defend: a deaf character is again the focus, but this time, as some critics wrote, Medoff forces emotions and risks banality. The same problems disabled *The Majestic Kid*, in which Medoff returned to the milieu of *When You Comin' Back Red Ryder?* to explore the persistent attractions of a mythic Wild West.

Try these:
▷William Inge (especially *Bus Stop*), Robert Sherwood's *The Petrified Forest* and Ed Graczyk's *Come Back to the Five and Dime, Jimmy Dean, Jimmy Dean* for plays about small-town America roadside gatherings; Lanford Wilson's *Balm of Gilead* for a more harrowing vision of coffee shop regulars; ▷Phil Young's *Crystal Clear*, ▷Brian Clark's *Whose Life Is It Anyway?*, and ▷Bernard Pomerance's *The Elephant Man* for comparative treatments of disability; Graeae, for a British company of disabled performers whose approach to disability is decidedly upbeat.

MERCER, David [1928–80]
British dramatist

Plays include:
The Buried Man (1962), *The Governor's Lady* (1965), *Ride a Cock Horse* (1965), *Belcher's Luck* (1966), *After Haggerty* (1970), *Flint* (1970), *White Poem* (1970), *Duck Song* (1974), *Cousin Vladimir* (1978), *Then and Now* (1979), *No Limits to Love* (1980)

The son of an engine driver in a working-class Northern family, David Mercer trained at art school. Heavily influenced at certain periods in his life by R.D. Laing (he had a mental breakdown in 1957) and marxism, his work reflects a disturbingly penetrating analysis of the individual in relation to society, with a critical judgement that left him politically unaligned and increasingly subject to attacks by left-wing critics. As such he brought a variety of perspectives to bear on situations ranging from the ▷Orton-esque comedy of *Flint* (about an agnostic vicar and a suicidal young girl) to the examination of infantilism in *Ride a Cock Horse* (in which a writer finds himself regressing emotionally following three unfortunate encounters with women). In *After Haggerty*, the title character – Godot-like – never arrives; instead the stage is occupied by a drama critic and, at times, an American woman. His fondness for disorienting monologues is echoed in *Duck Song*, a philosophical pastiche set in the home of a wealthy artist. *Cousin Vladimir* is a 'whither England?' piece, pitting a morally neutral Russian dissident against an acute and incisive Englishman; whereas *Then and Now* examines the mounting despair felt by two people seen at two points in their lives – aged twenty and fifty. Mercer's stage success was surpassed by his acclaim on television and film, and his screenplay for Karel Reisz's film *Morgan!*, about an eccentric artist hovering on the brink of insanity, is a classic of the 1960s.

Try these:
▷Peter Shaffer (especially *Equus*) for exaltations of passion over reason; ▷David Hare (especially *Plenty*), ▷Howard Brenton (especially *The Weapons of Happiness*), ▷Michael Frayn's *Benefactors* for left-wing disillusionment and lapsed idealism; ▷David Edgar's *Maydays* for another encounter between a dissident and the English; ▷David Pownall's *Master Class* for another treatment using artistic freedom of the individual against political dogma; ▷Stoppard for a more right-wing view.

MERRIAM, Eve [1916–]
American dramatist, writer

Plays include:
Inner City (1972), *Lady Macbeth of Westport* (1972), *Out of Our Father's Houses* (1975, based on her anthology of journals and letters, *Growing Up Female in America*, *The Club* (1977), *Viva Reviva* (with music

by Amy D. Rubin, 1977), *At Her Age* (1979), *Dialogue for Lovers* (1980), *Sweet Dreams* (with music by Helen Miller, 1981)

Eve Merriam first came to public attention in 1972, with the musical, *Inner City*, an adaptation of her book *The Inner City Mother Goose*, but it is *The Club* that earned her a reputation as a playwright. Set in a private men's club in 1903, *The Club* is notable for its use of female actors to portray male roles. As staged by Tommy Tune, this 'chamber musical,' featured provocative, androgynous costumes lampooning male patriarchal stereotypes. The idea of male impersonators functions as a teaching device that illuminates 'the unspoken, under-the surface texture and emotions of life between the sexes.' Merriam does not advocate replacing all male roles with females, however. She intentionally chose male director Tommy Tune and stage manager Gene Taylor to avoid the exclusivity criticised in the play. As a result of her efforts, she has garnered the reputation of being a writer who combines poetry, feminist values, and entertainment in her work.

She continues these themes – and the use of music – in her next play, *Viva Reviva*. This 'musical awakening' consists of four sections, which use the characters of Eve, Penelope, Ophelia, and Joan of Arc to illustrate the oppression of women. This time, Merriam adds male counterparts – Adam, Ulysses, and Hamlet – using male performers to make her feminist point. At *Her Age* commissioned by the Theatre for Older People, addresses the problems of ageing. This 1979 production featured post-performance discussions with Betty Friedan and Lydia Bragger. Merriam's most recent work is *Dialogue for Lovers*, a dramatic adaptation of Shakespeare's sonnets performed with Estelle Parson and Fritz Weaver in 1980 and *Street Dreams*, a significant re-working of the musical *Inner City* in 1981.

Try these:

▷Caryl Churchill's *Cloud Nine*, which shows how stereotypical social forces and determine the roles women play and *Top Girls* (1982) and *Fen* (1983) for their portrayal of women trying to assert themselves in a man's world; ▷Sarah Daniels' *Beside Herself* for female archetypes; Britain's Age Exchange as a company concerned with the experience of older people; Split Britches as a company also

using androgyny and women playing male roles in a different vein, so too do Charabanc. See also ▷Lesbian Theatre and ▷Women in Theatre.

MEYER, Marlane   [1953–]
American dramatist

Plays include:
Etta Jenks (1987), *Kingfish* (1988), *Geography of Luck* (1989)

With three plays Marlane Meyer has developed a distinctive playwriting style that has been recognised in various competitions (the Susan Smith Blackburn Prize in New York and the South Coast Repertory Playwriting Competition in California), and has received critical acclaim on both coasts of the United States and for *Etta Jenks*, in Britain. Meyer's writing might seem best suited to cinema's naturalism but productions have eschewed the realistic and gritty nature suggested by her characters (pornographic film actresses and drugged-out male prostitutes) for a representational style that evokes a sense of fable. Meyer is less interested in specific issues like pornography and prostitution and more interested in the moral, social and ethical questions that the existence of these societal extremities represent. Meyer is disarming because she does not offer judgement about the situations or characters but allows the audience to draw their own conclusions.

Etta Jenks
Hollywood is the quintessential symbol of the rags-to-riches myth that pervades American ideals. *Etta Jenks* is the story of one young dream-filled woman who buys into that myth and believes she can become a film star if she can produce a good audition tape. For her the prize is worth any cost, including becoming a pornographic film actress in order to pay for the tape. The play is a parable about life being manipulated for business purposes. *Etta Jenks* symbolises a culture in which identity has become a commodity and individuality so devalued that prostitution, at least for Meyer, is an apt symbol for contemporary life. The play extends that idea to a chilling conclusion as Etta Jenks is co-opted by the pornographic business, exploiting it to buy the murder of her former producer. She ends the domination that ruled her not with compassion and true self-assertion but by being ruthless.

Try these:
▷Sarah Daniels' *Masterpieces* for another treatment of pornography; ▷Kay Adshead's *Thatcher's women*; ▷Peter Terson's *Strippers* for the economics of the sex industry. Ariel Dorfman's *Death and the Maiden* which shows the female protagonist wreaking an awful revenge on a possible, one-time oppressor; for more female turning of the tables, Euripides' *The Bacchae* and Bryony Lavery's *Kitchen Matters* which gives it a homphobic twist.

MIDDLETON, Thomas   [1580–1627]
English Renaissance dramatist

Plays include:
A Mad World, My Masters (1606), *A Chaste Maid in Cheapside* (1611), *The Roaring Girl* (with ▷Thomas Dekker; 1611), *A Fair Quarrel* (with ▷William Rowley; 1617), *Women Beware Women* (1621), *The Changeling* (with Rowley; 1622). [Middleton is now often credited with writing *The Revenger's Tragedy* (1607), previously ascribed to ▷Cyril Tourneur, under whose name it is discussed in this book.]

The current interest in themes of gender, class and power has made Middleton a more widely staged dramatist than ever before, since his plays are particularly concerned with female psychology and preoccupied with the relationship between love, duty and money. His Citizen Comedy, *A Chaste Maid in Cheapside* has been seen as one of the theatre's richest investigations of the topics of money, sex and society but his best known works are the two tragedies *Women Beware Women* and *The Changeling* in which he again treats the relationship between money, sex and power. A recent RSC production of *The Roaring Girl* showed the continued relevance of this fictionalised account of the life of Moll Cutpurse, based on a real woman who scandalised early 17th-century society by her non-conformist ways (see ▷Dekker for more on *The Roaring Girl*).

The Changeling
There are no great affairs of state at stake in *The Changeling*, no kingdoms fall, no royal houses die out. It is far more of a domestic tragedy than many of the great Renaissance tragedies and it is very much a play about lack of perception and failure, sometimes deliber-

ate, to understand the probable results of actions. In particular, the heroine, Beatrice-Joanna, fails to see that playing on the malcontent De Flores' passion for her in order to get him to rid her of her unwanted betrothed in favour of another man is unlikely to be without consequences for her own future freedom of action and she becomes sucked into the vortex of passion which brings them both to their deaths. There is the usual Renaissance pattern of dumb shows, dropped handkerchiefs, severed fingers, dances of madmen and so on, but it is almost all still credible in modern terms (with the exception of the virginity test potions) and the result is a powerful unmasking of not only individual psychology but also, particularly in the subplot, of the constraints which determine the subordinate status of women within society.

Try these:
The modernity of Middleton's interests has encouraged contemporary dramatists to adapt his work, notably ▷Barrie Keeffe with his modern version of the comedy *A Mad World, My Masters* and ▷Howard Barker with his rewriting of the later parts of *Women Beware Women*; most Renaissance dramatists used revenge plots and malcontent figures – ▷Shakespeare's *Hamlet* is the most famous example of both, and there are notable examples in ▷Tourneur and ▷Webster; for modern equivalents of *The Roaring Girl*, ▷Timberlake Wertenbaker's *New Anatomies* and *The Grace of Mary Traverse*; ▷Aphra Behn for a late-seventeenth-century female view of similar themes.

MILLER, Arthur   [1915–   ]
American dramatist

Plays include:
The Man Who Had All the Luck (1944), *All My Sons* (1947), *Death of a Salesman* (1949), *The Crucible* (1953), *A View From the Bridge* (1955), *A Memory of Two Mondays* (1955), *After the Fall* (1964), *Incident at Vichy* (1964), *The Price* (1968), *Fame* (1970), *The Creation of the World and Other Business* (1972), *Up From Paradise* (1974), *The Archbishop's Ceiling* (1977), *The American Clock* (1980), *Two-Way Mirror* (1984), *Danger: Memory!* (1987), *The Ride Down Mt. Morgan* (1990)

Helen Mirren as Moll Cutpurse, the heroine, in Barry Kyle's 1983 RSC production of Thomas Middleton and Thomas Dekker's *The Roaring Girl*

The son of a clothing manufacturer hard hit by the Depression, Miller, a native New Yorker, established his reputation as a social dramatist in the tradition of Ibsen with *All My Sons*, a surprisingly timely tale of World War II venality that up-ends the cosy world of small-town America in which it is set. *Death of a Salesman*, his Pulitzer Prize-winning parable about the failure of the American dream, remains his most popular play. *The Crucible* – an exposure of McCarthyism in 1950s America filtered through the witch trials of 17th-century Salem, Massachusetts – is perhaps his most politically charged play. *A View from the Bridge* contrasts private morality and public pressure in the story of a Brooklyn longshoreman, Eddie Carbone. *After the Fall* attracted attention for gossip-related reasons: to what extent could the suicidal Maggie in Miller's play be read as the writer's portrait of his late wife, Marilyn Monroe? (An acclaimed 1990 revival of the play at the ▷National Theatre with a black actress, Josette Simon, in the lead role helped diminish the Monroe connection.) The prices people pay for choices they have made is an obsessive Miller theme, made explicit in *The Price* and also in his recent *Danger: Memory!*, in which efforts to forget pain cost people their memories.

Miller's reputation in the United States has not held up in recent decades, though he continues to be highly regarded in Britain, where several superior stagings of his plays – including ▷Alan Ayckbourn's 1987 production of *A View From the Bridge* with Michael Gambon, David Thacker's immaculate and sensitive rendering of *The Price* and *Two-Way mirror*, and Howard Davies' 1990 production of *The Crucible* for the National – have cemented his superstar status. (His latest play, *The Ride Down Mt. Morgan*, received its premiere at the National in 1990.) Miller's self-conscious use of language (sometimes compared to ▷O'Neill's in its linguistic shortcomings) certainly falls short of ▷Tennessee Williams' lyricism, and he is frequently criticised for the cumbersome metaphors and pontifical tendencies of much of his writing. Still, Miller's unceasing attention to questions of public and private integrity have distinguished his career and rightly earned him the respect of theatregoers on both sides of the Atlantic.

Death of a Salesman

Despite its portentous subtitle, 'Certain Private Conversations in Two Acts and a Requiem', Miller's play is still capable of packing a wallop – its regular appearance on the American and British regional circuits attests to its undiminished emotional power. Willy Loman, a pathetic and potentially tragic American Everyman, loses his job at age 63 and kills himself in a last-ditch effort to raise the money his family needs. At once particular and general, lean and overripe, linear and abstract in its cross-cutting in time, Miller's play is one of the profoundest examinations yet of the American dream. As the major American drama of the 1940s, *Death of a Salesman* engendered several major critical appraisals, mostly centering on whether the play ranks as a modern tragedy. Many critics have taken exception to the designation of tragedy, finding the play morally clichéd and Loman's character lacking the insight generally expected of a tragic hero. Nonetheless, Miller's interweaving of the realistic and poetic in the play, and his rich characterisations still have wide appeal. Lee J. Cobb's performance as Willy Loman in the 1949 premiere is considered definitive, though a controversial 1984 revival starring Dustin Hoffman received considerable attention. A production of the play in China prompted Miller's 1984 memoir, *Salesman in Beijing*.

Try these:
▷Ibsen, ▷G.B. Shaw ▷Clifford Odets and ▷Lillian Hellman for a variety of dramatic moralists; ▷Donald Margulies's *The Loman Family Picnic* for a black comedy about a Jewish salesman's family. ▷David Mamet (especially *Glengarry Glen Ross*), ▷Marlane Meyer, ▷Sally Nemeth, for soured visions of the American dream.

MILNER, Ron(ald)   [1938–]
American dramatist

Plays include:
Life Agony (1965), *Who's Got His Own* (1966), *The Warning: A Theme for Linda* (1969), *Jazz Set* (a play with music by Max Roach, 1974), *What the Wine-Sellers Buy* (1974), *Going Away Party* (1974), *Seasons Reasons* (a-capella musical, 1980), *Crack Steppin'* (a 'rhythm and blues opera,' 1982) *Don't Get God Started* (musical with music by Marvin Winans, 1987), *Checkmates* (1987), *Roads of the Mountaintop* (1988)

Since the 1960s, Ron Milner has been an articulate spokesperson for the Black theatre movement in America. He is not only a

Michael Gambon (Eddie Carbone) and Suzan Sylvester (Catherine, his niece) in the National Theatre's production of Arthur Miller's *A View from the Bridge*, directed by Alan Ayckbourn, Cottesloe, February 1987. It subsequently transferred to the Aldwych Theatre

writer, but an admitted proselytizer, and seeks to reveal the historic and current problems faced by Blacks in the United States. Milner encourages the work of playwrights and co-founded The Spirit of Shango Theatre in his birthplace, Detroit, Michigan, to give substance to his belief that Black artists should work with their roots in their own communities. His first play, *Who's Got His Own*, which was directed by Lloyd Richards at the American Place Theatre, concerns a Black family which is all but destroyed by the anger and grief they experience at the hands of an uncaring white world. *What the Wine-Sellers Buy* evokes some feminist controversy, as it suggests that Black women, though defined by the men in their lives, often exert negative influence on the Black male community. The play, nevertheless, also embodies the writer's most enduring theme that moral choices are not only possible, but positive. *Seasons Reasons* concerns a man imprisoned in the 1960s and released in the 1980s, only to find that his once-radical friends are now members of the 'establishment.'

Milner's often draws upon jazz, gospel, and blues, feeling that music can express everything inherent in Black culture. In *Jazz Set*, using music written and performed by Max Roach, each musician becomes a character who becomes one with his or her instrument. 'I try to find a way to blend music with drama-otherwise, the drama is European. Black culture is ritualistic.' Milner's musical, *Crack Steppin'*, is subtitled 'a comic book operetta in Rhythm and Blues.' *Don't Get God Started*, a gospel musical centering on a group of born-again Christians, relies even more heavily on music. Billed in its 1987 New York production as 'a revivalist event with an old time religious fervor, it is a powerful combination of gospel and theatre.

With *Cheekmates*, Milner comes to terms with the 'kill whitey' mentality of the 1960s. The four characters probe issues beyond Black/White conflict such as the 'generation gap' and 'Yuppie values' through the perspective of Black America. Milner's two married couples show the changing importance of job, women, and material gain in the lives of everyday citizens; they exemplify the issue of competitiveness in modern marriage and how deeply it contrasts with the marriages of generations past.

Milner has also published a novel, *The Life of the Brothers Brown*, which was awarded a John Hay Whitney Fellowship, and several short stories. Milner prefers working in Detroit, where he feels the theatre atmosphere is more relaxed. He is currently working on a screenplay about the young James Brown and a new play. *The Trial of William Freedman*, based on the story of a Black man in the 1880s tried for the murder of a white family.

Try these:
▷Ntozake Shange, especially . . . *for colored girls who have considered suicide/when the rainbow is enuff* (1975) and *Spell #7* (1979) for their oppositional view of male/female relationships in the Black community, also Lorraine Hansberry's *Raisin in the Sun* (1959), which Milner himself claims to have been a strong influence; ▷Albee's *Who's Afraid of Virginia Woolf?*, for married couples across the generation gap; ▷Felix Cross and Dennis Scott for black British concern with ritual.

MINGHELLA, Anthony   [1954–]
British dramatist

Plays include:
Child's Play (1978), *Whale Music* (1981), *A Little Like Drowning* (1984), *Two Planks and a Passion* (1984), *Love Bites* (1984), *Made In Bangkok* (1986).

Of Italian parentage, brought up on the Isle of Wight, Minghella, a former lecturer at Hull University, has established himself as a leading young dramatist capable of an impressive breadth of themes and periods. Even if his stage plays failed to cement his reputation, his TV work (*Living with Dinosaurs*, *What if it's Raining?*, *The Storyteller*) went on to firmly establish him in Hollywood's eyes (his recent film, *Truly, Madly, Deeply* with Juliet Stevenson, Alan Rickman and Bill Paterson already being highly acclaimed). *Made In Bangkok*, is his best-known play, in light of its 1986 West End run and its 1988 American premiere in Los Angeles. In *A Little Like Drowning*, an episodic flashback drama about an Italian family uprooted to England, a conversation between the elderly Nonna and her granddaughter Anastasia gives way to a series of pained recollections about her now-dead husband, Alfredo, who left her for an English mistress. Domestic discord continues in *Love Bites*, about a family reunion that disintegrates into recriminations. *Two Planks and a Passion* shifts the scene to 1392 and to preparations in York for a Passion play at the Feast of Corpus Christi, a religious event turned all too secular by the greed and avarice of a community suddenly visited by Richard II. *Made In Bangkok* continues Minghella's interest in issues of ethical and moral compromise, but he remains, as of now, a writer whose intentions outstrip his achievements.

Made In Bangkok

Commissioned by Michael Codron for a commercial engagement, *Made In Bangkok* was a risky venture about sexual exploitation that must have surprised tourists who thought it would be a spicy follow-up to *No Sex Please, We're British*. Five Britons arrive on an 'Eastern Promise' holiday in Asia – one woman, Frances, and four sex-starved men – only to find that geographical displacement leads to its own emotional truth-telling as the men are revealed to be rapacious wolves and Frances becomes an all-too-obvious authorial stand-in. An extended essay about exploitation, the play is too smart to be prurient itself, but it never quite packs the punch Minghella seems to assume it will, and Frances' moralistic editorialising ('It's got nothing to do with Bangkok; it's to do with us,' she decides, sensibly) is a bit wearisome.

Try these:
▷Stephen Lowe, ▷Caryl Churchill and ▷Dusty Hughes for a similar kind of peculiarly English staccato rhythm; Mark Brennan's *China* for sexual exploitation closer-to-home in a Soho hostess bar; ▷Robert Bolt's *A Man For All Seasons* for the sort of conventional history play *Two Planks and a Passion* reacts against; Julia Schofield's *Love On the Plastic*, ▷Marlane Meyer's *Etta Jenks*, ▷Kay Adshead's *Thatcher's Women* and ▷Peter Terson's *Strippers* as plays about the sexual exploitation of women; ▷Michael Wall's *Amongst Barbarians* for another view of British excursions in the Far East; ▷Peter Nicol's *Poppy*.

MITCHELL, Julian   [1935–]
British novelist, dramatist and historian

Plays include:
Half-Life (1977), *The Enemy Within* (1980), *Another Country* (1981), *Francis* (1983), *After Aïda* (originally *Verdi's Messiah*; 1986)

Mitchell is best known for *Another Country* (filmed with Rupert Everett as the iconic gay/rebel) which explored the link between sexual identity and political awareness in a British public school setting, echoing the background of the MI5 spy Guy Burgess. Critics were less kind to his bio-piece on St Francis of Asissi, *Francis*, which smacked somewhat of unimaginative school's radio, unable to match his sharp political edge in religious ideology.

Try these:
▷Alan Bennett's *The Old Country* and *An Englishman Abroad* for secret agents; *Saint Joan* is the most popular theatrical saint; ▷Shakespeare's *Henry VI*, ▷Shaw, ▷Brecht, ▷Terson, and ▷Anouilh for good examples.

MNOUCHKINE, Ariane   [1938–]
French director and dramatist, founder-member and manager of the Théâtre du Soleil

Key productions include:
Les Clowns (1969), *1789* (1970), *1793* (1972), *L'Age d'Or* (1975), *Méphisto* (1979), ▷Shakespeare's *Richard II* (1981) and *Henry IV* (1984), *L'Histoire Terrible Mais Inachevée de Norodom Sihanouk, Roi du Cambodge* (1985), *L'Indiade* (1987), *Les Atrides* (1990/91)

Mnouchkine is one of the most important French directors, and demonstrates what can be done with a devoted company, one production every two years, a substantial subsidy, and very considerable talent. The Théâtre du Soleil was founded in 1964 as a theatre co-operative, and the early successes included Gorki's *Philistines* and Arnold Wesker's *The Kitchen*, but they are best known for four *créations collectives* – improvised and devised plays – *Les Clowns, 1789, 1793,* and *L'Age d'Or. 1789* used all the devices of popular theatre to look at the people's view of the French Revolution: clown techniques, puppets of all sizes, fairground turns, a narrator like a fairground barker, and a set with a ring of five small stages and the audience standing in the middle. For *L'Age d'Or*, the story of a Moroccan immigrant worker in contemporary France, the whole theatre was filled with sand shaped into four large hollows, in which the audience sat in close proximity to the actors. More recent productions have all used a large, square acting area, with such scenery as there is round the edges, faced by a simple raked auditorium.

Since 1975 the Théâtre has made a film on the life of Molière, put on Mnouchkine's adaptation of *Méphisto*, and worked on some colourful Shakespearean productions in a style based on Kabuki and Kathakali. These techniques have also been applied to texts written from and with the company by the radical feminist writer ▷Hélène Cixous: two substantial historical plays on the terrible story of Sihanouk and Cambodia, and on the partition of British India. The most recent marathon has been a translation of Aeschylus' *Oresteia* trilogy converted into a four-part, two-day work by the addition of Euripides' *Iphigenia in Aulis*.

The company is based in a disused munitions factory beyond the end of the métro at Vincennes, to which they have attracted consistently large audiences, though perhaps not the popular audience which their techniques seem to invite. There has also been a hilarious one-man parody of Mnouchkine's directing style running in Paris – *Ariane ou l'Age d'Or*, by Philippe Caubère – not something that commonly happens to directors.

Try these:
▷Peter Brook, for inventive direction and use of space, though Mnouchkine is more politically committed; ▷Goethe's *Faust*, for Mephistopheles; Jerome Savary's *Le Grand Magic Circus* also uses theatre space in its totality; Peter Stein in Germany and the radical Yugoslav Group, Red Pilot, are two of the many Europeans who use space imaginatively; ▷Andre Serban's *Greek Trilogy* for an environmental reworking of Greek sources; also Jan Fabre and Pina Bausch who are more performance art oriented; in Britain the equivalents, though different in scope, could range from Lumiere and Son, to Welfare State to the ▷National Theatre's ▷promenade performances, or ▷Ann Jellicoe's community theatre.

MOFFATT, Nigel   [1954–]
Jamaican dramatist

Plays include:
Mamma Decemba (1985), *Lifetime* (1985), *Celebration* (1986), *Walsall Boxed In* (1987)

Poet, musician, songwriter (in 1983, he recorded with ex-Jam and Style Council lead singer Paul Weller, and has played the folk club circuit). Moffat now lives in the West Midlands. *Mamma Decemba*, written for Temba, won the Samuel Beckett award for 1986. Moffatt's play centres on the disillusionment of Caribbean immigrants with 'the home country', seen through the eyes of two older women, Mamma Decemba and her friend. But in *Mamma Decemba*, written in patois though the play is set in 'inner-city England', Moffatt has created a unique character whose shifts of mood and impenetrable grief as she mourns her recently deceased husband are handled with a sensitivity that goes beyond the individual and gives the play a universal appeal.

Moffatt has also been part of the National Theatre's studio workshops out of which came two plays *Tony* and *Rhapsody 'N Black 'N' White* performed to invited audiences. *Tony* subsequently appeared at the Oval under the title of *Thriller* in a version not approved of by the author.

Try these:
▷Caryl Phillips, ▷Mustapha Matura, ▷Edgar White for other plays on the theme of disillusionment with the mother country. ▷Winsome Pinnock for a female perspective.

MOLIÈRE
(Jean-Baptiste Poquelin)   [1622–73]
French dramatist and actor-manager

Plays include:
Les Précieuses Ridicules (*The Affected Ladies*; 1658), *L'École des Femmes* (*The School for Wives*; 1662), *Don Juan* (1665), *Le Misanthrope* (*The Misanthrope*; 1666), *Le Tartuffe* (*Tartuffe*; written 1664, produced 1667), *Georges Dandin* (1668), *Le Bourgeois Gentilhomme* (*The Would-be Gentleman* or *The Bourgeois Gentleman*; 1671), *Les Fourberies de Scapin* (*The Tricks of Scapin* or *Scapino*; 1671), *Les Femmes Savantes* (*The Learned Ladies*; 1672), *Le Malade Imaginaire* (*The Hypochondriac* or *The Imaginary Invalid*; 1673)

Molière was the eldest son of a wealthy Paris tapestry merchant in the King's service, and was well educated with a view to following his father's occupation. Instead, however, he went off with a troupe of actors, and toured in the provinces for fifteen years before making any success in Paris. This apprenticeship, and having to share the Palais-Royal theatre for half the week with an Italian *commedia dell'arte* troupe, gave him a very thorough theatrical grounding. He became France's most complete man of the theatre; he was as good a comic actor as he was a comic dramatist. He produced his own plays and managed his company against strong attacks from the respectable (though he enjoyed the firm support of Louis XIV), and he died with his make-up on. His output ranges from knockabout farce to conversation pieces, to political satire, to Court spectacles with elaborate machinery, to subtle comedies of character, all happily still holding the stage. His only failure was a heroic drama, *Don Garcie de Navarre*; being disinclined to waste, he salvaged some of the text and used it for Alceste's more lofty sentiments in *The Misanthrope*.

Molière's plays (like ▷Shakespeare's) can survive almost anything a director feels like doing to them. British directors tend to be more respectful of the text than Planchon or Vitez, but in recent years they have moved *Scapino* to modern Italy, with motorbikes (Young Vic 1970, starring Jim Dale); *The Misanthrope* to de Gaulle's France (National Theatre 1973 and 1989, in ▷Tony Harrison's elegant rhymed couplets) and to modern literary London (Neil Bartlett's version for Red Shift, 1988-9, with Alceste as a cantankerous Scot); and in Jatinder Verma's version of *Tartuffe*, to Moghul India (Royal National Theatre, 1989-91), all with considerable success.

The Misanthrope

Q. Will the noble, uncompromising, universally admired Alceste win his lawsuit despite his refusal to butter up the judges and his inability not to tell the truth about the awful verses of the powerful Oronte? A. No. Q. Will he marry the brilliant, beautiful, bitchy Célimène or the quiet, devoted Eliante? A. Neither. Célimène cannot face the thought of all that rustic high-thinking, and Eliante very sensibly decides that she will be happier with Alceste's more worldly and less demanding friend Philinte. The rest is just brilliant conversation. The world divides into those who think Alceste is Molière's funniest creation, and those (like Rousseau) who are shocked that Molière should have held up to ridicule this virtuous and Rousseau-like man.

Try these:
▷Racine for seventeenth-century French theatre, though they were on bad terms; English Restoration comedy (eg ▷Ether-

ege, ▷Wycherley) has much in common with Molière; ▷Christopher Hampton's *The Philanthropist* is an 'answer' to *The Misanthrope*; ▷Bulgakov's *Molière* and David Hirson's *La Bête*, a contemporary verse comedy about a Molière-like troop of actors.

MOLNAR, Ferenc   [1878–1952]
Hungarian dramatist

Plays include:
Liliom (1909), *The Guardsman* (1910), *The Swan* (1914), *The Play in the Castle* (as *The Play's the Thing* in the USA; 1924), *Olimpia* (1927), *The Good Fairy* (1931)

Beginning as a writer of farces and light-hearted satirical comedies of Hungarian city life but later gaining international success, Molnar is known less by name than by his work. *The Devil* (1907), a reworking of the Faust theme, was an early success; *The Wolf* surfaced in the West End in 1973 with Judi Dench; *The Swan* is best known through a Grace Kelly/Alec Guinness film version and *Liliom* in its musical adaptation *Carousel*. ▷Tom Stoppard reworked *The Play in the Castle* as *Rough Crossing* (▷National Theatre 1984) with initially disastrous results – changing the setting to a transatlantic liner, adding a parody musical (with a score by André Previn), complicating the plot and turning an elegant trifle into a heavy-handed wreck. Although the P. G. Wodehouse version for Broadway is much closer to the spirit of the original Stoppard's version has become popular in the USA. In the original version a young composer overhears his fiancée in a passionate exchange with another man; to save the situation a playwright dashes off a short play (a pastiche of one by Sardou) to convince the composer that all he heard was a snatch of a rehearsal. Molnar's touch is almost always light and his work often has elements of fantasy as in the father's return to earth in *Liliom* and the usherette's dream adventures in *The Good Fairy*.

Try these:
His work has been adapted by ▷Frank Marcus and ▷Tom Stoppard; Nicolle Freni's *Brooklyn E5* for a lesbian variation involving the return of a ghostly (and benevolent) father; ▷J. M. Barrie's *Mary Rose* for returning ghosts; ▷Anouilh, ▷Giraudoux for elements of fantasy.

MORNIN, Daniel   [1956–]
Northern Irish dramatist

Plays include:
Mum and Son (1981), *The Resting Time* (1981), *Kate* (1983), *Short of Mutiny* (1983), *Comrade Ogilvy* (1985), *The Murderers* (1985), *Built on Sand* (1987), *Weights and Measures* (1988), *At Our Table* (1991)

Belfast-born Mornin spent three years in the navy and travelled extensively in Asia and North Africa before coming to rest in London and deciding to become a writer. *Short of Mutiny* was in fact his first play. A sort of 'navy lark' below stairs with, for these days, a large cast (over twenty), it suffered from being produced in a post-Falklands context but was admired for its authenticity of crew life, social dynamics and observation about class and the wretchedness of life aboard for those at the wrong end of command. Mornin really came to prominence with his trio of plays about Belfast. As though trying to find answers to his own inner questions, the three plays have tried to explore the complex strands of the conflict, its effects on Irish people and how those strands go on being perpetrated. *Built on Sand*, a non-naturalistic piece that uses flashbacks, is as much a study in political cynicism as it is about young Belfast journalist Andrew's obsession with finding answers to the murder of his girlfriend; and *Kate* which tries to show the daily pressures of living in Belfast, is as harrowing in its depiction of the young, sullen son, already 'lost' and committed to violence and the loyalist paras, as it tries to be optimistic in its portrait of Kate, determined to get a typing qualification despite life falling apart all around her. *The Murderers* is the violent, inevitable end of the conundrum, going behind the scenes of a bloody sectarian killing, to reveal the same bigotry that both IRA and Loyalist leaders in *Built on Sand* feed off, and which leads to the killings being seen as part of some atavistic male initiation rite. Though *The Murderers* won the 1985 George Devine award, *Kate* is the one that lingers in the mind and may prove more durable.

Try these:
▷Christina Reid, ▷Ann Devlin, ▷Marie Jones, Rona Munro's *Bold Girls*, for more plays on Belfast and its effect on women; ▷Seamus Finnegan for historical and social explorations of Northern Ireland conflicts; ▷Stephen Lowe's *Seachange*

has particular affinities in its flashback style though Lowe's was to do with the Falklands; ▷Louise Page, ▷Robert Holman's *Lost* in *Making Noise Quietly* for more post-Falklands reprises, both army and navy; Tom McClenaghan's *Submariners* for navy crews under pressure; ▷Willis Hall's *The Long and the Short and the Tall* for inter-ranks service strife; Terry Johnson's *Imagine Drowning*, Tony Marchant for further explorations of the roots of violence.

MORRISON, Bill   [1940–]
Northern Irish dramatist, actor and director

Plays include:
Please Don't Shoot Me When I'm Down (1969), *Patrick's Day* (1972), *Tess of the D'Urbervilles* (1971; from Thomas Hardy), *Conn and the Conquerors of Space* (1972), *Sam Slade is Missing* (1972), *The Love of Lady Margaret* (1973), *The Irish Immigrant's Tale* (1976), *The Emperor of Ice Cream* (from Brian Moore; 1977), *Flying Blind* (1977), *Ellen Cassidy* (1978), *Dr Jekyll of Rodney Street* (1979), *Scrap!* (1982), *Cavern of Dreams* (musical with Carol Ann Duffy; 1984)

Morrison's greatest success is *Flying Blind*, one of a number of plays produced during a fruitful association with the Liverpool Everyman. Set in contemporary Belfast it uses broadly farcical mechanisms and devices – overheard conversations, inopportune exits and entrances, frustrated seductions, robings and disrobings – to present a portrait of a society impotent to solve its problems (the fact that none of the men can achieve an erection is metaphorically as well as farcically appropriate). The old certainties and convictions have given way to male withdrawal into the safer world represented by the music of Charlie Parker or to the fanaticism of the paramilitaries. Everyone is 'flying blind' without navigational aids, including the Protestant paramilitary who has to keep taking off his hood because he can't see without his glasses and the female babysitter who wants to borrow *Fear of Flying*. This powerful, disturbing and funny play ends in a welter of gunfire, urine, death and reconciliation which defies conventional theatrical expectations, just as the characters' lives have been forced out of conventional moulds by the political situation.

Try these:
The issues raised have counterparts in plays by ▷Sean O'Casey and ▷Brian Friel; ▷Joe Orton provides an example of the extension and subversion of the boundaries of farce in *Loot* and *What the Butler Saw*; Hector MacMillan's *The Sash* offers a Scottish angle on the Irish situation; ▷Marie Jones' *Somewhere Over the Balcony* also takes a farcical, surreal approach to present day Belfast; for other Belfast-touched subjects ▷Ann Devlin, ▷Seamus Finnegan, ▷Christina Reid, ▷Daniel Mornin, Allan Cubitt.

MORTIMER, John   [1923–]
British   dramatist,   journalist,   novelist, barrister

Plays include:
The Dock Brief (1957), *What Shall We Tell Caroline* (1958), *Lunch Hour* (1960), *The Wrong Side of the Park* (1960), *The Judge* (1967), *Come as You Are* (1970; comprising: *Mill Hill, Bermondsey, Gloucester Road, Marble Arch*), *A Voyage Round My Father* (1970), *Collaborators* (1973), *Heaven and Hell* (1976; comprising *The Fear of Heaven, The Prince of Darkness*, later retitled *The Bells of Hell*), *The Lady From Maxim's* (1977; from ▷Feydeau), *A Little Hotel on the Side* (1984; from ▷Feydeau)

Despite a very Establishment and traditional background, Mortimer has consistently espoused liberal positions in his writing and involvement in theatre. An enormously prolific writer, whose television series include the tremendously popular *Rumpole of the Bailey*, Mortimer remained until recently a working lawyer and has been a key figure in anti-censorship debates, giving testimony which was active in abolishing the censorship power of the Lord Chamberlain and speaking out against the attacks on ▷Howard Brenton's *The Romans in Britain*. There is very little danger of his own plays suffering censorship, however; his own writing is, for the most part, very gentle and often nostalgic.

The Dock Brief, the first play which really made his name, went through the process that has been true of many of Mortimer's plays, first written for radio, it was then staged, and finally televised. *Voyage Round My Father* is an autobiographical account of Mortimer's

father, a lawyer who resolutely denied his own blindness. It is a powerful and moving study of a man who is clearly monstrous in some aspects but who is, nonetheless, drawn with enormous affection. The play is almost an elegy for him, and for Mortimer's stalwart mother who forebore his father's eccentricities with enormous patience. First produced as a radio play, it was then staged in a final version at the Haymarket theatre, and later televised with Laurence Olivier as the father.

Try these:
▷Feydeau, whom Mortimer has translated with enormous success; ▷John Osborne whom Mortimer acknowledges as an influence; ▷De Filippo's *Ducking Out* and ▷Edgar White's *The Nine Night* both have central, *monstres sacrés* father figures, as does ▷Eugene O'Neill's *Long Day's Journey into Night*.

MOTTON, Gregory   [1962–]
British dramatist

Plays include:
Rain (1984), *Chicken* (1987), *Ambulance* (1987), *Downfall* 1988), *Looking at You (Revived) Again* (1989), *The Life of St Fanny* (1990)

Gregory Motton's work is primarily concerned with the harsh world of those living on the edges of society – the homeless, destitute and the handicapped, both physically and emotionally. He is a poetic writer, sometimes compared to ▷Samuel Beckett in their common lack of naturalism and easy intelligibility. His world is peopled with lost souls, frequently crippled physically – as with the wife in *Looking at You* – or emotionally, as with Pedro in *Ambulance*. In *Ambulance* his characters are the homeless of any city for whom an ambulance light is not a bringer of safety and warmth but something that terrifies and probably brings trouble. The story centres on Ellis, an alcoholic tramp who finds a dead baby and believes it is the one she herself lost 20 years earlier. The baby takes her on a journey into the past. *Looking at You (Revived) Again* follows the journey of an Irish vagrant, returning to his native country, and his relationships both with a young girl, whom he meets on the road and who hopes he will fall in love with her, and his wheelchair-bound, embittered wife who presides over his old home. Both plays are about the nature of obsession and despair, but Motton is also able to imbue the language with poetry and wit. Depicting a brutal world where dreams and aspirations are already a thing of the past, his plays have been described as 'bafflingly opaque'. Gregory Motton is a playwright who, having taken on Beckett's mantle, like him leaves his audience either rapturous or furious.

His new translation of Strindberg's *Ghost Sonata*, for Opera Factory (1990) turned up in a double bill with the opera of the same name by Aribert Reimann.

Try these:
▷Gorki, for similar visions of social outcasts and yearning; ▷Tunde Ikoli's *The Lower Depths* for a multi-racial East End version; ▷Jim Cartwright for another version of contemporary disenchantment; ▷Harold Pinter for characters as menacing symbols of external reality; ▷Tennessee Williams for a contrasting American treatment of the loss of dreams; ▷Dermot Bolger for a contemporary Irish native returning to Dublin.

MROZEK, Slawomir   [1930–]
Polish dramatist and cartoonist

Plays include:
Police (1958), *Charlie* (1961), *Out at Sea* (also known as *The Ship-Wrecked Ones*; 1961), *The Party* (1962), *The Enchanted Night* (also known as *What a Lovely Dream*; 1963), *Tango* (1964), *Emigrés*(1975), *The Hunchback* (1976), *A Summer's Day* (1983)

Mrozek is probably one of the best known Eastern European playwrights in the West, if only because he found himself there after protesting about Poland's role in the occupation of Czechoslovakia; his passport was withdrawn, but he managed to escape to Paris. Jan Kott, the eminent Polish critic now living in the USA, has written brilliantly on Mrozek, elucidating what may seem, to the uninitiated, an alien universe. His plays are often absurdist in style, but the background is not so much a meaningless universe as an irrational and arbitrary totalitarian state, and his tone is satirical and sardonic rather than despairing. The first Mrozek work done in English was Martin Esslin's adaptation of a short story, *Siesta*, for radio in 1963. Two

other Mrozek plays have appeared in recent years: *Emigrés*, a two-hander between AA the Intellectual and XX the Worker, both exiles in a sordid basement somewhere in the free world, fantasising and bickering on New Year's Eve; and *A Summer's Day* (at London's Polish Theatre in 1985), another two-handed philosophical tug-of-war between Sux, an over-achiever, and Unsux, an under-achiever, both of whom wish to commit suicide; there is an intervening lady (who goes off with Sux, of course). There are plenty more of his plays for enterprising directors to try: Detroit Repertory Theatre staged *Charlie* and *Out at Sea* during the 1988–9 season.

Tango, in ▷Tom Stoppard's adaptation, is probably Mrozek's most familiar work. In this play, questions of freedom and authority in the modern state are raised through the metaphor of an anarchic family with an intellectual but authoritarian son who is trying to reform it; he fails to maintain control, and brute force takes over in the form of Eddie the butler. The play, besides being full of logical paradoxes and knotty arguments of the Stoppard kind, is also very funny.

Try these:
▷Vacláv Havel for another Eastern European playwright with kindred themes and techniques; ▷Tom Stoppard for *Professional Foul*, *Every Good Boy Deserves Favour*, and *Squaring the Circle*, which treat similar themes; ▷Brecht's *Conversations in Exile* has similarities to *Emigrés*; Witold Gombrowicz; ▷Czeslaw Milosz; Janusz Glowacki's *Cinders* was co-adapted by ▷Hanif Kureishi; ▷Pam Gems adapted Stanislawa Przybyszewska's *The Danton Affair*.

MÜLLER, Heiner   [1929–]
German playwright and director

Plays include:
The Scab (1956), *The Construction Site* (1957), *The Correction* (1958), *Herakles 5* (1966), *Philoctetes* (1966), *Oedipus Tyrant* (1966), *The Horatian* (1968), *Mauser* (1970), *Germania Death in Berlin* (1971), *Macbeth* (1972), *The Battle* (1974), *Hamletmachine* (1977), *Quartet* (1981),

*Despoiled Shore Medeamaterial Landscape
with Argonauts* (1984), *Civil WarS Act IV*
(1984)

Heiner Müller's unique political theatre transcended even the Berlin Wall. The most produced playwright in both Germanys over the
last decade, he now must redefine his dialectic
in the face of national unity. His family chose
to move to the West, but Müller stayed in the
East, where his plays (many of which explore
the problems of a failed socialist utopia) were
banned from 1961 to 1973. His life, politics,
and art reflect the schizophrenia of the divided
German nation.

Heir to ▷Bertolt Brecht's position as premier German playwright, Müller served as dramaturg at the Berliner Ensemble from
1970–1975. His early works are Brechtian
Lëhrstucke (teaching plays), and his poetic
drama, like Brecht's, finds its roots in
▷expressionism; but he goes far beyond
Brecht's parable formula as a means of
expressing the political and historical contradictions of the world. His mature plays abandon conventional plot, dialogue, and
characterisation; instead, they are collages
that he calls 'synthetic fragments' in which
disparate scenes and metaphoric visions are
juxtaposed non-sequentially to create meaning
through clashes of image and text. Müller
suggests the director actively confront the
script and add elements that compound the
levels of meaning. This disjuncture between
words and actions has attracted the collaboration of Robert Wilson who created several
mise en scènes, including *Civil WarS Act IV*,
around Müller texts. Although Müller often
directs his own work, numerous other post-
modern directors are drawn to his image-
laden plays, and 1990 witnessed a theatre festival in Frankfurt devoted solely to productions of Müller's work.

Many of Müller's plays are deconstructions
of classical texts or historical dramas.
Germania Death In Berlin presents violent images and themes from Prussian history and
mythology. In this kaleidesceope of German
history, Müller chronicles the brutalization of
the German people, in which Nazism is seen
as the natural culmination of Prussian militarism. Here, Goebbels gives birth to Hitler's
child which turns out to be a thalidomide
wolf. Although he has spent a good deal of
time in the United States, Müller, hailed as
the most important playwright since
▷Samuel Beckett in Europe, is still relatively
little known by the American or British
publics which appear to prefer more traditional forms of theatre.

Try these:
▷Robert Wilson and Peter Sellars for
post-modern direction; ▷Büchner for influences on style; Erwin Piscator for early
lëhrstuck; Pina Bausch and Martha Clarke
for powerful stage imagery.

MUNRO, Rona   [1959–]
Scottish playwright

Plays include:
The Bang and Whimper (1982), *The
Salesman* (1982), *Fugue* (1983), *The Bus*
(1984), *Watching Waiters* (1984), Off the
Road (1988), *The Way To Go Home* (1987),
Bold Girls (1990)

Munro was born in Aberdeen though she now
lives in Edinburgh. Her work has been largely
Scottish based – besides her stage plays, she
has been a regular contributor to various
Scottish radio and television series, as well as
young people's theatre. Like her compatriot,
▷Liz Lochhead, she also performs her own
material and comedy sketches. As a playwright, however, her plays show an arresting
and penetrating line of psychological enquiry
and an interesting willingness to experiment
with forms.

Fugue, her first full-length play (presented
at the Traverse in Edinburgh and subsequently in New York), is about a young
girl's retreat into herself and her past with
poetic and pastoral overtones, and revealed
preoccupations which she has continued to
explore and develop with deepening intensity.
Watching Waiters, for example, commissioned
by BBC Radio Scotland, is a tense, powerful
journey into the female psyche – a confrontation by a woman, possibly on the verge of a
breakdown, with her inner state of being
(strong images of being trapped behind glass)
and connections between, vulnerability, self-
image and the sensuality of food and sex. Part
nightmare, part investigation, like the best of
therapies (it even has an alter ego interroga-
tor), it confronts past ghosts in order to move
forward to self-affirmation.

Intimations of ghosts are also present in her
most recent play for ▷7:84 Scotland, *Bold
Girls*, which won the 1990 Susan Blackburn
Award for best women's play. Ostensibly it is
a heart-warming albeit familiar tale of Belfast

women struggling against the odds to keep house and home together when menfolk are taken away (to prison or killed), but Munro's treatment endows the play with something more than mere melodrama. Subtly, she builds a complex pattern of relationships which ultimately reveal the ghosts as being the illusions and self-deceptions that women employ to sustain the reality about their relationships with men, which otherwise might not be tenable. Women's solidarity is also shown to be highly vulnerable under such strains and far from straightforward.

Try these:
▷Sarah Daniels' *Beside Herself* and Marsha Norman's *Getting Out* for plays that employ an alter ego to investigate areas of the female psyche; ▷Sharman Macdonald for more Scottish scrutiny of mother–daughter relationships at close quarters; ▷Marie Jones' *Beyond the Balcony* and ▷Christina Reid's *Joyriders* for other plays which, like *Bold Girls* use Belfast's Divis Flats for its central location; Reid's *Tea in a China Cup* for more pictures of generations of women and attitudes to community; Spare Tyre, for a women's group who started out looking at the relationship of women to their self-image and their *Pouring It Out* about women and friendship; ▷Pam Gems and ▷Nell Dunn for earlier examples of women struggling to find solidarity; Tony Roper's *The Steamie* is another Scottish writer's portrait of women together–in Glasgow's bath-houses; ▷Women in Theatre.

MURRAY, Melissa   [1954–]
British dramatist, poet

Plays include:
Bouncing Back with Benyon (with Eileen Fairweather; 1977), *Hot Spot* (1978), *Belisha Beacon* (with Eileen Fairweather; 1978), *Hormone Imbalance* (revue; 1979), *Ophelia* (1979), *The Admission* (1980), *The Execution* (1982), *The Crooked Scythe* (1982–3), *Coming Apart* (1985), *Body-cell* (1986)

Melissa Murray's output reflects the diversity of styles women playwrights have adopted in the past decade in the search for ways of expressing the female experience: revue (*Hormone Imbalance*, a surreal gay cabaret), agit-prop (*Bouncing Back with Benyon*, a pro-

abortion piece), blank verse (*Ophelia*, a parody of Shakespeare seen from a lesbian feminist perspective), rhyming verse (*The Crooked Scythe*) and historical epic (*The Execution*). They have had their share of brickbats (women's writing is frequently criticised for being either too aggressive or too humourless, too unfocused or too benign). However, *Coming Apart*, which won the Verity Bargate award, showed the best and the worst of Murray's style: a certain untidiness in the overall plot – the interaction of four characters, trapped in memories of the past in a Berlin boarding house – but a haunting, elusive quality capable of evoking a disturbing sense of paranoia, fear and disorientation, and a considerable sympathy for the vulnerable and isolated. Murray touched on this theme in a different way in the earlier *The Admission*, an angry forty-minute piece about society's approach to treating women and mental illness. *Body-cell* combines these themes of isolation and society's controlling techniques in the portrait of a female political prisoner in Durham prison, confined to solitary for disruptive behaviour, and her increasing withdrawal from human contact as a result of it.

Try these:
For states of isolation ▷Ayshe Raif's *Another Woman*, ▷Botho Strauss' *Great and Small*, and ▷Barry Collins' *Judgement*; for women and mental illness, ▷Tony Craze's *Shona*, ▷David Mercer's *In Two Minds*, ▷Alan Ayckbourn's perhaps over-praised but nonetheless moving *A Woman in Mind*, Charlotte Perkins Gilman's Edwardian account of a wife's deterioration, *The Yellow Wallpaper*, and ▷David Edgar's *Mary Barnes*; for images of women in prison, Clean Break and ▷Jacqueline Holborough; ▷Marsha Norman's *Getting Out* for an American comparison.

MUSIC-HALL/VARIETY IN BRITAIN
Music-hall and variety flourished in Britain for almost a hundred years, starting in the early to mid-nineteenth century in pubs and song and supper rooms, and gradually developing into vast Empires and Alhambras with twice-nightly programmes. The large halls gradually closed after World War I and the coming of cinema, but music-halls, and variety acts on radio, lingered on until after World War II. Nostalgia lingers still, mostly

because of the marvellous songs that were generated and the associated myth of a lively, subversive and essentially working-class culture.

There are two legacies from the music-hall to the current legitimate stage: one is its direct influence on plays, as in the use of authentic songs in *Oh What a Lovely War* to counterpoint the facts about the war, the extended use of a second-rate music-hall act in John Osborne's *The Entertainer* to make points about the state of England, and the use of techniques of cross-talk dialogue and comic monologue by playwrights such as ▷Beckett and ▷Pinter. The other legacy stems from nostalgia and the glamour that has always been attached to the 'Idols of the Halls': various one- or two-person shows and plays based on the lives and actions of real music-hall figures, such as Max Miller, Flanagan and Allen, and above all Marie Lloyd. The best so far is probably ▷Alan Plater's *On Your Way, Riley!* (Theatre Royal, Stratford; 1982), which neatly counterpoints the stage personae and sketches of Arthur Lucan and Kitty McShane with their Strindbergian marital battles. There will no doubt be more such plays – there were plenty of remarkable people in the halls. The interesting and invigorating thing about current variety entertainment is that it is often alternative cabaret, with individual stand-up acts, comic or musical or both, that has the closest affinity with music hall. Variety also still flourishes in larger pubs and clubs throughout Britain.

Try these:
▷Trevor Griffiths' *Comedians* for would-be stand up comics and the aggressive use of comedy as a tool of social criticism; ▷Peter Nichols' *Privates on Parade* for a concert party; ▷cabaret.

MUSSMANN, Linda   [1947–]
American writer and director

Productions include:
Room/Raum (1978), *Is the Dialogue Read* (1983), *Fresh Starts* (1984), *Avoidance and Peculiar* (1985), *Civil War Chronicles*, 1986–1989, *M.A.C.B.E.T.H.* (1990)

As founder/writer/director of Time & Space Limited in 1973, Mussmann experiments with the formal aspects of drama, challenging its meaning. Influenced by Gertrude Stein, Mussmann foregrounds and heightens perceptual understanding with an emphasis upon sounds, rhythms, intonations and voices. *M.A.C.B.E.T.H.* is a one-woman performance of the deprivations of Lady Macbeth. From 1979 to the present, Mussmann has adapted *Danton's Death* in various ways, with the most recent version being a radio play in which two women's voices speak in English/French/German in a montage technique of fragmentation and quotation that explores ▷Büchner's conception of the ideal and the real, of revolution and counter-revolution. The *Civil War Chronicles*, a massive project made up of four plays, examines narrative structure and meaning as history. Space and time is disrupted, the past becomes a continuous present in which traditions of historical representation are questioned. An 'official history of man' is revised by the personal thoughts of a female participant who continually re-contextualizes incidents through a journey of public and private landscapes of the femine.

Try these:
Dr. Faustus Lights the Lights, by Gertrude Stein, for a similar aesthetic that questions the politics of justice; *Katana*, by Japanese playwright Kikue Tashiro, in which the stylisation of the East meets the formal experimentation of the West; ▷Bernard Pomerance's *Quantrill in Lawrence* for another version of the American Civil War; ▷Brian Friel's *Translations* for multilingual approaches to history; ▷Nancy Reilly for another experimenter in dramatic forms, especially in *Assume the Position* which explores narrative forms as against Performance Art; ▷Shakespeare's *Macbeth*; Helen Cooper's *Mrs Ganguin* and *Mrs Vershinin*, Melissa Murray's *Ophelia* for female angles on male classics.

 n

NATIONAL THEATRE, THE

As Sir Peter Hall, the artistic director who took the company into the South Bank, said: 'for 150 years, the radicals of the theatre have been fighting for a National Theatre: they have collected money for it, given up their careers for it, and spent their energies in a most prodigal and altruistic way for it'. After many false starts work on a National Theatre building designed by Denys Lasdun, and comprising three auditoria, finally began under the Labour Minister for the Arts, Jennie Lee, in 1969, and the first theatre opened to the public in 1976.

Although the building and siting of a National Theatre took a long time, a National Theatre Company had been in existence since 1963 under the directorship of Laurence Olivier, and the Old Vic theatre was for many years the base for the National Theatre. The Old Vic company had been founded by Lilian Baylis, an enormously influential theatrical manager whose aim was to bring art and culture to the people, and who was instrumental in establishing national opera and ballet companies in Britain. Without her there would have been no National Theatre. Her efforts are rewarded at the National with a terrace in her name 'The Baylis Terrace'.

The National Theatre is now made up of three auditoria, a proscenium theatre, the Lyttleton (named after Lord Chandos, the National Theatre Board's first chair), the largest, the open stage Olivier (after Laurence Olivier), and the versatile workshop space, the Cottesloe (after the first Chair of the South Bank Theatre Board). The original plan was that the Lyttleton should concentrate on new writing, touring and retrospective seasons, the Olivier should continue the work of the Old Vic company and that the Cottesloe should be a space for new and experimental drama. In fact, government cutbacks and underfunding meant that the National was not in a position to take many risks, although the separately run studio (based in the Old Vic annexe) still attempts to meet its experimental obligations

with continuing workshops, encouragment of young writers, and studio workshops. There were exceptions: Bill Bryden's tenure developed a 'promenading' style in the Cottesloe which produced several outstanding productions culminating in Tony Harrison's adaptations of the The Mysteries, a truly outstanding cycle of mystery plays that showed just what a national subsidised theatre could do. On the whole the National has, in these straitened years, tended to work with tried and tested actors, directors and texts, often picking up on the proven successes of fringe theatre. Richard Eyre has expanded this policy further, encouraging an even wider representation of talent, including Jatinder Verma and the Théâtre de Complicité. Under Peter Hall's tenure, the National Theatre's strength lay in its revivals of neglected European classics by writers such as ▷Schnitzler and ▷von Horváth, first-rate productions of British and American classics, and visits by major foreign companies.

The Olivier, though proving a more challenging space than perhaps envisaged, has nonetheless produced its own share of memorable new plays including ▷David Hare's and ▷Howard Brenton's *Pravda*, ▷Ayckbourn's *Chorus of Disapproval*, ▷Christopher Hampton's *Tales from Hollywood*, and Tony Harrison's *The Trackers of Oxyrhynchus*.

One of the successes of Sir Peter Hall's regime was to establish in the ungainly concrete building a sense of popular hubbub with pre-theatre music in the foyer and outdoor summer activities on the terraces, to add to a well-stocked bookshop, continual theatre exhibitions and all-day restaurant facilities.

NELSON, Richard [1950–]
American dramatist

Plays include:
The Killing of Yablonski (1975), *Conjuring an Event* (1976), *Jungle Coup* (1978), *The Vienna Notes* (1978), *Bal* (1979), *Rip Van*

Winkle or The Works (1981), *The Return of Pinocchio* (1983), *An American Comedy* (1983), *Between East and West* (1984), *Principia Scriptoriae* (1986), *Some Americans Abroad* (1989), *Sensibility and Sense* (1989), *Two Shakespearean Actors* (1990)

Chicago-born Nelson is one of the few American playwrights to address political issues in the manner of British writers like ▷David Hare or ▷Howard Brenton; indeed, he says his interest in 'primarily social' themes can be 'lonely' for an American writer, and in recent years his work has found more of an audience in Britain than in the United States. Nelson has written both large sweeping works (his four-hour *Rip Van Winkle* plays like a parody of *Faust* crossed with *Peer Gynt*) and more focused two-character dramas such as *Between East and West* (about a Czech director and his wife experiencing culture shock in New York) and he frequently makes use of titles above his scenes for ironic or distancing effect. His embrace of private and public concerns no doubt prompted the producers of *Chess* to call on him when they needed someone to revise their troubled musical's book, but how Nelson will fare amidst the shark-like climate of Broadway – an environment he has so far eschewed – remains to be seen. He is perhaps best known for *The Vienna Notes*, a comedy about the contradictions between the glamorous public image of an American senator and the corrupt man within. The tensions between appearance and reality also surface in *Some Americans Abroad*, a recent work about tweedy American literature professors infatuated with an England that doesn't exist. Both plays also examine the varied ways we manipulate language and obstruct communication, a favourite Nelson theme that is also at the centre of *Conjuring an Event* (about journalism), *Principia Scriptoriae* (featuring writers caught in a right-wing police state), and *Sensibility and Sense*, with its many heated debates about the alleged distortions in one character's memoirs. Nelson carries the self-reflexive approach one step further in one of his latest plays, *Two Shakespearean Actors*, which is set during the Astor Place riot instigated by the rivalry between two 19th-century Macbeths – the Briton William Charles Macready and the American star, Edwin Forrest.

Nelson is also a prolific adapter and translator, especially of work by other politically concerned writers: ▷Dario Fo, ▷Brecht, and ▷Molière.

Principia Scriptoriae

An ambitious if flawed work set in an unnamed Latin American country, the play starts in 1970 under a right-wing government, moving to 1985 under a new leftist regime. Enmeshed in the political shift are two writers who find themselves on opposite sides of the ideological fence: the Cambridge-educated Ernesto, a Latin American dissenter who returns in the second act as the secretary to the Minister of Culture, and Bill, a middle-class American midwesterner who believes that 'you can't ever stop asking yourself questions'. Nelson's play ultimately poses more questions than it answers, but it's refreshing to see a writer reaching beyond his nation's boundaries in an attempt to consider how other nations breathe, speak, and think.

Try these:
▷Clifford Odets and ▷Arthur Miller are earlier writers with an overt social conscience; ▷David Hare's *A Map of the World*, Donald Freed's *The Quartered Man*, and ▷Dusty Hughes' *Jenkins' Ear* for contrasting treatments of contemporary *realpolitik;* ▷Manuel Puig's *Kiss of the Spider Woman*, ▷Trevor Griffiths' *The Party*, ▷David Hare's *Fanshen*, ▷Harold Pinter's *One for the Road* and ▷Samuel Beckett's *Catastrophe* are contemporary treatments of similar themes. ▷Bulgakov's *Black Snow*, ▷Lumiere and Son's *Why is Here there and Everywhere now?*, ▷Rose English and Nancy Reilly's *Assume the Position* for other disparate treatments of the nature of theatre.

NEMETH, Sally   [1960–   ]
American dramatist

Plays include:
Modern Lit (1982), *Pagan Day* (1985), *Holy Days* (1983), *Mill Fire* (1990), *Spinning into the Blue* (1990)

Chicago-born, Sally Nemeth's output has been small but highly significant. As is often the way of things, her rating appears to be higher in Britain than in her own native land.

A writer who places women at the centre of her plays but whose feminism is more subtle than overt, she writes sparely but with tremendous reverberative power, particularly on the inner emotional topographies of individuals at the sharp end of life's struggles.

The play that put her on the map in Britain was *Holy Days* – a taut, slice-of-life saga set in the US southern dust-bowl in the early part of this century. Stark, mean and bare, as was Nemeth's writing, Brian Stirner's immaculate and atmospheric 1988 production for London's tiny Soho Poly theatre translated Nemeth's naturalism into an experience that bit deep into the soul as its characters – two married couples – stoically carved out a meaning to their lives in the face of bitter odds and bereavement. The production won three London Fringe awards and has subsequently been performed in New Zealand and Dublin.

Nemeth, who founded her own company, Chicago New Plays in 1984 because 'we wanted to have more writers' control' was previously writer in residence at Pennsylvania's Bloomsbury Theatre Ensemble. Her following play, *Mill Fire* –another journey into the dark hinterland of grief, loss, anger and the patterns of marital need – was commissioned by Chicago's Goodman Theatre where she has also been writer in residence and later transferred to New York by Women's Project, the group set up over a decade ago to advance the work of women dramatists. Recent works have included *Spinning into the Blue*, commissioned by California's South Coast Rep – a play with abortion at its core, though not about abortion, insists Nemeth, in which the process of healing through anger and 'giving it up' is a central theme, and *Water Play*, an experimental piece for the Mark Taper Forum's New Works Festival.

Mill Fire

A relentless and sensual study of the response of Marlene, a young widow whose husband burned to death in a mill fire, Nemeth's focus is centred on Marlene's unassuageable grief and her anger at the indifference of the institution which controls the lives of those in the mill town. As with *Holy Days*, the dialogue is terse and uncompromising as she paints a hard-edged portrait of the brutality and banality of the minor's marriages and their prospects (Nemeth's father was himself a steel worker). The play is at once realistically structured yet unconventional in its use of flashbacks and the use of a Greek-like chorus of mill wives to reflect and comment.

Try these:
▷Marlane Meyer's *Etta Jenks* for a similarly unsentimental view of the options available to women; Darrah Cloud's adaptation of *Old Pioneers* and her play *The Stick Wife*; ▷Sean O'Casey, ▷Athol Fugard for earlier wirters with similar sympathies about women's lot; Steinbeck's *The Grapes of Wrath* for the original story of southern dust-bown American Depression.

NESTROY,
Johann Nepomuk   [1801–62]
Austrian actor, singer and dramatist

Plays include:
Einen Jux will er sich machen (*He's Out for a Fling*; 1842)

Nestroy's range of talents was even wider than ▷Molière's (his first professional appearance was as Sarastro in *The Magic Flute*) and his seventy-seven surviving plays (most of them satirical comedies) still hold the stage in Vienna, but little of his work has so far been translated into English. However, *Einen Jux will er sich machen* (itself based on two English farces) forms the basis both of ▷Thornton Wilder's successive versions, *The Merchant of Yonkers* (1938) and *The Matchmaker* (1954) (musicalised as *Hello, Dolly!*, 1963), and of ▷Stoppard's *On the Razzle* (▷National Theatre, 1981). Stoppard dealt with the problem of translating the rich Viennese dialect by ignoring it altogether, omitting sub-plot, comic songs, and local references, and letting his own line in outrageous wordplay enliven a good basic farce plot about two shop assistants having a stolen day out on the town (Vienna, of course).

Try these:
▷Horvàth, for adding a political element to Nestroy's folk play tradition; ▷Labiche's *La Cagnotte* for the theme of country folk having a day out on the town (Paris, of course).

NEW PLAYWRITING IN BRITAIN
A constant source of new writing is the life-blood of good theatre. Playwrights who end up as household names on British television frequently start off plugging their wares round

the fringe, pub and small touring companies. Unfortunately, the steady decline in public subsidy for theatre in Britain over the past decade, has had a particular effect on the commissioning of new work. Companies that used to be regular supporters and commissioners of new writing – such as the ▷RSC or the ▷National Theatre and many of the regional theatres such as Sheffield, Nottingham, Bristol and Leicester – find themselves struggling to survive at all and reluctant to be adventurous and support the new and challenging. In the past two years, since the *Guide*'s first edition, several small companies committed to new writing – Foco Novo and Joint Stock, for example – have been forced to close.

New plays are, of course, always a financial risk: larger companies like the RSC and the Royal National Theatre perhaps have more to lose with a new writer in their large auditoria than a small pub on the fringe circuit. On the other hand, they also have more funds at their disposal. On the whole, the major companies do not have as good a record as they might in encouraging new writing across the social spectrum, although new writers used to emerge through ▷RSC commissions and the National has such established names as ▷Tom Stoppard, ▷Christopher Hampton, ▷Alan Ayckbourn, ▷David Hare and ▷Howard Brenton. However, new writers from the Asian or West Indian communities (or the Irish or gay communities for that matter – ▷Sarah Daniels' *Neaptide* being a notable exception) have not found their way on to the National's stages, leading not surprisingly to cries of 'cultural apartheid'. This has been slightly ameliorated under Richard Eyre with his invitations to guest companies such as Tara Arts, Gay Sweatshop and Théâtre de Complicité to play at the National. For the past few years, the National has run a studio wing (first under director ▷Peter Gill, now under John Burgess) which has been nurturing new writers such as Mick Mahoney, Debbie Horsfield, Jacqueline Holborough, Jim Cartwright, and Sharman Macdonald. On the whole, therefore, new writing tends to test its muscles and make its mistakes away from the limelight (the Edinburgh Traverse still has a fine record on this score) and small-scale touring companies such as Gay Sweatshop, Paines Plough, Red Shift, Bristol Express, Foco Novo, Women's Theatre Group, Monstrous Regiment, Siren, Temba, 7:84 Scotland, and the Irish companies, Charabanc

and Field Day, have shouldered much of the responsibility for new writing. Certain London fringe theatres too have fine records for seeking out and championing new writing – the Soho Poly, the Bush, the Old Red Lion, the Oval House, Drill Hall, Riverside, the Orange Tree at Richmond and the Hampstead Theatre. But pre-eminently the ▷Royal Court has been at the forefront of new writing for well over 30 years. Some of the most innovative uses of texts have emerged through the multi-media, performance-art companies such as Hilary Westlake and Lumière and Son, Claire McDonald and Pete Brooks with Impact, and the Nottingham-based Dogs in Honey. New companies seem constantly to spring up to produce individual plays, but as project funding becomes the norm they disappear as quickly, and we are left with a similar situation as existed before 1956, where new writing relied on individual entrepreneurial producers such as Michael Codron (who introduced Pinter, Beckett, Stoppard to West End audiences. In the 1970s, Ian Albery was one of the few theatre managers to inject a little experimentation into the West End with transfers of Dario Fo's *Accidental Death of an Anarchist* and *Can't Pay Won't Pay* by the fringe company, Belt and Braces.

Among playwriting schemes to encourage new writing, particularly from women and black writers, are the Soho Poly's Verity Bargate award, the Royal Court's Young Playwriting Scheme. (Andrea Dunbar, ▷Ayshe Raif and the founders of Theatre of Black Women, Bernadette Evraisto and Patricia Hilaire are just a few to have started their careers through the scheme), and the Albany's Second Wave festival of new writing for young women (which has already produced a writer of promise in April de Angelis). The Royal Exchange's Mobil Playwriting competition has also proved its worth with the emergence of Iain Heggie and Robin Glendinning through its auspices. New sponsors are stepping in to some extent, Barclays Bank for example, with its 'New Stages' initiative. The Playwrights' Co-operative, New Playwrights Trust, Bristol Express and ▷Red Shift have also staged development and research schemes, readings and workshops to encourage new writing. Declining subsidy means new writing faces a precarious future. But it is impossible to judge how many new plays are not now being written, or are being restricted to only two or three characters to fit tighter budgets.

The feeling is that there is less good writing around now in Britain, not because there are fewer new plays but because the ones that are produced aren't very well written. Whatever hidden causes that implies, the result does seem to mean that not only are there fewer new playwrights emerging but the qualitative change in the kind of plays produced – more supine, less challenging to the status quo – that we predicted in the first edition has already begun to take hold. The spirited anarchy of the 1970s and early 1980s seems well and truly dead.

Try these:
New Playwrights Trust now acts as a co-ordinating centre for new writing; see also New Playwriting in the USA.

NEW PLAYWRITING IN THE USA
Play development in America began with George Pierce Baker, who began teaching a playwriting course at Harvard University in 1905. His work attracted a number of promising writers, chief among them ▷Eugene O'Neill. In 1925 Baker became head of Yale University's new Department of Drama; he is a forefather of the playwriting programme at Yale School of Drama, where many American dramatists receive their advanced training and launch their professional careers.

Established during the Depression by an act of Congress, the Federal Theatre Project at its peak employed 10,000 people at theatres in 40 states. Better known for the collective and ephemeral creations known as Living Newspapers than for new plays of lasting significance, the project, which lasted just four years (1935–9), set a precedent for government support of dramatic writing. Today the National Endowment for the Arts (NEA), created in 1965, is among the leading funders of new stage writing, through its fellowships for playwrights.

In 1949 Howard Lindsay, together with a handful of colleagues successful in the commercial theatre, founded an organisation to assist emerging playwrights. Today New Dramatists is thriving, and playwrights across the USA seek to become one of the group's forty members. Once chosen, a writer may hold membership for five years, and receives benefits ranging from theatre tickets and midtown-Manhattan accommodation to readings, workshops and script circulation. Even more important, perhaps, is the national exposure, the encouragement of being chosen by a committee of one's peers, the opportunity to know other good playwrights. The Playwrights' Center of Minneapolis, founded in 1971, is the most important of the similar organisations in other parts of the USA.

As head of the Ford Foundation's programme in support of the arts, authorised in 1957, W. MacNeil Lowry soon became a leading figure in the expansion of opportunities for American playwrights. For two decades the foundation poured millions of dollars of support into non-profit theatres throughout the United States in an attempt to create an alternative to the New York commercial theatre. Starting in 1958, the Foundation's Program for Playwrights backed productions of selected scripts. Following Ford's lead, in 1971 the Rockefeller Foundation launched its own Playwrights-in-Residence Program, which both supported writers financially and connected them with theatres to encourage productions of their plays. The development of hundreds of professional theatres across the country, most of whom stage at least one new play a year and some many more, has been the single most important factor in the development of new writing for the stage.

One of the early steps in the Ford Foundation's far-seeing programme of philanthropy was the establishment in 1961 of Theatre Communications Group, the national organisation of non-profit-making professional theatres. This communications centre for the decentralised American theatre became in time and among other things a publishing house. Before the launching of TCG's Plays in Progress series in 1979 plays that had not been successful in New York rarely found their way into print. By the mid-1980s, when TCG stepped up its book publication programme and began including plays in its *American Theatre* magazine, the link between success on New York's commercial stage and publication had been at least partially severed.

The off-Broadway and off-off-Broadway ferment of the 1960s having subsided, by the 1970s New York City was no longer the source of much of the country's new writing (although Playwrights Horizons, the New York Shakespeare Festival, Manhattan Theater Club and Circle Repertory Company are among the notable exceptions to this trend). Before the decade ended notable new plays were coming from such theatres as the

Mark Taper Forum in Los Angles and Actors Theatre of Louisville, whose Festival of New American Plays introduced ▷Beth Henley and ▷Marsha Norman, along with many other writers, to critics from around the country and abroad. Other plays were being developed in summer workshops like the National Playwrights Conference, which since 1965 has taken place annually at the O'Neil Center in Connecticut.

As Broadway possibilities kept shrinking through the 1980s, other kinds of opportunities – contests, residencies, commissions, workshops – continued to expand. But by the start of the 1990s major programmes for playwrights were disappearing or being cut back, and the value of others increasingly questioned. The Ford and Rockefeller foundations have moved on to other causes. The NEA, which has always had to fight to maintain its level of funding, has recently been under assault by right-wing forces who detect 'obscenity' in some of the art it has supported. Arts agencies in such key states as Massachusetts and New York are having their funding slashed as a result of bad economic time. Overwhelmed by unsuitable and often just plain bad plays, many theatres no longer accept unsolicited manuscripts. The Dramatists Guild has more than 7,000 members; some think it serves neither individual writers nor the American theatre to encourage everyone who shows a glimmer of talent. There is more and more talk of plays being 'developed to death' through endless rounds of readings and work-shops without promise of a full production. Some theatres are beginning to see that it is more important to sustain one or two playwrights over time than to work so hard to come up with a hit play.

Many would agree with critic Robert Brustein that 'there are more talented playwrights around the theatre today than at any other time in our history.' The programmes that have supported new writing for the theatre deserve credit. But for all they have done, it is still inordinately difficult for these talented writers to maintain a career in the American theatre.

Try these:

Theatre Communications Group's Plays in Process series circulates new scripts before they are published elsewhere. *The Dramatists Guild Quarterly* and TCG's *Dramatists Sourcebook* list opportunities for playwrights; the annual Newsday/ Oppenheimer Award for 'Best New American Playwright' is regularly given for a play produced outside the commercial mainstream; see also ▷New playwriting in Britain.

NICHOLS, Peter   [1927–   ]
British dramatist

Plays include:
A Day in the Death of Joe Egg (1967), *The National Health* (1969), *Forget-Me-Not-Lane* (1971), *Chez Nous* (1974), *The Freeway* (1974), *Harding's Luck* (1974), *Privates on Parade* (1977), *Born in the Gardens* (1979), *Passion Play* (USA: *Passion*; 1981), *Poppy* (1982), *A Piece of My Mind* (1986)

Nichols was born in Bristol, trained as an actor with the Bristol Old Vic and worked there until he was called up to National Service in the RAF and went to India and Malaya, a crucial experience for *Privates on Parade* which is set in a song and dance unit in Malaya. *A Day in the Death of Joe Egg*, Nichols' first stage play, is probably still the play with which he is most associated. It is openly autobiographical, drawn from the experience of his own disabled daughter. The play employs bitterly funny backchat between the father and mother, and brings in jazz and tap dance, in its exploration of the strains on a relationship of living with what the father calls a 'human parsnip'. Nichols writes very unsettling comedies, even the tragic subject of *A Day in the Death of Joe Egg* is handled with a bitter wit and he has taken a delight in experimenting with popular forms, often using an improbable form to make a satirical point. *The National Health* deals with a hospital ward full of patients who are in pain or dying, and puts them together with a hospital romance. *Privates on Parade* uses the form of the revue show to explore army life and the British presence in Malaya. *Poppy* uses ▷pantomime and ▷music hall to chart the British involvement in the Chinese Opium Wars, and has a wonderful alienation effect: the pantomime horse gets shot. *Poppy* also employs a pantomime sing song, in which a character uses all the pantomime devices to encourage the audience to sing along, only to confront them with the awareness of the racist and imperialistic implications of what they are singing. *Passion Play* is an elegant and witty dissection of middle-class adultery which gains extra resonance through the device of representing the characters' normally unspoken thoughts by other actors.

His most recent play *A Piece of My Mind* was a bitter comedy about his own difficulties with writing, and his resentment that his challenging and uncomfortable comedy was not more successful. Unsurprisingly it was badly reviewed, but contains some bravura writing and effects. According to Nichols: 'To make an audience cry or laugh is easy – they want to . . . this is only worth doing if one thereby catches a whiff of life, a true tang of the bitter mixture we all have to drink.'

Try these:
▷Alan Bennett, ▷Arnold Wesker and ▷John McGrath are among the (male) playwrights for whom National Service was a significant experience; ▷Tom Stoppard appears thinly disguised as Miles Whittier (a pun!) in *A Piece of My Mind*; ▷Graeae has affinities with Nichols in their ability to laugh at their own disabilities ▷Joe Orton shares Nichols' sense of the macabre in humour.

NORMAN, Marsha   [1947–]
American dramatist

Plays include:
Getting Out (1977), *Third and Oak* (comprising *The Laundromat* and *The Pool Hall*; 1978), *Circus Valentine* (1979), *'Night Mother* (1982), *The Holdup* (1983), *Traveler in the Dark* (1984), *Sarah and Abraham* (1988), *The Secret Garden* (book of the musical; 1991)

The Kentucky-born daughter of an estate agent, Marsha Norman has made a reputation as one of the United States' pre-eminent contemporary female playwrights on the basis of two widely known plays, *Getting Out*, her debut play commissioned for the Actors Theater of Louisville, and *'Night Mother*, which became a film co-starring Sissy Spacek and Anne Bancroft. The former is a terse and aggressive, if schematic, account of a woman's

re-assimilation into society after an eight-year prison term, with two actresses representing the central character at different phases of her life: the incarcerated, wilder Arlie and her maturer self, Arlene. *'Night Mother* premiered at Actors Theater of Louisville before moving to the The American Repertory Theater in Cambridge, Massachusetts and Broadway. It won the 1983 Pulitzer Prize (Norman won the first Susan Smith Blackburn prize the same year) and was seen at Hampstead in 1985. Its harrowing portrait of the suicidal but pragmatic Jessie Cates and her panic-stricken mother (originally played to great acclaim by Kathy Bates and Anne Pitoniak) ruthlessly up-ends the American family-in-crisis play. In telling its story to the onstage ticking of six clocks, *'Night Mother* is an unusual instance of a play whose stage time equals real time. *Traveler in the Dark* premiered at The American Repertory Theater, but fared less well with the critics. Norman is one of several regionally oriented playwrights (such as ▷Beth Henley and ▷David Mamet to move into the American theatrical mainstream in recent years.

Try these:
▷Tennessee Williams' *The Glass Menagerie*, Paul Zindel's *The Effect of Gamma Rays . . .*, ▷Louise Page's *Real Estate* are some of the many plays showing mothers and daughters locked in combat; Greek tragedy (particularly *Medea*) and ▷Ibsen's *Hedda Gabler* for dramas with an inexorable pull towards an event we cannot imagine happening that nonetheless shatters us when it does; ▷Thomas Babe, ▷Wallace Shawn for the willed aggression of the writing; ▷David Mamet for a comparable sense of the weight of silence, and the use of real time, also in ▷Lanford Wilson's *Talley's Folly*; Clean Break for treatments of women in prison; ▷O'Neill's *Strange Interlude* for an earlier example of an expressionistic treatment of the protagonist's inner life; ▷Miller's *Death of a Salesman* is a previous generation's look at a suicide in the making.

 O

O'BRIEN, Richard
Australian actor, composer, lyricist, director
and dramatist

Plays include:
The Rocky Horror Show (1973), *Top People*
(1984)

Richard O'Brien was responsible for one of
the great cult successes of the 1970s and one of
the great cult failures of the 1980s. *The Rocky
Horror Show*, a camp combination of transvestism, the Frankenstein story and music, began
at the Royal Court Theatre Upstairs and has
now achieved a kind of independent existence
of its own, virtually impervious to criticism,
as much a cultural monument in its own way
as ▷Agatha Christie's *The Mousetrap*. Its
initial success owed much to the energy and
commitment of its first cast who included Tim
Curry, Julie Covington and O'Brien himself
but it has now become equally its audience's
property with people regularly dressing up as
their favourite characters, joining in the songs
and dialogue, throwing confetti at the wedding and so on. There are, particularly in the
USA, conventions and fan clubs and the
whole camp cult has become a phenomenon
that transcends the bounds of theatre or of
cinema (the film version, made in 1975 with
many of the original cast, has much the same
effect as the stage version). *Top People* was an
unmitigated disaster that deservedly lasted
less than a week in London.

Try these:
For aspects of camp ▷Joe Orton, the
deliciously outrageous Bloolips and the
superb drag/performance artist, ▷Ethyl
Eichelberger; for contrast, Tilda Swinton's
trans-sexual male in the socialist-surreal
Man to Man by Manfred Karge; for
Frankenstein variations, ▷April De
Angelis' *Breathless*, ▷Graeae; the physi-
cality and energy of *The Rocky Horror
Show* can also be found in the work of

▷Steven Berkoff, ▷Performance Art and
some ▷cabaret artists.

O'CASEY, Sean   [1880–1964]
Irish dramatist

Plays include:
The Shadow of a Gunman (1923), *Juno and
the Paycock* (1924), *The Plough and the
Stars* (1926), *The Silver Tassie* (1928),
Within the Gates (1933), *The Star Turns
Red* (1940), *Purple Dust* (1940), *Red Roses
for Me* (1942), *Cock-a-Doodle Dandy*
(1949), *Bedtime Story* (1951), *The Bishop's
Bonfire* (1955), *The Drums of Father Ned*
(1960)

One of the great dramatists of the twentieth
century, O'Casey is best remembered for the
early Dublin plays but his later exuberant,
equally politically conscious, tragi-comic
epics deserve as wide an audience as the so-
called Dublin Trilogy (*The Shadow of a
Gunman*, *Juno and the Paycock*, *The Plough
and the Stars*). O'Casey, largely self taught,
and politically active, was initially fostered by
the Abbey Theatre but ▷Yeats' rejection of
The Silver Tassie, which now seems astonish-
ingly misguided, led to O'Casey's departure
from Ireland and a career marked by further
controversy and misunderstanding. *The Silver
Tassie* is an anti-war play which extends
O'Casey's dramaturgy into a highly stylized
quasi-liturgical second act; the mixture of
styles suggests the difference between the normal world and the world of the war. O'Casey's
socialism, his hatred of priestly influence in
Ireland and his ceaseless experimentation with
form all contributed to his relative eclipse in
the professional theatre and it is surprising
that, in an era more receptive to large-scale
non-linear political work, some of the later
plays have yet to be given major productions.
Cock-a-Doodle Dandy in particular deserves a
wider audience, with its life-size dionysiac
Cock struggling against the forces of repres-

sion in the form of capitalism and the church which attempt to quell the human spirit. Not that the earlier plays have outlived their welcome: O'Casey's presentation of the heady contradictions of the struggle for Irish independence is still horribly relevant to the present, not only in terms of an understanding of the intractability of that situation, but also in more general terms of an analysis of the sheer messiness and mixture of impulses and dynamics in any political situation.

Juno and the Paycock

A brilliant mixture of the comic and tragic which takes in the abduction and murder of Juno's son (Johnny) who has informed on a Diehard colleague, her unmarried daughter Mary's pregnancy and attitudes to it, the posturings of her feckless husband (the Paycock of the title), the apparent rise in the social status of the family as the result of a supposed inheritance, and its collapse when the will turns out to have been badly drafted. There are major issues here about the poisoned inheritance of Ireland, the importance of received attitudes in determining people's responses to both political and personal issues, the role of women in both sustaining and fracturing male vanities; but they emerge for us in truly epic style as we are faced with a necessity for practising complex seeing and thinking above the flow of the action as well as with it. The final scene, with the room stripped of furniture, Juno and Mary departed to Juno's sister's, Johnny dead, and the drunk and oblivious Paycock telling his pal Joxer that the whole world is 'in a terr . . . ible state o' . . . chassis', is a fine example of O'Casey's ability to present contradictions simultaneously and in memorable theatrical form.

The Plough and the Stars

Set during the Easter Rising of 1916, The Plough and the Stars is more directly concerned with great political events than Juno and the Paycock, but the focus is still largely on ordinary people and their reactions to events; although some of Padraic Pearse's speeches are spoken by the Voice in Act Two, he is not identified by name. Again we have a tenement setting, an assortment of representative characters and the mixture of the comic and the tragic, but here the mood is darker and the dispossession of the Irish is clearer. The play ends in another fine dramatisation of contradiction, with Dublin burning as two English soldiers sit drinking tea and singing

'Keep the Home Fires Burning' in the room from which the Irish inhabitants have been expelled; the hope embodied in the women and the pregnancy in Juno has been snuffed out in this play by death and by madness, and the men are generally as ineffectual as before.

Try these:
O'Casey declared that he was influenced by ▷Shakespeare and ▷Boucicault; ▷Joe Corrie and ▷Brecht's theatre have much in common with O'Casey's; Frank McGuinness' Observe the Sons of Ulster Marching Towards the Somme also deals with the Irish and World War I; ▷Brendan Behan had much of the energy, if less of the discipline, of O'Casey; ▷Sherriff's Journey's End, ▷Willis Hall's The Long and the Short and the Tall and Theatre Workshop's Oh What a Lovely War offer different accounts of war; ▷Howard Brenton and ▷David Edgar have something of the same energy and willingness to experiment in order to make political points; of the many writers now writing about Northern Ireland, ▷Ann Devlin's Ourselves Alone, ▷Seamus Finnegan's North, and ▷Marie Jones's Gold in the Streets attempt to show the intractable contradictions of the situation in all their socio-politico-religious complexity.

ODETS, Clifford   [1906–63]
American dramatist

Plays include:
Awake and Sing (1935), Waiting For Lefty (1935), Till the Day I Die (1935), Paradise Lost (1935), Golden Boy (1937), Rocket to the Moon (1938), Night Music (1940), Clash By Night (1941), The Big Knife (1949), The Country Girl (1950), The Flowering Peach (1954), The Silent Partner (written in 1937; produced posthumously in 1972)

'I would say that I have shown as much of the seamy side of life as any other playwright of the twentieth century, if not more', the Philadelphia-born Odets once commented. And as a chronicler of moral malaise, Odets is hard to beat, even when his chosen milieus (as in the Beverley Hills playroom of The Big Knife) deceptively evoke a ▷Noël Coward comedy, not a scabrous indictment of the 'noisy, grabbing world' of Hollywood. Odets was the star dramatist of the Group Theatre –

Harold Clurman, Cheryl Crawford and Lee Strasberg's 1931–41 New York enterprise that grew out of the Theatre Guild – and his keystone early plays *Waiting For Lefty* and *Awake and Sing* were both premiered there. Although his plays can seem melodramatic and ponderous, at their best their moral vigour is stirring, and they provide notable acting opportunities, particularly of a dry, hard-boiled sort. *Golden Boy*, a play about a violinist-turned-boxer that makes genuine individuals out of archetypes was memorably revived at the ▷National Theatre in 1984 by director Bill Bryden, with American actress Lisa Eichhorn as Lorna and Jack Shephard in top form as the manager, Fuseli. Generally, British interest in Odets is due to Robin LeFevre, who staged variable revivals of *Rocket to the Moon*, *The Country Girl*, and *The Big Knife* in 1982, 1983, and 1987, respectively.

Waiting For Lefty

A taxi union votes to go on strike in Odet's landmark 1935 drama, as important for its radical Socialist form as for its message. Produced by the Group Theatre and directed by its co-founder, Harold Clurman, the staging planted actual cabbies in the audience, which gave a charge to the final rallying cry, 'Strike!' The Lefty of the title, one of the union leaders, never arrives, but Odets uses the drivers and their families to launch an assault on capitalism in the kind of denunciation of avarice that few American playwrights have fielded since. The play is didactic agit-prop, to be sure, but also testimony to an era in American playwriting when plays were seen to make a difference – not marginalised, escapist 'entertainments' as they are all too often viewed now, despite genuine inheritors of Odets' vision like Arthur Miller and ▷David Mamet.

Try these:
The early plays of ▷Eugene O'Neill (especially *The Hairy Ape*) and Marc Blitzstein's folk opera *The Cradle Will Rock* for both subject matter and experimental form; ▷Beckett's *Waiting for Godot*, ▷David Mercer's *After Haggerty* for other plays where the title character never appears ▷David Rabe's *Hurlyburly* for later, equally bitter writing about Hollywood;

▷Arthur Miller and ▷David Mamet for comparable emphases on the playwright as conscience.

OFF- AND OFF-OFF-BROADWAY

Mary Henderson, in her fine illustrated book *Theater in America* (Abrams, 1986), finds the first use of the term 'Off Broadway' in a 1937 annual theatre reference book. However, alternatives to the more popular (and expensive) entertainments theatregoers find on Broadway had been available for decades.

Two groups grew out of the intellectual ferment of Greenwich Village around 1914–15: the Washington Square Players and the Provincetown Players, whose devotion to the theatre experiments and radical subjects (for that time) seem artistic forebears of the Off- and Off-Off-Broadway movements in the 1950s and 1960s. These companies produced the early plays of Eugene O'Neill and Susan Glaspell (among the founders of Provincetown Players) as well as work by Theodore Dreiser and Zona Gale.

The Living Theatre (the late Julian Beck and Judith Malina's radically experimental troupe) perhaps provided the most stunning and certainly the most publicized alternative to Broadway. Their productions of Jack Gelber's *The Connection* (1959) and Kenneth H. Brown's *The Brig* (1961) are not only seen as seminal moments in the development of Off-Broadway but in the history of American theatre as a whole. The Living Theatre, followed by Joseph Papp's New York Shakespeare Festival, and Circle in the Square founded by Jose Quintero, Ted Mann, and others, all remain active today, although in different forms, sizes, and with somewhat altered missions. They prove good samples, however, of the alternatives Off-Broadway provided: experimental, ensemble work; revivals of Shakespeare performed in an 'American style'; and new works by contemporary playwrights.

Today, Actors' Equity Association offers theatres an 'Off Broadway' contract, one whose assignees include Circle Repertory Company, Manhattan Theatre Club, New York Shakespeare Festival, and Playwrights Horizons. These theatres, and smaller companies like Second Stage, Ensemble Studio Theatre, and INTAR Hispanic Arts Center, have become the artistic homes to a large contingent of the USA's best known playwrights, including Lanford Wilson, Terrence

McNally, Beth Henley, George C. Wolfe, John Patrick Shanley, Christopher Durang, Wendy Wasserstein, Michael Weller, Richard Greenberg, Leslie Lee and Maria Irene Fornes, to name a few. Other companies like CSC Repertory Ltd./The Classic Stage Company (a recent production of *Arturo Ui* starred John Turturro) and SoHo Repertory focus on interesting revivals of neglected classics.

However, because the larger Off Broadway theatres are now firmly established as 'institutions' with solid reputations, the younger up-and-coming writers, performers, directors, and designers continue to gravitate to Off-Off-Broadway venues. This movement toward smaller, less financially taxing theatre spaces, in which productions may be mounted with a minimum of resources, continues a trend that began in the early 1960s. In fact, some of the 'established' playwrights mentioned above, like Irene Fornes and Lanford Wilson, first wrote for these theatres during this period.

Of course, these venues weren't always theatres, properly speaking. Two of the best known 'theatres' from Off-Off Broadway's hey-day in the 1960s, were the Greenwich Village coffeehouses Caffe Cino, where Joe Cino invited all sorts of writers and performers to take over the tiny stage, and Ellen Stewart's Cafe La Mama, which in its present incarnation as La Mama Etc. is one of the scene's most vital institutions, continually presenting an array of important American and international theatre artists like Harvey Fierstein, Jean-Claude van Itallie, Tadeusz Kantor, and Andre Serban. Other notable alternative spaces included St. Mark's Church-on-the-Bouwerie, where some of Sam Shepard's early performance pieces were presented by Theatre Genesis and a former garage in which Richard Schechner gathered together a group of theatre artists to produce his environmental stagings (many of these artists still work in there as the Wooster Group).

The late 1970s saw a flowering of a new kind of Off-Off Broadway performance genre, in which artists mixed media and messages in such experimental outposts for performance art as the Franklin Furnace (now defunct), the Kitchen, P.S. 122, and HOME for Contemporary Theatre and Art. Of course, actors, writers, and directors with a more mainstream mindframe continued to showcase their work through continuous low-budget productions of classics, revivals, and assorted new plays, much of them forgettable.

This theatrical fringe activity has spawned mirror images in larger American cities since the 1980s. There are 'Off-' and 'Off-Off-Broadways' in Los Angeles, San Francisco, and Chicago, for example, cities where Actors' Equity has created the equivalents of New York's Showcase Code and Mini contract so that theatre artists and producers can mount more experimental and/or small-budget productions while using professional actors. Almost every major city has a Performance Art venue or two as well.

In general, the last 30 years have seen a tremendous explosion of American theatrical production, playwriting, and experimentation, partly fueled by the low-budget, experimental aesthetic that came to prominence in the Off- and Off-Off Broadway theatres in New York during the 1950s and 1960s. As theatre becomes more and more decentralized in the USA, and notwithstanding recent attacks by conservative forces and intense economic pressures, the phenomenal growth of Off- and Off-Off Broadway theatre during the last three decades – in New York and other cities – should continue into the 21st century.

Try these:
▷African-American Theatre; ▷British Theatre Companies; ▷Resident Theatre in the USA.

OLIVE, John   [1949–]
American dramatist

Plays include:
Minnesota Moon (1979), *Clara's Play* (1981), *Standing on My Knees* (1981), *The Voice of the Prairie* (1987), *Killers* (1988)

John Olive's life has been a blend of midwestern American values and cultural urbanity. Born in Japan, Olive was educated and has spent most of his life in Minnesota, where many of his plays are set. His earthy character is the core for his plays and, though one might expect his creations to have limited appeal, they have been produced in New York, at the 1979 Edinburgh Festival, at the Humana New Play Festival and in numerous regional theatres. *Minnesota Moon*, produced in 100 different venues, is exemplary. It presents two young men as they share an evening near an old farmhouse drinking beer, reminiscing and dreaming; one is off to college and the other to stay in the small town. Both *Clara's Play* and *Voice of the Prairie* explore the same predicament. *Clara's Play* brings together an ageing woman, attached to a crumbling Minnesota farm, and a young Norwegian handyman bound for a life in the West. *Voice of the Prairie* crosses ideals in time rather than personalities, as radio players recollect travels of an earlier generation, intersecting people and values from past and present. Olive has expanded his dramaturgy with plays that are solid entertainment (*Killers*), provocative psychological inquiries (*Standing on My Knees*) and ventures into film, television, radio and opera libretti. He continues to live in Minnesota.

Standing On My Knees

Paranoid schizophrenia, the intriguing mental disorder that manifests the nether region between illusion and reality, can serve as good drama since conflict need not exist between characters but between personalities of an infirm mind. That is precisely the concept which drives *Standing On My Knees*, a story of Catherine, a recovering schizophrenic poet. Hungry for a genuine connection with reality, she falls in love with a young businessman. Still she remains a hair's breadth away from the pit; her sanity maintained through a delicate balance of drugs and psychotherapy. Her true self is realised within her poetry but to fulfil her muse would be a risk of relapse. This is Olive's most adventuresome playwriting. It is not a regional anecdote nor an exploitative pseudo-psychocurative for a complex illness. It is grounded enough in the terrible realities of schizophrenia to become a useful, though perhaps extreme, metaphor about the tribulations of the creative artist.

Try these:
▷Tennessee Williams' *Glass Menagerie* for a delicate balance; ▷Tom Kempinksi's *Duet for One*, ▷Nicholas Wright's *Mrs Klein* for mental anguish; ▷Tony Craze's *Shona* and ▷David Edgar's *Mary Barnes* for outright portrayals of schizophrenia. ▷Hugh Whitemore's *Stevie*, ▷Susan Glaspell's *Alison's House*; ▷Howard Barker's *Scenes from an Execution* for female creative artists; Kevin Kling and John Klein for Minnesota-based dramatists; Tony Craze and David Edgar for British dramatists who have also dealt with the subject of schizophrenia.

O'MALLEY, Mary   [1941–]
British dramatist

Plays include:
Superscum (1972), *A 'Nevolent Society* (1974), *Oh If Ever a Man Suffered* (1975), *Once a Catholic* (1977), *Look Out . . . Here Comes Trouble* (1978), *Talk of the Devil* (1986)

London born chronicler of north London and the London Irish, O'Malley saw an article in *The Stage* about a school-chum who was writing plays for the ▷RSC and she felt she could do as well. *Superscum*, about a man living well on social security, *A 'Nevolent Society*, about three Jewish boys in Stoke Newington and *If Ever a Man Suffered*, about incest in an Irish family in Cricklewood all followed quickly. But the big break came with *Once a Catholic*, which brought her a year's writer-in-residency at the ▷Royal Court. Semi-autobiographical and set in a north London convent school, our Lady of Fatima, her hysterically funny dig at Catholicism, damnation and the sexual stirrings of adolescent girls won her both the *Evening Standard* and *Plays & Players* awards as 'most promising playwright'. Cathartically, *Once a Catholic* seems to have been one way of O'Malley releasing herself from the oppression of school life which felt 'like a big black cloud hanging overhead' and where she was told, 'Mary O'Malley, you'll never be any good' (she was told to leave school at sixteen because she was always playing truant). 'Really it was an epitaph to the Irish living in England as I remember them in my youth and Catholicism as taught before the 2nd Vatican Council.' She continued in the same vein, to some extent in *Talk of the Devil*, a family saga with Ortonesque echoes with its mixture of sex, religion and death (including visitations from an imaginary Devil got up in black leather). Her early experiences as a young wife and mother, married to a Jew, and contemplating Judaic conversion also ended up as a television comedy *Oy Vey Maria*. *Once a Catholic*, with its emblematic Marys (all the girls are called Mary), however, remains her pièce de résistance – a rare and hilarious female expression of adolescent retaliation against

Catholic dogma and the authoritarianism and hypocrisy of school which should be compulsory viewing for every generation.

Try these:
For scenes from school life, Denise Deegan's Angela Brazil spoof *Daisy Pulls It Off*, Muriel Spark's classic Presbyterian variation *The Prime of Miss Jean Brodie*; for adolescent female yearnings, ▷Sharman Macdonald and ▷Wedekind's *Spring Awakening*; for a male Irish view, ▷Hugh Leonard's adaptation of James Joyce's *Portrait of the Artist as a Young Man* or for an English view, ▷Alan Bennett's *Forty Years On* and John Dighton's *The Happiest Days of Our Lives*; for a complete contrast, Adrienne Kennedy's *A Lesson in Dead Language* which uses visual imagery bordering on the grotesque to make its point about the education of young women; ▷Nigel Williams' *Class Enemy* and Bill Cain's *Stand Up* tragedy are contemporary versions of waste of potential in schools.

O'NEILL, Eugene   [1888–1953]
American dramatist

Plays include:
Beyond the Horizon (1920), *The Emperor Jones* (1920), *Anna Christie* (1921), *The Hairy Ape* (1922), *Welded* (1924), *All God's Chillun Got Wings* (1924), *Desire Under the Elms* (1924), *The Great God Brown* (1926), *Marco Millions* (1928), *Strange Interlude* (1928), *Lazarus Laughed* (1928), *Mourning Becomes Electra* (1931), *Ah! Wilderness* (1933), *More Stately Mansions* (1938), *The Iceman Cometh* (1939; performed 1946), *Long Day's Journey Into Night* (1940; performed 1956), *A Touch of the Poet* (1940), *A Moon For the Misbegotten* (1943)

One of the leading American playwrights of this (or any) century, Eugene O'Neill was born in New York, the son of the actor James O'Neill. His own tortured and often sorrowful upbringing prompted several of the greatest family dramas ever written – works that take a scalpel to the blood ties that bind, finding the inextricable link between pain and passion where affections hover precariously over the abyss. O'Neill came of age as a playwright with the Provincetown Players, contributing most of their significant works. Greatly influenced by the Greeks (his *Mourning Becomes Electra* is a New England reworking of *The Oresteia*) and by ▷Strindberg (in his ▷expressionist period), his plays can seem cumbersome and pedantic, and his aspirations occasionally exceed his achievement. Recently, however, European and American directors have taken a stylised approach to his works, finding poetry in what might have been pompous – Keith Hack with his staging of *Strange Interlude*, David Leveaux with *A Moon For the Misbegotten*, Germany's Peter Stein with *The Hairy Ape*, Patrick Mason with *Desire Under the Elms*, and Ingmar Bergman's *Long Day's Journey into Night*. (Of a somewhat different order, Elizabeth LeCompte and ▷The Wooster Group incorporated a 16-minute version of *Long Day's Journey . . .* in their 1979 piece *Point Judith*.) The plays themselves avoid easy classification, whether tending towards the modernist (*Strange Interlude*, with its Faulknerian stream of consciousness) or the opaque (*The Great God Brown*), the surprisingly comic (*Ah! Wilderness*) or the ineffably sad (*Long Day's Journey . . .*). A four-time recipient of the Pulitzer Prize, O'Neill also became, in 1936, the first (and only) American playwright to win the Nobel Prize for literature.

The Iceman Cometh
Written in 1939 but not performed until seven years later, the play remains associated with its 1956 off-Broadway revival, which made the reputations of star Jason Robards and director Jose Quintero (the two re-teamed in 1985 for a commercially unsuccessful but critically acclaimed Broadway staging). A 1990 production by Robert Falls and the Goodman Theatre in Chicago was widely considered a major new interpretation of the play. *The Iceman Cometh* shows O'Neill at both his most ponderous and his most profound, as his lumbering symbolism and sometimes archaic language (the Biblical 'cometh' of the title) yield before the cumulative majesty of a text which does not let the audience out of its grip until both they and the characters have been brought up short by the death of their collective illusions. Set in Harry Hope's saloon in 1912, the play is a devastating evening of pipe dreams gone sour, with Hickey as the Virgil of the occasion leading us through this bar-room *Inferno*. With a large cast (nineteen) and a long running-time (about five hours), the play has both marvellous vignettes and rending

monologues, and it highlights the emphasis on personal truth-telling that would obsess O'Neill through all his late plays.

Long Day's Journey Into Night
O'Neill's patterning of family pathology – a lifelong interest spanning the Oedipal tensions of *Desire Under the Elms* and the father/daughter relationship of *A Touch of the Poet* – reaches its most lacerating pitch in this play written 'in blood and tears', but not performed until 1956, three years after the author's death. The most directly autobiographical of O'Neill's plays, it plunges directly to the heart of familial darkness in its account of a single day amongst the tormented Tyrone clan: the Irish-born father James, the miserly paterfamilias feeding on his memories as a stereotyped matinee idol; his morphine-addicted wife Mary; and their two sons, the ruthlessly honest drinker Jamie and his younger brother Edmund, O'Neill's unsparing vision of himself as a young, tubercular artist. The roles are as challenging as any in the English-language theatre, and actors as diverse as Laurence Olivier, Robert Ryan, Jack Lemmon and Earle Hymen have taken on the part of the father, while Florence Eldridge and Constance Cummings were two notable Marys.

Try these:
▷Shakespeare (especially *King Lear*), ▷Ibsen (especially *Ghosts*) for distilled family tragedies; E.A. Whitehead's *Alpha Beta*, ▷Edward Albee's *Who's Afraid of Virginia Woolf?* for more recent domestic plays which have a cathartic effect; ▷Athol Fugard for one of the best of a large battalion of plays portraying a portrait of the artist-as-a-young-man (*'Master Harold' . . . and the Boys*); ▷Tennessee Williams' *Cat on a Hot Tin Roof*, and ▷Lillian Hellman's *Little Foxes* for probing treatments of 'mendacity'; ▷Gorki's *The Lower Depths* for earlier images of barflies; ▷Ibsen's *The Wild Duck* for another treatment of the saving lie.

ONE-PERSON SHOWS
It may be no coincidence that in Britain, the period of cuts in arts funding has also seen a proliferation of one-person shows, the cheapest possible form of a company. The Perrier fringe awards of the last few years at the Edinburgh Festival have been dominated by one-person shows and stand-up comics. In the USA the tradition of one-person shows reaches back to the inimitable monologuist Ruth Draper but also now incorporates stand-up comedians like Eric Bogosian, Whoopi Goldberg, John O'Keefe and Lili Tomlin.

Within the one-person format there is a huge range of possibilities. One-person shows can be used to present a biographical study of a single individual. Queen Victoria, the Russian Revolutionary Alexandra Kollontai, Emlyn Williams as Dickens, Miriam Margolyes as Dickens' women, Michael Pennington as ▷Chekhov, Frances de la Tour's memorable evocation of ▷Lillian Hellman in ▷William Luce's *Lillian*; and in the States, Julie Harris as Emily Dickinson, Robert Morse as ▷Truman Capote and Hal Holbrook as Mark Twain are just a few of those recently portrayed. They can also be used for more overtly political reasons: Jack Klaff (*Nagging Doubts*) and Pieter Dirk-Uys (*Adapt or Dye*) each employed the one-man show to present an indictment of South Africa; in which each played a number of characters as did Cordelia Ditton whose 35-character tour de force in *About Face* (compiled with Maggie Ford) conjured up the protagonists of the 1984 Miners' Strike in England. The extended monologue *Swimming to Cambodia* by ▷Spalding Gray has one the same for American involvement in Vietnam.

One-person shows can also present particular texts: Alec McCowen with *St Mark's Gospel*, Kerry Shale with the whole of John Kennedy Toole's novel *A Confederacy of Dunces* (in which Shale played fifteen characters), Eileen Atkins' superlative portrayal of Virginia Woolf's *A Room of One's Own* (seen on both sides of the Atlantic), the truly eccentric genius of ▷Ken Campbell or John Sessions' *Napoleon* in which voices ranged from popular characters in the British soap *EastEnders* (Angie and Den) to Sir Laurence Olivier.

Simon Callow devised a performance of ▷Shakespeare's sonnets as a ▷National Theatre Platform Performance; and in a tightly structured performance which appeared to be an informal conversation with the audience, Ian McKellen's *Acting Shakespeare* offered an insight into the making of the actor and his own approach to Shakespearean verse.

Many women performers have recently used the monologue which has ranged from play form (Ruth Harris's *The Cripple*) to the more unspecifiable categories of Rose English, Karen Finley and the female impersonator Ethyl Eichelberger.

▷Samuel Beckett and ▷Alan Bennett, in very different ways, are also master exponents of the monologue (funnily enough, many of them for women, and Bennett's owing a good deal to Joyce Grenfell). Dramatic monologues have also been used very successfully by many writers including ▷Barry Collins (*Judgement*), ▷Alan Drury (*The Man Himself*) and by ▷Franca Rame (*The Mother, Female Parts*) and ▷Berta Freistadt *Woman with a Shovel* to make fiercely feminist points.

Maurice Chevalier was a huge hit in London with his one man shows, and Ruth Draper became an important name in the 1930s and 1940s with her one woman shows. So too the irreplaceable Joyce Grenfell whose comic sketches, like Ruth Draper's, tread a fine line between comedy/mimicry/impersonation and the stand-up comic routine. (Maureen Lipman's one-woman show based on Joyce Grenfell, *Re: Joyce*, was a great success both in London and at The Long Wharf in Connecticut.) Victoria Wood is the contemporary equivalent.

Which leads us finally to housewife superstar, Dame Edna Everage, the ultimate one-person show (though vintage comics Ken Dodd and Frankie Howerd and Julian Clary – London's latest fashion fad – might have something to say about that). Holding court at London's largest theatre, Drury Lane, cajoling an entire audience to wave their 'gladdies' and, as an apotheosis, rising to the ceiling on a fork-lift truck, he exemplifies (and satirises) the power that the single performer can still gleefully exercise over an audience.

Try these:
▷cabaret for more on one-person performers; ▷Robyn Archer.

ORTON, Joe   [1933–67]
British dramatist

Plays include:
The Ruffian on the Stair (broadcast 1964; staged 1966), *Entertaining Mr Sloane* (1964), *Loot* (1965), *The Erpingham Camp* (televised 1966; staged 1967), *The Good and Faithful Servant* (televised 1967; staged 1971), *Funeral Games* (televised 1968; staged 1970), *What the Butler Saw* (1969)

Orton shocked delighted audiences by offering taboo subjects discussed in dialogue of the greatest propriety by characters moving through plots of sometimes Byzantine contrivance. He claimed to draw incident and dialogue straight from life, making full use of the phraseology and platitudes of official jargon, the contrived headlines of the tabloid press and the euphemisms of pretentious respectability. His characters adopt the moral values of the world as he observed it – a police inspector is by nature corrupt, a man is expected to have an affair with his secretary, a psychiatrist is himself habitually deranged, exceptional genital endowment is a natural feature of a heroic statue (even of Winston Churchill). Though the audiences that gave Orton West End success probably dismissed this as a world of high camp fantasy, its parallels can be found in the pages of the daily and Sunday papers. Orton is not setting out a critique of society he is simply holding a mirror up to it. Nevertheless, the humour of his plays does come largely from this apparent dislocation, in which the socially unacceptable is treated as the commonplace, authority figures are stripped of their disguises and all is orchestrated with the physical and coincidental mechanisms of farce. Orton is unlikely really to shock you, most audiences will lap up his apparently outrageous naughtiness – but take him seriously and you will find that today's world is even nearer to the world he created.

It is now almost impossible to view Orton's work without remembering his own life, so graphically described in John Lahr's *Prick Up Your Ears* and the film based on it, and recorded in Orton's own diaries, but his promiscuous cottaging and murder by his male lover affected his work only in bringing it so suddenly to an end. *Entertaining Mr Sloane*, in which an attractive young murderer thinks he has captivated a woman and her brother into giving him a cushy life but finds the tables turned and himself trapped as their sexual toy, is perhaps his most accomplished play. *The Good and Faithful Servant* shows a compassion not evident in his other work and a more conscious criticism of the way in which society treats its nonachievers.

Loot

Basically a parody of a stock detective play, *Loot* presents a pair of young male lovers who have robbed a bank and hide the loot in the coffin of one boy's mother – who had been murdered by her nurse who plans to marry the father before disposing of him in turn. A bent detective, posing as a Water Board official, completes the main cast. Contrasts between the manner of the dialogue (often quite formally stylised) and the substance of the situation, opportunities for hilarious business with the body to prevent discovery, and other farce devices keep the laughs coming. In the end everyone gets a piece of the share-out except the murdered woman's husband, the only truly innocent, who is hauled off to jail to take the rap. Or is he actually the most culpable for his blindness to the corruption of the world around him and his complicity in preserving the facades of respectability?

Try these:
▷Ray Cooney; ▷Alan Ayckbourn's *Absurd Person Singular* and *Bedroom Farce* for more abrasive comedies of suburbia; ▷Alan Bennett's *Habeas Corpus* and *Enjoy* for darker shades of grey along Orton lines; ▷Pinter for that strange mixture of menace amid the mundane; ▷Harry Kondoleon and ▷Charles Ludlam for American farcical plays.

OSBORNE, John   [1929–]
British dramatist

Plays include:
The Devil Inside Him (with Sheila Linden; 1950), *Personal Enemy* (with Anthony Creighton; 1955), *Look Back in Anger* (1956), *The Entertainer* (1957), *Epitaph for George Dillon* (with Anthony Creighton; 1958), *The World of Paul Slickey* (1959), *A Subject of Scandal and Concern* (1961), *Luther* (1961), *Plays for England: The Blood of the Bambergs, Under Plain Cover* (1963), *Inadmissible Evidence* (1964), *A Patriot for Me* (1966), *The Hotel in Amsterdam* (1968), *Time Present* (1968), *West of Suez* (1971), *A Sense of Detachment* (1972), *The End of Me Old Cigar* (1975), *Watch it Come Down* (1975)

Born in London of what he describes as 'impoverished middle-class' parents, John Osborne worked as journalist for a number of trade magazines before he became an Assistant Stage Manager and acted in repertory companies (an experience he draws on in *The Entertainer*).

Osborne's *Look Back in Anger* seemed to mark a watershed between the theatre of the 1930s and 1940s, and the new 'contemporary style' of the 1950s and 1960s which developed at the Royal Court and at the Theatre Royal, Stratford East. In a contemporary review Kenneth Tynan described it as 'the best young play of its decade' and journalists christened a whole group of new writers as the 'Angry Young Men'; they included ▷Arnold Wesker and ▷John Arden among the dramatists.

Osborne's first stage plays were collaborations; *Personal Enemy* was banned by the Lord Chamberlain because of its homosexual elements. *Look Back in Anger*, sent to George Devine in response to an advertisement in *The Stage* for new plays for the English Stage Company was Osborne's first produced play. Previously turned down, according to Osborne, by twenty-five managers and agents, it was the only play elicited from the advertisement which was considered worth a production. Osborne, previously unknown, was hailed by one critic as 'the voice of our generation', and became the first of the many 'discoveries' of the Royal Court's policy of a Writer's Theatre. It was the first of the Royal Court plays to be recognised internationally, and toured to the USSR in 1957 as part of the World Youth Festival. Osborne thus became a significant figure in turning international attention to the developments in new British drama.

His next play *The Entertainer* explored the 'state of England' through the music hall act of a shabby song and dance man. Laurence Olivier had expressed interest in performing in an Osborne play, after *Look Back in Anger*, and although the ESC committee were uncertain about staging it, Olivier's participation clinched the production. It was a smash hit, transferred to the West End, and was turned into a film directed by Tony Richardson. The

Court also produced *Epitaph for George Dillon*, which Osborne had written with Anthony Creighton four years prior to *Look Back in Anger*. Osborne wrote the part of Baron von Epp in *A Patriot for Me* for George Devine, but the play was censored by the Lord Chamberlain, and could only be staged as a club production. This led to the Court's decision to become a club theatre until the Theatres Act of 1968 made it no longer necessary.

Tony Richardson, the first director of *Look Back in Anger*, said of Osborne: 'He is unique and alone in his ability to put on the stage the quick of himself, his pain, his squalor, his nobility – terrifyingly alone.' Unfortunately the 'Angry Young Man' of the 1950s has soured in middle age (as the title of his 1981 autobiography *A Better Class of Person* suggests).

Look Back in Anger

Although it may not be the best of Osborne's plays, nor the best play of his generation of writers, it has come to stand as a key text for modern British drama. It came to express a widespread disillusion with post-war England, and contains a central statement of frustration from its anti-hero Jimmy Porter, which became a cry for a whole generation: 'there aren't any good brave causes left'. Jimmy Porter became the epitome of the Angry Young Man in his harangue on contemporary values. Jimmy is the single figure who dominates the stage, his bitterness the point of identification for the audience. His wife, the middle-class Alison, takes the brunt of his onslaughts, spending much of the play ironing, and taking abuse from Jimmy before finally leaving. The play ends with Alison's return, and the two cling together, addressing each other in child's language in an attempt to forge some kind of intimacy. Jimmy's treatment of Alison is now far harder to endorse than it was in the 1950s, and the play has therefore now lost some of its power. The play's setting and form is very social realist, the dingy bedsit where Jimmy and Alison live gave rise to the term 'kitchen sink' drama. Osborne himself has described *Look Back in Anger* as 'a formal, rather old fashioned play', and in retrospect, it is. Osborne has written a sequel, *Déja Vu*, in which Jimmy's views are apparently modified. It has not yet been staged.

Try these:
Osborne 'couldn't abide' ▷Ionesco's plays and used to quarrel with George Devine about the ▷Royal Court's productions of them; ▷John Arden, ▷Arnold Wesker and ▷Willis Hall were categorised with Osborne as 'Angry Young Men'; ▷Arthur Miller saw *Look Back in Anger* as the play which launched a new realism in a theatre that had been 'hermetically sealed from reality'; ▷Tony Craze's male protagonist in *Angelus* is a Jimmy Porter for the 1980s; Osborne's misogyny has ▷Strindbergian elements; ▷Trevor Griffiths' *Comedians* is very different treatment of stand-up comedy from *The Entertainer*.

OSTROVSKY, Alexander Nikolayevich [1823–86]
Russian dramatist

Plays include:
The Bankrupt (later *It's All in the Family*, or *A Family Affair*; 1848), *Stick to Your Own Sleigh* (1853), *The Storm* (1859), *The Scoundrel* (or *Diary of a Scoundrel*; 1868), *The Forest* (1871), *Artists and Admirers* (1881)

Ostrovsky was the virtual founder of the Russian theatre. He wrote forty-seven plays, many more than ▷Gogol or ▷Turgenev, and unlike them was a professional man of the theatre. He studied at Moscow University but failed Roman Law, and then worked as a clerk in the commercial courts until he was forced to resign in 1851 after the publication of his second play, *A Family Affair*. Although the play was banned, Ostrovsky's readings of it were a wild success in intellectual high society in Moscow, and this made his name. It, and his liaison with a charming but plebeian actress, also got him cut off without a penny, and he spent the next few years as a well-respected but very poor literary hack in Moscow. The first of his plays to be performed was *Stick to Your Own Sleigh* (ie 'know your place') in 1853, and from then until his death in 1868 he was Russia's most important playwright. His plays range from broad comedies to the nightmare tragedy *The Storm* (which is the source for Janacek's *Katya Kabanova*). They are all set in more-or-less contemporary Russia, sometimes back-dated to appease the censor, and are all vigorously critical of the society they depict, actors being the only group shown in a consistently favourable light.

A Family Affair

The censor said it all: 'A rich Moscow merchant deliberately declares himself bankrupt. He transfers all his property to his clerk, whose interests he hopes to identify with his own by marrying him to his daughter. Being as great a rogue as himself, the clerk accepts daughter, property and money and then allows his father-in-law to be thrown into a debtors' prison. All the characters in the play – the merchant, his daughter, the lawyer, the clerk and the matchmaker – are first-rate villains. The dialogue is filthy. The entire play is an insult to the Russian merchant class.'

Try these:

▷Gogol's *The Government Inspector*, for an earlier satire on corruption in provincial Russian society; ▷Isaac Babel's *Marya*, for a later one. ▷Jonson's *Volpone* for satire on greed and over-reaching plotters; ▷Ayckbourn and ▷de Filippo for modern critical social comedies.

OTWAY, Thomas   [1652–85]
English dramatist

Plays include:

Alcibiades (1675), *Don Carlos* (1676), *Titus and Berenice* (after Racine; 1676), *The Cheats of Scapin* (based on Molière; 1676), *Friendship in Fashion* (1678), *The History and Fall of Caius Marius* (1679), *The Orphan; or, The Unhappy Marriage* (1680), *The Soldier's Fortune* (1680), *Venice Preserv'd; or, A Plot Discovered* (1682), *The Atheist; or, The Second Part of the Soldier's Fortune* (1683)

Otway began his theatrical career as an actor but suffered from such stage fright at his undistinguished debut that he switched to play writing. *Don Carlos* is written in rhyming couplets, other plays in blank verse. Otway became known as 'the tragedian of love' but although his work was popular he died in penury. From its premiere until the mid-nineteenth century his most successful play, *Venice Preserv'd*, was probably revived more frequently than any other play not by Shakespeare and it still has considerable theatrical power. A bleak blank verse tragedy about the family and the state, loyalty and personal honour, and sexual politics, it includes a scene of grotesque comic sexuality and self abasement by a masochistic nobleman, echoing the corruption of the Venetian state against which the protagonists Pierre and Jaffeir plan revolt. *The Orphan*, once almost as popular as *Venice Preserv'd*, is seldom revived today but *The Soldier's Fortune*, a typical example of Restoration comedy, is occasionally staged.

Try these:

For other post-Restoration writers of verse tragedy whose work is still staged, ▷Dryden and ▷Shelley; other Restoration comic dramatists are ▷Aphra Behn, ▷Congreve, ▷Etherege and ▷Wycherley; for more satire on sexual abasement, *Nana*, in Olwen Wymark's adaptation and, for a high camp lesbian variety, Split Britches' stylish *Dress Suit to Hire*; (*Caius Marius* is an adaptation of ▷Shakespeare's *Romeo and Juliet*).

OVERMYER, Eric   [1951–]
American dramatist

Plays include:

Native Speech (1984), *On the Verge, or The Geography of Yearning* (1985), *In Perpetuity Throughout the Universe* (1988), *In a Pig's Valise* (1989), *Mi Vida Loca* (1990), *Heliotrope Bouquet* by Scott Joplin and Louis Chauvin (1991)

Overmyer has been writing for the theatre since his undergraduate days at Reed College. Although he made his home in New York, and served at one time as the literary manager at Playwrights Horizons, most of his plays have been performed first at Center Stage in Baltimore where he has held the position of Associate Artist since 1984. His plays display his 'lifelong obsession with the American language'. Although critics have compared him to ▷Tom Stoppard, he resists the comparison. He feels that his playing with words and visual images, although based on intuitive and subjective thought processes, has as its aim serious social and cultural commentary. Overmyer has pointed out that *In Perpetuity* deals with the resurgence of anti-Asian and anti-semitic prejudices in the USA. However, *In a Pigs Valise* is a film noir spoof with music; *Native Speech* is a post-apocalyptic vision mainly told through the hip renegade radio broadcasts of a character called Hungry

Mother; and *Heliotrope Bouquet* . . . is a lyrical memory play about the jazz great of the title. His scripts have virtually no stage directions and suggest a style of acting that is not naturalistic. Aesthetically, he is moving towards a more poetic drama, attempting to weaken the shackles with which narrative binds the dramatic text. Overmyer has also managed to write for two highly toured television series: *St. Elsewhere* and *Sisters*.

On the Verge

This playful comedy begins with the image of three intrepid Victorian lady explorers on a beach. The ladies become caught up in an erudite and unconventional play on words. As their imaginative flight begins to take wing, they find themselves hurled through time and space only to arrive on the banal shores of 1950s America. Their startling journey makes it possible for them to find the uncommon in the commonplace. They ponder the changes that have taken place in the modern world making thought-provoking and hilarious associations when confronted with such artifacts as Cool Whip and 'I Like Ike' buttons. Overmyer utilises character, situation, and humour to introduce serious thoughts about time and relative values of different civilisations. *On the Verge* is Overmyer's best-known work and has had more than thirty productions.

Try these:
▷J.B. Priestley's *Time and the Conways* for time shifts; ▷Caryl Churchill and ▷Timberlake Wertenbaker for inventive use of time and language; for prejudice ▷Peter Flannery's *Singer*, ▷Hanif Kureishi's *Borderline*, ▷Michael Abbensetts, ▷Derek Walcott, ▷Charles Fuller.

OWENS, Rochelle   [1936–]
American dramatist and poet

Plays include:
The String Game (1965), *Istanboul* (1965), *Futz* (1968), *Homo* (1966), *Beclch* (1966), *Kontraption* (1971), *He Wants Shih* (1971), *The Karl Marx Play* (1973), *K.O. Certaldo* (1975), *Emma Instigated Me* (1976), *The*

Widow and the Colonel (1977), *Mountain Rites* (1978), *The Writer's Opera* (1979), *Chucky's Hunch* (1981), *Who Do You Want Peire Vidal* (1982), *The Mandrake* (1983)

Brooklyn-born Owens belongs to the school of formally innovative and iconoclastic playwrights associated with the rise of off-Broadway in the 1960s – people who had a highly emotive, deeply contradictory attitude to the theatre, a medium whose form they tended to admire even as they distrusted or alienated the audience. (Owens has said that she sees theatre as a 'life-sustaining force' for a public that 'wishes to be summoned from its sleep'.) Her best-known work, *Futz*, made into a controversial 1969 film directed by the original director of *Hair* (Tom O'Horgan), is – in the words of New York critic Michael Feingold – 'the keystone play of the decade'; it's a violent piece about a man, Cyrus Futz, in love with a pig, Amanda, and the menage à trois between the two of them and a woman, Marjorie Satz. Images of excess and shock often figure in her work: *Beclch*, a play about four white adventurers in Africa, includes a lethal cockfight; in *String Game*, a priest chokes to death on spaghetti among a community of Eskimos he has just chided for thinking erotic thoughts. *The Karl Marx Play* is, in many ways, her freest and funniest work – a surrealist pastiche in which the black jazz musician, Leadbelly, Friedrich Engels and his wife wait for Marx to write *Das Kapital*.

Try these:
▷Amiri Baraka, ▷Lorca for theatre as ritual; ▷Jean-Claude Van Itallie's *America Hurrah* for benchmark avant-garde American plays of the 1960s, *Futz*-style; early ▷Arthur Kopit ▷Rosalyn Drexler and ▷Maria Irene Fornes, ▷Jack Gelber for hallucinogenic, surreal drama; ▷Caryl Churchill and ▷David Lan's *A Mouthful of Birds* for another disturbing pig image; adaptations of Orwell's *Animal Farm* for a political parable of porcine dimensions; ▷Nick Darke's *The Monkey* for a less successful handling of the animalistic menage à trois; ▷Susan Yankowitz's *Slaughterhouse Play* and Adrienne Kennedy's *A Rat's Mass* offer further theatrical images of the grotesque; for British equivalents, ▷Women in Theatre and ▷Bryony Lavery.

OYAMO
(Charles F. Gordon)
American playwright

Plays include
Breakout (1972), The Juice Problem (1974), The Resurrection of Lady Lester (1981), Mary Goldstein and the Author (1981), A Hopeful Interview with Satan (1989), The Return of the Been-To (1989), In Living Color (a play with music by Olu Dara, 1989), The Stalwarts (1990), Let Me Live (a play with music by Olu Dara, 1991)

Charles F. Gordon's adopted name, OyamO, meaning 'Black man with typewriter,' explores the idea of what it means to be a Black artist in modern society.

OyamO is a graduate of the Yale School of Drama and the founder of his own theatre company The Black Magicians. He is now an Associate Professor of Theatre and English at the University of Michigan. He is currently working on a new play for the Theatre of the First Amendment in Virginia and a stage adaptation, Black Orpheus, for the Crossroads Theatre Company, both scheduled for completion in 1991–92. Originally a writer of poetry, short stores, and a children's book, OyamO began in the 1970s to work with the Lafayette Theatre and the Negro Ensemble Company. He eventually returned to Harlem, believing that 'getting support from the Black community means giving support to the Black community.' He sees Afro-Americans struggling for a sense of their own destiny amidst cultural, political and economic oppression.

This theme is strongest in the author's earlier plays. In Breakout, two young Black convicts challenge the repressiveness of society; the 'breakout' of the title is as much an escape from the urban slums as it is from the penal system. Oyamo's interest in Black African identy compelled him to travel extensively in Africa during the early 1970s, where he discovered that, as an Afro-American, 'he's a child who's been taken away from home and made into a completely different kind of person. He goes back home, and no one recognizes him.' The Return of the Been-To is a dramatic odyssey chronicling such a trip. Told in dramatic encounters, OyamO explores the differences and similarities between African and American Black identities. With The Resurrection of Lady Lester. OyamO in 1981 begins to use music and historic characters: Resurrection, subtitled 'a poetic mood song', is based on the legend of noted jazz musician, Lester Young. The play employs transformations, time clisions, and multiple casting to provide a kaleidoscopic view of the impact of racism on the artistic gifts of Black musicians. OyamO's most recent drama, Let Me Live, returns to the prison setting of Breakout to portray the wrongful imprisonment of Black union leader Angelo P. Herndon in 1932. In Let Me Live, the protagonist's fellow inmates have been imprisoned on exaggerated charges, and Herndon himself is subjected to a kangaroo court, stressing the oppressive and unfair plight of the Black at the hands of white society. In this and other plays of the late 1980s, OyamO uses vivid movement and lively jazz music by Olu Dara as a pulsing dramatic lifeblood.

Try these:
Ntozake Shange's ... for colored girls who have considered suicide/when the rainbow is enuff (1975) provided strong influence – and leading actress Lorey Hayes – for OyamO's Mary Goldstein. See also Lanie Robertson's Lady Day at Emerson's Bar and Grill (1986) for its interweaving of music and movement to vivify dramatic action; Ronald Milner, George C. Wolfe for other Black Americans using jazz music in a variety of ways; ▷Willie Russell's Shirley Valentine, Dario Fo and Franca Rame's One Woman Plays for women trapped in roles with some resemblance to Mary Goldstein.

P

PAGE, Louise [1955–]
British dramatist

Plays include:
Want-Ad (1976), *Lucy* (1977), *Tissue* (1978), *Hearing* (1979), *Housewives* (1981), *Salonika* (1982), *Falkland Sound/Voces de Malvinas*; (1983), *Real Estate* (1984), *Golden Girls* (1984), *Beauty and the Beast* (1985), *Goat* (1986), *Diplomatic Wives* (1989)

A London-born writer now living in Sheffield, Page was a leading light of the 'second wave' of young women playwrights of the early 1980s. A graduate of Birmingham University's drama course (where she was taught by ▷David Edgar), she has been writer-in-residence at the Royal Court, a Fellow in Drama and TV at Yorkshire Television, and Associate Director at Theatre Calgary in Alberta, Canada.

Something of a minimalist and a writer of spare dialogue, her plays reflect a generation of women where feminism is assumed, if not overt. Her plays have ranged from the unpredictable and surreal time-warp of *Salonika* to the hermetic domesticity of *Real Estate*, and the large-scale and ambitious re-working of the old fairy tale *Beauty and the Beast*. An early play, *Tissue*, touches sensitively on the trauma of a young woman facing breast cancer whilst the later *Golden Girls*, about women and sport, takes a leaf out of ▷Caryl Churchill's book in tackling women and ambition. This issue is also touched on in the earlier *Real Estate*, an unflattering picture of post-feminist woman and the selfishness of daughters, in which the mother definitely has the last and better word – mother/daughter relationships are a recurring theme in Page's work. Much of her reputation, however, rests on *Salonika*, with which she won the 1982 George Devine award at the age of twenty-four. *Salonika* is a surrealistic account of the effect of World War I on a widow returning to the Grecian beach where her husband had

died sixty-five years earlier (he re-appears during the course of the play), and on her elderly spinster daughter. Critics hailed it as 'haunting' and a remarkably mature piece of work on the themes of futility and the frictions of mother/daughter relationships. Her plays have been produced all over the world, in New Zealand, the USA, Denmark, Greece, Australia, Norway.

Try these:
For 'ghosts' of other generations brought on stage, see Greg Cullen's *Taken Out*, ▷Stephen Lowe's *Seachange*, ▷T.S. Eliot's *The Family Reunion*, ▷J.M. Barrie's *Mary Rose*, ▷Ibsen's *Ghosts*, ▷Edward Bond's *Summer*; for the friction of mother/daughter relationships, ▷Ayshe Raif, ▷Julia Kearsley, ▷Sharman Macdonald; for images of the post-feminist woman ▷Caryl Churchill's *Top Girls*, ▷Jacqueline Holborough's *Dreams of San Francisco*; ▷Deborah Levy's *Heresies*.

PANTOMIME
Pantomime can mean any kind of dumb-show in which words are replaced by gesture and body signals, whether entertainment or communication. In Britain it is now specifically used to describe a traditional Christmas entertainment, usually loosely based on a fairy-tale or well-known children's story, featuring lavish sets, songs, dances, humour and farcical episodes. There will usually be an element of cross-dressing, with the romantic male lead – the 'Principal Boy' – played by an attractive woman and a comic female role – the 'Dame' – by a male comedian. The Principal Boy is not a male impersonator, but the sex reversals are usually deemed to allow greater liberties to be taken in humour without causing offence.

With the nineteenth-century rise of the music hall, variety artists, acrobats and speciality acts began to appear in pantomime and characters and plots were shaped to allow them to display their particular skills. The pattern continues today, with pop stars in leading roles, television comic double-acts as the broker's men in *Cinderella* or a conjurer playing a magician. To enable the casting of male pop singers some 'breeches' roles have recently been played by men but spectacle, romance, popular cultural references and songs – including a segment for the audience to sing along with – are still the hallmark of the popular pantomime. Complaints that comedians use too much blue material for a family audience have led to calls for a return to old standards, but pantomime humour has always included a certain amount of bawdy.

Pantomimes are still great money spinners, running anything from a week at Christmas right through to Easter, and often supporting the losses of the rest of the year. Many theatres now offer a 'children's play' as well, but it is inconceivable that panto will not survive even in its current 'watered down' version. Ironically, one of the best traditional pantomimes is staged annually by the innovative ▷Glasgow Citizens' Theatre. Cheryl Moch's *Cinderella, The Real True Story* (1987) and ▷Gay Sweatshop's *Jingle Ball* (1976) have both subverted the tradition by having Cinderella fall in love with a woman, no great elaboration when you consider the 'Principal Boy' is usually played by a woman anyway – but enough to set certain newspapers baying for blood!

Try these:
Contemporary plays that owe something to the pantomime tradition are ▷Peter Nichols' *Poppy*, ▷Caryl Churchill's *Cloud Nine*, ▷Louise Page's *Beauty and the Beast*; Theatre Workshop's *Oh What a Lovely War* uses the pierrot show, ▷Trevor Griffiths' *Comedians*, the stand up comic, and ▷John Osborne's *The Entertainer*, the music hall; Dame Edna Everage as a grotesque, wildly popular manifestation of cross-dressing satire. USA artists that have stretched the boundaries of traditional pantomime include Bill Irwin, San Francisco Mime Troop, and Bread and Puppet Theater.

PARKER, Stewart   [1941–88]
Northern Irish dramatist

Plays include:
Spokesong (1975), *Catchpenny Twist* (1977), *Kingdom Come* (1977), *I'm A Dreamer, Montreal* (1979), *The Kamikaze Ground*

Staff Reunion Dinner (1979), *Nightshade* (1980), *Iris in the Traffic Ruby in the Rain* (1981), *Blue Money* (1984), *Heavenly Bodies* (1984), *Northern Star* (1984), *Pentecost* (1987), *Lost Belongings* (1987)

Born in Belfast, educated at Queen's University, Parker received a number of awards. including the Evening Standard Award in 1977, a Thames Television Bursary in 1977, and the Banff International TV Festival Prize in 1985. With a skilful grasp of the surreal effects of everyday speech, and an obvious delight in word-play, Parker's plays are fast-moving, openly surreal, and very entertaining, although they frequently deal with the serious issues of the Troubles and their consequences for the lives of individuals. He repeatedly asserts that there is a force for life and independence which transcends political slogans and allegiances. In *Catchpenny Twist* the main characters are forced out of Ireland by violence and killed by a terrorist bomb in a foreign airport, but in the end their dreams of songwriting fame seem vastly superior to those of the politically 'enlightened' who condemn them for the irrelevance of their lives to the historic cause. In *Northern Star* Parker attempts a theatrical tour de force in a study of Irish history through the lives of its greatest playwrights from ▷Sheridan to ▷Beckett, a breathtaking exercise in skill and imagination with an operatic use of theatrical styles to present the response of each dramatist to his particular period.

Spokesong
Spokesong charts a family history through twentieth-century Ulster, in which a tenuous survival of individual eccentricity over political violence and faceless bureaucracy finally blossoms, despite the dehumanising forces ranged against it. Frank struggles to maintain the family bicycle-shop against threats of redevelopment, the car-culture, and the bombs of terrorists, and battles with his hostile brother Julian for the hand of the beautiful Daisy. Interwoven with Frank's story is that of his grandparents. The bicycle and its adherents take on symbolic value as the preservers of humanity, hope and simplicity, and Daisy finally rescues Frank from defeat and despair. The play is effectively allied to music hall and the 'good night out' philosophy, with songs, illustrative episodes and emphatic good nature underlining its central theme.

Try these:
▷Sean O'Casey for his sagas of Irish family life; ▷Seamus Finnegan, ▷Daniel Mornin and ▷Christina Reid for varying views of the Troubles; Charabanc who share a similar ebullience of spirit in the face of dehumanising forces; ▷George C. Wolfe's *The Colored Museum* for a parallel to *Northern Star*.

PATERSON, Stuart   [1954–   ]
Scottish playwright

Plays include:
Apetalk (1981), *Secret Voice* (1982), *Beowulf* (1982), *Merlin the Magnificent* (1982), *Fighting Talk* (1983), *Confessions of a Justified Sinner* (1983), *The Snow Queen* (1983), *Clean Sweeps* (1984), *Germinal* (1984), *In Traction* (1985), *Mr Government* (1986), *Beauty and the Beast* (1987), *The Cherry Orchard* (1989), *Cinderella* (1989), *George's Marvellous Medicine* (1990)

Though Stuart Paterson has been responsible for several masterly adaptations for the adult stage – *Beowulf* and *Confessions of a Justified Sinner* amongst them – his wider reputation has so far been gained on the strength of his plays for children. These divide, roughly, into one-acts for use in schools by Theatre in Education groups and full length versions of familiar fairy tales or legends which many repertory theatres prefer as a seasonal alternative to traditional ▷pantomimes. One element is common to both – Paterson's flair for making huge and complex questions of moral good and evil not just accessible to a young audience but positively entertaining for them – and the adults lucky enough to be with them in the theatre, gulpingback the tears as surrounding tinies stand in the aisles willing the Beast to live. . . .

The value of family ties and of loyal chums is a recurring theme in Paterson's work. Putting material gain, or one's ego, before keeping faith with those who are kind and caring results in come-uppance – usually of a risible, slapstick nature – while forgiveness of those who have 'erred and recanted' is mandatory. The tenor of the magical adventure plays, like *Merlin the Magnificent* and *The Snow Queen*, is that other people *matter* and that true happiness is not bought or got by vicious means. This message was given piquant reinforcement in *Cinderella*. The romantic Cinders does not marry her Prince; she discovers that he saw her only as another beautiful acquisition and so she goes off with the kitchen boy who had fallen in love with her when she was dressed in rags and covered in grime!

His first full-length, original play for adults, *Mr Government*, unfortunately didn't really come off. A more intimate setting than the Edinburgh Lyceum might have helped, but the script, with its troubled scenario of a returning brother opening up old family wounds was at once too ambitious and perhaps heartfelt in its forays through emotional landscapes.

Try these:
▷Pantomime; Myles Rudge's versions of fairy tales translate the conflict between good and evil into easily recognisable instances of sibling rivalry, reckless greed, obstinacy and laziness that strike cords with youngsters; for other British playwrights writing for children, try ▷David Holman, ▷David Wood, ▷Penny Casdagli and ▷Nona Shepphard; ▷Theatre for Young Audiences; ▷Wendy Kesselman's *Becca* for malevolent sprites in cupboards similar to that in *Secret Voice*; for adult re-arrangements of *Cinderella*, try Glowacki's *Cinders* and ▷Drew Griffiths' and Cheryl Moch's *The Real True Story of Cinderella*; Stephen Sondheim's musical *Into the Woods* also refashions a number of children's fairy stories for an adult audience in terms of acquiring knowledge through the lessons ('woods') of life.

PERFORMANCE ART IN BRITAIN

Performance Art is almost as much of a catch-all term as 'Theatre of the Absurd'; RoseLee Goldberg defines it as 'live art by artists', which is far too wide. It could be defined as something that happens before an audience and does not fit under the labels of theatre, ballet, opera, music, or strip-tease, though it may contain elements of all these. It is more a matter of visual artists turning to performance as a means of expressing their ideas than of anything to do with conventional theatre. The visual image is almost always central, though often accompanied or contradicted by complicated soundtracks using the latest technology. It often uses a variety of media, including

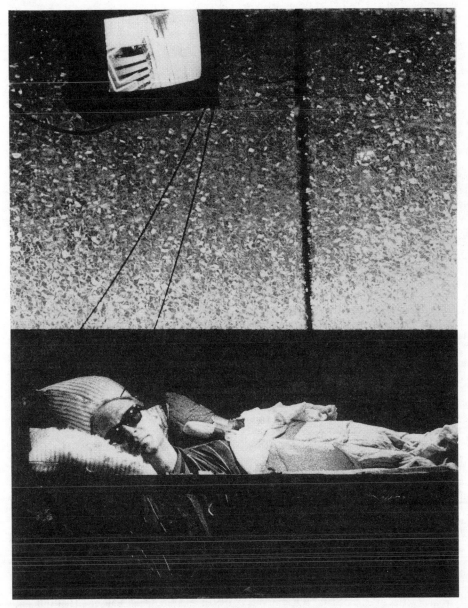

The Wooster Group's extraordinary *The Road to Immortality (Part Three)*: Frank Dell's 'The Temptation of Saint Antony'

music and dance, video, film and slides. The term has become current only since the 1970s, when the form began to be institutionalised, especially in the USA, in festivals, performance courses in art colleges, and specialist magazines.

It is difficult to write about Performance Art productions in standard critical terms, because they tend to be experimental and open-ended, and groups by definition wish to subvert standard art forms. Their ancestry can be traced to Italian Futurism, the Dada movement, Surrealism, and the Jarry-Apollinaire-Artaud line, but this does not add much precision to the discussion. The 'Happening' made popular in the late 1950s and early 1960s in the USA by artists such as Allan Kaprow (who coined the term) and Claes Oldenburg is clearly related, but was on the whole more anarchic and spontaneous; Performance Art productions tend to be carefully planned, even in the variable bits (witness The People Show). The line is often hard to draw – the term Performance Art has been used to encompass a range of projects from Welfare State's vast outdoor shows, through the ambitious large-scale works of ▷Robert Wilson and of Richard Foreman's Ontological-Hysteric Theatre, Martha Clarke and Pina Bausch's ritualistic and imaginative dance theatre, to Miranda Payne hanging alone from a wall in the Riverside Studios in her *Saint Gargoyle*. The only constants seem to be that the event is probably non-linear, that unexpected juxtapositions will occur, and that any number of media may be brought into play.

The difficulty of defining precisely what Performance Art is remains a constant source of debate and discussion. Certain it is, however, that it went through something of a renaissance in Britain in the 1980s with Geoff Moore's Cardiff based *Moving Being* company. Rational Theatre and Impact were two other influential groups of the time, whose members subsequently went on to form other conglomerations of like-minded artists. Another early and influential group was *Lumiere & Son* founded in 1973 by Hilary Westlake and David Gale whose 1980 *Circus Lumiere*, presented in a tent, showed the potentially popular appeal of Performance Art whilst later works such as *Brightside* and *Panic* confirmed the power and beauty of musical electronic scores. Welfare State, IOU (an offshoot from Welfare State) and the next generation, of Bow Gamelan (recycling junk into

musical instruments) and particularly Station House Opera's breeze block 'installation' *Bastille Dances* have continued the trend of outdoor spectacle and are now hugely popular, despite initially being very much in the margins.

In the 1980s, too, there was a profound movement against text, a recreation to the intensely literary traditions of British theatre. Deconstruction and fragmentation were keynotes, often using overlapping musical and textual sound, visual images and movement in repetitious and rigorously disciplined physical sequences, achieving a kind of hallucinatory state. By the late 1980s, the work of Dogs in Honey, from the Midlands Group in Nottingham and the Sheffield-based Forced Entertainment, heavily influenced by Impact, were signalling a clearer comment on the fragmentary nature of high-technology and its urban wastelands. In as much as Peformance Art's raison d'etre is concerned with the primacy of its performers (unlike actors reinterpreting Hamlet, these performers are the only interpreters of this work at this moment), and the performing of *real work in real time*, individual performance artists have highlighted other, more personal goals. There are the *living paintings*, installations of Stephen Taylor Woodrow, working off visual art traditions but adding a human dimension; there is Rose English, exploring language and the nature of theatre from a visual, Performance Art perspective; and there is the work of women like Rose Garrard, Bobby Baker and Sylvia Ziranek, involving sculpture, installations, and 'real time' work in the kitchen or around food, exploring a post-feminist aesthetic and language in the area of Performance Art. The work too, of Annie Griffin and Neil Bartlett still obtains much of its driving power from its adherence to strong visual images and acknowledgement of Performance Art principles of subversion of established forms. It would also certainly be true to say that in the past five years in Britain, women and gay artists have lead the way in responding to contemporary issues.

In the final analysis, it would be hard, though, to over-emphasise the influence of British Performance Art by outside practitioners; American Jim Haynes at the Traverse in the early 1960s (later at the Arts Lab in London), Joseph Beuys, also in the mid 1960s, and later Pina Bausch. That influence is also due to the support of such far-seeing promoters as Ritsaert ten Carte of the Mickery

Theatre in Amsterdam, who was the commissioning agent behind many of the groups eventually seen in London at the ICA (including Belgian Jan Fabre, whose 5–8 hour productions were tests of stamina for his audience as much as they were lessons in iconoclasm). Under John Ashford, in the mid 1980s, the ICA became *the* showcase for Performance Art both international and domestic. In recent years, it has also been a platform for the National Review of Live Arts – an annual showcase for the best of young performance artists from around Britain – initiated ten years ago by, amongst others Nikki Millican, now in charge of Glasgow's Third Eye (who originally commissioned Neil Bartlett's *A Vision of Love Revealed in Sleep*). It was also at the ICA that Robert Lepage's work was first seen in Britain.

Try these:
▷Claire MacDonald, ▷Neil Bartlett, ▷Deborah Levy and ▷Rose English as British performance artist/performers/writers; LIFT for a bi-ennial festival which often includes groups with strong Performance Art ingredients; ▷Ken Campbell for other streams of anarchy; ▷Spalding Gray and the Wooster Group for American examples.

PERFORMANCE ART IN THE USA

Traditionally, Performance Art has been the prerogative of visual artists, who saw performance as a means of extending the conventional mediums of paint, canvas and wood to include the human body (usually their own) and its potential for action, and adding the dimension of time to a discipline previously restricted to the two dimensions of the plane or the three spatial dimensions of volume.

Visual art based Performance Art, which went from strength to strength in the 1970s and early 1980s with artists such as Hannah Wilke, Collette, Chris Burden and Vito Acconci seems peculiarly quiet on the American scene with the exception of multi-person performance groups such as San Francisco's Science Research Laboratory who make theatrical spectacles which centre on machine-based wizardy and Blueman, a four-man performance group which creates musically-based art theory conscious cabaret.

Since 1985, solo Performance Art in America has enlarged its artistic territory to include work with a literary base. The innovative pioneers of this development, ▷Spalding Gray and ▷Eric Bogosian are actors whose creative abilities could not be bound by a traditional acting career. Instead of developing into directors or playwrights, both men broke ground by creating solo performances that played at art houses and performance spaces across America.

This formal innovation contained a contextual one. The most shining example can be found in the work of monologist ▷Spalding Gray who, instead of presenting a formal text with fictional characters whom he inhabited for a performance, began to play himself, presenting his personal and professional history as a form of entertainment. In his performance pieces he deconstructs roles he has previously played in the theatre and then recontextualises these roles into more expensive autobiographical accounts of his personal history. In *Monster in a Box*, his latest monologue, he plays the role of a narrator from Thornton Wilder's *Our Town*, re-enacting his experience of how the critics panned his performance.

Though many performance artists work exclusively in the solo form, many others alternate between solo work and larger multi-person commission pieces; and though American Performance Art has experienced a 'literary invasion', it continues to accommodate artists from every discipline and often aids in developing multi-disciplined artists. In movement work, Ann Carlson and Elizabeth Streb. From stand-up/club circuit beginnings artists like Karen Finley, Ann Magnuson and Reno continue to flourish.

The variety of work which has been called 'performance art', and the different forms which that work has taken is extensive. The breadth of field which the term no attempts to take in is so wide that its use as a term for tri-culture exploration of a Chinese and French Canadian family. a sub-category of visual art is effectively redundant. To all intents it now acts as a generic term to describe a range of time-based activities including the various theatres described elsewhere.

In 1990, the experimental theatre companies which rose to prominence in the 1970s and 1980s continue to dominate the scene with very few young companies vying for attention. The Wooster Group, under the artistic direction of Elizabeth LeCompte, are America's most dazzling example of postmodern experimental theatre. LeCompte and the company are still interested in the deconstruction of classic found texts such as *Long Day's Journey into Night*, *Our Town*, *The Cocktail Party*, *The Crucible*, and most recently, *The Three Sisters*. These deconstructions are embedded in a performance structure that includes dance, video, contemporary texts and autobiographical episodes. Mabou Mines, whose members include ▷Lee Breuer, Joanne Akailitis and Ruth Malezchech, recently staged a production of *King Lear*, with a woman playing Lear, set in the deep south. Richard Foreman works with Ontological Hysterical Theater as a poet/playwright generating his own text and then creating a theatrical vocabulary via performers who are represented as the population in a discontinuous (in subject matter) playing field. The Players orchestrate a connected web of profundities, thus invoking the power of a singular artistic mind.

Although distinctions between experimental theatre and Performance Art are largely redundant, in some aspects these distinctions still operate. Each survives on and operates within a completely different funding structure and way of working. The groups mentioned above are well funded by the National Endowment for the Arts, and maintain and run the business of theatre as any company would. Solo performance artists receive one third the amount of federal funding and often create work in the privacy of their own homes instead of a traditional rehearsal space. Conversely, the solo show is an attractive touring package and can be more often supported at smaller festivals and art houses than the large experimental theatre companies, who need a higher production rate.

Try these:
See also Performance Art in Britain.

PHILLIPS, Caryl   [1958–]
Caribbean dramatist

Plays include:
Strange Fruit (1979), *Where There Is Darkness* (1982), *The Shelter* (1983)

'Cass' Phillips was born in St Kitts but was brought up in Leeds and Birmingham, before going to Oxford University to study English Literature. His plays express the generational conflicts and bitter reproaches of that generation of young blacks brought up in Britain but with deep roots in Caribbean culture, the most powerful statement of which is *Strange Fruit*, a tragic tale of disillusionment and lives blighted by race. *Where There is Darkness* is another passionate treatment of a similar theme: a West Indian father, successfully settled in this country as a social worker, is on the point of returning to the Caribbean. The conflict between him – chauvinistic, aggressive and clearly intended by Phillips as symbolic of racism's brutalising effect – and his quieter son who is about to thwart his father's ambitions, reflects wider social ills and is drawn with great persuasion and subtlety. *Shelter*, on the other hand, a more schematic treatment of colonialism and its repercussions, contrasts 18th and 20th-century relations between the sexes (the first half has a white woman-black man/master-slave *Robinson Crusoe* type twist to it) but is less successful in creating credible human beings.

Apart from his stage output, Phillips has been prolific in every other writing medium with films, novels, television documentaries, radio (plays, and interviews including an extended one with ▷James Baldwin) and extensive lecturing. He now lives in St Kitts.

Strange Fruit
Premiered at the Sheffield Crucible in 1980 and revived frequently since, *Strange Fruit* is one of the landmarks of British black theatre. Centred around a schoolteacher, Vivien Marshall, and her two sons, it is a graphic, painful account of a family caught between two cultures, tearing each other apart as they fight out their destinies; the mother still upholding white values, one son opting for Rastafarianism, the other ultimately rejecting everything the mother (ie 'mother country') has stood for. *Strange Fruit* offers no optimistic ending; its naturalism is raw, and angry. Far from unique in its theme of disillusionment with the old country, it remains one of the most potent expressions of it.

Try these:
Many of the major black Caribbean writers have dealt with the theme of disillusionment with the old country including ▷Mustapha Matura, ▷Edgar White, Felix Cross, ▷Barry Reckord; ▷Tunde Ikoli's *Scrape Off the Black* focuses on two brothers; ▷Derek Walcott's *Pantomime* is another twist on the Robinson Crusoe theme; ▷Arthur Miller's *A View From The Bridge* has the father protagonist as a complex victim/aggressor; Nigel Moffatt and ▷Winsome Pinnock are a new generation who

have been concerned with disillusionment; ▷Hanif Kureishi's *Borderline* examines living on the borderlines of cultures from an Asian perspective; ▷Karim Alrawi's *A Child in the Heart* is equally concerned about mixing cultures; see also ▷Ntozake Shange, ▷George Wolfe's *The Colored Museum* and Kalamu Ya Salaam's *Black Love Song No 1* for satirical accounts of how white society has created 'the black image'.

Try these:
▷Feydeau for well-crafted farces; ▷Dumas fils and ▷G. B. Shaw for plays about the 'woman with a past' – *Mrs Warren's Profession* is partly an attack on the glamorising of that attractive figure; ▷Goldsmith's *She Stoops to Conquer* for another comedy that partly hinges on the age of a stepson.

PINERO, (Sir) Arthur Wing
[1855–1934]
British dramatist

Plays include:
The Magistrate (1885), *The Schoolmistress* (1886), *Dandy Dick* (1887), *The Second Mrs Tanqueray* (1893), *The Benefit of the Doubt* (1895), *Trelawney of the 'Wells'* (1898), *The Gay Lord Quex* (1899), *His House in Order* (1906)

During his lifetime, Pinero was most renowned for his 'problem plays', above all *The Second Mrs Tanqueray* which starred Mrs Patrick Campbell. These, despite the skill of their construction, have virtually died with the problems they dealt with. However, *Trelawney of the 'Wells'* remains a charming if sentimental picture of the mid-Victorian theatre, in which the passage of time has made the realistic characters seem stagey and the theatrical characters seem drawn from life; and his excellent farces are still regularly revived. *The Magistrate* has elements in common with ▷Feydeau's *A Little Hotel on the Side* – the visit to the dubious hotel in Act II by most of the characters, unknown to each other, the police raid, the desperate attempts to avoid discovery – but the taboos that are transgressed, this being nineteenth-century England, are not sexually oriented; Mr Poskett, a metropolitan magistrate, is merely trying to conceal the fact that he has been taken for a night out by his stepson, and Mrs Poskett is trying to hide the fact that this stepson, who is thought to be a precocious fourteen, is actually nineteen, she having lied about her age. Similarly, in *Dandy Dick*, the dreadful secret that involves the Dean of St Marvells in a night in prison is merely that he has placed a bet on a horse to save his tottering spire (and he doesn't even win the bet); but the nimble plotting and the lively dialogue can still effortlessly keep our attention.

PINNOCK, Winsome
[1961–]
British dramatist

Plays include:
A Hero's Welcome (rehearsed reading, 1986, revised version, 1989), *The Wind of Change* (1987), *Leave Taking* (1987), *Picture Palace* (1988), *A Rock in Water* (1989), *Talking in Tongues* (1991)

London-born Pinnock is a young, black playwright who has come to the fore with remarkable speed and whose stature now seems to be growing with every commission. *Picture Palace*, commissioned by the Women's Theatre Group, was an entertaining if slightly untidy attempt to look at the difference between celluloid fantasy and real-life experiences (Pinnock's examples were four young cinema usherettes) – a structure that enabled her to explore the theme that was much in vogue amongst young women writers in the late 1980s male violence. Far more theatrically accomplished was *A Hero's Welcome*, produced by the Women's Playhouse Trust, which was runner-up in the 1990 Susan Smith Blackburn Awards. A rites of passage piece set in Jamaica in 1947, it tackled the familiar territory of emigration to the 'mother country' through the aspirations of young Jamaicans setting off for England, and the return to Jamaica of a young black soldier at the end of World War II. Its unsentimental but sensitive characterisation of both men and women, young and old, showed Pinnock's growing maturity and sensitivity to personal interiors which *A Rock in Water* (about civil-rights leader Claudia Jones – worthy but more of a docudrama) lacked. *Leave Taking* is an account of conflicts between a Jamaican mother who settled in Britain and the two daughters she raised here. As much a search for identity as a study in the generation gulf and sibling rivalries. Pinnock again mixed contemporary feelings with older, ritual beliefs in the person of the obeah woman, a symbol of continuity and tracing of roots which many recent black playwrights, from ▷Edgar White to ▷Derek Walcott, have reclaimed.

Try these:
▷Caryl Phillips' *Strange Fruit*, Nigel Moffatt's *Mamma Decemba* for more first-generation immigrant mother figures; Felix Cross for ritual; ▷Jackie Kay for emotionally transforming journeys; ▷Noël Greig, and ▷Martin Sherman's *Bent* for gay examples: ▷Sarah Daniels' *Masterpieces*, ▷Clare McIntyre's *Low Level Panic* for further essays into male violence and the female image; ▷Hilary Westlake's *Panic* for Lumière is a superb multi-media piece about panic attacks of all kinds; ▷Tasha Fairbanks' *PULP* for Siren, a Marlowesque, lesbian thriller treatment of images, choices, compromises and survival – their *Curfew* was an out-and-out separatist solution; ▷Gregory Motton, a contemporary male voice treats dreams and fantasies very differently; ▷Catherine Hayes for mothers and daughters and sibling rivalries; Zindika's *Paper and Stone*, and *Mother* by the Women's Troop of the Black Mime Theatre for two explorations of young black British women and mothers in the 1990s.

PINTER, Harold   [1930–]
British dramatist, actor, director

Plays include:
The Room (1957), *The Birthday Party* (1958), *The Hothouse* (written 1958; staged 1980), *A Slight Ache* (1959), *The Dwarfs* (1960), *The Dumb Waiter* (1960), *The Caretaker* (1960), *A Night Out* (1960), *The Collection* (1961), *The Lover* (1963), *Tea Party* (1965), *The Homecoming* (1965), *The Examination* (1966), *The Basement* (1967), *Landscape* (1968), *Silence* (1969), *Night* (1969), *Old Times* (1971), *Monologue* (1973), *No Man's Land* (1975), *Betrayal* (1978), *Family Voices* (1981), *Other Places* (1982, made up of *Family Voices*, *Victoria Station*, *A Kind of Alaska*), *One for the Road* (1984), *Mountain Language* (1988)

Although Pinter has not written a full-length play since 1978, his distinctive theatrical voice remains a major force in the contemporary repertory. He has become notorious as the writer of dialogue with lengthy pauses; 'Pin-teresque' has come to mean the dialogue of evasion. He has been claimed as a British exponent of the Theatre of the Absurd, although his plays often begin from an ostensibly naturalistic context, which breaks down into a threatening, and sometimes surreal world. The plays are often structured around the intrusion of a menacing stranger into an apparently safe world, who then becomes a catalyst for the return of the repressed. The theatre critic Irving Wardle has termed Pinter's work the 'Comedy of Menace'. Pinter has said that his fascination with oblique communication was something that he learned as a Jew bought up in an anti-semitic area of London, where evasion was a means of survival.

Born in the East End, the son of a Jewish tailor, Pinter worked as an actor before turning to writing. The first London production of a Pinter play was received with criticial incomprehension, and was a commercial disaster. *The Birthday Party*, in which two menacing figures threaten the banality of a seaside boarding house, was variously described in the national papers as: 'half-gibberish', 'puzzling' a 'baffling mixture'. Consequently, *The Dumb Waiter* had its first performance in Hamburg, and it was not until *The Caretaker* in 1960 (and revived in 1991 with equal success) that Pinter was recognised as a major writer.

All the plays sound an enigma, the threat in them is all the more frightening for never being directly explained. Pinter's work has been interpreted in a host of different ways; among other theories, Freud and the Bible have been hauled in to account for their obscurity, but Pinter resolutely insists that the plays mean no more than they say: 'I can sum up none of my plays. I can describe none of them, except to say: That is what happened. That is what they said. That is what they did.'

Pinter is also a major film writer, whose credits include *The Servant* (1963), *The Quiller Memorandum* (1966), *The Go-Between* (1971), *The French Lieutenant's Woman* (1981) and *The Handmaid's Tale* (1990).

Old Times
With many of the characteristic Pinteresque themes, this play is concerned with power within relationships, with possessiveness over people and territory, with the fraudulence of memory, and the subtexts of social dialogue. The play is organised around an intrusion into an established relationship, an intrusion

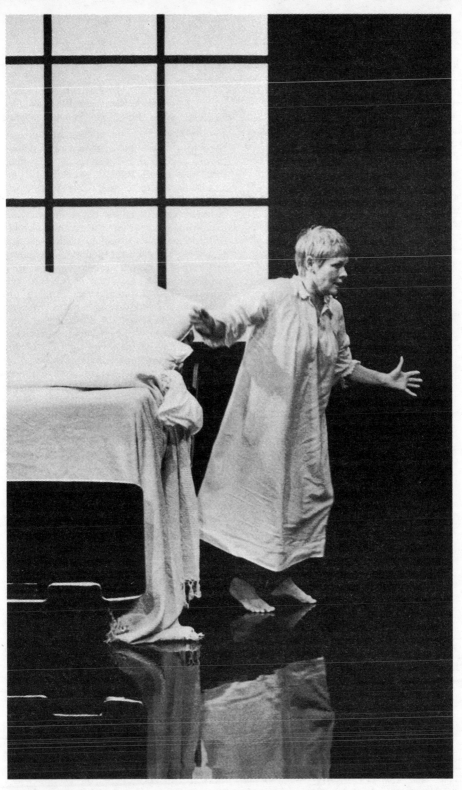
Harold Pinter's *A Kind of Alaska*, directed by Peter Hall, National Theatre, 1982. Judi Dench waking from virtually a lifetime of catatonia

which invokes the tensions, contradictions and power relations between a married couple, which had remained unspoken. The environment of the play initially appears to be a safe haven from the world, an attractive middle-class home, inhabited by an attractive, articulate couple, until Anna arrives to stay with her old friend Kate and her husband, Deeley. Over the course of the play, a power struggle between Anna and Deeley emerges, and it becomes clear that both are battling for Kate. Their conflict is fought over the memory of the past; each character reminisces about their shared experiences, but each has a very different version of events. The play does not have the menacing violence of *The Birthday Party* or *The Caretaker*, but is nonetheless very unsettling; it offers no help in untangling the 'truth' of the past, but suggests, like *Betrayal*, the slipperiness of truth, of memory and of language.

Try these:
▷Terence Rattigan, who interpreted *The Caretaker* as an Old Testament allegory; ▷Ionesco for similarities to *The Birthday Party*; ▷Beckett shares Pinter's refusal to analyse his plays and his paradoxical precision of language but ambiguity of meaning; ▷Joe Orton for an extension of the mundane into Surrealism, ▷Tom Stoppard for his interest in the fraudulence of memory; ▷Manuel Puig's *Mystery of the Rose Bouquet* as a multi-faceted exercise in memory; ▷Michel Tremblay's *Albertine in Five Times* for a Proustian play; Elizabeth Bowen's *The Heat of the Day* (adapted for Shared Experience) also explores the slipperiness of language and betrayal and was actually adapted by Pinter himself into a film for television; ▷N. F. Simpson, a Pinter contemporary and exponent of the British vein of Absurdism.

PIRANDELLO, Luigi   [1867–1936]
Italian dramatist

Plays include:
The Vise (1898), *Scamander* (1909), *Sicilian Limes* (1910), *Liola* (1916), *Right You Are – If You Think So* (1917), *Cap and Bells* (1917), *The Pleasure of Honesty* (1917), *Man, Beast, and Virtue* (1919), *Mrs Morli, One and Two* (1920), *Six Characters in Search of an Author* (1921), *Henry IV* (1922), *Each In His Own Way* (1924),

Diana and Tuda (1926), *The New Colony* (1928), *Lazarus* (1929), *Tonight We Improvise* (1930), *To Find Oneself* (1932), *When Someone is Somebody* (1933), *No One Knows How* (1934), *The Mountain Giants* (1937)

Born into a wealthy Sicilian family with a history of liberal and revolutionary beliefs, Pirandello attended the Universities of Rome and Bonn. His father was bankrupt by 1904, and his wife suffering from mental disorder, obsessed with the notion that Pirandello was unfaithful. He continued to live a miserable and withdrawn life until his wife was consigned to a mental institution in 1919. During this period of withdrawal he began writing plays, and in the early 1920s he achieved considerable fame, winning the support of Mussolini and world-wide acclaim. He won the Nobel Prize in 1934. Pirandello's influence is particularly powerful on the Theatre of the Absurd. His plays are about a deeply perplexing, frequently hostile universe populated by characters who are themselves inconstant; he is fascinated by the masks people adopt in altering social circumstances, by the possibilities of multiple personality and the relativity of truth. Again and again his plays return to themes of deception and self-deception, entangling the audience in nets of paradox. The surface naturalism of his style of writing serves to heighten the contradictions which beset his characters, who are generally speaking unspectacular minor bourgeois figures rather than Promethean heroes. The plays have an obvious intellectual appeal; Pirandello's great achievement is to make them also highly theatrical.

Six Characters in Search of an Author
A rehearsal in the theatre is disrupted by the unexpected intrusion of a strange family group, who claim to be characters from an incomplete play. In the hope that the actors can finish the work, the family act out scenes from their life, but these prove full of contradiction and contention. The Father has become estranged from his wife early in their marriage, he has brought up their son in isolation, while she has lived with the man she loved and had three children by him. The Father interprets this as proof of his benevolence; the Wife accuses him of ruthless self-interest, cruelty and lechery. The Father confesses that he encountered the Daughter in a brothel. The Stepdaughter blames the Father for her life of shame. The Son turns his back

both on the Father and the rest of the family. Then the Little Girl is discovered drowned, and the Younger Boy kills himself. In the horrified confusion which follows in the theatre, the family insist that the events witnessed have been real, while the actors insist that they must be illusion.

Try these:

▷Tom Stoppard, and ▷Thomas Kilroy for similar interest in role-playing; ▷Anouilh's *The Rehearsal* has Pirandellian influences; ▷Noël Greig's *Angels Descend on Paris* and Siren's *PULP* are two gay plays that deal in sexual role-playing; Don Hale's *Every Black Day* mixes fiction and real-life episodes; ▷Günter Grass' *The Plebians Rehearse The Uprising* plays with the notion of the play-within-the-play from a political perspective; for plays about theatrical illusion, and identity ▷Shakespeare's *Hamlet* (the 1987 ▷National Theatre production of *Six Characters* made *Hamlet* the play the actors were rehearsing) and *A Midsummer Night's Dream*; for other dramatists of the Absurd, ▷Genet and ▷Ionesco.

POLIAKOFF, Stephen   [1952–]
British dramatist

Plays include:
A Day With My Sister (1971), *Lay-By* (1971; with ▷Howard Brenton, ▷Brian Clark, ▷Trevor Griffiths, ▷David Hare, Hugh Stoddart and ▷Snoo Wilson), *Berlin Days* (1973), *The Carnation Gang* (1974), *Clever Soldiers* (1974), *Heroes* (1975), *Hitting-Town* (1975), *City Sugar* (1975), *Strawberry Fields* (1977), *Stronger Than The Sun* (1977), *Shout Across The River* (1978), *American Days* (1979), *The Summer Party* (1980), *Breaking The Silence* (1984), *Coming In To Land* (1987), *Playing with Trains* (1989), *Sienna Red* (1991)

Although he began writing plays in 1969 Poliakoff first came to prominence with *Hitting Town* and *City Sugar*, by the understated precision with which he evoked the sham comforts of anonymous shopping malls, fast-food outlets and motorway service areas, while exploring readily identifiable, unlikeable and deeply alienated characters. He is particularly effective in capturing the curious absence of real passion in people smothering in webs of superficiality, and the sense of conscious distress behind even the most glibly

desperate – exemplified by the radio DJ in *City Sugar*. The plays are notable for a strong sense of isolation and of communication replaced by half-hearted buzz-words and slogans. He conveys – rather suprisingly given his settings – an accurate sense of particular physical spaces, underlined by their actual emptiness: public spaces deserted at night; the enclosed but lonely world of the late-night radio phone-in; surveillance cameras and unseen observers render even his most aggressive characters exposed and vulnerable. In *Strawberry Fields* a brother and sister romanticise themselves as renegades and guerrillas, but they seem to be in flight from nothing more tangible than their own imagined fears of pursuit. His most recent plays have seen an expansion away from urban blight. In *Breaking the Silence* a scientist-inventor (based on Poliakoff's own grandfather) on the run from the Russian Revolution is holed up with his family in a railway carriage. In *Coming in to Land* another political refugee, a Polish woman seeking asylum in Britain, is the focus for a study on the nature of oppositional attraction, bureaucracy, immigration and East and West. Poliakoff's concerns have also transferred very effectively to television, particularly in *Caught on a Train* which starred Peggy Ashcroft. Poliakoff takes up the theme of neglect of inventors in modern Britain in *Playing with Trains* and returns to an earlier theme – incest between siblings – first mooted in *Hitting Town*, for his 1991 film, *Close My Eyes*.

Try these:

Jonathan Gems, ▷Len Jenkin and ▷Gregory Motton are contemporary writers whose characters are equally in flight; ▷Eric Overmyer's *Native Speech* for desperate DJs; ▷Tom Stoppard for political dissidents; ▷Robert Bolt's *Flowering Cherry* for portraits of grandiose dreamers sacrificing their families as in *Breaking the Silence*. Alexandr Gelman's *We the Undersigned* also takes place in a Russian railway carriage.

POLLOCK, Sharon   [1936–]
Canadian dramatist

Plays include:
Compulsory Option (1971), *Walsh* (1973), *And Out Goes You* (1975), *The Komogata Maru Incident* (1976), *Blood Relations* (1980)

Pollock, who also works as a director and actress and writes plays for children, is perhaps best known for *Blood Relations*, inspired by the true story of Lizzie Borden who, according to popular rhyme 'took an axe/ And gave her mother forty whacks' and then gave her father forty-one (she was actually acquitted of murdering them but it makes for a less interesting rhyme!). In Pollock's version whodunnit is less important than why it was done: the claustrophobic tensions, repressions, and slow violences of family life, are refracted through the device of having her story acted out ten years after the historical events by her actress friend while the 'real' Lizzie plays the role of the family maid. Women have come to the fore in Pollock's later plays but she has always been interested in the borderlines between normal and abnormal behaviour, the central and the marginal in a culture, as in the historically based *Walsh*, in which the Mountie Major of the title is torn between the values of his government and those of Sitting Bull, and *The Komagata Maru Incident*, in which a government agent who is himself of mixed race is sent aboard a ship full of Asian refugees who are being refused entry into Canada. Her work deserves to be more widely seen outside her native country.

Try these:
▷Michel Tremblay and ▷George Walker, for other Canadian dramatists; ▷Genet's *The Maids* and ▷Wendy Kesselman's *My Sister in This House* both based on an actual case, are also concerned with role playing and family tensions leading to murder; parent killing is a staple of drama from Orestes in ▷Aeschylus's *Oresteia*, Oedipus in ▷Sophocles' *Oedipus Rex*, Hamlet in Shakespeare's *Hamlet* to ▷Stephen Bill's *Curtains*; ▷Arthur Kopit's *Buffalo Bill and the Indians* is another meditation on the Red Indian/white culture clash; see Thomson Highway for views from the native Indian side.

POMERANCE, Bernard   [1940–]
American dramatist

Plays include:
Foco Novo (1972), *Someone Else Is Still Someone* (1974), *The Elephant Man* (1977), *Melons* (1985)

A Brooklyn-born long-time London resident, Pomerance seems – on the basis of his few widely seen plays – to be drawn to dialectics often at the expense of powerful writing. In *Foco Novo*, which gave its name to the theatre troupe Pomerance helped to found, an unnamed Latin American military dictatorship pits its citizens against the state, the guerilla outsiders against the technologically obsessed Americans. *The Elephant Man*, his best-known play, is based on a true life story in which a Victorian doctor, an anatomist named Treves, finds his definition of normality challenged by the Elephant Man of the title, a physically deformed, dream-obsessed visionary. *Melons*, set in a New Mexico melon patch in 1906, has its own would-be Treves: Carlos Montezuma, an Indian rights activist torn between the new world of the American colonialist and the ageless rituals of the native Indians. Pomerance's moral and ethical concerns are laudable, but he remains a playwright who may, perhaps, be creatively hamstrung by the burden of a monster hit.

The Elephant Man
In twenty-two short scenes with titles, Pomerance has written a major play that goes beyond prurient interest in its hunched, malformed central figure to touch on matters of faith, romance, and theatricality itself. To the left of the stage stands a strapping, well-built actor, who, as the description of his character is heard, assumes the stooped posture and slurred diction of the grotesquely misshapen John Merrick, labelled 'the elephant man' by nineteenth-century circus owners who used him as a freak attraction. A compassionate but career-minded physician, Treves, takes Merrick under his wing, undergoing a painful self-analysis that strips bare Victorian preconceptions about normality and the parameters of faith. The play features a superb part for a woman – the actress Mrs Kendal, who offers Merrick his one brief moment of eros. A raging success both in Britain and on Broadway, the play sparked interest in its subject, and a 1980 film was made with the same title, bypassing Pomerance's text.

Try these:
▷Peter Shaffer's *Equus* for doctor-patient conflict as metaphor; ▷Arthur Kopit's *Indians* for stage treatment of an often-ignored area; ▷Richard Nelson for his spare, enunciatory style and a shared interest in history and politics; ▷Maria

Irene Fornes' *The Conduct of Life* for another treatment of Latin-American brutality.

POWNALL, David   [1938–]
British dramatist and novelist

Plays include:
Crates on Barrels (1975), *Ladybird, Ladybird . . .* (1975), *Music to Murder By* (1976), *Richard III Part Two* (1977), *Barricade* (1977), *Motocar* (1977), *An Audience Called Edouard* (1978), *Livingstone and Sechele* (1978), *Beef* (1981), *Master Class* (1983), *The Viewing* (1987), *King John's Jewel* (1987), *Dark Star* (1987)

Pownall, co-founder of the touring company Paines Plough, is an inventive dramatist who characteristically yokes together apparently disparate material to create plays in which the audience is invited to enjoy itself by engaging with complex issues and the deconstruction of received patterns of thinking. His main interests so far have been in politics, history, the arts, music, and Africa. *Music to Murder By* combines both music and history in its study of the composer Peter Warlock reincarnating himself as the sixteenth-century composer Gesualdo in order to, literally, kill his writing block; *Motocar*, set in a mental hospital in Zimbabwe just before independence, is a powerful evocation of history and the relationship between personal and public madness; *Richard III Part Two*, a meditation on the construction and uses of history, begins with George Orwell telling us about *1984* and switches to an Orwellian present in which the Ministry of Sport is about to market its new game 'Betrayal' about Richard III and the Princes in the Tower. *An Audience Called Edouard* starts with the actors on stage in the attitudes of Manet's painting *Déjeuner sur l'herbe* with Manet supposed to be out front in the audience painting the scene; add to this the arrival of an incognito Karl Marx and we have a potent brew. After the success of *Master Class*, Pownall's touch seems to have deserted him, at least as far as the critics were concerned. *The Viewing*, in which a mysterious potential house buyer turns out to be God come to stop a blind scientist from destroying the world, was generally thought to be emptily portentous, and *King John's Jewel*, in which we see a different John to the normal version, seemed to be too static for many tastes. With Pownall there is always the chance that the material brought together will fail to gel, but when it does he can be one of the most exciting and entertaining dramatists around.

Master Class
In an imagined encounter in 1948 Stalin, Prokofiev, Shostakovich and Zhdanov engage in debate about the right formula for socialist music, but the terms of the debate are skewed by the composer's knowledge that Stalin can simply have them killed if they don't fall into line. Stalin equates artistic freedom, atonality and lack of melody with political irresponsibility: the people need uplifting with simple music they can understand to get them through the aftermath of war and the composers have a duty to provide it. The whole relationship between the state and the individual is brought into play in a way that is both entertaining and chilling, particularly at the end of the first act when Prokofiev is asked to choose his favourite record and Stalin proceeds systematically to destroy the record collection so that the second act is played on a visual and aural carpet of broken music.

Try these:
▷Snoo Wilson is like Pownall with the brakes off; ▷Terry Johnson's *Insignificance* brings together mythic figures in a similar way to much of Pownall's work, but without the time shifts; ▷Peter Parnell's *Romance Language* uses historical figures in a very different way; ▷Tom Stoppard's *Every Good Boy Deserves Favour* also tackles the theme of music in Russia, as does ▷Michael Wilcox's *78 Revolutions*; ▷C.P. Taylor's *Good* does the same for Nazi Germany; ▷Shakespeare's *Richard III* is the effective starting point for modern popular attitudes to Richard; ▷J.B. Priestley's *An Inspector Calls* is the best modern God-in-disguise play.

PRIESTLEY, J.B.
(John Boynton)   [1894–1984]
British dramatist, novelist, commentator and essayist

Plays include:
The Good Companions (with Edward Knoblock, from his own novel; 1931), *Dangerous Corner* (1932), *Eden End* (1934), *Time and the Conways* (1937), *I Have Been Here Before* (1937), *When We Are Married*

(1938), *Music at Night* (1938), *Johnson Over Jordan* (1939), *Desert Highway* (1943), *They Came to a City* (1943), *An Inspector Calls* (1945), *The Linden Tree* (1947), *Summer Day's Dream* (1950), *The Scandalous Affair of Mr Kettle and Mrs Moon* (1955)

Priestley wrote forty-seven plays (including one for Pollock's toy theatres), an opera libretto, films, television and radio plays and twenty-eight novels – quite apart from a much greater number of books of travel, political comment, literary biography etc. Most of his plays are carefully plotted and mainly conventional in form, even allowing for the split, serial and circular theories of time which shape the three 'time plays': *Dangerous Corner*, *Time and the Conways* and *I Have Been Here Before*. More unconventional in breaking out of the domestic box set are: *Johnson Over Jordan*, which follows its protagonist through the fourth dimension of immediate after-death; *Music at Night*, which explores the thoughts and lives of the audience at a concert; *They Came to a City*, which pictures a socialist utopia; and *Desert Highway*, written for army actors, which shows a tank crew marooned in the desert with a flash-back to their prototypes in ancient times. Priestley was much more adventurous than most dramatists being performed on Shaftesbury Avenue at the time, but he quite consciously sought to work within the limits acceptable to contemporary audiences; while experimenting in one direction he felt, 'it is dangerous to try and advance on all fronts at once'. Nevertheless, although the demands he makes may be slight compared with those some dramatists make of audiences, even his lightest comedies embody a critique of society and behaviour and a presentation of ideas beyond the humour and narration of their surface. Their optimism now dates his more overtly political pieces, but *Time and the Conways*, the comedy *When We Are Married* and *An Inspector Calls* are frequently revived and may outlive much contemporary writing.

An Inspector Calls

A totally believable middle-class Yorkshire household is visited by a detective – originally created rather enigmatically by Ralph Richardson, though there is no reason why he should not be much more mundane in manner – who is investigating the death of a young woman. As the background to the tragedy is revealed, the circles of responsibility and guilt

spread to affect almost everyone. At the end of the play, the announcement of the visit of a detective inspector questions the detective's real identity and reveals the play as a metaphor for our own failure to accept our responsibility to others.

Try these:
Harold Brighouse, ▷Keith Waterhouse and ▷Willis Hall and, ▷Willy Russell for other plays rooted in the North of England; ▷Somerset Maugham's *For Services Rendered* for a critique of conventional values within a traditional form; ▷Trevor Griffiths and ▷Arnold Wesker as socialist dramatists who tend to work with available forms; ▷Edward Bond and ▷Howard Brenton as socialist dramatists who use more radical approaches; ▷Brecht for communal responsibility; ▷Enid Bagnold for domestic revelations; ▷Ronald Harwood's *The Dresser* and ▷David Mamet's *A Life in the Theater* for other views of theatre life.

PROMENADE PERFORMANCES

This is an expression originally used to describe concerts, like the annual London series begun by Henry Wood in 1895, at which the audience is free to walk about. It is today sometimes used of special low-price performances which aim to attract new audiences and for which they must queue on the day. Since 1977, when the term was borrowed by the ▷National Theatre as less off-putting than saying that audiences had to stand, it has been used to describe performances such as the Bill Bryden productions of *The Mysteries* which played to popular and critical success (1977–85), and Keith Dewhurst's adaptation of *Larkrise to Candleford*. The promenade style has been used for such widely acclaimed productions as Le Théâtre du Soleil's *1789* (1970), an ▷RSC production of ▷Arthur Miller's *The Crucible*, André Serban's *Trojan Women*, Irene Fornes' *Fefu and Her Friends*, ▷Ann Bogart's *No Play No Poetry . . .* and much of her other work, ▷Ann Jellicoe's community plays and numerous ▷Shakespeare productions including Peter Stein's Berlin *As You Like It*. It can take two quite different forms: in one the audience and actors share a performance area, with the action flowing through the space; in the other the action moves on from place to place, the audience following from one location to another. In both cases some seating is usually provided for those not wishing to stand for the whole performance.

The processional form may exploit actual locations, indoor or outdoor, through which it passes or it may move through specially created environments. The ▷RSC's *The Dillen* (1983 and 1985), based on the life of a Stratford man, actually wound its way through the town. En Garde Arts productions have taken place in New York's Central Park, the city's meat-packing district, and on a Greenwich Village sidewalk. Bread and Puppet Theatre have frequently used processional forms to draw audiences into participation, and Welfare State is one of the British groups that have used a trail both to provide a series of dramatic and visual experiences and to increase awareness of the environment itself. Audiences can be offered a multitude of animate and inanimate images, in addition to human performers, and the extent of communication will depend upon the keenness of their observation. Interaction in this form may be more with the environment than with performers. Even when outdoor promenades encompass large territories, performance elements and any simultaneous, as opposed to sequential, experience will limit the number of participants. Many were turned away from events such as Lumière and Son's *Deadwood* at Kew Gardens.

Plays presented in promenade style within a limited theatrical space force audience and actors to share that space. As the action moves from one area to another the audience change their perspective and probably their position. The spectator chooses his or her constantly changing relationship with the action, as opposed to the passivity of a fixed seat. Offering a literal contact with the actors that is the extreme opposite of fourth-wall theatre, promenade performance paradoxically both emphasises the theatrical nature of the event and reinforces empathic involvement.

Try these:
▷Nick Darke's *Ting Tang Mine*, ▷David Edgar's *Entertaining Strangers* and ▷Jim Cartwright's *Road* are recent promenade productions; *Tony 'n' Tina's Wedding* and *Tamara* are two events at which the audience intermingles with the actors. See also ▷Ann Jellicoe, ▷Community Theatre, ▷Adaptations and Adapters.

PUB/CAFÉ THEATRE IN BRITAIN

Café theatre in Britain is almost non-existent – with the honourable exceptions of London's Canal Café Theatre in Little Venice and La Bonne Crêpe in Battersea – but pub entertainment is much more common. Entertainment in pubs comes in three kinds: the most basic is the band at one end of the bar, which is primarily there to encourage the clientèle to do their drinking in this pub rather than any other. The second type is the large room with a stage at one end, and often a bar down one side, where a charge is made for admission but drinking is an expected part of the evening. This is very much the way the ▷music hall started, but it is now the homeland of the 'alternative cabaret' circuit, above all of stand-up comics of both sexes, but may also include singers, comic groups and the odd poet. The third type, pub theatre proper, is mainly a London phenomenon except during festivals in other towns. In intent and principle it is related to venues such as the Donmar Warehouse or the Cottesloe, and makes up a large proportion of the London fringe (analogous to the kind of performance spaces which house the activities of New York's off-off-Broadway). There are other sources for such rooms – 'studios' in modern theatre or arts complexes, made-over church or drill halls – but pubs tend to have the cheapest ones. They also have the advantage that you can take your beer with you, as in the music halls, which makes for a pleasant informality.

The type of performance seen in these London pub theatres varies with the management. Some have strong managements and highly individual repertories; others are just 'venues', open to anybody who can put down the money, and liable to close as quickly as they opened. Of those with a more or less continuous programme, such as the Man in the Moon, the Old Red Lion and the King's Head, the Bush is the most well-established example of pub theatre. Its record of discovering new writers and consistently high production standards is comparable to that of the ▷Royal Court. In the past few years it has put on plays by ▷Snoo Wilson, ▷Doug Lucie, ▷Franz Xaver Kroetz, and ▷Sam Shepard, and 'discovered' many more authors, including ▷Nick Darke, ▷Terry Johnson, ▷Beth

Henley, ▷Sharman Macdonald, and ▷Julia Kearsley. The Gate, Notting Hill, has survived Lou Stein and Giles Croft's departures continuing to find and present rare foreign classics (anything from *Don Gil of the Green Breeches* by Tirso de Molina to Marie-Luise Fleisser's *Ingolstadt* plays) and recently mounted a much acclaimed Women in World Theatre season. However, *the* pub theatre success story so far must be the Orange Tree in Richmond, where Sam Walters' steady run of successes, ancient and modern, British and foreign, but all unusual, has enabled him to build his own ▷theatre-in-the-round (square, actually) across the road from the original pub.

Try these:
▷Cabaret

PUIG, Manuel   [1932–90]
Argentine novelist, dramatist and film director

Plays include:
Kiss of the Spider Woman (1981), *Mystery of the Rose Bouquet* (1981), *Under the Mantle of Stars* (1982)

Puig studied at film school in Rome and became a successful novelist before having his first play produced. *Kiss of the Spider Woman*, based on his own novel, is widely known from the film version which he also directed. Both this and *Mystery of the Rose Bouquet* are two-handers for contrasting characters, offering marvellous opportunities for actors, and exploring stormy and intricate relationships. Puig uses these small-scale pieces to reflect the culture in which they are set and perhaps suggests – in the transformation which the interaction works on each character – a possibility of social change. Both are set in enclosed worlds, *Mystery of the Rose Bouquet* in an expensive health clinic where a rich and mischievous old woman who has already sacked four nurses, and the poor, apparently unqualified nurse who is now looking after her, begin to find a pattern of similarity in their lives. As they relive their memories of sadness, failure and sometimes of roses, they both torment

and rehabilitate each other. As in his novels, such as *Betrayed by Rita Hayworth*, the character's imagination and fantasies are explored, thus lifting his plays out of strictly naturalistic forms.

Kiss of the Spider Woman
Kiss of the Spider Woman is set in an Argentinian prison cell where a camp window-dresser, found guilty of fooling around with a fifteen-year old, is shut up with a macho, Marxist revolutionary and promised release if he can pry secrets from him. As affection and dependence develop between the men, climaxing in physical consummation, the fey-gay who escapes from reality in reliving B-picture romances (oblivious to their fascist background and ideology) learns that caring for individuals is not enough, accepts social responsibility and recognises his own integrity, while the revolutionary learns reciprocal respect and the value of the individual. This is a homosexual love story, a study of power – not only of authority over the individual but between the prisoners themselves – and an argument for the innocence of love. It demolishes conventional bourgeois values while skilfully embroiling the audience in the conflicts of loyalty and betrayal.

Try these:
For other imprisoned homosexuals, John Herbert's *Fortune and Men's Eyes*, ▷Genet's *Deathwatch*, ▷Martin Sherman's *Bent*; for studies of power relationships ▷Harold Pinter's *One for the Road* and *No Man's Land*, ▷Beckett's *Endgame* and *Catastrophe*; Michele Celeste's *Hanging the President* for a South African variation; for contrasting two-handed female relationships, ▷Catherine Hayes' *Skirmishes*, Holly Hughes' *Dress Suits to Hire* (Split Britches); Win Wells' *Gertrude Stein and Companion*, Claire Tomlin's *The Winter Wife* (about Katherine Mansfield and her companion, Ida Baker, and *Fallen Angel and The Devil Concubine*, a post-colonial, Caribbean setting featuring two female tramps, one black, one white.

 r

RABE, David [1940–]
American dramatist

Plays include:
The Basic Training of Pavlo Hummel
(1971), *Sticks and Bones* (1971), *The
Orphan* (1973), *In the Boom Boom Room*
(1973), *Streamers* (1976), *Goose and Tom-
Tom* (1980), *Hurlyburly* (1984), *Those the
River Keeps* (1991)

A tough, gritty, often abrasive writer who
bides his time between plays, Rabe is distinguished by his trilogy about the Vietnam
War. This begins with the untidy *The Basic
Training of Pavlo Hummel*, continues on to the
stark, ironic *Sticks and Bones* and climaxes
with the altogether startling *Streamers*, one of
the great American plays of the 1970s. Set in
1965 in a Virginia army barracks, the play
makes the scabrous point that we carry war
with us, that war is an internal condition
which occasionally finds an external release. It
takes its title from the word for a parachute
which fails to open, but the play itself floats on
a bloody and pained compassion for all of
society's victims. This natural state of aggression finds its peace-time equivalent amongst
the Hollywood sharks who populate
Hurlyburly, a sour and rancid end-of-the-
world play which is as flowery and overwritten as *Streamers* is swift and sharp.

Those the River Keeps, Rabe's first play in
six years, premiered in early 1991 under the
author's direction at McCarter Theater in
Princeton, New Jersey. Phil, a character from
Hurlyburly, an emerging actor in Los Angeles,
is trying desperately to break with his gangster
past. His new-found stability and young marriage, however, are dramatically threatened
by the arrival of Sal, a hit-man and former
friend. The play, which features long conversations about the past, is concerned with the
dangerous magnetism of one's personal history, and with the difficulties of starting anew.
Not on a level with Rabe's earlier plays, *Those
the River Keeps* lacks sharp focus and firm

pacing, and the women's roles are severely
underwritten. Certain passages, apparently
intended to be intensely lyrical, are incoherent. It is to be hoped that Rabe will continue
working on *Those the River Keeps*.

Try these:
▷Genet's *Deathwatch*, Miguel Pinero's
Short Eyes for similar dramas of enclos-
ure; ▷Thomas Babe for often jagged,
sometimes over-literary language; for
Vietnam plays, James Duff's *The War at
Home* traces the experience without illumi-
nating it, ▷C.P. Taylor's *Lies About
Vietnam* links the public problem with the
personal, the Vietnam Veterans
Ensemble's *Tracers* and Emily Mann's *Still
Life* provide haunting documentary-like
responses; plays about the LA malaise are
also often second-rate (Nick Darke's *The
Dead Monkey* for example); try ▷John
Steppling's *The Dream Coast* instead.

RACINE, Jean [1639–99]
French dramatist and historiographer-royal

Plays include:
Le Thébaïde (*The Theban*; 1664), *Alexandre
le Grand* (*Alexander the Great*; 1665),
Andromaque (*Andromache*; 1667), *Les
Plaideurs* (*The Litigants*; his only comedy;
1668), *Britannicus* (1669), *Bérénice* (1670),
Bajazet (1672), *Mithridate* (*Mithridates*;
1673), *Iphigénie* (*Iphigenia*; 1674), *Phèdre*
(*Phaedra*; 1677), *Esther* (1689), *Athalie*
(*Athalia*; 1691)

Racine was orphaned at the age of four, and
brought up at Port-Royal by the Jansenists; he
escaped them for most of his adult life, but
they got him in the end. A good scholar and
an admirer of the Greek dramatists, he took
naturally to the neo-Aristotelian rules that
▷Corneille found so constricting; his relentless dramas run their course in twenty-four
hours or less, in one location, with no sub-

plots to lessen the intensity. His characters manage to combine uncontrollable passion, self-interest, and a merciless lucidity; the restrictions of the rhymed Alexandrine couplets and the limited vocabulary help to channel the force of the events. After the comparative failure of *Phèdre*, Racine was reconciled with Port-Royal, and wrote no more secular plays; the last two, on Biblical subjects, were written for Madame de Maintenon's school for young ladies at St Cyr, but the subjects are from the Old Testament, and the doom is just as inevitable. It used to be the received wisdom that Racine's plays were not successful in English because they were impossible to translate, but recent productions have disproved this.

Phèdre

This is based on ▷Euripides' *Hippolytus*, but with concessions to the seventeenth-century French taste for *vraisemblance*; Hippolyte spurns his stepmother's forbidden love because he is in love with Aricie rather than because he is vowed to Diana, and the gods are obsessionally present in the characters' minds rather than appearing on the stage. The tension rises inexorably and logically from scene to scene; as often in Racine, if you pray to the gods your prayer is always answered (such as Thésée's prayer to Neptune to kill his son), but by then it is not what you want at all.

Try these:
▷Corneille for seventeenth-century French tragedy and for the neo-Aristotelian rules, also for influence of the Greek dramatists (though ▷Corneille preferred subjects from Roman history); ▷Euripides, from whom he borrowed the plots of *Phèdre* and *Iphigénie*; ▷Molière for a seventeenth-century comic French dramatist.

RAIF, Ayshe   [1952–   ]
British dramatist

Plays include:
Cafe Society (1981), *Another Woman* (1983), *A Party for Bonzo* (1985), *Fail/Safe* (1986), *Caving In* (1989)

Of Turkish-Cypriot parentage, Raif is a superb observer of emotional currents, with an ear for dialogue that is angry, and painful in its accuracy. Her plays thus far have been firmly embedded in the school of naturalistic drama – domestic, two- and three-handers showing life at the sharp end of urban existence: single women in lonely bed-sits (*Another Woman*), marriage torn apart by the effects of unemployment (*A Party for Bonzo*), and the repressive bonds that can tie mother/daughter relationships in knots (*Fail/Safe*). Though the plays are bleak, there is often a mordant humour at work which has yet to be fully unleashed. Some critics have found her work to be closer to television drama, which she has also written. Her stage plays, thus far, have all been presented at the pint-sized Soho Poly although she has also been writer-in-residence at the Theatre Royal, Stratford East for whom she completed two commissions including an adaptation of ▷Michel Tremblay's *Les Belles-Soeurs* (*The Sisters-in-Law*).

Try these:
For female monologue about isolation/ alienation, see Jacqui Shapiro and Meera Syal's *One of Us*; ▷Franz Xaver Kroetz's *Request Programme*, ▷Melissa Murray's *Bodycell*, ▷Botho Strauss' *Great and Small*, Barry Collins' *Judgement* for comparative states of isolation; Polly Teale's *Fallen*; for relationships between mothers and daughters, ▷Julia Kearsley, ▷Sharman Macdonald; for marriage under stress, ▷Strindberg, ▷Albee's *Who's Afraid of Viginia Woolf?*, ▷Ted Whitehead's *Alpha Beta*, ▷David Spencer; for frustrated daughters, ▷Catherine Hayes' *Skirmishes*.

RAME, Franca   [c 1930–   ]
Italian actress, dramatist

Plays include:
The Mother, and in collaboration with ▷Dario Fo *It's All Bed, Board & Church* (1977, also known as *All House, Bed and Church* or *Female Parts* or *One Woman Plays* and comprising *Waking Up*, *Same Old Story*, *A Woman alone*, and *Medea*), *Tomorrow's News*, *Ulrike Meinhof*, *I Don't Move*, *I Don't Scream*, *My Voice is Gone* (1983; also known as *The Rape*), *The Open Couple* (1986–87)

The fame of this remarkable actress-cum-playwright, daughter of one of the last of Italy's companies of strolling players, has been inextricably linked with that of Italy's premier political free-thinking socialist and satirist ▷Dario Fo, with whom she collaborated on several plays, and ran their own company/ collective, La Commune.

A physical performer of enormous energy and dynamism, Rame's monologues reflect equally that emotional intensity and her political commitments. Her plays have focused on a variety of women's issues, often as a result of her own experiences, and are testaments to the various forms of women's oppression in Italian society – from the state, the church and men. *The Mother* and the co-written *Ulrike Meinhof* and *Tomorrow's News* arose directly out of her activism on behalf of political prisoners; *The Rape* is an account, all the more chilling for its economy and understatement, of an attack on Rame herself motivated, she believes, by political opponents. Likewise, *Female Parts*, a series of monologues (co-written with Fo), based on conversations with a range of Italian women, reflects their problems in a subversive mix of styles from the bitterly ironic and farcically anarchic to feminist reappropriation of fairy-tales and the Medea myth, and has struck a common chord with female audiences from Japan to Brazil. *The Open Couple*, again co-written with ▷Fo, from whom she has now split, is yet a further example of the comic and grotesque as a couple come to grips with the painful truths and double standards of extra-marital relationships.

The Mother and The Rape

These are classic Rame monologues, often performed together. Both are blatant but bravura pieces of feminist agit-prop, descriptive reconstructions in which simplicity is the keynote. A minimum of props is used – just a chair – but the emotional contents speak for themselves and the cumulative effect can be shattering. In *The Mother*, the mother's account of a young terrorist's trial and sentence recreates not only the intensity of maternal feelings and their chilling climax, but instills a growing sense of society's collective responsibility towards the young man and his fate. Similarly, *The Rape* is a simple step-by-horrific-step description of a young woman being gang raped and tortured (with a cigarette) which is as powerful a statement about male violence – ▷Sarah Daniels notwithstanding – as you are likely to see.

Try these:

▷Ayshe Raif's *Another Woman*, for a British equivalent of the solo woman; Dacia Maraini's *Dialogue Between a Prostitute and one of her Clients* as an exercise in engaging audiences directly in the subject of prostitution; for a surreal account of rape, Eve Lewis' *Ficky Stingers* (which with ▷Louise Page's *Tissue* is an equivalent double bill of fear, anger and pain); ▷Brecht's *The Mother* for contrast; ▷Jane Wagner and Lily Tomlin's *Search for Signs of Intelligent Life* and Willy Russell's *Shirley Valentine* for more watered-down feminism performed solo; Ariel Dorfman's *Death and the Maiden* examines the emotional repercussions and feelings of revenge in the aftermath of rape and torture as does William Mastrosimone's *Extremities*, if more dubiously.

RATTIGAN, Terence (Mervyn)   [1911–77]
British dramatist

Plays include:
French Without Tears (1936), *After the Dance* (1939), *While the Sun Shines* (1943), *Flarepath* (1942), *Love in Idleness* (1944), *The Winslow Boy* (1946), *Playbill* (*The Browning Version* and *Harlequinade*; 1948), *Adventure Story* (1949), *Who is Sylvia* (1951), *The Deep Blue Sea* (1952), *The Sleeping Prince* (1953), *Separate Tables* (1954), *Variation on a Theme* (1958), *Ross: a Dramatic Portrait* (1960), *In Praise of Love* (*Before Dawn* and *After Lydia*; 1974), *Cause Célèbre* (1977)

A master craftsman in plot construction and writing telling dialogue, Rattigan first gained fame with *French Without Tears*, a bright comedy about would-be candidates for the Civil Service learning French at a French resort. He maintained his light touch through plays such as *The Sleeping Prince*, an Olivier/ Viven Leigh vehicle about a middle-aged prince falling in love with a chorus girl, which Olivier filmed with Marilyn Monroe as *The Prince and the Showgirl*. In the late 1950s Rattigan's obvious commercial appeal led enthusiasts of the work of ▷John Osborne and the new generation of more politically motivated dramatists to dismiss his work as irrelevant. Nevertheless, Rattigan, working within the format of the well-made play, tackled issues far deeper than those of conventional Shaftesbury Avenue entertainment, though he presented them with a skill that avoided alienating the respectable, middle-class, middle-aged theatre-goer whom he personified as 'Aunt Edna'.

In *Flarepath* he explored the strains on Battle of Britain flyers and their civilian friends and families; in the factually based *The Winslow Boy* his subject was the wrongful dismissal from a military academy of a boy accused of stealing a postal order; and in *The Browning Version* he examined the pressure on a teacher being forced into retirement with his wife unfaithful and even the pupil who seems to share his ideals abandoning him. *In Praise of Love* tackled incurable illness and *Cause Célèbre* was based on a famous case of a woman and her lover, who murdered her husband. *The Deep Blue Sea*, originally written as a story of male homosexuals following a tragedy concerning an actor with whom Rattigan was in love, touches tragic heights in its presentation of a woman leaving her husband for a man who does not return her love. Rattigan's understanding of the pain of relationships transcends sexual orientation, although *Adventure Story*, a psychological study of Alexander the Great, makes no attempt to explore the Alexander-Hephaiston relationship. Presumed homosexual rape is a central element in *Ross*, a presentation of T.E. Lawrence after Arabia, but the removal of censorship did not bring any overt exploration of his own sexuality to Rattigan's work.

Separate Tables

This is a double-bill (*Table by the Window* and *Table Number Seven*, both set in the same Bournemouth private hotel and with the same subsidiary characters), with each play offering a contrasting role for the leading lady and leading man. The first presents a drunken Labour ex-junior minister unexpectedly confronted with the ex-wife who divorced him for cruelty but for whom he still feels passionately. The second has a bogus major, bound-over on a charge of insulting behaviour in a cinema and shows reactions to his exposure, especially that of a repressed spinster with a bullying mother whom he has befriended. As in much of Rattigan's work, a comparatively slight idea is enriched by a deep understanding of the needs and inadequacies of human relationships. In his original review Ken Tynan regretted 'that the major's crime was not something more cathartic than mere cinema flirtation', but supposed 'the play is as good a handling of sexual abnormality as English playgoers will tolerate'. This was in the days of the Lord Chamberlain's censor-

ship, and in fact Rattigan is said to have originally intended the charge to be a homosexual one.

Try these:
▷Somerset Maugham and ▷Tennessee Williams for similar treatments of homosexual themes; ▷Leslie Lee's *Black Eagles* for another perspective on World War II fliers; ▷Brian Clark's, *Whose Life Is It Anyway?* for a play about incurable illness; many British comedies for jokes at the expense of funny foreigners, from ▷Shakespeare's *The Merry Wives of Windsor* onwards (Larry Shue's *The Foreigner* provides a twist on this genre).

RECKORD, Barry
Jamaican dramatist

Plays include:
Adella (1954; revised version, *Flesh to a Tiger*; 1958), *You in Your Small Corner* (1960), *Skyvers* (1963), *Don't Gas the Blacks* (1969), *A Liberated Woman* (1970), *Give the Gaffers Time to Love You* (1971), *X* (1972), *Streetwise* (1984)

A black Jamaican, educated at Oxford, which he left in 1952, Reckord's first play centres on a woman in a Jamaican slum trying to choose between white medicine and local magic to save her dying baby. Insulted by the white doctor with whom she has begun to fall in love it ends melodramatically with her killing both her baby and the black 'shepherd' doctor in a parallel of her people's struggle to throw off both superstition and white domination. Reckord's other work for the stage, however, has been more concerned with class than colour. *You in Your Small Corner* shows a black bourgeois Brixton family in which the successful mother looks down on the local poor whites; and in his best-known play, *Skyvers*, set in a London comprehensive school, the pupils react violently against the social inadequacy of their parents and teachers and the suppression of talent and lack of opportunity. Although his next two plays present, in *Don't Gas the Blacks*, a black couple in which the wife has a black lover, and, in *A Liberated Woman*, a black couple in which the wife has a white lover, he is concerned less with racism as such than with personal freedom and sexual politics. Refusal to compromise on the forthright content of his work aborted several proposed productions of new plays in recent years, both on stage and on television.

X

Produced by Joint Stock at the Royal Court, *X* is a two-hander in which an Oxford don is visited in his college rooms by his daughter, a believer in the ideas of Wilhelm Reich. She strips preparatory to taking a shower and then settles down to an increasingly outspoken conversation with her father, in which they both describe their sexual disappointments and she reveals the 'X' of the title: a suppressed sexual longing for her father. In the premiere production some lines were played for laughs which made for an uneasy shift to the strong meat of the argument.

Try these:
▷Errol John, ▷Derek Walcott, ▷Edgar White, ▷Trevor Rhone for Caribbean-located plays; ▷Michael Abbensetts, ▷Mustapha Matura, ▷Caryl Phillips for plays about British blacks with roots in the Caribbean; ▷Barrie Keeffe and ▷Peter Terson for failures in the educational/social system; ▷Mary O'Malley and ▷Christopher Durang for a contrasting comic swipe at the Catholic educational system, and ▷Wedekind's *Spring Awakening* for a study of school children; ▷Trevor Griffiths for a writer influenced by Wilhelm Reich; ▷Sophocles' *Oedipus*, ▷John Ford's *'Tis Pity She's a Whore*, ▷Shelley's *The Cenci*, Michel Tremblay's *Bonjour, Bonjour* for quite different treatments of incest.

REDDIN, Keith   [1956–]
American dramatist, actor

Plays include:
Throwing Smoke (1983), *Life and Limb* (1983), *Desperadoos* (1989), *Rum and Coke* (1985), *Highest Standard of Living* (1986), *Big Time* (1987), *Plain Brown Wrapper* (1987), *Nebraska* (1989), *Life During Wartime* (1990)

New Jersey-born Keith Reddin has been called the 'Yuppie Playwright,' but his works actually speak sharply against the politics and pop culture of the 1980s. Merging historic settings and actual events with contemporary social and political issues, Reddin writes classic idea plays with an over-present layer of comedy. His first full length play, *Life and Limb*, follows a disabled Korean War veteran as he returns to alcoholism and marital separation in his suburban New Jersey home; Reddin mingles such serious issues with a spoof of 1950s family life, mirroring scenes from television's *I Love Lucy* and imitating the pace of *The Honeymooners*. He sees this blend as an effective medium, saying 'I want to take a tough look at the society of the '50s, but at the same time I never want to bore anyone.'

In *Rum and Coke*, Reddin uses the thirty-year-old Cuban Bay of Pigs incident to reflect on current US foreign policy in Latin America, following a young Yale graduate who encounters conflict between his ethics and his duty to the Central Intelligence Agency. *Highest Standard of Living* follows the studies and travels of a Columbia doctoral student in Moscow and after his return to New York, echoing the style of Russian theatre that preceeded Stalin's crackdown on artistic freedom and combining political issues with humorous culture-clash jokes and an Act II tone reminiscent of Hollywood spy thrillers. Echoing the stark savage atmosphere of ▷David Mamet's *Edmond*, *Big Time* illustrates the deterioration of personal relationships in the world of big business. The play is a sad look at the spoiled, self-centred American generation of the 1980s, where success and money claim priority.

The New Jersey veteran in *Life and Limb*, the Yale graduate in *Rum and Coke*, and the travelling doctoral student in *Highest Standard of Living* all seem to reflect Reddin's own upbringing, experiences, and idealistic search for hope in a cruel world. Paul in *Big Time* is caught up in the pace-money-drug fever of the business world, but he's also an idealist, a man who loves his work, fights for his girl, and believes in hard work. Reddin also includes in each new play a character from the previous one, perhaps aiming subconsciously to carry themes and issues from one play to the next; the villanous Tod Cartmell of *Life and Limb* re-appears in *Rum and Coke*, while the CIA recruiter Roger Potter in *Rum and Coke* returns as the American diplomat of the same name in *Highest Standard of Living*.

Try these:
▷Howard Brenton's *The Churchill Play*, and *The Romans in Britain*, ▷Howard Barker's *Alpha Alpha*, and *That Good Between Us*, for their juxtaposition of historic events with current politics. Reddin

himself acknowledges the influences of ▷David Hare, and ▷Dario Fo. See also the plays of Doug Lucie *Progress*, and *Fashion*, which are less hopeful but criticize society even more harshly; Stephen Jeffreys and Martin Crimp for more puncturing of 'yuppie' moves.

REID, Christina   [1942–]
Northern Irish dramatist

Plays include:
Tea in a China Cup (1984), *Did You Hear the One About The Irishman . . .?* (1984), *Dissenting Adults* (1985), *Joyriders* (1986), *The Belle of the Belfast City* (1989), *My Name, Shall I Tell You My Name* (1989)

Christina Reid, one of a number of fine playwrights to have emerged from Northern Ireland in the past ten years, is an unsentimental, sardonic chronicler of the domestic minutiae by which communities pass on attitudes. Reid does not use the Belfast troubles as the centrepiece of her plays, but their existence is never very far away, controlling and determining destinies. *Tea in a China Cup*, for example, takes an irreverently humorous if painful look at matriarchal influences in the daily, domestic rituals of one working-class Protestant family over a 50-year span. *My Name, Shall I Tell You My Name*, a delicate two-hander about a grandfather, a survivor of the Somme and member of the Orange Order and his granddaughter, also highlights the way views become entrenched through history and family. A fiercely pacifist play, it was equally a beautifully crafted study in human relationships, and a cry of anguished despair. *Joyriders*, on the other hand, took a tougher, almost surreal tone to show the effect of the present troubles on four young no-hopers from Belfast's notorious Divis Flats, paralleling their lives with those in ▷O'Casey's *Shadow of a Gunman*. *The Belle of the Belfast City* which won the 1987 George Devine award was commissioned by the Tricycle Theatre but was postponed when the theatre was burnt down in 1987. Since then Reid's radio play, the bitterly comic essay on death and dying *The Last of a Dyin' Race*, has turned up in a wonderful television version for Channel Four. She was also writer-in-residence at London's Young Vic for 18 months which produced one play *Lords, Dukes and Earls* and where she scripted the Youth Theatre's improvised show, *Young, Free and Single*.

Try these:
For other images of Belfast, ▷Ann Devlin's *Ourselves Alone*, like *Tea in a China Cup*, focuses on women-centred responses to their environment; also ▷Daniel Mornin, ▷Seamus Finnegan, and particularly Marie Jones's *From the Balcony* for Charabanc, also set in Belfast's Divis Flats, for another, even wackier view of confronting everyday madness with madness; ▷Rona Munro's *Bold Girls* also examines the effects on women of living in Belfast.

RESIDENT THEATRE IN THE USA
The prevailing wisdom goes that the USA's 'national theatre' cannot be contained in any one institution. Instead, the USA's diverse geography and multi-ethnic society is represented by a 'national theatre' consisting of the eclectic network of not-for-profit regional and resident theatres spread across the country. These companies range from large multi-million dollar institutions – the Mark Taper Forum, the New York Shakespeare Festival, the Guthrie Theater – to a variety of smaller organizations, some of which may or may not use Actors' Equity contracts, like Pan Asian Repertory, Mixed Blood in Minneapolis, Seattle's Alice B., the Bilingual Foundation for the Arts in Los Angeles, the Cocteau Repertory in New York City – and whose respective concerns may focus on Asian-American issues, multiculturalism, gay and lesbian works, Spanish-language productions, and neglected European classics.

What these theatres, and the hundreds of others like them, share is the designation 'not-for-profit.' This doesn't mean that an institution won't occasionally end up in the black after a season; some may be quite profitable, especially if a show successfully transfers to a commercial venue (Joseph Papp's NYSF is said to have flourished for years off the revenue from its production of *A Chorus Line*). The not-for-profit designation refers to a tax status the Internal Revenue Service bestows on an applicant theatre. In return, the theatre agrees to reinvest all profits back into the organization. Virtually all of these companies rely on a mixture of federal, state, and local government subsidy; foundation, individual, and corporate contributions; and ticket sales.

Theatre Communications Group, the national service organization that caters to this sector of American theatre, counts over 300 member theatres. The largest of these are the more than 80 LORT theatres (League of Resident Theatres), who negotiate their performers' contracts with the Actors' Equity Association. Most large cities in the USA have at least one LORT theatre and some have several. In New York, Circle in the Square and Lincoln Center Theater are the best known (however, they are designated 'Broadway' theatres in terms of Tony Award voting, a status Roundabout Theatre, another New York LORT member, will enjoy when it moves uptown to Times Square in 1991). In 1986, for the first time, more actor 'work weeks' were tallied in LORT theatres than under the standard Broadway 'Production' contract, one indication of resident companies' vital role in American theatre.

Most people will agree that the regional theatre 'movement' began about 30 years ago, when the Ford Foundation, under the leadership of W. MacNeil Lowry, began funding theatres outside New York in earnest. He also created Theatre Communications Group (TCG) to serve as a central support organization for these far-flung efforts. From 1963, when Tyrone Guthrie trekked west to Minneapolis to found the theatre that bears his name, to the end of the decade, many of the USA's major theatre institutions were created: Center Stage in Baltimore, Seattle Repertory Theatre and Trinity Repertory Theatre (1963); Actors Theatre of Louisville, The American Place Theatre, Hartford Stage Company, and South Coast Repertory (1964); the Long Wharf Theatre in New Haven and Studio Arena Theatre in Buffalo (1965).

Of course, there were earlier pioneers: Cleveland Play House began operations in 1915 and the Goodman Theatre, started as a theatre school, was founded in 1925; in 1947 Margo Jones started Theatre 47 in Dallas and premiered new work by a young playwright named Tennessee Williams; her assistant Nina Vance established the Alley Theatre in Houston that same year, and three years later Zelda Fichandler jumpstarted Arena Stage in the nation's capitol; Joe Papp's New York Shakespeare Festival and the Milwaukee Repertory Theatre sprang to life in 1954.

From modest beginnings, mounting productions in old movie houses and from the back of flatbed trucks, these theatres now serve as the artistic backbone of theatre pro-duction in the USA. For the last 15 years, virtually every winner of the Pulitzer Prize for drama originated at a not-for-profit institution either in New York (*A Soldier's Play*, Negro Ensemble Company; *A Sunday in the Park with George*, Playwrights Horizons) or at a regional theatre (*Glengarry Glen Ross*, the Goodman Theatre in Chicago; *Crimes of the Heart*, the Actors Theatre of Louisville).

In effect, Broadway has become a commercial showcase for successful West End productions and these institutions' work. Almost all American nonmusical offerings on Broadway originate in LORT theatres, and some musicals as well are tested on resident theatres' subscription audiences, a comingling of not-for-profit and commercial theatre production that has made some theatre observers and professionals queasy.

The past few seasons have seen highly acclaimed transfers – the Tony Award-winning adaptation of *The Grapes of Wrath* (the Steppenwolf Theatre in Chicago); *Our Country's Good* (Hartford Stage Company); *Burn This* (Mark Taper Forum and Circle Repertory Company); all of August Wilson's plays (starting at Yale Repertory Theatre and continuing on to several LORT theatres); and *I'm Not Rappaport* and *The Heidi Chronicles* (Seattle Repertory Theatre) – to name but a few of the more prominent examples.

More modest resident theatres across the USA work under a Small Professional Theatre or Letter of Agreement contract until they either become large enough to pay LORT contract wages or fold; those that cater to children and teens work under a TYA (Theatre for Young Audiences) contract; and Equity recognizes a number of other theatrical forms that include dinner theatres and touring and resident stock companies. Altogether, these companies offer American performers, directors, and designers a wide range of theatrical experience, and they combine to create a national theatre that mirrors the diversity of the audiences they serve.

Try these:
TCG publishes biennial reference guides to their member theatres called *Theatre Profiles*; the annual series by John Willis, *Theatre World*, details cast lists and production teams for each season on Broadway, ▷Off-Broadway, and at major resident theatres; ▷British Theatre Companies.

RHONE, Trevor   [1940–]
Jamaican dramatist

Plays include:
Not My Fault, Baby (1965), *The Gadget* (1969), *Smile Orange* (1970), *Comic Strip* (1973), *Sleeper* (1974), *School's Out* (1975), *Old Story Time* (1979), *Two Can Play* (1980), *Everyman* (1981), *The Game* (1982)

Born in Kingston, Jamaica, Rhone went to Britain in the 1960s (where he studied at the Rose Bruford College) but returned to Jamaica disappointed with the roles offered to him as a black actor, which he later said didn't begin to express black lives. Out of this frustration eventually came the impetus to write plays that did, and a desire to set up a theatre in Jamaica. In 1965, with some colleagues, (including director Yvonne Brewster), he set up the Barn Theatre (in the beginning the garage of a friend's home) with a mix of both Caribbean and non-Caribbean plays.

Now one of Jamaica's leading playwrights, he is best known outside his own country for comedies like *Smile Orange*, *Two Can Play* and *School's Out*. Rhone specialises in broad situation comedy (one of his role models is ▷Alan Ayckbourn) written with great verve and energy, inside which often lurk shrewd observations about Jamaican life. At his best, Rhone's language and comic timing are hugely enjoyable, but all too often his comic touch (or the way the productions are played) is allowed to swamp his sharper insights, leaving an impression simply of comic stereotypes. *Old Story Time*, considered to be Rhone's best play, proves he can be something considerably more; *Smile Orange*, a farcical treatment of tourists getting taken for a ride, also has something serious to say about Third World economics and methods of survival; *School's Out*, for all its playful characterisation is also a fairly pessimistic, highly critical portrait of the inadequacies of the Jamaican educational system, and reactionary attitudes that inhibit its change. *Two Can Play* is by far his most popular play and has been performed all over the world.

Two Can Play
Unlike *School's Out* this play shows the possibilities for human growth and is an enjoyable if sentimental two-hander on the old theme of marriage, given a new twist to do with female enlightenment (although Rhone has commented that the imbalance in the marriage was partly the wife's fault for not confronting

her husband sooner with her dissatisfactions!). Gloria and Jim are undergoing a crisis in their marriage; Gloria is the down-trodden, family organiser, Jim the usual male chauvinist. Gloria goes north to the USA to make a marriage of convenience (the two are planning on emigration to escape the Jamaican political unrest of the 1970s) and her return triggers a re-assessment and process of re-discovery for them both. Heart-warming and funny, the comedy can be overplayed (and its ending defies belief after what has gone before) but it clearly has appeal and should be around for some time to come.

Try these:
For more sparring couples, and resurgent wives, ▷Sarah Daniels' *Ripen Our Darkness* and *The Devil's Gateway*; for more acid marital conflicts, ▷Ted Whitehead's *Alpha Beta*; for other Caribbean writers, ▷Derek Walcott, ▷Edgar White, ▷Errol Hill.

RIBMAN, Ronald   [1932–]
American dramatist

Plays include:
Harry, Noon and Night (1965), *The Journey of the Fifth Horse* (1966), *The Ceremony of Innocence* (1967), *Passing Through From Exotic Places* (1969), *Fingernails Blue as Flowers* (1971), *The Poison Tree* (1976), *Cold Storage* (1977), *Buck* (1983), *Sweet Table at Richelieu* (1987)

The critic Gerald Weales has called Ribman 'One of our best and least appreciated dramatists'. Most of Ribman's plays have been produced by the American Place Theatre, an off-Broadway theatre founded by Wynn Handman devoted to literary plays. Ribman is neither traditional nor avant-garde, but has a doctoral degree in English literature and a passion for language. His characters are verbal and articulate, and his plays pose serious moral dilemmas which end frequently with unanswered questions. One could say Ribman expresses the theme of man's inhumanity to man, but this kind of simplistic reduction is unworthy of the material and fails to take into consideration his consistent presentation of victims who are often self-victimised. *Buck* deals with a pornographic film director who attempts to break away from his gangster bosses and create socially meaningful art. His artistic protests are linked to his rebellion against a court ruling which denies him visiting rights to his son. Although both protests are doomed to failure, Buck's rebellion reveals that he has not lost the capacity to feel.

Cold Storage

Cold Storage, by far Ribman's most successful play, ran both on and off Broadway. It is a black comedy about a pair of wheelchair-bound patients contemplating death. Armenian Joseph Parmigian and Jewish Richard Landau are cancer patients. The older Parmigian diabolically needles his younger companion. Landau becomes irritated and professes that his youth spent in a Nazi death camp has made him indifferent to life. Parmigian helps Landau to discover that what he takes for indifference is guilt – a guilt which has robbed Landau of life. The revelation provides the opportunity for Landau and Parmigian to share stories and come together. Their laughter begs the question whether the two men can sustain their courage. During the play, we see Landau's indifference begin to crumble and wonder whether Parmigian's wit is as centred as it seems.

Try these:
▷Peter Flannery's *Singer*, Barbara Lebow's *A Shayna Maiden* and Jon Robin Baitz's *The Substance of Fire* for the aftermath of the Holocaust; Jon Robin Baitz's *Substance of Fire* for another Holocaust survivor suffering guilt; ▷Sarah Daniels' *Masterpieces* and *Etta Jenks* by Marlane Meyer for the pornography industry; ▷C.P. Taylor's *Good* for moral dilemmas presented wittily.

RICE, Elmer   [1892–1967)
American dramatist, director and producer

Plays include:
On Trial (1914), *The House in Blind Alley* (1916), *The Iron Cross* (with Frank Harris; 1917), *A Diadem of Snow* (1918), *For the Defense* (1919), *It Is the Law* (1922), *Wake Up, Jonathan!* (with Hatcher Hughes; 1921), *The Adding Machine* (1923), *Close Harmony* (with Dorothy Parker; 1924) *Cock Robin* (with Peter Barry; 1928), *Street Scene* (1929), *The Left Bank* (1931), *Counsellor-at-Law* (1931), *We, the People*

(1932), *Flight to the West* (1940), *A New Life* (1943), *Dream Girl* (1945), *The Winner* (1954), *Cue for Passion* (1958)

In Elmer Rice's career, passion and pragmatism reached an uneasy balance. The passion is that of a democratic leftist working for social causes; the utility is that of a theatre professional eager to make a good living.

Born Elmer Leopold Reizenstein, the son of a poor New York bookkeeper, Rice showed an early talent for language, logic and theatre. After working his way through law school, he quit his first legal job to write *On Trial*. This thriller murder melodrama, the hit of the 1914 season, is the first American play to use the technical device of the flashback.

Rice's next few plays show the influence of ▷Ibsen and ▷Shaw: they deal with progressive causes, including child labour reform, women's rights and the Russian Revolution. Unable to find producers, he returned to writing courtroom melodramas and other popular entertainments. For the rest of his career, he would alternate serious, experimental work with crowd-pleasing melodramas and comedies: he never succeeded in uniting the two.

The 1920s gave Rice his greatest artistic successes. *The Adding Machine*, a dark, expressionistic work, presents the universe as a heartless corporate enterprise in which human beings are mere raw material. *Street Scene* depicted life in New York's slums by revolving a number of subplots around a melodrama of love and murder. (A 1947 musical version of *Street Scene*, with lyrics by ▷Langston Hughes and music by Kurt Weill, is still occasionally performed.)

Street Scene was the first of the many plays which Rice was to produce and direct. In the late 1930s, he organised the New York office of the Federal Theatre Project, the Roosevelt Administration's programme to employ out-of-work theatre people. There he played a central role in the development of the Federal Theatre's 'living newspapers', agitprop presentations of contemporary social problems. For the remainder of his career he continued alternating between commercial and experimental work.

Try these:
For a 19th-century image of New York's slums, *The Poor of New York*, by ▷Dion Boucicault; for other urban decay, ▷John Gay's *The Beggar's Opera*, and

▷Brecht's and Weill's *Threepenny Opera*; for American ▷expressionism, ▷Eugene O'Neill's *The Emperor Jones*; for another expressionistic look at an automated society, Sophie Treadwell's *Machinal*.

ROCHE, Billy   [1949–]
Irish dramatist

Plays include:
A Handful of Stars (1988), *Poor Beast in the Rain* (1989)

Roche hails from Wexford, in the Irish Republic, where he still lives. He won the John Whiting Award for his first play, *A Handful of Stars*, and the Thames Television Best Play award for his second, *Poor Beast in the Rain*. Both were produced at the Bush Theatre and a third play is being planned to complete the Wexford Trilogy. Roche's characters have been sidelined from their dreams and tend to live in the mist of memory. But he treats each one with amused affection – nowhere more so than in *A Handful of Stars*, a funny, playful tale of initiation into manhood, a Wexford *Rebel Without a Cause*.

Poor Beast in the Rain
Set in a Wexford betting shop, Danger Doyle coincidentally chooses the weekend of the All-Ireland hurling finals to return home to attempt to convince the adolescent daughter of the woman he ran away with ten years before to go to live with them in London. It finally doesn't seem to matter much whether or not the girl leaves the safety of a small town for the uncertainty of the metropolis. But Roche produces two hours of sparkling dialogue in the mouths of the six beautifully rounded characters.

Try these:
▷John Osborne's *Look Back in Anger* for an earlier anti-hero; ▷J.M. Synge's *Playboy of the Western World* for another young, Irish anti-hero; ▷Brian Friel's *Dancing at Lughansa* is a gentle tragicomedy in which, among other things, the protagonist tries to persuade his sweetheart to leave her rural life to go away with him; for another quite different-toned contemporary Irish playwright, see Frank McGuinness.

ROWLEY, William   [c 1585–1626]
English Renaissance dramatist

Plays include:
A Fair Quarrel (c 1615), *The Witch of Edmonton* (1621), *The Changeling* (1622)

Rowley, who was a comic actor, is noted for his collaborative works with others and probably had a hand in the writing of some fifty plays. His own works are not revived, but *The Changeling* and *A Fair Quarrel* (both with ▷Middleton) and *The Witch of Edmonton* (with ▷Ford and ▷Dekker) are still performed.

ROYAL COURT THEATRE
Beginning as a way of finding a London home for productions from the Tor and Torridge Festival, the English Stage Company was the idea of playwright Ronald Duncan, who involved businessmen Neville Blond and Greville Pike and theatre manager Oscar Lewenstein. To run it they invited actor-director George Devine (previously associated with the Young Vic School and company) and Tony Richardson (then a television director) who earlier in the 1950s had themselves tried to start a company to present the kind of plays not put on by West End managements. After proposals for other theatres fell through, they acquired a lease for the Royal Court, Sloane Square, and in 1956 opened with *The Mulberry Bush*, commissioned from novelist Angus Wilson. Duncan, himself a poet, had originally thought of this as a home for verse drama, but although the company has always been a champion of new writing this was not one of Devine's interests. The plays presented subsequently have included many by writers politically far to the left of Duncan; members of the new company were soon carrying its banner in early demonstrations against nuclear warfare. The third production of the new company, presented within five weeks of opening, was ▷John Osborne's *Look Back in Anger*, which had an immediate impact on British audiences and theatre workers, difficult to imagine today, and was closely linked to the general exasperation of young people at the time of Suez and the Hungarian rising.

Although the company has staged some classic revivals, it has mainly been an important venue for new writing, introducing to London, and sometimes to the world, such dramatists as ▷Arnold Wesker, ▷John Arden, ▷Ann Jellicoe, ▷David Storey,

▷Edward Bond, ▷Charles Wood, ▷Christopher Hampton, ▷Howard Barker, ▷Howard Brenton, ▷David Hare, ▷N.F. Simpson, ▷Harold Pinter and ▷Michael Hastings, and presenting such overseas writers as ▷Brecht, ▷Beckett, Sartre, ▷Ionesco and ▷Sam Shepard. Although the company is no longer unique in producing new work, the growth of opportunities for new writers owes much to its existence.

It was the English Stage Company which encouraged leading actors to take the risk of appearing in the 'new drama', with Peggy Ashcroft in ▷Brecht's *The Good Person of Sezchuan*, Laurence Olivier in ▷John Osborne's *The Entertainer* (1957), and John Gielgud and Ralph Richardson in ▷David Storey's *Home* (1970). It also established such directors as William Gaskill, Lindsay Anderson, John Dexter and Peter Gill. After Devine, Bill Gaskill took over the running of the company (1965–77), followed by Oscar Lewenstein, Nicholas Wright and Robert Kidd, Stuart Burge and, since 1979, Max Stafford-Clark.

The company played an important role in the fight against stage censorship, turning itself into a club for the presentation of ▷Osborne's *A Patriot for Me* because of its homosexual theme, and standing up against heavy criticism over plays such as ▷Edward Bond's *Saved*, although Jim Allen's *Perdition* was cancelled in 1987 before it opened, after a fierce onslaught from outside the theatre and disquiet from the Board (it eventually appeared elsewhere in 1988).

In 1969 the old rehearsal room at the top of the theatre, reclaimed from use as a night club, was opened as the Theatre Upstairs to provide a home for visiting fringe companies and the company's own more experimental work. Productions have ranged from ▷Richard O'Brien's *The Rocky Horror Show* (1973) to ▷Jim Cartwright's *Road* (1986). This intimate, adaptable space is now an important national venue which has premiered new plays by many of today's leading dramatists including ▷Sarah Daniels, ▷Timberlake Wertenbaker, ▷Daniel Mornin, ▷Louise Page, Nick Ward, ▷Hanif Kureishi and ▷Sue Townsend. The theatre also runs a Young People's Theatre Scheme, not only encouraging playgoing among the young but also offering them opportunities for workshops and productions of their scripts which have produced a whole new crop of writers, particularly among young black women.

The fact that the Royal Court no longer stands alone as a theatre for new writing is a measure of its success in its aims, but recognition of the artistic and critical importance of the Royal Court's activities has been a hard-won victory, and even that achievement is insufficient to guarantee financial stability. As a consequence the company not only enters into more co-production arrangements with regional theatres, but also survives thanks to a generous exchange deal with New Yorker Joe Papp, some of whose Public Theatre productions are exchanged with those of the Royal Court.

Try these:
Among the companies and venues particularly associated with new writing are The Soho Poly, Red Shift, Paines Plough, Hampstead, the Bush and the Tricycle; see also ▷New Playwriting in Britain.

RSC (Royal Shakespeare Company)

The Royal Shakespeare Company is now to be found on two main sites, one the Shakespeare Memorial Theatre at Stratford-upon-Avon, and the other the Barbican Theatre in London. The Barbican has two stages, one main stage and one smaller space, The Pit; while Stratford has three; the main auditorium, the more intimate The Other Place, and The Swan Theatre.

The idea that there should be a memorial theatre for ▷Shakespeare based at the Bard's birthplace at Stratford-upon-Avon predated the theatre and the company by several centuries. David Garrick staged a jubilee celebration in 1769, and the Shakespeare Memorial Theatre was finally built there in 1879 on a site provided by local brewer Charles Flower, and staged an annual festival of ▷Shakespeare's work. The Gothic splendours of that building fell victim to a fire in 1926 (the remains now house the Swan). The currently used building at Stratford was opened in 1932.

In 1960 the company (under the directorship of Peter Hall) acquired its first London base at the Aldwych Theatre, transferring its productions for seasons in London, and began regularly to tour internationally. It took the name The Royal Shakespeare Company in 1961, although it had had a Royal Charter since 1925. Peter Hall expanded the repertoire to include contemporary plays, aiming for a company in which the techniques and discipline of classical drama would inform the performance of modern work, while modern work would inject a contemporaneity to the productions of classical plays.

Two important innovations by the RSC in the 1960s considerably enhanced the vitality of British theatre. ▷Peter Brook's Theatre of Cruelty season, influenced by ▷Artaud and Grotowski, explored European dramatists and new techniques in theatre, which led to the development of the play *Marat/Sade*, and to a film (*Tell Me Lies*) based on the RSC production *US*. In 1964 Peter Daubeny instituted the World Theatre Season at the RSC's home at the Aldwych, which was an unprecedented opportunity to see international theatre companies. Trevor Nunn joined as Joint Aristic Director in 1968.

In 1982 the company moved from the Aldwych and its new writing base at the Warehouse to the theatres in the Barbican Centre, a complex built and managed by the Corporation of the City of London. The Barbican Theatre, designed in collaboration with Peter Hall and John Bury, then Head of Design at the RSC, has a versatile main stage (with lots of stage effects), and a smaller theatre space, The Pit.

The RSC has been severely underfunded, and the lack of government support for the arts over the past decade has not allowed for the experimentation which was so influential in the 1960s. Nonetheless it has continued to expand – some might say too much so, to the detriment of its overall quality – with a large repertoire of plays each year as well as making regular tours in Britain, visits elsewhere, and small-scale tours. Some of their most exciting work has in fact come from the smaller theatres with The Other Place (TOP) consistently serving up the most varied and challenging productions of Shakespeare and new plays. The Swan too has also seen some lively and much welcomed revivals of Ben Jonson, Aphra Behn, Thomas Heywood, Shakespeare and Fletcher and James Shirley.

But the cornerstone of the RSC's work remains Shakespeare. Their productions can sometimes suffer from the demands of having to produce the plays year in, year out, but many exciting and innovative productions still exhilarate audiences. These have included Trevor Nunn's chamber version of *Macbeth*; Bill Alexander's 1950s' *Merry Wives of Windsor*; Howard Davies' world-weary *Troilus and Cressida*; Adrian Noble's *As You Like It*

with Juliet Stevenson and Fiona Shaw as Rosalind and Celia and Alan Rickman as Jacques; Terry Hands' celebrated *Much Ado About Nothing* with Derek Jacobi; Deborah Warner's *Titus Andronicus* Nicholas Hytner's *Measure for Measure* with Josette Simon as Isabella and Anthony Sher's *Richard III* directed by Bill Alexander.

Nunn and Caird's 1981 production of *Nicholas Nickleby* in which ▷David Edgar adapted Dickens' novel in collaboration with the company was a stunning two-part work which despite initially cool critical reception became a major success and toured to packed houses.

It also marked a shift in RSC direction in encouraging large-scale, musically based productions: *Kiss Me Kate* and *Les Misérables* have followed. After Nunn's resignation as Artistic Director, Terry Hands tended to go for the broadly popular because of considerable financial pressure and pushed increasingly into commercial sponsorship. (The illfated musical *Carrie* proving the nadir of this policy.) Adrian Noble's new regime, however, looks well to start afresh – his *Henry IV* parts 1 and 2, with ▷Robert Stephens' sombre, bitter Falstaff confirming a company coming home to its roots.

Try these:
▷John Mortimer is one of the Governors of the RSC; Heidi Thomas, ▷Timberlake Wertenbaker, ▷Louise Page, ▷Nick Darke ▷Doug Lucie are among the new writers who have been commissioned by the RSC recently. The ▷National Theatre, Royal Court, Manchester's Royal Exchange and ▷Glasgow Citizens' Theatre for other British large-scale operations; ▷Peter Brook's *The Mahabharata* as a contrasting style of large-scale production; see also ▷Mnouchkine for contrast; Stratford Ontario in Canada is another ▷Shakespeare-based repertory.

RUDET, Jacqueline   [1962–]
British dramatist

Plays include:
Money to Live (1984), *God's Second in Command* (1985), *Basin* (1985)

Born in London's East End but brought up in Dominica, Rudet started out as an actress before forming her own group, Imani-Faith, to provide theatre for and about black women.

However, her first play, *Money to Live* was actually presented by the Black Theatre Co-op and proved a success with public and critics alike despite Rudet's own reservations about the way the production had been directed. A naturalistic writer with a television sense and lively line in dialogue she made a dazzling debut with the hard-hitting *Money to Live*, a domestic drama about stripping that tackled its subject with a rare lack of cant and undisguised anger at men who see women only as sexual objects. Although the relationship between love, sex and money is not a new subject, Rudet's treatment of it, in the context of a young, black female, and the timelessness of its theme probably ensures it will turn up regularly in future repertoires, because the play is as much about getting through in hard times as it is about 'being a black play'. *Basin* however, has no such equivocation; a conversation piece, it is openly about the love and communality between black women with Rudet's sparky dialogue providing some easy humour amongst the sometimes tense encounters as three friends work out the meaning of friendship.

Try these:
▷Peter Terson's *Strippers* for a rather more complex, and debatable treatment of the subject; ▷Pam Gems' *Treats* is set in a strip-club; ▷Kay Adshead's *Thatcher's Women* and Julia Schofield's *Love on the Plastic* also look at the economic pressures and moral hypocrisies around prostitution; ▷Jackie Kay's *Chiaroscuro* for another play about black women exploring friendship, lesbianism and labels; ▷Winsome Pinnock is another contemporary black playwright; see also New Playwriting in Britain.

RUDKIN, (James) David   [1936–]
British dramatist

Plays include:
Afore Night Come (1960), *Burglars* (1970), *The Filth Hut* (1972), *Cries from Casement as His Bones Are Brought to Dublin* (1973), *Ashes* (1973), *No Title* (1974), *The Sons of Light* (1976), *Sovereignty Under Elizabeth* (1977), *Hansel and Gretel* (1980), *The*

Triumph of Death (1981), *Space Invaders* (1983), *Will's Way* (1984), *The Saxon Shore* (1986)

Rudkin was hailed as a major playwright when *Afore Night Come*, already produced while he was an Oxford student, was taken up for production by the ▷RSC in 1962. The play touches on themes which are developed in his later work such as concern for the countryside, abhorrence of atomic weapons, chemical and other pollution, the idea of homosexuality as a natural and innocent manifestation of love and an awareness of English-Irish confrontation while his dialogue is both richly poetic and steeped in the rural, Anglo-Saxon dialects of his own area around the Black Country and Worcestershire. In *Afore Night Come* the continuity with the past seems ominous and evil but in other work, such as the television play *Penda's Fen* the past (in the persons of King Penda and Sir Edward Elgar) seems to be in guardianship, though the more recent *White Lady* showed nature overwhelmed by deadly petrochemicals.

Rudkin comes from a revivalist background but his plays question the ideology of sectarian religion and seek a closer communion with the natural world. His plays can be bafflingly dense with allusions to Christian and pre-Christian mythologies as in *The Sons of Light*, a complex science-fantasy fable which operates on many levels. Dedicated to the late Dr Robert Ollendorf, a Reichian therapist, it is divided into three sections linked to the stages of the Christian mythology of the 'Harrowing Hell' and involves the reclamation of a young girl from schizophrenia and a subterranean colony of workers into self-awareness – a resurrection of both the individual and the culture from spiritual and religious repressions.

Afore Night Come remains the most accessible of Rudkin's major stage works. More complicated structures appear in *Ashes*, a searingly painful account of an infertile couple's attempts to have a child (a fairly blatant – and equally anguished – metaphor for the violence and sterility of the Northern Ireland situation) which also offers political, anthropological and psychological viewpoints. *The Triumph of Death*, partly about Martin Luther is concerned with the way that organised Christianity seeks power through association with established forces.

Rudkin's adaptations and translations include ▷Euripides' *Hippolytus* (1978),

▷Genet's *Deathwatch* and *The Maids* (1987), ▷Ibsen's *Peer Gynt* (1983), and *When We Dead Awaken* (1990). Librettos include Schoenberg's *Moses and Aaron* (1965) and Gordon Crosse's *The Grace of Todd* (1969). The most characteristic of numerous television plays are perhaps *Penda's Fen* and *White Lady* and he has written screenplays for *Mademoiselle*, *Farenheit 451*, *Testimony* and *December Bride*.

The Sons of Light

The Sons of Light was worked on over eleven years (1965–76) resulting in an 8–9 hour play which was reshaped to about three hours playing time and then further cut for the published text as performed by the RSC in 1977. Dedicated to the late Dr Robert Ollendorf, a Reichian therapist, of whom the character Nebewohl is a portrait in reverse, it is divided into three main sections linked to the stages of the Christian mythology of the 'Harrowing of Hell'. A complex science-fantasy fable which operates on many levels, it is set on a Scottish island ruled by a 'Benefactor' operating a religion of vengeance. Beneath the earth is a factory colony of workers kept from rebellion by a promise of heaven. Here a new pastor and his sons arrive, one of whom eventually descends among the workers, reawakens their self-awareness and destroys the subterranean complex to reclaim the island for its inhabitants. This is parallelled by the reclamation of a young girl from schizophrenia – a resurrection of both the individual and the culture.

Try these:

▷Trevor Griffiths and ▷Barry Reckord for Reichian influences; ▷David Edgar's *Mary Barnes* for contemporary treatment of schizophrenia; ▷Tony Craze's *Shona*, for Caribbean exploration of pre-Christianity; ▷Felix Cross' *Mass Carib* and *Blues For Railton*; ▷John Osborne's *Luther*, for writers of dialect see Caryl Churchill's *Fen*, Nick Ward's *Apart from George*, Elizabeth Bond's *Farrowland*; John Arden and Margaretta D'Arcy for similar antipathies to the British establishment. For another image of infertility, see Lorca's *Yerma*; for Irish anguish, see Sean O'Casey, Daniel Mornin, Seamus Finnegan, Christina Reid etc; for images of illness onstage, see Sophocles' *Philoctetes*, Peter Nichols' *A Day in the Death of Joe Egg*, Lucy Gannon; for moral disgust, Anouilh, Beckett; Shakespeare's *Titus Androndicus* for equally gory physical detail.

RUSSELL, Willy   [1947–]
British dramatist, song-writer and singer

Plays include:
Keep Your Eyes Down (1971), *Sam O'Shanker* (1972; musical version 1973), *When the Reds* (1972), *Tam Lin* (1972), *John, Paul, George, Ringo and . . . Bert* (1974), *Breezeblock Park* (1975), *One for the Road* (originally *Painted Veg and Parkinson*; 1976), *Stags and Hens* (1978), *Educating Rita* (1979), *Blood Brothers* (1981; musical version 1983), *Our Day Out* (1983, from 1977 TV play), *Shirley Valentine* (1986)

One of the most often produced contemporary dramatists, Russell's work is closely linked with Liverpool (he was born in nearby Whiston) and the Everyman Theatre which mounted his first professional production and has commissioned other plays from him, including *John, Paul, George, Ringo and . . . Bert*. This musical about the Beatles brought him national success and was called 'a powerful statement about innocence and corruption that is also an hilariously funny evening out'. Such a balance between comment and exhilarating entertainment can be found right through Russell's work. *Educating Rita*, a two-hander about a middle-aged lecturer and a 'raw-diamond' working-class woman student – especially in its film version – put Russell on the international map. Russell himself left school at fifteen, returning to college years later because he had decided to become a teacher and a playwright, although the play probably owes as much to his regional background and time spent as a ladies' hairdresser. He is totally unpatronising about the working class, and his female characters are particularly vivid. In both *Educating Rita* and *Shirley Valentine* – a Liverpudlian monologue with marvellous jokes (but little feminist consciousness) – he makes use of minimal resources, but he is equally adept at handling large groups of characters. A good example is *Stags and Hens* (filmed as *Dancing Thru' the Dark*), in which bride and groom, each with their own friends on a last, prenuptial night out both choose the same club for their celebration. In this shrieking, puking

world, with major sections set in the lavator-
ies, Russell is no outsider and audiences can
share both the fun and pain of his characters at
grass-roots level.

Blood Brothers
Loosely based on the old 'Corsican Brothers'
story of twins brought up in different classes,
Blood Brothers has a superb creation in the
character of the working-class mother. It is a
deeply felt picture of different social backgrounds, although its middle-class characters
are perhaps less convincing than the working-
class, despite the parable-like nature of its

overall construction. The songs are able to
succeed outside the show, but they are an
integral and necessary part adding to our
understanding of the characters. A smash hit
that offered a social document disguised as
melodrama.

Try these:
For Manchester, ▷Waterhouse and Hall's
Billy Liar, Hobhouse, ▷Delaney; ▷Alan
Bleasdale; ▷John Godber's *Bouncers* for
a graphic, funny, but essentially damning
portrait of British yobbism at play.

 S

SACKLER, Howard [1929–1982]
American dramatist

Plays include:

Uriel Acosta (1954), *The Yellow Loves* (1959), *A Few Inquiries* (1964), *The Pastime of Monsieur Robert* (1966), *The Great White Hope* (1967), *Goodbye, Fidel* (1980), *Semmelweiss* (1981)

Born in New York, Sackler started out as a poet and worked on films throughout his life, but he remains best known for his 1967 play *The Great White Hope*, a thinly fictionalised account of the celebrated African-American boxer Jack Johnson, who became the world heavyweight champion in 1908. First performed at Washington DC's Arena Stage, the sprawling epic launched the career of James Earl Jones. Further acclaimed on Broadway, on film, and in two separate London productions, the play is socially and ethically exemplary; as drama, however, it has dated. Sackler was writing from the viewpoint of undigested late-1960s' white liberal guilt, and too many of the play's would-be challenges to the audience have more to do with assuaging Sackler's own uneasy conscience than with any genuine assault on the fourth wall. His follow-up plays were equally episodic, but nowhere near as successful, particularly *Goodbye, Fidel*, a rambling saga about a patrician Cuban widow about to be exiled from a country in tumult.

Try these:
▷Arthur Miller for social conscience; ▷James Baldwin and ▷Lorraine Hansberry for other representations of black experience from before the Black Power era; ▷August Wilson, Charles Fuller, George C. Wolfe for contemporary black treatments of racism; ▷Louise Page's *Golden Girls* for a rare account of

women and sport and racism; ▷Athol Fugard for a contrasting white playwright tackling large issues of racism and social awareness with a more authentic voice.

SAROYAN, William [1908–81]
American dramatist

Plays include:

My Heart's in the Highlands (1939), *The Time of Your Life* (1939), *Love's Old Sweet Song* (1940), *The Beautiful People* (1941), *Across the Board on Tomorrow Morning* (1942), *Talking to You* (1942), *Hello, Out There* (1942), *Get Away Old Man* (1943), *The Cave Dwellers* (1957), *Sam the Highest Jumper of Them All* (1960)

After the successes of his first two plays Saroyan's career appeared to be as bright and positive as the characters in his plays (*Time of Your Life* won both the New York Drama Critics' Circle Award and the Pulitzer Prize). However, his lack of discipline as a playwright and erratic behaviour as a collaborator made it impossible for him to develop his talents. Critics became tired and suspicious of his easy optimism during World War II, and later his impressionistic characters seemed out of place with the revelations of Nazi atrocities. Not until twelve years after the war did another Saroyan play, *The Cave Dwellers*, win a Broadway mounting. *The Cave Dwellers*, depicting a collection of misfits occupying a theatre slated for demolition, seemed to fit in with the Theatre of the Absurd vogue. However, Saroyan's sentimental ending betrayed the play's anachronistic point of view. A recent attempt by Joseph Papp to revive Saroyan's work *The Human Comedy* in musical form again revealed the same problem.

The Time of Your Life

The habitués of Nick's Saloon on the San Francisco waterfront are a fascinating lot of exuberant misfits: Joe, a young loafer with money and a good heart; Tom, his disciple and errand boy; Kitty, the whore with the heart of gold; Kit Carson, an old Indian-fighter; Willy, the pinball maniac; Harry, a natural-born hoofer; an Arab harmonica-player; and a Negro, a boogie-woogie pianist. Into this company comes a group of society slummers and later Blick, heel and head of the Vice Squad. Blick intends to arrest Kitty, but first he intends to force her to strip. In the ensuing action, Carson shoots Blick and the pinball machine spouts coins and flashes forth 'American Destiny'. Arab says, 'No foundation. All the way down the line': an apt description of Saroyan's comedy. Still, the play has been frequently revived with success on both sides of the Atlantic. Produced as a period piece, it continues to please audiences.

Try these:

▷Eugene O'Neill's *The Iceman Cometh* is *the* saloon-bar tragedy; Robert Patrick's *Kennedy's Children* uses a bar-room setting; ▷Osborne's *The Entertainer* for decay in the theatre; ▷Arthur Kopit's *Indians*; ▷Kaufman and Hart for commercially successful warm-hearted plays.

SARTRE, Jean-Paul   [1905–80]
French philosopher, novelist and dramatist

Plays include:
Les Mouches (*The Flies*; 1943), Huis Clos (*No Exit, Vicious Circle* or *In Camera*; 1944), *Vicious Circle* or *No Exit, Les Mains Sales* (*Crime Passionnel, The Assassin* or *Dirty Hands*; 1948), *Le Diable et le Bon Dieu* (*The Devil and the Good Lord*, or *Lucifer and the Lord*; 1951), *Kean* (from Dumas père; 1953), *Les Séquestrés d'Altona* (*Altona* or *Loser Wins*; 1959)

Play writing was never Sartre's main occupation, but he had a high degree of success with it, and his plays and his philosophy interact in an interesting manner. His first known play is *Bariona*, a nativity play which he wrote while in a prisoner-of-war camp in 1940, and staged there with the help of priests; it was a semi-disguised anti-colonialist play about the occupation of Judaea. He subsequently favoured a 'theatre of situations' rather than a psychological theatre, with characters defined by their actions rather than their intentions, the better to explore his ideas about existentialism and the possibility of individual freedom. *The Flies* shows Orestes accepting full responsibility for the killing of Aegisthus, rather than being a prey to fate, as in the Greek versions; it also has overtones of French attitudes, including Sartre's own, to the Nazi occupation. *In Camera* (or *No Exit*), or with its gradual revelation that the scene is hell, and its three characters who have lived in 'bad faith' must stay there for eternity, is perhaps his best bit of construction. In *The Devil and the Good Lord* the hero manages to achieve 'authenticity' in his actions (of which Sartre approved) by rejecting in turn attempts to be thoroughly evil or thoroughly good. By the time he reached *Altona*, however, Sartre had given up hope about man's ability to choose how to act, and adopted a Marxist perspective towards what seems to be the development of post-war Germany but is in fact a metaphor for the French war in Algeria.

Sartre's plays were important in opening the post-war French drama to serious subjects, and in persuading playwrights to engage with politics and philosophy, but they were not experimental in form. For Sartre, anti-capitalism implied no break with Aristotelian models of theatre; unlike ▷Brecht, he used fairly conventional and illusionistic forms of playmaking, though his characters do now seem to talk a lot. ▷Ionesco called his plays political melodramas, but this underestimates their complexity and ambiguity.

Kean

Kean is a reworking of Dumas père's Romantic drama, with substantial additions, and it is the play that displays most clearly Sartre's idea of theatre. Kean's ontological insecurities impel him to assume identities not his own (for he has none); at the same time, his free access to both princes and people gives him and others the illusion that it is easy for genius to move up in a class-ridden world. His constant awareness of his own psychological and social paradoxes allowed Sartre to turn theatre against itself without using Brechtian techniques of disjunction. Kean is also a marvellous part for a bravura actor.

Try these:

Camus for French plays with philosophical content; ▷John Arden and ▷Margaretta D'Arcy for *The Business of Good Government*, another Nativity play with a political message; ▷Pirandello, for the questioning of the distinction between acting and life; ▷Brecht for anti-capitalist plays with non-Aristotelian forms.

effect, ▷Liz Lochhead's *Mary Queen of Scots* for a contemporary Scottish perspective.

SCHILLER, Johann Christoph Friedrich von   [1759–1805]
German dramatist and poet

Plays include:
Die Räuber (The Robbers or *The Highwaymen*; 1782), *Fiesco* (1782), *Kabale und Liebe (Intrigue and Love*; 1784), *Don Carlos* (1787), the *Wallenstein* trilogy (1798–9), *Maria Stuart (Mary Stuart*; 1800), *Wilhelm Tell (William Tell*; 1804)

Schiller, the son of an army surgeon, was a young military doctor himself when his first play *Die Räuber* appeared – though safely set in the sixteenth century, it was an instant success for its contemporary revolutionary appeal, its *Sturm und Drang* claims for the rights of the individual, and its doubling of the parts of the good and bad brothers. He went on to become one of the major German verse playwrights, a professor of History at the University of Jena, and a close friend of ▷Goethe; but he never had quite enough money to live on, and never quite achieved respectability. *Maria Stuart* has the characteristics of all Schiller's 'historical' plays – powerful language, long aria-like speeches, dramatic confrontations, and a somewhat cavalier attitude to historical fact. The 'big scene' is a meeting between Mary Stuart and Elizabeth Tudor which never happened, and both queens are courted by a vacillating Lord Leicester. It makes a splendid, somewhat operatic play (and indeed a fine opera by Donizetti); but its success in southern Britain is perhaps inhibited by the national difficulty in taking seriously a play which casts Elizabeth I as villainess. However it has done well at the Edinburgh Festival (1958 and 1987) and at the Glasgow Citizens' (1985, in Robert David Macdonald's translation).

Try these:
▷Goethe for eighteenth-century German verse tragedy; ▷Dario Fo for a similar failure to understand Elizabeth I, ▷Corneille and ▷Racine for French classical tragedy; ▷Shakespeare's history plays also take liberties with historical fact for dramatic

SCHISGAL, Murray   [1926–]
American dramatist

Plays include:
The Typists (1960), *The Tiger* (1960), *Luv* (1964), *Fragments* (1967), *The Basement* (1967), *Jimmy Shine* (1968), *A Way of Life* (1969), *An American Millionaire* (1974), *All Over Town* (1974), *Twice Around the Park* (1982), *Road Show* (1987)

Since he launched his playwriting career in London in 1960 with a series of one-act plays at the British Drama League, New York-born Schisgal has written fifty plays – many of them little-known one-acts – and a variety of television shows and films, pre-eminently the Oscar-winning smash *Tootsie* (1982). His first New York success, *Luv*, is a three-character absurdist farce in which the suicidal Harry Berlin meets former schoolmate Milt Manville, who decides to unload his wife Ellen on the hapless Harry. The play once thought to make Schisgal 'a household word', it prompted critic Walter Kerr's dubious encomium that *Luv* was better than *Waiting For Godot*. In his 1968 *Jimmy Shine*, a comic vaudeville about despair, a failed abstract painter looks back on a life of frustration and fantasy. *All Over Town*, a Feydeau-esque farce set amidst Manhattan neurotics, is a mixed-identity comedy in which a canny black delivery boy called Lewis is mistaken for an unemployed, lusty white youth called Louie Lucas. *Road Show* is a comedy about midlife crisis, centring on two high school lovers who meet twenty years on.

Schisgal's career is associated with certain performers who have repeatedly appeared in and/or directed his plays, including the husband/wife team of Eli Wallach and Anne Jackson, who brought his two one-act plays, *Twice Around the Park*, to the Edinburgh Festival in 1984, and Dustin Hoffman, who played Jimmy Shine and directed *All Over Town*.

Try these:
▷Neil Simon (especially *The Prisoner of Second Avenue*) ▷Jules Feiffer, Herb Gardner (*I'm Not Rappaport*) for New York neuroticism and urban misadventures;

▷Arthur Kopit's *Oh Dad, Poor Dad . . .* for ▷Ionesco-influenced hi-jinks comparable to *Luv*; ▷Beckett.

SCHNITZLER, Arthur   [1862–1931]
Austrian dramatist

Plays include
Anatol (1893), *Liebelei* (*Dalliance*; 1895), *Das Weite Land* (*Undiscovered Country*; 1911), *Reigen* (*La Ronde*; 1902), *Der Einsame Weg* (*The Lonely Road*; 1904)

Schnitzler, the son of a rich Jewish doctor, studied medicine and psychoanalysis in late-nineteenth century Vienna, and his plays about the Viennese permissive society combine light comedy, satire, voyeurism, and apparent disapproval in an uneasy but appealing mixture. The plays are predictably popular today: ▷Tom Stoppard's free translations *Undiscovered Country* and *Dalliance* appeared at the ▷National Theatre in 1979 and 1985 respectively. In 1982, as soon as *La Ronde* came out of copyright, there were three staged versions and one televised version of it within three months (though, interestingly enough, nothing since). The play was carrying more expectations that it can live up to, and Schnitzler's other plays seem more likely to hold the stage in future. *La Ronde* is a series of ten episodes (the Prostitute picks up the Soldier; the Soldier seduces the Chambermaid; the Chambermaid seduces the Young Gentleman . . . the Count picks up the Prostitute). Its first performance in Berlin in 1920 was greeted with shock-horror and prosecutions of all concerned; it had a similar reception in Vienna in 1921, as did Max Ophüls' film version in 1950, though the film is far less sour and realistic than Schnitzler's original.

Try these:
▷Wedekind's *Lulu* for erotic cynicism, ▷Molnár for Austro-Hungarian comedy, but with quite a different tone; ▷Nestroy for another Viennese dramatist translated by ▷Tom Stoppard; ▷Noël Greig's *Angels Descend On Paris* for more sexual role-playing; ▷Genet's *The Maids* and *The Balcony* for role-playing taken to a high art; and for the High Priest of them all, ▷Lindsay Kemp.

SELLARS, Peter   [1957–]
American director

Wunderkind or enfant terrible, this self-styled cultural provocateur has set the opera world afire or aghast depending on one's point of view. Determined to find twentieth century contexts for classical opera to drive home a political point of view, Sellars has set *Cosi fan Tutte* in a neon-lit roadside diner, *Don Giovanni* in Spanish Harlem, *The Marriage of Figaro* in the Trump Tower, Haydn's *Armida* in Viet Nam, and Handel's *Orlando* in outer space. With his usual cultural hyperbole, Sellars talks of the union of traditionalists with the avant-garde to create illuminating revisions of the classics. He spouts wagnerian thought as ideology, seeing opera as 'the artwork of the future . . . the gesamtkunstwerk in which with all the new technology there will be radical changes'. His international reputation grows, and his radical directorial approach is gaining mainstream acceptance as demonstrated by the Trio of Mozart operas he directed for Austrian television. *Nixon in China* proved the feasability of using modern history as a subject for opera.

Sellars' short-lived terms as artistic director for theatre at the John F. Kennedy Center showed that his perturbing post-modern classicism leaves no quarter for public comfort. Empty houses greeted his grandiose mise en scenes. His 'high concept' productions are combinations of visual beauty, staggering profundity, and tedious boredom . . . the result of self-indulgent over-extensions of a single brilliant insight. Uncompromising genius or daring maverick, Sellars has forced the opera world to expand its vision.

Try these:
▷Peter Brook for avant-garde treatment of traditional operas; Robert Wilson and Philip Glass for contemporary opera and Elizabeth LeCompte for avant-garde directional concepts; ▷Mnouchkine; ▷Performance Art.

SENECA, Lucius Annaeus
[c 4 BC – 65 AD]
Roman philosopher and dramatist

Plays include:
Medea, Phaedra, Agamemnon, Oedipus, Thyestes

Seneca's verse plays were almost certainly not intended for the public stage but scholars disagree as to how (if at all) they were performed at Nero's court – the view that they were intended for dramatic recitation seems to owe something to their long rhetorical speeches, and something to so-called 'unstageable' scenes such as the reassembling of Hippolytus' dismembered body by his father. However, their static action and bloodthirsty plots were a major influence on the Elizabethan playwrights (eg Shakespeare's *Titus Andronicus* and ▷ Kyd's *The Spanish Tragedy*). Artaud, who regarded Seneca as the greatest Classical dramatist and the nearest in approach to his projected Theatre of Cruelty, planned to stage his own adaptation of *Thyestes* in 1934. The most important major production of a play by Seneca was ▷ Peter Brook's *Oedipus*, in a version by Ted Hughes, at the Old Vic in 1968. The production combined a powerful and direct text, filled with violent images of bloodshed and horror, delivered in a distanced monotone by largely static actors; complex choral work broken up into separate sounds and rhythms, wails and hums and hisses, accompanied by electronic music; and a light political dusting of possible references to Vietnam. It was an interesting mixture of the Artaudian and the Brechtian, and was received with respect (though it was said of ▷ Brook that he had 'gradually become the purveyor of avant-garde clichés to the mass audience').

Try these:
▷ Shakespeare for *Titus Andronicus*; ▷ Euripides, ▷ Racine for versions of the Hippolytus/Phaedra story; ▷ Artaud for the Theatre of Cruelty; ▷ Robert Wilson, whose *Civil Wars* include a section based on Seneca's Hercules plays.

SHAFFER, Anthony (Joshua)   [1926–]
British dramatist and novelist

Plays include:
The Savage Parade (1963), *Sleuth* (1970), *Murderer* (1975), *Widow's Weeds* (1977), *The Case of the Oily Levantine* (also known as *Who Done It*; 1979)

Only *Sleuth* has gained both critical and popular acclaim. *Sleuth* is both a clever and intricate thriller and a parody of the genre. The protagonist is even a thriller writer, who plans to avenge himself on his wife's lover. With a construction like a series of chinese boxes it demonstrates great technical skill. Though the

characterisations never attempt to rise above those of the conventional thriller, they offer the opportunity for bravura performances. *The Savage Parade*, originally given only a Sunday night peformance but more recently revived, offers a very different topic: the secret trial of a Nazi war criminal in Israel.

Shaffer wrote the screenplay for *Sleuth* and he has also collaborated on a number of novels with his twin brother, ▷ Peter Shaffer.

Try these:
Robert Shaw's *The Man in the Glass Booth* for another play about the trial of a war criminal; ▷ Tom Stoppard's *The Real Inspector Hound* for another thriller parody; Ira Levin's *Deathtrap* for a similar kind of plot; ▷ Christopher Hampton's *The Portage to San Cristobal of A.H.* for a play about the Israelis and war criminals; see also ▷ Thrillers.

SHAFFER, Peter   [1926–]
British dramatist

Plays include:
Five Finger Exercise (1958), *The Private Ear* (1962), *The Public Eye* (1962), *The Royal Hunt of the Sun* (1964), *Black Comedy* (1965), *White Lies* (1967), *The Battle of Shrivings* (1970), *Equus* (1973), *Amadeus* (1979), *Yonadab* (1985), *Lettice and Lovage* (1987)

Born in Liverpool and educated at Cambridge, Peter Shaffer is most interesting for what he is *not* – he is not a British resident, he is not politically motivated, and he is not interested in screenwriting, at a time when most playwrights are at least two out of the three. Instead, the New York-based Shaffer perpetuates infinite variations on a theme: the conflicts between reason and faith/mediocrity and genius/man and God, as examined from a variety of historical viewpoints. In *The Royal Hunt of the Sun*, the debate occurs between Atahualpa and Pizarro, the Inca and the atheistic Spanish conqueror of Peru. In *Equus*, it is a clash between a psychoanalyst and his charge – a self-tormenting doctor devoid of passion and the patient who has committed an extraordinary act of passion and violence. *Amadeus*, which became an acclaimed Oscar-winning film in 1984, shifts the argument to the creative arena, as it pits the aberrant genius Wolfgang Amadeus Mozart against the decent but uninspired court composer

Antonio Salieri, who may or may not have poisoned him. In all three plays, Shaffer weds his argument to a strong sense of the theatrical, not to mention an underlying repressed homo-eroticism. The former, if not the latter, forsook him in the Biblical *Yonadab*, an *Amadeus*-like tale of envy drawn from the Old Testament's Second Book of Samuel.

Shaffer has written comedy, as well, including four plays for Maggie Smith: *The Private Ear*, *The Public Eye*, *Black Comedy*, and his most recent, *Lettice and Lovage*, in which the two heroines enact their own variant on Shaffer's obsessive opposition of the eccentric outsider (Lettice) and the social conformist (Lotte). Is Shaffer a great playwright or merely a clever manipulator of the middlebrow? The verdict is out on that, but one thing is clear: Shaffer has a highly developed sense of the market second to none.

Equus

A stable boy blinds six horses after a frustrated sexual liaison in Shaffer's award-winning play, which was a huge hit both in London (with Alec McCowen) and on Broadway (with Anthony Hopkins and – among others – Richard Burton, later in the run) in John Dexter's mightily theatrical, swift production. Burton starred in Sidney Lumet's ill-fated 1977 film, where the realism of the genre mitigated the thesis of the play. How could one put any stock in Dr Dysart's envy for the tormented Alan, when we had just seen, in full blood-drenched realism, the climactic episode which was supposed to have triggered such thoughts? The film has the odd effect of rendering hollow and emptily rhetorical what on stage is a verbal thrill: the agony between the self-laceratingly literate Dysart and his semi-articulate, disturbed young patient – a tension between the realms of intellect and passion that is a thematic constant for this playwright.

Try these:
▷David Mercer for celebrations of the rebel; John Peielmeier's *Agnes of God*, ▷Bernard Pomerance's *The Elephant Man* for plays that pit doctors against patients, and definitions of normality against an unhingement that may be preferable; for historical sweep, ▷Robert Bolt's *A Man for All Seasons*, ▷John Whiting's *The Devils* and by contrast,

▷Nick Dear's debunking *The Art of Success* for a similar and shocking reassessment of an artist.

SHAKESPEARE, William   [1564–1616]
English Renaissance dramatist

Plays:
Henry VI, Parts II and III (1591), *The Comedy of Errors* (1592), *Henry VI, Part I*, *Richard III* (1593), *The Two Gentlemen of Verona* (1593), *The Taming of the Shrew* (1594), *Titus Andronicus* (1594), *Love's Labour's Lost* (1595), *A Midsummer Night's Dream* (1595), *Richard II* (1595), *Romeo and Juliet* (1595), *King John* (1596), *The Merchant of Venice* (1596), *Henry IV, Parts I and II* (1597), *Much Ado About Nothing* (1598), *As You Like It* (1599), *Henry V* (1599), *Julius Caesar* (1599), *The Merry Wives of Windsor* (1600), *Twelfth Night* (1600), *Hamlet* (1601), *All's Well That Ends Well* (1602), *Troilus and Cressida* (1602), *Measure for Measure* (1604), *Othello* (1604), *King Lear* (1605), *Macbeth* (1606), *Antony and Cleopatra* (1607), *Timon of Athens* (1607), *Coriolanus* (1608), *Pericles* (1608), *Cymbeline* (1609), *The Winter's Tale* (1610), *The Tempest* (1611), *Henry VIII* (1613; with ▷Fletcher), *The Two Noble Kinsmen* (1613; with Fletcher)

Shakespeare was a dramatist, actor, poet, land and theatre owner. He wrote most of his plays for the company of which he was part owner, and worked in all the popular genres of his time. He also wrote *Cardenio* with Fletcher (now lost) and probably part of *Sir Thomas More*. Many other Renaissance places have been attributed to him, often on scanty or non-existent evidence. The strongest recent claims have been made for *Edmund Ironside* and *Edward III*.

Shakespeare's plays based on English history cover the period from *King John* to *Henry VIII* and include two tetralogies (*Richard II*, *Henry IV, Parts I and II*, and *Henry V* form one and *Henry VI, Parts I, II, and III*, and *Richard III* the other), which are extremely effective when performed as a group (as done by the ▷RSC in John Barton's adaptations under the title of *The Wars of the Roses* in the 1960s and re-adapted in 1988 by ▷Charles Wood as *The Plantagenets*), even though they are perfectly viable as individual plays. The English Shakespeare Company has gone one further than the RSC in staging both tetralogies in tandem with considerable success. *Richard III* and *Henry V* have always attracted bravura interpretations, as has Falstaff in *Henry IV*. Shakespeare also wrote four plays drawn from Roman history (*Titus Andronicus, Julius Caesar, Antony and Cleopatra, Coriolanus*). *Julius Caesar* and *Antony and Cleapatra* form a linked pair, although the politics of *Julius Caesar* is exclusively social where that of *Antony and Cleopatra* is also sexual. *Titus Andronicus* is a fine example of revenge tragedy, considered unstageable until ▷Peter Brook showed the way with Laurence Olivier in 1955, but now a fairly regular sighting. *Coriolanus* is sometimes seen as a political vehicle – through there is dispute about whether its sympathies lean right or left – sometimes as a psychological study of mother-son relations and of repressed homosexual attraction between Aufidius and Coriolanus.

Shakespeare's comedies are almost exclusively of the romantic kind with 'boy meets girl/loses girl/finds girl' plots in which the young women, who are generally presented as intelligent, witty, down-to-earth, practical, resourceful and highly desirable, navigate their way through many complications (often associated with the fact that they are disguised as men) in order to arrive at marriages to men whose claim to our approval is that the women love them. Even in the most romantic plays there is a subplot to distance us from the romantic goings on. Bottom and his fellow amateur actors in *A Midsummer Night's Dream* provide incidental satire on the whole business of putting on a play and on the idea of romantic tragedy. In *Twelfth Night*, Malvolio's comic humiliation can easily turn into something that sours the whole romantic impulse of the play. Jacques compares the stream of couples about to get married at the end of *As You Like It* to the animals entering the Ark and, of course, Shylock in *The Merchant of Venice*, sometimes seen as a tragic hero, is always likely to cast a disturbing shadow over the romantic comic mood of the play's final act. In *All's Well That Ends Well* and *Measure for Measure* there are similar tensions between the dynamics and conventions of comedy, the events portrayed, and the means of characterisation, which lead them to be dubbed 'problem plays'. Similarly, *Troilus and Cressida* is a resolutely unheroic look at the Trojan war, which plays off its presentation of the sordid against the implied heroic image of a mythical period.

The tragedies *Othello, Hamlet, Macbeth*, and *King Lear* have traditionally been regarded as the peak of Shakespeare's achievement and their heroes as amongst the greatest challenges for actors. Interpretations of the plays, and the parts, have differed greatly but there generally has been more interest recently in giving full weight to other characters, rather than concentrating simply on the hero. The group of tragi-comedies or romances Shakespeare wrote at the end of his career (*Pericles, Cymbeline, The Winter's Tale*, and *The Tempest*) are noteworthy for their epic dramaturgy and refusal to be bound by naturalistic probability.

Shakespeare is one of the greatest challenges for directors, designers and actors who adopt a wide variety of approaches, from the reverent to the iconoclastic. There is one tradition which attempts to give the full texts in an approximation of Renaissance stage conditions, and this tends to mean elaborate costumes, few lighting changes and an emphasis on verse speaking, all of which can quite easily become funereal. At the other extreme there is the jazzy update in which the text is heavily cut and altered, the period and setting are anywhere and nowhere and the whole thing becomes a vehicle for an imposed directorial concept. Most modern productions avoid the worst excesses of either approach but use the full resources of the modern theatre and attempt to bring out themes and issues which are at least latently present in the plays. Certain plays are particularly open to interpretation, such as *The Taming of the Shrew*, which is a battleground – crudely – between those who believe that Shakespeare supported Petruchio in violence against women and those who see it as a play in which the only two lively characters deserve one another. A thoroughgoing feminist interpretation still has problems with this play, as evinced by the all-female production at the Theatre Royal, Stratford East in 1985 (though it was in fact the work of a male director).

Declan Donnellan's productions for England's Cheek by Jowl seem, on the whole, to have been able to tread a fine balance between a modernist and popular approach while still retaining respect for the text. Kenneth Branagh's Renaissance Company was set up to dive away from the director-dictatorship that actors like Simon Callow and Branagh feel have dominated the past twenty years of British theatre, and it has seen productions by the likes of Judi Dench and

Shakespeare goes West: A.J. Antoon's Wild West setting for Shakespeare's *The Taming of the Shrew*, New York Shakespeare Festival production, 1990. With Morgan Freeman as Petruchio, Tracy Ullman as Kate

Geraldine McEwan. The company has perhaps erred on the side of taking too many liberties but still has come up with a refreshing and invigorating *Twelfth Night*. Its *King Lear* and *A Midsummer Night's Dream* toured the United States in 1990, and Branagh's film of *Henry V*, (which he directed and starred in) has proved to be one of the most successful cinematic Shakespeares, supplanting the Olivier version in the hearts of many. Michael Bogdanov and Michael Pennington's English Shakespeare Company's history cycles, too, have found a way of escaping from the hidebound, with a Henry V that adopts a World War I, war-weary irreverence, while Anthony Quayle's Compass touring company steered a fairly traditional line.

Despite the director-dominated atmosphere of the RSC, at its best its productions are hard to beat and its record bears witness to a solid stream of productions that have acquired a legendary stamp - from the early 1960s Peter Hall/John Barton history plays, Brook's landmark *King Lear* and *A Midsummer Night's Dream* (though even he had a slump with his last RSC production, *Antony and Cleopatra*), to John Barton's many textually subtle interpretations (a marvellous *Much Ado About Nothing* with Judi Dench and Donald Sinden, and his classic *Troilus and Cressida* with Ian Holm and Dorothy Tutin). Trevor Nunn, Terry Hands, Adrian Noble and Bill Alexander have all had their share of successes and failures - Noble's *Henry V* with Kenneth Branagh, and Bill Alexander's *Merry Wives of Windsor*, Hand's *Much Ado* with Derek Jacobi, and Nunn's cycle of the Roman history plays have all carved out a place in theatrical history. With the exception, however, of the late Buzz Goodbody, and until Deborah Warner's arrival, women as directors of Shakespeare at Stratford have been conspicuous by their absence. At the ▷Royal National Theatre, Peter Hall's mid-life *Antony and Cleopatra*, with Anthony Hopkins and Judi Dench, received rave attention but seemed like a recall of the 1960s. In the summer of 1988, ▷Temba's Alby James also produced a Cuban-set *Romeo and Juliet* which augurs well for some new multi-racial interpretative slants. One of the most notable of these was Peter Brook's multicultural *Tempest*, performed in 1990 at his centre in Paris. Yvonne Brewster's all-black Anthony and Cleopatra in London will also go down in theatre history - not least for its fine verse speaking.

On the American side of the Atlantic, Shakespeare has been well served by a host of energetic directors and companies. Some of the best productions have built on the tradition of bold conceptual work inaugurated by Orson Welles and his 'voodoo' *Macbeth* and *Julius Caesar* set in Fascist Italy. Lee Breuer and Mabou Mines created a fascinating gender-reversed *King Lear* set in Georgia of the 1950s, with Ruth Maleczech as Lear. Former Mabou Mines member JoAnne Akalaitis has also recently become a significant director of Shakespeare, staging a controversial *Cymbeline* in 1989 and *Henry IV, Parts I and II* in 1991 as part of Joseph Papp's ongoing Shakespeare marathon, The New York Shakespeare Festival's ambitious plan to stage all of Shakespeare over the course of several years. (They were about half-way finished in 1991). Other important offerings in the marathon have been playwright/director ▷Steven Berkoff's *Coriolanus* and Kevin Kline's own production of *Hamlet*, the latest Shakespeare role for the actor who also won praise for his Benedick, Richard III, and Henry V. All of NYSF's productions are notable for their commitment to non-traditional casting. Denzel Washington's Richard III and Morgan Freeman's Petruchio are recent examples. Dustin Hoffman received his own kudos for his Shylock in Peter Hall's Broadway production of *The Merchant of Venice*.

Outside New York, regional theatres have contributed several major interpretations of Shakespeare, and some directors, like Michael Kahn at the Shakespeare Theatre at the Folger Library in Washington DC and Mark Lamos at Hartford Stage Company, have earned reputations as artists particularly suited to his work. At the Guthrie Theatre in Minneapolis, Garland Wright mounted both parts of *Henry IV* in 1990 and the prominent lighting designer Jennifer Tipton offered her *Tempest* in 1991. John Hirsch, the late artistic director of the Stratford Festival in Ontario, mounted a news-making *Coriolanus* for San Diego's Old Globe (it featured many references to the Iran–Contra scandal). In addition, since the 1960s there has been a rapid proliferation of summer Shakespeare festivals all over the USA.

The director ▷Robert Wilson, famous for his visually adventurous productions, staged his first Shakespeare in 1990 – a *King Lear* in Frankfurt, featuring the famous German actress Marianne Hoppe as Lear. Romanian-born Liviu Ciulei directed *A Midsummer*

Bradley Whitford and Janet Zarish in Mark Lamos' stunningly visual production of *A Midsummer Night's Dream*, Hartford Stage Company, 1988

Night's Dream in the United States in 1987, with music by Philip Glass. There have also been some important visits of foreign companies that will surely have an effect on American approaches to Shakespeare: a Soviet Georgian theatre presented their *Lear* in 1990, under the direction of Robert Sturua. Andrzej Wajda's *Hamlet IV*, from Poland, was a provocative experiment in gender reversal (following Sarah Bernhardt and Jane Lapotaire, Hamlet was played by a woman). And Ingmar Bergman's version of *Hamlet* won many admirers when it played in New York in 1988.

Try these:
For other Renaissance dramatists ▷Beaumont, ▷Chapman, ▷Fletcher, ▷Ford, ▷Thomas Heywood, ▷Jonson, ▷Kyd, ▷Marlowe, ▷Marston, ▷Massinger, ▷Middleton, ▷Tourneur, ▷Webster; for adaptations/reworkings of Shakespeare see ▷Dryden's and Davenant's *The Tempest*; ▷Charles Marowitz's collage versions of several plays; Peter Ustinov's *Romanoff and Juliet*; the musical *West Side Story* is an updating of *Romeo and Juliet* to New York, and *Kiss Me Kate* is a reworking of *The Taming of the Shrew* into a clever showbiz musical in which the offstage lives of the stars parallel the story of their musical adaptation of *The Shrew*; ▷Arnold Wesker's *The Merhant* is a counterargument to *The Merchant of Venice*; ▷C.P. Taylor's *Ophelia*, ▷Melissa Murray's *Ophelia*, Lee Blessing's *Fortinbras* and ▷Tom Stoppard's *Rosencrantz and Guildenstern Are Dead* are each rather more than *Hamlet* through the eyes of the supporting cast, as, in its way, is ▷W.S. Gilbert's *Rosencrantz and Guildenstern*; ▷Howard Brenton's *Thirteenth Night* reworks *Macbeth* and his *Pravda* (with ▷David Hare) draws on *Richard III*; Barbara Garson's *MacBird* was a 1960s reinterpretation featuring President Lyndon Johnson as the title character; ▷Edward Bond's *Lear* reassesses Shakespeare's, and his *Bingo* reassesses Shakespeare himself; ▷Howard Barker's own response to *King Lear* is *Seven Lears*; ▷Barrie Keeffe's *King of England* is an Afro-Carribean/East End transposition; ▷Terence Rattigan's *Harlequinade* is set during rehearsal of *Romeo and Juliet*; ▷Shaw disliked *Cymbeline* so much he produced an

'improved' final act in *Cymbeline Refinished*; ▷Alfred Jarry's *Ubu Roi* contains elements of *Macbeth* and several other Shakespeare plays; ▷Kleist's *The Schroffenstein Family* is a version of the *Romeo and Juliet* story; the Martiniquan writer Aimé Césaire's *A Tempest* turns the Shakespeare original into a biting commentary on colonialism; German dramatist Heiner Müller's *Hamletmachine* is one of the most powerful pieces of theatre in recent years, and was especially compelling in Robert Wilson's 1986 staging; ▷Richard Nelson's *Two Shakespearean Actors* for a portrait of Edwin Forrest and William Charles Macready, rival nineteenth-century stars; ▷Brecht (Shakespeare's world had a major influence on his dramaturgy, and one of Brecht's last plays was a reworking of *Coriolanus*); ▷Alan Ayckbourn for theatrical inventiveness and risk-taking; ▷Beckett for striking theatrical images; composers from Berlioz to Prokofiev, Tchaikovsky to Cleo Laine have drawn on Shakespeare.

SHANGE, Ntozake   [1948–]
American dramatist

Plays include:
for colored girls who have considered suicide when the rainbow is enuf (1974), *where the mississippi meets the amazon* (1977), *Spell No 7* (1978), *A Photograph: Lovers-in-Motion* (1979), *Black and White Two-Dimensional Planes* (1979), *Boogie Woogie Landscapes* (1980), *It Hasn't Always Been This Way* (1981), *Savannahland* (1981), *Bocas* (1982), *Betsey Brown* (reading; 1982 and, with Emily Mann, full production; 1986), *The Jazz Life* (1984), *Take Off From A Forced Landing* (1984), *from okra to greens* (1985), *Ridin' the Moon in Texas* (1986), *Betsy Brown* (musical, 1991)

Creator of the long running Broadway show (*for colored girls who have considered suicide when the rainbow is enuf*), Ntozake Shange is a South Carolina-born poet, professor and performer, author of over 25 stage productions, and several novels and books of poetry, defies categorisation. Shange rejects the term 'playwright' as irrelevant to the way she thinks and works.

Shange is a poetic/political writer in the best sense of the 'personal is political' school of feminist writing, and her 'choreopoems', as

Ian McKellen's Richard III, a political gangster for our times and equally, the centrepiece of Richard Eyre's vibrant contemporary production of *Richard III* (Royal National Theatre, 1990/91, London and World Tour)

she calls some of her performance pieces, combine words, music and dance as integral components in expressing the realities of black life on stage. Greatly influenced by the women's movement and California's radical women's presses, both *for colored girls* and *Spell No 7* – Shange's best-known works – contain shattering accounts of racial humiliations and pain but balance the anger and images of victimisation with communal celebration and pride. *for colored girls* started out as a handful of Shange's poems in a Berkeley bar before developing into the innovative music-theatre piece which moved to Broadway following a highly successful stint at the Public Theatre in New York. It is a consciousness-raising account of the trials, tribulations and, importantly, endurance of black American womanhood. The highly acclaimed production was subject to some criticism of its images of black males (similar to the censure of Alice Walker for *The Color Purple*). *Spell No 7* is a more bitter, ironic comment on the images, internalised self-hatred and stereotyping of black entertainers. Productions of Shange's works in Britain have not fared particularly well, partly due perhaps to the difficulties of transplanting cultural references and colloquialisms to another clime.

None of Shange's later work has met with the enthusiasm which greeted *for colored girls*. Some have found her dialogue too rhetorical, her anger too insistent, and the structure of her pieces too loose, but her contribution to the creation of a black feminist theatrical aesthetic has been groundbreaking.

Try these:
▷Pam Gems' *Piaf* for a play whose colloquial language had similar problems of understanding when it made the transatlantic crossing; George Wolfe's *The Colored Museum*, Kalamu Ya Salaam's *Black Love Song No 1* are bitter satires on the theme of black stereotypes (the former even satirizes Shange); Adrienne Kennedy's *A Lesson in Dead Language* deals with young women's education through a vivid, almost grotesque visual image; Suzi Lori Parks matches Shange's elliptical lyricism while adding a cutting-edge contemporaneity. Many recent musicals have used the black woman as victim as their central theme particularly, and seemingly endlessly, about Billie Holliday,

Lady Day (with Dee Dee Bridgewater); ▷Amiri Baraka, ▷Lorraine Hansberry, ▷Langston Hughes, Zora Neale Hurston and Alice Childress as contrasting and influential black playwrights; ▷Jackie Rudet's *Basin* for a British expression of black women's shared history; Jackie Kay's *Chiaroscuro*.

SHANLEY, John Patrick   [1950–]
American   dramatist,   screenwriter   and director

Plays include:
Saturday Night at the War (1978), *Welcome to the Moon* (six short plays; 1982), *Danny and the Deep Blue Sea* (1984), *Savage in Limbo* (1985), *The Dreamer Examines his Pillow* (1986), *Women of Manhattan* (1986), *Italian American Reconciliation* (1988), *The Big Funk* (1990)

Films include:
Five Corners, Moonstruck, Joe versus the Volcano

This Bronx-born, Academy Award-winning writer first earned notice with the Circle in the Square production of *Danny and the Deep Blue Sea* (starring John Turturro), which remains his most acclaimed play. Here, confused and troubled working-class characters, programmed to self-destruct after years of emotional deprivation, struggle to find wisdom and salvation through love. This was the first of four autobiographical plays (*The Dreamer Examines his Pillow, Savage in Limbo*, and *Italian American Reconciliation* were the others) which explore how a man learns emotional responsibility and confronts the demands of a loving relationship. His plays are often romantic melodramas, and Shanley openly admits targetting 'the big, big emotions', as well as using his writing as pragmatic personal therapy. Shanley captures New York speech rhythms and ethnic local color. He admits his personal longing for the Italians' connection to the body, and creates Italian-American characters possessed of the Irish gift of the gab. His later plays push the limits of realism, and *The Big Funk* is openly absurdist in style.

Moonstruck, his Academy Award-winning screenplay, explored familiar themes. Characters who substitute the safety of empty relationships for the risks of true love and passion learn to take love's leap of faith and

Antony Sher's extraordinary performance as Richard III in Shakespeare's play was the centrepiece of the RSC's 1984 Stratford and 1985 Barbican seasons. *Richard III* was directed by Bill Alexander

acquire self-knowledge through the process. His films sport the humour, objectivity and large sweep that his plays often lack.

Try these:
Michael Gazzo for families in crisis; Terence McNally's *Frankie and Johnny in the Clair de Lune* for another play featuring two down-and-out New Yorkers battling through their emotions; ▷David Mamet for aggressive male characters; McNally's *Frankie and Johnny . . .* for emotionally frigid lower-class lovers; ▷Jules Feiffer and ▷John Osborne for struggling relationships; ▷Tom Kempinksi for autobiographical angst.

SHAPIRO, Jacqui   [1961–]
British dramatist

Plays include:
Family Entertainment (1981), *Thicker Than Water* (1981), *I'm Not a Bloody Automaton You Know!* (1982) *Sharon's Journey* (1981); *One of Us* (1983), *Up The Garden Path* (1983), *Trade Secrets* (1984), *Dead Romantic* (1984), *Three's a Crowd* (1985), *Dance Gazer* (1985), *How Odd of God* (1986), *Winter in the Morning* (1988)

Though Shapiro once confessed she had been writing ever since she could remember, and had several one-act plays and monologues performed whilst at Manchester University, it was her first major play, *One of Us*, that brought her to public prominence. Winner of a Yorkshire Television award in the 1983 National Student Drama Festival this one-woman monologue that took on racism as seen through the eyes of a Birmingham Asian girl was performed with great panache by Meera Syal (who also co-wrote it) and is notable for its sharp social observation about prejudices and the pressures imposed on a young Asian girl battling for independence – spry, funny and tragic all at the same time.

Trade Secrets, for the Women's Theatre Group, tackled pornography and violence and an imagined world without men, but its fragmentary structure and characterisations left something to be desired; *Dead Romantic* (a Soho Poly commission) was, however, a snappy comedy of recognisable 'ideological' angsts getting in the way of physiological lust! *Winter in the Morning*, taken from Janina Bauman's horrific account of life for Polish Jews under the Nazis in the Warsaw Ghetto,

succeeded best in the way it translates its adolescents' yearnings to the stage and as a reminder of the distortion of human values under extreme conditions. The cabaret-within-a-play, caricaturing Hitler and money-grabbing Ghetto Jews alike, was more problematical.

Try these:
▷Harwant Bains' *The Fighting Kite* gives another image of the young Asian woman's bid for independence; ▷Sue Townsend's *The Great Celestial Cow* looks at cross-cultural pressures on Asian women in Britain; ▷Sharman Macdonald and Lynda Barry's *The Good Times Are Killing Me* for more female adolescent growing pains; ▷Sarah Daniels's *Masterpieces* is *the* rad fem play on pornography and violence; Siren's *Curfew* dealt more surreally with a world without men; ▷Clare McIntyre's *Low Level Panic* and ▷Winsome Pinnock's *Picture Palace* contrast romantic dreams and marketed images with more frightening day-to-day realities; ▷Terry Johnson's *Unsuitable for Adults*, Jack Klaff's *Cuddles* and ▷Pam Gems' *Loving Women* deal with the difficulties of feminism and heterosexual tangles; ▷Barry Collins' *Judgement* looks at the corruption of human values under extreme pressures; see also the plays of Jean-Claude Grumberg Joshua Sobol's *Ghetto*, George Tabor is *Mein Kampf Farce*, and Roxane Shafer's *Adam and Eve, The Raging Angels*, Julia Pascal's *Theresa*, and Wendy Kesselman's *I Love You, I Love You Not* for others, and various treatments on WWII and the Holocaust.

SHARED EXPERIENCE
British touring company

See under Mike Alfreds.

SHAW, George Bernard   [1856–1950]
Irish dramatist, critic

Plays include:
Widower's Houses (1892), *Arms and the Man* (1894), *Candida* (1897), *The Devil's Disciple* (1897), *The Man of Destiny* (1897), *You Never Can Tell* (1899), *Captain Brassbound's Conversion* (1900), *Mrs Warren's Profession* (1902), *John Bull's Other Island* (1904), *The Philanderer*

(1905), *Caesar and Cleopatra* (1907), *Man and Superman* (1905), *Major Barbara* (1905), *The Doctor's Dilemma* (1906), *Getting Married* (1908), *The Shewing Up of Blanco Posnet* (1909), *Press Cuttings* (1909), *Misalliance* (1910), *The Dark Lady of the Sonnets* (1910), *Fanny's First Play* (1911), *Overruled* (1912), *Androcles and the Lion* (1913), *Pygmalion* (1913), *Great Catherine* (1913), *The Music Cure* (1914), *O'Flaherty VC* (1917), *Heartbreak House* (1920), *Back to Methuselah* (1922), *Saint Joan* (1923), *The Fascinating Foundling* (1928), *The Apple Cart* (1929), *Too True to Be Good* (1932), *On the Rocks* (1933), *Village Wooing* (1934), *The Simpleton of the Unexpected Isles* (1935) *The Millionairess* (1936), *Cymbeline Refinished* (1937), *Geneva* (1938), *In Good King Charles's Golden Days* (1939), *Buoyant Billions* (1948), *Far Fetched Fables* (1950), *Why She Would Not* (1957)

George Bernard Shaw, among the most widely produced of playwrights, and prolific man-of-letters (he published major essays on ▷Ibsen and Wagner as well as many on political and artistic issues of the day), won the Nobel Prize for literature in 1925, and refused a peerage on principle. An active Socialist for most of his life, he was a leading member of the Fabian Society, a co-founder with Sidney and Beatrice Webb of the *New Statesman*, helped to establish the London School of Economics, and was a leading figure in the campaign for a ▷National Theatre.

It is often claimed that Shavian theatre sacrifices dramatic effect and characterisation for the sake of ideas, but with the hindsight of post-Brechtian theatre, Shaw can be seen as an innovator in bringing a challenging theatre of ideas to the West End and to theatres all over the world. The skill that Shaw always demonstrates with paradox becomes dialectical drama in his most successful plays.

Born in Dublin of Anglo-Irish parents, Shaw worked briefly in an estate agent's office before moving to London in 1876. He became a music critic and also reviewed books and the visual arts, before moving into drama criticism for the *Saturday Review*, producing some of the wittiest and wisest reviews ever of theatre. Through his reviewing Shaw gained a thorough awareness of the forms of contemporary theatre which informs his own writings: *Heartbreak House* and *Major Barbara* play with the conventions of dramatic form,

while *The Fascinating Foundling* is a pastiche of contemporary commercial West End theatre writing. His first critical and commercial success came with *Arms and the Man*, a comedy with a moral; a contemporary reviewer described Shaw as 'the most humourously extravagant paradoxer in London' (no mean praise, since ▷Oscar Wilde was a contemporary contender for the title). Besides their inventiveness and wit, Shaw's plays consistently dealt with controversial and often taboo subjects; in 1893 *Mrs Warren's Profession* (her profession of brothel keeper is not respectable) was banned by the Lord Chamberlain, and was not produced until 1925 (the year in which Shaw's Nobel prize had unequivocally established him as a Grand Old Man of the British theatre). *Candida* was written as a response to ▷Ibsen's *A Doll's House*, and Ibsen's philosophy of naturalistic theatre became an informing influence on Shaw's work. Ibsen's exploration of non-realist forms in *Peer Gynt* was also influential: *Back to Methuselah* demonstrates the mix of fantasy, allegory and historical breadth that is an important aspect of Shaw's later (and less often produced) writings.

Man and Superman established Shaw as one of the most important of contemporary dramatists, and initiated a period of Shaw's most popular (both then and now) plays: *Major Barbara*, *Pygmalion*, *Saint Joan* and *Heartbreak House*. Shaw was very much involved with the staging of his plays; his stage directions are thorough and copious, and each play has a substantial preface. Shaw is perhaps most widely known through the musical version of *Pygmalion*, which with the libretto of Alan Jay Lerner became *My Fair Lady*.

Major Barbara

Major Barbara is a play which explores the nature of charity and wealth. Subtitled a 'discussion in three acts', the play puts contemporary debates about poverty on stage, and subjects them to dramatic investigation. The first act appears to be a standard 'drawing room comedy', as Lady Britomart and her son Stephen display conventional wit and discuss the marriages of the family daughters; the appearance of a long lost father completes the apparent conventional melodrama. However, Major Barbara, one of the daughters, is a Major in the Salvation Army, committed to the battle against poverty, while her father, Undershaft, is an arms manufacturer and a staunch defender of capitalism. In the next act, the curtain rises on a Salvation Army housing shelter (a real challenge to contemporary West End theatre audiences used to drawing room comedy), and the play confronts Barbara with the fact that her concept of 'charity' rests on a capitalist system. Undershaft demonstrates that he financially supports the shelter, and that it is funded from the profits of breweries; a paradox that overturns the Salvation Army principle of teetotalism. In the final act Barbara and her academic lover Cusins confront Undershaft in a debate about the nature of poverty. Their debate is not a simple one, each employs unexpected arguments, and Undershaft effectively wins. Barbara finally comes to the realisation that her philosophy of faith, hope and charity depends upon the capitalism espoused by Undershaft, and accepts his patronage. The questions raised by the play remain unanswered, however: while Barbara may accept Undershaft, the audience is reminded that his philosophy of a charity made possible by wealth and profit is based on his manufacture of lethal weaponry. *Major Barbara* demonstrates that concepts of 'morality', 'liberty' and 'redemption' can only be abstractions in the face of poverty, and that what is necessary is an economic system based on the principle, as Shaw says: 'to each according to their needs, from each according to their means.' While the play was very much written in response to contemporary topical debates about poverty, its arguments remain potent.

Try these:
▷Oscar Wilde, for a shared background and a very different approach to theatre; ▷Strindberg was a major figure for Shaw, in championing a theatre of ideas; Shaw appears as a character in ▷Hugh Whitemore's play *The Best of Friends*; ▷John McGrath shares Shaw's commitment to using dramatic form for socialist ideas; ▷Brecht, whose *The Good Person of Szechuan*, like *Major Barbara*, explores the interdependence of charity and capitalism; ▷Trevor Griffiths is another dramatist who extends contemporary dramatic forms to socialist ends; ▷Edward Bond ▷Howard Brenton and ▷Howard Barker tend to be more formally innovative; ▷Karim Alrawi's *A Child in the Heart* and Jonathan Falla's *Topokana Martyr's Day* are contemporary examples of plays which confront the paradoxes of charity in relation to the Third World.

SHAWN, Wallace   [1943–]
American dramatist and actor

Plays include:
Our Late Night (1975), *A Thought in Three Parts* (1977), *Marie and Bruce* (1979), *The Hotel Play* (1981), *My Dinner With André* (with André Gregory; 1981), *Aunt Dan and Lemon* (1985), *The Fever* (1990)

Although celebrity-spotters recognize him through bit parts in a number of films, Shawn has developed into one of America's most unpredictable and subversive dramatists since he started writing plays in 1971. Whether epic (*The Hotel Play*) or intimate (*My Dinner With André*), seemingly straightforward or sinuously ironic, Shawn's plays get under the skin in a way audiences may not even realise until several days after the event. Often premiered in London at the Royal Court, they may move on to Joe Papp's Public Theatre off-Broadway, where, during the run of *Aunt Dan and Lemon*, New Yorkers could be found nightly arguing whether Shawn himself *agreed* with the play's ostensibly profascist stance. His targets are the nightmarishness of domesticity – the couple who can't stop firing invective at one another in his one-act *Marie and Bruce* – as well as hypocrisy disguised as doing-good, and the ceaseless quest for meaning in a society hell bent on its own extinction. *The Fever*, a monologue delivered by Shawn on a bare stage, perhaps best distils the anxiety and guilt suppressed by most well-to-do American liberals when confronted by third world poverty. Unfortunately, his ideas often exceed his craft, and none of his plays has yet found the shape to make them truly ignite; indeed, their shapelessness often seems to be part of the point. If he can wed his imagination to a stricter control of form, he might come up with the seismic blast of a play which he has so far promised but never delivered.

Aunt Dan and Lemon
Overlong yet underwritten, at once wordy and evasive, *Aunt Dan* is a fascinating jumble of a drama about the relationship between a charismatic American don at Oxford, Aunt Dan, and the sickly young Leonora (Lemon) whom she befriends. A lifelong voyeur whose seemi-

ngly calm exterior belies a moral blankness inside, Lemon invites the audience into her sickroom only to lead us into a disquieting diatribe against the cult of compassion, in which the Nazis' extermination of the Jews is seen as a mere extension of our annihilation of cockroaches. The tone of the play is its most elusive aspect, and Shawn gives his actors and his director wide room to manoeuvre. Still, the writing itself remains maddeningly opaque; this is a dark treatise on moral pathology that can't quite illuminate the troubled and troubling people at its core.

Try these:
▷David Mamet and ▷Jules Feiffer for cutthroat dissections of the American psyche; ▷Strindberg and ▷Edward Albee (especially *Who's Afraid of Virginia Woolf?*) for images of marital malaise; ▷Michael Frayn's *Benefactors* for the underside of idealism; ▷Spalding Gray for powerful monologues that catch the jangling, frayed nerve ends of our societies.

SHELLEY, Percy Bysshe
English radical and poet   [1792–1822]

Plays include:
The Cenci (1819)

The Romantic poet cast several of his works in dramatic form but only *The Cenci* seems ever to have been performed and that long after his death. A five-act drama in sub-Shakespearean style, it retells a true story Shelley had heard in Rome; Beatrice Cenci is raped by her father, an establishment figure protected by Church and society, and eventually murders him. Its theme of incest was probably a reason why it was not staged for so long. Although it is not a great play it is much better than Byron's or Tennyson's attempts at writing for the stage and occasional revivals, such as the Bristol Old Vic production seen at London's Almeida Theatre in 1985, demonstrate its theatrical vitality.

Try these:
For modern verse plays ▷T.S. Eliot and ▷Christopher Fry; ▷Howard Brenton's *Bloody Poetry* and ▷Ann Jellicoe's *Shelley* for plays about Shelley; ▷Artaud's is the most famous production of a version of *The Cenci*; Shelley's dramaturgy was much influenced by the Renaissance dramatists – ▷John Ford's *'Tis Pity She's a Whore* is probably the most famous Renaissance treatment of incest; for contemporary treatments of incest ▷Barry Reckord's *X* and ▷Michel Tremblay's *Bonjour, Bonjour*, for a black American feminist version, Adrienne Kennedy's surreal account, *A Rat's Mass*.

SHEPARD, Sam   [1943–]
American dramatist and actor

Plays include:
Cowboys (1964), *The Rock Garden* (1964), *La Turista* (1967), *The Tooth of Crime* (1972), *Curse of the Starving Class* (1978), *Buried Child* (1978), *Suicide In B-Flat* (1978), *Seduced* (1979), *True West* (1980), *Fool For Love* (1983), *A Lie of the Mind* (1986), *Savage/Love* (1979), *States of Shock* (1991)

Is Sam Shepard the pre-eminent dramatic observer of the American myth, or the greatest exemplar of it? Whatever one's stance, the Illinois-born playwright has achieved a near-legendary status through a combination of his commanding laconicism and more than two decades of plays which defy classification as they move from the overtly fantastical (some of his early one-act plays) to long, piercing reveries about families rent asunder (*A Lie of the Mind*). The most successful American playwright never to have had a work produced on Broadway, Shepard eschews the tidy dramatics and often pat psychology that make Broadway hits, and his plays tend to take place in the American equivalent of the Outback, far from the East Coast swells. Shepard is the poet par excellence of the American mythic imagination and its debased frontier mentality. Drawing from such diverse (and generally non-literary) sources as popular music (rock 'n' roll, jazz, country & western), sci-fi, Hollywood Westerns and the beat poets, his early plays offer intensely theatrical pastiches of legend and actuality. When *Suicide in B-Flat* first opened at Yale Repertory Theatre, one critic characterised it as 'a free-form jazz opus by Ornette Coleman to a text by Wittgenstein translated by Abbott and Costello.' His track record off-Broadway and in London, though, has been exemplary; indeed, his *Tooth of Crime*, an intriguing 'style war' between two rock musicians, Hoss and

Crow, was written during Shepard's London residency (at the Bush) in the early 1970s.

Many of his middle-period plays mix comic absurdism with Pinter-style game-playing; his Pulitzer Prize-winning *Buried Child* takes the form of a homecoming, as a man and his girlfriend return to the family farm in Illinois. In *True West*, two brothers in a Southern California suburb squabble and swap identities, while taking potshots at American myth-making, both Hollywood-style and otherwise. *A Lie of the Mind* posits two families, one in California, the other in Montana, separated by a mileage that is spiritual not spatial. 'I don't think it's worth doing anything unless it's personal,' Shepard says, and despite his increasing fame as a film star and matinee idol, his work shows no signs of accommodating itself to the mob he has never courted. This was reaffirmed by his first stage play in years, *States of Shock*, that had a limited, sold-out off-Broadway run at the American Place. It featured a pair of crazed Vietnam veterans (portrayed by John Malkovich and Michael Wincott) who do their best to bring the insanity of war home to a roadside restaurant occupied by an all-American middle-aged couple. The man's response to the war is masturbation while his wife remains demure and distant. The play's images resonated loudly as the USA was in the midst of the Gulf War.

Shepard has also appeared as a screen actor in *Days of Heaven, Resurrection, The Right Stuff, Raggedy Man, Fool For Love, Baby Boom*, and – opposite his wife, Jessica Lange – *Frances, Country, Crimes of the Heart*, and *Far North*.

Fool For Love

'You're gonna erase me', May tells her former lover Eddie when they re-encounter one another in a motel room on the edge of the Mojave Desert, and Shepard's play is about exactly that – the threat of emotional erasure generated by a love so combustible that it doesn't know its own limits. A long-running success off-Broadway and a West End transfer from the ▷National Theatre, the four-character drama set in Shepard's favoured terrain, the American southwest, epitomises this playwright's method: at once violent and oblique, highly charged and digressive. The play has been described both as a *Phaedra* on amphetamines and a visceral but ultimately empty vehicle for actors. Whatever one's response, there's no denying Shepard's ability

to elicit a charge from his re-examination of the ethos of the American cowboy, as the romantically ravaged Eddie lassoes bedposts instead of the woman with whom he should have never become entangled.

Try these:
▷Harold Pinter, ▷David Mamet for their juxtaposition of violent spoken encounters with equally violent and abrupt silences; Lyle Kessler's (*Orphans*), ▷Strindberg's *Miss Julie* for another study of explosive sexual attraction, ▷Botho Strauss' *The Tourist Guide*; ▷Megan Terry, ▷Jean-Claude Van Itallie, Maria Irene Fornes for other American experimentalists of the 1960s; Greek tragedy for the ultimate family curse plays; ▷O'Neill for archetypal 'family as battlefield' plays; Mac Wellman for improvisational approach to language and disposable culture.

SHEPPHARD, Nona   [1950–]
British playwright and director

Plays for children include:
Off the Rails (1979), *Getting Through* (1985), *Beulah's Box* (1986), *The Last Tiger* (1984)

Other plays include:
Robyn Hood (1988), *The Snow Queen* (1989)

The author, since 1979, of 27 plays (and director of more than 40), Shepphard has a warmth of perception and robustness of style that make her work both a popular and a sustaining experience for young audiences. Her plays span the age ranges. *Beulah's Box*, for instance, written for the Quicksilver Theatre Company, was targetted at 8 to 10 year olds. It tells the story of a sad, wordless creature, put upon by a mean employer, who crawls through a mysterious box and finds a world of contrasts, colour, individuality and a wealth of languages. Reinforced by quirky and flexible set designs, it uses multilingualism as evidence of strength rather than as a perfunctory duty.

Getting Through, written for Theatre Centre, provided girls about to move on, at the age of 12, to senior school with useful bolstering. Caz' greatest ambition is to build a radio transmitter – not a project for a girl, so she's told. Despite feeling alone and vulnerable in a new environment, she sticks to her guns. Interestingly, *Getting Through* had its mirror counterpart in *Over and Out*, written by Shepphard with ▷Bryony Lavery, and produced in tandem. In this, another Caz, in a science fiction world, escapes from the drab and unsympathetic world of the Norms and makes contact, via a transmitter, with Caz of the first play. Both these plays form the basis of a book to be published by Bodley Head.

Robyn Hood and *The Snow Queen*, Shepphard's two pantomimes, have also been the high spots of the Christmas season at the Drill Hall, exuding a wicked humour and subverting gender roles with a robustness which is clearly as appealing to adult audiences as her children's plays are to younger audiences.

Try these:

▷Wendy Kesselman, ▷Penny Casdagli, Susan Zeder, Timothy Mason, ▷David Wood and ▷David Holman are other dramatists writing for children; see also ▷Theatre for Young Audiences; ▷Women in Theatre.

SHERIDAN,
Richard Brinsley   [1751–1815]
Irish dramatist, theatre manager and politician

Plays include:
The Rivals (1775), *St Patrick's Day; or, the Scheming Lieutenant* (1775), *The Duenna* (comic opera; 1775), *A Trip to Scarborough* (1777), *The School for Scandal* (1777), *The Critic; or, a Tragedy Rehearsed* (1779), *Pizarro* (1799)

Son of a Dublin actor-manager and a playwright-novelist, Sheridan was intended for a career at the Bar, but his elopement and marriage to Elizabeth Linley brought him need of money and led to him writing *The Rivals*, based on his observation of society at Bath and his own experiences.

Sheridan bought David Garrick's share of Drury Lane in 1776 and managed the theatre for over twenty years, though after becoming a Member of Parliament in 1780 he devoted most of his writing skills to speeches in the House. Sheridan watched Drury Lane burn down in 1809 from an inn opposite, remarking: 'Can not a man take a glass of wine by his own fireside?' He became more and more beset by money troubles and when he died in Savile Row in 1815 there were bailiffs at the

door. His plots are fast moving and his dialogue witty and though without the sexual explicitness of Restoration dramatists, his plays have much in common with their comedy of manners. Although his characters often have identifying names in the tradition of ▷Jonson – Snake, or Lady Sneerwell (in *The School for Scandal*) for instance – they are nevertheless rounded creations rather than mere caricatures. They include the famous Mrs Malaprop (in *The Rivals*). *The Critic* is a burlesque of the contemporary stage which has not lost its point and is occasionally revived, while *The Rivals* and *The School for Scandal* have won a permanent place in the repertoire. Undoubtedly his finest work, *The School for Scandal* play presents the arrival from the country of Lady Teazle, a naive young wife, and her exposure to, and education in, London Society, against a background of intrigue and a parallel plot concerning an inheritance involving virtuous and corrupt brothers. The 'screen scene' in which her much older husband, Sir Peter, discovers Lady Teazle in hiding must rank with the Malvolio letter scene as amongst the finest in English comedy. Sheridan's most popular work in his own times was *Pizarro*, a spectacular reworking of a German play.

Try these:

▷G.B. Shaw's *Pygmalion* offers some parallels between Professor Higgins and Sir Peter learning to accept a lively young woman; ▷Farquhar shows society, earlier in the century, visiting the provinces; ▷Aphra Behn's *The Lucky Chance* and ▷William Wycherley's *The Country Wife* for earlier and more robust treatment of town/country conflicts; ▷Goldsmith's *She Stoops to Conquer* for a contemporary version; ▷Tom Stoppard's *The Real Inspector Hound* is a modern play about critics.

SHERMAN, Martin   [1938–]
American dramatist

Plays include:
Passing By (1972), *Cracks* (1973), *Bent* (1977), *Messiah* (1981), *When She Danced* (1984), *A Madhouse in Goa* (1987)

Born in Philadelphia, and educated at Boston University, Sherman was resident playwright at Playwrights' Horizons in New York from 1976–77 before going to England where his

Passing By was one of half a dozen plays in the 1975 lunchtime season of gay plays put on by Ed Berman at the Almost Free. Sherman is probably best known however for *Bent*, a play about the Nazi persecution of homosexuals, one of the plays that arose out of ▷Gay Sweatshop's production of *As Time Goes By* which looked at homosexual persecution in three different periods.

Bent subsequently turned up at the Royal Court and on Broadway with some star names – Ian McKellen and Tom Bell in Britain, Richard Gere and briefly Michael York on Broadway – and scored considerable success. It has gone on to be performed all over the world.

His follow-up play *Messiah*, a parable of redemption set in 1665 Poland in the period following the Cossacks' massacre, was less well received. However, both *When She Danced* the story of dancer Isadora Duncan's marriage to the Russian Sergei Esenin in 1923 Paris and *A Madhouse in Goa* have had better luck (Vanessa Redgrave appeared in both in the West End). A writer with a style that mixes the florid and spare – sometimes an uncomfortable combination – two of the early plays, *Passing By*, a pre-AIDS play dealing with illness and the support men can give to each other, and *Cracks*, are included in Methuen's Gay Plays series.

Bent

One of the early plays to show gays in a sympathetic and unsensationalistic light, *Bent* used two quite distinct styles: a first half of a *Boys in the Band* type bitchery and a second act set in Dachau with a Beckettian-type duologue between the central character, the tormented Max, and his lover, Horst. This may be partly due to the fact that though ostensibly set in the 1940s, the play is informed by and exudes a 1970s Gay Liberation consciousness and is therefore as much concerned with issues of changing personal politics as it is with historical perspective. Two exchanges also stand out; Max's scene with his elderly, discreet Uncle Freddie and, later, the verbally arrived-at orgasm between the two incarcerated men.

Try these:

▷Drew Griffiths; ▷Noël Greig for *As Time Goes By* and his *Angels Descend On Paris* for a different treatment of homosexuals under Nazi repression; ▷Manuel Puig's *Kiss of the Spider Woman* for its exploration of homosexuality in a South American political and prison setting; ▷Lanford Wilson, ▷Harvey Fierstein, ▷Larry Kramer, William Hoffman and Neil Bell as other American playwrights who write unabashedly gay plays; ▷Hugh Whitemore's *Breaking the Code* for homosexuality British-style during World War II; *Cabaret*, for glimpses of pre-War gay politics in Germany, ▷Genet's *Deathwatch*, for another treatment of prison and homosexuality.

SHERRIFF, R.C. (Robert Cedric)   [1896–1975]
British dramatist and novelist

Plays include:
Journey's End (1928), *Badger's Green* (1930), *St Helena* (1935), *Miss Mabel* (1948), *Home at Seven* (1950)

Sherriff is virtually a one-play author, though his other plays were competent Saturday Night Theatre fodder, and he had a long and lucrative career as a screenwriter (*The Dam Busters*, *Mrs Miniver*, *Goodbye Mr Chips*). *Journey's End* was first put on as a Sunday night production by the Stage Society (with the little-known Laurence Olivier playing Captain Dennis Stanhope), and in spite of doubts about the commercial prospects of a realistic play about World War I, it ran and ran (though without Olivier, who had gone into *Beau Geste* instead). The tension between the public school ethos (which the play accepts) and the grinding horror of trench warfare at its worst, produces one of the 'strongest' plays ever written, and it works surprisingly well whenever revived. It is frequently put on by amateur groups in Britain, in spite of the problems inherent in making a dug-out collapse at the end (see Michael Green, *The Art of Coarse Acting*), and was revived in London in 1988 with Jason Connery and Nicky Henson as the two young captains.

Try these:

▷Sean O'Casey's *The Silver Tassie* for a very different Expressionist treatment of the war zone; ▷Willis Hall's *The Long and the Short and the Tall*, Leslie Lee's *Black Eagles*, and ▷Terence Rattigan's *Flare Path* deal with World War II; ▷Noël Greig's *Poppies* is a fiercely pacifist play, seen from a gay perspective; the crop of post-Falklands plays, by ▷Tony Marchant, ▷Louise Page, ▷Robert Holman (*Making Noise Quietly*) and Greg Cullen, all make their anti-war points in various ways; Theatre Workshop's *Oh What a Lovely War*, remains *the* World War I testament; ▷Emily Mann's *Still Life*, ▷Terence McNally, ▷David Rabe, ▷Stephen Metcalfe, ▷Romulus Linney. ▷Megan Terry for Vietnam.

SHIRLEY, James   [1596–1666]
English Renaissance dramatist

Plays include:
The Traitor (1631), *Hyde Park* (1632), *The Gamester* (1633), *The Cardinal* (1641)

Like Heywood, Shirley owes his current theatrical status to the ▷RSC's Swan theatre and its policy of producing forgotten but lively plays by ▷Shakespeare's near contemporaries, in his case *Hyde Park*, which appears not to have been staged for some 300 years before the 1987 revival. In his own time, after leaving the Anglican priesthood on his conversion to Catholicism, Shirley was a popular and prolific dramatist but his work has suffered in the general theatrical neglect of the plays of this period. *The Traitor* and *The Cardinal* are very much in the revenge tragedy tradition with plots reminiscent of ▷Kyd, ▷Shakespeare, ▷Tourneur, ▷Webster and ▷Middleton; the comedies are very much concerned with contemporary manners and London life, using locations, characters and themes that are more familiar to us in their post-Restoration forms. *Hyde Park* proved to be stageworthy and it would be interesting to see *The Gamester* with its double bed trick in which a man pays off gambling debts by allowing the winner to take his place in bed with the woman he was about to commit adultery with; his wife later informs him that she has taken the other woman's place, but it all turns out not to have happened and decorum of a kind is maintained.

Try these:
For the comedies ▷Jonson and ▷Middleton, ▷Behn, ▷Etherege and ▷Wycherley as immediate predecessors and successors; the other forgotten dramatists of the pre-Civil War period are Richard Brome and William Davenant; ▷Shakespeare uses the bed-trick in both *Measure for Measure* and *All's Well that Ends Well*; and ▷Middleton and ▷Rowley use the same device in their tragedy *The Changeling*.

SHUE, Larry   [1946–85]
American dramatist and actor

Plays include:
The Nerd (1981), *The Foreigner* (1985), *Wenceslas Square* (1988), *Grandma Duck Is Dead*, *My Emperor's New Clothes*

Larry Shue's untimely death (in a plane crash as he was about to join the New York cast of the musical, *The Mystery of Edwin Drood*), ended his developing careers in playwriting and acting. In 1977 Shue joined the Milwaukee (Wisconsin) Repertory Theater acting company and only four years later *The Nerd* reached Broadway. Both *The Nerd* and *The Foreigner* demonstrate Shue's reliance on situation and character-based humour. Neither play broke new ground and whether Shue would have grown as a playwright is merely conjecture. Indeed, critics were not kind to *The Foreigner* and the New York production of *Wenceslas Square* was lauded more for Jerry Zaks' direction than for Shue's writing. Whether *Wenceslas Square* will become popular in regional theatres like his first plays is somewhat doubtful since Eastern Europe is no longer the closed culture depicted in the play.

Wenceslas Square
Wenceslas Square dramatises an incident from Shue's life. It follows a college theatre professor and his protegé on their trip to Czechoslovakia. The professor has visited the country as a college student during the Dubček regime. His return serves as research for a book about the effects of the Soviet repression upon the arts. Both the professor and the student are political neotypes and are shocked by the lack of free speech and thought that had marked the Professor's earlier visit. The contrast is punctuated by the professor's flashbacks and by the apparent self reflection that the professor sees in his young student. Shue incorporates humorous devices used in his other plays – mistaken identify and communication problems for example – and he includes a melancholy tone that makes the audience aware of the consequences of artistic repression. The play became anachronistic after 1989 when the Soviet leadership in

Czechoslovakia was replaced with a more liberal government headed by onetime dissident ▷Vaclav Havel.

Try these:
▷Tom Stoppard for similar themes; ▷David Edgar's *The Shape of the Table* for the end of the Cold War; ▷Richard Nelson's *Some Americans Abroad* and ▷Brian Friel's *Translations* for cultural dissonances.

SIMON, Neil   [1927–]
American dramatist

Plays include:
Come Blow Your Horn (with his brother Danny; 1961), *Little Me* (book of the musical; 1962), *Barefoot In the Park* (1963), *The Odd Couple* (1965; revised, 1985), *Sweet Charity* (book of the musical; 1966), *The Star-Spangled Girl* (1966), *Plaza Suite* (1968), *Promises, Promises* (book of the musical; 1968), *The Last of the Red Hot Lovers* (1969), *The Gingerbread Lady* (1970), *The Prisoner of Second Avenue* (1971), *The Sunshine Boys* (1972), *The Good Doctor* (1973), *God's Favorite* (1974), *California Suite* (1976), *Chapter Two* (1977), *They're Playing Our Song* (1979), *I Ought To Be In Pictures* (1980), *Fools* (1981), *Brighton Beach Memoirs* (1983), *Biloxi Blues* (1985), *Broadway Bound* (1986), *Jake's Women* (1988), *Rumours* (1989), *Lost in Yonkers* (1991)

The most successful living American playwright, the New York-born Simon is also, unsurprisingly, the only living American playwright to have a Broadway theatre named after him. After beginning as a television sketch writer for Phil Silvers and, briefly, Tallulah Bankhead, Simon has written roughly one play or musical libretto a year since the early 1960s, and almost all have been commercial – if not critical – successes. (*The Good Doctor*, adapted from eleven ▷Chekhov tales, was the rare example of the opposite.) He is a screenwriter of distinction, with both original scripts and adaptations of his own plays. Steeped in snappy repartee and one-liners Simon has often been criticised for sacrificing psychological truth to the convenient punch line and glossing over difficult situations (alcoholism in *The Gingerbread Lady*, a widower's bereavement in *Chapter Two*) in time for a tidy final curtain. His recent autobiographical trilogy, spanning three alliteratively titled plays, has attempted to rectify that, but each has its soft and sentimental patches as well as, it should be said, its charms. Critics hailed *Lost in Yonkers* as Simon's deepest work, and it won the Pulitzer Prize for Drama as well as that year's Tony Award for best play.

Brighton Beach Memoirs
This is the play in which the old Neil Simon can be said to give way to the new, and the first in Simon's tripartite portrait of himself as a young man that also includes *Biloxi Blues* and *Broadway Bound*. 'The world doesn't survive without families,' announces Kate, the mother in the play, and Simon gives us an extended family of seven eking out a living in the Brighton Beach section of Brooklyn on the eve of World War II. Fifteen-year-old Eugene, a chirpy adolescent discovering baseball, girls and writing, is clearly Simon's alter ego, but more interesting are the adults – his mother, father, and spinsterish Aunt Blanche – all of whom are written in warm, rich hues. The play is undoubtedly cosy – Simon is not ▷Eugene O'Neill – but at its best it's an evocative memory play, as pleasing as a faded family snapshot you've had for years.

Try these:
▷Eugene O'Neill and ▷Tennessee Williams for earlier, harder-edged views of families, and ▷Arthur Miller's *Death of A Salesman* for the prototype of the father in *Brighton Beach*; ▷Wendy Wasserstein and Donald Margulies as younger Jewish humorists; ▷Alan Ayckbourn mostly for contrast; ▷Sharman Macdonald for scenes of adolescents growing up; ▷Marguerite Duras for plays about memory of a more elliptical kind; ▷Athol Fugard for the formation of the artist as a young man.

SIMON, N.F.
(Norman Frederick)   [1919–]
British dramatist

Plays include:
A Resounding Tinkle (1957), *The Hole* (1958), *One Way Pendulum* (1959), *The Cresta Run* (1965), *Was He Anyone?* (1972)

N.F. Simpson was first a bank clerk and then an English teacher in adult education; in 1957 he won third prize in *The Observer* playwriting competition with *A Resounding Tinkle*.

He has perhaps suffered from being over-analysed as an Absurd dramatist and classed as less 'serious' than ▷Ionesco; however, his plays are beginning to be revived (eg *One Way Pendulum* by Jonathan Miller at the Old Vic, 1988). His logical paradoxes and flow of verbal invention are ultimately more like ▷Gilbert and Lewis Carroll than ▷Ionesco. It is difficult to forget Arthur Groomkirby in *One Way Pendulum*, expounding his utterly convincing reasons for having to train these weighing machines to sing the Hallelujah Chorus so that he could take them to the North Pole and melt the ice around it, but it is probably a mistake to go through Simpson's work for profound thoughts about the desperation of the Human Condition.

Try these:
▷Ionesco for word-play and surreal situations; ▷Alfred Jarry and (more politically inclined) ▷Snoo Wilson for similar approaches to theatre.

SMITH, Dodie   [1895–1990]
British dramatist, novelist

Plays include:
Autumn Crocus (1931), *Service* (1932), *Bonnet over the Windmill* (1937), *Dear Octopus* (1938), *I Capture the Castle* (1954)

Dodie Smith is probably most remembered for her children's novels *A Hundred and One Dalmations* (later made into a Disney film) and *I Captured the Castle*, which was itself to become a stage play. Nonetheless, she was one of the most fashionable playwrights of her generation, and her influence still firmly hovers over the West End. Her first professionally produced play was *Autumn Crocus*, a Tyrolean romance, and her most successful was *Dear Octopus*. Described by Smith in her autobiography as 'a play of lamplight, candlelight, firelight, sunset deepening into twilight . . . a play of youth and age', the Octopus of the title is the family, brought together for a Golden Wedding celebration. Though now rarely peformed (*Dear Octopus* does sometimes surface) Dodie Smith's work typifies the notion of the 'well-made play' for the West End. Her plays are domestic, if sophisticated, comedies in three acts, delivered with a certain wit and charm. As the drama of the 1930s comes up for reassessment her work may well be due for a revival at any moment.

Try these:
For other 'well-made plays' ▷Lillian Hellman, ▷Terence Rattigan, ▷Galsworthy, ▷Alan Ayckbourn; her contemporaries include ▷J.B. Priestley; ▷Enid Bagnold and ▷N.C. Hunter for similar approaches.

SOBOL, Joshua (Yehoshua)   [1939–]
Israeli playwright

Plays include:
Soul of a Jew (Weininger's Night) (1982), *Ghetto* (1984), *Adam* (1988), *The Jerusalem Syndrome* (1988), *Underground* (1989), *Ghetto*, *Adam*, and *Underground* comprise his Ghetto Triptych

Born in Israel, Joshua Sobol was educated in Paris at the Sorbonne and began writing short stories before turning to the stage and television. He has been a playwright-in-residence and Co-Artistic Director of the Haifa Municipal Theatre and writes passionately and expansively on issues facing Israelis as Jews, reflecting the schizophrenia in the Israeli personality torn between the residual paranoia of the Holocaust and a macho belief in their own supremacy and power. Sobol's play *Soul of a Jew* deals with the final hours of Jewish philosopher Otto Weininger and his struggles with Zionism, anti-Semitism, and his Jewish identity. The title itself can be found in 'Hatikva,' the Israeli national anthem. Weininger ultimately commits suicide at age 23, unable to find a resolution of this conflict. As a result, *Soul of a Jew* was extremely controversial, and there were repeated, though unsuccessful, attempts to censor it. The play has received high praise, however, at the Edinburgh Festival, Washington, D.C.'s Kennedy Center, at the Chicago International Festival, and in New York City in 1988.

Sobol's most frequently-produced work is *Ghetto*, a drama about the theatre run by a company of actors in the Jewish ghetto in Vilna (now Vilnius, Lithuania) from Janauary 1942 until its liquidation by the Germans in September 1943. Using diaries, historical evidence, and actual accounts of the survivors, Sobol combines cabaret-style songs and satire to create a play-within-a-play depicting the daily struggle of the Jewish company to endure and survive in the ghetto. *Ghetto*, the first to be written in Sobol's 'Ghetto Tryptich,' has received critical acclaim worldwide, in productions in Berlin, London, Chicago, Washington, Los Angeles, New York, and even Vilna.

Sobol's 1988 play, *The Jerusalem Syndrome*, is perhaps better known for the political stir it caused than as a dramatic work. Written originally in 1987 but not produced until a year later, the play opened in Tel Aviv as part of Israel's 40th Anniversary celebration. Sobol clearly means to parallel the historic plight of Palestinians and Jews by juxtaposing a ragged group of actors dramatising the Jewish revolt against the Romans in 66 AD with today's Palestinians in the Occupied Territory. Disturbing to Israelis, it engendered a heated debate in the Knesset. The play was allowed to open, but its shocking scenes (including a Jewish soldier shooting a refugee woman) caused demonstrations, interrupted performances, and police arrests of nearly 150 people in the theatre. In Haifa, nearly 30,000 of the theatre's subscribers walked out. Under the pressure of censorship, both Sobol and Artistic Director Gedalia Besser were forced to resign.

Sobol has since completed his 'Ghetto Tryptich' with the plays *Adam* and *Underground*. The latter, focusing on the problems of a medical ward in the Vilna ghetto, was given its first European productions in Oslo, Bonn, and Wuperthal in 1989 and its first American production at the Yale Repertory Theatre in 1991 under the direction of Adrian Hall. Having progressed from a documentary-like style in his earlier works, Sobol now feels his work to be best described as 'expressionist.'

Try these:
▷Expressionism; for socially-concerned drama set in a backdrop of war or violence, see Sidney Kingsley's *Dead End*, and *The Patriots*, Robert Sherwood's *Abe Lincoln in Illinois*, and *There Shall Be No Night*, and Maxwell Anderson's *Winterset*; ▷O'-Casey's *The Silver Tassle*, *Oh What a Lovely War!*, C.P. Taylor's *Good* for disturbing visions of war; ▷Synge, ▷O'Casey, ▷Bond, Gogol for trouble with censors; Sobol had written one of the pieces in *Consequences*, a Foco Novo commission unstaged because of the company's demise, together with ▷Howard Brenton, ▷Nell Dunn, ▷Trevor Griffiths,

▷Tunde Ikoli, ▷Nigel Williams, ▷Snoo Williams, and ▷Olwen Wymark; David Lan translated The National Theatre's version of *Ghetto*; Jean-Claude Grumberg for a Parisian-based Jewish dramatist who has also written a trilogy based on some of his own war-time experiences.

SOPHOCLES [496–406 BC]
Greek dramatist

Surviving plays include:
Ajax (c 442), *Antigone* (c 441), *Oedipus the King* (c 429), *Philoctetes* (c 409), *Oedipus at Colonus* (406), *Women of Trachis* (date unknown), *Electra* (date unknown)

Sophocles is credited with the introduction of a third actor to Greek drama, thus widening the possibilities of the dramatic conflict; also with introducing those mysterious revolving scenic devices, the *periaktoi*. He is said to have won eighteen prizes at the Festival of Dionysus, and to have written over a hundred plays altogether. Aristotle based his account of tragedy in *The Poetics* on Sophocles, thus influencing his successors for centuries, and the British crime novelist Dorothy L. Sayers claimed him as the originator of the detective story. Freud's reading of the Oedipus story is central to the development of psychoanalysis.

The 1980s saw some extremely interesting adaptations of Sophocles' plays in the US. Often, his works were transferred not just to different historical epochs, but to different cultures.

Engendered by the *Oedipus* cycle is *Gospel at Colonus*, adapted and directed by ▷Lee Breuer, with music by Bob Telson. As described by Breuer, *Gospel* is an 'oratorio set in a black Pentecostal service, in which Greek myth replaces Bible story . . . sung, acted and preached by the characters of the 'play' – Preacher, Pastor, Evangelist – who take the roles of the oratorio – Oedipius, Theseus, Antigone.' *Gospel at Colonus* won an Obie award for Outstanding Musical for the 1983–4 season and after touring worldwide, moved to Broadway in 1988. Writing in *Newsweek* after the Broadway opening, Jack Kroll said, 'This is one of the most marvellous shows of the decade . . . a triumph of reconciliation, bringing back together black and white, pagan and Christian, ancient and modern in a sunburst of joy that seems to touch the secret heart of civilization itself.'

Alaska's Perseverance Theatre produced a

Thomas Derrah as Kittel, a young Nazi officer, Ford Rainey as Dr Gottlieb in Joshua Sobol's *Underground*, Yale Repertory Theatre, 1991

fascinating version of *Antigone*, set in the tiny Inuit fishing village of Toksook, on the west coast of that state. *Yup'ik Antigone* adapted and directed by Dave Hunsaker in 1984, consisted of a small cast of Inuit natives who performed in Yup'ik, a language that had never before been heard on mainland theatrical stages. The Greek choruses were replaced with Eskimo chant-songs, native dances, legends and creation myths. The stark production featured traditional masks, costumes made of animal skins and traditional sculptural elements. *Yup'ik Antigone* ran at La Mama in New York, among other mainland venues.

In 1986, Peter Sellars directed Robert Auletta's adaptation of *Ajax* for the short-lived American National Theatre in Washington DC and it later moved to the La Jolla Playhouse. Set at the Pentagon after a Latin American war, this version features Ajax as a renowned general who has gone mad after having been betrayed. The title role was played by Howie Seago, a leading actor from The National Theatre of the Deaf. In an interview with *Drama Logue* Sellars said, 'We see a hero who refuses to listen. Having passed a certain boundary of pride, he now cannot hear the voices who are desperate to save him. . . . Given a military and given a system of government, it's impossible to have them act morally, which brings us to the obvious question: when is something or someone heroic and when does it cross the line into immorality?'

In 1987, twenty-six years after its composition, the Ezra Pound and Rudd Fleming adaptation of *Elektra* had its world premier at New York's Classic Stage Company, under the direction of Carey Perloff. Set in a mental home, the production referred to the fact that Pound did this translation while interned at St. Elizabeth's, after having pleaded an insanity defense to the charge of treason. The production was generally praised for its clarity and intelligence. The cast featured Pamela Reed in the title role and Nancy Marchand as Klytemnestra. Pound's jazzy, gangster-film-like use of colloquial language – in which, for example, the letter 'g' is dropped from all gerunds, and 'ya' frequently replaces 'you' – nettled a number of critics who held that it cheapened the original and diluted theatrical intensity.

Oedipus the King

This story of the stranger who becomes King of Thebes by solving the riddle of the Sphinx and marrying the widow of the late king, only to find, after relentlessly interrogating one man after another, that the sins which have brought the plague to Thebes are his own, and that he has killed his own father and married his mother, has one of the most tightly knit and relentless plots in the history of drama. The power of the dialogue may be lost in translation, but the impeccable construction means that the play is effective in any language.

Try these:
▷Aristophanes, ▷Euripides, ▷Aeschylus and Menander for surviving Greek plays; ▷Berkoff and Tony Harrison for modern British versions of Greek subjects. ▷Anouilh for updating *Antigone* to deal with the theme of collaboration in war-time France, ▷Giraudoux for a version of *Electra*, ▷Cocteau and Nigerian Ola Rotimi for a version of the Oedipus story; the Living Theatre for an idiosyncratic use of the Antigone story; ▷Robert Wilson for a version of *Oedipus at Colonus*; Seamus Heaney's *The Cure at Troy* his plangent and moving plea for reconciliation (on the far side of revenge) in Northern Ireland is based on *Philoctetes*.

SOYINKA, Wole (Arkinwande Oluwole)   [1934–]
Nigerian dramatist, novelist, poet

Plays include:
The Swamp Dwellers (1958), *The Lion and the Jewel* (1959), *The Invention* (1959), *A Dance of the Forests* (1960), *The Trial of Brother Jero* (1960), *Camwood on the Leaves* (1960), *The Strong Breed* (1964), *Kongi's Harvest* (1964), *The Road* (1965), *Madmen and Specialists* (1970), *Jero's Metamorphosis* (1973), *The Bacchae: A Communion Rite* (from ▷Euripides; 1973), *Death and the King's Horseman* (1975)

Soyinka was born in Western Nigeria and studied at the Universities of Ibadan and Leeds. He spent several years after graduation in London, a period when he was closely associated with the Royal Court; between 1958 and 1959 he read plays for them. Soyinka became a member of the Writer's group led by William Gaskill and Keith Johnstone, and the Court put on the first production of a Soyinka play (*The Invention*)

(L–R) Mark Lutz and Howie Seago in Robert Auletta's adaptation of Sophocles' *Ajax*, directed by Peter Sellars, American National Theatre, 1986

in 1959 as a Sunday Night performance, directed by Soyinka himself.

Soyinka returned to Ibadan as a Research Fellow in Drama in 1960 and went on to become a powerful and influential figure in African theatre developing a dramatic voice which reflected Nigeria's recent political history in a voice influenced by both African culture and western literary traditions: as such, he was the founder of the 1960 Masks Theatre. But in 1967 he was arrested for alleged activities in support of Biafra by the Federal Government, and held as a political prisoner for two years. On his release, Soyinka became Director of the Drama School at the University of Ibadan, and later Research Professor. He has continued to work in Nigeria, although he has travelled internationally with his writing. *Madmen and Specialists* was first staged at The National Playwrights Conference at the Eugene O'Neill Theatre Center in the USA. In 1973 Soyinka was an Overseas Fellow at Churchill College, Cambridge, and in that year he wrote *Death and the King's Horseman*, probably his best-known play to date. Since 1975, he has been Professor of Comparative Literature at Ife. He was awarded the Nobel Prize for Literature in 1986.

Death and the King's Horseman

A powerful fable aimed at British colonialism, *Death and the King's Horseman* is based on an actual event that took place at Oyo in Nigeria in 1945 involving the interrupted ritual suicide of the King's Horseman. Nigerian custom dictated that a favoured servant should follow his master after his death. A British colonial officer however orders Jinadu, the Horseman, to be arrested and Jinadu's son, in the end, takes his own life. Employing dance, mime, music and folklore, it is a rich expression of Yoruban culture as much as it is engages with ideas of honour, leadership and colonial ignorance. Interestingly, the play was coolly received in Nigeria, respectfully in the UK (in the Royal Exchange's 1990 production) and with some enthusiasm in the US.

Try these:
▷Edward Bond, ▷Ann Jellicoe, ▷Arnold Wesker were also members of George Devine's Writer's group, set up at the Royal Court in 1958; Yemi Ajibade, another Nigerian playwright, whose *Fingers Only* is set in a small Nigerian town; ▷Maureen Duffy also draws on

▷Euripides' *The Bacchae* for her *Rites*; as does ▷Bryony Lavery for *Kitchen Matters*; Ola Rotimi's *The Gods Are Not to Blame* is a reworking of *Oedipus* in Yoruban terms.

SPENCER, David   [1958–   ]
British dramatist

Plays include:
Releevo (1987), *Space* (1987), *Blue Hearts* (1989), *Killing Cat* (1990)

One of the most promising of new playwrights to emerge in the late 1980s, Spencer's first play *Releevo*, won the 1986 Verity Bargate award and almost universal acclaim. A bleak and blistering account of a young working-class couple's marital break-up, it was the latest in a long line of wide-eyed, baleful chronicles of the nuclear family and its fall-out in the late 1980s. Subsequent plays have been no less uncompromising. All performed at the Soho Poly, which was responsible for bringing his plays to public prominence (he has also been writer in residence at the National Theatre under the Thames TV Bursary Scheme), his second play, *Space*, dealt with domestic violence and battered wives whilst *Killing the Cat* (another Verity Bargate winner) touched on alcoholism and incest (between father and daughter and brother and sister).

Described thus baldly, Spencer's plays may sound harrowing. Painful they certainly are but the plays are also shot through with compassion and a poetic realism that borders on despair. Written in a sparse but pungent Yorkshire dialect, the emotional violence his characters endure inspires a sense of sadness. By Spencer's own admission, his experience of theatre was minimal. Brought up in Halifax but now living in Germany, he trained as a scientist but became disillusioned with science's inability to explain things emotionally. To all intents and purposes, he is a graduate of adult education writing courses (at the City Lit in London where he took classes, in poetry, short story, and modern fiction), turning to plays because, he said, he liked to write in the first person but had problems with characters' interior thoughts. His scientific training has left him with a reductionist mind – 'Life's an expression of fundamental forces' and a deeply deterministic – some might say, pessimistic – outlook on human behaviour.

Space

Focussing on a young single parent mother, Pam, and her boyfriend Dean, *Space* is an attempt to look at the roots of violence and its impact on individuals. Pam has a young son, Kenny who is witness to scenes of violence between Pam and Dean. As with his later play, *Killing the Cat*, Spencer is concerned with the imprisonment of individuals by their past and by patterns of behaviour perpetuated through family ties – in *Space*, exacerbated by conditions of economic and spiritual impoverishment. Pam has already been a victim of violence, and the play suggests her gravitational pull towards that kind of behaviour again though there are also glimmers of awareness and hopes of change. In an interview, Spencer admitted it was his own reactions to violence, the potential for it in his own relationships that was one of the driving forces behind the play (he has also written a film script in Berlin with his girl friend, Sylvia Ludat, on a similar theme). *Space* was performed in a workshop presentation as part of a New York/Soho Poly play-reading exchange.

Try these:
▷Andrea Dunbar, ▷Ayshe Raif and ▷Julia Kearsley for domestic working-class ruptures; ▷David Storey for an older generation of northern family dramas; ▷Tony Marchant's *The Attraction* and ▷Terry Johnson's *Imagine Drowning* for other treatments of the roots of violence; ▷Nick Ward's *Apart from George* and ▷Michel Tremblay's *Bonjour, Bonjour* for hints of incest; for plays within a play (like *Killing the Cat*), see ▷Pirandello's *Six Characters in Search of an Author* and *Henry IV*, ▷Anouilh's *The Rehearsal*, and Tremblay's *The Real World*; for onstage presentation of a younger self, Marsha Norman's *Getting Out* and ▷Sarah Daniels' *Beside Herself* offer parallels with Spencer's *Killing the Cat*.

STANISLAVSKI, Konstantin
[1865–1938]
Russian director, actor, teacher

Writings include:
My Life in Art (1924), *An Actor Prepares* (1926) *Stanislavski Rehearses 'Othello'* (1948) *Building a Character* (1950)

Stanislavski is probably the most influential figure on performance and acting in Western theatre: his methods still form the basis of much British and American drama school training and his Moscow Arts Theatre has inspired the philosophies of many of the most important twentieth-century companies.

Stanislavski was born in Moscow and began in the theatre working with amateur companies. He was much influenced by the company formed by the Duke of Saxe-Meiningen, which is usually regarded as the first in which an ensemble of actors developed productions under the auspices of a director. As he says in *My Life in Art*: 'I was always looking for something new, both in the inner work of the actor, in the work of the producer and in the principles of stage production.' In 1897, he became the founder of the Moscow Arts Theatre with Vladimir Nemirovich-Danchenko, and developed his ideas with a regular company of actors. After their first tour to Germany, Stanislavski resolved to set down his findings about acting methods, and to construct a theory of dramatic technique. He felt that the principles of acting developed by actors, directors and teachers had never been organised, so he devised a 'system'. The Stanislavskian 'method' proposed training and rehearsal for the actor in which the actor 'became the part' and lived it not only on the stage, but in preparation for performance. The principle was that the actor should explore all aspects of the character, often through improvisation: his or her history, attitudes and way of behaving outside the frame and events of the play should be as much a part of the actor's knowledge as the lines and responses in the play. The aim was to acquire what Stanislavski termed 'inner realism', to 'be' rather than to 'do' a character. His system is based on two main parts; inner and outer work of actors on themselves and the inner and outer work of the actor on the part.

Unfortunately, only part of Stanislavski's theories was available in translation for many years and led to an over emphasis on the 'inner' element of the method. This accounts for some of the ways in which American interpretations of the Method differed from the Russian original. Stanislavski's was the informing principle of Lee Strasberg's enormously influential Actors' Studio, which trained such diverse performers as Marilyn Monroe, Shelley Winters and Marlon Brando. Strasberg taught a Method that put more emphasis on psychology and emotions than on the body and voice. It was this focus on the actor's own life that led Strasberg's rival, Stella Adler, to form her own studio, where she taught students to prize the play's world over their own psychic one. Adler, who studied with Stanislavski in 1934, had, like Strasberg, been a member of the Group Theatre before she started teaching. The Group, founded by her husband Harold Clurman, used Stanislavski's Moscow Arts Theatre as its model, and from 1931 to 1941 produced over twenty plays, among them works by the then-unknown ▷Clifford Odets. It also launched the careers of three actors who went on to be important teachers of the Method in their own right, Morris Carnovsky, Robert Lewis, and Sanford Meisner.

Try these:
Much of what ▷Brecht has to say about acting in *The Messingkauf Dialogues* is a direct rebuff to Stanislavskian methods; ▷Joan Littlewood was influenced by Stanislavski and by Brecht; see ▷Mike Leigh for the use of improvisation to create plays.

STOPPARD, Tom   [1937–]

Plays include:
A Walk on the Water (television 1963, staged 1964; revised as *The Preservation of George Riley*, 1964, and as *Enter a Free Man*, 1968) '*M' is for Moon Among Other Things* (1964), *The Dissolution of Dominic Boot* (1964, radio), *The Gamblers* (1965), *Rosencrantz and Guildenstern are Dead* (1966), *Albert's Bridge* (1967, radio), *The Real Inspector Hound* (1968), *If You're Glad I'll be Frank* (1969), *After Magritte* (1970), *Where are They Now?* (1970, radio), *Dogg's Our Pet* (1971), *Jumpers* (1972), *Artist Descending a Staircase* (1973, radio), *Travesties* (1974), *Dirty Linen* (1976), *New-foundland* (1976), *Every Good Boy Deserves Favour* (1977), *Night and Day* (1978), *Dogg's Hamlet, Cahoot's Macbeth* (1979), *The Real Thing* (1982), *Hapgood* (1988)

Stoppard is among the most fashionable of contemporary playwrights; 'Stoppardian' is now used as a term for the display of verbal wit and intellectual games. His work is always full of verbal fireworks, intellectual references and literary jokes. Most of his plays are constructed around elaborate conceits; *Jumpers* puts a philosophical discussion of logic together with a troupe of acrobats; *Every Good Boy Deserves Favour* has a full scale orchestra

on stage in a play about Soviet dissidents; *Hapgood*, relates the complexities of spying and double agents to nuclear physics. This method of highly improbable juxtaposition owes a lot to Surrealism, and, in *After Magritte*, Stoppard wrote a play around the elements of a Magritte painting (umbrellas, bowler hats, skies, etc) located in a suburban household.

Born in Czechoslovakia, Stoppard was brought up in Singapore, and moved to England in 1946. He began writing as a journalist in Bristol, and became involved in drama through his theatre reviewing. Very much influenced by ▷John Osborne's *Look Back in Anger*, and recognizing that in the late 1950s: 'The theatre was suddenly the place to be', he resigned his job and moved to London, in a period at which the new influences of European and Absurdist theatre were hitting the London stage. His first plays were written for radio and television, but it was *Rosencrantz and Guildenstern are Dead* which first brought him to attention. The play, a sideways look at *Hamlet* from the perspective of two minor characters, intercuts their discussions while off-stage in *Hamlet*, with scenes and events from ▷Shakespeare's play. First produced at the Edinburgh Festival, it was taken up by the National Theatre and staged in London to wide acclaim. In the 1970s, Stoppard was involved with Ed Berman and the Interaction Group, with whom he developed *Dogg's Our Pet*, and the West End success *Dirty Linen*. He is an accomplished adapter of Mrozek, ▷Schitzer, ▷Nestroy, ▷Molnar, and ▷Havel. His own more recent work has largely gone straight to the West End.

His television plays *Squaring the Circle* (about Solidarity and Lech Walesa) and *Professional Foul* are both set in Eastern Europe, and take up the questions of political dissidence under Communism which he raised in *Every Good Boy Deserves Favour*.

Travesties
Travesties is based on the actual historical oddity that Lenin, the Dadaist poet Tristan Tzara, and James Joyce must have been in Geneva in the same period. The events of the play and imagined meeting of the three are recounted by a minor British consular official whose major memory of the time is that he played a minor part in an amateur production of *The Importance of Being Earnest*. The three historical figures are thus cast into characters

from *The Importance of Being Earnest*, and their work and influence is intercut with scenes from Wilde's play. The comedy of *Travesties* does very much depend on the recognition of the literary references, audiences for the play tend to have an air of self-congratulation for getting the jokes, but it is (unlike some of Stoppard's other work) more than an exercise in displays of intellectual wit. It is too a poignant study of the self-aggrandisement of the consul, and a suggestive exploration of memory, and of versions of historical events.

Try these:
▷Ionesco for logic games; ▷Beckett's *Waiting for Godot* is drawn on heavily for *Rosencrantz and Guildenstern are Dead*; ▷Pirandello and ▷Ayckbourn for theatrical games; ▷David Pownall's *Master Class* for another look at Russian musical totalitarianism; ▷Eric Overmyer for another dramatist in love with language.

STOREY, David [1933–]
British dramatist, novelist

Plays include:
The Restoration of Arnold Middleton (1966), *In Celebration* (1969), *The Contractor* (1969), *Home* (1970), *The Changing Room* (1971), *Cromwell* (1973), *The Farm* (1973), *Life Class* (1974), *Mother's Day* (1976), *Sisters* (1978), *Early Days* (1980), *Phoenix* (1984), *The March on Russia* (1989/90)

Storey, the son of a Wakefield miner, is one of the generation of Northern working-class writers who emerged into what was known at the time as the second wave of new dramatists (following the first wave of the *Look Back in Anger* generation). Storey was trained at Wakefield School of Art, and later at the Slade (an experience he draws on in his play *Life Class*). He then worked at a number of jobs, including a stint as a professional rugby league player (an experience reflected in *This Sporting Life* and *The Changing Room*). He began writing as a novelist with *This Sporting Life*, (his sixth novel *Saville*, won the Booker Prize), and went on to become one of the most commercially successful of the Royal Court 'house writers' winning numerous awards including the New York Drama Critics Awards for *The Contractor*, *Home*, and *The Changing Room*. Storey is perhaps the best known exponent of contemporary slice of life kind of drama. Several of his plays are concerned with men at work and a recurrent device is the progression of work in real time over the course of the play: the building of a tent in *The Contractor*, or a rugby match (with complete team) in *The Changing Room*.

Storey's first play, *The Restoration of Arnold Middleton* written in 1958, was disinterred for production by Lindsay Anderson during the filming of *This Sporting Life* in 1960. According to Storey, the play was not even typed at that point.

At the Royal Court, the professional partnership between Anderson and Storey was confirmed with the production of *In Celebration*. Anderson went on to direct *The Contractor*, *Home* and *The Changing Room* at the Court, and all transferred to the West End.

Home is in fact an atypical Storey play in that its setting is far from concrete – merely four chairs and a table and an encounter between four elderly people. Neither this nor the dialogue give many clues as to the context; according to John Gielgud (whose first appearance at the Royal Court was in this play) the text intrigued 'but somewhat mystified me'. Storey has said 'Halfway through the writing I discovered it was taking place in a lunatic asylum'. More in keeping with the usual Storey style was *In Celebration*, a searching essay on traditional family relationships, set in a northern mining family, and following the return home of three sons for their parents' 40th wedding anniversary. A grim exercise in fraternal truth-telling, more skeletons ooze from the cupboard in Storey's later sequel, *The March on Russia* in which the same couple, the Pasmores, are once more the focus, this time on their 60th anniversary. Again directed by Lindsay Anderson, this elegy for the post-war British working class – one which seems to speak of their displacement and spiritual vacuum despite material benefits – is proof, for some, of Storey at his vintage best. For others, it seemed like a voice from another age, now gone.

Try these:
▷David Mercer whose career followed a similar trajectory and who also trained at the Wakefield Art School; ▷David Williamson's *The Club*, ▷John Godber's *Up'N'Under* and ▷Louise Page's *Golden Girls* for the sporting life; ▷Harold Pinter's *No Man's Land*; ▷Edgar White's *The*

Bootdance is set in a mental hospital; ▷Dürrenmatt's *The Physicists*, ▷Peter Weiss' *Marat/Sade*.

STRAUSS, Botho   [1945–]

German dramatist, poet, novelist, translator, drama critic

Plays include:
(*The Hypochondriacs*; 1972), (*Familiar Faces*), (*Great and Small* or *Big and Little*; 1978), *The Park* (1983), *Tourist Guide* (1986).

Strauss is one of Germany's most prodigiously talented men-of-letters. A contemporary of film-maker Rainer Werner Fassbinder, and Austrian playwright Peter Handke, his disenchantment with modern society and anti-naturalistic style seem to have frequently been misunderstood in Britain (though in Germany, he is hailed as a considerable talent, not least for the work he has done as adaptor/translator with the Schaubühne's director Peter Stein). In Britain, *Great and Small*, the story of Lotte, the rejected wife turned baglady who embarks on an epic and losing battle for love and affection, *Tourist Guide*, a re-working of timeless themes about intellect versus feeling, and the destructive power of erotic love, and *The Park*, *A Midsummer Night's Dream* misanthropically updated, and adventurously staged by Sheffield's Crucible theatre in February 1988, have been greeted with less than general enthusiasm. (A plan to produce them at The Old Vic during Jonathan Miller's directorship, and aborted by David Mirrisch The Old Vic's owner led to Miller's ultimate resignation.) Perhaps the German sensibility does not travel well, or something has been lost in translation. Either way, Strauss remains an elusive, potent European voice railing against contemporary urban society and its selfish materialism.

Try these:
For another image of the female encountering society, ▷Timberlake Wertenbaker's *The Grace of Mary Traverse*; ▷Strindberg's *Miss Julie* and ▷Sam Shepard's *Fool For Love* for other themes of erotic love; ▷Willy Russell's *Educating Rita* for passion and intellect; for bleakness, ▷Beckett, and urban bleakness, see Gregory Motton.

STRINDBERG, August   [1849–1912]

Swedish dramatist, novelist, poet, essayist

Plays include:
Hermione (1869), *The Travels of Lucky Per* (1882), *The Father* (1887), *Miss Julie* (1888), *Creditors* (1888), *To Damascus* (trilogy; 1898–1901) *The Stronger* (1890) *Playing with Fire* (1892), *Advent* (1898), *Gustaf Vasa* (1899), *Erik XIV* (1899), *Easter* (1900), *The Dance of Death* (1900). *A Dream Play* (1902), *Swan White* (1902), *The Ghost Sonata* (1907) *The Storm* (1907), *The Burnt Lot* (1907)

Strindberg's dramatic imagination is immensely powerful. Although his plays variously comprise historical drama, fairy tale, fantasy and symbolism he is most associated with a claustrophobic world of embittered relationships, repressions and embattled psyches. His plays' preoccupations with sexuality, irrationality and with the family as a site of struggle can make them seem like dramatisations of Freud's case studies.

Born in Stockholm, Strindberg studied medicine and worked as an actor, a journalist and a librarian. His three marriages all ended in divorce, and he held a great bitterness towards women which he explores over and over again in his plays. Throughout his life Strindberg was beset by periods of insanity (he would probably now have been diagnosed a manic depressive), an experience he wrote about in his painful autobiography, *A Madman's Defence*.

His first plays were historical dramas and rural fairy tales, both preoccupations he explored throughout his writing life. His historical plays, however, take their events as dramatic frames from which to draw metaphors which explore issues of power. In 1882 the fairy play *The Travels of Lucky Per* moved him towards an exploration of fantasy.

Strindberg was much influenced by Zola's espousal of a 'naturalism' in art. *The Father*, *Miss Julie*, *Creditors* and *The Stronger*, all plays which explore sexuality and power, through a struggle of wills, are a significant part of the naturalist enterprise, although Strindberg has his own particular version of naturalism, which edges very close to symbolism; the plays are full of symbolic images and props, their situations fraught with symbolic resonance.

In *The Stronger*, two women confront one another, but only one speaks, with the growing realisation that the woman she is addressing is the source of her own husband's infidelity. The 'psycho-dramas' of this period developed into full scale fantasy plays in Strindberg's late work. *A Dream Play* and *The Road to Damascus* eschew any attempt at realism, in order to explore a form in which, in Strindberg's words: 'imagination spins and weaves new patterns: a mixture of memories, experiences, unfettered fancies, absurdities and improvisation'.

Although Strindberg has often been cast as a virulent misogynist (and his writings are indeed full of scathing accounts of women), he is so obsessed with questions of power and gender that his plays are very open to feminist readings.

Miss Julie

An extraordinary play about power, sex and class set on a Midsummer's Eve in the kitchen of a nobleman's house. As the evening winds on, the daughter of the house Julie seduces the man-servant Jean, and they resolve to run away together. The play charts the shifts in their power relations. Julie begins with all the cards because of her social position, but once she has given herself sexually, she is lost and her class power means nothing in the face of Jean's sexual power. She appeals to Jean, who urges her to kill herself and the play ends with Julie leaving the stage, with the clear intent of suicide. Jean is left to face the class power of Julie's father. According to Strindberg, the play conformed to his development of new forms, in its pattern of 'three art-forms', 'the monologue, the mime and the ballet'. The ballet occurs at the moment of the consummation: a group of peasants sing a Midsummer's Eve drinking song, and point up the class positions that are being negotiated in the offstage bedroom. Jean's fiancée, the servant Kristin, opens the play with a mime of her domestic duties, in which the class difference with Julie is established.

Try these:
The Wanderings of Lucky Per echoes ▷Ibsen's *Peer Gynt*; ▷G.B. Shaw was much affected by Strindberg's new 'theatre of ideas', cross-class sexual attraction is a mainspring of *Arms and the Man*; ▷Genet is among the writers to have exploited the form of dream and fantasy drama that Strindberg forged and both ▷Expressionism and ▷Theatre of the Absurd can be seen as owing a great deal to Strindberg; ▷Shakespeare's *A*

Midsummer Night's Dream also deals with Midsummer sexual attraction; ▷Botho Strauss' *The Tourist Guide* is a bleak modern meditation on the destructiveness of obsessive sexual attraction; Fassbinder's *The Bitter Tears of Petra von Kant*, is in the tradition of Strindberg's obsession with power games in sexual attraction.

SYNGE, J.M.
(John Millington)   [1871–1909]
Irish dramatist

Plays include:
In the Shadow of the Glen (1903), *Riders to the Sea* (1904), *The Well of the Saints* (1905), *The Playboy of the Western World* (1907), *The Tinker's Wedding* (1909), *Deidre of the Sorrows* (1910)

Synge played a significant part in the creation of the Abbey Theatre with ▷Yeats and ▷Lady Gregory, both as manager and as dramatist. His plays are centred on the life and beliefs of Irish peasant communities in the west and in the Aran Islands, which he visited on ▷Yeats' advice, but there is also a strong underpinning from Christian and Classical sources. Synge's most famous play is *The Playboy of the Western World*, partly because of the riots associated with its first production but mainly because of its assured handling of its tragi-comic theme. The contrast between 'a gallous story and a dirty deed' lies at the heart of the different reactions to Christy's two apparent parricides, one safely performed far away and glamorised in the telling, the other done in full view of the community, both on stage and in the audience. With the loss of Christy, Pegeen Mike is left to the humdrum spirit-sapping of her previous existence and our responses are divided: Christy and his father are reconciled and Christy has matured, which suggests comedy; Pegeen Mike is left trapped and aware of her loss, which suggest self-knowledge purchased at almost tragic cost.

Try these:
▷Mustapha Matura's *Playboy of the West Indies* is a sparkling adaptation of the play to the Caribbean; ▷Sean O'Casey's dramatisation of the urban Irish in *The Plough and the Stars* also caused a riot at the

Abbey Theatre; *Playboy* is a comic reworking of the Oedipus story, as is ▷Edward Bond's *Saved*; the Orcadian George Mackay Brown's *The Stormwatchers* is reminiscent in tone and subject matter of *Riders to the Sea*; ▷Caryl Churchill's *Fen* includes a version of the story that provides the plot of *The Shadow of the Glen*; ▷Christina Reid's *Joyriders* opens with the joyriders watching a scene from *The Shadow of the Glen* and then develops the parallels further.

t

TALLY, Ted [1952–]
American dramatist

Plays include:
Terra Nova (1977), *Night Mail and Other Sketches* (1977), *Word of Mouth* (1978), *Hooters* (1978), *Coming Attractions* (1980), *Little Footsteps* (1986)

A Yale graduate who has, in turn, taught playwriting at the Yale Drama School, Tally made his reputation early on with *Terra Nova*, a fascinating historically-based drama which seems to bear little thematic or stylistic relation to his subsequent works. Set in 1911–12, the play tells the true story of Englishman Robert Scott's race to the Antarctic against Roald Amundsen, the Norwegian. But the play charts more a metaphysical than a physical contest, as Tally displays an unusual historical and temporal breadth. Few people would associate that play with the author of *Hooters*, a four-character comedy about sexual competition on a Cape Cod beach, distinguished by repeated use of the defamatory 'jerkwad!' Most recently, Tally has turned to contemporary satire on society (*Coming Attractions* strikes out at media manipulation) and the family and (the targets in *Little Footsteps* are domestic). While both plays are deftly written, each seems a bit *easy*, and one wishes Tally a return to the challenges he earlier posed himself.

Try these:
▷Jules Feiffer as an elder statesman satirist, and Jonathan Reynolds, James Lapine and ▷Christopher Durang as a newer breed working in the same bright, deliberately comic book-like style; ▷Terence Rattigan's *Ross* (about T. E. Lawrence) and *Bequest to the Nation* (Nelson and Lady Hamilton) and ▷Howard Brenton's *Scott of the Antarctic* are other plays about 'heroes'; ▷Barry Collins' *The Ice Chimney* for its climbing anti-hero, Maurice Wilson.

TAYLOR, C.P. (Cecil) [1929–1981]
British dramatist

Plays include:
Allergy (1966), *Bread and Butter* (1966), *Lies About Vietnam* (1969), *The Black and White Minstrels* (1972), *You Are My Heart's Delight* (1973), *Gynt* (1973), *Schippel* (1974; from Sternheim; later known as *The Plumber's Progress*), *Bandits* (1976), *Walter* (1977), *Ophelia* (1977), *Some Enchanted Evening* (1977), *Peter Pan and Emily* (1977), *And a Nightingale Sang* (1978), *Withdrawal Symptoms* (1978), *Peter Pan Man* (1979; originally as *Cleverness of Us*, 1971), *Bring Me Sunshine, Bring Me Smiles* (1980; as *The Saints Go Marching In*), *Good* (1981)

Taylor's premature death only months after the initial success of the ▷RSC production of *Good*, robbed the British theatre of an extraordinarily versatile and talented dramatist who had been grossly undervalued in his lifetime. Born in Glasgow, but long time resident in the Northeast, Taylor wrote some fifty plays for virtually every type of theatre – from the local village to the West End, via ▷community theatre, television and the ▷RSC. Much of his work, from his first play to his last, included music, and his wry imagination and capacity for what ▷Brecht called 'complex seeing' is exemplified in *Ophelia*, which is *Hamlet* from Ophelia's viewpoint, or *Withdrawal Symptoms* which parallels its heroine's drug withdrawal treatment with the pangs of withdrawal from empire. ▷J. M. Barrie was the inspiration for *Peter Pan Man* and *Peter Pan and Emily* in which Peter Pan becomes involved with a Newcastle working-class family. It is typical of the paradoxical nature of Taylor's career, and of the split in theatre-going audiences, that the majority of those who went to see Harry Secombe in the retitled *The Plumber's Progress* and the majority of those who went to see *Good* would have been extremely unlikely to recognise him as the author of both plays.

Good

Taylor's last play was notable for its willingness to confront the banality of evil in its study of its protagonist's gradual drift into Nazism through all the daily minor compromises, adjustments and accommodations which take him from being an emotional advocate of euthanasia in his fiction to advising on giving the Final Solution a caring façade. We can see the terrible seductive power of Nazism as something which offers the protagonist (given a fine performance by Alan Howard in the original RSC production) the possibility of a fixed position in a sea of moral uncertainties and doubts. The idea that public postures have the configuration of private derangements achieves a memorable form: throughout the play he is haunted by snatches of music, so that the discovery that the prisoners' band which greets him at Auschwitz is real represents his complete surrender to the inverted logic of the Third Reich.

Try these:
▷Peter Nichols' *Poppy* covers similar imperial ground to *Withdrawal Symptoms*, but more noisily and with less certainty of tone; ▷David Pownall's *Master Class* and ▷Tom Stoppard's *Every Good Boy Deserves Favour* also examine the relationship between totalitarianism and music; ▷Peter Barnes' *Laughter* is another Auschwitz 'comedy'; *And a Nightingale Sang* covers similar war-time working-class territory to ▷Stephen Lowe's *Touched*; ▷David Edgar's *Destiny* is another study of fascism, British style; Julia Pascal's *Theresa* for Nazi collaboration in Britain.

TAYLOR, Tom   [1817–80]
British dramatist

Plays include:
Masks and Faces (1852; with Charles Reade), *To Oblige Benson* (1854), *Still Waters Run Deep* (1855), *Our American Cousin* (1858), *The Overland Route* (1860), *The Ticket-of-Leave Man* (1863), *New Men and Old Acres* (1869)

Taylor was a Professor of English at London University, a civil servant and, in later years, editor of *Punch*. He wrote over seventy plays, few of which are now performed. *Our American Cousin* and its star part, Lord Dundreary, might be worth reviving, but the unfortunate connection with President Lincoln probably still militates against it.

The Ticket-of-Leave Man

Although *The Ticket-of-Leave Man* is by no means the best of Victorian melodramas (why doesn't someone revive Henry Arthur Jones' *The Silver King*?), it is for some reason the most frequently performed on the London stage. This is possibly because of its apparent social message about the problems of the rehabilitation of a man with a prison record, although the issue is completely fudged because our hero did not commit the crime in the first place. There is some unusual interest in the fact that the villain has the same problem, but the real attraction is Hawkshaw, the detective, and his mastery of disguise.

Try these:
▷Boucicault, for nineteenth-century melodrama; ▷John Galsworthy's *Justice*, for a more realistic picture of the effects of prison.

TERRY, Megan   [1932–]
American, writer, director, teacher

Plays include:
Calm Down Mother (1964), *Hothouse* (1964; produced 1974), *Ex-Miss Copper Queen on a Set of Pills* (1964), *Comings and Goings* (1966), *Viet Rock* (1966), *The Gloaming, Oh My Darling* (1966), *Nightwalk* (1973; with ▷Sam Shepard and ▷Jean-Claude van Itallie), *Approaching Simone* (1974), *Hothouse* (1974), *Babes in the Bighouse* (1974), *Brazil Fado* (1977), *American Kings English for Queens* (1978), *Attempted Rescue on Avenue B* (1979), *Amtrak* (1988); collaborations with Jo Ann Schmidman: *X-rayed late* (1984), *Sea of Forms* (1987), *Walking Through Walls* (1987), *Babies Unchained* (1989)

Hailed by American critic Helene Keyssar as the 'mother of American feminist drama', Terry, who has written over sixty plays, deserves greater recognition in Britain and the USA. One of the major contributors to Joe

Chaikin's Open Theatre in the late 1960s and early 1970s, she made her name with the American public with the now famous anti-war *Viet Rock* (the *first* rock musical), in a double bill with Open Theatre colleague ▷Jean Claude van Itallie's *America Hurrah*. The production made history, partly because of its anti-war stance, but also for the style of its presentation, which built on Chaikin's improvisational group work and Terry's favoured 'transformation' techniques – a way of looking at women's lives and theatre technique that informs much of her work.

Her concerns have ranged over a wide spectrum of issues covering sexism, violence, the materialism of American society, and political confusion, but the excitement of her work has been both in her gestural use of language and in the physical and theatrical immediacy of her *mise-en-scène*: sudden Brechtian changes of tempo; visual metaphors; satiric parodies culled from popular culture; lots of music (again often satirising familiar cultural references); gender swapping (in *Babes in the Bighouse* and in *Viet Rock* Terry used male actors to interpret females roles and vice versa).

Since 1970, she has been writer-in-residence at the Omaha Magic Theatre in Nebraska with Jo Ann Schmidman, the company's founder. The two collaborate on at least one musical a year, usually more. One work every year deals with a theme of particular import locally, for which the artists do research in the community. While deeply rooted in Nebraska, Omaha Magic tours its productions regionally and nationally.

For some enterprising women's theatre group a revival of any of Terry's works, such as *Babes in the Bighouse*, about women in prison (one of the big successes at OMT), or the equally challenging *Approaching Simone* (about the remarkable life of French philosopher Simone Weil who committed suicide by starving herself to death), might pay exhilarating dividends.

Try these:
▷Caryl Churchill's *Cloud Nine*, ▷Susan Yankowitz's *Slaughterhouse* for gender-bending; Clean Break for other images of women in prison; ▷Pam Gems' *Dusa, Fish, Stas and Vi*, ▷Maureen Duffy's *Rites* for collections of women; for American anti-war images, Emily Mann's *Still Life*, James Duff's *The War At Home*, the

Vietnam Vets Ensemble's *Tracers*; for searing poetic language, feminist politics, and inventive production concepts, ▷Ntozake Shange and Karen Malpede.

TERSON, Peter   [1932–]
British dramatist

Plays include:
The Mighty Reservoy (1964), *Zigger Zagger* (1967), *Mooney and His Caravans* (1968; TV version 1966), *The Apprentices* (1968), *Spring-heeled Jack* (1970), *The 1861 Whitby Lifeboat Disaster* (1971), *But Fred, Freud is Dead* (1972), *Cul de Sac* (1978), *Strippers* (1984)

A working-class Geordie, Terson trained as a teacher after National Service and taught games for ten years, while collecting rejection slips for his early plays. In 1964 *A Night to Make the Angels Weep* began a close association with Peter Cheesman and his Stoke Victoria Theatre-in-the-round. Since then his output has been prolific (sixteen plays for Stoke alone in the following ten years) for both theatre and television. Equally at home with a two-hander, such as *Mooney and His Caravans* or *The Mighty Reservoy*, and the large casts of the National Youth Theatre, for whom he has written extensively, his plays often show an allegorical opposition of traditional or rural life and 'progress', but his greatest characteristic is the fluency of his dialogue and his ear for working-class speech. In his plays for the National Youth Theatre Terson has shown the ability to respond to ideas and individual talents coming from the company to rapidly create new material. His earliest plays, set in the Vale of Evesham, where he then lived, all have an air of menace. *The Mighty Reservoy* charts the relationship of the keeper of a new reservoir and a more educated, town-bred visitor who is drowned in Act Three but whose spirit apparently returns to warn the drunken keeper of a crack in the reservoir. The reservoir becomes a dark obsession for the characters and several critics have described their relationship with it as 'Lawrencian'. Many later plays reflect the style developed at Stoke for local documentary drama, including narration and rapid changes of locale. *Strippers*, a provocative examination of the downside of Thatcherism which shows working-class women taking to stripping as a response to the economic collapse of the North East, raises as many questions about the way to present female exploitation as it answers about sexism and male double standards.

Zigger Zagger

His first play for the National Youth Theatre, *Zigger Zagger* brought both Terson and the NYT to public notice and is still his best known work. A football crowd on the terraces surrounds the action played out before it of the dead-end prospects of a football-mad teenager. Naturalistic scenes are framed by songs and interjections from the terraces but these reinforce the overall content rather than providing a Brechtian alienation, though the criticism of a society which presents such no-hope prospects is implicit. Full of vitality, it eschews any false sentiment and is as objectively critical of working-class parents and soccer stars as it is of probation officers and the establishment.

Try these:
▷David Rudkin, especially in *Afore Night Come*, has also recorded the brooding menace behind the tranquility of rural Worcestershire; ▷John Byrne's *The Slab Boys* follows the problems of the developing adolescent in a tale about apprentices; ▷Barry Reckord's *Skyvers* for educational critique; ▷Kay Adshead, in *Thatcher's Women*, and Julia Schofield, in *Love On the Plastic*, also investigated the relationship between Thatcherism, unemployment in the North, and the sexual exploitation of women; ▷Debbie Horsfield for a football trilogy based around four female football fans; Robert Ardley for aquatic ghosts.

TESICH, Steve   [1942–]
American dramatist, screenwriter

Plays include:
The Carpenters (1970), *One on One* (1971), *Lake of the Woods* (1971), *Baba Goya* (1973; later revised and staged as *Nourish the Beast*), *Gorky* (1975), *The Passing Game* (1977), *King of Hearts* (1977, author of book for musical), *Touching Bottom* (1978, comprised of 3 one acts, *The Road*, *A Life*, *Baptismal*), *Division Street* (1980), *The Speed of Darkness* (1988), *Square One* (1990), *Commencement Exercises* (1991)

Although Steve Tesich is best known as a screenwriter, his roots are in the theatre, and it remains his chief focus and interest. Born Stoyan Tesich in Yugoslavia, the playwright arrived in America at the age of fourteen with little English and an immigrant's objectivity. In his plays and films, Tesich captures with lifesize characters the hopes and disappointments of the 'American Dream'. *The Carpenters* concerns a radical son whose plan to kill his working-class father receive a twist of fate when he is unexpectedly killed by his father. In plays like *One on One*, which focuses on racial tension, Tesich uses music, black humour, and purposeful exaggeration; in both *The Carpenters* and *Lake of the Woods* the dramatic action is built on conflict, whereas his later plays evolve from character.

In these later plays, like *Baba Goya*, Tesich uses the family as a special symbol of America, a warm and convincing portrait of hope filled with humour and compassion. An idealistic streak runs throughout these works, which seem to remind people that they are better 'deep down' than they seem. *Speed of Darkness* focuses on family of a different sort: two Vietnam veterans who share a dark secret as they meet again in South Dakota twenty years after their service. Tesich's first play in almost a decade, it is a stylistic departure, one that probes more realistically in the style of ▷Arthur Miller or ▷Robert Anderson. The play's two antagonists are direct opposites as characters, one a seemingly-successful businessman, the other a menacing drifter. Tesich now has lost his immigrant's idealism; he strongly criticizes America's involvement in Vietnam. His disillusion is continued in *Square One*, which presents almost-soulless characters who meet, marry, breed, and part. These cold characters exhibit Tesich's mourning for 'a time when people cared and felt.'

Despite his emphasis on screenwriting in the 1980s, Tesich adamantly maintains his loyalty to the theatre, noting, 'Once you write for the stage, you never give it up, no matter what else you do.' His next play, *Commencement Exercises*, is scheduled for the Goodman Theatre in Chicago in 1991.

Try these:
▷Arthur Miller's *All My Sons* (1947) and *American Clock* (1979), ▷Trevor Griffiths's *Sam Sam* for their use of family to make a political statement; ▷Frank Galati's 1989 adaptation of *The Grapes of*

Wrath by John Steinbeck for a similar sense of a strong, core family and its personal battles fought against a backdrop of troubled American landscape; ▷Emily Mann's *Still Life* for another Vietnam play.

THEATRE FOR YOUNG PEOPLE IN BRITAIN

Several unhelpful spectres haunt the world of theatre for younger audiences: a chronic lack of resources, a long-established assumption that young people need theatre solely at Christmas-time, and low status within the profession – all adding up to playwright David Wood's bitter though pithy comment of its being seen as the home of 'beginners, cranks and failures'.

But despite all that, there have been signal developments in post-war years. Frequently these have been due to the work of committed individuals who have determinedly swum against the tide: Caryl Jenner, for instance, who, in 1947, packed her Unicorn Theatre Company into the back of a van and set out to tour professional theatre for young people nationally; Brian Way who, in 1953, took the equally visionary step of taking the new Theatre Centre and quality professional theatre into schools.

Both ventures have thrived. The Unicorn – settled since 1967 in the Arts Theatre near Leicester Square – produces regular seasons of adventurous work. Determined to buck the trend that saw young people as less important theatre-goers, it has commissioned and mounted work by mainstream writers like Ted Hughes, Roald Dahl, Ken Campbell, James Thurber, Joan Aitken and many more. But it has, as importantly, helped to develop younger writers like Charles Way, Penny Casdagli and Lisa Evans whose 1988 play *The Red Chair*, set in revolutionary China, brought the Unicorn its second annual award from Drama Magazine.

Theatre Centre has also matured. It is now part of a widespread Theatre-in Education movement that has been responsible for some of the most exciting theatrical work of the last twenty years. TiE work has a distinctive flavour. Traditionally it has dealt with issues – ecological disaster in David Holman's *Drink the Mercury* for Merseyside Young People's Theatre; Britain's imperialist past and its contemporary effects in Leeds TiE's *Raj* (devised by the company); AIDS and homophilia in Noel Greig's stunning *Whispers in the Dark* for Theatre Centre. The work is stylistically inventive. Peripatetic, needing to adapt itself to varying school spaces and audiences, it has acquired a flexible character. Doubled-up roles (often across gender and racial lines) and the creative use of minimal sets and props have forced audiences to use their imaginations. They have also, it could be argued, taken theatre back to the urgency of living roots.

TiE has not been the only aspect exploring new territory. Excellent small touring companies like Pop-Up Theatre and Oily Cart have sketched out their own area. One of the most consistently interesting, Quicksilver, has produced a series of vivid and sturdy pieces that, like *Mr Biff the Boxer* and *Beulah's Box* combine cheerful inventiveness with underlying humanity. Polka Theatre, the only other venue beside the Unicorn specifically for young audiences, opened its doors in Wimbledon in 1980. A remarkably pretty theatre, it has the gilded decorated feel of a fairground. Since Vicki Ireland became its director in 1988, it has concentrated on finding a style that could go beyond text, incorporating elements of visual and physical theatre as well as music.

The scope today of theatre for younger audiences is wider than it has ever been. Large-scale touring productions, like those of Whirligig and Vanessa Ford, have toured elaborate if traditional, adaptations of well-known classics like Dahl's *Charlie and the Chocolate Factory* and C.S. Lewis's Narnia books. Establishment theatres like the Royal National Theatre and Royal Shakespeare Company have directly addressed younger audiences with wonderfully staged productions of *The Wind in the Willows* and *The Wizard of Oz*; at a lower profile, the National has started sessions specially designed for under 5s, following in the pioneering footsteps of the Children's Theatre Association. Direct involvement with theatre is also strong, with the growing network of youth theatre companies.

The growth is tentative and not always consistent in quality. It suffers from a low profile, existing away from the main critical arena. It is now also threatened by recession-based cutbacks that have seen a diminution in arts going into schools, the closure of companies like York Young Peoples Theatre and the shutting up of small-space studios in many regional reps.

Try these:
David Holman, David Wood, Penny Casdagli, Nona Shepphard for British playwrights of children's work; see also ▷Theatre for Young People in the USA.

THEATRE FOR YOUNG PEOPLE IN THE USA

Theatre for young people in the United States most often manifests itself through adaptations of classic children's literature and fairy tales such as *Jack and the Beanstalk*, *The Wind in the Willows* and *Cinderella*. However, in the last ten to fifteen years, theatre professionals have been inspired to create plays and performance pieces for young people that deal with provocative contemporary issues – war, urban violence, the plight of the homeless and AIDS. University theatre programmes have started to offer graduate degrees specifically for those who want to work in theatre for young audiences. Part of this growth may be attributable to national organisations such as the American Alliance for Theater and Education which publishes *Youth Theater Journal*. Unfortunately, this publication and its competitors – *Dramatics* and *Plays: The Drama Magazine for Young People* – often focus on conventional plays, seemingly unaware of the more innovative work taking place.

Theatre for young people is usually directed toward two different age groups: the pre-high-school set and the turbulent teenage years. Some of the theatres which have managed to avoid condescending to young people are ensemble groups that incorporate other mediums. The Paper Bag Players, for example, imagine their bodies as life-size puppets, trees, books and rocks to stage (among other things) an adaptation of Benjamin Britten's *Noye's Fludde*, and a Kabuki play called *A Box of Tears*.

There are a few large not-for-profit theatres scattered across the USA whose programming is predominantly, if not exclusively, geared toward young audiences. Seattle Children's Theatre has produced plays by Israel Horovitz and adapted Judy Blume for the stage. In 1987 they mounted a version of the cartoon *Rocky and Bullwinkle*, as well as an adaptation of ▷Molière's *The Would-be Gentleman*. The Children's Theatre Company, based in Minneapolis, with an annual budget of well over three million dollars and over 80 full-time staff members, produces adaptations of classics like *Tom Sawyer*, and new work such as *The Children of Belfast*, a sentimental melodrama set in Northern Ireland. The Honolulu Theatre for Youth produces standard children's fare like *Charlotte's Web*, but explores the Pacific Rim cultures with original shows like *Maui the Trickster* (1988) and *Song for the Navigator* (1985). Other similar institutions include Theatre IV in Virginia, Stage One: Louisville Children's Theatre in Kentucky, and TheatreWorks/USA, based in New York City. Theatres such as the Center for the Puppetry Arts in Atlanta and the National Theatre for the Deaf in Connecticut perform their own brands of theatre for an audience in large part composed of young people.

Other theatre groups perform mostly improvisational or community-based work. The Living Stage Theater, an offshoot of Washington DC's Arena Stage, is an ensemble that creates pieces that encourage the participation of their audiences, giving voice to the concerns of young people who don't usually see theatre: underprivileged, Spanish-speaking, deaf and physically handicapped children. In 1987 for example, Living Stage produced and toured *Images*, a play about a boy with cerebral palsy meeting the challenge of living in a non-disabled society. In Chicago, the Free Street Theater does only community-based work, such as their 1989 piece *Project!*. Sponsored by the Chicago Housing Authority, the work was set in Chicago's disastrous Cabrini Green housing project and dealt with gangs, urban violence and teenage sexuality in an aggressive rap style. *Project!* was eventually made into a television special.

Cornerstone Theater, founded by an itinerant group of Harvard graduates, creates original adaptations of classics in small towns across the USA, often corralling members of each community into collaborating on the performances. They created a production of *Romeo and Juliet* in a Mississippi town and set the action in the high school. Local teens, drawn from the black and white populations, portrayed members of the Montague and Capulet 'gangs', thereby working through their feelings of racism with ▷Shakespeare's help. Director/writer Peter Brosius, an artistic associate at the Mark Taper Forum in Los Angeles, has received critical acclaim for his work with young audiences. His plays, for both the pre-teen and high-school sets, have dealt with divorce, sexual pressures, race relations and death. *A Family Album* (1986) explores how fantasy can be a refuge from reality's problems, while *School Talk* is a frenetic but tough examination of teenagers' lives, staged in LA-area high schools.

In New York, Theatre for a New Audience, with an outreach program to 5,000 public school students, insists that the quality of its productions appeal to both adults and youth. The company backs up its pledge by hiring such innovative directors as Julie Taymor and Bill Alexander to stage its Shakespeare offerings.

Unfortunately, such examples are exceptions to the rule – most often young people's theatre is given minority status, both by theatre professionals (the pay scale for young people's contracts is often less than that for a comparably sized 'adult' theatre) and by audiences at large. Until American theatre artists take theatre for young people more seriously, the medium will continue to fight a losing battle against television, film and MTV for the audiences of the future.

Try these:
▷Theatre for Young People in Britain; ▷Ann Jellicoe; ▷Community Theatre; ▷Ann Devlin and ▷Christine Reid for Irish plays.

THEATRE-IN-THE-ROUND

This is the name given to a performance when the acting area occupies a central position with audience on all sides of it. An alternative name is arena theatre, or arena staging, though confusingly this has been used to describe a stage which projects into the audience and is only partly surrounded by them, as in John English's Arena Theatre Company, which pioneered this kind of staging in Britain in the 1940s. (Zelda Fichandler continued the tradition in the USA with the founding of her Washington DC-based theatre Arena Stage.)

▷Artaud was already proposing this kind of theatre in the 1920s (though his work was not published until 1938) and by the mid-1930s 'in-the-round' was already one of the audience-actor configurations being used by the Realistic Theatre in Moscow.

In Britain the development of this form of staging owed much to Stephen Joseph, who first created a temporary theatre in one of London University's halls of residence and then made a permanent base in Scarborough in 1956, where the theatre is now named after him. The Victoria Theatre, Stoke-on-Trent, and the Royal Exchange, Manchester, are major British theatres-in-the-round, but many studio theatres, such as the ▷National Theatre's Cottesloe and the RSC's Pit are sometimes used in this form. In most cases the seating rises in banks above the stage level so that everyone can see well.

In the USA, the Arena Stage in Washington DC, founded by Zelda Fichandler in 1950, is, along with Circle-in-the-Square in New York, the best example of theatres that regularly stage plays-in-the-round. For years, many audiences could have the in-the-round experience when touring companies would perform in large tents, taking their example from one-ring circuses.

Settings for in-the-round productions are not necessarily circular in shape and are carefully designed to create an appropriate atmosphere and indication of location without obscuring the view of any section of the audience; appropriate furniture can often make important points. However, this does not preclude spectacle – as in productions such as *Moby Dick* at Manchester, where the rigging and deck of Ahab's ship were transformed into the heaving body of the whale. The smaller theatres, with only two or three rows of seating, create what Glen Hughes called a feeling of 'being *in* the play' (this is particularly true of Sam Walters' small but beautiful Grange Tree Theatre at Richmond), and although this may not be so strong in a larger auditorium the focus of concentration of the audience around the acting space greatly increases the link between actor and audience. In the early days of the form, directors often kept the action irritatingly fluid so that no part of the audience saw an actor's back for long. With confidence, it was realised that this was not necessary and, with the exception of minute and subtle gestures that can only be seen from one side, there is no need for special echoing or duplication. Audiences take in the whole scene and learn through body language and reactions from other characters, even when they cannot see a face. When it is essential that a single actor address the whole audience, positions outside the central area at the head of gangways can be usefully dominant.

Anyone who has never been to a performance where they can see other members of the audience across the stage may take a few minutes to adjust to the situation, but most people find an in-the-round performance more involving than one on a proscenium stage. Since the audience sits on all sides there are no 'best seats', though people may have preferences as to whether they like to sit right next to the acting space or further back.

THOMAS, Dylan [1914–1953]
Welsh poet

Drama:
A Child's Christmas in Wales (1950), *Under Milk Wood* (1954)

Anglo-Welsh poet Dylan Thomas was born in Swansea, and wrote his poetry while living precariously at Laugharne and in London, earning money from articles, broadcasts and film scripts, and eventually from lecture tours in the USA, on one of which he died.

Under Milk Wood is probably the most famous radio play in English (well, Anglo-Welsh), but it has very little plot and very little conflict. It is more of a descriptive piece, opulently written and often very funny, about the inhabitants of Llareggub, that Platonic ideal of a Welsh coastal village, read by two narrators and a series of actors, mostly in monologue. It is more often staged in the USA than Britain where it is generally thought of as better heard than seen. Brian Abbott's *Milk Wood Blues*, at the Lyric Hammersmith in 1987, featured Thomas losing the original manuscript of *Under Milk Wood* on a Soho pub crawl (with interventions from Douglas Cleverdon and from Big Bill Broonzy and his guitar), but tended to become just an ingenious *Portrait of the Artist as a Drunken Poet*.

Try these:
▷Artaud, whose life has also become mythical and a matter for plays; ▷Emlyn Williams, *The Druid's Rest*, for another relentlessly picturesque view of the Welsh; Edgar Lee Master; ▷Thornton Wilder's *Our Town* does the same for middle America; ▷Jim Cartwright's *Road*, has been called a 'radicalised *Under Milk Wood* for the 1980s'; Edward Kamau

Braithwaite's *Mother Poem,* presented by Temba, is a Barbadian equivalent; for other ways of using monologues, see ▷Michel Tremblay.

THRILLERS
Excitement is an essential element of theatre, and the thriller genre exploits the excitement of suspense and our pleasure at being vicariously frightened; often, but not always, thrillers involve a murder story. The Elizabethan *Arden of Faversham* or ▷Webster's *Duchess of Malfi* certainly have plent of suspense and capacity to frighten an audience, and a line of development can be traced through crime melodramas and the French 'Grand Guignol' plays, but the modern notion of a thriller has become inextricably linked with that of the detective novel. This does not make every detective story a thriller – the crime or attempted crime will almost certainly be murder, and the circumstances that either the murder is still to be committed or further murders are to be expected. The audience may already know the murderer's identity while the characters are ignorant of the danger of their situation – the suspense lies in whether they will find out in time to be able to outwit him or her.

Wilkie Collins (1824–89) can be called the inventor of the modern crime novel, and he also wrote his own dramatic version of *The Moonstone* and *The Woman in White*. Thereafter thrillers became a popular form in the twentieth-century theatre, especially between the wars. Edgar Wallace (1875–1932) had a long run of successes with thrillers such as *The Ringer, The Case of the Frightened Lady*, and *On the Spot* (the last responded well to revival in the West End in 1984, with Simon Callow in the Charles Laughton role). Other plays from this period that are frequently revived include Patrick Hamilton's *Rope* (1929) and *Gaslight* (1939), and ▷Emlyn William's *Night Must Fall* (1935). After the thirties ▷Agatha Christie came to dominate the genre; her plays have run in the West End for the last fifty years – *The Mousetrap* never stops running – and her detective stories steadily continue to be adapted for the stage and television.

The thriller, however, does not currently seem to be doing quite so well in commercial terms as the farce. Rupert Holmes' *Accomplice* was a recent Broadway failure. However clever their plots, the social background to some pre-war plays may seem alien to modern audiences, who respond happily to parodies on the form such as ▷Tom Stoppard's *The Real Inspector Hound* and ▷Anthony Shaffer's *Sleuth*. The comedy thriller, such as Joseph Kesselring's *Arsenic and Old Lace*, is perhaps an easier subject for revival.

TOURNEUR, Cyril   [c 1575–1626]
English Renaissance dramatist

Plays include:
The Revenger's Tragedy (1606; attributed to Tourneur 1656), *The Atheist's Tragedy* (1610)

There is now considerable scholarly doubt about the 1656 attribution of *The Revenger's Tragedy* to Tourneur, with ▷Middleton being the favoured alternative author, in which case Tourneur becomes even more of a shadowy figure. He was in the service of the Cecil family and died after being put ashore from a returning naval expedition to Cadiz. To add posthumous insult to injury, the manuscript of another play was lost in the eighteenth century, when it was used by a cook, apparently to line a pie dish, a fate it shared with a number of other unique manuscripts. *The Atheist's Tragedy* has been described as 'hilarious', particularly in view of the fact that the protagonist D'Amville has to accidentally brain himself as he attempts to execute the hero; it is not likely to become a staple of the contemporary theatre, although its stylistic diversity and changes of mood might be successfully tackled by an adventurous company. *The Revenger's Tragedy*, authorship controversy notwithstanding, has had several productions in Britain and America since 1965 when it was revived professionally at the Pitlochry festival. The most memorable production was Trevor Nunn's 1966 ▷RSC revival which made Alan Howard a star and gave full weight to the play's satirical theatricality. Most of the conventional elements of revenge tragedy are here: the long delayed revenge, rape, the skull of a dead woman used to poison the man responsible for her death, incest and the culminating masque which leads to multiple deaths. But there is also a strong sense both of the corruption of the world of *Realpolitik* and of the corruption of the revenger who has to move in that world to achieve revenge.

Try these:
Most Renaissance dramatists used revenge plots and malcontent figures – ▷Shakespeare's *Hamlet* is the most famous example of both, but ▷Kyd's *The Spanish Tragedy* started the vogue for revenge and there are notable examples in ▷Chapman, ▷Ford, ▷Marston, ▷Middleton, ▷Shakespeare (*Titus Andronicus*) and ▷Webster; amongst contemporary dramatists ▷Peter Barnes has a gift for the wittily macabre that recalls Tourneur.

TOWNSEND, Sue   [1946–]
British dramatist and novelist

Plays include:
Womberang (1979), *The Ghost of Daniel Lambert* (1981), *Dayroom* (1981), *Bazaar and Rummage* (1983), *Captain Christmas and the Evil Adults* (1982), *Groping For Words* (revised as *Are You Sitting Comfortably*; 1983), *The Great Celestial Cow* (1984), *The Secret Diary of Adrian Mole aged 13³/4* (1984)

The phenomenal success of her best-known creation, Adrian Mole, has tended to overshadow the fact that Townsend, suburban lower middle-class mother of four, ex-hot-dog stall and garage forecourt manager, youth club worker and one-time Thames television writer-in-residence at Leicester's Phoenix Theatre, has more than schoolboy strings to her bow.

Townsend writes with a droll, down-to-earth kind of humour that now and again takes on a surreal and surprisingly angry edge – as in *Womberang*, a comic-vitriolic swipe at the bureaucratic inadequacies of the National Health Service set in the normally stock situation of a hospital waiting-room, with its wonderfully vituperative working-class rebel, Rita Onions. *Groping for Words* also sets up the unprepossessing sit-com of an evening class in adult literacy, but turns it, with warmth and humanity, into quite a grim political warning about the link between illiteracy, frustration and the pent-up anger of society's underclass. *The Great Celestial Cow*, a fantasy-carnival for Joint Stock based on Townsend's observations of the Asian community in her home town of Leicester, and intended to break down the stereotype of the 'passive' Asian woman, unfortunately was too broad for some, and ended up inadvertently reinforcing the images it was supposed to be cracking. *The Secret Diary of Adrian Mole aged 13³/₄* (which started out life as an unsolicited radio script, then became a best-selling book before becoming a musical and a television series) and its sequel *The Growing Pains of Adrian Mole* will probably remain Townsend's enduring legacy. Of Mole, her spotty adolescent who turns his consistently cool eye on the antics of adult passion, Townsend wrote, somewhat prophetically: 'I wanted to put down what it was like for a certain type of person in 1981 – a class of person that's now deserting the Labour Party – and get it all down in detail because things are changing.'

Try these:
For school-oriented views of adolescence ▷Mary O'Malley's *Once a Catholic* and Denise Deegan's *Daisy Pulls It Off;* ▷Harwant Bains' *The Fighting Kite* explores a young man's dual identity as a British Asian; few plays have advanced the disjunction of the Asian woman from her roots, but ▷Hanif Kureishi's *Borderline* covers some of the ground and ▷Jacqui Shapiro's monologue, *One of Us*, comes even closer; for contrasting hospital images, ▷Louise Page's *Tissue* and ▷Tony Marchant's *Raspberry;* ▷Peter Nichols' *The National Health* for a much more expanded and satirical account of the NHS; ▷Asian Theatre.

TRAVERS, Ben   [1886–1980]
British novelist and dramatist

Plays include:
The Dippers (1922), *The Three Graces* (1924), *A Cuckoo in the Nest* (1925), *Rookery Nook* (1926), *Thark* (1927), *Mischief* (1928), *Plunder* (1928), *A Cup of Kindness* (1929), *A Night Like This* (1930), *Turkey Time* (1931), *Dirty Work* (1932), *A Bit of a Test* (1933), *Chastity, My Brother* (1936), *O Mistress Mine* (1936), *Banana Ridge* (1938), *Spotted Dick* (1940), *She Follows Me About* (1945), *Outrageous Fortune* (1947), *Runaway Victory* (1949), *Wild Horses* (1952), *Corkers End* (1968), *The Bed Before Yesterday* (1975)

Travers' first plays were adaptations of his own novels but from 1925–1933 he became the 'house dramatist' for the Aldwych Theatre, London, with a succession of meticulously constructed farces written to exploit the talents of actor-manager Tom Walls (hero), Ralph Lynn (hero's friend), Robertson Hare (hen-pecked husband), Winifred Shotter (heroine) and Mary Brough (Amazonian female). Creating vehicles for the same team does make his characters somewhat predictable, but his plots are inventive, within the basic requirements of farce. Travers himself considered ▷Feydeau's type of farce far too mechanical and that everything should be absolutely true to life – though today it now seems a rather stylised 1930s kind of reality! His farces preserve the proprieties and restore the status quo – though, as in *Plunder* for instance, that may include an acceptance of corruption and duplicity. Their tension comes from fear of scandal and the conflict between the outbreak of sexuality and its suppression. On the page they present numerous appalling bad jokes, puns and non-sequiturs which can only be hilarious if played with conviction and precise timing.

In his last play, *The Bed Before Yesterday*, liberated from the Lord Chamberlain's censoring hand, he made explicit what had previously had to be conveyed implicity. A prude, put off sex by her first bridal night and having survived two marriages without it, finds herself an impoverished widower to marry for company. Intrigued by hearing other women describe sexual passion she then demands it – and gets totally turned on! Though a relatively slight piece, it encapsulates a whole cycle of sexual experience from puritan rejection, through intrigue, experiment, awakening and infidelity, to final conjugal conviviality – and presents it from the woman's point of view.

Try these:
▷Feydeau and ▷Labiche as the acknowledged masters of French farce; English farce is itself the subject of ▷Michael Frayn's *Noises Off;* ▷Joe Orton's *Loot* and *What the Butler Saw* owe much to Travers; Ray Cooney is the contemporary master of English ▷farce.

TREMBLAY, Michel   [1942–   ]
French Canadian dramatist

Plays include:
Le Train (*The Train;* 1964); *Les belles-soeurs* (*The Sisters-in-law;* 1965); *La Duchesse de Langeais* (*The Duchess of Langeais;* 1969), *A Toi pour toujours, ta Marie-Lou* (*Forever*

Yours, Marie-Lou; 1971), *Hosanna* (1973), *Hello, là, bonjour*, or *Bonjour, Bonjour* (*Hello, There, Hello*; 1974), *Sainte Carmen de la Main* (*Carmen of the Boulevards*; 1976), *Damneé Manon, Sacrée Sandra* (*Sandra/Manon*; 1977), *L'Impromptu d'Outremont* (*The Impromptu of Outremont*; 1980), *Les anciennes odeurs* (*Remember Me*; 1981), *Albertine in Five Times* (1984), *Le Vrai Monde?* (*The Real World*; 1986), *La Maison Suspendue* (1990)

French Canadian Michel Tremblay is by now one of Canada's most exportable assets as well as one of its most acclaimed sons at home. A prolific novelist as well as playwright, he was brought up in a working-class family in Montreal's impoverished East End, a fact which reflects itself over and over again in his plays. Reminiscent of ▷Tennessee Williams in his domestic and female obsessions (not surprisingly Tremblay has translated several plays of Williams), Tremblay's heightened, voluptuous prose style, absorption with guilt, sexual fantasy and homosexuality also recalls ▷Jean Genet and at his best is as exciting, though without the misogyny. A taut two-hander about ecstasy, sacred and profane, *Sandra/Manon* is the last in a cycle of plays developed from *The Sisters-in-law* dealing with three sisters: Marie Lou in *Forever Yours, Marie-Lou* (considered Tremblay's masterpiece); her older sister Carmen in *Saint Carmen of the Boulevards*, and finally the younger sister Manon.

Of the other, more recent plays, *Albertine in Five Times* continues Tremblay's exploration of women and their lives, being a lyrical, multifaceted view of a mother, ageing from thirty to seventy (and played by five different actesses, at least in the British version). Somewhat deterministic in its never-ending cycle of woes, it is nonetheless a sensitive representation of the lives of Montreal working-class women, even if its static monologue structure seems more appropriate to radio than stage – a fault that could certainly not be laid at the door of Sandra/Manon, which, adventurously, played with notions of gender and fantasy to thrilling effect. *The Real World*, by contrast, a fairly self-conscious 'making-of-the-artist-as-a-young-man', with its seething resentments and claustrophobic family discord (a familiar Tremblay theme, particularly emphasised in the earlier play, *Bonjour, Bonjour*), strikes a more naturalistic note even whilst seeming to experiment with

notions of reality and fantasy by repeating scenes through the eyes of different members of the family.

Try these:
Monologues have become a popular technique in modern naturalistic drama – ▷Jim Cartwright's *Road*, ▷Clare McIntyre's *Low Level Panic*, ▷Nick Ward's *Apart from George* are among recent plays which have utilised it effectively to express internalised thoughts; Robert Patrick's *Kennedy's Children* also uses monologues in a multi-faceted way; ▷Shakespeare got there sooner, of course, and his soliloquies in such plays as *Richard III*, *Hamlet*, *Macbeth* are the perfect vehicle for contrasting the levels of action – the inner thoughts of the protagonist and what is going on, on-stage; for three sisters, ▷Shakespeare's *King Lear* and ▷Chekhov's *Three Sisters*; for an alternative feminist version, *Lear's Daughters* by Elaine Feinstein; see Neil Simon, Hugh Leonard for other artists-in-the making, for claustrophobic households, try Lilian Hellman, Wendy Kesselman;s *My Sister in this House* David Storey and Ayckbourn for British equivalents.

TRIANA, José   [1933–]
Cuban dramatist

Plays include:
El Major General, (*The Major General*; 1956), *Medea En El Espaio*, (*Medea in the Mirror*; 1960), *El Parque de la Fraternidad*, (*Fraternity Park*; 1961), *La Casa Ariendo*, (*The Burning House*; 1962), *La Muerte del Neque*, (*The Death of Neque*; 1963), *La Noche de los Asesinos* (produced as *The Criminals* in London in 1967), *Worlds Apart* (1986)

A Cuban playwright who has lived in Paris since 1979, José Triana is known in Britain for two plays – *The Criminals* and *Worlds Apart* – produced by the ▷RSC over a twenty-year period. An impressionistic drama about three children who may or may not have murdered their parents *The Criminals* was the first Cuban play to be seen in Britain, and its raw, violent mix of reality and fantasy shocked some observers; others took its ▷Genet-like theatrics metaphorically, drawing an implicit analogy between familial oppression and that of the state. In *Worlds Apart*, set in Cuba between 1894 and 1913, a sprawling family saga unfolds against the background of political upheaval. With his interest in incident-filled family yarns told in a discursive, dream-like fashion, Triana recalls great Latin American novelists like Marquez and Borges more than his playwriting peers, although the sagas can get bogged down in *Dallas*-style soap operatics at the expense of dramatic finesse.

Try these:
▷Genet, ▷Lorca, and (more recently) ▷Wendy Kesselman's *My Sister In this House* for often violent enactments of social ritual, both in and outside the family; ▷Eduardo Machado and Maria Irene Fornes for Cuban-born playwrights with dream-like lyricism. ▷Jack Gelber's *The Cuban Thing* and ▷Howard Sackler's *Goodbye, Fidel* for American treatments of a country in tumult.

TURGENEV, Ivan Sergeivich

[1818–83]
Russian anarchist and dramatist

Plays include:
The Bachelor (1849), *A Poor Gentleman* (1851), *A Month in the Country* (written 1850; performed 1872)

Born the son of an impoverished nobleman in Orel, central Russia, Turgenev is one of the great nineteenth-century masters of psychological realism, on a par with Flaubert and George Eliot, and the pre-eminent forebear of ▷Chekhov, who would further refine Turgenev's incisive sense of character. He travelled extensively through Europe, befriending many of the leading writers of his time. Turgenev's own stage reputation rests on *A Month in the Country*, a romantic drama about an idle provincial wife who falls in love with her son's tutor. George F. Walker's adaptation of his novel *Fathers and Sons* has had many productions in the USA. ▷Brian Friel's adaptation of the same novel has been less successful in Britain.

A Month in the Country
One of the most frequently revived Russian plays after the work of ▷Chekhov, this play bears many similarities to that other master playwright. The story of the indolent Natalya's infatuation with her son's tutor, the play is also – like *The Cherry Orchard* – a portrait of a shifting society, emblematised both in the Trofimov-like tutor, Belyaev (a spiritual cousin to the celebrated nihilist, Bazarov, in *Fathers and Sons*), and in Natalya's Lopakhin-like husband, Islayev, with his triple interest in the forces of progress, mechanisation, and the psychology of the workers. A languid witness to romantic evasions in which she participates and a world in flux in which she does not, Natalya herself recalls Yelyena from *Uncle Vanya*, and the play has proven a fine showcase for both Ingrid Bergman in London and Tammy Grimes in New York.

Try these:
▷Chekhov and ▷Gorki for later Russian playwrights who offer both acute insights into character and varying degrees of political comment on Russian society on the eve of change; ▷Goldoni's *Villeggiatura* trilogy, ▷Peter Shaffer's *Five Finger Exercise*, and (for a musical bent) Stephen Sondheim's *A Little Night Music* for comparable depictions of romantic goings-on in a country setting; ▷Arthur Miller for fathers and sons.

 **u**

UHRY, Alfred [1937–]
American lyricist and dramatist

Plays include:

Here's Where I Belong book for musical; 1968), *The Robber Bridegroom* (book for musical; 1978), *Swing* (book for musical; 1980), *America's Sweetheart* (book for musical; 1985), *Driving Miss Daisy* (1987)

Born in Atlanta, Alfred Uhry began his theatrical career as a lyricist, first attracting notice with *The Robber Bridegroom*, a collaboration with composer Robert Waldman. Inspired by a 1942 novella by the Southern writer Eudora Welty, a demure, faintly gothic tale about a thief who robs people with a much good-humoured zest as he courts their affection and love, the musical was a big success when it moved to Broadway, where it established the career of its star, Barry Bostwick. It didn't earn Uhry himself nearly so much praise as did his first play, *Driving Miss Daisy*. The off-Broadway theatre Playwrights Horizons first produced it in 1987, and the play made such an impact that it quickly spawned touring companies to Chicago and London. After winning the Pulitzer Prize in 1988 it became one of the most produced plays of the American regional theatre.

A small play, acutely observed and restrained, *Driving Miss Daisy* spans twenty-five years in the life of a widowed Jewish woman in Atlanta, starting the year she acquiesces to her son's demand that she hire a chauffeur. The new employee, a black man named Hoke, at first finds himself unwelcome and uncomfortable around the brittle Daisy: she won't have anyone pointing out to her that she's no longer as able and independent as she once was. Before long, however, Daisy finds herself cherishing Hoke's off-hand wit and warm attentiveness, and they stay together as car models change, their eyesight deteriorates, and racial politics starts to intrude upon their idyll.

Some have rightly faulted Uhry for predictability and gratuitous references to the civil rights movement, but (remarkably, given its premise) this is not a sentimental play. Uhry is sure about what to put in and leave out in the pair's conversations, where to end scenes before they start to cloy, how long to make his play. And it doesn't seem so mechanical in performance, where fine actors can bring spontaneity and add to its charms. That seemed to be the consensus, at least, of the movie industry, which heaped praise (and Oscars) on Uhry's film version (after initially keeping their distance when it was proposed) and especially on its two stars, Jessica Tandy (who won an Oscar) and Morgan Freeman. (Freeman, along with Dana Ivey, performed in the stage version.)

Try these:
▷Tennessee Williams and ▷Beth Henley for plays infused with the atmosphere of the American South, which share some of Uhry's lyricism; ▷Athol Fugard, who dramatises the friction between blacks and whites in a contrasting way; other writers associated with Playwrights Horizons (▷Ted Tally, ▷Christopher Durang, ▷A.R. Gurney, jr) for a sense of the range of the theatre that first produced *Driving Miss Daisy*.

V

VANBRUGH, John [1664–1726]

English dramatist, soldier and architect

Plays include:
The Relapse (1696), *The Provoked Wife* (1697)

Vanbrugh's adventurous life included several spells as a soldier, a stay in the Bastille after being arrested in France as a spy, an attempt at theatrical mangagement, and designing Blenheim Palace. He also found time to adapt plays from the French (including several by ▷Molière) and finished two of his own. *The Relapse* takes over the characters from Colley Cibber's *Love's Last Shift* and deploys them in a complicated intrigue plot involving town/country contrasts, secret marriages, impersonation and mistaken identity. Although the continued success of both plays probably owes as much to their farcical elements (the humiliation of and satire at the expense of the aptly named Lord Foppington in *The Relapse* and the transvestite antics of Sir John Brute in *The Provoked Wife*), perhaps their most interesting feature is the presentation of unhappily married couples in which the faithful wife resists the temptations of a potential lover. In a period when divorce was practically non-existent Vanbrugh's refusal to adopt the mix-and-match 'happy' ending solution favoured by some of his contemporaries leaves his comedies curiously unresolved. There is an open ended realism about his endings which suggests that they are resting points rather than conclusions. In the first version of *The Provoked Wife* Sir John wore a clerical costume rather than women's clothing for his drunken frolics; the scenes were probably altered in response to complaints about their disrespect to religion, but they are more thematically appropriate in their revised form.

Try these:
Vanbrugh's comedies can be compared instructively with those of the other writers of Restoration comedy, ▷Aphra Behn, ▷Congreve, ▷Etherege, ▷Farquhar, ▷Otway and ▷Wycherley and with later exponents of comedy of manners such as ▷Goldsmith, ▷Sheridan, ▷Oscar Wilde, ▷Noël Coward, ▷Neil Simon; ▷Doug Lucie; ▷Alan Ayckbourn's pictures of marriage are reminiscent in some ways of Vanbrugh; ▷Pinero's *The Magistrate* offers another pillar of society in court as a result of drunken misdeeds.

VAN ITALLIE, Jean-Claude [1936–]

Belgian-born American dramatist

Plays include:
War (1963), *Almost Like Being* (1964), *I'm Really Here* (1964), *The Hunter and the Bird* (1964), *Where Is De Queen* (1965), *Motel* (1965), *Interview* (1966), *America Hurrah* (1966), *The Girl and the Soldier* (1967), *The Serpent: A Ceremony* (1968), *Take A Deep Breath* (1969), *Photographs: Mary and Howard* (1969), *Eat Cake* (1971), *The King of the* ▷*United States* (1973), *Nightwalk* (with ▷Megan Terry and ▷Sam Shepard; 1973), *A Fable* (1975), *Bag Lady* (1979), *The Tibetan Book of the Dead* (1983), *The Traveller* (1987) *Ancient Boys* (1991).

Jean-Claude van Itallie was a central figure in the off-Broadway explosion of the 1960s. As a writer for the Open Theatre in New York City he structured his plays around the company's actor-centred improvisational work while infusing them with social and political awareness. His 1966 trilogy of social alienation, *America Hurrah*, is still considered one of the key works of the decade. Van Itallie is better known of late for his ▷Chekhov translations, notably his version of *The Cherry Orchard* which was used in Andrei Serban's celebrated

1977 production at New York's Lincoln Center. Elsewhere, Van Itallie has experimented with breaking down the expected form and structure of drama, eschewing conventions of plot in favour of archetypal situations (the story of the Garden of Eden and temptation in *The Serpent*) or anarchic satire (*Eat Cake*, a brief but telling assault on American consumerism). Recently, his original works have become more pedestrian. His 45-minute monologue *Bag Lady* never gets inside its peripatetic character's head, and *The Traveller* (first seen at the Mark Taper Forum in Los Angeles and later in a revised version at the Haymarket Theatre in Leicester), based on the stroke and aphasia of his friend and former colleague Joseph Chaikin, too often sacrifices hoped-for lyricism to obvious dramaturgy. In *Ancient Boys*, Van Itallie's most recent work, a theatre designer discovers he has AIDS, prompting an exploration of individual and planetary disease, and the hope of salvation through art.

Try these:
▷Megan Terry and ▷Sam Shepard for playwrights influenced by Joseph Chaikin's Open Theatre; Susan Yankowitz, another Chaikin devotee, wrote *Night Sky*, inspired by her mentor's aphasia as well. ▷Lorca and ▷Wole Soyinka for emphasis on theatre as ritual; Rochelle Owens's *Futz* for a seminal American play of the 1960s along the lines of *America Hurrah*; ▷De Filippo's *Ducking Out*, ▷Julia Kearsley's *Under the Web* and ▷Arthur Kopit's *Wings* for plays featuring stroke victims; ▷Larry Kramer's *Normal Heart*, William Hoffman's *As Is*, ▷Harry Kondoleon's *Zero Positive* for plays about AIDS.

VINAVER, Michael   [1927–]
French dramatist and novelist

Plays include:
Aujourd'hui ou Les Coréens (*The Koreans*, 1956), *Iphigénie Hotel* (1960), *Par-dessus bord* (*Overboard*; 1972), *Les Travaux et les Jours* (*A Smile on the End of the Line*; 1979), *Chamber Theatre* consists of

Dissident, il va sans dire – *Dissident, Goes Without Saying* – and *Nina, c'est autre chose* – *Nina, It's Different* 1978)

Michel Vinaver (whose real name is Michel Grinberg) is one of the most important contemporary French playwrights. He began as a novelist, but has concentrated on plays since 1955, except for a long gap in the 1960s when his work for the Gillette company came first (they never seem to have found out about his second life, and their reactions to his unflattering pictures of international companies are not recorded). His first play *The Koreans* was put on by Roger Planchon in 1956, and shows alternately a group of French soldiers and some Korean villagers, with the events of the war reported and distanced; his second, *Iphigénie Hotel*, similarly shows the coming to power of de Gaulle unreliably transmitted by radio to a group of tourists cut off in a hotel in Mycenae. Planchon also put on *Overboard*, his first play after the twelve-year gap, an epic treatment of the fortunes of a toilet roll company, shown from multiple viewpoints, with hilarious juxtaposing of various styles of discourse. Vinaver is now a full-time playwright, and his later plays like *A Smile On the End of the line*, set in the Customer Service Department of a small, traditional firm whose staff are about to be replaced by computer technology tend to show the lives and work of ordinary people, often employed in a big company, with the main events that affect them happening off stage. His plays are neither didactic nor naturalistic. The seemingly banal snatches of dialogue overlap and fragment, and the complex interweaving becomes clearer in performance than on the page. He says he regards theatre as 'a way of making the familiar very strange'.

Try these:
See ▷Kroetz for the 'théâtre du quotidien' (theatre of everyday life), but his political commitment is more overt; Vaclar Havel's Vanek plays and Alexandr Gellman's *We the Undersigned*, and *A Man with Connections* also focus on working lives, though with different emphases; Jerry Sterner's financial comedy, *Other People's Money* concerns a traditional firm on the brink of take-over.

W

WACKLER, Rebecca   [1949–   ]
American dramatist

Plays include:
Tent Meeting (with ▷Levi Lee and ▷Larry Larson; 1983), *Nicholas De Beaubien's The Hunchback of Notre Dame* (with Levi Lee 1984); *Wild Streak* (1986), *The Gospel of Mary* (with Ron Short; 1989)

Rebecca Wackler, born in Anchorage, Alaska, took an undergraduate degree at Florida State University, and currently lives in Atlanta where she co-founded the Southern Theatre Conspiracy with Levi Lee in 1979. As an actor, director and playwright, she is prominent in Atlanta theatres, but became more widely appreciated for her collaboration on *Tent Meeting*, a kind of surreal mystery farce in which a self-proclaimed preacher drags his beleaguered son, daughter and deformed grandchild – who might be the new Christ – from Arkansas to Saskatchewan. The three authors have toured their mockingly humorous satire internationally. Although she acts in films and commercials for a living, Wackler considers her playwriting the artistic thread which gives her life direction. Humour, even painful humour, has been one means through which she has tried to discover and dramatise truth in her plays. Myths and legends attract her imagination and she is currently working on a play which will use the Medea legend in exposing truth through an unspecified use of the Hedda Nusbaum–Joel Steinberg murder trial in New York City.

The Gospel of Mary
The discovery in Egypt in 1945 of the gnostic gospels allowed theologians a new and Eastern view of Christianity. The concept that Wackler develops rests upon the recognition that Mary Magdalene has her own gospel and that she was also a disciple of Christ. Although humour is present, this play involves a more serious story in which trials and tribulations are used to provoke truth.

Try these:
▷Timberlake Wertenbaker's *The Love of the Nightingale* for reworking legends; ▷Caryl Churchill's *Top Girls*, ▷C.P. Taylor's *Ophelia*, Helen Cooper's *Mrs Vershinin*, ▷Melissa Murray's *Ophelia*, Elaine Feinstein's *Lear's Daughters* for women written out of history.

WALCOTT, Derek   [1932–   ]
St Lucian dramatist

Plays include:
Ti-Jean and His Brothers (1957), *Dream on Monkey Mountain* (1967), *The Joker of Seville* (1974; from Tirso de Molina), *O Babylon!* (1976), *Pantomime* (1977; produced 1987), *Remembrance* (1977; produced London 1987), *Beef No Chicken* (1982), *The Isle is Full of Noises* (1982), *To Die for Grenada* (1986), *Steel* (collaboration with composer Galt MacDermot; 1991)

Walcott is one of the Caribbean's most important playwrights and men of letters. A recent volume of poetry, of which, *Omeros*, a book-length epic, has won him considerable acclaim. However, so far only a handful of his nearly three dozen plays have been seen in the United States or Britain though he holds a professorship of poetry and literature at Boston University. The fact that Walcott's plays are known at all in the UK must largely be due to the personal drive and initiative of director Yvonne Brewster. She worked with Walcott at the Trinidad Theatre Workshop, which he founded in 1959 (he moved to Trinidad after graduating from the University of Jamaica) to produce his own work as well as other Caribbean and foreign plays. Brewster has directed at least two of the plays, *Pantomime* and *O Babylon!*, and *Remembrance* was part of the 1987 Black Theatre Season in

London. His work has also been produced regularly in the USA by the Negro Ensemble Company, Joseph Papp's New York Shakespeare Festival, and the Yale Repertory Theatre. The now-defunct Hudson Guild Theatre in New York mounted a production of *Pantomime* in 1986, which was well received.

Walcott's plays, as with those of many other Caribbean writers, are an attempt to find ways and means to expressing the richness of their cultural legacies. Rhythms of speech are important; so too is the use of music, ritual, myth and drumming. *Dream on Monkey Mountain* is regarded as a West Indian classic, an allegory about myth and history. *Remembrance* is a smaller-scale study of the legacies of colonialism, focused on the character of Albert Perez Jordan, teacher and fantasist. It is an affectionate, almost sentimental portrait of a far from sympathetic character irrevocably influenced by British rule (especially literature and war-time experiences) but left behind by time – a sort of epitaph to a dying breed. *O Babylon!*, on the other hand, is a hymn to Rastafarianism that takes a hefty, ironical swipe at cracking capitalism, Kingston style, with additional music by Galt MacDermot of *Hair* fame. *The Last Carnival* portrays the crisis of a French Creole colonial family as it comes to terms with the rising Black Power movement. An uncertain future also preoccupies the small town in *Beef, No Chicken*, a strong portrait of the corruption that often comes with progress. Like *Pantomime*, Walcott's 1983 play *A Branch of the Nile* has a theatrical setting: a Port-of-Spain troupe nearly falls apart from internal conflict.

Pantomime

This is probably Walcott's most accessible play and certainly one of his most popular. A neat twist on the Robinson Crusoe theme, Walcott's white master and black servant prepare a play to greet the tourists coming to visit the island of Tobago, but with the white hotel-owner and one-time actor playing Man Friday. The device reaps a rich comic harvest in its own right, as well as gleefully giving vent to some painful historical taboos for the black community about race, gait and language. Indeed, one of its most enthusiastic receptions has been in Cardiff, where the implications about holding on to language were hugely appreciated by Welsh-language supporters in the audience.

Try these:
▷Brian Friel's *Translations* for another play about language as an instrument of invasion; ▷Ntozake Shange, who also sees language as a symbol of oppression; ▷Caryl Phillips' *The Shelter* is another, less successful version of the Robinson Crusoe theme; ▷Mustapha Matura's transplanted *Three Sisters, Trinidad Sisters*, is a poignant portrayal of British imperial legacies; see also his *Playboy of the West Indies*; Rastafarianism is the consciousness behind ▷Edgar White's *Lament for Rastafari*; ▷Michael Hastings' *The Emperor* sees Haile Selassie in a rather different light; ▷Edgar White's *The Nine Night*, ▷Felix Cross' *Mass Carib* and Dennis Scott's *Echo in the Bone* all use ritual to greater or lesser effect, Scott and Cross also with graphic references to slavery; Earl Lovelace's Trinidad-set *The New Hardware Store* is an implicit attack on capitalism (the oppressed reproducing oppressive lifestyles) though social comedy.

WALKER, George F.   [1947–]
Canadian dramatist

Plays include:
The Prince of Naples (1972), *Ambush at Tether's End* (1972), *Sacktown Rag* (1972), *Bagdad Saloon* (1973), *Beyond Mozambique* (1975), *Zastrozzi* (1977), *Gossip* (1977), *Ramona and the White Slaves* (1978), *Filthy Rich* (1979), *Rumours of Our Death* (1980), *Theatre of the Film Noir* (1981), *Science and Madness* (1982), *The Art of War* (1983), *Better Living* (1986), *Nothing Scared* (1988), *Love and Anger* (1989)

One of Canada's most prolific playwrights, Walker was instrumental in the alternative theatre movement of the 1970s. Many of his plays have been premiered at Toronto's Factory Theatre Lab, with which he has been closely associated throughout his career. His plays are regularly produced outside Anglophone Canada, particularly in the United States and Great Britain. Walker's first works derived from the European absurd tradition, a point of departure that became less and less obvious as he developed as a writer. *Beyond Mozambique*, his earliest widely known play, takes off from the B-movie and is concerned with popular culture. Walker displays no fear, or contempt, for pop culture; on the contrary, he is fascinated by it and makes no attempt to draw a line of demarcation between it and so-called 'high culture'. Stage presences include Rita Hayworth, ▷Chekhov, Nelson Eddy and Victor Hugo. Walker also likes to mix different places and historical epochs within a work: *Ramona and the White Slaves*, set in an opium den in Hong Kong after World War I, is a prime example.

Zastrozzi, which explores our fascination with evil in an exuberantly Neo-Gothic setting, was a break-through work for Walker. Based on an encyclopedia description of Shelley's novelette of the same title, this play did much to establish Walker outside Canada as a playwright of note. It is action-packed, in a Grand Guignol manner, and features male-female sword-fights. Like earlier work, *Zastrozzi* comprises elements that may at first seem strange bedfellows: gothic melodrama, B-movies, moral concerns and silly stage business. The New York premiere was directed by Andrei Serban at Joseph Papp's Public Theatre.

Walker tends to write clusters of plays on a particular theme or devoted to a particular character. The 'Power Plays' (*Gossip*, *Filthy Rich* and *The Art of War*) hinge on Tyrone Power, a novelist *manqué*, obsessed with politics. *Criminals in Love*, *Better Living* and *Beautiful City*, all set in Toronto's East End, could also be considered a trilogy.

Criminals in Love, which won the Governor's Award in 1984, returns to Toronto's East End, the terrain of Walker's first plays. A continuation of the nature/nurture, destiny/free-will debates, the play is a farce that breaks the generic mold.

Nothing Sacred is Walker's adaptation of Turgenev's *Fathers and Sons*. As described by the author, the work is 'a Canadian comedy, not a Russian tragedy'. It has won numerous awards, including four Dora Awards, and has been widely produced within and without Canada.

Try these:
▷Michel Tremblay, a prolific Quebecois playwright who shares some of Walker's thematic concerns and rootedness to a particular urban environment; ▷Brecht, for theatrical techniques, especially as regards *The Art of War*; David Freeman, Larry Fineberg, John Palmer, Larry Kardish are also associated with Factory Theatre Lab.

WALL, Michael   [1951–91]
British dramatist

Plays include:
Japanese Style (1984), *Blue Days* (1987), *Imaginary Wars in England* (1987), *Amongst Barbarians* (1989)

Michael Wall's career as a writer in the 1980s followed a near-classic pattern of fringe work, radio plays (which included several of his stage plays), the odd one-off television drama and contributions to long-running series. Having studied English at university he worked at a variety of jobs including being a grave-digger and a sales assistant at Harrods. His extensive travel experience provides the material for much of his work. He rose to prominence with his play *Amongst Barbarians*, which won the Mobil Play Competition in 1988 and received productions both at the Royal Exchange Theatre, Manchester and at the Hampstead Theatre, London. It concentrates on the reactions of two families who arrive in an Asian country in an attempt to save their sons who are about to be executed for drug running. The behaviour of the Westerners is infinitely more barbaric and uncivilised than the Asians whom they so self-righteously brand as savage. The questions raised are those of culture, civilisation and who is really a 'barbarian'.

Try these:
▷Gorki's *Barbarians* asked a similar question; ▷Anthony Minghella's *Made In Bangkok* followed Westerners as they travel to the Orient with an equally jaundiced eye; ▷Robin Glendinning and ▷Iain Heggie are other Mobil Play winners.

WANDOR, Michelene   [1940–]
British dramatist, poet, fiction writer and theoretician

Plays include:
The Day After Yesterday (1972), *Spilt Milk* (1972), *To Die Among Friends* (1974), *Penthesilea* (1977; from ▷Kleist), The Old Wives' Tale (1977), *Care and Control* (1977; scripted for ▷Gay Sweatshop), *Floorshow* (1977; with ▷Caryl Churchill, ▷Bryony Lavery and David Bradford), *Whores D'Oeuvres* (1978), *Scissors* (1978), *AID Thy Neighbour* (1978), *Correspondence* (radio 1978; staged 1979), *Aurora Leigh* (1979; from Elizabeth Barrett Browning),

The Blind Goddess (1981; from Toller), *The Wandering Jew* (1987; with ▷Mike Alfreds, from Eugene Sue)

Michelene Wandor's unique position is well summed up by Helene Keyssar: 'More than any single figure, Wandor is responsible for articulating and supporting the interaction of feminism, theatre, socialism and gay liberation in Britain.' Active in the reborn women's movement from its earliest days – *The Day After Yesterday* attacks the sexism of the Miss World contest, *Care and Control* is about the issue of lesbian mothers having custody of their children – Wandor has made significant contributions at both the theoretical and the practical level, as one of the few theatre practitioners with a strong academic background. As editor of the first four volumes of the Methuen anthologies of *Plays by Women*, she has made a significant body of women's dramatic writing available to those who were unable to see the plays in their first productions and as author of *Understudies, Carry on Understudies* and *Look Back in Gender*, she has documented and analysed the undervalued contribution of women to the contemporary theatre, and the representation of women in the theatre.

A prolific radio dramatist, she has never achieved comparable critical success in the theatre: the ▷National Theatre production of *The Wandering Jew* lasted for over five hours and, despite ▷Mike Alfreds' acknowledged gifts with novel adaptations and Wandor's successful radio adaptations of Dostoyevsky, Austen and H.G. Wells, the general view was that the novel simply was not up to it. *Aurora Leigh* is a fine adaptation of Elizabeth Barrett Browning's verse novel that deserves a wider audience, and some of the earlier work, such as *Whores D'Oeuvres*, a fantasy about two prostitutes stranded on a makeshift raft on the Thames after a freak storm, is well worth reviving as more than a historical curiosity. It is probably worth pointing out that *AID Thy Neighbour* is an attempt at a comedy about contemporary attitudes to the family focused on the question of Artificial Insemination by Donor, not a play about AIDS.

Try these:
▷Adaptations and Adapters; Monstrous Regiment and Mrs Worthington's Daughters have staged Wandor's work; ▷Women in Theatre, ▷Lesbian Theatre, ▷Gay Sweatshop, ▷Women Dramatists

for more on the issues Wandor confronts in her theoretical as well as her theatrical writings; ▷Sarah Daniels' *Neaptide* for another lesbian custody case; ▷Kay Adshead's *Thatcher's Women* for a recent play about prostitution.

WARD, Nick [1962–]
British dramatist and director

Plays include:
Splendid Isolation (1986), *Apart from George* (1987), *The Strangeness of Others* (1988)

Nick Ward has come a long way very quickly. Born in Geelong, Australia, but brought up in East Anglia, by the age of 25 he had already won the George Devine Award (for *Apart from George* and *The Strangeness of Others*), been commissioned by the ▷Royal Court and ▷Royal National Theatre and made his mark sufficiently as a director to be signed up for a BBC contract. At Cambridge (he graduated in 1984 with an English degree) he ran two experimental theatre companies. He also spent a year at the Bristol Film School, under David Puttnam, making a number of short features and documentaries. He was 'spotted' by ▷Peter Gill in 1985 after *Eastwood*, a piece he wrote, directed and designed (based on the D.H. Lawrence short story, *Odour of Chrysanthemums*), won an Edinburgh Fringe 'First'. *Apart from George*, the play that brought him national attention, was the third project Ward had completed at Gill's National Theatre Studio (where he also directed a production of ▷David Spencer's *Space* as well as doing his own translation of ▷Strindberg's *Ghost Sonata*).

Interviewed around the time of *Apart from George*, Ward is reported to have said that he very quickly discovered how few words were needed to make a point. *Apart from George* and *The Strangeness of Others* seem to bear out both the strengths and weaknesses of that. There is no-one like Ward for evoking a particular time and place. In *Apart from George*, it was the bleak and dour East Anglian Fens; in *Strangeness*, the 'faceless, heartless' belly of the beast that is contemporary London. In *Apart from George*, the economy of words, subtle accentuation of physical gesture and nuances and plangent violin accompaniment created an unforgettable picture. Comparisons with ▷Caryl Churchill's *Fen* were obvious, and certainly the same sense of claustrophobic intensity and domestic misery brought on by geographical isolation were present. But Ward's central figure of George, the farm labourer made redundant, his dumb inability to communicate his despair and the repercussions on his wife and daughter (intimations of incest) were distinctively his own. The formula seemed to work less well in Ward's essay on the bitter, love-lorn metropolis. While Lyn Gardner, in *City Limits*, called it 'a brilliant impressionistic portrait', and *The Guardian's* Michael Billington, 'a poet's vision of urban life', the tenor and framework of his dialogue seemed this time to draw only irritation. Whether it was the desperation expressed by his collection of oddballs and down-and-outers or as another reviewer noted, 'the banality of their thoughts', it is hard to say. Discretion, it's said, can sometimes be the better part of valour. So brevity, it's true, can also be its soul. However, the current fad for ellipsis in new British writing betokens a more confused state: on the one hand, rich distillation; on the other, obfuscation and sterility.

Try these:

Elizabeth Bond's *Farrowland* for rural gloom; Sally Nemeth's *Holy Days* for a superb evocation of time and place – the American Dust Bowl in the Depression – and more domestic rural tragedies; ▷David Spencer, ▷Jacqueline Holborough, Paul Godfrey, ▷Debbie Horsfield, ▷Sharman Macdonald, ▷Sarah Daniels, Michael Mahoney for other young writers who have passed through the National's studio wing under ▷Peter Gill and John Burgess; ▷Martin Crimp and Peter Gill himself, for British contemporaries economical with their words; ▷Gregory Motton's *Chicken*, Tim Firth's *Cardboard City*, *Heaven* by American Sarah Aicher (a victim of the Lockerbie disaster) for more contemporary scenes of London's urban angst; George Tabori's *Mein Kampf: Farce* for more tramps, German and Jewish variety; ▷Gorki's *The Lower Depths* for the definitive 'tramp' play.

WASSERSTEIN, Wendy   [1950–]
American dramatist

Plays include:

Any Woman Can't (1973), *When Dinah Shore Ruled the Earth* (with ▷Christopher Durang; 1975), *Montpelier Pizzazz* (1976), *Uncommon Women and Others* (1977), *Isn't It Romantic?* (1981; revised 1983), *Tender Offer* (1983), *Miami* (1986), *The Heidi Chronicles* (1988)

The most commercially successful contemporary woman playwright in the USA, Wendy Wasserstein first came to prominence with *Uncommon Women and Others*, originally begun as a one-act play for Wasserstein's graduate thesis at the Yale School of Drama and later expanded to full length for its 1977 New York premiere (a television adaptation with an all-star cast was aired the following year). *Uncommon Women*, in which a group of women friends reminisce about their college years and the directions their lives have taken since, was quickly established as a favourite on the regional theatre circuit. The play was followed up by *Isn't It Romantic?*, the story of the friendship between a 28-year-old Jewish homebody and an elegant WASP. The comedy was a financial and critical success for Playwrights' Horizons, the off-Broadway venue which has developed several Wasserstein projects, including her 1986 musical-in-progress *Miami*, about a Long Island family on holiday in Florida. In *The Heidi Chronicles*, her 1988 Pulitzer Prize-winning Broadway hit (originally produced by Seattle Repertory Theatre), Wasserstein returned to the issues of women's choices as she followed the progress of Heidi Holland from high school to approaching middle age, with detours for college, consciousness-raising, career moves and childbearing questions.

Wasserstein has an ear for the hilarities of everyday dialogue and an ability to tap into the emotional insecurities facing many women of her generation. Detractors have found her humour too flashy and insubstantial, and feminist critics have generally eschewed her self-deprecating heroines. Born in Brooklyn to Jewish emigrés from central Europe, Wasserstein is frequently asked about the autobiographical elements of her writing. She plays down the parallels while acknowledging that 'to this day I receive phone calls [from my mother] whose opening lines a writer could spend months inventing.'

Try these:

▷Neil Simon as a commercial comic playwright drawing from Jewish family experiences; ▷Christopher Durang, ▷Albert Innaurato, A.R. Gurney as other

Joan Allen (foreground) and Peter Friedman in Wendy Wasserstein's *The Heidi Chronicles*, directed by Daniel Sullivan, Playwrights Horizons

Playwrights' Horizons authors who write often about family pressures; ▷Caryl Churchill's *Top Girls*, ▷Nell Dunn's *Steaming* for a gathering of women; Clare Booth Luce's *The Women*; and for contrast ▷Pam Gems' *Dusa, Fish, Stas and Vi*; ▷Maria Irene Fornes' *Fefu and Her Friends*; ▷Beth Henley's small-town Southern sensibility contrasts with Wasserstein's urban Northern one; ▷Simon Gray's *Common Pursuit* for an Oxbridge contrast to *Uncommon Women*; Wendy Kesselman for another American-Jewish dramatist of somewhat different sensibility.

WATERHOUSE, Keith   [1929–]
British dramatist

HALL, Willis   [1929–]
British dramatist

Joint plays include:
Billy Liar (1960), *Celebration: The Wedding and the Funeral* (1961), *England, Our England* (revue; 1962), *All Things Bright and Beautiful* (1962), *Say Who You Are* (1965), *The Card* (musical from Arnold Bennett's novel; 1973)

Yorkshiremen from Leeds, these dramatists have worked both independently and together and are best known for their well-constructed, accurately observed studies of north-country life, frequently showing their characters' attempts to escape – actually or in fantasy – from their surroundings. However, one of their biggest commercial successes, *Say Who You Are*, is a farce set in Knightsbridge and other major successes have been *Saturday, Sunday, Money* and *Filumena*, both adaptations of Neopolitan plays by ▷Eduardo De Filippo.

Hall had already had productions – especially *The Long and the Short and the Tall* (1958), a moving play about a trapped group of soldiers and their Japanese prisoner in Malaya – and Waterhouse had published novels before their collaboration on the stage version of his *Billy Liar*. Both separately and together they have produced a number of screenplays (including *The Long and the Short and the Tall* (1961), *Whistle down the Wind* (1961), *A Kind of Loving* (1963) *Billy Liar* (1963)), radio and television plays and series, and revue material.

There is no typical Hall and Waterhouse play as far as subject matter is concerned. What you can expect is assured handling of naturalistic details, fresh and original writing in a sound structure and at least one role that is a gift to the actor. Waterhouse's latest success, *Jeffrey Bernard is Unwell* (1989), is just such a gift. Based on the writings of its eponymous hero, a journalist with *The Spectator*, well known for his alcoholic adventures, it was a great success for Peter O'Toole. *Bookends* was less completely successful in its presentation of a friendship maintained by letters.

Try these:
▷J. B. Priestley for earlier and middle-class Yorkshire comedies; ▷Alan Bennett for similar accurate depiction of Yorkshire life, though often less naturalistic in structure (especially *Worm's Eye View*); ▷David Storey for similar naturalistic portrayals of northern and working-class life in the 1960s and early 1970s; ▷R.C. Sherriff's *Journey's End*, ▷Terence Rattigan's *Flarepath* and ▷Arnold Wesker's *Chips with Everything* for some of the many different views of conscript life; ▷Osborne's *Inadmissible Evidence* for phantasmagoric self-destruction; ▷Tom Kempinski's *Separation* for a long-distance relationship.

WEBSTER, John   [c 1580–c 1632]
English Renaissance dramatist

Plays include:
The White Devil (1612), *The Duchess of Malfi* (1613)

Webster, the son of a London coachmaker, had a legal training which may explain the number of trial scenes in his plays, and he probably wasn't a full-time professional dramatist. Although he did write plays about London life, his reputation rests on the two revenge tragedies set in Italy which bear out ▷T.S. Eliot's remark that he 'was much possessed by death/And saw the skull beneath the skin'. This emphasis on corruption and death – in *The Duchess of Malfi* the Cardinal's mistress dies after kissing a poisoned Bible – still encourages some people to side with ▷George Bernard Shaw, who described Webster as the 'Tussaud laureate'. *The White Devil* and *The Duchess of Malfi*, both based on Italian history, are characterised by lavish use of violent and macabre deaths, adultery, dumb shows and apparitions; but they bring a new emphasis to the presentation of the tragic female protagonist since their central figures are victims of events rather than initiators of them, sacrifices to the power of patriarchy who pay the price for stepping out of line.

The Duchess of Malfi

The bare bones of the plot might seem to support the charge that Webster was simply out to give his audience a quick thrill through gruesome effects and sensational plotting. After all, the widowed Duchess makes a secret second marriage to her steward Antonio, thus incurring the wrath of her two corrupt brothers, Ferdinand and the Cardinal, who engineer plots to torment her and destroy the marriage, with the result being a final body count of ten. Not only is the number of deaths high even by the generous standards of the Renaissance but there is a heady mix of mistaken murders, dances of madmen, tableaux of wax dummies, apparently severed hands and lycanthropy to go with it. But throughout the play there is a sense of the Duchess and Antonio as 'ordinary' people attempting to make sense of and to live 'normal' lives in a world which has no fixed positions or moral absolutes, in which good intentions are no salvation, and from whose absurdity there is no escape. Even in a bad production the play has the virtues of good melodrama, but in a brilliant one, such as Adrian Noble's 1980 production for the Manchester Royal Exchange with Helen Mirren as the Duchess, Pete Postlethwaite as Antonio, Mike Gwilym as Ferdinand, Julian Curry as the Cardinal and Bob Hoskins as the malcontent Bosola who does most of the dirty work, the play's resolute refusal to be bowed by corruption and pervasive evil emerges very clearly.

Try these:
Plays by ▷Samuel Beckett and ▷Edward Bond for that curious sense of an optimism that refuses to be bowed by the harshness of life; plays by other Renaissance dramatists, particularly ▷Chapman, ▷Ford, ▷Marlowe, ▷Marston, ▷Middleton and ▷Shakespeare (especially *Measure for Measure* where Isabella is confronted by a similar atmosphere of changing moral absolutes) for the use of Machiavellian villains, revenge plots and malcontents; ▷Brecht's *Galileo* and ▷Hochhüth's *The Representative* for questionable cardinals;

Robert Daniel Macdonald's *Webster* takes a supposed look back-stage at the Webster ménage.

WEDEKIND, Frank   [1864–1918]
German dramatist

Plays include:
Spring Awakening (1891), *The Earth Spirit* (1895), *The Marquis of Keith* (1900), *Pandora's Box* (1903)

Wedekind had a profound effect on the development of twentieth-century German drama. It is fair to regard him as an originator of ▷Expressionism: his deliberate use of non-naturalistic and symbolic devices, his exaggerated and caricatured characterisation, and his deployment of ▷music hall and ▷cabaret technique, clearly influencing Toller, Kaiser, and ▷Brecht.

Wedekind's first play, *Spring Awakening*, was immediately controversial, both by its theme – adolescent sexuality and adult repression – and its anti-naturalistic style. His later plays continued to concern themselves with sex and society, and Wedekind was widely regarded as a scandalous libertine and anarchist. In fact, his work is very much concerned with morality, and his later work has a strongly religious flavour.

His plays display a major preoccupation with the clash between the irresistable force of Life – most strongly experienced as sex – and the immovable object of bourgeois hypocrisy and 'respectability'. In *Spring Awakening* the adults prefer the destruction of their children to a public admission of the facts of life, in the so-called 'Lulu' plays – *The Earth Spirit* and *Pandora's Box* – Lulu destroys a series of representative bourgeois males through her uninhibited but essentially innocent enjoyment of sex before her death at the hands of a madman. The power of Wedekind's writing is such that his plays continue to disturb and shock. They were still being refused a performing licence in Britain in the 1960s.

Spring Awakening
Stiefel, a fourteen-year old boy, commits suicide rather than face his parents after failure at school. His diaries are found to contain a graphic account of sex written by another boy, Gabor. Horrified respectability expels Gabor from school for possessing this knowledge, and then sends him to a reformatory when his innocent and childishly ignorant girlfriend is

found to be pregnant. The girl's mother forces her to have an abortion, and she dies as a result. Escaping from the reformatory, Gabor grieves over her grave and is confronted with Stiefel's ghost, exhorting him to join the other children in death. A strangely positive conclusion is reached, however, by the intervention of a mysterious figure who convinces Gabor that he must not abandon life.

Try these:
Wedekind's personal quarrel with Gerhart Hauptmann played a part in his reaction against Naturalism; ▷Strindberg was another major precursor of Expressionism; Wedekind's controversial frankness about sex parallels ▷Ibsen's; Wedekind influenced Surrealism and the Theatre of the Absurd; ▷Peter Barnes' *The Ruling Class* has parallels with the 'Lulu' plays, ▷Howard Brenton's *Romans in Britain* scandalised the moral majority with its naked buggery, intended as a metaphor for imperialism; ▷Bond's *Saved* still shocks with its baby-battering violence, a device used by the playwright to show the dehumanising effects of capitalism.

WEISS, Peter Ulrich   [1916–82]
Czechoslovakian-born Swedish painter, novelist, director and dramatist

Plays include:
The Persecution and Assassination of Jean-Paul Marat as Performed by the Inmates of the Asylum of Charenton under the Direction of the Marquis de Sade (1964), *The Investigation* (1965), *The Tower* (1967), *Discourse on the War in Vietnam* (1968), *Song of the Lusitanian Bogey* (1968), *How Mr Mockingpott was Relieved of his Sufferings* (1968), *The Insurance* (1969), *Trotsky in Exile* (1971), *Holderlin* (1971)

Born in Czechoslovakia of German parents and resident in Sweden from 1939, Weiss was an intensely political writer with a considerable range. *The Investigation* is a documentary based on the 1964 War Crimes Trial at Frankfurt, *The Insurance* a surrealist allegory, *Song of the Lusitanian Bogey* a record of an uprising in Angola and its suppression by the Portuguese. His work often attracted controversy – attempts to suppress *Discourse on the War in Vietnam* in Berlin, outrage at *Marat/Sade* (as his first play is frequently called) in London – but no one could deny that his plays

have a strong theatrical power as well as a forceful message.

Marat/Sade, which brought him an international reputation through the historic ▷Artaud-influenced 1964 ▷RSC production by ▷Peter Brook (a *tour de théâtre* difficult to match), is exactly what the full title describes. In an introduction ▷Brook says: 'Everything about [the play] is designed to crack the spectator on the jaw, then douse him with ice-cold water, then force him intelligently to assess what has happened to him, then give him a kick in the balls, then bring him to his senses again.' Brook's production gave one little chance to come back to one's senses but the play does include a variety of arguments about revolutionary violence and an ironic picture of the revolution tamed by the new Empire but very likely to re-emerge.

Try these:
▷Büchner's *Danton's Death*; ▷Mnouchkine's *1789*, ▷Pam Gems' *The Danton Affair* are all treatments of the French Revolution; ▷Hochhüth is concerned with similar issues, especially in *The Representative*; the Wooster Group is one of the few companies still attempting political, social and physical theatre on a comparable scale; ▷Robert Wilson; ▷Peter Brook.

WELLER, Michael   [1942–]
American dramatist

Plays include:
Moonchildren (1970), *Fishing* (1975), *Loose Ends* (1979), *The Ballad of Soapy Smith* (1983), *Ghost On Fire* (1985), *Spoils of War* (1988), *Lake No Bottom* (1990)

Weller is the leading chronicler of the generation of Americans who came of age in the 1960s. His knack for bright, outrageous dialogue and his ability to draw sympathetic, three-dimensional characters can be found in all of his works for the theatre. Although he has departed from his depiction of the socially committed, college-educated (Klondike gold-rush hucksters in *The Ballad of Soapy Smith*), he is most at home dealing with these characters. Weller's three major plays (*Spoils of War, Moonchildren, Loose Ends*) form a loosely linked trilogy. In his first play, *Moonchildren*, set in the 1960s, Weller drew a sympathetic picture of the Vietnam-era youth counterculture. In *Loose Ends*, which culminates in the 1970s, Weller focuses on Paul and Susan, who meet in the Peace Corps and later become affluent. They pay a high price for their success and lose touch with their ideals and each other. *Spoils of War*, the last play written, deals with the 1950s. This is Weller's most autobiographical work. The central character is a teenager who tries to re-unite his divorced parents. The plays share the themes of a loss of continuity in relationships and the inability to express genuine feelings within a relationship. *Lake No Bottom*, a three character drama, tells the story of an author who turns on his mentor and critic by writing a successful trashy novel. He is also having an affair with the critic's wife. The play explores the layers of subterfuge and deception that Weller believes are a part of the interdependent relationship between artist and critic. Critics have compared Weller to ▷Chekhov, although Weller's approach to narrative is more cinematic (Weller wrote screenplays for *Hair* and *Ragtime*). Weller populates his plays with writers, photographers, literary critics, filmmakers and cartoonists. These characters share the playwright's interest in reflective commentary. Weller has been successful off-Broadway and in the regional theatres.

Try these:
Robert Patrick's *Kennedy's Children*, ▷Doug Lucie's *Progress*, ▷Deborah Levy's *Heresies* for contemporary societies and their roots; ▷Howard Barker's *Scenes from an Execution*, ▷David Pownall's *Masterclass*, ▷Tom Stoppard's *The Real Inspector Hound* for artists and critics; ▷Simon Gray, ▷Martin Crimp as further contemporary chroniclers with a bitter taste.

WELLMAN, Mac John   [1945–]
American dramatist

Plays include:
Fama Combinatoria (1975), *The Memory Theatre of Giordana Bruno* (radio play; 1977), *Dog in the Manger* (adaptation from ▷De Vega; 1982), *Phantomnation* (1983), *The Professional Frenchman* (1984), *Harm's Way* (radio play; 1984), *Energymen* (1985), *The Bad Infinity* (1985), *'1951'* (1986), *Cleveland* (1986), *Dracula* (1987), *Albanian Softshoe* (1989), *Sincerity Forever* (1990), *Crowbar* (1990), *Terminal Hip* (1990)

Mac Wellman, one of America's most prolific and eclectic writers, has written radio plays, edited anthologies (*7 Different Plays*, 1986, and *Theatre of Wonders*, 1984), and taught playwriting. Most importantly, he has worked with particular theatres or artists to develop scripts. Wellman's work often features unusual word play and construction. A brief section from *Terminal Hip* is a good example: 'Any damn fool can winterize the octagon./ Any bojar walloon can strip the pentagon/ of its fluffy stuff and egg the wax./ Any airhead can play air guitar on X/ the beefy sand dollar hoohah . . .' His untraditional style has brought the accusation of sacrilege, as in *Sincerity Forever* a play that drew the ire of ultra-conservative Donald Wildmon and Senator Jesse Helms during their crusade to abolish National Endowment for the Arts funding for controversial artists. Wellman's literary non-conformity represents the fringe of American writers, but his 1990 confrontation with Wildmon and Helms was a stance championed by traditional venues and artists as well.

Crowbar
As a 'site specific' play, dependent upon a particular geographic location for contextual meaning, *Crowbar* was conceived for and then performed in New York's Victory Theatre just a month before its demolition. Constructed at the turn of the century by Oscar Hammerstein, the playhouse had been home to noted productions including some of David Belasco's. The building's history fuels *Crowbar*, a play set during the intermission of James A. Hearn's *Sag Harbor*, the production that opened the theatre. A man searches for his daughter during the intermission and links the physical exploration of the Victory Theatre with historical anecdotes. It is a more conventional script than others by Wellman, but *Crowbar's* experimental intent is not diminished. The play's limited run added political poignancy about the selling of New York's theatrical and social heritage.

Try these:
▷Performance Art; Welfare State for environmental stagings; ▷Tom Stoppard's *The Real Inspector Hound*; ▷Sheridan's *The Critic*, ▷Jonson's *Bartholomew Fair*, ▷Pirandello's *Six Characters* for theatre-set plays.

WERTENBAKER, Timberlake

Anglo-French-American dramatist, now resident in Britain

Plays include:
The Third (1980), *Case to Answer* (1980), *Breaking Through* (1980), *New Anatomies* (1981), *Inside Out* (1982), *Home Leave* (1982), *Abel's Sister* (with Yvonne Bourcier; 1984), *The Grace of Mary Traverse* (1985), *The Love of a Nightingale* (1988), *Our Country's Good* (loosely based on Thoman Keneally's *The Playmaker*; 1988), *Three Birds Alighting in a Field* (1991)

Although Timberlake Wertenbaker is American by birth, and French educated, her work has all been created within the British theatre. Her most successful plays, *The Love of the Nightingale* and *Our Country's Good*, offer an exhilarating contrast in their treatment of theatrical techniques. Like ▷Caryl Churchill she has shown a persistent interest in how notions of normality and self are constructed and many of her plays contain a Faustian bargain in which knowledge is purchased at the expense of innocence. *Abel's Sister* (co-written with the disabled Yvonne Bourcier) is quite remarkable for its insights into both physical disability and, through its attendant characters of Vietnam veteran and young jaundiced radicals, emotional and spiritual disability. *The Grace of Mary Traverse*, on the other hand, is a picaresque eighteenth-century gallop with Faustian undertones – what price knowledge? – but also, and primarily, an exploration of the possibilities for women when they step outside their own environment. Wertenbaker had already engaged with this topic in *New Anatomies*, a sprawling, ambitious account of two rebellious women who broke the conventions of gender by dressing in male attire: the nineteenth-century explorer Isabelle Eberhardt and the music hall performer Vesta Tilley. *Our Country's Good* owed its success at the ▷Royal Court, in Australia and the West End to its reaffirmation of the power of theatre to change lives and influence people for the better. The play, based on Thomas Keneally's novel *The Playmaker*, shows convicts from the First Fleet staging the first theatrical production in Australia, ▷Farquhar's *The Recruiting Officer*. The play uses familiar backstage situations to debate the aesthetics and politics of the theatre and the philosophy of punishment, and the original production used devices such

as cross-casting, multiple doubling and onstage changes of identity to further the debate about the relationship between environmental and genetic influences on character and behaviour. *The Love of the Nightingale* is a powerful and spare reworking of the myth of Philomel and Procne, which includes a staging within the play of the Phaedra story and an enactment of Bacchic rituals. Its use of the theatre within its design relates dialectically to that in *Our Country's Good*, where theatre is regarded in terms of its power to transform the performers, rather than its audience. *Nightingale* is much more concerned with the making of myths, the power of language, gender roles, and the role of fantasy in more negative terms. Here the power of theatre is questioned alongside a powerful exploration of the construction of male and female roles. With these two plays Wertenbaker established herself as one of Britain's most challenging and intellectually stimulating dramatists. In 1991, as well as a new play, *Three Birds Alighting in a Field*, she has translated three plays by Sophocles – *Oedipus the King*, *Oedipus at Colennus* and *Antigone*, under the title of *The Thebians* – for the RSC.

Try these:
For women in male clothes, ▷Shakespeare's *Twelfth Night* and *The Merchant of Venice*, ▷Middleton and ▷Dekker's *The Roaring Girl*; for 'history' plays with contemporary parallels, ▷Howard Barker's *Victory* and *The Castle*; ▷Nick Dear's *The Art of Success*; ▷Goethe's *Faust* for the philosophical knot; for images of disability, Graeae, Theatre of Black Women's *The Cripple* and ▷Peter Nichols' *Day in the Death of Joe Egg*, ▷Phil Young's *Crystal Clear* and ▷Mark Medoff's *Children of a Lesser God*; Wertenbaker has very successfully translated ▷Marivaux and ▷Mnouchkine's *Mephisto*; ▷Euripides for *The Bacchae*; ▷Racine for *Phèdre*; ▷Trevor Griffiths' *Comedians* for backstage debates about the function of art.

WESKER, Arnold   [1932–   ]

British dramatist

Plays include:
Chicken Soup with Barley (1958), *Roots* (1959), *I'm Talking About Jerusalem* (1960) (these three plays forming *The Wesker*

Ron Cook and Lesley Sharp discuss their plight as two convicts in Timberlake Wertenbaker's *Our Country's Good*, Royal Court, 1988 (later West End)

Trilogy), The Kitchen (1959), *Chips with Everything* (1962), *The Nottingham Captain* (1962), *Menace* (1963), *Their Very Own and Golden City* (1965), *The Four Seasons* (1965), *The Friends* (1970), *The Old Ones* (1972), *The Wedding Feast* (from Dostoevski; 1974) *The Journalists* (1975), *Love Letters on Blue Paper* (1976), *The Merchant* (1977), *Caritas* (1981), *One More Ride on the Merry Go Round* (1981, produced 1985), *Sullied Hands* (1981, produced 1984), *Mothers* (1982), *Annie Wobbler* (1983), *Whatever Happened to Betty Lemon* (1986)

Born in Stepney, the son of Jewish emigrés, Wesker worked as a furniture maker's apprentice, as a carpenter's mate, plumber's mate, farm labourer and bookseller's assistant and for four years after National Service in the Royal Air Force as a pastry cook, an experience he draws on in *Chicken Soup with Barley* and *The Kitchen*. In 1956 he took a film course and began writing film scripts and for the theatre.

Much of his early writing is very autobiographical, ▷John Arden has termed it 'autobiography in documentary style'; *The Wesker Trilogy*, firmly set in an East End world of the Jewish family, uses a form of social realism to depict working-class life. *Chicken Soup with Barley* charts the experience of the Kahns, a Jewish family in the East End over twenty years, beginning in 1936 with the threat of Moseley's Blackshirts, and ending with the 1956 Soviet invasion of Hungary. These events are experienced from within a domestic world; the play traces the decline of the family, a group of people who come to stand for the disillusion of the post-war generations, as their hopes for the future turn to a loss of faith. The play was enormously influential. In the last play of the trilogy, *I'm Talking about Jerusalem*, Wesker returns to the Kahn family; the Jerusalem of the title represents the hopes of the future in the face of the failure of socialist idealism (a reference to the call 'Next Year in Jerusalem!' of the Passover ritual). In *Chips With Everything* Wesker began to move away from a strictly naturalist form, and employed folk and popular song, a device he was to pursue in his later plays. Wesker's more recent work has tended to move away from the broad chronology and canvases of his earlier work. In *Caritas* he explores the phenomenon of a fourteenth-century woman anchorite (a religious mystic and recluse) who

literally walls herself up in a cathedral wall. *Annie Wobbler* and *Mothers* take the form of dramatic monologue. His *The Merchant* is an intelligent reworking of ▷Shakespeare's *The Merchant of Venice* from a Jewish viewpoint.

Try these:
▷John Osborne as the first of the generation of 'Angry Young Men'; John McGrath also forged alliances with the labour and Trade Union movements and generated labour support for the arts; ▷Harold Pinter and Wesker share an East End Jewish background; ▷Robert Bolt was imprisoned with Wesker for their anti-nuclear protest; ▷John Arden for a while also shared their pacifism; ▷Debbie Horsfield for a contemporary writer who has written a trilogy – on young women and football; ▷Michel Tremblay uses monologue techniques in *Albertine in Five Times*; ▷Shelagh Delaney's *A Taste of Honey* and ▷David Storey as other exponents of social realism; ▷Andrea Dunbar, ▷Jim Cartwright, ▷Karim Alrawi, and ▷Tony Marchant as modern equivalents.

WESLEY, Richard   [1945–]
American dramatist

Plays include:
The Black Terror (1971), *Gettin' It Together* (1972), *Strike Heaven on the Face* (1973), *Goin' Thru Changes* (1973), *The Past Is the Past* (1973), *The Sirens* (1974), *The Mighty Gents* (originally called *The Last Street Play*; 1974), *Cotillion* (book for the musical, with Woodie King, jr; 1975), *On the Road to Babylon: A Musical Journey* (book for the musical; 1979) *The Dream Team* (book for the musical; 1985), *The Talented Tenth* (1989)

Born in Newark, New Jersey, and witness to its history of radical turmoil in the 1960s, Wesley has become one of the most politically controversial playwrights of his generation. Influenced, as a young writer, by ▷Amiri Baraka and Ron Milner, Wesley writes unsentimental realism, often fiercely philosophical and moral, and concerned with the ways in which social conditions and history affect identity. From 1968 to 1973 Wesley was a member of the New Lafayette Theatre, the prominent Harlem company, where he worked with ▷Ed Bullins, helped edit the theatre's magazine, and served as playwright-in-residence. He came to the attention of Joe Papp in 1971, and The New York Shakespeare Festival produced Wesley's first full-length play, *The Black Terror*. A meditation on revolution, the play presents a black terrorist who has begun to question the usefulness of violence, and yet can't quite propose satisfactory alternatives. The play won Wesley the Drama Desk Award for most promising playwright.

Wesley's second major play, originally called *The Last Street Play* when it opened at the Manhattan Theatre Club, the off-Broadway company most associated with Wesley's recent work, became *The Mighty Gents* when it moved to Broadway. It could be a companion piece to *The Black Terror*, for in it Wesley again asks what happens after the revolutionary fire has gone out. Here, members of a black gang confront the unhappy truth that they're no longer powerful and vital players in Newark's streets. Anxious to recapture their youthful glory, but also to break out of the suffocating conditions of their past and become adults, the men are eloquent spokesmen for the diverse frustrations of the disenfranchised. The play also allowed Wesley to display his gift for imagining a broad range of characters, each finely observed, distinct, yet closely engaged with one another.

Wesley became a favourite Hollywood screenwriter after this play, scripting *Uptown Saturday Night*, *Let's Do it Again* and *Fast Forward*. He also wrote books for several musicals before premiering his most recent play, *The Talented Tenth*, at the Manhattan Theatre Club in 1989. One critic called it 'a black *Big Chill*', for it protrayed a group of 'buppies' (Wesley's term for black yuppies). Wesley says he grew exhausted with writing about the street and wanted to focus on those who escaped its dangers: the title refers to W.E.B. DuBois' term for the ten percent of black Americans able to save the others from 'contamination and death'. Wesley's talented tenth – Harvard graduates, business executives and Republicans among them – are guilty about their privilege, their detachment from most of their fellow African-Americans, yet unsure about how to bring the much-needed change to their lives. The play marked a considerable shift for Wesley and, for audiences used to ▷August Wilson, made him difficult to classify. Part of the uncertainty about Wesley's artistic identity comes from his own desire constantly to redefine the nature of so-called black writing: 'Black

playwriting is stagnating,' Wesley wrote in 1972, at the start of a career spent jostling it back to life. And in 1989 he said to an interviewer who asked about the origin of *The Talented Tenth*, 'we'd written about drugs, about prostitution, about alienated youth. There had to be some new territory to be limned.'

Try these:
▷Amiri Baraka, ▷Ed Bullins, Charles Fuller for writers with similarly uncompromising social consciences; ▷Ntozake Shange and ▷Adrienne Kennedy for plays treating issues of black identity in a less naturalistic way; ▷Richard Nelson and ▷David Rabe for other kinds of politically informed writing; J.E. Gaines, Clay Goss, Martie Charles, Ron Milner (along with Baraka and Bullins) as writer from whom Wesley says he draws his 'strongest inspiration'; ▷Mustapha Matura, ▷Tunde Ikoli, ▷Alfred Fagon, ▷Felix Cross, for British equivalents.

WHITE, Edgar   [1947–]
Caribbean dramatist, born in Monserrat

Plays include:
The Mummer's Play (1970), *The Wonderfule Yeare* (1970), *Seigsmundo's Tricycle* (1971), *Little Orfeo's Lay* (1972), *La Gente* (1973), *The Black Women* (1977), *Masada* (1978), *Lament for Rastafari* (1979), *Trinity* (1981), *The Nine Night* (1983), *Redemption Song* (1984), *The Boot Dance* (1984), *Moon Dance Night* (1987)

Poet, dramatist, Edgar White studied at City College in New York and has had many plays produced there, including five by Joe Papp's Shakespeare Festival Theatre: *The Mummer's Play* (1970), *The Wonderfule Yeare* (1970), *Seigsmundo's Tricycle* (1971), *La Gente* (1973), and *Les Femmes Noires* (or *The Black Ladies*; 1974).

He went to Britain in the 1960s and was involved with the seminal gathering of black actors, musicians and directors at the Keskidee Centre in north London. White writes particularly of disillusionment and of the quest for roots back in the Caribbean with a mixture of dry humour, sorrow and sometimes dreamy romanticism; his plays invariably introduce elements of mysticism and ritual into realistic settings as well as frequent references to Rastafarianism.

Two of White's most popular plays, *The Nine Night* and *Redemption Song*, deal with the return and disillusionment of the exile. In *Redemption Song*, a richly ironic title in itself, Legion, a young dreamer and poet, returns home to claim his inheritance after his father's death, only to find he is as much of an outcast as he was in Britain. Legion is in limbo-land and, as White has written, stands for a generation of young immigrants, brought to Britain when small, but lost and rejected by both cultures as adults. White tends to concentrate, though by no means exclusively, on the experiences of males; *Moon Dance* which focused on a smart, urbanised black woman from London returning to the Caribbean for a holiday seemed more like caricature. However, this aspect of White's writing, and of other black writers, can provoke a variety of responses from outrage to guffaws of instantaneous identification, depending on the cultural background of the audience.

The Nine Night

The Nine Night (it refers to a Jamaican funeral ritual used to help a troubled soul pass to paradise) opens and closes this domestic comedy that highlights the disillusionment of those who went to Britain regarding themselves as British and Britain as 'the mother country' until they started to live there. In the central figure of Hamon, the troubled spirit – 'a Black Alf Garnett only with some brains' (John Connor, *City Limits*) – on the eve of returning to the Caribbean with his son, White has created a character rich in comic pretensions as well as pathos (loss of illusions is also mirrored in loss of power in the home). His fanatical love of cricket – there is a wonderful scene where Hamon and his old friend drunkenly recreate the first West Indies Test victory over England – symbolises a whole generation cast of mind and old 'adopted' values in conflict with the harsher ones of contemporary England. His son, brought up in England, prefers football to cricket.

Try these:
The Nine Night bears strong similarities to Steve Carter's *Eden*; ▷Derek Walcott's *Oh Babylon* is a rock hymn to Rastafarianism; ▷Felix Cross and David Simon's *Blues for Railton* is a highly successful marrying of the Caribbean past and British present – Dennis Scott's impressively wide-ranging exploration of black history and oppression *An Echo in the*

Bone also uses the ritual of the Nine Night; ▷Mustapha Matura, ▷Caryl Phillips, and ▷Nigel Moffatt for plays dealing with disillusionment; ▷Trevor Rhone for caricature; for cultural contrast ▷Ayckbourn and for more images of patriarchy in retreat, ▷De Filippo's *Ducking Out*; ▷Black Theatre in Britain.

WHITEHEAD, Ted (Edward Anthony)   [1933–   ]
British dramatist

Plays include:
The Foursome (1971), *Alpha Beta* (1972), *The Sea Anchor* (1974), *Old Flames* (1975), *Mecca* (1977), *The Man Who Fell in Love with His Wife* (1984)

Whitehead worked in various manual jobs, in advertising and as a teacher, before becoming a full-time writer in 1971 when he was resident dramatist at the Royal Court. His television adaptations of Fay Weldon's *The Life and Loves of a She-Devil* (1987) and of ▷Strindberg's *Dance of Death* (1984) are indicative of his dominant interest in sexual politics, particularly of the obsessive kind. His work is always closely observed and often comic, but there is an edge of uneasiness to the comedy as his characters engage in mating rituals and other games. In *The Foursome* he charts a brief sexual relationship between two couples and in *The Sea Anchor* the emphasis is on promiscuity and the nature of marriage. *Alpha Beta* is a raw battle of the sexes and a misogynistic tirade against marriage. His most recent stage play, *The Man Who Fell in Love with His Wife*, is a revised version of his 1980 television play *Sweet Nothings*, in which a man becomes obsessed with what his wife is doing when she goes to work outside the home after twenty years of childcare and domesticity; the result is that she rediscovers herself and he crumbles into pathological jealousy.

Old Flames

Most of Whitehead's stage work is naturalistic in tone and texture, and he puts this to good use in *Old Flames* which develops from a comedy of manners opening, with a man being put out to find that the woman who has invited him to dinner has also invited his ex-wives and his mother, into a kind of gothic farce as he discovers he is the menu. After the interval, and the dinner, the women sit around talking freely about their lives to one another in a way that is still rare in drama. Inevitably, the static nature and almost monologue quality of the second act has given rise to cries of lack of dramatic interaction, but the value placed on women's discourse is more than adequate compensation.

Try these:
▷ Euripides' *The Bacchae* for women eating men; ▷ Caryl Churchill's *Top Girls* for another all-female meal that worried some critics; ▷ Strindberg for sexual politics; ▷ Ibsen's *A Doll's House* for an earlier strained marriage; ▷ Willy Russell's *Stags and Hens* for contemporary mating rituals; ▷ Jacqui Shapiro's *Dead Romantic*, Jack Klaff's *Cuddles* as more recent examinations in the sexual politics arena.

WHITEMORE, Hugh   [1936–]
British dramatist

Plays include:
Stevie (1977), *Pack of Lies* (1983), *Breaking the Code* (1986), *The Best of Friends* (1988)

A list of Hugh Whitemore's stage plays gives little indication of his versatility or distinguished career as a television and film writer – with such credits as the screenplay for *84 Charing Cross Road*, a Writers Guild award for a television adaptation of *Cider with Rosie* (1971) and *Country Matters* (1972), as well as a clutch of television drama series. His stage plays, not surprisingly, show an equal craftsmanship, like an old Chippendale, with the same attention to detail. His portrayal of the Palmers Green poet Stevie Smith (*Stevie*) was as much a pinpointing of the minutiae of suburban claustrophobia as the makings of a poet. In *Pack of Lies*, suburbia again sets the scene for a microscopic examination of emotional destruction, with the Jacksons, who befriended and then betrayed the Portland Spy case spies, the Krogers. In *Breaking the Code*, about Enigma code-breaker and homosexual Alan Turing, ideas of loyalty and national expediency are again explored alongside homosexuality. His most recent play, *The Best of Friends*, a celebration of friendship, dramatising the correspondence between ▷ G.B. Shaw, Sir Sydney Cockerell and the Abbess of Stanbrook in Worcester, was an

exercise in elegance with a glittery cast including Sir John Gielgud. Both *Pack of Lies* and *Breaking the Code* successfully transferred to Broadway (with Derek Jacobi repeating his much praised role as Turing).

Pack of Lies
Set in 1961 with the Portland Spy case as its background, Whitemore chose to focus not so much on the Krogers as the way the suburban couple, the Jacksons, were drawn into a web of deceit by MI6, and the effect on them. A subtle study in the pain of betrayal, of conflicting loyalties between friends and country, and of how the lives of ordinary people can be ruthlessly destroyed, it breathed new life into the old soap opera form and became a compelling drama, particularly in the hands of Judi Dench and Michael Williams. *Pack of Lies* started out as a British television play and was also turned into an American television film (1986) (with Ellen Burstyn, Alan Bates and Teri Garr).

Try these:
▷ Simon Gray, ▷ Julian Mitchell also specialise in the 'well-made' play and deal in loyalties and things British; ▷ Alan Bennett's *The Old Country* for betrayal and homosexuality; for images of ageing mothers, ▷ Julia Kearsley's *Under the Web*, ▷ Ayshe Raif's *Fail/Safe*; Laclos' *Les Liaisons Dangereuses* (adapted by ▷ Christopher Hampton) is entirely based on letters, but dramatised letters have been less frequent than anthologies, which over the years have formed the basis of solo performances about specific poets and writers (eg ▷ Oscar Wilde in Michael McLiammoir's *The Importance of Being Oscar*; Michael Pennington's *Anton Chekhov*).

WHITING, John   [1917–63]
British dramatist

Plays include:
Conditions of Agreement (1948), *A Penny For A Song* (1951; revised 1962), *Saint's Day* (1953), *Marching Song* (1954), *The Gates of Summer* (1956), *The Devils* (1961);

and staged posthumously, *Conditions of Agreement* (1965), *No More A-Roving* (1975)

His death from cancer at forty-five cut tragically short one of the most intriguing playwriting careers of the post-war period, as John Whiting, who began his career as a RADA-trained actor, showed a facility for both gentle comedies of character (*Penny For A Song*) and large-scale and brutal tragedy (*The Devils*). In between came *Saint's Day*, about an 83-year-old poet, Paul Southman, at odds with the literary society that has scorned him, and *Marching Song*, a story of political disaffection filtered through the individual tale of one Rupert Foster, a war criminal invited to commit suicide by the chancellor of a newly powerless country (Britain?). None of his plays, except for *The Devils*, was particularly well reviewed during his life, and the intriguing characters of *Penny For A Song* – in which an English coastal community awaits a Napoleonic invasion – only began to be appreciated following a 1962 revival, one year before his death.

The Devils

The Devils, commissioned by Peter Hall for the ▷RSC at the Aldwych, established Whiting as a major dramatist capable of a Jacobean richness of language, epic scope and bold, often shocking stage imagery. Based on Aldous Huxley's *The Devils of Loudun*, the play tells of the supposed 'possession' of a group of nuns in a seventeenth-century French priory. Sister Jeanne, a hunchback abbess, succumbs to an infectious hysteria, and leads the accusations that the lecherous priest, Grandier, is in league with the devil. A 1971 film adaptation by Ken Russell, starring Vanessa Redgrave and Oliver Reed, was expectedly over the top.

Try these:
▷Robert Bolt's *A Man For All Seasons*, ▷Arthur Miller's *The Crucible* for contrast; ▷Edward Bond (especially *Lear* and *The War Plays*) and ▷Howard Barker for the hair-raising intensity of the images and the elevated prose; ▷Jean Anouilh, ▷Rolf Hochhüth's *Soldiers* for studies in disillusionment akin to *Marching Song*.

WILCOX, Michael   [1943–]
British dramatist

Plays include:
The Atom Bomb Project (1975), *Grimm Tales* (1975), *Roar Like Spears* (1975), *Phantom of the Fells* (1977), *The Blacketts of Bright Street* (1977), *Pioneers* (1977), *Dekka and Dava* (1978), *Rents* (1979), *Accounts* (1981), *Lent* (1983), *78 Revolutions* (1984), *Massage* (1986)

Wilcox, a former teacher who lives in Northumberland, is probably best known for his plays about the gay community, although he has also tackled nuclear (in both the atomic and family senses) themes in *The Atom Bomb Project*, and reassessed folk tales in *Grimm Tales* and *Dekka and Dava*, which is a Newcastle version of *Hansel and Gretel*. His initial breakthrough came with *Rents*, a study of Edinburgh rent boys in which the staccato, episodic presentation represents the fragmented nature of their lives. He followed this with *Accounts*, in which the homosexual theme is only one element in an altogether gentler account of both literal and figurative balancing the books, in an English hill farming family in the Scottish Borders. *Lent* is similarly gentle on the surface, with its picture of a boy spending his Easter holiday virtually alone in his prep school, although under the surface Michael Billington detected a lament for the Peter Pan-like inability of British men to mature fully. In *78 Revolutions* Wilcox used two Americans attempting to record singers in the Russian Imperial Opera in the early days of recording as a means of investigating various kinds of cultural clash, but the enterprise turned into something more like an illustrated recital and lecture on the technicalities of recording. More controversial is *Massage*, in which Wilcox tackles questions of paedophilia. Wilcox also edits Methuen's *Gay Play* volumes.

Try these:
Wilcox acknowledges ▷C.P. Taylor's influence and there are similarities between their interests in, for example, Peter Pan and retelling old stories; ▷Stewart Parker's *Spokesong* shares *Massage's* bicycle shop setting; ▷David Pownall's *Master Class* and ▷Tom Stoppard's *Every Good Boy Deserves Favour* also deal with the theme of music in Russia; ▷C.P. Taylor's *Good* uses music in its investigation of Nazism; Wilcox's *Phantom of the*

Fells is a reworking of ▷J.M. Synge's *In the Shadow of the Glen*; for rather different versions of schooldays, ▷Julian Mitchell's *Another Country* and Denise Deegan's *Daisy Pulls It Off*; Gay Sweatshop; ▷David Rudkin for another version of *Hansel and Gretel*.

WILDE, Oscar Fingal O'Flahertie Wills [1854–1900]
Irish dramatist, poet, essayist, novelist

Plays include:
Vera (1882), *The Duchess of Padua* (1891), *Lady Windermere's Fan* (1892), *A Woman of No Importance* (1893), *An Ideal Husband* (1895), *The Importance of Being Earnest* (1895), *Salomé* (1896)

Wilde's father was an ear surgeon, his mother an Irish nationalist who wrote political pamphlets and poetry. A graduate of Trinity College Dublin and later Oxford University he emerged from both as a brilliant scholar and had his first book of poetry published in 1881. With Walter Pater Wilde became a focal point for the Aesthetic movement, popularising Pater's gospel of 'the ecstasy of beauty'. ▷Gilbert and Sullivan parodied his style in *Patience* with their portrayal of Bunthorne, a 'very, very sensitive young man', waving a lily. He produced his first play *Vera* in New York, which flopped; *The Duchess of Padua*, a verse drama, produced in New York in 1891, was no more successful but the 1892 London production of *Lady Windermere's Fan* was acclaimed and established Wilde as the darling of *fin de siècle* London. *A Woman of No Importance* and *An Ideal Husband* confirmed Wilde's position. His reputation was however precarious; celebrated for his social dramas and comedies, his novel *The Picture of Dorian Gray* was branded as 'immoral', his play *Salomé* banned by the Lord Chamberlain; the first night of his most successful play *The Importance of Being Earnest* was the evening on which the Marquess of Queensberry, father of his lover Lord Alfred Douglas, accused Wilde of being a sodomite. Arrested and tried for homosexuality, Wilde was sentenced to the maximum penalty of two years hard labour. While in prison he wrote *De Profundis* and his major poem, *The Ballad of Reading Gaol*. Released in 1897, a declared bankrupt, he moved to France where he lived until his death in Paris from meningitis.

The Importance of Being Earnest
Subtitled 'A Trivial Comedy for Serious People', Wilde's last major play has been described as 'the wittiest comedy in the English language'. Structurally, the play is a brilliant inversion and extension of theatrical conventions, with the elements of farce and melodrama thrown together to the point of absurdity. The plot of mistaken identity, long lost brothers, frustrated romance and foundlings, is couched in the sophisticated and urbane wit of contemporary London society. According to Max Beerbohm: 'the fun depends on what the characters say, rather than on what they do; they speak a kind of beautiful nonsense, the language of high comedy, twisted into fantasy.' For ▷Shaw, however, 'three acts of studied triviality, however brilliant, are too much.'

Try these:
▷Joe Orton, ▷Alan Bennett and ▷Noël Coward share with Wilde a camp wit and a sardonic awareness of the hypocrisies of conventional society manners; the elegant wit of Wilde's comedy owes a great deal to the eighteenth-century comedy of manners, (writers such as ▷Congreve, ▷Goldsmith and ▷Sheridan); ▷Tom Stoppard takes *The Importance of Being Earnest* as the structure for his play *Travesties*.

WILDER, Thornton [1897–1975]
American dramatist

Plays include:
The Trumpet Shall Sound (1927), *The Long Christmas Dinner* (1931), *Pulman Car Hiawatha* (1931), *The Happy Journey to Trenton and Camden* (1931), *Our Town* (1938), *The Merchant of Yonkers* (1938), *The Skin of Our Teeth* (1942), *The Matchmaker* (1954; revised version of *The Merchant of Yonkers*), *A Life in the Sun* (1955), *Three Plays for Bleecker Street* (1962)

A three-time Pulitzer Prize-winner, Wilder paints an often affectionate but astute picture of small-town American life, finding in the minutiae of experience the electrically charged matter of drama. Often mistaken as bland and cosy, Wilder can be surprisingly subversive both in form and content, and pain never lies far outside the borders of any of his scenes. In *The Long Christmas Dinner*, for example, a family gathering slowly reveals its darker shades until the would-be festivity has an air of melancholy more akin to James Joyce's *The Dead* than, even, comparable scenes in ▷Neil Simon's *Brighton Beach Memoirs*. Catastrophe defines the human experience in *The Skin of Our Teeth*, a play which sees the history of mankind as a litany of encounters with chaos. Even the celebrated *Our Town* finds some sadness in its pastoral landscape. Wilder was, however, capable of a great laugh and in *The Matchmaker*, which inspired the legendary musical *Hello, Dolly!*, he wrote a classic farce about a woman who becomes engaged to the same penny-pinching man she has been trying to match up with somebody else.

Our Town

Beginning in Grover's Corners, New Hampshire, on a determinedly ordinary day in 1901, Wilder's Pulitzer Prize-winning play is one of the most often produced – and, perhaps, misunderstood – American plays in America, where it is seen as the theatrical equivalent of apple pie by people who overlook its depth. Embracing fourteen years over its prologue and three acts, the play is an exalted chronicle of the everyday – Wilder's attempt, as he puts it, 'to find a value above all price for the smallest events of our daily life'. Those events may be small, but they are significant, and Wilder takes a scalpel to human psychology in a way that restores an often lacking immediacy to matters of love and loss. Innovative in form, the play is both abstract and utterly realistic, with its use of a Stage Manager to act as narrator and chorus, and the inexorable progression of its three acts, entitled 'anti-illusionary', 'love and marriage', and 'death'. The story is about two families, the Webbs and the Gibbses, but it's Everyfamily, of course, as well – this is *our* town – Wilder makes clear, and his incisive and loving play is both the quintessential comment on Americana and the perfect by-product of it. A Broadway musical – entitled *Grover's Corners*, and written by the men who wrote *The Fantasticks* – has been kicking around American regional theatre for years but has yet to open in New York. *Our Town* has become a favourite in the repertory of Washington DC's Arena Stage, with stage and television actor Robert Prosky as a definitive Stage Manager. On the less orthodox side, New York's experimental troupe ▷The Wooster Group appropriated portions of the play in its 1981 opus *Route 1 & 9*, and the

imagistic director ▷Robert Wilson has recently expressed interest in commandeering it.

Try these:
▷Chekhov, ▷Lanford Wilson (especially *The Rimers of Eldritch* and his narrative use of Matt in *Tally's Folley*) and ▷Dylan Thomas' *Under Milk Wood* for ensemble pieces strongly allied to a sense of place and a similarly gentle yet tough-minded tone; ▷Shaw's *Back to Methusaleh* for the sweep of history; ▷Mark Medoff and ▷Sam Shepard for modern, often absurdist variants on Wilder's small-town reveries; A.R. Gurney's *The Dining Room* as a 1970s WASP update of *The Long Christmas Dinner*; ▷Jim Cartwright's *Road* for a lethal contemporary British version of *Our Town*; ▷Alan Ayckbourn's *The Norman Conquest* trilogy for another cataclysmic account of Christmas dinner; *The Matchmaker* and ▷Stoppard's *On the Razzle* are ultimately derived from John Oxenford's *A Day Well Spent* and ▷Johann Nestroy's *Einen Jux Will er Sich Machen*.

WILLIAMS, (George) Emlyn

[1905–1987]
British dramatist, actor and director

Plays include:
A Murder Has Been Arranged (1930), *The Late Christopher Bean* (1933; from Sidney Howard's 1932 play of the same name, itself a version of René Fauchois' 1932 hit *Prenez Garde à la Peinture*), *Spring 1600* (1934), *Night Must Fall* (1935), *The Corn is Green* (1938), *The Light of Heart* (1940), *The Druid's Rest* (1944), *The Wind of Heaven* (1945)

Night Must Fall, a 'psychological thriller' – about the cheerful pageboy with a head in his hatbox, and the old lady in the wheelchair whom he doesn't quite murder – still has a good deal of theatrical force, and is the only play by Welsh-born Williams that is likely to wear well – except perhaps his genial comedy of Welsh public house life, *The Druid's Rest*, which is full of affectionately drawn Welsh characters of the kind he was brought up with. His other plays, including the more famous autobiographical *The Corn is Green*, are marred by being too 'well-made' and too sentimental, though it might still work if the schoolmistress were played as a battleaxe, as she was by Sybil Thorndike. His two volumes of autobiography, *George* (1961) and *Emlyn* (1970), give as vivid a picture of life in North Wales, Oxford, and the London theatre of the 1920s and 1930s as one is likely to find, and could be effectively dramatised, perhaps as a one-person show of the kind that he himself did so well.

Try these:
▷Terence Rattigan for well-crafted plays partly based on autobiographical material; ▷Agatha Christie for thrillers; ▷Thrillers.

WILLIAMS, Heathcote   [1941–]
British dramatist

Plays include:
The Local Stigmatic (1965), *AC/DC* (1970), *Hancock's Last Half-Hour* (1977), *The Immortalist* (1977), *At It* (1982; part of *Breach of the Peace*)

Williams is one of the key figures of the counter-cultural landscape as the Founding Editor of *Suck* and the author of *AC/DC*, which was greeted as 'seminal to the seventies'. Williams' work is generally concerned with individuals at the margins of existence in a world that is hostile to the individual and to non-conformism in any form. Much of *AC/DC* now seems trapped in a kind of period aspic with its two schizophrenics and three hippies, its relentless energy and its linguistic violence, though it is itself critical of the ways in which hippiedom had become another form of conventional behaviour; the attack on 'psychic capitalism', the way in which the media set a conformist and coercive mindscape, is still as relevant as ever but the contemporary theatre has moved on to more detailed analyses of the ways agendas are set. *Hancock's Last Half-Hour* is likely to be revived more frequently, not only because it offers a fine part for an actor but because its meditation on the nature of the self, the relationship between performers and their audiences, the role of the media in creating and destroying individuals, and the meaning of comedy and of fame is more readily accessible. Williams' 1964 book *The Speakers*, about Speakers' Corner in Hyde Park where individuals put forward often bizarre socio-politico-religious theories to whoever will listen, was successfully dramatised by Joint Stock.

Try these:
▷Snoo Wilson for works not entirely dissimilar to *AC/DC*; ▷Artaud for a highly physical idea of theatre; Bill Gaskill compared Williams to ▷Congreve on the strength of *AC/DC*; *Hancock's Last Half Hour* is one of many theatrical meditations on the role of the performer and of comedy, including Colin Bennett's *Hancock's Finest Hour*, ▷Trevor Griffiths' *Comedians* and ▷John Osborne's *The Entertainer*, *The Local Stigmatic* is reminiscent of early ▷Pinter and ▷Albee's *The Zoo Story*.

WILLIAMS, Nigel   [1948–]
British dramatist, novelist and screenwriter

Plays include:
Double Talk (1976), *Class Enemy* (1978), *Easy Street* (1979), *Sugar and Spice* (1980), *Line 'Em* (1980), *Trial Run* (1980), *WCPC* (1982), *The Adventures of Jasper Ridley* (1982), *My Brother's Keeper* (1985), *Country Dancing* (1986)

A versatile writer who has won awards for his fiction, translated ▷Genet, and works for the BBC, Williams made his initial impact as a gritty presenter of claustrophobic urban tensions in the classroom drama *Class Enemy* but has branched out into political farce (*WCPC*) and analysis of myth-making and the co-option of the past in *Country Dancing*. Society has already given up on Williams' group of streetwise teenagers in *Class Enemy* as they mark time at school but he reveals the mixture of individual needs and aspirations beneath their surface of malcontent bravado. The bleakness of this world is continued into the sexual politics of *Sugar and Spice*, the racial politics of *Trial Run*, and the confrontation between pickets and the army in *Line 'Em*. There is more comedy in *WCPC* and *The Adventures of Jasper Ridley* but it remains based on a firm sense of the absurd waste and endemic corruption of society, even if the use of cartoon techniques and caricature sometimes give rise to accusations of being patronising: in *WCPC* a straight policeman's mission to arrest cottaging gays spirals into farce, as first he discovers his sergeant in highly suspicious circumstances and is then frustrated in his attempts to bring him to 'justice' by the discovery that virtually everyone else in the force is involved in a gay conspiracy; Jasper Ridley is a picaresque hero in the Candide mould whose adventures include being sponsored by Prince Charles as Unemployed Young Person of the Year. In *My Brother's Keeper* we have family tensions at a dying old actor's bedside and in *Country Dancing* Williams examines the folk song collector Cecil Sharp as he gathers songs from an old man just before World War I, using Sharp's antiquarian interests to make points about the function of song and the need to reclaim the past from myths which reduce its contradictions and sentimentalise its hardships.

Try these:

▷Debbie Horsfield, ▷Hanif Kureishi, Michael Mahoney, and ▷Barrie Keeffe for images of contemporary urban life ▷C.P. Taylor's *Good*, ▷David Pownall's *Master Class*, ▷Tom Stoppard's *Every Good Boy Deserves Favour* for other variations on the musical theme; ▷Eugene O'Neill's *Long Day's Journey into Night*, ▷Tunde Ikoli's *Scrape Off the Black*, ▷Catherine Hayes' *Skirmishes* for combative siblings; ▷Timberlake Wertenbaker's *The Grace of Mary Traverse* for contemporary female picaresque: ▷Peter Flannery's *Our Friends in the North* and ▷G. F. Newman's *Operation Bad Apple* for peculiar police procedures; for pickets and the army ▷John Arden's *Serjeant Musgrave's Dance*; ▷Joe Orton's *Loot* for realism spiralling off into farce.

WILLIAMS, Samm-Art   [1946–   ]
American dramatist and actor

Plays include:

Welcome Back to Black River (1975), *The Coming* (1976), *Do Unto Others* (1976), *A Love Play* (1976), *The Last Caravan* (1977), *Birds Don't Sing* (1977), *Home* (1979), *The Sixteenth Round* (1980), *Friends Sing* (1977), *Home* (1979), *The Sixteenth Round* (1980), *Friends* (1983), *Bojangles* (book for musical; 1985), *Eyes of the American* (1985), *Eve of the Trial* (after ▷Chekhov) in *Orchards* (1986), *Cork* (1986)

Born in Burgaw, North Carolina, Williams knew from an early age that he wanted to write for the theatre. Upon graduating from college in 1968, he joined Philadelphia's Freedom Theatre where he got acting as well as writing experience. In 1974 he joined the Playwrights Workshop of the Negro Ensemble Company in New York, the company that later premiered his first plays as part of its 'season within a season', and for which he acted in many productions.

Williams is best known for *Home*, which won the John Gassner Playwriting Award from the Outer Critics' Circle, Most Provocative New Play by an American, and a Tony Award nomination for Best Play. The play, which has autobiographical elements, concerns a young black man who leaves his native South and goes North. He has said the idea for *Home* came to him while on a Greyhound Bus heading South one Christmas. In an interview with *The New York Times*, after the play moved to Broadway, Williams said he considered himself 'the pioneer generation that is going to have to start the new things rolling. The old, angry young black man is now the hungry young black man. Not that he is not angry, not that you do not want things to change. But there are so many things we wrote about in the past that are just old hat. Now we've got to show a different side of black life style. You know, all black characters don't have to be heroes. All black men do not have to be black macho, strong leaders of the household, knocking everybody down on stage. You can have very sensitive, very kind, very gentle, kinds of black men.'

Williams maintains that black writers should not isolate themselves. *Birds Don't Sing* is about two Polish sisters who, after surviving Hitler's regime, went to live in the USA. *Friends*, not a wholly successful work, is about a romantic triangle involving a woman whose two lovers are blind and unaware that they are competitors.

Cork, which takes its title from the burnt substance used by 19th-century minstrels to darken their faces, is at once an exploration of negative black stereotypes and a homage to the entertainers who, for complex reasons, helped to perpetuate some of them. *Cork* is set in a contemporary West End theatre where Randy Madison, a black playwright and actor, has won his first critical acclaim and substantial financial compensation. He is visited in his dressing room by the ghost of a legendary black minstrel who asks him to cancel one performance in honour of American minstrels. 'You don't have to use cork,' the ghost tells Madison, 'I wore it for you.'

Try these:
Steve Carter, for similarly gentle treatment of black life; ▷Lorraine Hansberry, Charles Gordone, Richard Wesley, ▷Ed Bullins, Lonnie Elder III, ▷Amiri Baraka for contrasting techniques, settings and viewpoints; ▷Phil Young's *Crystal Clear* for blind lovers; ▷Ntozake Shange's *Spell No 7* for more allusions to black minstrels and ▷George C. Wolfe for the challenging of black stereotypes.

WILLIAMS, Tennessee (Thomas Lanier)   [1911–1983]
American dramatist

Plays include:
Battle of Angels (1940), *The Glass Menagerie* (1944), *A Streetcar Named Desire* (1947), *Summer and Smoke* (1948), *The Rose Tattoo* (1951), *Camino Real* (1953), *Cat On A Hot Tin Roof* (1955), *27 Wagons Full Of Cotton* (1955), *Orpheus Descending* (1957), *Suddenly Last Summer* (1958), *Sweet Bird of Youth* (1959), *Period of Adjustment* (1960), *Night of the Iguana* (1961), *The Milk Train Doesn't Stop Here Anymore* (1962), *The Gnädiges Fräulein* (1966), *Kingdom of Earth* (also called *The Seven Descents Of Myrtle*; 1968), *Small Craft Warnings* (1972), *Outcry* (1973), *The Red Devil Battery Sign* (1975), *Vieux Carré* (1977), *A Lovely Sunday for Crève Coeur* (1979), *Clothes For A Summer Hotel* (1980), *Something Cloudy Something Clear* (1981)

The Mississippi-born son of a travelling salesman who, to quote from *The Glass Menagerie*, 'fell in love with long distance', Williams turned his own poignant life into the material for some of the most rending and luminous plays of our time. His father was cool, remote and given to calling him 'Miss Nancy' (Williams was gay); his unstable mother a rector's daughter, and his sister Rose the victim of a lobotomy in 1937. After a nervous collapse himself at age twenty-three, Williams spent much of his life in various stages of ill health, and he frequently wrote about people (often women) on the brink of a breakdown – most memorably Blanche DuBois, in *A Streetcar Named Desire*, but also Zelda Fitzgerald in his late play *Clothes for a Summer Hotel*. He is famous for his emotional honesty, but some of his most interesting plays are tinged with the

grotesque, filled with foreboding, and often darkly comic. *Suddenly Last Summer* and *The Gnädiges Fräulein* are dazzling, weird examples, and *Orpheus Descending*, usually dismissed as overblown, became a magnificent experience in Peter Hall's 1989 London and Broadway version, with Vanessa Redgrave as Lady. The production initiated something of a Williams renaissance in the States: among the more notable productions were a Broadway *Cat on a Hot Tin Roof* with Kathleen Turner and, at some stylistic remove, *Belle Reprieve*, a collaboration between the American lesbian company, Split Britches, and the English drag troupe, Bloolips. Loosely adapted from *Streetcar*, it played to general acclaim in London and New York in 1990 and 1991.

After repeated critical success on Broadway for over two decades, often in the company of his frequent collaborator, the director Elia Kazan, Williams' fortunes turned sour in the late 1970s and 1980s, as play after play met poor receptions only to turn up (often) to better notices in London's West End. His key themes are the physical ravages of time and the emotional ravages of deceit, and his plays often pit the sexes against one another on a continuum of regret in which both ravages take their toll: Blanche and Stanley in *Streetcar*, the alcoholic Brick and his wife Maggie the Cat in *Cat on a Hot Tin Roof*, the fading actress Princess Kosmonopolis and her young gigolo Chance Wayne in *Sweet Bird of Youth*. Critics often complained that his later plays were pale shadows of his earlier ones, leaving Williams the ironic embodiment of his own theme – a man victimised by memories of an earlier, more productive time.

The Glass Menagerie
A four-character work set in St Louis, this early memory play is an almost perfect miniature, which distills Williams' gift for transmuting autobiography into art. A talkative domineering mother, Amanda Wingfield, runs roughshod over her shy daughter, Laura, and her rebellious son, Tom. In an effort to kindle a romance for Laura, she invites to dinner one of Tom's workmates, Jim, The Gentleman Caller, only to watch her well-intentioned plans fall to pieces as cruelly as the glass figurine in the menagerie of the title. Written with a fragile delicacy, the play offers not only a haunting portrait of the playwright as a young man – the would-be poet Tom, who seeks solace in the cinema and bursts

with dreams of 'the moon' – but also a quartet of superb parts that have been cornerstones of many actors' careers, from the legendary Laurette Taylor (as Amanda) at its premiere to Jessica Tandy and Constance Cummings, and a wonderfully mercurial John Malkovich (as Tom) in Paul Newman's 1987 movie.

A Streetcar Named Desire

The play that brought Williams his first Pulitzer Prize (the second was for *Cat On a Hot Tine Roof* eight years later), *Streetcar* shows the playwright at his sweatiest and most fevered best. The neuraesthenic Blanche arrives in the 'Belle Reve' quarter of New Orleans to stay with her sister Stella, only to enter into a fraught battle of attraction and repulsion with Stella's bestial husband Stanley. A woman in need of constant pampering, Blanche has her illusions shaken by Stanley, who in turn feels his domestic territory to be at risk. A lyrical plunge into emotional territory that wipes both the characters and the audience out, the play ends as a showdown between two wounded, deceptively strong-willed souls, who find that the promised Elysian Fields where Stella lives hid a landmine of sorrow and pain.

Try these:
▷Susan Glaspell, ▷Michel Tremblay for hothouse atmospheres; Williams has been a pervasive influence on contemporary American playwrights; ▷Lanford Wilson and ▷August Wilson for their compassionate, graceful looks at often blighted lives; ▷Sam Shepard for his dissections of the peculiar landscape of the American family; and, amongst non-Americans, South Africa's ▷Athol Fugard, for his similarly sustained use of metaphor – he uses images of flames and candles in *Road To Mecca* the way Williams does in *The Glass Menagerie*.

WILLIAMSON, David   [1942–]
Australian dramatist

Plays include:
The Coming of Stork (1970), *The Removalists* (1971), *Don's Party* (1971), *Jugglers Three* (1972), *What If You Died Tomorrow* (1973), *The Department* (1974), *A Handful of Friends* (1976), *The Club* (1977, also known as *Players* and *The Team*), *Travelling North* (1979), *Celluloid Heroes* (1980), *The Perfectionist* (1982), *Sons of Cain* (1985), *Emerald City* (1987)

Williamson's plays are mainly dissections of Australian society that cast a sceptical eye on what he has described as its 'conformist philistine, sexist, and aggressive' aspects. For non-Australian audiences the danger is to assume that Williamson's studies are purely naturalistic, thus fuelling anti-Australian prejudice, for Australian audiences there is the danger that the delight of recognition may obscure the social criticism; in both cases these are the classic dangers of a socially aware comic drama. Williamson has tackled many significant topics from the roots of violence in *The Removalists*, through the fading dreams of youth in *Don's Party* to role swapping in an 'open' marriage in *The Perfectionist*. The British reception of *Sons of Cain* was perhaps typical: there was virtually unanimous praise for Max Cullen as a crusading newspaper editor, coupled with the usual journalists' refusal to admit any similarity between their own newspapers and the stage presentation of journalism and, more significantly, a rather dismissive attitude to a major Australian political scandal that formed the basis of the play on the grounds that it was parochial. *Emerald City*, his most recent play to appear in Britain and the USA, is an examination of the vexed relationship between popular appeal and artistic integrity; although Williamson appears to come down on the side of integrity at the expense of popularity the popular success of his own high-quality screenplays for *Gallipoli* (1981) and *The Year of Living Dangerously* (1983) suggests that another view is not untenable.

Try these:
▷Doug Lucie for contemporary dissections of British manners; ▷Keith Reddin for an American version; ▷David Storey's *The Changing Room* for a view of rugby league comparable to *The Club's* view of Australian Rules football; ▷Ron Hutchinson's *Rat in the Skull* for an analysis of police behaviour offering interesting parallels with *The Removalists*; ▷Thomas Babe's *Buried Inside Extra* for a contemporary American play about journalism, Stephen Wakelam's *Deadlines* and ▷Howard Brenton and ▷David Hare's *Pravda* for recent British thoughts on the subject; ▷Dario Fo and ▷Franca Rame's

Howard Davies' 1990 Broadway production of Tennessee Williams' *Cat on a Hot Tin Roof*, with Kathleen Turner as Maggie

The Open Couple for a different treatment of an 'open' marriage; for another Australian performer/writer ▷Robyn Archer.

WILSON, August   [1945–   ]
American dramatist

Plays include:
Ma Rainey's Black Bottom (1984), *Fences* (1985), *Joe Turner's Come and Gone* (1986), *The Piano Lesson* (1987), *Two Trains Running* (1990)

A black playwright born in Pittsburgh but living in St Paul, Minnesota, Wilson has rapidly established himself in a short time as a key American dramatist capable of the sustained lyricism of ▷Tennessee Williams. Having begun his career as a poet, Wilson writes distinctively eloquent and passionate waves of speech that subordinate conventional exposition to a sheer pleasure in the richness of language; and he's at his most interesting when he subverts one's expectations of naturalism, as in *Joe Turner's Come and Gone*. He is currently in the middle of a cycle of plays about black life in the twentieth century, one play about each decade. Already complete are works set in the 1910s, 1920s, 1930s, 1940s, 1950s and 1960s. To date all his plays have been directed by Lloyd Richards, until 1991 the dean of the Yale Drama School and artistic director of the Yale Repertory Theatre in New Haven, Connecticut. One critic has likened their collaboration to that between Tennessee Williams and Elia Kazan. Wilson and Richards hit the critical and financial big time with *Fences*, a family drama set in the Pittsburgh inner city in 1957 in the period just before America's simmering racial tensions came to the boil: it won Wilson the Pulitzer Prize. In *Joe Turner's Come and Gone*, perhaps Wilson's most mysterious and dark play, and influenced, he says, by the paintings of Romare Bearden, the experiences of black Africans are painfully set against those of their American descendants in a Pittsburgh boarding house. Wilson won his second Pulitzer for *The Piano Lesson*, which also confronts the past. It focuses on a family's attempt to understand the history of slavery and exorcise its pain. In Wilson's latest, *Two Trains Running*, which takes place in Pittsburgh a month after the assassination of Martin Luther King jr the denizens of a greasy spoon debate the efficacy of the civil rights movement.

Ma Rainey's Black Bottom

Although *Fences* enjoyed a longer Broadway run and has been bought for the screen by Eddie Murphy, *Ma Rainey's Black Bottom*, Wilson's first play, still seems to be his best (though *Joe Turner* also has its partisans). Set in a Chicago recording studio in 1927, *Ma Rainey* is a piercing look at American racism and bigotry – not just white against black but, significantly, black against black – coupled with snatches of American blues music that reflect on and recapitulate the drama. Despite having her name in the title, the legendary Ma Rainey herself is a secondary figure in the play; central to it are the four musicians in her band – Slow Drag, Levee, Toledo and Cutler – who weave a tale of beauty and pain perfectly in keeping with the power of the music they perform.

Try these:
▷Tennessee Williams and ▷Lanford Wilson for dramatic lyricism; ▷Lorraine Hansberry and ▷James Baldwin for earlier comparable treatments of black domestic life; ▷Arthur Miller for examinations of the American dream gone sour; ▷Mustapha Matura, ▷Hanif Kureishi for social acclimatisation; Heidi Thomas's *Indigo* for slavery; ▷Ronald Milner, ▷George C. Wolfe for integration of jazz into drama.

WILSON, Lanford   [1937–   ]
American dramatist

Plays include:
Balm In Gilead (1965), *The Sand Castle* (1965), *The Rimers of Eldritch* (1966), *Lemon Sky* (1970), *Serenading Louie* (1970), *The Great Nebula In Orion* (1972), *The Family Continues* (1972), *The Hot-l Baltimore* (1973), *The Mound Builders* (1975), *Brontosaurus* (1977), *Fifth of July* (1978), *Talley's Folly* (1979), *Thymus Vulgaris* (1981), *A Tale Told* (1981), *Angels Fall* (1982), *Talley and Son* (1985), *A Betrothal* (1986), *Burn This* (1987), *A Poster of the Cosmos* (1988)

A leading American writer for over twenty years, Lanford Wilson is an inextricable part of the history of off-Broadway. Born in Lebanon, Missouri, where many of his plays are set, Wilson moved to New York's Greenwich Village in 1962 and had his earliest one-act plays produced at the now-defunct

Remembering a late mutual friend, Samuel E. Wright and Samuel L. Jackson in August Wilson's *Two Trains Running* directed by Lloyd Richards, Yale Repertory Theatre's artistic director, 1990

Caffe Cino off-off-Broadway. In 1965, he and director Marshall Mason collaborated on *Balm In Gilead*, an exhilarating tapestry of New York low-life set in an all-night coffee shop; their partnership not only led to the founding of Circle Repertory Theatre off-Broadway – long Wilson's authorial base – but to a sustained partnership that has seen thirty-eight productions of eighteen Wilson plays over twenty-two years. A writer with a Chekhovian sense of human fallibility and compassion, Wilson is best known for his trilogy of works spanning thirty-three years in the various generations of the Talley family in Lebanon, Missouri, and two further plays are planned to complete an ambitious historical tapestry which will be known, collectively, as *The Wars In Lebanon*. The second play of the trilogy, *Talley's Folly*, is a sharp clever two-hander about Matt Friedman's courtship of young Sally Talley in 1944. It won Wilson the 1980 Pulitzer Prize, but the first play of the trilogy *Fifth of July*, is the most resonant. The third, the deliberately old-fashioned *A Tale Told*, has been revised to the newly titled *Talley and Son*. Wilson has also written well on topics beyond the Talley's Midwest farm: his underrated *Angels Fall*, set on a New Mexico mission, is one of the most piercing, yet unpolemical plays to date on the subject of nuclear fall-out. His 1987 *Burn This* is an affecting, if overwritten, piece about the relationship between a grief-stricken dancer and the volatile brother of her deceased lover.

Fifth of July

A homosexual who lost his legs in Vietnam might seem an unlikely figure to put at the centre of a comedy, but Wilson accomplishes the unexpected in *Fifth of July*, set on the day after American Independence Day in 1977. Ken Talley, the paraplegic schoolteacher who may or may not sell the Talley farmhouse, dominates this often rending, humane comedy about loss, acceptance, and maturation – a *Cherry Orchard* re-written for the post-1960s generation, with a casual acceptance of gay life that is gratefully free of cliché. The play has robust supporting roles (the singer Gwen is so strongly written that she can unbalance poorly directed productions), all put to the service of its author's keen-eyed sense of grace. Life may be painful or sad, but our best hope – this play tells us – is to make our own individual peaces and move on.

Try these:
▷Chekhov for comic rue tempered with wisdom; ▷Athol Fugard for particular emphasis on human charity and redemption; ▷August Wilson for another American playwright who uses story-telling to good advantage in his plays; ▷Howard Brenton's *The Genius*, ▷Nick Darke's *The Body*, ▷Robert Holman's *The Overgrown Path* for British plays on the nuclear issue; Emily Mann's *Still Life* for the effects of Vietnam on life at home, ▷Noël Greig's *Poppies* and Philip Osment's *This Island's Mine* for British counterparts where the gay issue is a part of the general action.

WILSON, Robert   [1941–   ]
American avant-garde dramatist and director

Key productions include:
The King of Spain (1969), *Deafman Glance* (1970), *KA MOUNTAIN AND GUARDenia Terrace* (1972), *The Life and Times of Joseph Stalin* (1973), *A Letter For Queen Victoria* (1974), *The $ Value of Man* (1975), *Einstein On the Beach* (1976), *I Was Sitting on My Patio This Guy Appeared I Thought I Was Hallucinating* (1978; with Lucinda Childs), *Death Destruction and Detroit* (1979), *The CIVIL warS* (1983), *Death Destruction and Detroit II* (1986), *Hamletmachine* (1986; after Heiner Müller), *Alcestis* (adaptation; 1986), *Quartet* (by Heiner Müller; 1988), *The Forest* (with David Byrne; 1988), *The Black Rider: the casting of the magic bullets* (with William S. Burroughs and Tom Waits; 1990) *When We Dead Awaken* (after ▷Ibsen; 1991)

Texas-born and trained as a painter and an architect, Robert Wilson is a leading figure of the international avant-garde, a visionary auteur director whose works have been seen in major opera houses in Europe, Berlin's Schaubühne and such recent American venues as New York's Brooklyn Academy of Music and the American Repertory Theatre in Cambridge, Massachusetts. Though potentially limited in scope and appeal (he tends to be more highly regarded in Europe than the USA), his work has reached a wide audience. Like some of his collaborators, notably Laurie Anderson and David Byrne, Wilson has transmuted heightened aestheticism into media celebrity.

Interested in the language of visual signs and signals, Wilson has an ambivalent relationship with scripted texts, claiming that they are incorporated only to be destroyed. For him, texts are interesting for their ambient significnce, for providing what he calls 'the weather, the atmosphere' of the occasion. Though he has turned his attentions more frequently of late to existing play scripts (such as ▷Ibsen's late spiritual drama *When We Dead Awaken* – which Wilson cut significantly), the spoken word is always subservient to the image. Characterised by precise and often slow-motion sequences of action, Wilson's imagistic productions (many of which he has chosen to call 'operas') create distinctive if occasionally droning dreamscapes. His evenings can be long – *The Life and Times of Joseph Stalin*, with a cast of fourteen, ran twelve hours; *KA MOUNTAIN AND GUARDenia Terrace* for 168 hours (a full week!) – but their rigours frequently fascinate, and few who saw *Einstein On the Beach*, his million-dollar project set to continuous music by Philip Glass, failed to be hypnotised by the seductive rhythms and repetitions throughout its five hours. As he has aged, both his chosen venues and his running-times have become more conventional, perhaps reflecting financial frustrations that have, for example, kept his ambitious project *The CIVIL warS* from reaching completion, despite its being considered for the 1985 Pulitzer Prize for Drama. Whatever the reason, Wilson's non-narrative theatre of free-association has had an indelible effect on theatrical form and function on both sides of the Atlantic.

Hamletmachine

Seen at the Almeida in 1987 as the lone British stop on a European tour, this 1986 piece serves to crystallise the Wilson experience. There's only one major difference – it's atypically short. At two hours without an interval, the play is a disturbing, often corrosive expansion upon East German playwright Heiner Müller's 1977 six-page version of ▷Shakespeare's *Hamlet*, and the production bespeaks Wilson's interest in what theatre evokes rather than what it means: the repeated sight of characters scratching their heads could serve to tease audience members searching for ready explication. References abound both to Ingmar Bergman and to ▷Beckett, as well as to Hamlet's problem – the curse of rationalism – in a society marked by revolution, genocide,

and the human potential for bestiality. The staging, at once deliberate and provocative, highly cerebral yet immediate, captures the Wilsonian paradox: theatre full of import and meaning which is best approached in a fluid, non-academic manner.

Try these:

▷Shakespeare and ▷Beckett; Peter Stein and Peter Sellars for contrast; ▷Lee Breuer and the Wooster Group for shared histories; Jan Fabre for a European equivalent; Ping Chong, Meredith Monk, Martha Clarke for other auteur theatre artists with strong visual and choreographic impulses; Wagner's *Gesamtkunstwerk* and Gordon Craig's ideal of director as master-artist, both Wilson's ideological forebears.

WILSON, Snoo (Andrew)   [1948–]

British dramatist and director

Plays include:
Pericles (1970), *Pignight* (1971), *Blow Job* (1971), *Lay By* (1971; with ▷Howard Brenton, ▷Brian Clark, ▷Trevor Griffiths, ▷David Hare, ▷Stephen Poliakoff, Hugh Stoddart), *Boswell and Johnson on the Shores of the Eternal Sea* (1972), *England's Ireland* (1972, with ▷Howard Brenton, Tony Bicât, ▷Brian Clark, ▷David Edgar, Francis Fuchs, ▷David Hare), *The Pleasure Principle* (1973), *Vampire* (1973), *The Beast* (1974; revised version as *The Number of the Beast*, 1982), *The Everest Hotel* (1975), *Soul of the White Ant* (1976), *England-England* (1977), *The Glad Hand* (1978), *A Greenish Man* (1978), *Flaming Bodies* (1979), *Spaceache* (1980), *Our Lord of Lynchville* (1983; revised as *Lynchville*, 1990), *Loving Reno* (1983), *The Grass Widow* (1983), *More Light* (1987), *Callas* (1990)

After writing and directing with Portable Theatre, Wilson worked as a script editor for the BBC and as a resident dramatist with the ▷RSC but, unlike his Portable contemporaries ▷David Hare and ▷Howard Brenton, he has never developed a sustained relationship with one of the major institutions. This probably relates to his eclectic and anarchic approach which, at its best, can juxtapose apparently discrete material and produce a theatrically exciting and spectacular event but can also lead to turgid self absorption and a lack of disciplined writing. Wilson's interest in the occult, magic, politics, fantasy, and all the paraphernalia of the counter-culture leads to, for example, Jung, Freud, Enoch Powell and a talking ox in *Vampire*; gorillas emerging from 'a huge eyeball in the corner of the theatre' to enact a character's subconscious impulses in *The Pleasure Principle*; a fascist sailing an oil tanker to the Bermuda Triangle in the hope of entering a time warp to encounter the Antichrist in a previous manifestation during the Wyoming cowboy strike of 1886; and ectoplasm, karma, piranha fish and marijuana in *The Grass Widow*. The occultist Aleister Crowley inevitably attracted Wilson's attention in *The Beast*; three girls sing from the top of Mount Everest to save the world from Communism in *The Everest Hotel*; a magician has an incestuous relationship with his daughter in *Loving Reno*; Jerry Falwell attempts to convert the Jews in *Our Lord of Lynchville*; a car crashes through a window in *Flaming Bodies*; a Pope dreams that Giordano Bruno asked ▷Shakespeare to revise *Il Candelaio* in *More Light* (presumably this may not be unrelated to Wilson's own aborted version of *Il Candelaio* for the RSC); and Maria Callas is given the Wilson treatment in *Callas*. Some of this may work well, some of it may leave you cold and it can be a close run thing between the two depending on the production and your own personal taste.

Try these:
▷Heathcote Williams' *AC/DC* is another example of early 1970s counter-cultural play making; ▷Barry Reckord's *X* is another modern treatment of incest; the extravagant imaginative quality of Wilson's work is generally reminiscent of ▷Peter Barnes, and *The Everest Hotel* of ▷N. F. Simpson's *One Way Pendulum*; Wilson has been described as a political absurdist – the link would be with ▷Jarry, ▷Genet and ▷Ionesco rather than ▷Beckett.

WODEHOUSE, P.G.
(Pelham Greville)   [1881–1975]
British humorous novelist, dramatist, librettist and autobiographer

Libretti include:
Miss Springtime (1916), *Have a Heart* (1917), *Oh, Boy!* (1917), *The Cabaret Girl* (1922), *Oh, Kay!* (1926), *Anything Goes* (1934), and one song (*Bill*) in *Showboat*

In partnership with Guy Bolton, Wodehouse wrote the book and lyrics of many of the most successful American ▷musicals of the 1910s and 1920s; in 1917 he had five shows running on Broadway at the same time, mostly with music by Jerome Kern. They are revived from time to time (though more for the music than the words). He adapted very few of his novels or stories for the stage, and none of the most Wodehousian ones (eg *Leave It To Psmith* (1930) rather than Wooster and Jeeves); subsequent attempts to do so have generally proved the soundness of his judgment. Andrew Lloyd Webber's only real failure to date has been his musical version of *Jeeves*, though there have been successful one-person shows such as *Jeeves Takes Charge* (1981, revived 1987 with Edward Duke). More modern styles of adaptation may solve the problem, and we may yet see Gussie Fink-Nottle's Speech Day oration to the boys of Market Snodsbury Grammar School before the horrified gaze of Bertie Wooster . . .

Try these:
▷Coward for a contrasting career

WOLFE, George C.   [1954–   ]
American dramatist

Plays include:
Up For Grabs (1975), *Block Party* (1976), *Back Alley Tales* (1978–9), *Paradise* (book and lyrics; 1985), *Queenie Pie* (libretto; 1986), *The Colored Museum* (1986), *Hunger Chic* (television play; 1989), *Jelly Lord* (1990), *Spunk*; adapted from three tales by Zora Neale Hurston (1990), *Blackout* (1991)

While his early plays explore what it means to grow up black and male in America, George C. Wolfe's most acclaimed work is *The Colored Museum* which moved his writing into the area of social satire. On this larger canvas, Wolfe examines the entire African-American experience. *The Colored Museum* takes the audience through twelve museum exhibits that come to life, debunking the myths and stereotypes of the African-American experience. Among the topics satirised are 'afro' wigs, *Ebony Magazine* as well as a spoof on *A Raisin in The Sun* called the *Last Mama on The Couch Play*. In the 'museum', Wolfe lampoons sensitive targets such as black aspirations to white middle-class life. Confident in his identity and style, Wolfe daringly mocks

(L–R) Keith David, Patty Holley, Phyliss Bailey, Regina Le Vert and (seated) Obba Babatundé in *Jelly's Last Jam*, George C. Wolfe's jazz musical based on the life of Jelly Roll Morton, 1991

the racist images that define and constrain African-Americans. In 1986, he received a CBS/Foundation of the Dramatists Guild Award in playwriting for *The Colored Museum*, which also won the 1987 George Oppenheimer/Newsday playwriting Award. The play was first presented by Crossroads Theatre in New Jersey and went on to productions in London at the ▷Royal Court Theatre and at The Public Theatre in New York. It was recently aired on PBS television. Satire is not Wolfe's only interest. *Queenie Pie*, for which he wrote the libretto, is a musical eulogy to Duke Ellington, while *Jelly Lord* does the same for Jelly Roll Morton. Joseph Papp recently named Wolfe to take over as one of three artistic supervisors at The Public Theatre. Wolfe's 1990 New York Shakespeare Festival productions included *Spunk*, adapted from the writings of Zora Neale Hurston, and ▷Brecht's *Caucasian Chalk Circle* set in Haiti. When asked why his production was not more political, Wolfe responded that being black and alive in America was already a political statement, and his work reflects this.

Try these:
▷OyamO's plays, especially *The Stalwarts* which satirises black middle-class families; ▷August Wilson's *Joe Turner's Come and Gone* and *Ma Rainey's Black Bottom* for how the music industry has treated black performers; also see ▷Lorraine Hansberry's *A Raisin in the Sun* for reference; ▷Brecht for epic theatre and Japanese Noh and Kabuki for directorial influences.

WOMEN DRAMATISTS
(Women writers pre 1945)

Although there have been women dramatists working regularly and successfully in the professional theatre since the late seventeenth century their work has tended to be marginalised, neglected and disparaged to a far greater extent than that of their male counterparts, both by their contemporaries and by posterity. ▷Aphra Behn, the Restoration dramatist, is the classic example of a woman whose personal and artistic reputation was subject to male attack in her own day and has been attacked almost continually since from a variety of mutually contradictory moral and artistic positions whereas her male contemporaries have suffered far less. But Behn is at least visible, partly because Virginia Woolf's cham-

pioning of her made her an obvious starting point for a theatrical reclamation of plays by women, while other women authors languish in, at best, footnotes and scholarly limbo. The actress Fidelis Morgan has played an important part in reclaiming women dramatists with her book *The Female Wits* (Virago, 1981), which made texts of plays by Behn, Catherine Trotter (1679–1749), Delarivière Manley (c 1667–1724), Mary Pix (c 1666–1709) and Susannah Centlivre (c 1669–1723) readily available to the general public. One practical result of the interest generated by the book was Annie Castledine's respectfully received 1987 Derby Playhouse production of Pix's *The Innocent Mistress* in an adaptation by Elizabeth Rothschild. No one has yet tried anything by the late seventeenth-century Duchess of Newcastle and most late eighteenth and nineteenth-century women writers still languish unperformed, although so too, it must be added in all fairness, do most male writers of those periods. Hannah Cowley (1743–1809), a contemporary of ▷Sheridan and ▷Goldsmith, wrote comedies which were regarded as among the best of their day. Elizabeth Inchbald (1753–1821) was another highly competent dramatist whose comedies could be worth revival. The campaign for women's voting rights in Britain at the beginning of the twentieth century led to a considerable number of essentially agit-prop plays, often performed at suffrage meetings, some of which have been revived very effectively in recent years. Among the short plays, Inez Bensusan's *The Apple* is a fine exposé of double standards and Evelyn Glover's *A Chat with Mrs Chicky* neatly reverses assumptions that the middle-class woman knows best. Among the longer plays *Votes for Women* (1907) by the actress/novelist Elizabeth Robins, best known as an early champion of ▷Ibsen, stands comparison with ▷Granville Barker in its handling of sexual politics and has a fine scene set on the edges of a Trafalgar Square Suffrage meeting where public and personal issues are entwined in a way reminiscent of the second act of ▷Sean O'Casey's *The Plough and the Stars. How the Vote Was Won*, by Cicely Hamilton and Christopher St John is a farce which extends the argument that women did not need the vote because men looked after them to its logical extreme; as more and more female relatives descend on the male householders of Britain to be 'looked after' so the men become more and more convinced of the need for female suffrage.

Hamilton and St John (whose real name was Christabel Marshall) were also involved with Edith Craig (daughter of Ellen Terry) in the 1914 staging of Hroswitha's *Paphnutius* in St John's translation. The significance of Craig's pioneering work in the theatre has been greatly undervalued; as ▷G. B. Shaw said, 'Gordon Craig [her brother Edward] has made himself the most famous producer in Europe by dint of never producing anything, while Edith Craig remains the most obscure by dint of producing everything'. Githa Sowerby's *Rutherford and Son*, produced by Craig in 1912, was revived successfully by Mrs. Worthington's Daughters in 1980, but there has so far been no interest in reviving the 1933 *Richard of Bordeaux* by Gordon Daviot (better known under another pseudonym, Josephine Tey) or anything by the mid-century dramatist Clemence Dane (pseudonym of Winifred Ashton).

Try these:
▷Medieval Drama for more on Hroswitha; ▷adaptations for female novelists/poets in stage adaptations; ▷Agatha Christie, ▷Lillian Hellman, ▷Susan Glaspell, ▷Dodie Smith, ▷Enid Bagnold as better known dramatists of previous generations; ▷Women in Theatre.

WOMEN IN THEATRE IN BRITAIN

Why still a special 'ghetto' entry for women in these so-called post-feminist times? In the first place, *post*-anything implies the achievement of an objective. With feminism, that is very far from the case. Despite two decades of struggle, equality of opportunity for women in theatre in Britain has yet to be achieved. Although women make up over 50% of audiences, and certainly a good deal more in terms of working personnel, women as writers, or directors in positions of power are still substantially fewer in number. Though a definite shift of consciousness is now noticeable – a response perhaps to two studies carried out in recent years by the Conference of Women Theatre Directors and Administrators and the Women's Playhouse Trust which confirmed the depth of discrimination against women – women are very far from being given equal status. Certainly, they are now more often to be found as directors at the ▷National Theatre or ▷RSC but are not, as yet, noted for the longevity of their stays.

Despite two decades of vigorous feminist campaigning, successful women playwrights, too, are still a rarity. Certainly a cursory look down the nominations for the prestigious Olivier Theatre awards for 1991 reveals women nominated in only two categories, and those the two for which men can certainly not apply: best actress and best supporting actress! Otherwise, no women as directors, designers, composers, or playwrights. Women and the way they work in the theatre still tend to be undervalued. The women in our Guide do, of course, reflect the strides some women playwrights have made. In Britain, ▷April de Angelis, ▷Caryl Churchill, ▷Sarah Daniels, ▷Bryony Lavery, ▷Debbie Horsfield, ▷Deborah Levy, ▷Louise Page, ▷Tasha Fairbanks, ▷Sharman Macdonald, ▷Clare McIntyre, ▷Winsome Pinnock, ▷Ayshe Raif, ▷Timberlake Wertenbaker bear witness to that. But since our first edition, only Churchill, Daniels, Macdonald and Wertenbaker have had plays put on in the West End or commissioned by the two major companies, the RSC and National Theatre.

These writers are, however, the tip of a much larger iceberg (though not as large as it was) of activity which is to do with the way women work, with feminism, with working collectively and, at another level, with power structures in society at large and theatre in particular. It also has to do with *how* women wish to write and whether they wish to adhere to the linear, Aristotelean principles which have dominated western theatre in the past 2,000 years.

Such is the decimation of the theatrical landscape of the past two years (in effect the accumulation of many more years of underfunding but also a sign of the ways social and political attitudes have changed) that there are far fewer women's groups (or groups in general) working collectively. The emphasis is much more on the individual. Still there are, thankfully, some women who still dare to risk their work being received with puzzlement, infuriation and controversy. But the cost is incresingly high. Better to go for safe entertainment if you wish to stay in the game. Women continue to bring their political commitment to their creativity at their peril.

Some groups which were set up for specific purposes, however, are still in the ring, for example, Clean Break, the ex-prisoners women's group, and Spare Tyre. Initially triggered by Susie Orbach's book *Fat Is A Feminist Issue*, Spare Tyre have brought a light-hearted revue-type approach to such subjects as compulsive eating, women's images and women's friendship (the latter a subject given a brilliantly surreal treatment by three female stand-up comics, Jenny Eclair, Julie Balloo and Maria McErlane in *Thirtysomehow*, a hit of the 1990 Edinburgh Festival Fringe). Sensible Footwear equally have made a name for themselves as a feminist performance group of sharp social observation and attack. Scarlet Harlets, as a radical feminist group with a highly physical style and organic approach to their material (they have used acrobatics, clowning, puppets and even fire-eating in their shows) have continued to develop; their recent pieces, *La Folie*, about madness and women, and the self-affirming study about female sexuality and fantasies in *Appetite of the Mind* both attest to a maturing professionalism. It is no coincidence perhaps that a particular visual flair was brought to *La Folie* by their collaboration with Anna Furse, formerly of the innovative but now defunct Blood Group and now with Paines Plough. Attempts to break out of the straitjacket of the purely verbal to find ways of expressing feminist perspective also lead to such groups as Siren, the lesbian feminist group, and ReSisters, who started off specifically looking at self-defence and have gone on to tackle women's refuges, women in the 1984 Miners' Strike (the remarkable *About Face* compiled from original research in the Nottinghamshire and Derbyshire coalfields by Cordelia Ditton and directed by Maggie Ford, in which Ditton played all 35 parts), and women and violence in ▷April de Angelis' *Women-in-law*.

Feminist polemics do not necessarily mean tedium, though sometimes it can; sorting out the good from the poor in experimental work when women are attempting to find new forms can make judging the result difficult. Much innovative women's work has disappeared for good, in particular the anarchic streak brought by Cunning Stunts, Beril and the Perils, and Burnt Bridges, whose exposé of the City, *Deals*, was an object lesson in group continuity finally paying off, though it was inevitably overshadowed by ▷Caryl Churchill's *Serious Money*. The hugely popular cabaret trio Fascinating Aida have also ceased, giving way to one of its progenitors, Dillie Kean, going gloriously solo – her off-beat humour, mimicry and singing talent deserve to put her on a par with Victoria Wood and French and Saunders.

Monstrous Regiment and the Women's Theatre Group, the doyennes of the circuit, endeavour still to encourage new writing with mixed success rate and Monstrous Regiment have bravely tried to look beyond British shores for inspiration (coming up with a particularly resonant piece with their 1990 production *Love Story of the Century*, taken from Finnish writer Marta Tikkannen's award-winning poem *Love Story of the Century* about her marriage and relationship with an alcoholic husband). Women in World Theatre has been the umbrella title under which the small Gate Theatre in London's Notting Hill enterprisingly and on a shoestring have introduced women playwrights from Russia, Germany, Africa and America never previously seen in Britain, to great critical acclaim – proof that the appetite and taste for women's work remains constant though a feminist aesthetic is harder than ever to pin down.

One of the most consistently daring directors has been Tessa Schneideman who, through her own company, Loose Change, has continued to stage plays with tremendous visual flair – again on next to no money – including plays by Carlos Fuentes (*Orchids in the Moonlight*), ▷Lorca (*Mariana Pineda*), Roxane Shafer (her extraordinary surreal exploration of Hollywood and Holocaust myths, *Adam and Eva: The Raging Angels*), Deborah Levy (*Naked Cake*) and Chilean playwright Antonio Skármeta (*Burning Patience*, about the Chilean poet Pablo Neruda). With the demise of such experimental groups as Blood Group, Hesitate and Demonstrate, Natasha Morgan's That's Not It, and Jude Alderson's irregular Sadista Sisters, times have clearly changed. Women's work, however, is built on the endeavours of the women who have gone before them, and if the message now seems neither so distinct nor the issues so clear-cut or defined as a decade ago (individualism and stand-up comedy replacing agitprop and collectivism), then that is also a reflection of the times. More positively it may also be a mark of how far we have come since the Women's Theatre Festival in the Spring of 1973, out of which came so many initiatives and so many of the writers, directors and performers who have formed the backbone of women's theatre in Britain in the past two decades (including Monstrous Regiment and the Women's Theatre Group). That Festival also included *Voices* by Susan Griffin – a stream-of-consciousness monologue of five different women's lives directed by Kate Crutchley, who as director at the Oval House has been a

Split Britches and Bloolips in *Belle Reprieve*, their cross-gender send-up of the Tennessee Williams classic, *A Streetcar Named Desire*. With Lois Weaver (l) as Stella, Peggy Shaw (c) as Stanley, Precious Pearl (née Paul) (r) as Mitch, and Bette Bourne (recumbent) as Blanche, London and New York, 1990/91

steadfast supporter of women's work – and *The Three Marias*, a dramatised reading of the true story of three Portuguese feminists imprisoned for their anti-Catholic views; two pieces of work that set the tone and agenda for so long.

To return to the beginning, women have made some advancement in the past five years. A number were directors of regional theatres – Jenny Killick, at the Traverse in Edinburgh, Clare Venables in Sheffield, Annie Castledine and Sue Todd in Derby, Sue Dunderdale at Greenwich, though all have now moved on (Venables in now in charge of Monstrous Regiment). Deborah Warner, Di Trevis, and a new generation, Phyllida Lloyd, Katie Mitchell and Jenny Killick are apparent at the RSC and the National. Jude Kelly is supremo at the new multi-million pound West Yorkshire Playhouse, Pip Broughton at Nottingham, Jenny Topper, formerly of the Bush, is now artistic director of the influential Hampstead theatre club in London, and Anna Furse of Paines Plough, one of the few remaining touring companies involved in new writing. Nikki Millican of Glasgow's Third Eye is proving a dynamic influence with her programme of commissions. LIFT, the biennial international London festival is run by two women – Rose de Wend Fenton and Lucy Neal – and the Magdalena Project in Cardiff continues to push the frontiers of women's theatre work ever forward, likewise Yvonne Brewster for Black Theatre in Britain. Julia Pascal's iconoclastic approach is one of the few making inroads in Europe. The theory goes that where there are women, there is a likelihood of women as writers being further encouraged, but Max Stafford Clark at the ▷Royal Court has encouraged women writers over a number of years. Meanwhile, the Women's Playhouse Trust, set up in the early 1980s out of a sense of frustration with the RSC and the National, in the hope of securing a building, has continued to bring on new plays by women writers (amongst them, ▷Clare McIntyre with *Low Level Panic*, ▷Winsome Pinnock's *A Hero's Welcome* and *Leave Taking* and ▷Sarah Daniels's *Beside Herself*). Under Jules Wright, they have run an impressive array of workshops on a variety of associated subjects to do with women and writing and, at last, in the Summer of 1991, acquired their own building.

Try these:
▷Lesbian theatre, ▷Cabaret, ▷Performance Art, Theatre of Black Women, Gay Sweatshop; ▷Women Dramatists, ▷New Playwriting in Britain and the USA; ▷Royal Court. The two studies mentioned in this entry are *The Status of Women in the British Theatre, 1982–1983* commissioned by Sue Parrish, published by the Conference of Women Theatre Directors and Administrators in 1984; and *What Share of the Cake?* by Caroline Gardiner, published by the Women's Playhouse Trust in 1987.

WOMEN IN THEATRE IN THE USA

It's just the same in the United States as it is in a lot of other places: though women outnumber men in the general population, in theatre audiences and as theatre workers, in the theatre they do not have equal power, equal status, equal work opportunities. On Broadway they never will – too much money, too much white male power. The real possibilities lie elsewhere.

Of course women have always been important to the American theatre as actresses, but a lack of true equality may be glimpsed in all kinds of details. In 1982 Ellen Burstyn became the first woman president of Actors' Equity Association in its sixty-year history. There are many fewer parts for women in any theatre season, and of the female roles, too few will have been written by women. These are among the reasons why actresses of the stature of Colleen Dewhurst and Joanne Woodward have complained that they can't find roles that interest them. 'Most roles for women are stupid, stereotypical, male-written and male-directed,' says Estelle Parsons. A playwright like Constance Congdon had a different problem; spending days auditioning glamorous actresses for plays about ordinary midwesterners, she couldn't find anyone she could believe in the roles. 'Actually the person I wanted to cast was the stage manager,' she sighed. Meanwhile, an avant-garde company like the Wooster Group must watch its male actors – Spalding Gray, Willem Dafoe, Ron Vawter – become film stars while its female actors (highly skilled, but hardly 'actresses') are unpursued. Until the concept of 'actress' is further eroded, the full range of women's lives can never be truly represented on most American stages.

In the United States women have from the first been well represented throughout the fields of costume and lighting design. However, at the top of the set-design field they are virtually non-existent. Marjorie Bradley Kellogg, who designed her first Broadway show in 1976, is the first woman scenic designer in 50 years to work there with any consistency. When in 1985 Kellogg's younger colleague Heidi Landesman won a Tony for her set for *Big River*, she was the first female scenic designer to be so singled out. Women are also scarce on many technical staffs, though a few theatres (Hartford Stage Company is one) employ a remarkably high percentage of female carpenters and electricians.

A ground-breaking survey conducted by a group of playwrights and directors in 1976 found that in 50 non-profit-making theatres receiving more than $50,000 a year in grants from public and private foundations, just 7% of the plays produced were written by women, and only 6% were directed by women. This Action for Women in Theatre report led to some improvement in the situation, though still not enough. A 1980 study showed that while 42% of the plays presented off-off-Broadway the previous season were directed by women, on Broadway it was only 4%. On the other hand, women directors have from the first been key figures in the regional theatre movement – Margo Jones, Nina Vance and Zelda Fichandler are its matriarchs – but even in this arena they are substantially under-represented. In recent years, however, a number of established non-profit-making theatres in the market for a new artistic director have appointed a woman to the post, thereby almost always increasing opportunities for other women artists at those theatres. In 1990 New York Shakespeare Festival producer Joe Papp announced that avant-garde director JoAnne Akalaitis, late of Mabou Mines, was his successor designate; whether or not she actually takes over, the choice was remarkable.

The Women's Project was launched by Julia Miles in 1978, partially in response to the 1976 survey. The Ford Foundation supplied a grant and the American Place Theatre, in midtown Manhattan, a home. Having mounted several dozen productions and several hundred readings by 1986, the project received a million-dollar grant from Kentucky heiress and playwright Sallie Bingham, enabling it to break with American Place, which had fallen on hard times. Hundreds of women playwrights and directors have been part of the organisation, and many have no doubt felt themselves encouraged, but the project's productions have never gained the respect the best of them deserved. For this reason most would prefer to have their work seen elsewhere.

After a flourishing of feminist theatre through the 1970s and into the 1980s, women's theatre generally seems to be on the wane. Women's Interart Theatre and the Women's Experimental Theatre in New York, and At the Foot of the Mountain in Minneapolis, once created notable work; now they are quiescent. Small groups like the three Native American sisters who make up Spiderwoman, or the trio known as Split Britches, have survived; the Cafe WOW remains the East Village home of ▷lesbian theatre. Women's theatre festivals still take place, but the energy of women theatre artists seems in the main to be found elsewhere.

In playwriting, opportunities for women appear to be increasing, however slowly. Fellowships for playwrights now go in substantial numbers to women. ▷Beth Henley, ▷Marsha Norman and ▷Wendy Wasserstein have won the Pulitzer Prize for drama in the last decade. The 1990 Humana Festival of New American Plays, the country's most prestigious such gathering, featured six plays by women and one by a man. Women's plays are being published in anthologies, in collections, as single volumes. Still, the daily reviewers almost never greet a woman's play with an enthusiasm comparable to that with which they receive their favourite plays by men. So long as most of the influential reviewers are men, this result is almost inevitable. And when these critics do champion a woman's play, it is almost always a comedy (Marsha Norman's *'night, Mother* is a notable exception) regarded by most women in theatre as insignificant and even, as in the case of Wendy Wasserstein's *The Heidi Chronicles*, not very good. Meanwhile the plays of a truly major writer like ▷Maria Irene Fornes remain little known and poorly understood. Most of the really interesting women writers are creating new forms, new kinds of plays, which are often inappropriately measured by old male standards.

Some of the most important makers of theatre in America are women: ▷Anne

Bogart, Martha Clarke, Meredith Monk, ▷Elizabeth Swados, Julie Taymor are names to conjure with. Elizabeth LeCompte, who shapes the work of the Wooster Group, may be the most brilliantly original of them all. Particularly powerful new work is coming from the field of Performance Art just now; the solo pieces of the shamanistic ▷Karen Finley and the wittily lesbian Holly Hughes are especially notable. Grounded in autobiography and openly sexual, both women's writings break through taboos, and their performances elicit right-wing outrage. Laurie Carlos, Robbie McCauley and Jessica Hagedorn – two black women and a Filipino – perform together as Thought Music and also create pieces independently, in every case providing poetic insight into their own lives and the cultures from which they come.

Try these:
▷Women dramatists, ▷Women in British theatre, ▷Lesbian theatre.

WOOD, Charles   [1932–]
British dramatist

Plays include:
Cockade (1963), *Don't Make Me Laugh* (1965), *Meals On Wheels* (1965), *Fill the Stage with Happy Hours* (1966), *Dingo* (1967), *H: or Monologues at Front of Burning Cities* (1969), *Welfare* (1970), *Veterans* (1972), *Jingo* (1975), *Has 'Washington' Legs?* (1978), *Red Star* (1984), *Across From the Garden of Allah* (1986)

Blackly comic views of the military and of filmmaking dominate the plays of Charles Wood, who began his career as a stage manager and designer, largely for ▷Joan Littlewood. Wood spent five years in the army in the 1950s, and the experience doubtless facilitated the writing of plays like *Dingo*, a satirical piece set in a German prisoner-of-war camp and focusing on two World War II heroes, and *Jingo*, set amongst the British army in Singapore in 1941. Survivors of film sets are heroes of a sort, too, and Wood has often written about the art form where he made most of his money. *Veterans*, which starred two great theatrical Sirs, John Gielgud and John Mills, focuses on two seasoned actors on the Turkey location shoot of a film; *Has 'Washington' Legs?* is a satire about a film being made of the American Revolution. His most recent plays, the Russian-set *Red Star*,

seen at the ▷RSC, and the West End comedy, *Across From the Garden of Allah*, a piece of anti-Hollywood bile that merely recycles better, similar treatments from novelists like Evelyn Waugh and Nathaniel West have been poorly received. The 1988 BBC television screening of *Tumbledown* excited a political controversy over the treatment of a young officer badly wounded in the Falklands.

Try these:
▷Beckett, for the speech rhythms of plays like *Dingo;* ▷Clifford Odets, ▷Kaufman and ▷Hart, ▷David Rabe's *Hurlyburly*, and ▷Nick Darke's *The Oven Glove Murders* for comic and/or bilious treatments of Hollywood and the film industry; ▷Anthony Minghella's *Made in Bangkok* for the Englishman abroad; ▷Willis Hall's *The Long and the Short and the Tall* and ▷Peter Nichols' *Privates on Parade* for contrasting accounts of the British army in World War II; ▷Louise Page's *Falkland Sound/Voces de Malvinas* for another view of the Falklands War.

WOOD, David   [1944–]
British dramatist

Plays include:
The Owl and the Pussycat Went to Sea . . . (1968), *The Plotters of Cabbage Patch Corner* (1970), *Nutcracker Sweet* (1977), *The Ideal Gnome Expedition* (1980), *Selfish Shellfish* (1983), *The See-Saw Tree* (1986)

A prolific and widely produced playwright, David Wood was dubbed 'the national children's dramatist' by Irving Wardle in *The Times*. His thirty or so musical plays include all the above and *The Meg and Mog Show*, which starred Maureen Lipman in its first production. Wood has also written copiously for films (the screenplay of *Swallows and Amazons*) and television (the series *Chish'n Fips* on ITV). His touring children's theatre company, Whirligig, formed with John Gould in 1979, has toured 11 of Wood's plays to over a million children.

They are notably well-crafted plays with strongly drawn characters (frequently, like the testy Pepper-pot in *The Gingerbread Man*, high in idiosyncrasy), a keen sense of dramatic tension, and a striking feel for the visual magnificence possible in theatre. *The Gingerbread Man*, for instance, takes place on the vastly magnified surface of a kitchen dresser, while the insect plotters of Cabbage Patch Corner fight their fight against insecticide (green before their time) in a garden that acquires a magical life of its own. If at times the suspicion of a formula play exists, it is outbalanced by Wood's colour, humour and sheer professionalism.

Try these:
▷David Holman, ▷Penny Casdagli, ▷Nona Shepphard for other playwrights writing for children; ▷Theatre for Young People in Britain.

WRIGHT, Nicholas   [1940–]
South Africa-born British dramatist

Plays include:
Changing Lines (1968), *Treetops* (1978), *The Gorky Brigade* (1979), *One Fine Day* (1980), *The Crimes of Vautrin* (1983), *The Custom of the Country* (1983), *The Desert Air* (1984), *Mrs Klein* (1988)

The South Africa-born Wright began his career as an actor and director before turning to playwriting in 1968 with *Changing Lines* at the Royal Court, where he worked as a casting director and – in 1976–7 – as joint artistic director. His plays show an impressive command of history and period. *Treetops*, set in Cape Town, draws upon his childhood as the youngest of three boys to emigrate from South Africa; and the African continent figures as well in *One Fine Day* (set on an East African coffee plantation), *The Custom of the Country* (racial acculturation in Johannesburg in the 1890s), and *The Desert Air* (a wartime satire set mostly in Cairo in 1942). *The Gorky Brigade* shifts the scene to Russia following the 1917 Revolution, and *The Crimes of Vautrin* – adapted from Balzac's *Splendeurs et Misères des Courtesans* – uses Paris in the 1830s to strike an anti-Thatcherite critique of a society worshipful of money and power. Wright's strengths are his intellectual curiosity and range; his weaknesses, a tendency towards overlength and caricature (for example, the opportunistic Colonel Gore in *Desert Air*).

Mrs Klein
In *Mrs Klein* Wright found a subject and a style that brought him major critical and popular success. A three-hander between female psychiatrists, including Melanie Klein and her daughter Melitta, it combines mother–daughter tensions, sibling rivalry, psychiatric case histories, soul baring, and a 'did he fall or did he push himself?' mystery. Klein's own important theoretical positions are subjected to destruction testing in Wright's subtle dramatisation of the contradictions of family life, as manifested in a family with a talent for the closest possible scrutiny of every nuance of speech or gesture.

Try these:
Plays by expatriate South Africans include Michael Picardie's *The Cape Orchard*, Yana Stajno's *Salt River*, ▷Ronald Harwood's *Tramway Road*; ▷David Hare (especially *Plenty*) for the vagaries of British colonialism; Olwen Wymark's *Nana* as an adapted nineteenth-century French novel used to lash out at Britain today; ▷Nick Darke's *Ting Tang Mine*, ▷David Edgar's *Entertaining Strangers* for use of nineteenth-century contexts to comment on Thatcherite Britain; ▷Tom Kempinksi for psychiatrists; ▷Strindberg for family life.

WYCHERLEY, William   [1640–1716]
English Restoration dramatist

Plays include:
Love in a Wood (1671), *The Gentleman Dancing Master* (1672), *The Country Wife* (1675), *The Plain Dealer* (1676)

Wycherley trained in the law but never practised, inherited one of Charles II's mistresses, married the Countess of Drogheda for her money and ended up in prison for her debts before settling down to burnish his literary reputation, which, however, rests on his plays and not on the verse to which he devoted the last thirty years of his life. The plays, robust, sexually explicit and satirical, are fine examples of what the term 'Restoration Comedy' has come to mean with their emphasis on the interrelationship of money, sex and power. But the really interesting point about Wycherley is that there is no obvious fixed authorial position for the audience to adopt. Wycherley used to be condemned, as many satirists are, for recommending the behaviour he presents in his plays; then he was praised for his celebratory presentation of a society in which the streetwise achieved their ends at the expense of those who failed to match their pretensions; now he seems to be a writer aware of the glitter and attractions of the life he presents but also aware of the void beneath. This comes over very clearly in *The Country Wife*, where the central character Horner is both hero and victim of the strategy which allows him unlimited sexual access to allegedly modest women but also condemns him to exhaustion as a provider of production line orgasms, particularly in the scene where a number of women exhaust Horner's supply of what is euphemistically called china.

Try these:
▷Molière's *Le Misanthrope* is a distant source for *The Plain Dealer*; there are similarities between Wycherley and the comedies of ▷Jonson as well as other Restoration comic writers such as ▷Aphra Behn, ▷William Congreve and ▷George Etherege; other writers of comedy of manners, such as ▷Goldsmith, ▷Sheridan, ▷Oscar Wilde, ▷Noël Coward, ▷Doug Lucie, ▷Keith Reddin; Wycherley's analysis of sex, class and power is reminiscent of ▷Joe Orton, and to a lesser extent, later ▷Alan Ayckbourn; ▷Edward Bond's *Restoration* uses conventions and themes derived from the practice of Restoration writers to make modern points.

WYMARK, Olwen   [1929–   ]
American playwright

Plays include:
The Technicians (1967); *Speak Now* (1971); *Find Me* (1977), *Loved* (1978); *Please Shine Down On Me* (1980); *Best Friends* (1981); *Buried Treasure* (1984); *Lessons and Lovers* (1985); *Strike Up The Banns* (1988)

Best known in recent years for adapatations of novels following the West End transfer of Zola's *Nana* by Shared Experience, Olwen Wymark's early plays (1967–70) were experimental in form, favourably compared to Beckett and described by Harold Hobson as 'atonal'. Born in America, Olwen Wymark came to Britain in the 1950s and married the actor Patrick Wymark, with whom she had four children. When she was widowed, she worked as a typist until Chattie Salaman of Common Stock Theatre Company encouraged her to write plays, and Gordon McDougal commissioned her to write regularly for television. In 1975 she became writer-in-residence at the Unicorn Theatre and wrote several children's plays, and in 1977 she became Gulbenkian Writer in Residence at Kingston Poly and wrote *Find Me*, about a disturbed young girl who ended up in Broadmoor. Based on a true story it was written as a result of extensive discussions with the real parents and improvisations with students, and used a cast of eight (including Sharman Macdonald before she started writing) switching roles constantly to elucidate and 'find' the personality of the central character.

Since then her plays have become more naturalistic, ('What's the point of writing Absurd theatre when nobody's surprised by it any more? Monty Python killed all that,' she says.) Usually they involve a central female character hitting out against the comfortable expectations of suburban family and friends. Cross-dressing, disguise and impersonation are subversive and liberating acts, often providing a catalyst for change and new insight. In *Loved*, two semi-real characters assume roles and engineer situations to provoke a reaction from an unresponsive husband and sister, while in her latest play, a comedy *Strike Up The Banns* (a later version of *Speak Now*), a bamboozled wife and mother dresses up as her husband's imaginary brother Rollo when her daughter's right-wing, moral crusading future father-in-law comes to dinner. Her husband retaliates by dressing up as Rollo's highly strung wife Lilian.

Since the success of *Nana* Wymark has been inundated with requests for adaptations, has worked extensively for television and radio and teaches on David Edgar's Playwriting course at Birmingham University. All this has left her little time for her own writing, but a new stage play is promised.

Try these:
See Adaptations and Adapters for other successful adapters, ▷Caryl Churchill and ▷Joe Orton for cross-dressing, Melissa Murray's *Bodycell*, David Edgar's *Mary Barnes* and Clean Break Company for other examples of young women in trouble; Ayckbourn for put-upon wives.

Y

YANKOWITZ, Susan [1941–]
American dramatist

Plays include:
Terminal (1969), *Transplant* (1971), *Sideshow* (1971), *Slaughterhouse Play* (1971), *Boxes* (1972), *Acts of Love* (1973), *Wooden Nickels* (1973), *American Piece* (1974), *Still Life* (1977), *True Romances* (1978), *Qui Est Anna Marx* (1978), *Baby* (1983), *A Knife in the Heart* (1983), *Taking Liberties* (1986), *Alarms* (1987), *Monk's Revenge* (1988), *Utterances* (1991)

New Jersey-born Yankowitz was an original member of Joe Chaikin's Open Theatre, one of the most influential groups in America's breakaway avant-garde theatre movement of the 1960s and 1970s, where company-created, physically intense, performer-centred styles of theatre held sway. Yankowitz collaborated on several texts with Chaikin, of which *Terminal* is the best known. An extraordinary and clinical exploration on death and morality, John Lahr said it sent 'audiences away thirsting for life'. The confrontational and highly controversial *Slaughterhouse Play*, written for Joseph Papp's Public Theatre, had as its central metaphor butchered meat and a slaughterhouse where the genitals of black men were sold to white men as prize meat. British audiences were introduced to Yankowitz with *Alarms*, written in response to the Chernobyl disaster. Presented in 1987 by ▷Monstrous Regiment, the play is part surreal thriller, part passionate anti-nuclear polemic. Though not her best work, it caught the agony of a contemporary Cassandra, in the character of a crusading obstetrician. In the USA, *Alarms* was produced by the Omaha Magic Theatre in 1988. Yankowitz's *Knife in the Heart*, a terrifying play about a boy who becomes an assassin, received further work at New York's New Dramatists in 1988–9. An accomplished novelist and screenwriter, Yankowitz wrote the script for *The Amnesiac*, and did the film adaptation of her novel *Silent Witness*. Her most recent effort, *Utterances*, was directed by Joe Chaikin for the Women's Project and Productions off-Broadway in the spring of 1991.

Try these:
Vladimir Gubaryev's extraordinary post-Chernobyl play, *Sarcophagus*; Cordelia Ditton and Maggie Ford's *The Day the Sheep Turned Pink* for another post-Chernobyl, documentary-style look at nuclear power, initiated *prior to* Chernobyl; ▷Deborah Levy's *Clam* is another anti-nuclear/sexual politics play; ▷Stephen Lowe's *Keeping Body and Soul Together*; for other feminist images of grotesquerie Adrienne Kennedy's *A Rat's Mass*, *A Lesson in Dead Language* and *Funnyhouse of a Negro*; ▷Caryl Churchill's *Owners* and Myrna Lamb's *The Butcher's Shop* for other slaughterhouse images; ▷Megan Terry also has close connections with Omaha Magic Theatre.

YEATS, W.B. (William Butler) [1865–1939]
Irish poet, dramatist, theatre manager and politician

Plays include:
The Countess Kathleen (1892), *The Land of Heart's Desire* (1894), *The Shadowy Waters* (1900), *Diarmuid and Grania* (1901; with George Moore), *Cathleen ni Houlihan* (1902), *The Pot of Broth* (1902), *Where There is Nothing* (1902; revised version with ▷Lady Gregory as *The Unicorn from the Stars*, 1907), *The Hour Glass* (1903), *The King's Threshold* (1903), *On Baile's Strand* (1904), *Deidre* (1906), *The Golden Helmet* (1908; revised version as *The Green Helmet*, 1910), *At the Hawk's Well* (1916), *The Dreaming of the Bones* (1919), *The Only Jealousy of Emer* (1919), *The Player Queen* (1919), *Calvary* (1921), *King Oedipus* (1926), *Oedipus at Colonus* (1927), *The*

Resurrection (1927), *Fighting the Waves* (1929), *The Words Upon the Window Pane* (1934), *The Herne's Egg* (1938), *A Full Moon in March* (1938), *The King of the Great Clock Tower* (1938), *Purgatory* (1938), *The Death of Cuchulain* (1939)

As well as being one of the great poets of the twentieth century, Yeats played a major part in establishing the modern Irish professional theatre through his managerial work at the Abbey and wrote throughout his life a series of mainly short plays, usually in verse, which are stylistically innovative, blending symbolist, oriental and Irish elements to create an art which, in his own words, does its work 'by suggestion, not by direct statement, a complexity of rhythm, colour, gesture, not space-pervading like the intellect but a memory and a prophecy'. Irish legend provides the material for most of the plays from the early personifications of Ireland in the figure of Cathleen ni Houlihan to his final play, *The Death of Cuchulain*, which is the culmination of a lifelong interest in the Red Branch cycle of folk tales. His concern for the supernatural also finds an outlet in the seance of *The Words Upon the Window Pane*, his play about Jonathan Swift. In many ways Yeats' interest in non-naturalistic use of sound, music, masks and colours anticipates much of the ▷Performance Art of the present but outside Ireland he is seldom produced professionally. The Cuchulain plays have been performed as a cycle and they offer a tempting proposition to an adventurous director in view of the success of ▷Peter Brook's *The Mahabarata*.

Try these:
▷J. M. Synge and ▷Sean O'Casey were originally staged at the Abbey under Yeats' aegis; ▷T.S. Eliot wrote the other most successful twentieth-century verse dramas – *Sweeney Agonistes* is particularly interesting to compare with Yeats; ▷Melissa Murray's *The Crooked Scythe* is a verse drama about the Black Death. Maxwell Anderson's verse dramas, especially *Mary Stuart*, were popular in the 1930s and 1940s.

YIDDISH AND JEWISH THEATRE IN THE USA

Yiddish theatre in America was an immigrant theatre which began with the first wave of eastern European Jewish immigrants in 1880.

Jewish-American theatre is an amorphous category descended from the dregs of Yiddish theatre, but it also includes anything vaguely Jewish – plays about Israel, plays by Jewish authors, plays about Jews – which loosely commutes traditional Jewish values into contemporary issues.

The first Yiddish-American plays were written by Abraham Goldfaden, one of the founders of Jewish theatre in Eastern Europe. Goldfaden began with popular folk elements, but eventually he transcribed them into scripts. Most of these – (*Shulamith* (1880), for example, and *Bar Kohkhba* (1883) – evoked the Jews' glorious past and anticipated a return to Jerusalem.

By the turn of the century, mystical-religious plays like Sholem Asch's *God of Vengeance* (1907) and S. Anski's *Dybbuk* were being performed in New York in both English and Yiddish. About a decade later, Sholem Aleichem was writing folkloric parables for The Yiddish Art Theatre, founded by Maurice Schwartz in 1918. The Yiddish Art Theatre toured Europe, and then Schwartz tried to open a Broadway theatre to perform European classics in Yiddish. But the Yiddish theatre had already begun its great decline as Jews became more assimilated. By the 1930s, Yiddish theatre in America was what most Jewish theatre is today: revivals, sometimes starring the ageing originals of the earlier theatre; musicals of a Borscht Belt quality, and Yiddish adaptations of Broadway hits.

After World War II, a number of Jewish playwrights began to write about the Holocaust. In 1959, Frances Goodrich and Albert Hackett adapted *The Diary of Anne Frank* for the stage. ▷Arthur Miller's *Incident At Vichy* (1965) also dealt with the Holocaust, but it tried to complicate the roles of heroes and villains. More recently, *A Shayna Maidel* (*A Pretty Girl*) tells the story of two sisters reunited 20 years after the war. *A Shayna Maidel*, written by Atlanta-based playwright ▷Barbara Lebow in 1985, goes beyond any clichés about ethnicity and deals with the sisters' personal losses.

In terms of Jewish-American theatre, or theatre that uses elements of Jewish culture but is performed in English, the most famous mainstream playwright is ▷Neil Simon; whose latest narrative play based on his New York childhood, *Lost in Yonkers*, opened on Broadway in 1991. More innovative is A Traveling Jewish Theater, which works out of San Francisco. ATJT, an ensemble made up of Helen Stofulz, Naomi Newman and Corey Fischer, stretches the spiritual and epistemological underpinnings of Jewish culture over a contemporary drum. In *Heart of the World*, for example, they examine the implications of child-rearing for mixed-marriage couples. There are still Jewish theatres in New York, Chicago and other major cities where there are large Jewish communities, but most of these mix a bland stew of classical Yiddish repertory performed in English and new plays in traditional forms. In New York, for example, Jewish Repertory Theater recently produced Paddy Chayevsky and revived some of Goldfaden's plays. In Skokie, Illinois, the National Jewish Theater tries to keep the heritage of Jewish theatre alive with similar mishmashes.

In the early 1980s, there was a renaissance of groups who focused on issues of Judaism, although many of them shared stylistic similarities with the 1960s radical theatre. Brooklyn's The Buttonhole Players, for example, adapted Jewish tales to a less explicit modern idiom, and the Vermont ensemble Barking Rooster uses circus arts and puppetry to weave a Cabbalistic web, much like a Jewish Bread and Puppet Theatre. But even these shows seem outdated, although perhaps it's too early to tell whether multiculturalism and the economic demands of a larger audience will force Jewish theatre to follow in Yiddish theatre's footsteps.

Try these:
▷ Arnold Wesker for a British involvement in specifically Jewish issues; ▷ Harold Pinter; ▷ Asian Theatre and ▷ Black Theatre for similar questions; ▷ C.P. Taylor's *Good*, Hochhüth's *The Representative*, ▷ Sherman's *Bent* for other Holocaust plays; Julia Pascal's *Theresa* for Nazi collaboration, British style.

YOSHIMURA, James   [1950–]
American dramatist

Plays include:
Lion Dancers (1976), *Stunts* (1977), *Mercenaries* (1982), *Ohio Tip-Off* (1983), *Union Boys* (1985), *In Transit* (1989)

Yoshimura is one of several Asian-American playwrights to achieve a long-overdue measure of visibility in the past decade. He was born in Chicago and graduated from the Yale School of Drama, where *Stunts* was his award-winning graduate thesis. *Mercenaries*, Yoshimura's professional debut, was produced by New York's Interart Theatre. An incisive and uncompromising portrait of 'unofficial' political policy making at its basest level, the play concerns three white American soliders of fortune, Vietnam veterans, who are being held prisoner on a Caribbean island following an abortive coup. The boorish and jingoistic grunts come off as cogs in an even uglier machine when an American envoy sent to monitor the situation agrees to their execution as part of face-saving deal. In later plays, Yoshimura returned to the themes of allegiances and divided loyalties within traditional male (though multiracial) enclaves: *Ohio Tip-Off* explores the lives of a group of minor-league basketball players; *Union Boys*, set in the reelroom of a Chicago newspaper office, details the tensions between lifelong buddies being sold out by the paper and by their own union.

Try these:
▷ Harold Pinter's *One for the Road* and ▷ Richard Nelson's *Principia Scriptoriae* for plays with similar *realpolitik* themes; Allan Havis' *Hospitality* and *Haut Gout* for more surreal treatment of political game-playing and cultural displacement; David Henry Hwang, ▷ Philip Kan Gotanda, R.A. Shiomi among many other contemporary Asian-American dramatists.

YOUNG, Phil   [1949–]
British director and dramatist

Plays include:
Crystal Clear (1983), *Kissing God* (1985), *Torpedoes in the Jacuzzi* (1987)

After winning the ▷ RSC Buzz Goodbody Award for Best Director at the National Student Drama Festival in 1976, Young went on to a career as a director in a variety of theatres including Leeds Playhouse, Leicester Haymarket and Croydon Warehouse. In 1983 he devised *Crystal Clear* through improvisation and workshops with a small group of actors. This play won an *Evening Standard* most promising playwright award. Since then he has worked on other projects in a similar style.

Crystal Clear

The play uses a naturalistic form to convey an intense and, at times, distressingly intimate sense of pressure, as Richard, an art dealer with diabetes, falls victim to the abrupt onset of blindness. Ironically, he is having a love-affair with Thomasina, who is blind. Their gentle and genuinely touching relationship is highlighted by visits from Richard's ex-lover Jane, who, after trying unsuccessfuly to maintain her previous place in his life, attempts to help him after his blindness. He drives her away, only to discover that Thomasina now rejects him, despite her feelings for him. In this way the defensive layers of politeness and passive acceptance which conceal the awful realities of life for the blind are stripped away to reveal the agony and desperation which lie beneath.

Try these:
▷Mark Medoff's *Children of a Lesser God* for deafness and its effects on personal relationships; ▷Brian Clark's *Whose Life Is It Anyway* comically raises painful questions, on terminal illness, responsibility and dignity; ▷Jean-Claude Van Itallie's *The Traveller* deals with aphasia (inability to make sense of words) with equal passion as well as beauty; Graeae for other more upbeat, images of disability.

 **Z**

ZALOOM, Paul   [1951–]
Performance artist, mime and puppeteer

Productions include:
The Fruit of Zaloom (1979), *Zalooming Along* (1980), *Zaloominations* (1981), *Crazy as Zaloom* (1982), *Creature from the Blue Zaloom* (1984), *The House of Horror* (1988)

In 1971, Zaloom began his career with a seven-year stint with The Bread and Puppet Theatre and has continued to appear at their annual festival in rural Vermont. From Peter Schumann, the German-born director of the troupe, Zaloom learned to combine political puppetry with epic theatre. But Schumann's lyricism reflected a European aesthetic, and Zaloom needed to create from an American sensibility. He uses crass objects, junk collected from trash piles, to parody the icons of our consumer culture. Zaloom can create the city of New York out of the disposable materials that symbolise our throwaway mentality: styrofoam packing products form the skyline, tattered cartons for slums, tiny yellow cowboy hats for taxis, the subway out of a tube of dirt, ambulances out of band-aid boxes. Zaloom plays the politicians as shiny apples and ghetto inhabitants as newspaper cut-outs chased by sock-puppet slumlords. A master pupeteer, Zaloom manipulates and animates these objects into scathing political satire accompanied by good-natured, high-spirited patter that turns object into metaphor.

Zaloom's performances are a hybrid form combing mime, clowning and puppetry, and he appears in theatres as well as at art galleries and mime festivals. His shows include crankies – hand-drawn movies on paper scrolled in a wooden box. These 'paper videos' are accompanied by satiric lectures on American society. Zaloom combines a Keaton-like mask, Punch and Judy verve, and surrealist humour into a style that serves his political message. His primitive methods

contrast with the increasing use of technology by other performance artists. His Theatre of Trash finds its roots in Dada's iconoclasm and he is the heir to Marcel Duchamp's irreverent cultural commentary.

Try these:
Peter Schumann for political puppetry; Erwin Piscator for Epic Theatre; Commedia dell'arte for broad humour; ▷ Alfred Jarry and Marcel Duchamp for irreverent satire; Futurists Tommaso Marinetti, Gilbert Clavel, Fortunato Depero, Enrico Prampolini and Giacomo Balla, and Dadaists Sophie Taeuber and Hans Arp for avant-garde puppetry; Buster Keaton, Marcel Marceau and Charles Chaplin for mime; Laurie Anderson for high-tech performance art; ▷ Performance Art.

ZEDER, Suzan L.   [1948–]
American dramatist and educator

Plays include:
Wiley and the Hairy Man (1972), *The Play Called Noah's Flood* (1972), *Step on a Crack* (1974), *Something with Jamie in the Title* (1975), *Osma of Oz: A Tale of Time* (1975), *Doors* (1980), *Mother Hicks* (1983), *An Evening at Versailles featuring: THE MISER* (1986), *The Death and Life of Sherlock Holmes* (1987)

Suzan Zeder is acknowledged for producing a new play form for young audiences. Refraining from adapting popular literature and stories, Zedar chose to focus her plays on real problems facing children. *Mother Hicks* deals with an orphaned girl's search for her real parents and birth name. *Wiley and the Hairy Man* examines a child's concept of mystery, magic and fear. And Zeder's most notable play, *Step on a Crack*, takes place in a contemporary setting with a girl adjusting to a new step-parent. Zedar's theatrical success has paralleled her educational career. She has held appointments in playwriting or child drama at Florida State University, University of Washington, University of Dallas and Southern Methodist University, and has conducted workshops or held guest lecturer positions at universities throughout the United States. Additionally, Zedar has an estimable record of scholarship with a number of articles about aspects of children's theatre. She is recognised for making the young person's theatrical experience extend beyond diversion and into issues of growth and maturation.

Step on a Crack

Step on a Crack was an early effort to address a difficult topic from a child's perspective and for an audience of children. Ellie, the central character, is ten and has lived as her father's only child for the six years since her mother's death. When her father remarries, Ellie rebels and retreats into a world of make-believe where she plays with imaginary friends. The play was one of the first to confront fantasy and illusion as an unworkable solution to the real source of a child's concern.

Try these:
▷David Wood, ▷David Holman, ▷Penny Casdagli, ▷Paul Zindel, ▷Wendy Kesselman as other writers for young people.

ZEPHANIAH, Benjamin   [1958–]
British poet and dramatist

Plays include:
Playing the Right Tune (1984), *Job Rocking* (1986), *Streetwise* (1990), *Delirium* (1990)

Born in Birmingham, brought up in Jamaica, educated in a number of reform schools and by a short spell in prison, rastafarian Benjamin Zephaniah first came to prominence as a uniquely talented performance poet, chanting unaccompanied indictments of the Handsworth riots and police brutality to brisk Afro-Caribbean rhythms in the early 1980s.

Initially reluctant to accept the label of poet ('I'm not white and I'm not dead'), his popularity and his interest in the rhythm and power of words quickly grew, and he has diversified into broadcasting, journalism, music and theatre writing. In the late 1980s, the prospect of his appointment to a poetry chair at Cambridge caused a storm in the tabloid press. Although he has published several books of poetry, he rightly insists that his verse works best when spoken or listened to live; as such, it seemed natural he should turn to the theatre. His theatre work is characterised by a high political awareness and a wish to get away from the sex comedies which constitute a large part of the theatrical fare served up for Black audiences. Although his popularity has brought acceptance from the cultural establishment, Zephaniah maintains that he is still angry and still wishes to change things. He sees his continuing work in theatre as just another part of his vocation 'to discover the poetry in everyday life.' He remains at the forefront of Black writing, and is one of the few writers today to can successfully write verse plays.

Streetwise

Zephaniah's verse play explores the different reactions of four Black Londoners to an attempt made by White Councillors to sanitise and bureaucratise the Notting Hill Carnival. The violent attitudes of posse-leader Angel are contrasted to the peaceful, celebratory stance of Val and the pessimism of Bingy, who just wants to walk away. The question of response takes on a new urgency when the cool-headed local hero Streetwise enters, badly beaten after a racist attack. The play frustrated many since it offered alternatives with no conclusions, and Zephaniah's words lost some of their power in the actors' delivery. Nevertheless, his achievement remains in bringing both verse and Black theatre to large, racially and socially mixed audiences.

Try these:
Amani Naphtali's *Ragamuffin*, another rastafarian playwright, was, amongst other things, a response to the London Broadwater Estate race riots; other contemporary black playwrights in Britain are Edgar Wallace, Nigel Moffatt, Michael Ellis, Winsome Pinnock and Trish Cooke;

Trevor Rhone's comedies are perhaps some of the work Zephaniah is reacting against; Caryl Churchill's *Serious Money* for a comparative use of verse; also Neil Bartlett's colloquial translation of Moliere's *The Misanthrope* for Red Shift; see also Black Theatre.

Try these:
Kenneth Koch's *George Washington Crossing the Delaware* and ▷George C. Wolfe's *The Colored Museum* for other American history lessons, comic book style; ▷Peter Nichols' *Poppy* for a panto-derived British variant; ▷Dario Fo for theatrical clowning; the 'New Vaudeville' movement in the US for related Performance Art, Ken Campbell for a British equivalent.

ZIGUN, Dick   [1953–]
American dramatist and producer

Plays include:
His Master's Voice (1977), *3 Unnatural Acts* (1978), *Red Letter Days* (1986), *Barnacle Bill the Husband* (1989), *Into the Night Life . . . A Coney Island of the Mind* (1990), *The Misadventures of Alice E. Neuman* (1990)

Dick Zigun grew up, as he likes to point out, in P.T. Barnum's hometown of Bridgeport, Connecticut; a coincidence entirely suited to Zigun's chosen metier as showman and pre-server of America's vaudeville heritage. In 1980, after graduating from Yale Drama School, Zigun founded Coney Island, USA, a museum and theatre company dedicated to reviving the parades, sideshows, live performances and exhibits that characterised the amusement park in its heyday. Zigun's own plays combine elements of carnival exhibitionism and avant-garde wayfaring in a unique fashion, frequently incorporating toys, found objects, sideshow performers and musical interludes in charting America's fascination with the sensational.

A Life in a Day: Lucky Lindy, the middle segment of *3 Unnatural Acts*, has received several independent productions at theatres around the US. It tells the story of Charles Lindbergh's life in cartoon shorthand, its 33½ brief scenes corresponding to the number of hours spent in the momentous Atlantic crossing. The play makes use of historical slides, audience singalongs, miniature props (Lindbergh's plane is a cheap toy jerked along a string from one side of the stage to the other) and a variety of Marx Brothers antics. The throwaway style is at once hilarious and lurid, belying the keenness of its underlying insights into one of the 20th century's major cultural icons.

ZINDEL, Paul   [1936–]
American dramatist, screenwriter and novelist

Plays include:
Dimensions of Peacocks (1959), *Euthanasia and The Endless Heart* (1960), *A Dream of Swallows* (1962), *The Effect of Gamma Rays on Man-in-the-Moon Marigolds* (1966), *And Miss Reardon Drinks A Little* (1971), *The Ladies Should Be in Bed* (1973), *The Secret Affairs of Mildred Wild* (1973), *Ladies At The Alamo* (1977), *A Destiny With Half Moon Street* (1981), *Ladies on the Midnight Planet* (1982), *Amulets Against The Dragon Forces* (1989)

Born in Staten Island, New York, Paul Zindel attended Wagner College, and became a high-school Chemistry teacher. He began his writing career with novels for and about teenagers. He went on to study playwriting with ▷Edward Albee who directed Zindel's first play off-Broadway. In the late 1960s Zindel was the playwright-in-residence at Houston's Alley Theatre.

The central theme of sensitive children dominated by demented parents, particularly the mother figure, runs through Zindel's plays. In *The Effect of Gamma Rays on Man-in-the Moon Marigolds*, his best-known work, we meet a dysfunctional family headed by an idiosyncratic, hateful widow living with her two daughters. The older daughter has passed the point of sanity while the younger one turns to a pet rabbit for love and comfort. The younger daughter's high-school science project, studying the effect of gamma rays on withering marigolds yields the metaphor for the decay of the family, as well as of the self. Some of the marigolds do blossom, offering a symbolic ray of hope. Critics called the play touching, honest and compassionate and it won the Pulitzer Prize for Drama, the New York Critics' Award and the Drama Desk Award in 1971.

In *Miss Reardon Drinks a Little*, Zindel continues the theme of eccentricity masking insanity. The play was coolly received despite its witty dialogue. Zindel is often criticised for an overly harsh view of women, but he stands by his work as an exorcism of personal experience, and maintains that for him, the view is valid.

Try these:

▷Tennessee Williams' *Glass Menagerie* and Arthur Miller's *Death of a Salesman* for dysfunctional family; ▷Pirandello's *Henry IV*, Witkewicz' *The Madman and The Nun* and ▷Dürrenmatt's *The Physicists* for explorations of sanity and madness; Berta Freistadt's *Chicken Licken* for more grotesque parents.

Acknowledgments

The authors would like to thank the many people without whose help and co-operation this book could not have been compiled. Especial thanks are due to: Mrs Foster at the British Theatre Association's reference library for her invaluable help in research; to Ian Herbert's *London Theatre Record* and his personal generosity in answering numerous queries; to all the agents (and some of the playwrights themselves) who supplied information, sometimes at very short notice; to innumerable press officers and literary managers; to the following for enlightening conversations – Yvonne Brewster, Alby James, Anton Phillips, Jim Hiley, Graeme Miller, David Benedict, Peter Hepple, Carl Miller, Lois Keidan, Jules Wright, Jonathan Lamede, Alan Pope, Sue Sanders, Lyn Gardner and Ros Asquith. Many thanks also go to Stephanie King, Wendy Wheeler, Kerry Shale, Carina Petter, Christine Page and Ursula Philips. For their advice on all aspects of American theatre, the authors and publisher would like to thank Tad Lathrop (Senior Editor, Back Stage Books) and John Istel. Particular thanks are due to Professor Mira Felner of Hunter College, New York for her invaluable support and assistance throughout the project.

William Duff-Griffin in Romulus Linney's *2*, Actors Theatre of Louisville, Spring 1990

Further reading

There are a vast number of books on theatre ranging from do-it-yourself manuals to theoretical works and studies of individual authors and directors. This list is made up of some of the books we found useful in writing this guide, both reference works and studies of specific topics which offer in depth coverage of individual issues.

Antonin Artaud, *The Theatre and its Double*, 1970

Eric Bentley (ed), *Theory of the Modern Stage*, 1968

C. W. E. Bigsby (ed), *Contemporary English Drama*, 1981

Gerald Bordman, *The Oxford Companion to American Theatre*, 1984

Edward Braun, *The Director and the Stage from Naturalism to Grotowski*, 1982

Peter Brook, *The Empty Space*, 1983

Peter Brook, *The Shifting Point*, 1988

Simon Callow, *Being an Actor*, 1984 and 1985

Sandy Craig (ed), *Dreams and Deconstructions; Alternative Theatre in Britain*, 1980

John Gassner and Edward Quin, *Reader's Encyclopedia of World Drama*, 1970

Phyllis Hartnoll (ed), *The Oxford Companion to the Theatre*, originally 1951, 4th ed 1983

Catherine Itzin, *Stages in the Revolution*, 1980

Catherine Itzin, *Directory of Playwrights, Directors, Designers 1*, 1983

Helene Keyssar, *Feminist Theatre*, 1984

Helen and Richard Leacroft, *Theatre and Playhouse*, 1984

David Ian Rabey, *British and Irish Political Drama in the Twentieth Century*, 1986

Constantin Stanislavski, *Creating a Role*, 1963

J. L. Styan, *Drama, Stage and Audience*, 1975

J. L. Styan, *Modern Drama in Theory and Practice*, 3 vols, 1981

William Tydeman, *The Theatre in the Middle Ages*, 1978

James Vinson (ed), *Contemporary Dramatists*, 1982

Michelene Wandor, *Carry on Understudies*, 1986

Michelene Wandor, *Look Back in Gender*, 1987

John Willett (ed), *Brecht on Theatre*, 1969

Contributors

Clare Bayley is theatre editor at *What's On* in London and has contributed reviews and features to *The Independent*, *The Guardian*, *The Observer*, *Vogue* and *City Limits* amongst others. She wrote the libretto for an opera, *The Waterfall* performed at the ICA in 1990 and extracts from her play *Eco Warrior* had a rehearsed reading at the Soho Poly in June 1990.

Annika Bluhm is the editor and compiler of *The Methuen Audition Book for Men* and *The Methuen Audition Book for Women*. She has recently compiled a collection of plays by the French–Canadian playwright Michel Tremblay with a full introduction placing his work in context. She works as a literary assistant.

Mary Brennan is the drama and dance critic of *The Glasgow Herald*. She has also written about theatre for *Drama* magazine, was on the editorial board of *Scottish Theatre News* and is a regular contributor to arts programmes on BBC Radio Scotland and the BBC World Service.

Alastair Cording is a professional actor. He has a Ph.D. from Glasgow University. He has taught there and at Strathclyde University, where for a number of years he was Assistant Director of the University Drama Centre. He is the editor of the second edition of Bloomsbury's *Actors Handbook*.

Eileen E. Cottis is Senior Lecturer in French and co-founder of, and former Course Tutor for, the MA in Modern Drama Studies at the Polytechnic of North London. She is a committee member of the Society for Theatre Research and a member of the International Federation for Theatre Research, and has written on French and English nineteenth-century theatre.

Nick Curtis is assistant editor of *Plays & Players* theatre magazine. He contributes theatre reviews to *Time Out* and features to *GQ*, *Harpers & Queen* and various other publications.

Luke Dixon is a writer, theatre director and celebratory artist who has created spectacular performance works across Europe. He is an advisor to many major arts bodies including the Arts Council of Great Britain and the London Arts Board.

Marguerite Feitlowitz is a freelance writer, editor, and translator who has published in *Theater*, *The Drama Review*, *Bomb*, *The American Voice*, *City Lights* and other magazines, newspapers and quarterlies. She edited and translated *Theatre Pieces: An Anthology by Liliane Atlan* (The Penkevill Publishing Co., 1985) and edited and translated *Information for Foreigners: Plays by Griselda Gambaro* (Northwestern University Press, 1991).

Mira Felner is a Professor of Theatre at Hunter College and The Graduate Center of the City University of New York. She received a Ph.D. in Drama from New York University and has acted and directed in New York and Paris. In addition to numerous journal and encyclopaedia articles, she is the author of *Free to Act: An Integrated Approach to Acting Technique* and *Apostles of Silence: The Modern French Mimes* which was named Outstanding Academic Book in Theatre, 1985–86 by *Choice*. She has been assisted in the preparation of entries for the Bloomsbury *Theatre Guide* by Nancy Grome, David Leichtman, Paul Nadler, Christine A. Pinkowicz, and Jennifer Stock.

Alexis Greene is an Adjunct Assistant Professor in the doctoral program in Educational Theatre at New York University. Articles and criticism by Dr. Greene have appeared in a variety of publications, including *The New York Times*, *American Film Magazine*, and *American Theatre Magazine*, where she is an affiliated writer and critic.

Trevor R. Griffiths is Director of Media and Interdisciplinary Studies at the Polytechnic of

North London, where he runs the MA in Modern Drama Studies and an undergraduate degree in Theatre Studies; he has reviewed theatre for *City Limits*, *The Scotsman* and the *Glasgow Herald*; while lecturing at Strathclyde University he played a prominent part in the award winning Strathclyde Theatre Group; he was Chair of the touring theatre company Foco Novo; his previous books are *Stagecraft* and the *Longman Guide to Shakespeare Quotations* (with Trevor A. Joscelyne).

Andrew B. Harris has chaired Theatre Departments at Southern Methodist University and Columbia University prior to his present position as Chair at Texas Christian University. He received his doctorate from Columbia University and did his undergraduate work at the University of Chicago. A writer member of New Dramatists (NYC), he is completing work on a volume entitled *Broadway Theatre* for Routledge.

Naseem Khan is a writer, broadcaster and freelance journalist and was Theatre Editor of *Time Out* and Fringe Editor of the British Theatre Association's *Drama* magazine. Her book, *The Arts Britain Ignores* (1976) published by the Arts Council, the Commonwealth Relations Commission and the Gulbenkian Foundation, first put Britain's ethnic minorities arts on the cultural agenda. She is a contributor to both the first and second edition.

Howard Loxton was an actor and stage manager in repertory and the West End before becoming a writer and editor and although he is also the author of a number of books on historical and natural history subjects theatre remains his greatest enthusiasm. Recent publications include an introduction to theatre for young readers and he is currently completing a book on promenade performances.

Walter J. Meserve is Distinguished Professor of Theatre and English at the CUNY Graduate School. Among his published books are *The Complete Plays of W.D. Howells*, 1960; *An Outline History of American Drama*, 1965; *An Emerging Entertainment: the Drama of the American People to 1828*, 1977; *Heralds of Promise: the Drama of the American People during the Age of Jackson, 1829–1849*, 1986. He has received a Fulbright Award, a

Rockefeller Award, three fellowships from the National Endowment for the Humanities and a Gugenheim Fellowship.

Kent Neely has been a member of the University of Minnesota theatre arts faculty and Managing Director of the University Theatre since 1977. His research has centred on such contemporary theatrical artists as JoAnne Akalaitis, Ushio Amagatsu, Lee Breuer, Ping Chong, David Henry Hwang, Tadashi Suzuki and Robert Wilson. Professor Neely's performance reviews and studies have appeared in *Theatre Journal*, *The Journal of Dramatic Theory and Criticism* and *High Performance* and he has presented papers at regional and national conferences. He teaches classes in dramatic appreciation, myth and modern performance and theatre management. Professor Neely also serves on the Board of Directors for the Association for Theatre in Higher Education and the Mid America Theatre Conference.

M. Elizabeth Osborn is a freelance editor, writer and dramaturg with a particular interest in contemporary American theatre and performance art. She has a Ph.D. from the University of Pennsylvania and is the editor of *On New Ground: Contemporary Hispanic–American Plays* and *The Way We Live Now: American Plays and the AIDS Crisis*, two anthologies published by TCG.

Janice Paran is on the editorial staff of *American Theatre* magazine. She teaches in the Drew University theatre department, and was, until the theatre's demise, the literary manager of The New Theatre of Brooklyn.

Deborah Philips teaches Literature and Women's Studies at the West London Institute of Higher Education. She once worked for Ray Cooney Productions. She was a co-founder of *Women's Review* and has written for *The Stage* and *City Limits*.

Christine A. Pinkowicz is a lecturer in the Hunter College Department of Theatre and Film and the Lehman College Department of Continuing Education and is a doctoral candidate in the City University of New York PhD Program in Theatre. She has an MFA in Arts Administration from Columbia University, has served as Director of Development for Circle In The Square Theatre, and writes on the inter-relationship between artistic mission and economic survival in the theatre. She has published articles in *Western European Stages* and *Theatre Times* and co-researched the book *Space to Create: The Theatre Community in Crisis*. Her *Real Estate Crisis in the New York City Not-for-Profit Theatre* has been used widely by city government and service organizations.

Judith Piper is an Assistant Professor of Performance in an interdisciplinary program in the School of Arts and Humanities at the University of Texas at Dallas. Her first book, *Staging Exceptional Worlds: The Subject of Performance*, will be published in 1992. It is the study of four performance artists, Ping Chong, Laura Sarabough, Alan Finneran, and Linda Mussmann, seen in the context of the cultural politics of identity. Her assistant during the preparation of her articles for Bloomsbury's *Theatre Guide* was Shiyuan Zhou.

Nancy Riley, writer, actress has worked with Richard Schechner (the Performance Group), Mabou Mines, Richard Foreman and the Wooster Group with whom she has created five theatre pieces. She has written a volume of poems, one full-length play (*Hoodwink*), three one-act plays, and a novel, *A Professional High* from which she has created and toured two one-woman performance pieces.

Marc Robinson is the associate editor of *American Theatre* magazine and a freelance critic based in New York. He contributes regularly to *The Village Voice*, *Performing Arts Journal*, and other publications.

Rachel B. Shteir is a freelance journalist living in New York. She recently received a Jerome Fellowship, an annual grant awarded by *American Theatre*/TCG for critical writing.

Carole Woddis is a freelance journalist, former theatre co-editor of *City Limits* and regular theatre reviewer for a number of publications. Prior to that she worked in the theatre for a number of years as a publicist (with the RSC, the National Theatre and the RoundHouse). She was co-author with Trevor R. Griffiths of the first edition of *The Bloomsbury Theatre Guide*; her book, *Sheer Bloody Magic: interviews with leading actresses*, was published by Virago in July 1991.

Matt Wolf is the London theatre critic for *The Associated Press* and *The Wall Street Journal* (Europe). He freelances regularly for *Harpers & Queen* and *The Times* in Britain and *The Chicago Tribune* and *The New York Times* in America.

Index